Affect Regulation

&

the Repair of the Self

The Norton Series on Interpersonal Neurobiology
Daniel J. Siegel, M.D., Series Editor

The field of mental health is in a tremendously exciting period of growth and conceptual reorganization. Independent findings from a variety of scientific endeavors are converging in an interdisciplinary view of the mind and mental well-being. An "interpersonal neurobiology" of human development enables us to understand that the structure and function of the mind and brain are shaped by experiences, especially those involving emotional relationships.

The Norton Series on Interpersonal Neurobiology will provide cutting-edge, multidisciplinary views that further our understanding of the complex neurobiology of the human mind. By drawing on a wide range of traditionally-independent fields of research—such as neurobiology, genetics, memory, attachment, complex systems, anthropology, and evolutionary psychology—these texts will offer mental health professionals a review and synthesis of scientific findings often inaccessible to clinicians. These books aim to advance our understanding of human experience by finding the unity of knowledge, or "consilience," that emerges with the translation of findings from numerous domains of study into a common language and conceptual framework. The series will integrate the best of modern science with the healing art of psychotherapy.

A NORTON PROFESSIONAL BOOK

Affect Regulation

&

the Repair of the Self

ALLAN N. SCHORE

W.W. Norton & Company
New York • London

For information about permission to reproduce
selections from this book, write to
Permissions, W. W. Norton & Company, Inc.,
500 Fifth Avenue, New York, NY 10110

Production Manager: Leeann Graham
Manufacturing by Haddon Craftsmen, Inc.

Library of Congress Cataloging-in-Publication Data

Schore, Allan N., 1943–
Affect regulation and repair of the self / Allan N. Schore.
     p.   cm.
    "A Norton professional book."
    Includes bibliographical references and index.
    Contents: v. 1 [no distinct title]–v. 2 Affect regulation and repair of the self.
    ISBN 0-393-704008-4 (set) — ISBN 0-393-70406-8 (v. 1) — **ISBN 0-393-70407-6 (v. 2)**
    1. Affective disorders. 2. Self. 3. Self psychology. I. Title.

RC537.S3848 2003
616.85′27 — dc21   2002038055

W. W. Norton & Company, Inc., 500 Fifth Avenue, New York, N.Y. 10110
www.wwnorton.com

W. W. Norton & Company Ltd., Castle House, 75/76 Wells St., London W1T 3QT

5 6 7 8 9 0

Dedication

To Beth, David, Suzy, and Amanda

Revelation

We make ourselves a place apart
   Behind light words that tease and flout,
But oh, the agitated heart
   Till someone find us really out

'Tis pity if the case require
   (Or so we say) that in the end
We speak the literal to inspire
   The understanding of a friend

But so with all, from babes that play
   At hide-and-seek to God afar
So all who hide too well away
   Must speak and tell us where they are.

Robert Frost

Contents

Acknowledgments

M Y ACTIVITIES in theoretical science now span two decades, but my work as a clinician continues over the last 35 years. Throughout my professional life I have remained extremely curious about the common mechanisms that allow for change within the human conscious and unconscious minds, yet I am still fascinated and surprised by the unique ways these unfold and are expressed within the context of an individual psychotherapeutic exploration. Much of my learning has come from these relational experiences with my patients, and I thank them for allowing me to share in this rich context of subjective knowledge of self and other.

Other relationships have also been a valuable source of clinical knowledge, those with my peers. Early in my writing career, dialogues with Henry Krystal, the late Michael Basch, Calvin Settlage, John Gedo, Ernest Wolf, Stanley Greenspan, Paul Gilbert, and especially Jim Grotstein were very supportive of my interdisciplinary perspective. Over the years I continue to be greatly enriched in ongoing dialogues with Peter Fonagy, Anne Alvarez, Miriam Steele, Ed Tronick, Jim Masterson, Frank Putnam, Althea Horner, Bob Stolorow, Beatrice Beebe, Lou Sander, Colwyn Trevarthen, Steve Seligman, Mary Sue Moore, Susan Coates, Liz Muir and the late Roy Muir, Phil Mollon, Jeremy Holmes, Pat Sable, Nicola Diamond, Mario Marone, Suze Orbach, Anni Bergman, Lotte Kohler, Diana Fosha, Graeme Taylor, Jack Panksepp, Russell Meares, Ellert Nijenhuis, Onno van der Hart, Kathy Steele, Paul Valent, Francine Shapiro, Dan Stern, Joe Lichtenberg, Bessel van der Kolk, and Dan Siegel. I send a special expression of warm regards to Sir Richard and Lady Xenia Bowlby.

I am also most appreciative of the opportunities that have been afforded me by a number of editors—Leo Goldberger, Arnold Richards, Michael Moskowitz, Catherine Monk, Carol Kaye, Steve Ellman, Howard Steele, Joy Osofsky, William MacGillivray, Judith Edwards, David Scharff, Shelly Alhanati, Jean Arundale, Vivian Green, Jean Carney, and Mark Solms. In light of my work as an integrationist, it is especially gratifying that I am now on the editorial staff and/or a reviewer for 15 journals in a spectrum of fields, including the *Journal of Neuroscience, Behavioral and Brain Sciences, Neuroscience & Biobehavioral*

Reviews, Journal of Abnormal Psychology, American Academy of Pediatrics Pediatric Update, Development and Psychopathology, Infant Mental Health Journal, Neuro-Psychoanalysis, Psychologist Psychoanalyst, and *Journal of Analytical Psychology.*

I would like to thank Murray Brown, the director of clinical training of the UCLA/San Fernando Valley Psychiatric Training Program and numerous third-year psychiatric residents for the many rich discussions of the applications of my work to child and adult clinical psychiatry. Countless dialogues with faculty members and doctoral students of the California Institute for Clinical Social Work have afforded me valuable opportunities to broaden my ideas about the scientific bases of psychotherapy and their clinical applications. Working over the years with so many talented psychologists, psychiatrists, psychoanalysts, clinical social workers, and marital and family therapists in my Study Groups in Developmental Affective Neuroscience and Clinical Practice has been a critical source of both lively case discussion, intellectual challenge, and further elaboration of my theoretical models. Again I express my deep gratitude to the talented staff at W. W. Norton, Andrea Costella, Michael McGandy, and especially Deborah Malmud, the most gifted and responsive editor I have worked with.

And, finally, once again, from the mind and the heart, to Judith.

Preface

THIS BOOK REPRESENTS the third volume of a triad on the critical relationship between affect regulation and the organization of the self. In my first book, *Affect Regulation and the Origin of the Self*, published in 1994, I outlined the principles of regulation theory. In that volume, after describing the psycho-neurobiological mechanisms by which the attachment relationship facilitates the development of the major self-regulatory structures in the infant's brain, I applied the developmental conception to models of psychopathogenesis and the psychotherapy process. In the companion to this volume, *Affect Dysregulation and Disorders of the Self* I have expanded the applications of regulation theory to developmental affective neuroscience and developmental neuropsychiatry. In this book, *Affect Regulation and Repair of the Self*, I offer further expositions in the fields of developmentally-oriented psychotherapy and developmental neuropsychoanalysis.

Over the course of what was known as the Decade of the Brain, neuroscience experienced a remarkable growth spurt in knowledge. This advance, due in part to new imaging technologies, occurred not only in cognitive neuroscience, but also in the burgeoning fields of affective and social neuroscience. The rich body of data that emerged from basic brain research, as well as from psychobiology and psychophysiology, was now, perhaps more so than any time before, relevant to clinicians. In the same period psychiatry was making significant advances in understanding the relationship between affect dysregulation and trauma, while psychotherapists, focusing on emotional processes, were generating more effective models for the treatment of early-forming self pathologies. Parallel to these trends, experimental and social psychology seriously addressed an area long seen as outside of their scientific province — the domain of emotion. Similarly, developmental psychology, through its intensifying interest in attachment theory, increased the amount of research on social and emotional development in human infancy.

But perhaps what best characterizes the advances of the last 10 years in the life sciences is the tremendous acceleration of interdisciplinary research. This has allowed for the integration of data from a spectrum of different fields of study, each of which is attempting to more deeply understand the human condition. A prime example of this trend is seen in the fact that affect regulation and dysregulation are a common area of intense interest to researchers in the psychological, biological, medical, and social sciences, as well as to clinicians in psychiatry, psychology, and social work.

The integration of psychological and biological data is seen in contemporary models of the self, and there is a growing consensus that its origin must be explained in terms of the complexities of developmental psychology and developmental neuroscience. The ontogenesis of the human mind is now thought to involve more than the emergence of increasingly complex cognitions. Affective processes appear to lie at the core of the self, and due to the intrinsic psychobiological nature of these bodily-based phenomena recent models of human development, from infancy throughout the lifespan, are moving towards brain-mind-body conceptualizations. These models are redefining the essential characteristics of what makes us uniquely human.

Indeed, within the last ten years a shift has occurred in science's focus regarding what it considers to be the essential attributes of the human condition. In an issue of the journal *Science*, Richard Davidson concluded, "The self and personality, rather than consciousness, is the outstanding issue in neuroscience. So much of our behavior emerges from processes to which we have little conscious access" (2002, p. 268). There is an intense interest in nonconscious processes, fundamental operations of the brain-mind-body that occur rapidly and automatically, beneath levels of conscious awareness. This specifically applies to the behavioral, cognitive, and particularly emotional processes that mediate the fundamental capacity for self-regulation.

The self-regulation of emotion is usually defined in terms of the conscious self-regulation of emotion, the set of control processes by which we influence, consciously and voluntarily, the emotions we have, when we have them, and how we experience and express these emotions. This conception — that we can change the way we feel by consciously changing the way we think — is a primary corollary of the current dominant field in psychology, that is cognitive psychology. A secondary postulate is that rational thinking and the "cooling" attentional strategy of distraction are the major coping mechanisms for dampening down the "hot" negative emotional consequences of a distressing experience. The adaptive function of the amplification of positive emotion and the fundamental bodily-based operations that lie at the foundation of emotional processes are usually not addressed.

However, in contrast to this model of the down-regulation of emotion processing by conscious operations, a large body of studies indicates that most moment-to-moment psychological processing occurs nonconsciously. The essential self-regulatory functions that allow us to appraise and adapt to personally meaningful changes in the environment occur largely at levels beneath conscious awareness. Indeed, both researchers and clinicians are converging on the findings that rapidly communicated nonconscious social emotional information is primarily processed and acted upon at the implicit rather than the explicit level. In their clinical practice, psychotherapists of all persuasions are focusing upon both negative and positive "hot" rather than "cool" cognitions, and asserting that modifications in implicit relational knowledge and unconscious internal representations are the major changes in the psychotherapy context.

Researchers in social psychology are also exploring the important differences between implicit and explicit learning, as well as the direct relevance of the former to specifically social cognition. Cognition means knowing the world, but it is usually misinterpreted to signify only conscious verbal knowing. Much of the exchange of essential subjective information in human relationships is nonverbal, and includes dynamic changes in facial expression, prosodic tone of the voice, touch, gesture, and bodily state. These operations are essential to the functioning of the implicit (as opposed to the explicit) self.

This dichotomy between the verbal-conscious and nonverbal-unconscious realms also applies to neuroscience's research into self-regulation. Current studies in cognitive neuroscience are for the most part investigating the brain substrates involved in the conscious, voluntary control of emotional states. For example, this line of research is delving into verbal reappraisal strategies, whereby we mentally talk to ourselves in order to regulate anxiety states. These operations are lateralized to the verbal left hemisphere, especially in prefrontal areas. But neurobiological research also demonstrates another form of emotion regulation strategy, one that does not involve an interpretative verbal component. This mechanism is lateralized to the right prefrontal areas, and is specifically accessed in states of very high or very low arousal associated with intense emotions. The data presented in the chapters of this volume indicate that this right lateralized affect regulating function is dominant for coping with the stress and uncertainty that is a fundamental accompaniment of the human condition.

Indeed, one of the major advances of the Decade of the Brain has been the rediscovery that "the brain" is in actuality two brains, two different processors of external and internal information. Studies are moving away from the familiar territory of the verbal left hemisphere and are charting the unique functions of the right hemisphere. Despite earlier controversies on affective laterality, a growing body of research cited in this volume demonstrates the general superiority of the right hemisphere for the expression and reception of both positive and negative emotions. Furthermore, this hemisphere is dominant for the implicit cognitive processing of facial, prosodic, and bodily information embedded in emotional communications, for attention, for empathy, and for the human stress response. These essential processes — central to both the regulation of homeostasis and the capacity to flexibly alter the internal environment to optimally cope with external perturbations — take place extremely rapidly, at levels beneath conscious awareness. Converging neuropsychologic and neurobiological data strongly suggest that the right hemisphere is critically involved in the maintenance of a coherent, continuous, and unified implicit sense of self.

A number of authors are pointing out that the concept of implicit and explicit dimensions of the self is a direct analogue of Freud's separation of the mind into unconscious and conscious levels. Indeed, contemporary neuropsychoanalysis is correlating the unique functions of the left and the right brains with the conscious and unconscious left and right minds. But due to the nature of psychoanalysis (the science of unconscious processes) it has always been most interested in the operations of the nonconscious realm, the province of primary process cognitions, the bodily-based drives, and the earliest primordial events that impact the developing mind-body. Freud's essential discovery was that this unconscious realm contained the major systems of human motivation that operate in everyday life, and that knowledge of the functional capacities of this unconscious system allows for a more comprehensive understanding and prediction of overt behavior than does a consideration of the conscious system. This principle is echoed in the *Affect Regulation* triad in the assertion that the implicit self is the key to a deeper understanding of personality and the problems of normal and abnormal behavior.

Just as the other sciences have been transformed in the last decade, so has psychoanalysis. Although many scientists have a conception of psychoanalysis frozen in time, as it existed in the early twentieth century, Freud's original theoretical and clinical models have been substantially updated and in some cases radically altered. Attachment theory, an outgrowth of psychoanalysis, is only one example — the concept of the centrality of the unconscious in everyday life was incorporated into Bowlby's nonconscious internal working models. But even Freud's characterizations of the unconscious inner world have been transformed. Instead of a repository of archaic untamed passions and destructive wishes, the unconscious is now seen as a cohesive, active mental structure that continuously appraises life's experiences and responds according to its scheme of interpretation. And in contrast to a static, deeply buried storehouse of ancient memories buried and silenced in "infantile amnesia," contemporary intersubjective psychoanalysts now refer to a "relational unconscious," whereby one unconscious mind communicates with another unconscious mind. In a number of upcoming chapters, I describe how this communication begins in early attachment experiences, which imprint the developing right brain, the biological substrate of the human unconscious.

I should point out that throughout this book the generic term "psychodynamic" can be exchanged for the term "psychoanalytic." Also "psychoanalyst" can be translated to "clinician." The reader will note that the term I use to describe the clinical approach to severe self pathologies is "developmentally-oriented psychotherapy." Not only psychoanalytic theory but psychoanalytically-oriented technique has changed in order to optimally meet the challenges and treat the deficits of individuals who at one time were seen to be refractory to psychotherapy. This treatment, guided by understandings from developmental psychoanalysis and its derivative attachment theory, is best achieved in other than a traditional clinical psychoanalytic context, that is, face-to-face. The focus is as much on process as content, and on the psychobiological rather than the mental state.

My identification with psychoanalysis specifically reflects my interests in the nonconscious realm, in modifying the patient's representational processes and internal object world, and in strengthening psychic structure in order to en-hance the capacity to organize affects and self-regulate the implicit as well as explicit self systems. These goals are no longer just within the domain of psychodynamic clinical models—indeed, they have been adopted by the larger group of eclectic clinicians. Also, I have no personal identification with any particular school of psychoanalysis. The essays in this book reappraise the works of a number of psychoanalytic pioneers and the chapters range across almost all of the subdisciplines of psychoanalysis, demonstrating that each emphasized the concept of regulation. Yet, despite their differences, all share "a fascination with the mysterious and marvelous transmutative power of conversation within a human dyad" (Auchincloss, 2002, p. 502).

But even beyond psychoanalysis, as a clinician-scientist my interest is in the commonalties of all psychotherapies—that is, the generic change process itself. The phenomena of transference and countertransference, once considered a hallmark of psychoanalysis, are now seen to be fundamental to all forms of psychotherapy. Furthermore, the criticial importance of the therapeutic rela-tionship, first discussed by Freud (1913/1958), is being validated in a large body of basic clinical research. Indeed, among the common elements of psychother-apy, the therapeutic alliance (i.e., the collaborative relationship between patient and the therapist) is most important to positive therapeutic outcome. It is now accepted that a primary component of the alliance is the emotional bond within the dyad of patient and therapist and so all schools of psychotherapy are now placing emphasis upon the affective aspects of the therapeutic relationship. All forms of clinical interpretative and noninterpretive technical interventions are mediated through this relational mechanism.

Thus, throughout this book, I focus on the underlying mechanisms by which the therapeutic relationship can alter the patient's internal structural brain sys-tems that nonconsciously and consciously process and regulate external and internal information, and thereby not only reduce the patient's negative emo-tional symptoms but expand his or her adaptive capacities. Contemporary clini-cal models suggest that the therapeutic alliance is a common element of all of the different therapy modalities, that it accounts for more of the variance of treatment outcome than treatment method, that affect dysregulation is a funda-mental mechanism of all psychiatric disorders, and that all psychotherapies show a similarity in promoting affect regulation. The principles outlined in the following chapters apply equally well to short-term as well as long-term treat-ment models.

If development fundamentally represents the process of change, then psy-chotherapy is, in essence, applied developmental psychology. The data in de-velopmental affective neuroscience and developmental psychoanalysis clearly demonstrate that in the critical early periods of life the maturing human brain/mind/body evolves to greater degrees of complexity within the context of an affect regulating relationship with another human being. This essential inter-personal component of a growth-facilitating developmental matrix clearly sug-gests that psychotherapeutic changes are mediated by aspects of the relationship of the patient and therapist. When effective, this cocreated dyadic system can facilitate the further development and organization of the patient's internal brain/mind/body systems. The brain sciences demonstrate that the adult brain retains plasticity, and this plasticity, especially of the right brain that is dominant for self-regulation, allows for the emotional learning that accompanies a successful psychotherapeutic experience.

Although there was initially anxiety among some clinicians that neuroscience would lead to reductionistic and over-simplified models of the complexities of human normal and abnormal behavior, as the following chapters demonstrate, a growing number of researchers are also becoming interested in the central role of affect regulation in psychotherapy. Neuroscientists are concluding that "the ability to modulate emotions is at the heart of the human experience [and] the use of emotional self-regulatory processes constitutes the core of several modern psychotherapeutic approaches" (Beauregard, Levesque, & Bourgouin, 2001, p. RC165), that the development of self-regulation "may be open to change in adult life, providing a basis for what is attempted in therapy" (Posner & Rothbart, 1998, p. 1925), and that "experts in neuropsychology and clinical psychology should play a leading role in developing the next generation of illness-specific and neural pathway-targeted psychotherapeutic techniques" (Post & Weiss, 2002, p. 647). The idea that pharmacology changes the brain and psychotherapy changes the mind is clearly outdated. Recent research cited in this volume shows alterations in brain function that accompany successful psychotherapeutic treatment. Indeed neuroimaging studies support the principle, "change the mind and you change the brain" (Paquette et al., 2003).

This work on regulation theory and on creating models that synthesize the interactions of biological and psychological data also attempts to integrate biological psychiatry with dynamic psychiatry. I suggest the field is now in a position to actualize the enormous potential of the biopsychosocial model. Just before the Decade of the Brain, George Engel, a major contributor to this integrative formulation, presciently wrote,

> It is not just that science is a human activity, it is also that the interpersonal engagement required in the clinical realm rests on complementary needs, *especially the need to know and understand and the need to feel known and understood.* . . . The need to know and understand originates in the regulatory and self-organizing capabilities of all living organisms to process information from an everchanging environment in order to assure growth . . . self-regulation, and survival. In turn, the need to feel known and understand originates . . . in the life-long need to feel socially connected with other humans. (1988, pp. 124–125)

The interpersonal engagement that occurs in psychotherapy represents a potent medium in which an individual self can subjectively experience the need to know and the need to feel known in a safe, emotionally-responsive context. Although psychotherapy has recently been devalued or at best undervalued, the art and the science of psychotherapy, of the careful study of the inner worlds of a multiplicity of psychopathologies, as well as the necessary self study involved in this profession, are as complex and rigorous as any other discipline in the experimental or applied human sciences. These skills are deepened by repeated careful observations of the external and internal patterns of resistances against, yet, possibilities for, change in a wide range of human psychopathologies, and take many years to craft. In addition to the subjective learning that comes from clinical experience, professional growth also involves a continual need to incorporate the new objective findings from not only the psychological, psychiatric, and social, but also the biological sciences.

Regulation theory is an effort in that direction. The theory focuses upon how the clinician can gain this new knowledge in order to more effectively use the explicit and particularly implicit self in order to treat, at close intersubjective range, a spectrum of early-forming disorders of the self. Over the last ten years these clinical populations have dramatically increased, and they now represent a significant proportion of the case load of most clinicians. In the following chapters I refer back to the neurobiological models of psychopathogenesis outlined in the companion volume to this book, *Affect Dysregulation and Disorders of the Self*, and elaborate the applications of regulation theory to the affectively-focused, developmentally-oriented treatment of infant, child, and adult attachment pathologies and severe personality disorders.

References

Auchincloss, E. L. (2002). The place of psychoanalytic treatments within psychiatry. *Archives of General Psychiatry, 59,* 501–502.

Beauregard, M., Levesque, J., & Bourgouin, P. (2001). Neural correlates of conscious self-regulation of emotion. *Journal of Neuroscience, 21,* RC165.

Davidson, R. J. (2002). Synaptic substrates of the implicit and explicit self. *Science, 296,* 268.

Engel, G. L. (1988). How much longer must medicine's science be bound by a seventeenth century world view? In K. L. White (Ed.), *The task of medicine: Dialogue at Wickenburg,* (pp. 113–136) Menlo Park, CA: Henry J. Kaiser Foundation.

Freud, S. (1958). Further recommendations on the technique of psychoanalysis: On the beginning of treatment. The question of the first communications. The dynamics of the cure. In J. Strachey (Ed. & Trans.), *Standard edition of the complete works of Sigmund Freud* (Vol. 12, pp. 122–144). London: Hogarth Press. (Original work published 1913)

Paquette, V., Levésque, J., Mensour, B., Leroux, J-M., Beaudoin, G., Bourgouin, P., & Beauregard, M. (2003). "Change the mind and you change the brain." Effects of cognitive-behavioral therapy on the neural correlates of spider phobia. *NeuroImage, 18,* 401–409.

Posner, M. I., & Rothbart, M. K. (1998). Attention, self-regulation, and consciousness. *Philosophical Transactions of the Royal Society of London B, 353,* 1915–1927.

Post, R. P., & Weiss, S. R. B. (2002). Psychological complexity: Barriers to its integration into the neurobiology of major psychiatric disorders. *Development and Psychopathology, 14,* 635–651.

PART I

DEVELOPMENTALLY
ORIENTED PSYCHOTHERAPY

CHAPTER 1

Interdisciplinary Research
as a Source of Clinical Models

A FTER REMAINING ALMOST UNCHANGED for most of psychoanalysis' first century, the central core of Freud's model of the mind is now undergoing a rapid and substantial transformation. The scaffolding of clinical psychoanalysis is supported by underlying theoretical conceptions of psychic development and structure, and it is these basic concepts that are now being reformulated. The elucidation of these metapsychological underpinnings is doing more than strengthening clinical models—it is enriching the intellectual climate of our discipline. More than anyone could have predicted, observational and experimental research of infants interacting with their mothers has turned out to be the most fertile source for the generation of heuristic hypotheses about not only early development but also psychic dynamics. Indeed, a deeper understanding of the fundamental processes that drive development, of why early experience influences the organization of psychic structure and how this structure comes to mediate emergent psychological functioning, of the origins of the human mind, is now within sight.

The question of why the early events of life have such an inordinate influence on literally everything that follows is one of the fundamental problems of not only psychoanalysis but of all science. How do early experiences, especially affective experiences with other humans, induce and organize the patterns of structural growth that result in the expanding functional capacities of a developing individual? A spectrum of disciplines—from developmental biology and neurochemistry through developmental psychology and psychoanalysis—share the common principle that the beginnings of living systems indelibly set the stage for every aspect of an organism's internal and external functioning throughout the lifespan. A developmental theory, a conception of the genesis of living systems, a model of self-organization, is found at the base of each and every domain of theoretical and clinical science. The data that is being generated by the current explosion in infant research is not only giving us a more detailed model of human development, it is also being rapidly absorbed into clinical models where it is radically altering the central concepts of psychoanalysis and psychiatry. At present all major theoreticians are placing developmental concepts at the foundation of their clinical models.

Using an expanding arsenal of different methodologies and studying different levels of analysis, multidisciplinary investigators are now inquiring into the incipient interactions the infant has with the most important object in the early environment—the primary caregiver. It is now very clear that this dialectic with the social environment is mediated by transactions of affect, and that this emotional communication is nonverbal. Human development cannot be understood apart from this affect-transacting relationship. Furthermore, these early social events are imprinted into the biological structures that are maturing during the brain growth spurt that occurs in the first two years of human life, and therefore have far-reaching and long-enduring effects (see Figure 1.1). In the November 1995 issue of the *American Journal of Psychiatry,* Eisenberg (1995) presented an article, "The *Social* Construction of the Human Brain" (italics added). It is well established that the accelerated growth of brain structure during "critical periods" of infancy is "experience-dependent" and influenced by "social forces." But neurobiology is unclear as to the nature of these "social forces."

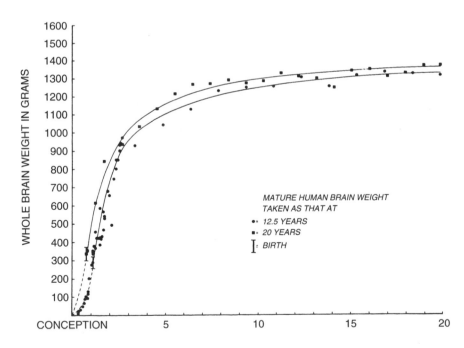

FIGURE 1.1. Growth of whole brain compared when mature weight is taken at 12.5 years and at 20 years. Note the accelerated growth in the first 2 years. (From Himwich, 1975)

FIGURE 1.2. Picture of Freud, age 53. (From Schore, 1997)

FIGURE 1.3. *Baby's First Caress*, by Mary Cassatt. (From Schore, 1997)

In fact, psychoanalysis has much to say about the "social forces" that influence the organization of developing "psychic structure." The period of early-forming object relations so intensely studied by psychoanalysis exactly overlaps the period of the brain growth spurt. The most important revisions of Freud's model in the latter half of this century have occurred in developmental psychoanalysis: Fairbairn (proclaiming that infants are not solely instinctually driven but object-seeking), Klein (exploring very early developmental events and primitive cognitive mechanisms), Winnicott (concluding that an infant can not be understood apart from its interaction with the mother), Bowlby (applying then current biology to an understanding of infant–mother attachment), Mahler (introducing observational research in psychoanalysis), Stern (focusing on interactive attunement mechanisms in the relationship), and Emde (emphasizing that the child's environment is the relationship with the primary caregiver).

There are few visual symbols in psychoanalysis. The symbol of "classical" psychoanalysis is a photograph of Freud's face (Figure 1.2), an icon of a monad, a single unit; an adult, conscious, reflective mind attempting to understand the realm of the dynamic unconscious that forms in early childhood; a man's face gazing inward; a representation of a paternal-oedipal psychology.

But there is one other visual symbol of "developmental" psychoanalysis that is familiar to us—the icon from the cover of Stern's (1985) book, *The Interpersonal World of the Infant* (Figure 1.3). Here we have a symbol of a dyad; two interlocking units; gazes between two faces, one of an adult female, the other of an infant; a representation of a maternal-preoedipal psychology. This is, of course, Mary Cassatt's *Baby's First Caress*, painted in 1890. The two figures form a compact and unified group; thus, the structure expresses a close maternal–infant relationship. The visual image conveys their Winnicottian intense engagement, a Bowlbyian image of bonding. How does the artist convey this? Yes, the curve of their arms suggest a loop, the baby touches the mother's face, the mother's hand is on the baby's foot—a closed system of linked bodies. But more than this, the heads are placed together; what unites them is the meeting of *direct glances between their eyes*.

My book, *Affect Regulation and the Origin of the Self* enlarged and concentrated on this focus. In this volume, I integrated new insights about interactive, relational processes from developmental and clinical psychoanalysis, current ideas about the origins of social functioning from the developmental sciences, recent data on emotional phenomena from the behavioral sciences, and the latest research on the limbic structures that support these functions from the brain sciences, in order to generate an overarching model of emotional development (Schore, 1994). A multidisciplinary approach is especially relevant to the investigations of the psychobiological mechanisms that underlie affective processes. In contrast to reductionism, my work presents a multilevel perspective that is guided by the tenet that development can only be explained by studying it simultaneously along several separate but interrelated dimensions ranging from the biological level of organization through the psychological, social, and cultural levels.

Drawing upon my book, as well as on an article in the interdisciplinary journal *Development and Psychopathology* (Schore, 1996), in this chapter I will present a brief overview of recent studies from a spectrum of disciplines that reveal more detailed and precise knowledge of early socioemotional development. This information about the ontogeny of the mind cannot be apprehended clinically, yet it is relevant and indeed essential to psychoanalysis. As you will soon notice, I am arguing that the appearance of the adaptive functions of the developing mind cannot be understood without also addressing the problem of the maturation of structures responsible for these functions. Changes in the child's behavior or in the child's internal world can only be understood in terms of the appearance of more complex structure that performs emergent functions. In describing the process of psychological structure formation, Rapaport declared, "We must establish how processes turn into structures, how a structure once formed changes, and how it gives rise to and influences processes" (1960, pp. 98–99). Freud's "structural theory" must not be abandoned but updated in terms of what we now know about brain–mind relationships. Psychoanalysis must now come to terms with structure, and although its models of psychic structure should not be reduced to neurobiology, they should be compatible with what is now known about structure as it exists in nature.

Toward that end, I will begin by offering a multilevel perspective of the structure–function relationships of an event central to human emotional development—the interactive creation of an attachment bond of affective communication between the primary caregiver and the infant. In the course of this I will outline psychobiological models of the mirroring process, symbiosis, and self object phenomena. I will then describe how these very same affect-transacting experiences specifically shape the maturation of specific structural connections within the brain that come to mediate both the interpersonal and intrapsychic aspects of all future socioemotional functions. Of particular importance is the organization of a hierarchical regulatory system in the prefrontal areas of the right hemisphere. Finally, I will begin to sketch out a few of the important implications of these results for contemporary theoretical and clinical psychoanalysis, which Cooper asserted is "anchored in its scientific base in developmental psychology and in the biology of attachment and affects" (1987, p. 83).

AFFECTIVE TRANSMISSIONS
IN MUTUAL GAZE TRANSACTIONS

Although much has been written about cognitive development in infancy, until very recently few studies have been done on emotional and social ontogeny. This development is closely tied into the maturation of sensory systems, especially visual systems. In fact, over the first year of life, *visual experiences play a paramount role in social and emotional development* (Blank, 1975; Fraiberg & Freedman, 1964; Hobson, 1993; Keeler, 1958; Nagera & Colonna, 1965; Preisler, 1995; Wright, 1991). In particular, the mother's emotionally expressive face is, by far, the most potent visual stimulus in the infant's environment, and the child's intense interest in her face, especially in her eyes, leads him/her to track it in space, and to engage in periods of intense mutual gaze. The infant's gaze, in turn, reliably evokes the mother's gaze, thereby acting as a potent interpersonal channel for the transmission of "reciprocal mutual influences." These sustained face-to-face transactions are quite common and can be of very long duration, and they mediate what Spitz (1958) called "the dialogue between mother and child." In fact, gaze represents the most intense form of interpersonal communication, and the perception of facial expressions is known to be the most salient channel of nonverbal communication.

Congruent with these findings, Kohut concluded that "The most significant relevant basic interactions between mother and child usually lie in the visual area: The child's bodily display is responded to by the gleam in the mother's eye" (1971, p. 117). There is now evidence that the mother's gleam is more than a metaphor. By 2 to 3 months, a time of increasing myelination of the visual areas of the infant's occipital cortex, the mother's eyes become a focus of her infant's attention, especially her pupils. Studies by Hess (1975) showed that a woman's eyes (and a man with children) dilate in response to the image of a baby, a response associated with the positive emotions of pleasure and interest. Furthermore, an infant will smile in response to enlarged pupils. Even more intriguingly, viewing enlarged pupils rapidly elicits dilated pupils in the baby, and dilated pupils are known to release caregiver behavior. The pupil of the eye thus acts as an interpersonal nonverbal communication device, and these rapid communications occur at unconscious levels. Hess concluded, "The fact that babies have large pupils, or respond with enlarging pupils in adult–infant interaction would in general assure al least a minimal degree of the infant–adult interaction that is necessary for the mental and emotional development of the child" (p. 106).

Mutual gaze interactions increase over the second and third quarters of the first year, and because they occur within the "split second world of the mother and infant" (Stern, 1977) are therefore not easily visible. This dialogue is best studied by a frame-by-frame analysis of film, and in such work Beebe and Lachmann (1988a) observed synchronous rapid movements and fast changes in affective expressions within the dyad (Figure 1.4). This affective mirroring is accomplished by a moment-by-moment matching of affective direction in which both partners increase together their degree of engagement and facially expressed positive affect. The fact that the coordination of responses is so rapid suggests the existence of a bond of unconscious communication.

This microregulation continues, as soon after the "heightened affective moment" of an intensely joyful full gape smile the baby will gaze avert in order to regulate the potentially disorganizing effect of this intensifying emotion (Field & Fogel, 1982, Figure 1.5). In order to maintain the positive emotion the attuned mother takes her cue and backs off to reduce her stimulation. She then waits for the baby's signals for reengagement. Importantly, not only the tempo of their engagement but also their disengagement and reengagement are coordinated. In this process of "contingent responsivity" the more the mother tunes her activity level to the infant during periods of social engagement, the more she allows him/her to recover quietly in periods of disengagement, and the more she attends to his/her reinitiating cues for reengagement, the more synchronized their interaction becomes. Facial mirroring thus illustrates interactions organized by ongoing regulations, and experiences of mutually attuned synchronized interactions are fundamental to the ongoing affective development of the infant.

These mirroring exchanges generate much more than overt facial changes in the dyad; they represent a transformation of inner events. Beebe and Lachmann (1988a) asserted that as the mother and the infant match each other's temporal and affective patterns, each recreates an inner psychophysiological state similar to the partner's. In synchronized gaze the dyad creates a mutual regulatory system of arousal (Stern, 1983) in which they both experience a state transition as they move together from a state of neutral affect and arousal to one of heightened positive emotion and high arousal. The mother's face, the child's "emotional" or "biological" mirror, has been described as reflecting back her baby's "aliveness" in a "positively amplifying circuit mutually affirming both partners" (Wright, 1991, p. 12). Stern (1985) referred to a particular maternal social behavior which can "blast the infant into the next orbit of positive excitation" and generate vitality affects.

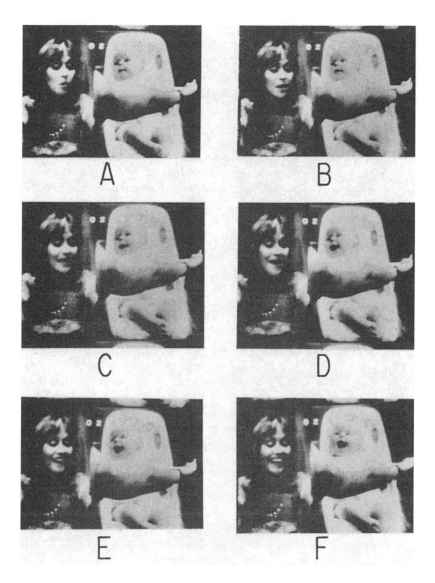

FIGURE 1.4. Photographic illustrations of a "mirroring" sequence. The mother and infant are seated face to face, and are looking at each other. At point (A), the mother shows a "kiss-face," and the infant's lips are partially drawn in, resulting in a tight, sober-faced expression. At point (B), .54 seconds later, the mother's mouth has widened into a slightly positive expression, and the infant's face has relaxed with a hint of widening in the mouth, also a slighly positive expression. At point (C), .79 seconds later, both the mother and the infant show a slight smile. At point (D), .46 seconds later, both the mother and the infant further widen and open their smiles. Again at points (E), .46 seconds later, and (F), .58 seconds later, both the mother and the infant further increase their smile display. Points (E) and (F) illustrate the infant's "gape smile." At point (F) the infant has shifted the orientation of his head further to his left, and upward, which heightens the evocativeness of the gape-smile. (From Beebe & Lachmann, 1988)

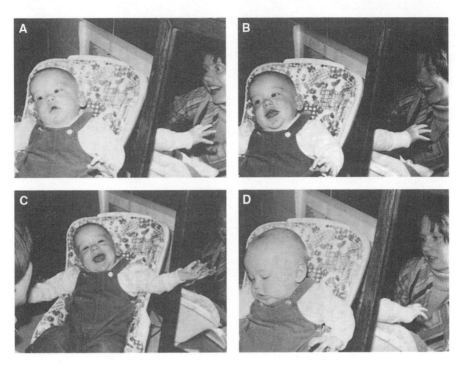

FIGURE 1.5. A typical sequence observed during "attuned" interactions of normal infants and their mothers: (A) The infant looks at the mother and the mother shows an exaggerated facial expression (mock surprise); (B) the infant and the mother smile; (C) the infant laughs, and the mother "relaxes" her smile; and (D) the infant looks away, the mother ceases smiling, and she watches her infant. (From Field & Fogel, 1982)

In order to enter into this communication, the mother must be psychobiologically attuned not so much to the child's overt behavior as to the reflections of his/her internal state. She also must monitor her own internal signals and differentiate her own affective state, as well as modulating nonoptimal high levels of stimulation that would induce supraheightened levels of arousal in the infant. The burgeoning capacity of the infant to experience increasing levels of accelerating, rewarding affects (enjoyment-joy and interest-excitement; Tomkins, 1962) is thus at this stage externally regulated by the psychobiologically attuned mother, and depends upon her capacity to engage in an interactive emotion communicating mechanism that generates these in herself and her child.

We know that the caregiver is not always attuned; indeed, developmental research shows frequent moments of misattunement in the dyad, ruptures of the attachment bond. In fact, over the course of time, especially as the baby becomes a mobile toddler, she shifts from a caregiver to a socialization agent, and in doing so she continues to use visual channels for emotional communication. Reciprocal gaze, in addition to transmitting attunement, can also act to transmit misattunement, as in shame experiences. The misattunement in shame, as in other negative affects, represents a regulatory failure and is phenomenologically experienced as a discontinuity in what Winnicott (1958) called the child's need for "going-on-being."

Prolonged negative states are too toxic for infants to sustain for very long, and although they possess some capacity to modulate low-intensity negative affect states, these states continue to escalate in intensity, frequency, and duration. How long the child remains in states of intense negative affect is an important factor in the etiology of a predisposition to psychopathology. Active parental participation in state regulation is critical to enabling the child to shift from the negative affective states of hyperaroused distress or hypoaroused deflation to a reestablished state of positive affect. In early development an adult provides much of the necessary modulation of infant states, especially after a state disruption and across a transition between states, and this allows for the development of self-regulation. Again, the key to this is the caregiver's capacity to monitor and regulate her own affect, especially negative affect.

In this essential regulatory pattern of "disruption and repair" (Beebe & Lachmann, 1994) the "good-enough" caregiver who induces a stress response in her infant through a misattunement reinvokes in a timely fashion her psychobiologically attuned regulation of the infant's negative affect state *that she has triggered*. The reattuning, comforting mother and infant thus dyadically negotiate a stressful state transition of affect, cognition, and behavior. This recovery mechanism underlies the phenomenon of "interactive repair" (Tronick, 1989), in which participation of the caregiver is responsible for the reparation of dyadic misattunements. In this process the mother who induces interactive stress and negative emotion in the infant is instrumental to the transformation of negative into positive emotion. It is thought that "the process of reexperiencing positive affect following negative experience may teach a child that negativity can be endured and conquered" (Malatesta-Magai, 1991, p. 218). Infant resilience is characterized as the capacity of the child and the parent to transition from positive to negative and back to positive affect (Demos, 1991). It is important to note that resilience in the face of stress is an ultimate indicator of attachment capacity (Greenspan, 1981).

These regulatory transactions underlie the formation of an attachment bond between the infant and primary caregiver. Attachment biology is thus the cement that provides what Freud (1917/1961 & 1963) called the "adhesiveness" of early object relationships. Indeed, regulatory processes are thought to be the precursors of psychological attachment and its associated emotions (Hofer, 1994), and psychobiological attunement is understood to be the essential mechanism that mediates attachment bond formation (Field, 1985a). In essence, the baby becomes attached to the modulating caregiver who expands opportunities for positive affect and minimizes negative affect. In other words, the affective state underlies and motivates attachment, and the central adaptive function of attachment dynamics is to interactively generate and maintain optimal levels of positive states and vitality affects.

THE NEUROBIOLOGY AND PSYCHOBIOLOGY
OF ATTACHMENT BOND FORMATION

According to Bowlby (1969), vision is central to the establishment of a primary attachment to the mother, and imprinting is the learning mechanism that underlies attachment bond formation. Furthermore, attachment is more than overt behavior, it is internal, "being built into the nervous system, in the course and as a result of the infant's experience of his transactions with the mother" (Ainsworth, 1967, p. 429) Emde (1988) asserted that the infant is biologically prepared to engage in visual stimulation in order to stimulate its brain. This brings us to another level of analysis—the neurobiological level. In this "transfer of affect between mother and infant" how are developing systems of the organizing brain influenced by these interactions with the social environment? Or, as Stechler and Halton put this question, what do we know of "the processes whereby the primary object relations become internalized and transformed into psychic structure" (1987, p. 823)?

The work of Trevarthen (1993) on maternal–infant protoconversations bears directly on this problem (see Figure 1.6). Coordinated with eye-to-eye messages

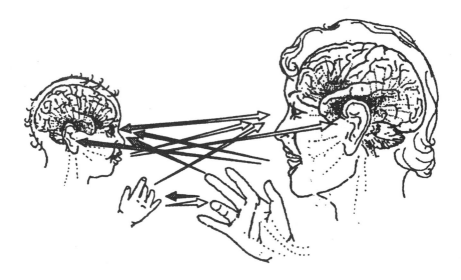

FIGURE 1.6. Channels of face-to-face communication in protoconversation. Protoconversation is mediated by eye-to-eye orientations, vocalizations, hand gestures, and movements of the arms and head, all acting in coordination to express interpersonal awareness and emotions. (From Aitken & Trevarthen, 1997)

are auditory vocalizations (tone of voice, "motherese") as a channel of communication, and tactile and body gestures. A traffic of visual and prosodic auditory signals induce instant emotional effects, namely excitement and pleasure builds within the dyad. But Trevarthen also focused on internal structure-function events. He pointed out that the engaged infant is interacting with the mother while she is in a state of primary maternal preoccupation (Winnicott, 1956), and that the resultant dyadic resonance ultimately permits the intercoordination of positive affective brain states. His work underscored the fundamental principle that the baby's brain is not only affected by these transactions, its growth literally requires brain–brain interaction and occurs in the context of a positive affective relationship between mother and infant. This interactive mechanism requires older brains to engage with mental states of awareness, emotion, and interest in younger brains, and involves a coordination between the motivations of the infant and the subjective feelings of adults.

Next question: What parts of the growing brain are affected by these events? I suggest that what is happening here is that the infant's right hemisphere, which is dominant for the child's processing of visual and prosodic emotional information and for the infant's recognition of maternal facial affective expressions, is psychobiologically attuned to the output of the mother's right hemisphere, which is involved in the expression and processing of emotional information and in spontaneous and nonverbal communication. The right cortex, which matures before the left, is known to be specifically impacted by early social experiences, to be activated in intense states of elation, and to contribute to the development of reciprocal interactions within the mother–infant regulatory system. The child is using the output of the mother's right cortex as a template for the imprinting—the hard wiring of circuits in his/her own right cortex that will come to mediate his/her expanding affective capacities. It has been said that in early infancy the mother is the child's "auxiliary cortex" (Diamond, Krech, & Rosenzweig, 1963). In these transactions she is "downloading programs" from her brain into the infant's brain. There is solid evidence that the parenting environment influences the developing patterns of neural connections that underlie infant behavior (Dawson, 1994).

Interactive transactions that regulate positive affect—in addition to producing neurobiological, structural consequences—are also generating important events at the psychobiological level. In describing the mother–infant experience of mutuality, Winnicott proposed that "The main thing is a communication between the baby and mother in terms of the anatomy and physiology of live bodies" (1989, p. 258). This physiological linkage is an essential element of Kohut's (1971) postulate that the crucial maintenance of the infant's internal homeostatic balance is directly related to the infant's continuous dyadic reciprocal interactions with selfobjects. Indeed, self-psychology is built upon a cardinal developmental principle—that parents with mature psychological organizations serve as "selfobjects" that perform critical regulatory functions for the infant who possesses an immature, incomplete psychological organization. This developmental psychoanalytic model is being confirmed by Hofer's (1990, 1994) psychobiological research, which demonstrates that in dyadic, "symbiotic states" the infant's "open," immature, and developing internal homeostatic systems are interactively regulated by the caregiver's more mature and differentiated nervous system. Self-objects are thus external psychobiological regulators (Taylor, 1987) that facilitate the regulation of affective experience (Palombo, 1992), and they act at nonverbal levels beneath conscious awareness to cocreate states of maximal cohesion and vitalization (Wolf, 1988).

We now can understand the mechanism of Kohutian "mirroring." The human face is a unique stimulus for the display of biologically significant information. Psychobiological studies of attachment show that in mutual gaze the mother's face is triggering high levels of endogenous opiates in the child's growing brain (Hoffman, 1987; Panksepp, Siviy, & Normansell, 1985). These endorphins, produced in the anterior pituitary, are biochemically responsible for the pleasurable qualities of social interaction and attachment as they act directly on dopamine neurons in the subcortical reward centers of the infant's brain that are responsible for heightened arousal (Schore, 1994). Stimuli that induce arousal exert a potent influence on developmental processes (Rauschecker & Marler, 1987). By promoting a symbiotic entrainment between the mother's mature and the infant's immature endocrine and nervous systems, hormonal responses are triggered that stimulate the child into a similar state of heightened central nervous system (CNS) arousal and sympathetic nervous system activity and resultant excitement and positive emotion. These findings support Basch's assertion that "the language of mother and infant consist of signals produced by the autonomic, involuntary nervous system in both parties" (1976, p. 766).

In the latter half of the first year, object seeking, which Modell (1980) defined as the sharing and communicating of affects, specifically revolves around the mother's face, and it is her expressive face that is searched for and recognized (Wright, 1991). High-intensity mirroring exchanges thus create a "merger" experience that acts as a crucible for the forging of the affective ties of the attachment bond. This interactive mechanism creates what Mahler, Pine, and Bergman called "optimal mutual cueing, a perfect fit of the dual unity" (1975, p. 204). Hofer stated that "in postnatal life, the neural substrates for simple affective states are likely to be present and that the experiences for the building of specific pleasurable states are likewise built into the symbiotic nature of the earliest mother–infant interaction" (1990, p. 62). The concept of symbiosis is now solidly grounded in developmental research, and it should be returned into psychoanalysis.

Trevarthen (1993) referred to "The self born in intersubjectivity: The psychology of an infant communicating." At 9–10 months occurs what he described as the emergence of "secondary intersubjectivity." Indeed, in the last quarter of the first year, the child's attachment experiences enable him/her to now share an intersubjective affect state with the caregiver (Lichtenberg, 1989). Beebe and Lachmann concluded that facial mirroring allows for "entering into the other's changing feeling state" (1994, p. 136). What is more, they asserted that these experiences are stored in what they termed "presymbolic representations." These interactive representations appear at the end of the first year, and in them the infant represents the expectation of being matched by and being able to match the partner, as well as "participating in the state of the other." This is also the identical time period when internal representations of working models of attachment are first encoded.

Attachment functions involve highly visual mechanisms and generate positive affect, and they mature near the end of the first year of life. These psychobiological experiences of attunement, misattunement, and reattunement are imprinted into the early developing brain. In this manner, "affects are at the crossroads of biology and history" (Modell, 1984, p. 184). Stable attachment bonds that transmit high levels of positive affect are vitally important for the infant's continuing neurobiological development (Trad, 1986). Main, perhaps the most influential current attachment researcher, concluded that "The formation of an attachment to a specified individual signals a quantitative change in infant behavioral (and *no doubt also brain*) organization" (italics added; 1993, p. 214). Do we now know what parts of the brain begin a critical period of structural growth at 10 to 12 months and are involved in attachment functions and in the regulation of affect?

THE MATURATION OF THE ORBITOFRONTAL CORTEX DURING MAHLER'S PRACTICING PERIOD (10–12 TO 16–18 MONTHS)

In my 1994 book, I offered evidence to show that dyadic communications that generate intense positive affect represent a growth-promoting environment for the prefrontal cortex, an area that is known to undergo a major maturational change at 10–12 months (Diamond & Doar, 1989). It is established that frontal lobe functioning plays an essential role in the development of infant self-regulatory behavior (Dawson, Panagiotides, Klinger, & Hill, 1992). There is also evidence to show that, in particular, orbital prefrontal areas (Figure 1.7) are critically and directly involved in attachment functions (Steklis & Kling, 1985). This cortical area plays an essential role in the processing of social signals and in the pleasurable qualities of social interaction. Attachment experiences (face-to-face transactions between caregiver and infant) directly influence the imprinting or circuit wiring of this system.

The orbital frontal cortex (so called because of its relation to the orbit of the eye; Figure 1.8) is "hidden" in the ventral and medial surfaces of the prefrontal lobe (Figures 1.9 and 1.10) and acts as a "convergence zone" where cortex and subcortex meet (Figures 1.10 and 1.11). It sits at the hierarchical apex of the limbic system, the brain system responsible for the rewarding-excitatory and aversive-inhibitory aspects of emotion (Figure 1.12). This "limbic cortex" also acts as a major control center over the sympathetic and parasympathetic

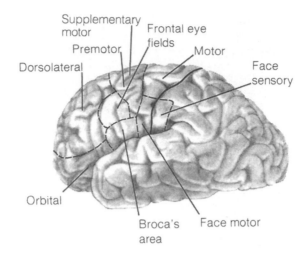

FIGURE 1.7. Approximate boundaries of functional zones of the human cerebral cortex, showing the dorsolateral and orbital prefrontal areas. (From Kolb & Whishaw, 1996)

branches of the autonomic nervous system (ANS), and thereby regulates drive and drive-restraint. Most significantly, in the cortex the orbitofrontal region is uniquely involved in social and emotional behaviors and in the homeostatic regulation of body and motivational states (Schore, 1994).

Due to its unique connections, at the orbitofrontal level cortically processed information concerning the external environment (e.g., visual and auditory stimuli emanating from the emotional face of the object) is integrated with subcortically processed information regarding the internal visceral environment (e.g., concurrent changes in the emotional or bodily self-state). Neuroanatomists describe that the function of this structure is involved with the internal state of the organism and is "closely tied to the synthesis of object-emotion relationships in a behavioral context" (Pandya & Yeterian, 1990, p. 89). Orbitofrontal areas subserve memory (Stuss et al., 1982) and cognitive-emotional interactions (Barbas, 1995), and are specialized to participate in the encoding of high-level, psychological representations of other individuals (Brothers & Ring, 1992). This system thus contains the operational capacity to generate an internalized object relation—that is a self-representation, an object representation, and a linking affect state (Kernberg, 1976)—or a representation of interactions that have been generalized (RIGS; Stern, 1985).

The orbital prefrontal region is especially expanded in the right cortex (Falk et al., 1990), the hemisphere that is dominant for selectively attending to facial expressions. Because the early maturing and "primitive" right cortical hemisphere (more than the left), contains extensive reciprocal connections with limbic and subcortical regions, it is dominant for the processing, expression, and

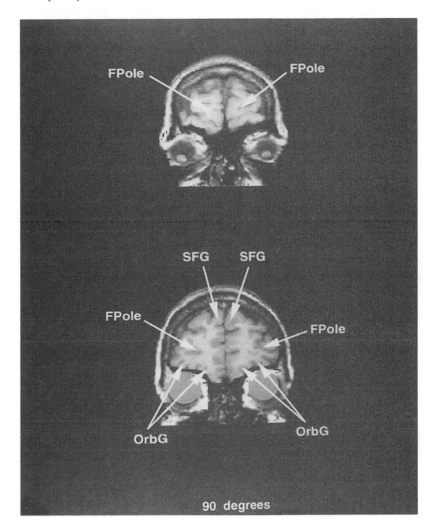

FIGURE 1.8. Computerized reconstruction of magnetic resonance (MR) imaging of a coronal section of the human brain. Notice orbital gyri. (From H. Damasio, 1995)

regulation of emotional information (Joseph, 1988). This hemisphere mediates pleasure and pain (an essential concern of Freud's ideas about affect) and the intrinsically more biologically primitive emotions that serve fundamental motivational and social communication functions. These primary emotions are nonverbal affects that are spontaneously expressed on the face (Buck, 1993). They appear early in development, are expressed in universally recognizable configurations of facial movements, are correlated with differentiable autonomic activity, and arise quickly and "automatically." Autonomic nervous system (ANS)

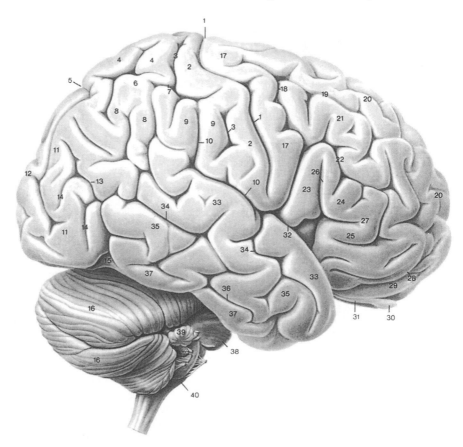

FIGURE 1.9. Lateral view of the human right hemisphere. Note the position of the orbital sulci (28) and gyri (29) in the frontal undersurface. (From Nieuwenhuys, Voogd, & van Huijzen, 1981)

control occurs quite rapidly—it begins within under 1 second and reaches full development in 5 to 30 seconds. Automatic emotional processes are thus involuntary, effortless, and operate outside conscious awareness.

This prefrontal region comes to act in the capacity of an executive control function for the entire right cortex, the hemisphere that modulates affect, nonverbal communication, and unconscious processes. Early object relational experiences are not only registered in the deep unconscious, they influence the development of the psychic systems that process unconscious information for the rest of the lifespan. In this manner, the child's first relationship, the one with the mother, acts as a template for the imprinting of circuits in the child's emotion-processing right brain, thereby permanently shaping the individual's adaptive or maladaptive capacities to enter into all later emotional relationships.

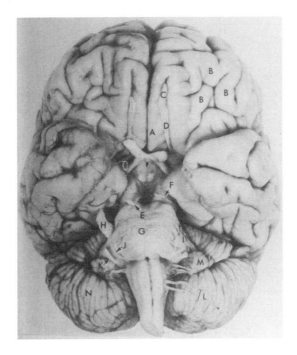

FIGURE 1.10. Photograph of the base of the human brain showing orbital gyri and sulci at sites labeled B. (From Watson, 1977)

Most intriguingly, the activity of this "nondominant" hemisphere, and not the later-maturing "dominant" verbal-linguistic left, is instrumental to the capacity of empathic cognition and the perception of the emotional states of other human beings (Voeller, 1986). The right brain plays a superior role in the control of vital functions supporting survival and enabling the organism to cope actively and passively with stress and external challenge. Indeed, the right brain is thought to contain the essential elements of the self system (Mesulam & Geschwind, 1978; Schore, 1994).

The right hemisphere contains an affective-configurational representational system, one that encodes self-and-object images unique from the lexical-semantic mode of the left (Watt, 1990). According to Hofer (1984b), internal representations of external human interpersonal relationships serve an important intrapsychic role as "biological regulators" that control physiological processes. These internal representations that contain information about state transitions (Freyd, 1987) enable the child to self-regulate functions that previously required the caregiver's external regulation. There is agreement that the encoding of strategies of affect regulation is a primary function of internal working models of attachment (Kobak & Sceery, 1988) and that security of attachment fundamentally relates to a physiological coding that homeostatic disruptions will be set right (Pipp & Harmon, 1987). Wilson and colleagues

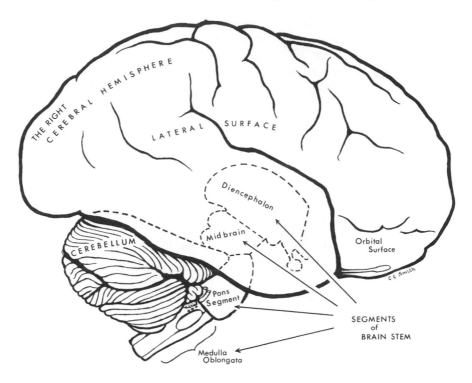

FIGURE 1.11. Relationships of brain stem structures to the orbital surface of the right hemisphere. (From Smith, 1981)

(1990) concluded that the experience of being with a self-regulating other is incorporated into an interactive representation. Of particular importance is the emergent capacity to access the complex symbolic representations that mediate evocative memory, because this allows for self-comforting during and subsequent to interactive stress (Fraiberg, 1969).

Regulated and unregulated affective experiences with caregivers are thus imprinted and stored in early-forming procedural memory in the orbital prefrontal system and its cortical and subcortical connections as interactive representations. Current studies indicate that the development of parental representations and the development of self-representations occur in synchrony (Bornstein, 1993b), that internal representations develop epigenetically through successive developmental stages (Blatt, Quinlan, & Chevron, 1990), and that developmental gradations of representational capacity have important implications for affective development (Trad, 1986). It relevant to note that the infant's memory representation includes not only details of the learning cues of events in the external environment, but also of reactions in his/her internal state to changes in the external environment.

The orbitofrontal system, which Goleman (1995) called "the thinking part of the emotional brain," plays a major role in the internal state of the organism (Mega & Cummings, 1994), the temporal organization of behavior (Fuster, 1985), and the appraisal (Pribram, 1987) and adjustment or correction of emotional responses (Rolls, 1986), that is, affect regulation. In fact, it is one of the few brain regions that is "privy to signals about virtually any activity taking place in our beings' mind or body at any given time" (Damasio, 1994, p. 181). It acts as a recovery mechanism that efficiently monitors and autoregulates the duration, frequency, and intensity of not only positive but also negative affect states. This allows for a self-comforting capacity that can modulate distressing psychobiological states and reestablish positively toned states. The essential activity of this psychic system is thus the adaptive switching of internal bodily states in response to changes in the external environment that are appraised to be personally meaningful. This emergent function, in turn, enables the individual to recover from disruptions of state and to integrate a sense of self across transitions of state, thereby allowing for a continuity of experience in various environmental contexts. These capacities are critical to the emergence, at 18 months, of a self-system that is both stable *and* adaptable, a working definition of a dynamic system (Lewis, 1995).

Infant observers report the emergence, at 18 months, of a "reflective self" that can take into account one's own and others' mental states, an achievement that is an essential step in emotional development (Fonagy, Steele, Steele, Moran, & Higgitt, 1991). In the course of the second year the infant acquires

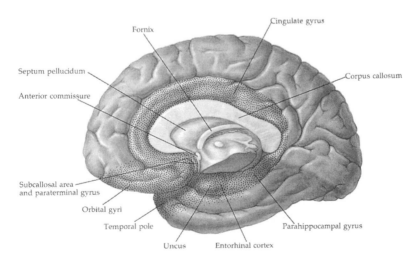

FIGURE 1.12. Midsagittal view of the right cerebral hemisphere, with brain stem removed. The limbic association cortex is indicated by the dotted region. Note the orbital gyri. (From Martin, 1989)

the capacity to generate a "theory of mind" in which an individual imputes mental states to self and to others and predicts behavior on the basis of such states (Bretherton, McNew, & Beeghly, 1981). The orbital cortex matures in the middle of the second year, the end of Mahler's practicing period, a time when the average child has a vocabulary of 15 words. The core of the self is thus nonverbal and unconscious, and it lies in patterns of affect regulation.

IMPLICATIONS FOR
PSYCHOANALYTIC METAPSYCHOLOGY

The nature and dynamics of this regulatory system that critically participates in the adaptive functions of mediating between the external environment and the internal milieu and in balancing external reality with internal desires is relevant to the identification of psychoanalytic "psychic structure." Freud hypothesized in his *Project for a Scientific Psychology* (1895/1966) that excitation from sources within and outside of the individual might be regulated by processes essentially within the individual (Schore, 1997a). Hartmann (1939) proposed that development, in essence, represents a differentiation in which primitive regulatory factors are increasingly replaced or supplemented by more effective and adaptive regulatory factors. Decades later he, along with Loewenstein (Hartmann & Loewenstein, 1962), and then Schafer (1968), theorized that the transformation of external regulations into internal ones essentially defined the internalization process. In his last work, Kohut (1984) concluded that early self–self object relationships allow for the maternally influenced creation of structure involved in drive-regulating, integrative, and adaptive functions previously performed by the mother. Mahler and colleagues (1975) described a psychic structural system involved in the self-regulation of affect and therefore autonomous emotional functioning appears in the middle of the second year. And Settlage and his colleagues (1988) conceptualized development as a progression of stages in which emergent adaptive self-regulatory structures and functions enable qualitatively new interactions between the individual and his/her environment.

Furthermore, this drive-modulating system is identical to a controlling structure, described by Rapaport (1960) more than 40 years ago, that maintains constancy by delaying press for discharge of aroused drives. Holzman and Aronson wrote that Freud "might have had some interest in contemporary neuropsychological studies of the frontal lobes in providing the organic infrastructure for channeling drives" (1992, p. 72). In his book, *Descartes' Error*, Damasio, a neurological researcher, argued that emotions are "a powerful manifestation of drives and instincts," and emphasized their motivational role: "In general, drives and instincts operate either by generating a particular behavior directly or by inducing physiological states that lead individuals to behavior in a particular way" (1994, p. 115). Psychobiological and neurobiological studies of emotion thus strongly indicate that the concept of drive, a phenomenon at the frontier between the psychic and somatic, must be reintroduced as a central construct of psychoanalytic theory.

The essential role of the orbitofrontal cortex in emotional-cognitive processes is now being explored by brain-imaging techniques that allow us to image function as well as anatomy, to literally visualize "images of mind" and transient subjective states. For example, a positron emission tomography (PET) study demonstrated that when normal subjects silently fantasize dysphoric affect-laden images of object loss (e.g., imagining the death of a loved one), increased blood flow and activation is recorded in the orbital prefrontal areas specifically (Pardo et al., 1993). In other words, we now can operationalize an online, real-time representation of an internal object relation. Interestingly, the PET scans of females revealed orbitofrontal activity in both hemispheres, while males showed only unilateral activation, and more of the females than males experienced tearfulness during the imagery. An even more recent PET study also showed that women display significantly greater activity in this affect regulating structure than do men, especially in the right hemisphere (Andreasen et al., 1994). These data indicate gender differences in the wiring of the limbic system, and may relate to differences in empathic styles or capacities of processing nonverbal affect between the sexes. This may bear on the question of why nature has psychobiologically equipped women to be primary objects, and may be relevant to the "maternalization of psychoanalysis."

In another functional neuroimaging study of introspective and self-reflective capacities, when subjects were asked to relax and listen to words that specifically describe what goes on in the mind (mental state terms such as *wish*, *hope*, *imagine*, *desire*, *dream*, and *fantasy*), a specifically increased activation of the right orbitofrontal cortex occurred (Baron-Cohen et al., 1994). And in another PET study, Andreasen, Zametkin, Guo, Baldwin, and Cohen (1995) reported that during focused episodic memory (the recalling and relating of a personal experience to another), an increase of blood flow occurs in the orbitofrontal areas. Right frontal activity specifically occurs when the brain is actively retrieving this personal event from the past. Even more intriguingly, this same inferior frontal region is activated when the subject is told to allow the mind to "rest." In this condition of uncensored and silently unexpressed private thoughts, the individual's mental activity consists of loosely linked and freely wandering past recollections and future plans. The authors concluded that this orbitofrontal activity reflects "free association" that taps into primary process!

With regard to yet another aspect of primary process activity, Solms, whose work on the organization of dreaming is at the interface of neurology and psychoanalysis, has presented neurological data indicating that the control mechanism of dreaming is critically mediated by anterior limbic orbitofrontal structures. He concluded, "These regions are essential for affect regulation, impulse control, and reality testing; they act as a form of 'censorship'" (1994, p. 60–61). Normal activity in this brain system during sleep allows for the processing of information by symbolic representational mechanisms during dreaming, while failures in regulatory functioning caused by overwhelming experiences causes a breakdown in dreaming, disturbed sleep, and nightmares.

IMPLICATIONS FOR PSYCHOANALYTIC CONCEPTIONS OF PSYCHOPATHOLOGY

There is compelling evidence, from a number of separate disciplines, that all early-forming psychopathology constitutes disorders of attachment and manifests itself as failures of self and/or interactional regulation (Grotstein, 1986). According to Grotstein, the fundamental pathology of these patients, who frequently manifest some form of neurobiological impairment, traces back to a failure of "good-enough attachment and bonding." As a consequence of an inability to gain access to maternal modulation of their affective states, Grotstein found that patients experience a lifelong "inability to self-regulate, to receive, encode, and process the data of emotional experience they are subjected to" (1990, p. 157). Furthermore, it appears that the "lack of differentiation between self and other results because of the semipermeability of physiological regulation between infant and mother" (Pipp, 1993, p. 194).

Indeed, borderline personalities exhibit an inability to self-regulate and lack the capacity to form "stable" self- and object representations (Grotstein, 1987). Narcissistic personalities, although developmentally more advanced, also exhibit insecure attachments (Pistole, 1995) and manifest an impairment of self-esteem regulation and a disturbance in the representation of self in relationship to others (Auerbach, 1990). Such personalities never developmentally attain a psychic organization that can generate complex symbolic representations that contain information about transitioning out of stress-induced negative states. Instead, they frequently access pathological internal representations that encode a dysregulated self-in-interaction-with-a-misattuning-other.

I propose that the functional indicators of this adaptive limitation are specifically manifest in recovery deficits of internal reparative mechanisms. This psychopathology is manifest in a limited capacity to modulate the intensity and duration of affects, especially biologically primitive affects like shame, rage, excitement, elation, disgust, and panic-terror, and it may take the form of either under- or overregulation disturbances. Such deficits in coping with negative affects are most obvious under challenging conditions that call for behavioral flexibility and adaptive responses to socioemotional stress. This conceptualization fits well with recent models that emphasize that loss of ability to regulate the intensity of feelings is the most far-reaching effect of early trauma and neglect (van der Kolk & Fisler, 1994), and that this dysfunction is manifest in more intense and longer lasting emotional responses (Oatley & Jenkins, 1992). I suggest that these functional vulnerabilities reflect structural weaknesses and defects in the organization of the orbitofrontal cortex, the neurobiological regulatory structure that is centrally involved in the adjustment or correction of emotional responses.

For some time, psychoanalysis has speculated that developmental disorders reflect a defect in an internal psychic structure, but it has been unable to identify this structural system. I believe that the orbital prefrontolimbic system is this psychic structure, and further maintain that every type of early-forming disorder involves, to some extent, altered orbital prefrontal limbic function (Schore, 1996). Anatomical studies highlight the unique developmental plasticity of the prefrontal limbic cortex, and this property has been suggested to mediate its "preferential vulnerability" in psychiatric disorders (Barbas, 1995). Indeed, recent research (mostly brain-imaging studies) shows evidence for impaired orbitofrontal activity in such diverse severe psychopathologies as autism (Baron-Cohen, 1995), schizophrenia (Seidman et al., 1995), mania (Starkstein, Boston, & Robinson, 1988), unipolar depression (Mayberg, Lewis, Regenold, & Wagner, 1994), phobic states (Rauch et al., 1995), posttraumatic stress disorder (Semple et al., 1992), drug addiction (Volkow et al., 1991), alcoholism (Adams et al., 1995), and borderline (Goyer, Konicki, & Schulz, 1994) and psychopathic (Lapierre, Braun, & Hodgins, 1995) personality disorders.

IMPLICATIONS FOR PSYCHOANALYTIC CLINICAL THEORY

A theoreticial perspective centered in developmental psychoanalysis, psychobiology, and neurobiology emphasizes the salience of early affective phenomena, and the emergent paradigm created by this interdisciplinary integration also has significant implications for clinical models of psychoanalysis, whose focus of primary study has been described as "human emotional development and functioning" (Langs & Badalamenti, 1992). Indeed, "affect theory is increasingly recognized as the most likely candidate to bridge the gap between clinical theory and general theory in psychoanalysis" (Spezzano, 1993, p. 39). Krystal (1988) underscored the fundamental principle that the development and maturation of affects represents the key event in infancy. Knapp argued that "Optimal regulation is a goal of maturation, including therapeutic maturation. Dysregulation is a therapeutic target" (1992, p. 247) The psychotherapy of "developmental arrests" (Stolorow & Lachmann, 1980) is conceptualized as being directed toward the mobilization of fundamental modes of development (Emde, 1990) and the completion of interrupted developmental processes (Gedo, 1979).

In early preverbal development, the infant constructs internal working models of the attachment relationship with his/her caregivers, and these representations, permanently imprinted into maturing brain circuitries, determine the individual's characteristic approach to affect modulation for the rest of the lifespan. The restoring into consciousness and reassessment of these internalized working models, suggested by Bowlby (1988) to be the essential task of psychoanalytic psychotherapy, is identical to Kernberg's assertion that that unconscious, nonverbally communicated "units constituted by a self-representation, an object-representation, and an affect state linking them are the essential units of psychic structure relevant for psychoanalytic exploration" (1988b, p. 482). These interactive representations are stored in the right hemisphere that contains an affective-configurational representational system and is dominant for the processing of emotional information.

The direct relevance of developmental studies to the psychotherapeutic process derives from the commonality of interactive emotion-transacting mechanisms in the caregiver–infant relationship and in the therapist–patient relationship. The essence of development is contained in the concept of "reciprocal mutual influences" (Schore, 1996). Early preverbal maternal–infant emotional communications that occur before the maturation of the left hemisphere and the onset of verbal-linguistic capacities represent contingently responsive affective transactions between the right hemispheres of the members of the dyad. Yet, the "non-verbal, prerational stream of expression that binds the infant to its parent continues throughout life to be a primary medium of intuitively felt affective-relational communication between persons" (Orlinsky & Howard, 1986, p. 343). A young infant functions in a fundamentally unconscious way, and unconscious processes in an older child or adult can be traced back to the primitive functioning of the infant (Fischer & Pipp, 1984). Unconscious processes are, of course, most clearly revealed and expressed in transference-countertransference interactions that are characterized, according to Stolorow, Brandchaft, and Atwood (1987), by "mutual reciprocal influence." Freud's statement that "everyone possesses in his own unconscious an instrument with which he can interpret the utterances of the unconscious of other people" (1913/1958a, p. 320) and Racker's (1968, p. 137) discovery that "Every transference situation provokes a countertransference situation" clearly imply a transactional model of the psychotherapeutic relationship.

Eisenstein, Levy, and Marmor (1994) described the importance, frequency, and variety of nonverbal communications that take place between therapist and patient. These communications are expressed in tone of voice, facial expression, and body posture, outside the realm of awareness of both, yet transference and countertransference reactions occur in response to these cues. Indeed, the authors concluded that this nonverbal exchange represents a major factor in the therapeutic process. Demos, from the perspective of infant research, cautioned us that psychoanalysis "overvalues verbal and symbolic modes of representation and undervalues nonverbal and presymbolic modes. It places language in a privileged position as the only reliable source of information about the inner experience of another" (1992, p. 208). In a paper on the critical role of nonverbal components in the clinical psychoanalytic process, Jacobs stated that mastering the art of understanding nonverbal communication is "like learning to become an accomplished baby watcher" (1994, p. 748). Krystal (1988) noted that the "infantile nonverbal affect system" continues to operate throughout life. I conclude that a deeper understanding of the interactive affect transacting mechanisms of the nonverbal, unconscious transference-countertransference relationship represents the frontier of clinical psychoanalysis.

There is a growing consensus that despite the existence of a number of distinct theoretical perspectives in psychoanalysis, the clinical concepts of transference (Wallerstein, 1990) and countertransference (Gabbard, 1995) represent a common ground. The deeper elucidation of the mechanisms that underlie these core phenomena therefore becomes an important goal. In my 1994 book I presented multidisciplinary evidence to support the proposal that nonverbal transference-countertransference interactions that take place at preconscious-unconscious levels represent right hemisphere-to-right-hemisphere communications of fast-acting, automatic, regulated, and unregulated emotional states between patient and therapist. The orbitofrontal cortex—intimately involved with internal, bodily, and motivational states—plays a preeminent role in this interactive mechanism. In fact, studies show that it functionally mediates the capacity of empathizing (Mega & Cumming, 1994) and inferring the states of others (Baron-Cohen, 1995), and of reflecting on one's own internal emotional states, as well as others (Povinelli & Preuss, 1995). Furthermore, this cortical area is essentially involved in the control of "the allocation of attention to possible contents of consciousness" (Goldenberg et al., 1989). This system is expanded in the right cerebral cortex that is responsible for the manifestations of emotional states (Ross, 1984) and unconscious processes (Galin, 1974; Wall, 1990).

IMPLICATIONS FOR A PSYCHOANALYTIC MODEL OF PSYCHOTHERAPY

A model of treatment that integrates developmental and clinical perspectives generates heuristic hypotheses about the underlying dynamic mechanisms that are involved in the psychotherapeutic experience, especially those involved in the "primitive emotional disorders" that characterize the early-forming right hemispheric impairments of "preoedipal" developmental psychopathologies (see appendix for an outline of psychotherapy principles). Of special importance to the psychotherapy process are early-forming representations of a dysregulated-self-in-interaction-with-a-misattuning-other, since these become unconscious templates of emotional relationships that mediate psychopathology. Such representations are imprinted predominantly with painful primitive affect that the developmentally impaired personality can not intrapersonally nor interpersonally regulate. As a result of this limitation, certain forms of external and internal affect-inducing input are selectively and defensively excluded from conscious processing.

A body of clinical and experimental evidence indicates that all forms of psychopathology have concomitant symptoms of emotional dysregulation, and that defense mechanisms are, in essence, forms of emotional regulation strategies for avoiding, minimizing, or converting affects that are too difficult to tolerate (Cole, Michel, & O'Donnell, 1994). However, it is just these strategies of affect regulation and pathogenic schemas of dysregulation that must be recognized and addressed in the transference-countertransference matrix. Such "latent" "sequestered" schemas are, according to Slap and Slap-Shelton (1994), egocentric, analogical, and visual. They are stored in the visuospatial right hemisphere that contains an analogical representational system (Tucker, 1992) and a nonverbal processing mode that are unaccessible to the language centers in the left (Joseph, 1982). From this realm that stores split-off parts of the self also comes transference projections that are directed outward into the therapist.

The pathology of early-forming developmental disorders is most clearly revealed under conditions of interpersonal stress. Though early painful experiences are buried in deep layers of the unconscious, during stress their effects are felt on the surface, especially at the interface where the self interacts with other selves, selves who are potential sources of dysregulation. A prime example of this occurs during the sudden rupture of the therapeutic alliance that accompanies the negative therapeutic reaction, a regressive worsening of the patient's condition following what seems to be adequate therapeutic management. "When one speaks hopefully to them or expresses satisfaction with the progress of treatment, they show signs of discontent and their condition invariably becomes worse" (Freud, 1923/1961b, p. 39). I suggest that in actuality this represents the therapist's misattunement to the patient's current state.

How might we understand the rapid disorganizing events of this clinical phenomenon? It is now thought that critical "cues" generated by the therapist, which are absorbed and metabolized by the patient, generate the transference (Gill, 1982), an activation of existing units of internalized object relations (Kernberg, 1980). These cues resemble the parents' original toxic behavior at heightened affective moments of misattunement, and they are processed by the patient's right hemisphere, which is preferentially activated under stress conditions (Tucker, Roth, Arneson, & Buckingham, 1977). Of particular importance are visual and auditory cues that were perceived during early self-disorganizing episodes of shame-humiliation, a common element of borderline and narcissistic histories (Schore, 1991).

Facial indicators of transference processes (Krause & Lutolf, 1988) are quickly appraised from the therapist's face in movements occurring primarily in the regions around the eyes and from prosodic expressions from the mouth (Fridlund, 1991) by the patient's right cortical mechanisms involved in the perception of nonverbal expressions embedded in facial and prosodic stimuli (Blonder, Bower, & Heilman, 1991). Such input generates "a series of analogical comparisons between distortions by the therapist ('misalliance') and the empathic failures and distortions of parents" (Watt, 1986, p. 61). This instantly activates right brain-imprinted pathological internal object relations and "hot cognitions" (Greenberg & Saffran, 1984), which program the patient's "hot theory of mind" (Brothers, 1995) that constructs others' evaluative attitudes and meaningful intentions. These early interactive representations encode expectations of imminent dysregulation. As a result, the patient's brain suddenly shifts dominance from a mode of left hemispheric linear processing to right hemispheric nonlinear processing.

Indeed, the right hemisphere is involved in the memorial storage of emotional faces (Suberi & McKeever, 1977) and is activated during the recall of autobiographical (Cimino, Verfaellie, Bowers, & Heilman, 1991) and early childhood memories (Horowitz, 1983; Joseph, 1992). The current interactive stress—similar in form to a very early misattuned, dysregulating transaction—instantly ruptures the attachment bond between patient and therapist. This sudden shattering of the therapeutic alliance thus represents a reconstruction of what Lichtenberg (1989) called a "model scene," and it induces the entrance into consciousness of a chaotic state associated with early traumatic experiences that is stored in implicit (Siegel, 1995) procedural memory and usually protected by "infantile amnesia." But now, due to state-dependent recall (Bower, 1981), the patient is propelled into a bodily state that psychobiologically designates a "dreaded state of mind" (Horowitz, 1987), thereby triggering "splitting" (the instant evaporation of the positive and sudden intensification of the negative transference). This "malignant transference reaction" manifest in rapid emotional activation and instability, reflects hyperarousal- or hypoarousal-associated alterations of limbic regions (McKenna, 1994). As a result of the subsequent rapid escalation of intense negative affect, the self disorganizes, either explosively or implosively. Neurobiological studies show that the emergence of strong affect during psychotherapy is accompanied by increased right hemispheric activation (Hoffman & Goldstein, 1981).

It is important to remember that this affective state is transmitted within the dyad. The therapist's resonance with this right brain state, in turn, triggers "somatic countertransference" (Lewis, 1992), and these "somatic markers" (Damasio, 1994) may be physiological responses that receive (or block) the patient's distress-inducing projective identifications. Sander referred to a "mutuality of influence," "a thinking that is oriented as much around the way the patient's signals influence therapist state as around therapist on patient state" (1992, p. 583). This dialectical mechanism is especially prominent during stressful ruptures of the working alliance that occur during "enactments," defined as those "events occurring within the dyad that both parties experience as being the consequence of behavior in the other" (McLaughlin, 1991, p. 611). The rapid-onset, dynamic events of the "negative therapeutic reaction" are thus an overt manifestation of the interaction of the patient's covert deep unconscious transference patterns with the clinician's covert deep unconscious countertransference patterns.

The working-through process at this point is a dyadic venture of interactive repair (Tronick, 1989) and depends very much upon the therapist's ability to recognize and regulate the negative affect within him- or herself. Ellman (1991) pointed out that although the handling of negative affect and the negative transference is the most difficult part of treatment, the therapist's tolerance and containment of negative states is an important contributor to the creation of analytic trust. The clinician's participation in the disruption and repair process (Beebe & Lachmann, 1994) is dependent upon and limited by his/her capacity to tolerate and cope with the patient's negative state that he/she has (unconsciously) triggered. This coping capacity is reflected in an ability, under stress, to self-regulate (contain) the projected negative affect, and thereby act as an interactive regulator of the shared negative state. In doing so, the therapist resonates with the patient's internal state of arousal dysregulation, modulates it, communicates it back prosodically in a more regulated form, and then verbally labels his/her state experiences.

The essential step in this process is the therapist's ability, initially at a non-verbal level, to detect, recognize, monitor, and self-regulate the countertransferential stressful alterations in his/her bodily state that are evoked by the patient's transferential communication. In doing so, the therapist must engage in a "reparative withdrawal"—a self-regulating maneuver that allows continued access to a state in which a symbolizing process can take place, thereby enabling the therapist to create a parallel affective and imagistic scenario that resonates with the patient's (Freedman & Lavender, 1997). According to these authors, the presence or absence of the therapist's recognition of his/her countertransferential bodily signals and his/her capacity to autoregulate the disruption in state caused by the patient literally determines whether or not the countertransference is destructive or constructive, "symbolizing" or "desymbolizing."

Thus, the active involvement of both members of the dyad in the process of disruption and repair is absolutely necessary for the patient's learning that a previously self-disorganizing state can be regulated (rather than further dysregulated) by an external object. The patient can now, in the presence of a reparative object, transition out of a previously avoided stressful state into one in which he/she can associate the nonverbal affect state with verbal processing. Researchers have shown that "The ability to express oneself in words during states of high emotional arousal is an important achievement in self-regulation" (Dawson, 1994, p. 358). Wolf (1991) held that, as a result of a successful repair process, the mutual reciprocal empathic bond between patient and therapist becomes stronger and less vulnerable to repeated disruptions. And Gedo wrote that working through, "the difficult transitional process whereby reliance on former modes of behavioral regulation is gradually superseded by more effective adaptive measures," is accomplished by "the mastery of affective intensities" (1995b, p. 344).

Unconscious affect and its regulation thus become a primary goal of the psychotherapy of preoedipal dynamics, especially a focus on the recognition and identification of affects that were never developmentally interactively regulated nor internally represented. Therapeutic interventions are directed toward the elevation of emotions from a primitive presymbolic sensorimotor level of experience to a mature symbolic representational level, a functional advance that is mediated by an increased flexibility of the patient's emotional control structures. In long-term work, with the internalization of the therapist's regulatory functions, the patient becomes capable of accessing a self-reflective position that can appraise the significance and meanings of a variety of emotional states. As Bach pointed out, this developmental achievement is expressed in the emergence of a higher-level integrative capacity that allows "free access to affective memories of alternate states, a kind of suprerordinate reflective awareness that permits multiple perspectives on the self" (1985, p. 179).

These functional advances reflect alterations in internal structures. In the neuropsychiatric literature Mender wrote that "psychoanalytic recall, through a reacquaintance with the most primitive and undifferentiated sources of human potential, can rejuvenate our range of neurobiological options" (1994, p. 169). I suggest that the mobilization of fundamental modes of development that occurs in psychotherapy reflects the organization of structural alterations in limbic circuitries that neurobiologically mediate the emergence of adaptive capacites. In psychoanalytic writings, Basch (1988) asserted that psychotherapy can facilitate the alteration and reworking of the patterns in the patient's nervous system that govern how he/she processes socioemotional information. In fact, it is now thought that specifically cortical and sensorilimbic connections are reworked in long-term dynamic psychotherapy (McKenna, 1994).

In concordance with this model, Spezzano (1993) proposed that:

> The analytic relationship heals by drawing into itself those methods of processing and regulating affect relied on by the patient for psychological survival and then transforming them. The mechanism of these transformations is the regulation of affect in a better way within the analysis than it was previously managed by the patient and the subsequent modification of what, in the classical language of structural change, might be called the patient's unconscious affect-regulating structures. (pp. 215–216)

Watt (1986) was even more specific—he speculated that the connections of the right frontolimbic cortex (a neurobiological structure involved in the regulation of primitive affects) are specifically reorganized by the psychoanalytic experience. Most intriguingly, these hypotheses about the nature of the internal structural system that is altered in psychotherapy has been corroborated in a PET imaging study demonstrating that patients show significant changes in metabolic activity in the right orbitofrontal cortex and its subcortical connections as a result of successful psychological treatment (Schwartz Stoessel, Baxter, Martin, & Phelps, 1996).

These results are supported by a large body of studies in the neurosciences indicating that although the effects of environmental experiences develop more rapidly and extensively in the developing than the adult brain, the capacity for experience-dependent plastic changes in the nervous system remains throughout the lifespan and, indeed, experience is necessary for the full growth of brain and behavioral potential (Rosenzweig, 1996). In fact, there is evidence that the prefrontal limbic cortex, more than any other part of the cerebral cortex, retains the plastic capacities of early development. The orbitofrontal cortex, even in adulthood, continues to express anatomical and biochemical features observed in ontogeny, and this accounts for its great plasticity and involvement in learning, memory, and cognitive-emotional interactions (Barbas, 1995). Such findings suggest that this particular system, with its capacity for utilizing and directing the psychobiological expression of learning encoded within the limbic system (Rossi, 1993), is a critical site of the psychic structural changes that are a product of a long-term, growth-facilitating psychotherapeutic relationship.

1997

CHAPTER 2

Minds in the Making: Attachment, the Self-Organizing Brain, and Developmentally-Oriented Psychoanalytic Psychotherapy

I T IS AN HONOR TO BE INVITED to present the Seventh Annual John Bowlby Memorial Lecture. Indeed, this is a double privilege, in that it follows another honor from last year, when I was asked to write the Foreword to the reissue of Bowlby's groundbreaking volume, *Attachment* (Bowlby, 1969b). In that work I surveyed, from a perspective at the close of what has been called "the Decade of the Brain," his far-sighted proposals about the biological and neurological nature of attachment (Schore, 2000c). Indeed, in a number of contributions I am describing how a spectrum of psychological and biological disciplines have adopted his ideas as the dominant model of human development available to science (Schore, 2000a, 2000i, 2000j, 2001, 2000b, 2000c).

Each of these fields of scientific inquiry, when documenting the origins of the theory, points to Bowlby's integration of ethology (the study of behavioral biology) and psychoanalysis. In a contemporary description of *Attachment*, Ainsworth wrote, "In effect what Bowlby has attempted is to update psychoanalytic theory in the light of recent advances in biology" (Ainsworth, 1969, p. 998). I suggest that in the more than 3 decades since the publication of *Attachment*, although the connections between attachment theory and science have deepened, those between itself and psychoanalysis, especially clinical psychoanalysis, have not. This situation is currently improving, however, due to the contributions of developmental psychoanalytic and psychological attachment research that demonstrate the clinical relevance of the concepts of mental representations of internal working models and reflective functions. Experimental and clinical attachment researchers are now describing, in detail, these two fundamental characteristics of "minds in the making," the theme of this meeting.

It has sometimes been forgotten that attachment theory is a direct outgrowth of Freud's developmental perspective, not just a repudiation of some of his early speculations. Indeed, in the very first paragraph of *Attachment*, Bowlby began his work with specific reference to Freud's fundamental goal of understanding early development. In his opening passage, he contrasted Freud's methodology for generating developmental hypotheses—analyzing the dreams and symptoms of adult neurotic patients and the behavior of primitive peoples—to his own, and stated, "Although in his search for explanation [Freud] was in each case led to events of early childhood, he himself only rarely drew for his basic data on direct observation of children" (1969a, p. 3). Expanding this latter theme is the focus of the book, yet in the final chapter he returned to a summary of developmental psychoanalytic concepts with a chapter titled, "The Child's Tie to His Mother: A Review of the Psychoanalytic Literature."

In this lecture I want to present some recent interdisciplinary advances that are forging tighter links between the common goals of classical psychoanalysis and attachment theory. It may appear surprising that the new developments that are recoupling Freud and Bowlby come from neuroscience. Yet this information bears upon a shared interest of the two most important contributors to a theory of the development of the early mind, specifically, an interest in internal psychic structure and how it is influenced by early relational interactions.

At the very outset of his first chapter, Bowlby (1969b) quoted Freud's (1915/1957d) final paragraph of *Repression*: "We must select first one and then another point of view, and follow it up through the material as long as the application of it seems to yield results." In ongoing writings I am presenting, from a psychoneurobiological point of view, a specification of the structural systems of the developing unconscious in terms of recent brain research. This work on "the origin of the self" (a phrase I deliberately used to evoke an echo of Darwin's phylogenetic speculations on "the origin of species") attempts to document the ontogenetic evolution of the neurobiology of subjectivity and intersubjectivity, which I equate with specifically the experience-dependent self-organization of the early-developing right hemisphere. In a 1997 article in the *Journal of the American Psychoanalytic Association* and another in 1999 in *Neuro-Psychoanalysis*, I suggested that the structural development of the right hemisphere mediates the functional development of the unconscious mind. And this year, in *Attachment and Human Development*, I offer further evidence to demonstrate that the right hemisphere is the repository of Bowlby's unconscious internal working models of the attachment relationship (Henry, 1993; Schore, 1994, 2000a; Siegel, 1999).

Taking this even further, in the following I want to suggest that an integration of current findings in the neurobiological and developmental sciences can offer a deeper understanding of the origins and dynamic mechanisms of the system that represents the core of psychoanalysis, the system unconscious. Psychoanalysis has been called the scientific study of the unconscious mind (Brenner, 1980), clearly implying both that the unconscious is its definitional realm of study and that this realm is accessible to scientific analysis. This has been so from its very inception. Although Freud was well aware of Darwin's groundbreaking biological concepts, the major science that influenced his thinking was neurology (Schore, 1997a). Despite the fact that he failed to produce "a psychology which shall be a natural science" in the *Project for a Scientific Psychology* (1895/1966), Freud transplanted its germinal hypotheses concerning the regulatory structures and dynamics of the system unconscious in the seventh chapter of his masterwork, *The Interpretation of Dreams* (1900/1953b).

As you remember, Freud predicted that there would someday be a rapprochement between psychoanalysis and neurobiology. A number of current rapidly expanding trends indicate that this convergence with the other sciences is now underway. Indeed, in this last year we have seen the appearance of a new journal, *Neuro-Psychoanalysis*, with a dual editorial board composed of both psychoanalysts and neuroscientists. The first issue centers on Freud's theory of affect, and in that journal I (1999a) presented evidence from both domains of science, the study of the brain and the study of the mind, to argue that the early developing right brain (or, as Ornstein [1997] called it, "the right mind") is the neurobiological substrate of Freud's system unconscious. Freud, of course, deduced that the unconscious system appears very early in life, well before verbal conscious functions. A body of research now indicates that the right hemisphere is dominant in human infancy, and indeed, for the first 3 years of life (Chiron et al., 1997).

Freud (1916–1917/1961 & 1963) described the unconscious as "a special realm, with its own desires and modes of expression and peculiar mental mechanisms not elsewhere operative." Due to its central role in unconscious functions and primary process activities, psychoanalysis has been intrigued with the unique operations of the early developing right brain for the last quarter of a century. In the 1970s, Galin (1974), Hoppe (1977), Stone (1977), and McLaughlin (1978), stimulated by the split-brain studies of the time, began to link up psychoanalysis and neurobiology by positing that the right hemisphere is dominant for unconscious and the left for conscious processes.

The relevance of hemispheric specialization to psychoanalysis continued in the work of Miller (1991), Levin (1991), and particularly Watt (1990), who offered data to show that the right hemisphere contains an affective-configurational representational system, one that encodes self-and-object images, while the left utilizes a lexical-semantic mode. In fact, current neurobiological studies are revealing greater right than left hemispheric involvement in the *unconscious* processing of affect-evoking stimuli (Wexler, Warrenburg, Schwartz, & Janer, 1992). Most intriguingly, a neuroimaging study by Morris, Ohman, and Dolan (1998) demonstrated that unconscious processing of emotional stimuli is specifically associated with activation of the right and not left hemisphere, and the reporter in the journal *Science* described this finding as indicating that "the left side is involved with conscious response and the right with the unconscious mind" (Mlot, 1998, p. 1006).

In an updated description of the unconscious, Winson concluded, "Rather than being a cauldron of untamed passions and destructive wishes, I propose that the unconscious is a cohesive, continually active mental structure that takes note of life's experiences and reacts according to its scheme of interpretation" (1990, p. 96). Notice his use of the term *structure*. Although psychoanalysis has used this term to describe internal cognitive *processes* such as representations and defenses, and content such as conflicts and fantasies, I suggest that *structure* refers to those specific brain systems, particularly right-brain systems, that underlie these various mental functions. In other words, the internal psychic systems involved in processing information at levels beneath awareness, described by Freud in his topographic (1900/1953b) and structural (1923/1961b) models, can now be identified by neuroscience.

A common ground of psychoanalysis, neurobiology, and psychology is an emphasis on the centrality of early development. In 1913 Freud proclaimed, "From the very first, psychoanalysis was directed towards tracing developmental processes. It . . . was led . . . to construct a genetic psychology" (1913/1958c, pp. 182–183). Continuing this tradition, I would argue that the most significant psychoanalytic contributor to our understanding of developmental processes was, indeed, Bowlby (Schore, 2000a, 2000c). As mentioned earlier, in *Attachment* he applied then-current biology to a psychoanalytic understanding of infant–mother bonding, and in so doing offered his "Project," an attempt to produce *a natural science of developmental psychology*. This volume focused upon one of the major questions of science, specifically, how and why do certain early ontogenetic events have such an inordinate effect on everything that follows? Bowlby's scientifically informed curiosity about this question envisioned the center stage of human infancy, on which is played the first chapter of the human drama, to be a context in which a mother and her infant experience connections and disconnections of their vital emotional communications.

Because these communications are occurring in the period of the brain growth spurt that continues through the second year of life (Dobbing & Sands, 1973), attachment transactions mediate "the social construction of the human brain" (Eisenberg, 1995), specifically the social emotional brain that supports the unique operations of "the right mind." Attachment is thus inextricably linked to developmental neuroscience. Stern wrote, "Today it seems incredible that until Bowlby no one placed attachment at the center of human development" (2000, p. xiii). I suggest that the great advances in our knowledge of early development have been the engine that has transformed contemporary psychoanalysis, which according to Cooper is "anchored in its scientific base in developmental psychology and in the biology of attachment and affects" (1987, p. 83).

In 1920, Freud proclaimed that *"the unconscious is the infantile mental life"* (1920/1955; italics added). This fundamental tenet is directly relevant to the topic of today's Bowlby Memorial Conference, Minds in the Making, and suggests that what particularly interests us here are *unconscious minds in the mak-*

ing. We now know that an infant functions in a fundamentally unconscious way, and unconscious processes in an older child or adult can be traced back to the primitive functioning of the infant. Knowledge of how the maturation of the right brain, "the right mind," is directly influenced by the attachment relationship offers us a chance to more deeply understand not just the contents of the unconscious, but its origin, structure, and dynamics.

In *Affect Regulation and the Origin of the Self* (1994), I described a number of psychoneurobiological mechanisms by which attachment experiences specifically impact the experience-dependent maturation of the right hemisphere. In a continuation of this work, (Schore, 2000a), I offered an overview of Bowlby's classic volume and argued that attachment theory is fundamentally a regulatory theory. In the following talk I want to offer some ideas about the *psychobiological* regulatory events that mediate the attachment process, and the *psychoneurobiological* regulatory mechanisms by which "the right mind" organizes in infancy.

In the latter part of this lecture I will suggest that regulation theory describes the mechanisms by which the patient forms an attachment, that is, a working alliance with the therapist. This construct—created to define the subtle, interactive dynamic relationship between patient and therapist—is the most important conceptualization of the common elements of the different therapy modalities (Horvath & Greenberg, 1994; Safran & Muran, 2000). Bradley (2000) pointed out that all psychotherapies—psychodynamic, cognitive-behavioral, experiential, and interactional—show a similarity in promoting affect regulation.

In other words, this information about attachment, regulation, and the emotion-processing right brain is describing the "nonspecific factors" that are common to all forms of clinical treatment, factors particularly accessed in developmentally oriented psychoanalytic psychotherapy (Schore, 2000b). The major contribution of attachment theory to clinical models is thus its elucidation of the nonconscious dyadic affect transacting mechanisms that mediate a positive therapeutic working alliance between the patient and the empathic therapist. Complementing this, the neurobiological aspects of attachment theory allow for a deeper understanding of how an affect-focused developmentally oriented treatment can alter internal structure within the patient's brain/mind/body systems. (Throughout the following, the term *psychoanalyst* is equated with *psychoanalytically oriented psychotherapist*).

THE NEUROBIOLOGY OF A SECURE ATTACHMENT

The essential task of the first year of human life is the creation of a secure attachment bond between the infant and primary caregiver. Indeed, as soon as the child is born it uses its maturing sensory capacities, especially smell, taste, and touch, to interact with the social environment. But at 2 months a developmental milestone occurs in the infant brain; specifically, the onset of a critical period in the maturation of the occipital cortex (Yamada et al., 2000). This allows for a dramatic progression of its social and emotional capacities. In particular, the mother's emotionally expressive face is, by far, the most potent visual stimulus in the infant's environment, and the child's intense interest in her face, especially in her eyes, leads him/her to track it in space, and to engage in periods of intense mutual gaze. The infant's gaze, in turn, reliably evokes the mother's gaze, thereby acting as a potent interpersonal channel for the transmission of "reciprocal mutual influences." It has been observed that the pupil of the eye acts as a nonverbal communication device (Hess, 1975a) and that large pupils in the infant release caregiver behavior (Figure 2.1).

According to Feldman, Greenbaum, and Yirmiya (1999):

> Face-to-face interactions, emerging at approximately 2 months of age, are highly arousing, affect-laden, short interpersonal events that expose infants to high levels of cognitive and social information. To regulate the high positive arousal, mothers and infants . . . *synchronize* the intensity of their affective behavior within lags of split seconds." (p. 223, italics added)

In this process of *affect synchrony*, the intuitive (Papousek & Papousek, 1995) mother initially attunes to and resonates with the infant's resting state, but as this state is dynamically activated (or deactivated or hyperactivated) she fine tunes and corrects the intensity and duration of her affective stimulation in order to maintain the child's positive affect state. As a result of this moment-by-moment state matching, both partners increase together their degree of engagement. The fact that the coordination of responses is so rapid suggests the existence of a bond of unconscious communication.

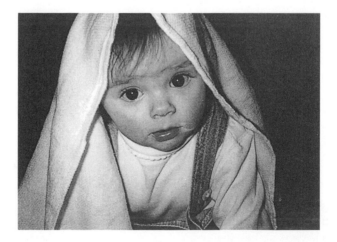

FIGURE 2.1. Notice the size of the pupils of this 9-month-old-infant, and the strong positive valence of the facial expression. (Photo courtesy of Suzy Schore)

In this interpersonal context of "contingent responsivity" the more the mother tunes her activity level to the infant during periods of social engagement, the more she allows him/her to recover quietly in periods of disengagement, and the more she contingently responds to his/her signals for reengagement, the more synchronized their interaction becomes. Lester, Hoffman, and Brazelton (1985, p. 24) stated that "*synchrony* develops as a consequence of each partner's learning the rhythmic structure of the other and modifying his or her behavior to fit that structure." The primary caregiver thus facilitates the infant's information processing by adjusting the mode, amount, variability, and timing of stimulation to its actual temperamental-physiological abilities. These mutually attuned *synchronized* interactions are fundamental to the ongoing affective development of the infant.

Reciprocal facial signalling thus represents an open channel of social communication, and this interactive matrix promotes the outward expression of internal affects in infants. In order to enter into this communication, the mother must be psychobiologically attuned not so much to the child's overt behavior as to the reflections of his/her internal state. In light of the fact that misattunements are a common developmental phenomena, she also must modulate nonoptimal high levels of stimulation that would trigger hyperarousal, or low levels that engender hypoarousal in the infant.

Most importantly, the arousal-regulating primary caregiver must participate in interactive repair to regulate interactively induced stress states in the infant. If attachment is interactive synchrony, stress is defined as an *asynchrony* in an interactional sequence, and, following this, a period of reestablished *synchrony* allows for stress recovery. In this reattunement pattern of "disruption and repair" the "good enough" caregiver who induces a stress response in her infant through a misattunement, self-corrects and in a timely fashion reinvokes her psychobiologically attuned regulation of the infant's negative affect state that she has triggered. The key to this is the caregiver's capacity to monitor and regulate her own affect, especially negative affect.

These regulatory processes are precursors of psychological attachment and its associated emotions. An essential attachment function is "to promote the synchrony or regulation of biological and behavioral systems on an organismic level" (Reite & Capitanio, 1985, p. 235). Indeed, psychobiological attunement, interactive resonance, and the mutual synchronization and entrainment of physiological rhythms are fundamental processes that mediates attachment bond formation, and attachment can be defined as the interactive regulation of biological synchronicity between organisms. (Schore, 1994, 2000a, 2000b, 2000h, 2001c)

To put this another way, in forming an attachment bond of somatically expressed emotional communications, the mother is synchronizing and resonating with the rhythms of the infant's dynamic internal states and then regulating the arousal level of these negative and positive states. Attachment is thus the dyadic (interactive) regulation of emotion (Sroufe, 1996). The baby becomes attached to the psychobiologically attuned regulating primary caregiver who not only minimizes negative affect but also maximizes opportunities for positive affect. Attachment is not just the reestablishment of security after a dysregulating experience and a stressful negative state; it is also the interactive amplification of positive affects, as in play states. Regulated interactions with a familiar, predictable primary caregiver create not only a sense of safety, but also a positively charged curiosity that fuels the burgeoning self's exploration of novel socioemotional and physical environments.

Furthermore, attachment is more than overt behavior, it is internal, "being built into the nervous system, in the course and as a result of the infant's experience of his transactions with the mother" (Ainsworth, 1967, p. 429). Next question: In this transfer of affect between mother and infant, what do we know of the processes whereby the primary object relations become internalized and transformed into psychic structure? The work of Trevarthen on maternal–infant protoconversations bears directly on this problem. He noted, "The intrinsic regulators of human brain growth in a child are specifically adapted to be coupled, by emotional communication, to the regulators of adult brains" (1990, p. 357). In these transactions, the *resonance* of the dyad ultimately permits the intercoordination of positive affective brain states. Trevarthen's work underscored the fundamental principle that the baby's brain is not only affected by these transactions, its growth requires brain–brain interaction and occurs in the context of an intimate positive affective relationship. These findings support Emde's assertion that "it is the emotional availability of the caregiver in intimacy which seems to be the most central growth-promoting feature of the early rearing experience" (1988, p. 32).

There is consensus that interactions with the environment during sensitive periods are necessary for the brain as a whole to mature. But we know that different regions of the brain mature at different times. Can we tell what specific parts of the growing brain are affected by these emotion transacting events? It has been observed that: "The emotional experience of the infant develops through the sounds, images, and pictures that constitute much of an infant's early learning experience, and are disproportionately stored or processed in the right hemisphere during the formative stages of brain ontogeny" (Semrud-Clikeman & Hynd, 1990, p. 198). A body of evidence shows that the right hemisphere matures before the left, a finding in line with Freud's assertion that primary process ontogenetically precedes secondary process functions.

The learning mechanism of attachment, imprinting, is defined as *synchrony* between sequential infant maternal stimuli and behavior (Petrovich & Gewirtz, 1985). I suggest that in these affectively *synchronized*, psychobiologically attuned face-to-face interactions the infant's right hemisphere, which is dominant for the infant's recognition of the maternal face and for the perception of arousal-inducing maternal facial affective expressions, visual emotional information, and the prosody of the mother's voice, is focusing her attention on and is therefore regulated by the output of the mother's right hemisphere, which is dominant for nonverbal communication, the processing and expression of facially and prosodically expressed emotional information, and the maternal capacity to comfort the infant. In support of this, Ryan and his colleagues, using electroencephalogram (EEG) and neuroimaging data, reported that "the positive emotional exchange resulting from autonomy-supportive parenting involves participation of right hemispheric cortical and subcortical systems that participate in global, tonic emotional modulation" (1997, p. 719).

There are clear experimental and theoretical indications that this emotional exchange also effects the development of the infant's consciousness (another factor primary to the theme here of "minds in the making"). Tronick and his colleagues described how microregulatory social-emotional processes of communication generate intersubjective states of consciousness in the infant–mother dyad. In such there is "a mutual mapping of (some of) the elements of each interactant's state of consciousness into each of their brains" (Tronick & Weinberg, 1997, p. 75). Tronick and his team (1998) argued that the infant's self-organizing system, when coupled with the mother's, allows for a brain organization that can be expanded into more coherent and complex states of consciousness. I suggest that Tronick was describing an expansion of what the neuroscientist Edelman (1989) called *primary consciousness*, which relates visceral and emotional information pertaining to the biological self to stored information processing pertaining to outside reality. Edelman lateralized primary consciousness to the right brain.

Thus, regulation theory suggests that *attachment is, in essence, the right-brain regulation of biological synchronicity between organisms.* Feldman and colleagues published a study entitled "Mother–Infant Affect Synchrony as an Antecedent of the Emergence of *Self-Control*" (1999, italics added). At the same time, Garavan, Ross, and Stein (1999) reported on a functional magnetic resonance imaging (fMRI) study, "Right Hemispheric Dominance of *Inhibitory Control*" (italics added). These data bear upon Bowlby's (1969a) assertion, 30 years ago, that attachment behavior is organized and regulated by means of a "*control system*" within the central nervous system.

MATURATION OF AN ORBITOFRONTAL REGULATORY SYSTEM

Bowlby hypothesized that the maturation of the attachment control system is open to influence by the particular environment in which development occurs. Current neurobiological studies show that the mature orbitofrontal cortex acts in "the highest level of *control* of behavior, especially in relation to emotion" (Price, Carmichael, & Drevets, 1996, p. 523) and plays "a particularly prominent role in the emotional modulation of experience" (Mesulam, 1998, p. 1035). The orbitofrontal regions are not functional at birth. Over the course of the first year, limbic circuitries emerge in a sequential progression, from amygdala to anterior cingulate to insula and finally to orbitofrontal (Schore,

1997b, 2000e, 2001b). And so, as a result of attachment experiences, this system enters a critical period of maturation in the last quarter of the first year, the same time that working models of attachment are first measured.

The orbital prefrontal cortex is positioned as a convergence zone where the cortex and subcortex meet. It is the only cortical structure with direct connections to the hypothalamus, the amygdala, and the reticular formation in the brain stem that regulates arousal, and through these connections it can modulate instinctual behavior and internal drives. But because it contains neurons that process face and voice information, this system is also capable of appraising changes in the external environment, especially the social, object-related environment. Due to its unique connections, at the orbitofrontal level cortically processed information concerning the *external* environment (e.g., visual and auditory stimuli emanating from the emotional face of the *object*) is integrated with subcortically processed information regarding the *internal* visceral environment (e.g., concurrent changes in the emotional or bodily *self* state). In this manner, the (right) orbitofrontal cortex and its connections function in the "integration of adaptive bodily responses with ongoing emotional and attentional states of the organism" (Critchley, Elliot, et al., 2000, p. 3033).

The orbitofrontal system is now described as "a nodal cortical region that is important in assembling and monitoring relevant past and current experiences, including their affective and social values" (Cavada, Company, Tejedor, Cruz-Rizzolo, & Reinoso-Suarez, 2000, p. 238). In a recent entire issue of the journal *Cerebral Cortex* on "The Mysterious Orbitofrontal Cortex," the editors concluded, "[T]he orbitofrontal cortex is involved in critical human functions, such as social adjustment and the control of mood, drive and responsibility, traits that are crucial in defining the 'personality' of an individual" (Cavada & Schultz, 2000, p. 205).

This frontolimbic cortex is situated at the hierarchical apex of an "anterior limbic prefrontal network" interconnecting the orbital and medial prefrontal cortex with the temporal pole, cingulate, and amygdala. This cortical-subcortical limbic network is involved in "affective responses to events and in the mnemonic processing and storage of these responses" (Carmichael & Price, 1995, p. 639). The limbic system is thought to be centrally implicated in the implicit processing of facial expressions without conscious awareness (Critchley, Daly, et al., 2000), in the capacity "to adapt to a rapidly changing environment," and in "the organization of new learning" (Mesulam, 1998, p. 1028). Current findings thus support Bowlby's (1969a) and Anders and Zeanah's (1984) speculation that the limbic system is the site of developmental changes associated with the rise of attachment behaviors. Indeed, it is held that "The integrity of the orbitofrontal cortex," the highest level of the limbic system, "is necessary for acquiring very specific forms of knowledge for regulating interpersonal and social behavior" (Dolan, 1999, p. 928).

The orbitofrontal system, the "Senior Executive" of the social-emotional brain, is especially expanded in the right cortex (Falk et al., 1990), and in its

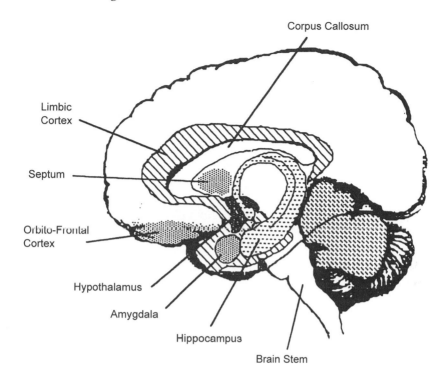

FIGURE 2.2. Limbic structures of the right hemisphere, lateral view. Cingulate is labeled limbic cortex. (From Trevarthen, Aitken, Papoudia, & Robarts, 1998)

role as an executive of limbic arousal it comes to act in the capacity of an executive control function for the entire right brain. This hemisphere, which is dominant for unconscious processes, performs, on a moment-to-moment basis, a "valence tagging" function, in which perceptions receive a positive or negative affective charge, in accord, as Freud speculated, with a calibration of degrees of pleasure-unpleasure. Recent studies have shown that the right hemisphere is faster than the left in performing valence-dependent, automatic, preattentive appraisals of emotional facial expressions (Pizzagalli, Regard, & Lehmann, 1999). It also contains a "nonverbal affect lexicon," a vocabulary for nonverbal affective signals such as facial expressions, gestures, and vocal tone or prosody (Bowers, Bauer, & Heilman, 1993; Snow, 2000), a finding directly relevant to Bowlby's (1969a, p. 120) speculation that in intimate settings human feelings are detected through "facial expressions, posture, tone of voice, physiological changes, tempo of movement, and incipient action."

The right hemisphere is, more so than the left, deeply connected into not only the limbic system but also both the sympathetic and parasympathetic branches of the autonomic nervous system (ANS) that are responsible for the

somatic expressions of all emotional states. For this reason, the right hemisphere is dominant for a sense of corporeal and emotional self (Devinsky, 2000;
Schore, 1994). Indeed, the representation of visceral and somatic states and the
processing of "self-related material" (Keenan et al., 1999) are under primary
control of the "nondominant" hemisphere. The ANS has been called the "physiological bottom of the mind" (Jackson, 1931).

The connections of the highest centers of the limbic system into the hypothalamus (the head ganglion of the ANS and anatomical locus of drive centers)
supports Freud's idea about the central role of drive in the system unconscious.
The fact that the right hemisphere contains "the most comprehensive and integrated map of the body state available to the brain" (Damasio, 1994, p. 66)
indicates that Freud's (1915/1957a) definition of "drive" as "the psychical representative of the stimuli originating from the organism and reaching the mind"
may be more properly characterized as reaching the "right mind" (Ornstein,
1997). It may also elucidate Freud's remark to Groddeck: "The unconscious is
the proper mediator between the somatic and the mental, perhaps the long-
sought 'missing link'" (Groddeck, 1977, p. 38).

For.the rest of the lifespan, the right brain plays a superior role in the regulation of fundamental physiological and endocrinological functions whose primary control centers are located in subcortical regions of the brain. Because
the hypothalamo-pituitary-adrenocortical axis and the sympathetic-adrenomed-
ullary axis are both under the main control of the right cerebral cortex, this
hemisphere contains "a unique response system preparing the organism to deal
efficiently with external challenges" (Wittling, 1997, p. 55), and thus its adaptive functions mediate the human stress response. It therefore is centrally involved in the vital functions that support survival and enable the organism to
cope actively and passively with stress (Sullivan & Gratton, 1999; Schore,
2001b). In support of Bowlby's speculation that the infant's "capacity to cope
with stress" is correlated with certain maternal behaviors (1969a, p. 344), the
attachment relationship directly shapes the maturation of the infant's right-
brain stress-coping systems that act at levels beneath awareness.

The right hemisphere contributes to the development of reciprocal interactions within the mother–infant regulatory system and mediates the capacity for
biological synchronicity, the regulatory mechanism of attachment. Due to its
role in regulating biological synchronicity between organisms, the activity of
this hemisphere is instrumental to the empathic perception of the emotional
states of other human beings (Schore, 1994, 1996, 1997c, 1998a, 1998b, 1998d,
1998g, 2002b). According to Adolphs and colleagues, "Recognizing emotions
from visually presented facial expressions requires right somatosensory cortices"
and in this manner "we recognize another individual's emotional state by internally generating somatosensory representations that simulate how the individual would feel when displaying a certain facial expression" (2000, p. 2683).
The interactive regulation of right brain attachment biology is thus the substrate
of empathy.

The right brain stores an internal working model of the attachment relationship that encodes strategies of affect regulation that maintain basic regulation and positive affect even in the face of environmental challenge (Schore, 1994). Because the right hemisphere is centrally involved in unconscious processes and in "implicit learning" (Hugdahl, 1995), this unconscious model is stored in right-cerebral implicit-procedural memory. Neuropsychological studies now also reveal that the right hemisphere, "the right mind," and not the later forming verbal-linguistic left, is the substrate of affectively laden autobiographical memory (Fink et al., 1996).

Psychobiological models refer to representations of the infant's affective dialogue with the mother that can be accessed to regulate its affective state (Polan & Hofer, 1999). The orbitofrontal area is particularly involved in situations in which internally generated affective representations play a critical role (Zald & Kim, 1996). Because this system is responsible for "cognitive-emotional interactions" (Barbas, 1995), it generates internal working models. These mental representations, according to Main, Kaplan, and Cassidy (1985), contain cognitive as well as affective components and act to guide appraisals of experience. Recent findings—that the orbitofrontal cortex generates nonconscious biases that guide behavior before conscious knowledge does (Bechara, Damasio, Tranel, & Damasio, 1997), codes the likely significance of future behavioral options (Dolan, 1999), and represents an important site of contact between emotional information and mechanisms of action selection (Rolls, 1996)—are consonant with Bowlby's (1981) assertion that unconscious internal working models are used as guides for future action.

According to Fonagy and Target (1997), an important outcome of a secure attachment is a reflective function, a mental operation that enables the perception of another's state. Brothers (1995, 1997) described a limbic circuit of orbitofrontal cortex, anterior cingulate gyrus, amygdala, and temporal pole that functions as a social "editor" that is "specialized for processing others' social intentions" by appraising "significant gestures and expressions" (Brothers, 1997, p. 27) and "encourages the rest of the brain to report on features of the social environment" (p. 15). The editor acts as a unitary system "specialized for responding to social signals of all kinds, a system that would ultimately construct representations of the mind" (p. 27). Neuropsychological studies have indicated that the orbitofrontal cortex is "particularly involved in theory of mind tasks with an affective component" (Stone, Baron-Cohen, & Knight, 1998, p. 651) and in empathy (Eslinger, 1998).

As previously mentioned, the orbitofrontal control system plays an essential role in the regulation of emotion. This frontolimbic system provides a high-level coding that flexibly coordinates exteroceptive and interoceptive domains and functions to correct responses as social conditions change; processes feedback information; and thereby monitors, adjusts, and corrects emotional responses and modulates the motivational control of goal-directed behavior. It thus acts as a recovery mechanism that efficiently monitors and regulates the duration, frequency, and intensity of not only positive but negative affect states. Damasio has emphasized that developmental neurological damage of this system in the first 2 years leads to abnormal development of social and moral behaviors (Anderson, Bechara, Damasio, Tranel, & Damasio, 1999).

The orbital cortex matures in the middle of the second year, a time when the average child has a productive vocabulary of less than 70 words. The core of the self is thus nonverbal and unconscious, and it lies in patterns of affect regulation. This structural development allows for an internal sense of security and resilience that comes from the intuitive knowledge that one can regulate the flows and shifts of one's bodily based emotional states either by one's own coping capacities or within a relationship with caring others. In developmental neurobiological studies, Ryan, Kuhl, and Ceci (1997) concluded that the operation of the right prefrontal cortex is integral to autonomous regulation, and that the activation of this system facilitates increases in positive affect in response to optimally challenging or personally meaningful situations, or decreases in negative affect in response to stressful events. Confirming earlier proposals for a central role of the right orbitofrontal areas in essential self-functions (Schore, 1994, 1996), current neuroimaging studies now demonstrate that the processing of self occurs within the right prefrontal cortices (Keenan et al., 2000), and that the self-concept is represented in right frontal areas (Craik et al., 1999).

The functioning of the "self-correcting" orbitofrontal system is central to self-regulation, the ability to flexibly regulate emotional states through interactions with other humans (interactive regulation in interconnected contexts via a two-person psychology) and without other humans (autoregulation in autonomous contexts via a one-person psychology). The adaptive capacity to shift between these dual regulatory modes, depending upon the social context, emerges out of a history of secure attachment interactions of a maturing biological organism and an early attuned social environment. The essential aspect of this function is highlighted by Westen (1997, p. 542) who asserted that "The attempt to regulate affect—to minimize unpleasant feelings and to maximize pleasant ones—is the driving force in human motivation."

THE RIGHT HEMISPHERE, ATTACHMENT THEORY, AND THE EMPATHIC RECEPTION OF UNCONSCIOUS EMOTIONAL COMMUNICATIONS

Earlier I described an optimal developmental scenario, one that facilitates the experience-dependent growth of an efficient regulatory system in the right hemisphere that supports functions associated with a secure attachment. On the other hand, growth-inhibiting environments negatively impact the ontogeny of self-regulatory prefrontal systems and generate attachment disorders, and such early disturbances of personality formation are mechanisms for the transmission of psychopathology. Recall Bowlby's well-known prediction that "In the fields of etiology and psychopathology [attachment theory] can be used to frame specific hypotheses which relate different family experiences to different forms of psychiatric disorder and also, possibly, to the neurophysiological changes that accompany them" (1978). Very recent neuropsychiatric research demonstrates that reduced volume of prefrontal areas serves as an "endophenotypic marker of disposition to psychopathology" (Matsui, Gur, Turetsky, Yan, & Gur, 2000, p. 155).

In a number of works I have provided clinical and neurobiological evidence to show that various forms of attachment pathologies specifically represent inefficient patterns of organization of the right brain, especially the right orbitofrontal areas (Schore, 1994, 1996, 1997b; see 2001c for a theory of trauma). Yet all share a common deficit: Due to the impaired development of the right-cortical preconscious system that decodes emotional stimuli by actual felt emotional responses to stimuli, individuals with poor attachment histories display empathy disorders, the limited capacity to perceive the emotional states of others. An inability to read facial expressions leads to a misattribution of emotional states and a misinterpretation of the intentions of others. Thus, there are impairments in the processing of socioemotional information.

In addition to this deficit in social cognition, the deficit in self-regulation is manifest in a limited capacity to modulate the intensity and duration of affects, especially biologically primitive affects like shame, rage, excitement, elation, disgust, panic-terror, and hopelessness-despair. Under stress such individuals experience not discrete and differentiated affects, but diffuse, undifferentiated, chaotic states accompanied by overwhelming somatic and visceral sensations. The poor capacity for what Fonagy and Target (1997) called "mentalization" leads to a restricted ability to reflect upon one's emotional states. Right-cortical dysfunction is specifically associated with alterations in body perception and disintegration of self-representation (Weinberg, 2000). Solms also described a mechanism by which disorganization of a damaged or developmentally deficient right hemisphere is associated with a "collapse of internalized representations of the external world" in which "the patient regresses from whole to part object relationships" (1996, p. 347), a hallmark of early forming personality disorders.

There is consensus that the psychotherapy of these "developmental arrests" is directed toward the mobilization of fundamental modes of development (Emde, 1990) and the completion of interrupted developmental processes (Gedo, 1979). This development is specifically emotional development. Recall Winnicott's dictum that the therapist must understand, at an intuitive level, specifically the emotional history of the patient: "In order to use the mutual experience one must have *in one's bones* a theory of the emotional development of the child and the relationship of the child to the environmental factors" (1971b, p. 3; italics added).

With patients, especially those manifesting early-forming attachment pathologies and therefore developmental disorders of self-regulation, the psychotherapeutic interaction functions as an attachment relationship. Recent models suggest that affect dysregulation is a fundamental mechanism of all psychiatric disorders (Taylor, Bagby, & Parker, 1997), that all psychotherapies show a similarity in promoting affect regulation (Bradley, 2000), and that the goal of attachment-focused psychotherapy is the mutual regulation of affective homeostasis and the restructuring of interactive representations encoded in implicit-procedural memory (Amini et al., 1996) (see appendix for an outline of psychotherapy principles).

In 1913, Freud proclaimed, "It remains the first aim of treatment to *attach* him [the patient] to it [the process of analysis] and to the person of the doctor" (Freud, 1913/1958a, p. 139). What can current ideas about attachment as the dyadic regulation of emotion and research on the right brain tell us about this process? The direct relevance of developmental attachment studies to the psychotherapeutic process derives from the commonality of interactive right-brain-to-right-brain emotion-transacting mechanisms in the caregiver–infant attachment relationship and in the clinician–patient therapeutic relationship (Schore, 1994, 1997c, 1998d, 1999h, 2002b, 2002e). A number of authors have pointed out the direct parallels between the clinical attributes of an effective therapist and the parental characteristics of the psychobiologically attuned intuitive caregiver of a securely attached child (e.g., Dozier, Cue, & Barnett, 1994; Holmes, 1993a; Sable, 2000; Schore, 1994).

Embedded in Freud's description of the aim of the treatment is the centrality of the concept of attachment to the operational definition of the therapeutic alliance. For a working alliance to be created, the therapist must be experienced as being in a state of vitalizing attunement to the patient; that is, the crescendos and decrescendos of the therapist's affective state must be in *resonance* with similar states of crescendos and decrescendos of the patient (Schore, 1994, 1997c). Studies of empathic processes between the "intuitive" attuned mother and her infant demonstrate that this affective *synchrony* is entirely nonverbal and that resonance is not so much with his mental (cognitive) states as with his psychobiological (affective-bodily) states. Similarly, the intuitive empathic therapist psychobiologically attunes to and resonates with the patient's shifting affective state, thereby co-creating with the patient a context in which the clinician can act as a regulator of the patient's physiology (Amini et al., 1996; Schore, 1994, 1997c).

The right-cortical hemisphere, which is centrally involved in attachment functions, is dominant for the perception of the emotional states of others, by a right-posterior-cortical mechanism involved in the perception of nonverbal expressions embedded in facial and prosodic stimuli (Schore, 1994, 1999a). It is also dominant for "*subjective* emotional experiences" (Wittling & Roschmann, 1993; italics added) and for *the detection of subjective objects* (Atchley & Atchley, 1998; italics added). The *interactive* "transfer of affect" between the right brains of the members of the mother–infant and therapeutic dyads is thus best described as *intersubjectivity*. So, what can current developmental neuropsychoanalysis tell us about psychotherapeutic intersubjectivity?

The right brain is centrally involved in unconscious activities, and just as the left brain communicates its states to other left brains via conscious linguistic behaviors, so the right nonverbally communicates its unconscious states to other right brains *that are tuned to receive these communications*. Freud asserted that "it is a very remarkable thing that the Ucs. of one human being can react upon that of another, *without passing through the Cs*" (1915/1957e, p. 194; italics added). He also proposed that the therapist should "turn his own unconscious like a receptive organ towards the transmitting unconscious of the patient . . . so the doctor's unconscious is able . . . to reconstruct [the patient's] unconscious" (1912/1958b, p. 115). He called the state of receptive readiness "evenly suspended attention." Bion (1962b) referred to "reverie" or "dream state alpha," clearly implying a right-brain state. Indeed, Marcus wrote, "The analyst, by means of reverie and intuition, listens with the right brain directly to the analysand's right brain" (1997, p. 238).

This same right brain-to-right-brain system was described in the neuropsychological literature by Buck (1994) as "spontaneous emotional communication":

> Spontaneous communication employs species-specific expressive displays in the sender that, given attention, activate emotional preattunements and are directly perceived by the receiver. . . . The "meaning" of the display is known directly by the receiver. . . . This spontaneous emotional communication constitutes a *conversation between limbic systems*. . . . It is a biologically-based communication system that involves individual organisms directly with one another: the individuals in spontaneous communication constitute literally a *biological unit*. (p. 266; italics added)

Buck (1994) emphasized the importance of specifically the right limbic system, and localized this biologically based spontaneous emotional communication system to the right hemisphere, in accord with other research that indicates a right lateralization of spontaneous gestures (Blonder, Burns, Bowers, Moore, & Heilman, 1995) and emotional communication (Blonder, Bowers, & Heilman, 1991). Earlier, I pointed to Bowlby's (1969a) speculation that human feelings are recognized through facial expressions, posture, tone of voice, physiological changes, tempo of movement, and incipient action.

Indeed, this right brain process lies at the heart of the nonverbal relational communications between patient and therapist. Lyons-Ruth (2000), a member of Stern's Study Group (1998a, 1998b), described the centrality of the "recognition process" that occurs in the "ordinary moments of change in psychoanalytic treatment": "[M]ost relational transactions rely heavily on a substrate of affective cues that give an evaluative valence or direction to each relational communication, and these communications are carried out at an implicit level of rapid cueing and response that occurs too rapidly for simultaneous verbal translation and conscious reflection" (Lyons-Ruth, 2000, pp. 91–92). Recall that the right hemisphere recognizes emotions from visually presented facial cues (Adolphs, Damasio, Tranel, Cooper, & Damasio, 2000), is specialized for "implicit learning" (Hugdahl, 1995), and performs rapid (80 msec) valence-dependent, automatic, appraisals of emotional facial expressions (Pizzagalli et al., 1999).

Furthermore, the right hemisphere uses an expansive attention mechanism that focuses on global features (while the left uses a restricted mode that focuses on local detail; Derryberry & Tucker, 1994), a characterization that fits with Freud's "evenly suspended attention." And, in contrast to the left-hemisphere's activation of "narrow semantic fields," the right hemisphere's "coarse semantic coding is useful for noting and integrating *distantly* related semantic information" (Beeman, 1998, p. 279), a function that allows for the process of free association. Bucci (1993) described free association as "following the tracks of nonverbal schemata," by loosening the hold of the verbal system on the associative process and giving the nonverbal mode the chance to drive the representational and expressive systems; that is, by shifting dominance from a left to right hemispheric state. In this manner, as Freud described, the clinician uses "the derivatives of the unconscious which are communicated to him to reconstruct that unconscious, which has determined the patient's free associations" (1912/1958b, p. 116).

I have suggested that if Freud was describing how the unconscious can act as "a receptive organ," Klein's concept of projective identification (Schore, 2000g, 2002b) attempts to model how an unconscious system acts as a "transmitter," and how these transmissions will then influence the receptive functions of another unconscious mind. Klein proposed that although this primitive process of communication between the unconscious of one person and the unconscious of another begins in early development, it continues throughout life. These moments of right-brain-to-right-brain communication represent an alignment of what Zeddies (2000) called the "nonlinguistic dimension" of the "relational unconscious" of both the therapist and the patient.

There is a growing consensus that despite the existence of a number of distinct theoretical perspectives in psychoanalysis, the clinical concepts of transference (Wallerstein, 1990) and countertransference (Gabbard, 1995) represent a common ground. In my ongoing work I propose that nonverbal transference-countertransference interactions that take place at preconscious-unconscious levels represent right-hemisphere-to-right-hemisphere communications of fast-acting, automatic, regulated, and dysregulated emotional states between patient and therapist. Transferential events clearly occur during moments of emotional arousal, and recent neurobiological studies indicate that "attention is altered during emotional arousal such that there is a heightened sensitivity to cues related to the current emotional state" (Lane, Chua, & Dolan 1999, p. 986).

Psychoanalytic research highlights the role of "fleeting facial expressions" that act as indicators of transference and countertransference processes (Andersen, Reznik, & Manzella, 1996; Krause & Lutolf, 1988; Schore, 1994, 1998d). These cues are nonconsciously appraised from movements occurring primarily in the regions around the eyes and from prosodic expressions from the mouth (Fridlund, 1991). Because the transference-countertransference is a reciprocal process, facially communicated "expressions of affect" that reflect changes in internal state are rapidly communicated and perceptually processed within the affectively synchronized therapeutic dialogue. This finding is relevant to the "reciprocal process," described by J. Munder Ross, in which the therapist has access to "the subliminal stimulation . . . that emanates from the patient" (1999, p. 95). In fact, these very same spontaneously communicated and nonconsciously perceived visual and auditory cues represent "the intrapsychic edge of the object world, the perceptual edge of the transference" (Smith, 1990, p. 225).

Only in a right hemispheric-dominant receptive state in which "a private self" is communicating with another "private self" can a self–self object system of spontaneous affective transference-countertransference communications be created. Fosshage (1994), a self-psychologist, noted that when the self object seeking dimension is in the foreground, the analyst must *resonate* at the deepest layers of his/her personality to be sufficiently available to the patient's developmental and self-regulatory needs. In other words, a state of resonance exists when the therapist's subjectivity is empathically attuned to the patient's inner state (one that may be unconscious to the patient), and this *resonance* then interactively amplifies, in both intensity and duration, the affective state *in both members of the dyad*. Sander (1992) stated that "moments of meeting" between patient and therapist occur when there are matched specificities between two systems in *resonance*, attuned to each other. Loewald (1986) described "resonances between the patient's and the analyst's unconscious."

Resonance phenomena are now thought to play one of the most important roles in brain organization and in central nervous system (CNS) regulatory processes (Schore, 2000e, 2002b). Although this principle is usually applied to the *synchronization* of processes within different parts of a whole brain, I have suggested that it also describes the resonance phenomena that occurs between the two right brains of the psychobiologically attuned mother–infant dyad. Thus, this also applies to the moments within the treatment process when two right brains, two emotion-processing unconscious "right minds" within the therapeutic dyad, are communicating and in *resonance*. Kantrowitz suggested that "it is in the realm of preconscious communication that the interwoveness of intrapsychic and interpersonal phenomena becomes apparent," and emphasized the importance of "attunement and *resonance*." (1999, p. 72; italics added).

This leads to the following proposals: Empathic *resonance* results from dyadic *attunement*, and its induces a *synchronization* of patterns of activation of both right hemispheres of the therapeutic dyad. *Misattunement* is triggered by a mismatch, and describes a context of stressful *desynchronization* between and destabilization within their right brains. Interactive *reattunement* induces a *resynchronization* of their right brain states. These brain-state shifts occur rapidly at levels beneath awareness. In other words, the two right-brain systems that process unconscious attachment-related information within the coconstructed intersubjective field of the patient and therapist are temporally coactivated and coupled, deactivated and uncoupled, or reactivated and recoupled. The unconscious minds and bodies of two self-systems are connected and coregulating, disconnected and autoregulating, or reconnected and again mutually regulating their activity. Recall self-regulation occurs in two modes, autoregulation, via the processes of a "one-person psychology," or interactive regulation, via a "two-person psychology."

IMPLICATIONS OF A PSYCHONEUROBIOLOGICAL MODEL OF EMOTIONAL DEVELOPMENT FOR CLINICAL PRACTICE

Even more specifically, during the treatment, the empathic therapist is consciously attending to the patient's verbalizations in order to *objectively* diagnose and rationalize the patient's dysregulating symptomatology. But he/she is also listening and interacting at another level, an experience-near *subjective* level, one that processes socioemotional information at levels beneath awareness. According to Kohut (1971), the empathically immersed clinician is attuned to the continuous flow and shifts in the patient's feelings and experiences. His/her "oscillating attentiveness" (Schwaber, 1995) is focused on "barely perceptible cues that signal a change in state" (Sander, 1992), in both patient and therapist, and on "nonverbal behaviors and shifts in affects" (McLaughlin, 1996). The attuned, intuitive clinician, from the first point of contact, is learning the nonverbal moment-to-moment rhythmic structures of the patient's internal states, and is relatively flexibly and fluidly modifying his/her own behavior to *synchronize* with that structure, thereby creating a context for the organization of the therapeutic alliance.

Freud (1915/1957a) asserted that the work of psychotherapy is always concerned with affect. Perhaps the most important clinical advances in this realm have come from those working in "the nonverbal realm of psychoanalysis" (e.g., Hollinger, 1999; Jacobs, 1994; Schore, 1994; Schwaber, 1998; Stern, Bruschweiler-Stern, et al., 1998; Stern, Sander, et al., 1998). The current emphasis in developmental studies on "heightened affective moments" and in emotion studies on "actual moments of experience" is mirrored in very recent psychotherapy research which is exploring "significant moments" in the therapeutic hour. And learning research on the importance of the implicit perception of affective information is echoed in the clinical principle, that in order for implicit affective learning to take place, the patient must have a vivid affective experience of the therapist (Amini et al., 1996).

Neurobiology is also delving into this theme—studies demonstrate the involvement of the right hemisphere in implicit learning (Hugdahl, 1995) and nonverbal processes (see Schore, 1994) and the orbitofrontal system in implicit processing (Rolls, 1996) and procedural (Rolls, 1996) or emotion-related learn-ing (Rolls, Hornak, Wade, & McGrath, 1994). Such structure-function relation-ships may elucidate how alterations in what Stern, Brucshweiler-Stern, and colleagues (1998) called nonverbal "implicit relational knowledge" are at the core of therapeutic change. In light of the central role of the limbic system in both attachment functions and in "the organization of new learning," the cor-rective emotional experience of psychotherapy, which can alter attachment pat-terns, must involve unconscious right-brain limbic learning.

But a dyadic-transactional perspective entails not only more closely examin-ing the patient's emotion dynamics, but also bringing the *therapist's emotions* and personality structure more into the picture. During a therapeutic affective encounter, the therapist is describing his/her psychobiological state of mind and the countertransference impressions made upon it by the patient's uncon-scious transference communications. These are expressed in clinical height-ened affective moments when the patient's internal working models are accessed, thereby revealing the patient's fundamental transferential modes and coping strategies of affect regulation (Schore, 1997c).

Gans described the "ever-deepening grasp of the patient's essence that can result from therapists' ongoing efforts to distill meaning from reactions caused or evoked in them by their patients" (1994, p. 122). These countertransferential reactions include the clinician's "visceral reactions to the patient's material" (Loewald, 1986, p. 278). Recall that attachment is fundamentally the right-brain regulation of biological synchronicity between organisms, and thus the empathic therapist's resonant synchronization to the patient's activated un-conscious internal working model triggers, in the clinician, the procedural pro-cessing of his/her autonomic visceral responses to the patient's nonverbal, nonconscious communications. In rupture and repair transactions (Beebe & Lachmann, 1994; Lewis, 2000; Schore, 1994) the therapist also utilizes his/her autoregulatory capacities to modulate and contain the stressful negative state induced in him/her by the patient's communications of dysregulated negative affect. The psychobiologically attuned therapist then has an opportunity to act as an interactive affect regulator of the patient's dysregulated state (see Schore, 2002b). This model clearly suggests that the therapist's role is much more than interpreting to the developmentally disordered patient either distortions of the transference, or unintegrated early attachment experiences that occur in inco-herent moments of the patient's narrative.

We need to go beyond objectively observing the disorganization of left-brain language capacities by dysregulating right-brain states and feeding this back to the patient in insight-oriented interpretations. Rather, we can directly engage and therefore regulate the patient's inefficient right-brain processes with our own right brains. On the part of the therapist, the most effective interpretations are based on the clinician's "awareness of his own physical, emotional, and ideational responses to the patient's veiled messages" (Boyer, 1990, p. 304). On the part of the patient, the most "correct understandings" can be used by the patient "only if the analyst is attuned to the patient's state at the time the interpretation is offered" (Friedman & Moskowitz, 1997, p. XXI). This interactive regulation allows the dyad to interactively hold online and amplify internal affective stimuli long enough for them to be recognized, regulated, labeled, and given meaning. This is an interactive context that supports a corrective emotional experience.

In light of the observation that "physical containment by the therapist of the patient's disavowed experience needs to *precede* its verbal processing" (Dosamantes, 1992, p, 362), the interactive regulation of the patient's state enables him/her to begin to verbally label the affective experience. In a "genuine dialogue" with the therapist, the patient raises to an inner word and then into a spoken word what he/she needs to say at a particular moment but does not yet possess as speech. But the patient must experience this verbal description of an internal state is heard, felt, and witnessed by an empathic other. In this manner the emotionally responsive aspects of the therapist's interventions are transformative for the patient.

This affectively focused therapeutic experience may literally alter the orbitofrontal system. A functional magnetic resonance imaging study conducted by Hariri, Bookheimer, and Mazziotta provided evidence that higher regions of specifically the right prefrontal cortex attenuate emotional responses at the most basic levels in the brain, that such modulating processes are "fundamental to most modern psychotherapeutic methods," that this lateralized neocortical network is active in "modulating emotional experience through interpreting and labeling emotional expressions," and that "this form of modulation may be impaired in various emotional disorders and may provide the basis for therapies of these same disorders" (2000, p. 48). This process is a central component of therapeutic narrative organization, of what Holmes (1993b, p. 150) called turning "raw feelings into symbols." Recall that the same "neocortical network" that "modulates the limbic system" is identical to the right-lateralized orbitofrontal system that regulates attachment dynamics.

As a result of such modulation, the patient's affectively charged but now regulated right-brain experience can then be communicated to the left brain for further processing. This effect, which must follow a right-brain-then-left-brain temporal sequence, allows for the development of linguistic symbols to represent the *meaning* of an experience, *while one is feeling and perceiving the emotion generated by the experience*. The objective left hemisphere can now coprocess subjective right-brain communications, and this allows for a linkage of the nonverbal implicit and verbal explicit representational domains. This in turn facilitates the "evolution of affects from their early form, in which they are experienced as bodily sensations, into subjective states that can gradually be verbally articulated" (Stolorow & Atwood, 1992, p. 42). The patient can reflect upon not only what external information is affectively charged and therefore personally meaningful, but how it is somatically felt and cognitively processed by his/her self-regulatory system.

The exploration for meaning is thus not in the content but in the very process of sensing and communicating emotional states. In a growth-facilitating therapeutic context, meaning is not singularly discovered but dyadically created. Focusing, at levels beneath and above awareness, not so much on cognitions as on the subtle or abrupt ebbs and flows of affective states and on rhythms of attunement, misattunement, and reattunement within the therapeutic dyad allows us to understand the dynamic events that occur within what Holmes (1993b) called "the spontaneous encounter of two solitudes." The essential mechanisms that regulate, in real time, the connections, disconnections, and reconnections of the inner worlds of the patient and the therapist are mediated by the transactions of the nonverbal transference-countertransference.

Brown asserted that the process of emotional development, as it continues in adulthood, brings the potential to observe and understand the processes of our own minds: "Adult affective development is the potential for self-observation and reflection on the very processes of mental functioning" (1993, p. 42). This involves not simply the affective content of experience but of the very processes by which affect comes into experience—how it is experienced by the self and what informs the self about its relationship to internal and external reality. As Brown noted, "Psychotherapy is one medium of adult affective development in the sense that it serves the purpose of disciplined conscious reflection on affective processes" (p. 56).

I suggest that Brown was describing a developmental progression in the patient's internal psychic structures, namely the orbitofrontal system that performs functions central to affect regulation (Davidson, Putnam, & Larson, 2000; Schore, 1994). This—"the thinking part of the emotional brain" (Goleman, 1995)—acts to "integrate and assign emotional-motivational significance to cognitive impressions; the association of emotion with ideas and thoughts" (Joseph, 1996) and in "the processing of affect-related meanings" (Teasdale et al., 1999). Because its activity is associated with a lower threshold for awareness of sensations of both external and internal origin, it functions as an "internal reflecting and organizing agency" (Kaplan-Solms & Solms, 1996). This orbitofrontal role in "self-reflective awareness" (Stuss et al., 1992) allows the individual to reflect on one his or her own internal emotional states, as well as others (Povinelli & Preuss, 1995). Furthermore, in light of recent interest of neuroscience in the "mind's eye" (Kawashima et al., 1995), I propose that the psychobiological operations of the right orbitofrontal system represent the "subjective lens of the mind's eye."

It is important to note that the right-hemisphere cycles back into growth phases throughout the lifespan (Schore, 1999a, 2002b, 2002e; Thatcher, 1994) and that the orbitofrontal cortex retains a capacity for plasticity in later life (Barbas, 1995), thereby allowing for the continuing experience-dependent maturation of a more efficient and flexible right frontal regulatory system within the growth-facilitating environment of an affect regulating therapeutic relationship. Although short-term treatment may allow the patient to return to a reregulated premorbid attachment pattern, over long-term treatment this neurobiological development may mediate an expansion of the patient's unconscious right mind and the transformation of an insecure into an "earned secure" attachment (Phelps, Belsky, & Crnic, 1998).

The infant literature clearly demonstrates that the nature of the mother's right brain-driven affective experiences powerfully influences the affects she acknowledges and attunes to in her child. This fundamental principle also applies to the therapeutic relationship. The therapist's use of his or her self in the treatment process of mutual reciprocal influences is expressed in his or her critical role as an affect monitor and regulator of the patient's shifting internal psychobiological states. Cycles of organization, disorganization, and reorganization of the intersubjective field occur repeatedly in the treatment process. Our own ability to "enter into the other's feeling state" depends upon our capacity to tolerate varying intensities and durations of countertransferential states marked by discrete positive affects, such as joy and excitement, and negative affects, such as shame, disgust, and terror. This range of our affect tolerance is very much a product of our own unique history of early indelibly imprinted emotionally-charged attachment dialogues, since it is these primordial interactive experiences that profoundly influence the origin of the self. For this reason, I believe personal psychotherapy is a prerequisite for anyone entering the field.

In a creative contribution, Holmes pointed out that our security mechanisms are biologically programmed and do not need to reach consciousness to be activated, and that these mechanisms, shaped by early attachments, provide for a "psychological immune system." Holmes (2002) contended,

> Just as a tropical diseases expert needs to be immunized against the organisms she is likely to encounter, so personal therapy for therapists can be seen as an immunization process, not just to protect them and their patients from themselves, but also to extend the range of experience that therapists can then draw on in working with clients. (p. 4)

A psychoneurobiological model of the attachment communications between patient and therapist indicates that in order to create an optimal working alliance, the therapist must access, in a timely fashion, both his/her own subjective, unconscious, intuitive, implicit responses, as well as his/her objective conscious, rational, theory-based explicit knowledge in the work (Renik, 1998). These applications of the advances in developmental psychoanalysis and neuropsychoanalyis to theoretical and clinical psychoanalytic therapeutic models support Bowlby's assertion, in his last writings, that "clearly the best therapy is done by the therapist who is naturally intuitive and also guided by the appropriate theory" (1991a, p. 16).

From a cognitive social neuroscience perspective, intuition is now being defined as "the subjective experience associated with the use of knowledge gained through implicit learning" (Lieberman, 2000, p. 109). Recall that right-hemispheric processes are central to implicit learning and that psychotherapy essentially alters and expands implicit relational knowledge. But in light of the intrinsic dyadic nature of attachment, this expansion occurs in the brain/mind/ bodies of both the patient and therapist. In his last work, Bowlby (1991b) described the therapeutic process as a "joint exploration." An attachment model grounded in both biology and psychoanalysis thus accounts for how a successful therapeutic relationship can act as an interactive affect-regulating context that optimizes the growth of two "minds in the making"; that is, increases in complexity in both the patient's and the therapist's continually developing unconscious right minds.

2001

Clinical Implications of a Psychoneurobiological Model of Projective Identification

W E ARE IN A PERIOD in which psychoanalysis and science are converging to produce more powerful explanatory models of the mind. This rapprochement may allow for a fresh approach to certain fundamental, yet heretofore seemingly impenetrable questions of human experience. A particularly intriguing problem that has been of interest to a number of different disciplines is the matter of how and why the mind first develops, and then continues to become more complex. If it is true that for most of this century this question has seemed to be beyond the province of scientific inquiry, it should be noted that even within psychoanalysis the early development of the mind was hardly addressed, if almost avoided by Freud. Perhaps more than any other of the psychoanalytic pioneers, it was Melanie Klein who established the formal theoretical and clinical explorations of the primitive mind. To this date, however, the findings of experimental science have offered little validation for many of Klein's hypotheses. In return, it should be noted, many of the followers of Klein have not been exactly inarticulate in expressing their antipathy for science.

Despite the controversies about Klein's theoretical constructs, her clinical concepts have offered valuable clues about working with developmentally disordered patients and primitive domains of the mind. This is true for perhaps her most important discovery, the clinically relevant yet theoretically enigmatic process of projective identification. Klein (1946) defined projective identification as a process wherein largely unconscious information is projected from the sender to the recipient. Although this primitive process of communication between the unconscious of one person and the unconscious of another begins in early development, it continues throughout life. This phenomenon also refers to a primitive unconscious defense mechanism that is a central focus of the treatment of child and adult developmental psychopathologies.

Psychoanalysis has been called the science of unconscious processes. Freud's major contribution to science was to emphasize the central importance of a continuously active unconscious mind in everyday life functions. Adaptive interactions with other humans take place on both conscious and unconscious levels, and in his work Freud began to model the state of mind of "evenly suspended attention" in which one could receive the unconscious communications of others. I suggest that if Freud (1912/1958b) was describing how the unconscious can act as "a receptive organ," Klein's concept of projective identification attempts to model how an unconscious system acts as a "transmitter," and how these transmissions will then influence the receptive functions of another unconscious mind. This clearly implies that unconscious systems interact with other unconscious systems, and that both receptive and expressive properties determine their communicative capacities.

In more recent clinical work, Joseph (1997, p. 103) stressed that "projective identification is, by its very nature, a kind of communication," a theme also emphasized by Alvarez (1997) and Mason (2000). Morrison (1986) wrote that it is "a communication to the recipient of what the unconscious fantasy *feels like*" (p. 59). Other authors assert that projective identification involves the projection of *affects* associated with self and object representations (Adler & Rhine, 1992). Ogden concluded "In projective identification, the projector by means of actual interpersonal interactions with the 'recipient' unconsciously induces *feeling states* in the recipient that are congruent with the 'ejected' feelings" (1990a, p. 79).

These clinical observations bear upon a long-debated issue concerning the specific nature of what is projected in this primitive communicative process. A commonly held belief is that Klein's sole emphasis was on the development of phantasy, on unconscious cognitions generated within the infant's mind. This seems to be inconsistent with current developmental research revealing that the infant's states are less cognitively complex and more bodily based and sensori-affective. Yet Brody (1982) asserted that Klein contributed to psychoanalytic thought when she described the intensities that *affects* can reach during infancy. Although most readers are familiar with her work on envy and gratitude, in 1943–1944 Klein published "On Observing the Behavior of Young Infants" and "Some Theoretical Conclusions Regarding the Emotional Life of the Infant." And more recently, in an article entitled "A New Look at the Theory of Melanie Klein," Stein proposed that: "The common thread running through all mental development, according to Klein, may be said to be that of *"regulation of feelings"* (1990, p. 508; italics added).

A major conclusion of my ongoing work on the "regulation of feelings" or "affect regulation" (Schore, 1991, 1994, 1996, 1997a, 1997b, 1997c, 1998a, 1998b, 1999b, 2000a, 2000c, 2000d, 2000e, 2000g, 2001b, 2001d, 2001f, 2002e) is that "primitive mental states" are much more than early-appearing "mental" or "cognitive" states of mind that mediate psychological processes. Rather, they are more precisely characterized as *psychobiological states*. Thus, those of us with a developmental framework are exploring not primitive states of mind, but primitive states of "mind-body." This developmental psychobiological perspective also suggests that affective states are transacted within the mother–infant dyad (Feldman, Greenbaum, & Yirmiya, 1999), and that this highly efficient system of somatically driven, fast-acting emotional communication is essentially nonverbal (Schore, 1997c). Current developmental research thus supports Grotstein's (1981) speculation, 20-plus years ago, that the state in which the therapist receives the projective identification is identical to maternal receptivity.

Thus, both clinical and developmental models of projective identification are now stressing the critical role of the communication of internal affective states and process, rather than cognitions and content. This conception fits with a general trend within psychoanalysis, articulated by Kantrowitz (1999, p. 72), who discussed the centrality of "intense affective engagements" and concluded, "It is in the realm of preconscious communication that the interwovenness of intrapsychic and interpersonal phenomena become most apparent." With respect to the communications embedded in projective identification, Ryle pointed out that this mechanism is essentially concerned with "the relationship between intrapsychic and interpersonal phenomena and with indirect forms of communication and influence" (1994, p. 107).

Indeed, projective identification, a process that mediates what Loewald (1970) called the transmission of "intrapsychic externalizations," is being seen as a "bridge concept" between classical and interpersonal psychoanalysis (Migone, 1995). But more than this, the concept is now linking developmental psychoanalysis with developmental psychology. An entire issue of the journal *Psychoanalytic Dialogues* (Seligman, 1999) was devoted to a "Symposium on Projective Identification Revisited: Integrating Clinical Infant Research, Attachment Theory, and Kleinian Concepts of Phantasy." Clinicians and theoreticians are also looking into the developmental sciences, as it has been suggested that a deeper understanding of projective identification may come from "the laboratories of infant researchers" (Stolorow, Orange, & Atwood, 1998, p. 723).

Taking this even further, I argue here that Klein's seminal concept links clinical psychoanalysis with not only developmental psychoanalysis and psychology, but also with developmental neuroscience, especially affective neuroscience. I have proposed (Schore, 1997a, 1999a, 1999c, 2000a, 2000c, 2002e) that the time is right for a rapprochement between psychoanalysis and neurobiology, and that this integration can lead to a deeper understanding of clinical phenomena. This is especially true of projective identification, which writers now describe as operating "in some mysterious way that we cannot begin to comprehend scientifically" (Sands, 1997a, p. 653). Towards that end, in this chapter I suggest that current findings from studies of the neurobiology of emotional development are particularly relevant to projective identification, an early appearing process that involves a "mutuality of *emotional* response" (Migone, 1995; italics added).

There is now a surge of research on emotional behavior, and an increasing number of studies on the psychobiology of affective states and the neurobiology of the emotion-processing right brain. The early-maturing right hemisphere is dominant for the first 3 years of life (Chiron et al., 1997) and is specialized for the processing of emotional information (see Schore, 1994, 1998b, 1999a, 1999c). This is due to the fact that this cortex, more so than the left, is anatomically connected into the limbic system, the brain network that "derives subjective information in terms of emotional feelings that guide behavior" (MacLean, 1985, p. 220). In fact, this hemisphere plays an essential role in the nonconscious appraisal of the positive or negative emotional significance of social stimuli via a mechanism similar to Freud's pleasure-unpleasure principle (Schore, 1999b). The right hemisphere is dominant for the perception of nonverbal emotional expressions embedded in facial and prosodic stimuli (Blonder, Bowers, & Heilman, 1991; George et al., 1996), even at unconscious levels (Wexler, Warrenburg, Schwartz, & Janer, 1992), for nonverbal communication (Benowitz et al., 1983), and for implicit learning (Hugdahl, 1995).

In parallel work, psychophysiological studies have focused an intense interest on the implicit perception of affective information transmitted by faces (Niedenthal, 1990), and in the distinct dynamic properties of "nonconscious" affect, which is relatively diffuse, more readily displaced, and yields stronger or less adulterated effect (Murphy, Monahan, & Zajonc, 1995). This "automatic emotion" operates in infancy and beyond at nonconscious levels (Hansen & Hansen, 1994), and such early automatic reactions shape the subsequent conscious emotional processing of a stimulus (Dimberg & Ohman, 1996). A body of research indicates that emotional face-to-face communications occur on an unconscious level (Dimberg, Thunberg, & Elmehed, 2000). I suggest that projective identification is a prime example of the "transmission of nonconscious affect" (Murphy et al., 1995, p. 600).

An integration of current developmental studies of infant–mother emotional communications, psychophysiological data on affective processing, and neurobiological research on the essential role of the right brain in emotional communications can offer us a deeper understanding of the mechanism of affective communications within projective identification. These right-brain-to-right-brain communications embedded within the attachment bond represent what Bion (1959) called "links" between mother and infant. Ornstein (1997) termed the unconscious right brain "the right mind," and so Bianchedi's assertion that "the mother's mind functions as a link" (Vergopoulo, 1996) described the link provided by *the mother's right mind.*

This rapidly expanding body of interdisciplinary studies can serve as a source pool for heuristic models of not only normal emotional development, but also of how disorganizing forces in the early social environment can interfere with maturational processes. The early social environment can positively and negatively influence the emergence of the early developing "primitive" (Tucker, 1992) right brain. Indeed, this hemisphere is dominant for affect regulation, and for generating coping strategies that support survival and enable the individual to cope with stresses and challenges (Schore, 1994; Sullivan & Gratton,

1999; Wittling & Schweiger, 1993). In contemporary psychodynamic models, defense mechanisms are defined as forms of emotional regulation strategies for avoiding, minimizing, or converting affects that are too difficult to tolerate (Cole et al., 1994). There is agreement that intrapsychic psychological defenses are best characterized as a subset of coping mechanisms (Rutter, 1987), and that the development of coping responses is dependent upon early experience (Levine, 1983).

There is a great deal of interest amongst clinicians in intense, primitive affects, such as terror and rage. But in recent work I have suggested that we must also deepen our understanding of the early etiology of the primitive *defenses* that are used to cope with—to autoregulate—traumatic, overwhelming affective states. An interdisciplinary approach can thus model how developing systems organize primitive defense mechanisms, such as projective identification and dissociation, to cope with interactive forces that induce intensely stressful states that massively disorganize the infant's homeostatic equilibrium (Schore, 2001a). Dissociation is a very early appearing survival mechanism for coping with traumatic affects, and it plays a critical role in the mechanism of projective identification (Schore, 1998c, 2000g, 2002d). Since these early events are imprinted into the maturing brain (Matsuzawa et al., 2001), where states become traits (Perry et al., 1995), they endure as primitive defense mechanisms. It has been observed that patients who utilize projective identification have "dissociatively cleansed" themselves of traumatic affects in order to maintain some form of relationship with narcissistically vulnerable others (Sands, 1994, 1997b).

In two seminal papers, Klein conjectured that defensive projective identification is associated with the massive invasion of someone else's personality (1955/1975) and represents an evacuation of unwanted parts of the self (1946). The use of a unique and restricted set of defenses in severely disturbed personalities has been long noted in the clinical literature. Indeed, a primary goal of treatment of such patients is to help them replace excessive use of projective identification with more mature defensive operations. Boyer described a group of patients who experienced an early defective relationship with the mother that resulted in a grossly deficient ego structure. Their excessive use of projective identification "very heavily influences their relationships with others as well as their psychic equilibrium. Their principal conscious goal in therapy is to relieve themselves immediately of tension. Often they greatly fear that the experience of discomfort is intolerable and believe that failure to rid themselves of it will lead to physical or mental fragmentation or dissolution" (Boyer, 1990, p. 304).

In writings on the "costs" of the characterological use of projective identification, Stark described, "Those patients who do not have the capacity to sit with internal conflicts will be in the position of forever giving important parts of themselves away, leaving themselves feeling internally impoverished and excessively dependent upon others" (1999, p. 269).

With this introduction, the following chapter is a continuation of a series of contributions directed toward elucidating the mechanisms that link early interpersonal processes with the organization of intrapsychic unconscious structural systems (Schore, 1994, 1996, 1997b, 1997c, 1998a, 1998b, 1999b, 2000a, 2000e, 2001b, 2002e). Specifically, I am proposing that knowledge of the experience-dependent maturation of the right brain ("right mind") offers us a chance to more deeply understand not just the contents of the unconscious, but its origin, structure, and dynamics. In these works I am attempting to demonstrate the power of regulation theory and a neuropsychoanalytic perspective to describe the covert mechanisms that underlie a variety of essential developmental and clinical phenomena.

As opposed to the customary strategy of presenting material from a specific case in order to elucidate a general clinical principle, this approach attempts to model common fundamental mechanisms of unconscious intrapsychic and interpersonal phenomena and then apply them to the therapeutic context of a specific case. This work specifically represents an exploration of the nonverbal, nonconscious realm, and therefore focuses on process more than verbal content. Models of the "hidden" mechanisms by which rapidly appraised alterations in the external social environment elicit patterns of dynamic changes of internal psychobiological states can offer a deeper understanding of the fundamental fast-acting mechanisms that occur within moment-to-moment interactions of the coconstructed therapeutic alliance (see appendix for an outline of psychotherapy principles).

Affect, both its regulation and dysregulation, play a central role in the infant–caregiver and patient–therapist relationship. Affect dysregulation is associated with stresses within the therapeutic alliance, and therefore it is important to understand the etiology and operations of early-developing yet enduring defense mechanisms that are mobilized by relational stress. Depending upon the attachment history, these coping strategies can be both adaptive and maladaptive, and therefore critical elements of psychopathogenesis. Clinical models derived from this psychoneurobiological perspective are targeted toward expanding psychoanalytic techniques to the more severe psychopathologies of both childhood and adulthood. Therapeutic regulation and not interpretation and insight is the key to the treatment of developmentally disordered patients who are not "psychologically minded." Forty-plus years ago Loewald stressed that "a better understanding of the therapeutic action of psychoanalysis may lead to changes in technique" (1960/1980, p. 222).

And so in the following, I describe projective identification as an early organizing unconscious coping strategy for regulating right-brain-to-right-brain communications, especially of intense affective states. Because affects are psychobiological phenomena and the self is bodily based, the coping strategy of projective identification represent not conscious verbal-linguistic behaviors but instead unconscious nonverbal *mind-body communications*. This information from developmental affective neuroscience and neuropsychoanalysis describes

the fundamental psychoneurobiological mechanisms that mediate the therapist's capacity to access unconscious communications in order to know the
patient "from the inside out" (Bromberg, 1991).

I then apply the model to a number of clinical issues, keeping in mind
Sander's dictum that in therapeutic exploration, "it is not the past we seek but
the logic of the patient's own state regulating strategies" (in Schwaber, 1990,
p. 238). It has been suggested that the nature of (neuro) development is "the
great frontier in neuroscience where all of our (psychoanalytic) theories will be
subject to the most acid of acid tests" (Watt, 2000, p. 191). The work presented
here not only supports Klein's concept; it highlights the fundamental role of
projective identification in both development and psychoanalytic treatment.

CURRENT UPDATINGS OF CLINICAL CONCEPTIONS
OF PROJECTIVE IDENTIFICATION

Klein originally described projective identification as the projection of an unwanted part of the self onto an important other, together with identification of
that part with the other. This is usually interpreted to mean the projecting out,
in a controlling way, of "bad," *negative* parts that could be dangerous to the
self into another person. However, a number of authors have emphasized
the fact that Klein also spoke about the role of projective identification in the
child's *positive* relationship with the mother, stating that this process also involves the projection of a much-valued part of the self into another. Muir noted,
"It was described initially as a defensive process but later she indicated that it
could be seen as a fundamental necessary and normal process in early ego
development" (1995, p. 247). Leiman (1994) pointed out that projective identification is involved in the "negative sphere of experience" *or* the "positive
sphere," the latter expressed in Winnicott's (1971) transitional experiences and
in the origin of play. Likierman (1988) wrote on "maternal love and positive
projective identification." And Sandler and Sandler (1996) discussed states of
"primary identification"—of moments in interpersonal interactions when the
boundary between self and object is lost. They argued that this is the essential
basis of the process of projective identification, and that it occurs in a "reciprocal love relationship" and is a significant basis for empathy.

These current conceptions represent an extension of Klein's (1946) original
assertion that the processes associated with projective identification are of vital
importance for the normal development as well as for abnormal object relations. But is was Bion who emphasized the central role of this mechanism in
all early developmental phenomena (Schore, 2001h). In a far-sighted work,
Bion (1962b) described that when mother and infant are adjusted to each other
the infant behaves in such a way that projective identification is a "realistic"
rather than defensive phenomenon, and that this is its normal condition and
function. This idea continues in the current literature, where the emphasis is
on the adaptive aspects of projective identification, and on more than just the

valence or the content of the projected material but rather on the underlying process of the communication of states.

A conception of mother and infant adjusting to each other's communications describes a model of mutual reciprocal influence. This clearly suggests that projective identification is not a unidirectional but a bidirectional, interactive process. The interpersonal component of projective identification has been advanced by clinical theoreticians such as Grotstein (1981) and Ogden who stated, "Projective identification does not exist where there is no interaction between projector and recipient" (1979, p. 14). Scharff (1992) referred to the "forgotten concept of introjective identification" and described the coupling between the linked processes of projective *and* introjective identification. Following these leads, Ryle (1994) referred to projective identification as a particular form of "reciprocal role procedures" that organize interactions with others, predict the role of the other, and combine action with affect, expectation, and communication. Again, the concept moves from a monadic, one-way ejection of intrapsychic contents to a dyadic, intersubjective communicative process.

Expanding upon this interactional principle, Muir (1995) integrated Klein's work with Mahler's and Bowlby's developmental models. In an important contribution, he demonstrated that projective identification represents a medium of "psychobiological connection" and that, indeed, it is the vehicle of the communication of positive symbiotic states and the transmission of attachment patterns. Muir contended that instead of just ridding oneself of unwanted parts into another person, this transpersonal process of projection of valued parts of the self is also used developmentally by the infant to induce nurturance and relationship behavior in the caregiver. These ideas are very similar to my own work, which indicates that psychobiologically regulated affect transactions that maximize positive and minimize negative affect cocreate a secure attachment bond between mother and infant (Schore, 1994, 1996, 1999i; 2000a, 2000d, 2001b). They also are concordant with attachment researchers who are now defining the central role of the attachment relationship, a mechanism that continues in dyadic interactions throughout the lifespan, as *the dyadic regulation of emotion* (Sroufe, 1996), a concept that mirrors Klein's lifelong interest in *the regulation of feelings* (Stein, 1990).

Current developmental models thus emphasize the fact that projective identification, both in the developmental and the therapeutic situations, is not a unidirectional but instead is a bidirectional process in which both members of an emotionally communicating dyad act in a context of mutual reciprocal influence. Although projective identification arises in the emotional communications within the mother–infant dyad, this "primitive" process plays an essential role in "the communication of affective experiences" in all later periods of development (Modell, 1994). These communications, however, have unique operational properties and occur in specified contexts. Authors emphasize that projective identification constitutes a mode of "primitive joint action" mediated by nonverbal signs (Leiman, 1994). Migone (1995, p. 626) held that instances of projective identification occur in "intimate or close relationships, such as the mother–child relationship or the patient–analyst relationship."

DEVELOPMENTAL STUDIES AND THE ORIGIN OF DISSOCIATION AND DEFENSIVE PROJECTIVE IDENTIFICATION

The ontogeny of both adaptive and defensive projective identification is deeply influenced by the events of the first year of life. Developmentally, "realistic" or "adaptive" projective identification is expressed in the "split-second world" (Stern, 1985) of the mother–infant dyad in the securely attached infant's expression of a "spontaneous gesture," a somatopsychic expression of the burgeoning "true self," and the attuned mother's "giving back to the baby the baby's own self (Winnicott, 1971a). This developmental mechanism continues to be used throughout the lifespan as a process of rapid, fast acting, nonverbal, spontaneous emotional communications within a dyad (Schore, 1994, 1997c).

As opposed to the interactive scenario of a secure attachment in which the caregiver contingently responds to the child's projective identifications, the insecurely attached child is often unable to induce affect-regulating responses and engage in empathic mutual regulatory processes because the other is not sufficiently attuned to the child's state and therefore unable to receive the infant's emotional communications (Schore, 1994, 1996, 1997b, 2001c). This prevents the establishment of a dyadic system in which the infant can safely project "valued" parts of the self into the mother (i.e., aspects of adaptive projective identification). The insecurely attached organizations of developmental personality disorders thus have a greater tendency to use defensive rather than adaptive projective identification. Doucet wrote, "I consider that projective identification works in two ways: a normal way, in which the analyst-mother takes into herself a part of the patient-child's emotional identity in order to return it to him in a detoxified and hence assimilable form, and a pathological way in which the negative aspects are so plentiful that projective identification operates to excess" (1992, p. 657).

More specifically, "primitive" personalities encode early traumatic experiences of being used as what Robbins called "a projection screen for repudiated elements of parental identity, rather than having the parent act as a mirror for integration, and differentiation of nascent aspects of itself" (1996, p. 764). These "negative maternal attributions" (Lieberman, 1997) contain an intensely negative affective charge, and therefore rapidly dysregulate the infant. According to Tronick and Weinberg, "When infants are not in homeostatic balance or are emotionally dysregulated (e.g., they are distressed), they are at the mercy of these states. Until these states are brought under control, infants must devote all their regulatory resources to reorganizing them. While infants are doing that, they can do nothing else" (1997, p. 56).

In fact, current developmental research is elucidating the effects of traumatic affect on the infant, and these studies are directly relevant to an understanding of the origins of projective identification (Schore, 1998e, 1998i, 1999f, 1999g, 2000g, 2002d). Perry and colleagues (1995) demonstrated that the infant's psychobiological response to trauma is comprised of two separate response patterns, hyperarousal and dissociation. These two patterns are extreme forms of, respectively, Bowlby's (1969), protest and despair responses to attachment ruptures. These dual responses also represent activation of the two components of the autonomic nervous system (ANS): first, the energy-expending sympathetic branch; and then, the energy-conserving parasympathetic branch (see Schore, 1994). The ANS has been called "the physiological bottom of the mind" (Jackson, 1931).

In the initial stage of threat, hyperarousal, an alarm reaction is initiated by the sympathetic nervous system, and a distress response, in the form of crying and then screaming, is expressed. This communication of negative affect also serves as an intense bid for interactive regulation. The infant's state of "frantic distress" or what Perry terms fear-terror is mediated by a significant release of the stress hormone corticotropin releasing factor, which in turn results in an increase in heart rate, blood pressure, respiration, and muscle tone, as well as hypervigilance. This dyadic transaction was described by Beebe as "mutually escalating overarousal": "Each one escalates the ante, as the infant builds to a frantic distress, may scream, and, in this example, finally throws up. In an escalating overarousal pattern, even after extreme distress signals from the infant, such as ninety-degree head aversion, arching away . . . or screaming, the mother keeps going" (2000, p. 436).

But a second, later-forming, longer-lasting reaction is seen in dissociation, a parasympathetic response of the ANS, in which the child disengages from stimuli in the external world and attends to an "internal" world. Traumatized infants are observed to be "staring into space with a glazed look." The traumatized child's dissociation in the midst of fear or terror involves numbing, avoidance, compliance, and restricted affect, mediated by high levels of behavior-inhibiting cortisol, pain-numbing endogenous opioids, and especially high levels of parasympathetic dorsal motor vagal activity in the baby's developing brain (Schore, 2001c). If early trauma is experienced as "psychic catastrophe" (Bion, 1962b), dissociation is "the escape when there is no escape" (Putnam, 1997), "a last resort defensive strategy" (Dixon, 1998).

This primary regulatory process of conservation-withdrawal (see Schore, 1994, 2001c) occurs in helpless and hopeless stressful situations in which the individual is hyperinhibited and therefore immobile in order to avoid attention by becoming "unseen," and it allows the infant to maintain homeostasis in the face of an internal state of accelerating hyperarousal. The dissociation from both contact with the external social environment and from the child's subjective physical experience is experienced as a discontinuity in what Winnicott (1958) called the child's need for "going-on-being," and Kestenberg (1985) referred to as a "dead spot" in the infant's subjective experience. The result is the constricted state of consciousness that is characteristic of dissociation.

I suggest that an infant with an early history of "ambient" (Mordecai, 1995) or "cumulative trauma" (Khan, 1974) must excessively utilize defensive projective identification in order to cope with all-too-frequent episodes of interactive stress that disorganize the developing self. The startled, traumatized infant's sudden state switch from sympathetic hyperarousal into parasympathetic dissociation is also reflected in Porges's characterization of "the sudden and rapid transition from an unsuccessful strategy of struggling requiring massive sympathetic activation to the metabolically conservative immobilized state mimicking death" (1997, p. 75).

Furthermore, in the first stage of trauma, hyperaroused terror and screaming are triggered by "negative maternal attributions," which is equated with Spitz's (1965) "psychotoxic" maternal care, manifest in an overdose of affective stimulation, and Klein's (1955/1975) "massive invasion of someone else's personality." The second stage, the dissociative strategy to counterregulate the hyperarousal, is expressed by "staring into space," and represents the mechanism that drives what Klein (1946) described as an "evacuation" of the self. These dual mechanisms were described in a child therapy case by Joseph: "When projective identification was operating so powerfully," the patient "started to scream," and then "stared through the window with a vacant, lost expression" (1997, p. 104).

In other words, the sudden, discontinuous, counterregulatory switch from an active state of sympathetic energy-expending, emotion-amplifying autonomic hyperarousal into an enduring passive state of parasympathetic energy-conserving, emotion-dampening hyperinhibition underlies the rapid onset of dissociation and represents the mechanism of projective identification as it operates in real time. The stressed child, with only primitive abilities to cope with the overwhelming arousal induced by relational trauma and at the limit of his or her fragile regulatory capacities, experiences intense affect dysregulation, projects a distressing emotional communication, and then instantly dissociates. States of autonomic hyperarousal are subjectively experienced as pain, and thus this strategy represents a psychobiological mechanism by which psychic-physical pain is instantly inhibited.

In these traumatic moments of marked discontinuities in the caregiver–infant relationship, the child's attempts to use other-directed regulatory behaviors (e.g., crying, expressions of fear) are often met with continuing dysregulation by the misattuning caregiver; that is, further abuse. They therefore must be inhibited, and so, for adaptive goals, the infant must resort to an autoregulatory strategy to modulate overwhelming levels of distress. Furthermore, this rapid shift from a mode of interactive regulation into a long-lasting mode of autoregulation that the infant must access in order to maintain homeostatic equilibrium during traumatic assaults is imprinted into the maturing limbic system (Schore,

1996, 1997b, 2001c). It therefore endures as a basic strategy of affect regulation, a characterological disposition to use defensive projective identification under conditions of interpersonal stress.

What is maladaptive about the psychic-deadening defense of dissociation is not only that the individual shifts into dissociation at lower levels of stress, but also that he/she finds difficulty in exiting the state of conservation-withdrawal. Once dissociated one stays in this massive autoregulatory mode for longer periods of time, intervals when the individual is shut down to the external environment, totally closed and impermeable to attachment communications, interactive regulation, and not incidentally, verbal interventions. Grotstein wrote that "the phenomenon of dissociation . . . is more widespread and universal than has hitherto been thought" (1981, p. 111).

There is a long history, dating back to Janet (1889), on the link between early trauma and dissociation. In a developmental study, Ogawa and colleagues (1997) offered evidence to show that early trauma more so than later trauma has a greater impact on the development of dissociative behaviors. Current brain research not only supports this connection, but deepens our understanding of why individuals exposed to early trauma tend to use dissociation at later points of stress. There is now a growing body of evidence indicating that the massive caregiver misattunement of abuse and neglect induces not only intense attachment ruptures but also severe dysregulation of the infant's nascent, fragile psychobiological systems (de Bellis et al., 1999; Karr-Morse & Wiley, 1997; Perry et al., 1995; Schore, 1997b), especially in the early-developing right hemisphere (Henry & Wang, 1998; Raine et al., 2001; Rotenberg, 1995; Schore, 1997b, 2001c). Furthermore, the primitive avoidant strategy of dissociation that is accessed in order to cope with this trauma (Liotti, 1992) is known to lead to permanent alterations in the maturing brain (Schore, 2001c; Weinberg, 2000), and these events, stored in implicit procedural memory, thereby increase the use of dissociation in later life (Siegel, 1996).

In the clinical literature, Stolorow and Atwood (1992) wrote of "affect-dissociating defensive operations," rooted in early derailments, in which central affect states are walled off because they evoked "massive malattunement" from the caregiving surround. They also asserted that psychopathological phenomena unfold within an "intersubjectve field that includes the analyst as a codetermining influence" (p. 189). I suggest that the mechanism of defensive projective identification is overtly expressed in a treatment context that resembles an early interactive derailment of an insecure attachment. This occurs in an affective transaction when the therapist exhibits a massive malattunement of the patient's disorganizing state. In this interactive context high levels of dysregulated affect, codetermined by both members of the dyad, are rapidly amplified within the intersubjective field. This interactive stress will trigger, in real time, the patient's dissociating defensive operations and the primitive avoidant defense mechanism of defensive projective identification.

PROJECTIVE IDENTIFICATION AS
RIGHT-BRAIN-TO-RIGHT-BRAIN
TRANSFERENCE-COUNTERTRANSFERENCE COMMUNICATIONS

In the developmental context, the mother of the securely attached infant psy-chobiologically attunes her right hemisphere to the output of the infant's right hemisphere in order to receive and resonate with fluctuations in her child's internal state. This bond of unconscious emotional communication, embedded in adaptive projective identifications, facilitates the experience-dependent maturation of the infant's right brain. Neuroscientists have noted that:

> Spontaneous communication employs species-specific expressive displays in the sender that, given attention, activate emotional preattunements and are directly perceived by the receiver. . . . The "meaning" of the display is known directly by the receiver. . . . This spontaneous emotional communication constitutes a *conversation between limbic systems.* . . . It is a biologically-based communication system that involves individual organisms *directly* with one another: the individuals in spontaneous communication constitute literally a biological unit. (Buck, 1994, p. 266; italics added)

Buck (1994) emphasized the importance of specifically the right limbic system, and localized this biologically based spontaneous emotional communication system to the right hemisphere, in accord with other research indicating a right lateralization of spontaneous gestures (Blonder et al., 1995), the control of spontaneously evoked emotional reactions (Dimberg & Petterson, 2000), and emotional communication (Blonder et al., 1991).

In earlier writings, I provided interdisciplinary data indicating that the "transfer of affect" within the intersubjective field of the caregiver and infant and patient and therapist represents transactions between the right hemispheres of the members of these dyads (Schore, 1994, 1996, 1997c, 1998b, 2000a, 2000c, 2002e). It is established that the "primitive affect system" (Gazzaniga, 1985) or what Krystal (1978) called the "infantile nonverbal affect system" is located not in the linguistic left hemisphere but instead in the right brain ("the right mind") of both infants and adults. This "primitive" hemisphere is dominant for the processing of nonverbal affects at unconscious levels (Wexler et al., 1992). The right brain is also involved in the reciprocal interactions that occur within the mother–infant regulatory system (Taylor, 1987), an essential interactive mechanism that induces the dominance of the right hemisphere for a sense of an emotional and corporeal self (Devinsky, 2000).

I suggest that the primitive mechanism of projective identification is an affect-regulating strategy that is used in spontaneous right-brain-to-right-brain communications, a preverbal bodily based dialogue between right-lateralized limbic systems, especially in intensely emotional contexts. This model supports both Bion's (1967) assertion that projective identification is the most important form of interaction between patient and therapist and Stark's (1999) proposal that it takes place all the time within families and couples. Neurobiological studies indicate that "while the left hemisphere mediates most linguistic behaviors, the right hemisphere is important for broader aspects of communication" (van Lancker & Cummings, 1999, p. 95). And psychophysiological studies have demonstrated that "long sequences of interactions between people may be partly determined by nonconscious perceptions and automatic responses on the part of both the sender and receiver. Their conscious understanding of what is going on in the interaction that they can formulate verbally, on the other hand, may be quite independent of this basic level of interaction" (Dimberg & Ohman, 1996, p. 177). These authors specifically implicate right-hemispheric processes in these events.

Due to its central role in unconscious functions and primary process activities, psychoanalysis has been intrigued with the unique operations of the right brain for the last quarter of a century (e.g., Galin, 1974; Hoppe, 1977; McLaughlin, 1978; Miller, 1986; Watt, 1986). Most neuropsychological studies of "the minor hemisphere" have focused solely on motor behaviors, visuospatial functions, and cognition, but only recently have neuroscientists delved into the fundamental activity of the right brain in the recognition of facially expressed nonverbal affective expressions (Kim et al., 1999; Muller et al., 1999; Nakamura et al., 2000; Narumoto et al., 2000). This research demonstrates that the right hemisphere is specialized for both the receptive processing (Blair et al., 1999) and expressive communication (Borod, Haywood, & Koff, 1997) of facial information during spontaneous social interactions, such as in "natural conversation" or within "interpersonal family communication" (Blonder et al., 1993). This hemisphere is also dominant for evaluating the trustworthiness of faces (Winston et al., 2002).

Furthermore, according to Adolphs and colleagues, "recognizing emotions from visually presented facial expressions requires right somatosensory cortices," and in this manner "we recognize another individual's emotional state by internally generating somatosensory representations that simulate how the individual would feel when displaying a certain facial expression" (2000, p. 2683). These right-lateralized operations thus allow for the adaptive capacity of empathic cognition and the perception of the emotional states of mind of other human beings (Perry et al., 2001; Schore, 1994, 1996, 2001b; Voeller, 1986).

The right brain processes information in a holistic fashion, and it can appraise facially expressed emotional cues in less than 30 milliseconds (Johnsen & Hugdahl, 1991), far beneath levels of awareness. Because the unconscious processing of affective information is extremely rapid (Martin et al., 1996), the dynamic operations of these processes cannot be consciously perceived. It is for this reason that brain research offers valuable data to psychoanalysis, "the science of unconscious processes" (Brenner, 1980). Psychoanalytic research highlights the importance of facial indicators of transference processes (Krause &

Lutolf, 1988), which are quickly appraised from the face in movements occurring primarily in the regions around the eyes and from prosodic expressions
from the mouth.

Because the transference-countertransference is a reciprocal process, facially
communicated "expressions of affect" that reflect changes in internal state are
rapidly communicated and perceptually processed within the affectively synchronized therapeutic dialogue. This finding is relevant to the "reciprocal process," described by Munder-Ross, in which the therapist has access to "the
subliminal stimulation . . . that emanates from the patient" (1999, p. 95). In
fact, these very same spontaneously communicated and rapidly perceived visual
and auditory cues are a central component of the nonverbal communication
in the psychoanalytic process and represent "the intrapsychic edge of the object
world, the perceptual edge of the transference" (Smith, 1990, p. 225).

In earlier work (Schore, 1994), I described this "perceptual edge of the
transference":

> It is now thought that critical "cues" generated by the therapist, which are
> absorbed and metabolized by the patient, generate the transference (Gill,
> 1982), an "activation of existing units of internalized object relations"
> (Kernberg, 1980). In recent theorizing on the neurobiological underpin-
> nings of this process, Watt (1986) proposes a "field effect" model, in which
> the activation of internalized object relations (unconscious, preverbal inter-
> nal working models) is triggered by the patient's perception of aspects of
> the interpersonal field that are external analogues of existing affect-laden
> self and object internal images (representations). More specifically, the
> transference crystallizes around perceived expressions of the therapist's per-
> sonality, therapeutic style, and behavior—in particular his/her "facial ex-
> pression" and "perceived tone of voice." Transference activation is
> intensified by "precipitating stresses in the environment that present some
> formal analog to the stored internal images" (p. 57), and the patient is
> especially sensitive to (biased towards) perceiving aspects of the treatment
> situation which resemble "the parent's original toxic behavior.
>
> The patient, according to Watt, is very "attuned" to alterations in the
> "bipersonal field" (Langs, 1976) which excite an emotional resonance
> within enduring internal object images. . . . This input generates "a series
> of analogical comparisons between distortions by the therapist ("misalli-
> ance") and the empathic failures and distortion of parents" (p. 61). Watt
> presents a number of persuasive arguments to show that the analogical
> cognition of the transference is organized by the analogical processing of
> the right hemisphere. (p. 450)

In describing the clinical correlates of this mechanism, psychoanalytic observers have noted: "In the treatment situation, the analyst is unconsciously
scanned for whatever characteristics might be gleaned that support a view of

him or her as similar to some internally pressing representation, owned or disowned by the patient" (Kantrowitz, 1999, p. 68). In this manner, "The transference illusion is not simply a false perception or a false belief, but the manifestation of the similarity of the subjective experience aroused by an event in the past and in the present" (Klauber, 1987).

The activation of a "malignant transference reaction," manifest in rapid emotional activation and instability, (McKenna, 1994), represents the expression of a spontaneous emotional expression of distress. The patient's distress communication, even though it may be extremely brief, is in turn perceived implicitly by the clinician as a countertransferential response. De Paola (1990) described a "special kind of communication that comes from the unconscious and is perceived unconsciously; this communication is reached through our countertransference feelings, aroused by the projective communication" (1990, p. 334). Again, in previous writings (Schore, 1994) on the psychophysiology of countertransference I stated:

> Countertransferential processes are currently understood to be manifest in the capacity to recognize and utilize the sensory (visual, auditory, tactile, kinesthetic, and olfactory) and affective qualities of imagery which the patient generates in the psychotherapist (Suler, 1989). Similarly, Loewald (1986) points out that countertransference dynamics are appraised by the therapist's observations of his own visceral reactions to the patient's material. (p. 451)

These data support Racker's (1968) assertion that every transference situation provokes a countertransference situation, Ogden's (1979) proposal that projective identification involves an interaction between projector and recipient, and Scharfs (1992) description of an alteration between "projective" and "introjective processes."

The reciprocal affective transmissions that occur between the interpersonal and intrapsychic spheres, the realms of a "two-person" and a "one-person" psychology, are fast acting, and these transactions occur within the temporal domain of microsecond reactions. Thus, in the clinical context, although it appears to be an invisible, instantaneous, endogenous unidirectional phenomenon, the bidirectional process of projective identification is actually a very rapid sequence of reciprocal affective transactions within the intersubjective field that is coconstructed by the patient and therapist.

More specifically, the disorganized and chaotic somatic components of dysregulated biologically "primitive emotions" are involved in projective identification. These biologically primitive emotions—excitement, elation, rage, terror, disgust, shame, and hopeless despair—appear early in development, are correlated with differentiable autonomic activity, arise quickly and automatically, and are processed in the right brain (Schore, 1994). This particular class of "primary" emotions are the "nonverbal" emotions in which Klein was interested, and they are specifically expressed in the rapid events of projective identification.

Right Hemisphere Attachment Trauma
and Defensive Projective Identification

The right hemisphere is specifically impacted by early attachment experiences—in fact, these object relational affect-communicating experiences facilitate its maturation (Henry, 1993; Schore, 1994, 1996, 1998a, 1998b, 2000a, 2000c, 2002e). In face-to-face interactions, the child uses the output of the mother's emotion-regulating right cortex as a template for the imprinting, the hard wiring of circuits in his/her own right cortex that will come to mediate his/her expanding capacities. In other words, the regulated emotional transactions of adaptive projective identification that promote a secure attachment have potential structure-inducing effects. They mediate "between intrapsychic and interpersonal phenomena" (Ryle, 1994) by acting as a medium for the transmission of "intrapsychic externalizations" (Loewald, 1970), thereby allowing for the organization of internal structural systems involved in the processing, expression, and regulation of emotionally charged information.

On the other hand, a history of cumulative relational trauma, or of frank abuse and neglect, represents a growth-inhibiting environment for the maturation of the right brain (Schore, 1997b, 2001b). The insecurely attached infant's all-too-common stressful experiences with a caregiver who chronically initiates but poorly repairs intense and long-lasting dysregulated states are incorporated in right-brain long-term autobiographical memory (Fink et al., 1996) as a pathological internal object relation, an interactive representation of a dysregulated-self-in-interaction-with-a-misattuning-object (Schore, 1997b, 1997c). In a recent overview, Gaensbauer concluded, "The clinical data, reinforced by research findings, indicate that preverbal children, even in the first year of life, can establish and retain some form of internal representation of a traumatic event over significant periods of time" (2002, p. 259).

This early representation includes "nonverbal presymbolic forms of relating" that "protect the infant from trauma and continue to be used by patients to avoid retraumatization" (Kiersky & Beebe, 1994, p. 389); that is, the right-brain defensive regulatory strategies of dissociation and projective identification. Experiences of early relational trauma (Schore, 2001b) restrain the manner in which coping responses occur at later points of stress: "The experience is then structure-bound, the present situation or certain aspects of it evoking only an already formed experience pattern with a fixed unchangeable repetitive structure. In that case, the experience is a "frozen whole" (Gendlin, 1970), and . . . the person experiences the same thing over and over" (Vanaerschot, 1997, p. 144). These representations, a primary source generator of Freud's repetition compulsion, are stored in the early-developing, "holistic" (Bever, 1975) right hemisphere (Schore, 1994).

Neuroscientists describe "early emotional learning occurring in the right hemisphere unbeknownst to the left; learning and associated emotional responding may later be completely unaccessible to the language centers of the brain" (Joseph, 1982, p. 243). From this realm that stores split-off parts of the self also come projections that are directed outward into the therapist. McDougall (1978) asserted that the patient who has suffered preverbal traumas transmits "primitive communications" that induce countertransferential emotional stated in the analyst. Similarly, Modell stated that in projective identification, "affects that are associated with the patient's past traumatic relationships are . . . projected onto the therapist, so that these affects are also experienced by the therapist" (1993, p. 148). A clinical study indicating that repression of traumatic events, intrusive imagery, and recollection of traumatic memories is related to right hemisphere functioning (Brende, 1982) is supported by neuroimaging studies showing the preeminent role of right hemispheric activity as traumatic emotional memories are activated (Rauch et al., 1996) and recalled (Schiffer et al., 1995).

It is well known that the infant's attachment system is activated when he/she is under stress, and this occurs even when the caregiver is the source of traumatic stress. Krystal noted that psychic trauma is the outcome of being confronted with overwhelming affect that produces "an unbearable psychic state which threatens to disorganize, perhaps even destroy all psychic functions" (1978, p. 82). This means that during the interpersonal transmission of a stressful state the child is also bidding the mother to interactively regulate this stress. Thus, at the "heightened affective moment" of the defensive projective identification, the child in the developmental context—as well as the patient in the therapeutic context—due to a failure of interactive regulation, is in a dysregulated and therefore intolerable state. Ogden (1990b) described how the projector (the patient) induces a feeling state in the other (the therapist) that corresponds to a state that the projector is unable to tolerate.

Because the right hemisphere is deeply connected into the limbic system (Joseph, 1996; Tucker, 1992) and the autonomic nervous system (Spence, Shapiro, & Zaidel, 1996), it is centrally involved in controlling vital functions supporting survival and enabling the individual to cope with stresses and challenges (Wittling & Schweiger, 1993). Defensive projective identification, an early-forming right-brain survival mechanism for coping with interactively generated overwhelming traumatic stress, is activated in response to subjectively perceived social stimuli that potentially trigger imminent dysregulation. I suggest that at the moment of the projection, the patient's disorganizing right brain (fragmenting self) switches from a rapidly accelerating, intensely dysregulated, hyperactive distress state into a hypoactive dissociated state.

In developmental psychoanalytic writings, Seligman postulated that projective identification arises in a developmental context "of asymmetrical influence, with both internal-structural and behavioral communicational aspects, in which one person pressures another to experience as part of herself something that the first person cannot accept within his own self-experience" (1999, p. 143). Ryle noted that the "force" of the projective identification "will be greatest where the reciprocal role pattern concerned carries a high affective charge and where the projector's sense of self is precarious" (1994, p. 111).

In the developmental psychopathology literature, Sroufe and his colleagues concluded that "the vulnerable self will be more likely to adopt dissociation as a coping mechanism because it does not have either the belief in worthiness gained from a loving and responsive early relationship or the normal level of defenses and integration that such a belief affords" (Ogawa et al., 1997, p. 875).

Developmentalists have also pointed out that "extreme" projective identification is associated with insecure attachments (Murray, 1991). Thus, for the rest of the lifespan, early-forming self-pathologies, which manifest right-hemispheric impairments (Schore, 1997b, 2001c), overutilize primitive defenses such as dissociation and defensive projective identification.

THE NATURE OF THE RECEPTIVITY REQUIRED FOR PROCESSING ADAPTIVE AND DEFENSIVE PROJECTIVE IDENTIFICATIONS

Developmental researchers studying the spontaneous affective transactions within the mother–infant dyad refer to "a mutual mapping of (some of) the elements of each interactant's state of consciousness into each of their brains. This mutual mapping process may be a way of defining intersubjectivity" (Tronick & Weinberg, 1997, p. 75). These authors contended that the infant's limbic system is centrally involved in such emotional communications. For the rest of the lifespan the right brain, which is more connected into the limbic system than the later-developing left, is especially involved in unconscious activities and spontaneous emotional communication. Because this hemisphere is dominant for "*subjective* emotional experiences" (Wittling & Roschmann, 1993; italics added), the interactive "transfer of affect" between the right brains of the members of the mother–infant and therapeutic dyads is thus best described as *intersubjectivity*. Furthermore, the cocreated dyadic amplification of state and alteration of consciousness that spontaneously occur in moments of intersubjective resonance of two "right minds" facilitate the cocreation of what Ogden called, "this third subjectivity," "the analytic third," the "unique dialectic generated by/between the separate subjectivities of an analyst and analysand within the analytic setting" (1994, p. 64).

Psychoanalysis has long been intrigued yet baffled by the mechanism of intersubjective unconscious communication. I suggest that just as the left brain communicates its states to other left brains via conscious linguistic behaviors, so the right nonverbally communicates its unconscious states to other right brains *that are tuned to receive these communications*. Freud asserted that the therapist should "turn his own unconscious like a receptive organ towards the transmitting unconscious of the patient . . . so the doctor's unconscious is able . . . to reconstruct [the patient's] unconscious" (1912/1958b, p. 115). He called the state of receptive readiness "evenly suspended attention" (p. 115). Sandler (1976) described the clinician's "free floating responsiveness."

Bion referred to "reverie," "that state of mind which is open to the reception of any 'objects' from the loved object and is therefore capable of reception of the infant's projective identifications whether they are felt by the infant to be good or bad" (1962b, p. 36). It is now thought that the mother's reverie processes the preverbal material contained in the infant's projective identifications (Bion, 1959, 1962b; Grotstein, 1981), and that "reverie is a unique experience of the therapist and is connected with countertransference" (Vaslamatzis, 1999, p. 433). Marcus noted, "The analyst, by means of reverie and intuition, listens with the right brain directly to the analysand's right brain" (1997, p. 238).

In pioneering integrations of psychoanalysis and neuroscience Miller speculated, "it is tempting to conceive of the role of the psychoanalyst in trying to understand the analysand's unconscious dynamics as including temporary suspension of left hemisphere rational-semantic cognition in order to foster a more psychodynamically meaningful 'right hemisphere-to-right hemisphere' interface between therapist and patient" (1986, p. 139). In other words, in a state of "regressive openess and receptivity" (Olnick, 1969), the therapist's right-brain countertransferential affective-receptive communications are tuned to the patient's right-brain transferential affective-expressive communications. Recall that the right brain plays a central role in the empathic perception of the emotional states of other humans (Miller et al., 2001; Schore, 1994; Voeller, 1986). Earlier clinical research demonstrates that more empathic therapists show a greater right frontal electrophysiological activation (Alpert et al., 1980).

Heimann, perhaps the first psychoanalyst to redefine the concept of countertransference, wrote, "The analyst's emotional response to the patient within the analytic situation represents one of the most important tools for his work. The analyst's countertransference is an instrument of research into the patient's unconscious" (1950, p. 74). More recently, Tansey and Burke asserted, "We view countertransference as an umbrella term encompassing the concepts of projective identification, introjective identification, and empathy" (1989, p. 41).

In more current literature, clinicians have observed that in projective identification "the receptive potential must already be present in the second person that has been perceived (out of awareness) by the initiator" (Park & Park, 1997, p. 144). Hammer described the receptive state in which the clinician can empathically resonate with the patient's unconscious communications: "My mental posture, like my physical posture, is not one of leaning forward to catch the clues, but of leaning back to let the mood, the atmosphere, come to me—to hear the meaning between the lines, to listen for the music behind the words. As one gives oneself to being carried along by the affective cadence of the patient's session, one may sense its tone and subtleties" (1990, p. 99). This description reflects the fact that the prosodic elements of communication such as rhythm, force, and tonality—more so than the linguistic elements of language—carry the affective messages within projective identifications. Right-cortical mechanisms are specifically involved in communicative pragmatics (van Lancker, 1997), and in the perception and memory of emotional words (Borod et al., 1992; Nagae & Moskovitch, 2002) and prosodic stimuli, the emotional tone of the voice (Ross, 1984; Walker, Daigle, & Buzzard, 2002).

The right hemisphere is specialized to process new information by comparing it directly with context information (Federmeier & Kutas, 1999). Kantrowitz (1999) offered a clinical example of "a transmission of one unconscious to another" within a therapeutic context:

> A patient mildly complains that her husband is urging her to dress in a more sexy manner. She rather likes the idea, doesn't really mind the slight pressure, but. . . . Here the analyst, sensing the patient's state and the quality and extent of her discomfort, spontaneously speaks the line of the sentence left unspoken: "Where will it end?" The patient sighs, "Exactly," and then elaborates, with greater nuance and detail, the worries that are stirred, the memories revived.
>
> Responses of this sort have referents that are recognizable. What had been registered that led me to complete my patient's thought in this manner? I had a context greater than the words recorded here, from which my response immediately emerged. My detailed knowledge of my patient meant not only that I had much more information than was provided by the moment, information enabling me to contextualize her material, but that I also was familiar with the *forms and nuances of her expression of affect.* I had been attuned to a *certain tone and timbre in her voice* suggestive of tension, anxiety, possibly excitement. But none of these thoughts were consciously present when I spoke. Only in retrospect, on reflection, could I account for what seemed at that moment to be my spontaneous completion of her thought. At that time, my comment might have been described simply as empathic. (p. 74; italics added)

Recall Klein's (1946) original definition of projective identification as a process wherein largely unconscious information is projected from the sender to the recipient.

The psychological orientation that allows for a receptivity to defensive projective identification is usually described in terms of a capacity to receive the patient's disavowed negative states. It is important to note that for certain personalities positive states need to be disavowed, and this points to the important function of adaptive projective identification in the treatment of preoedipally disordered, insecurely attached patients, especially those who present with anhedonic symptomatology. Seinfeld underscored the long-term psychopathogenic effects of "the lack of actual positive experiences in the patient's early life that would serve as *receptors* for the taking in of later positive relations" (1990, p. 11; italics added). The internalization of positive relations is required for the co-construction of the positive transference. This suggest that the positive affective transferential-countertransferential communications embedded within projective identifications may act as a primary interactive mechanism by which the therapeutic alliance is forged.

The Central Role of Bodily States in Projective Identification

In the early stage of treatment, the therapist is consciously attending to the patient's verbalizations in order to objectively diagnose and rationalize the patient's dysregulating symptomatology. But he/she is also listening and interacting at another level, an experience-near subjective level, one that processes socioemotional information at levels beneath awareness. The attuned, intuitive therapist, from the first point of contact, is learning the moment-to-moment rhythmic structures of the patient and is relatively flexibly and fluidly modifying his/her own behavior to fit that structure. In order to do this "the analyst must have the ability to allow a certain 'fluctuation' of his internal objects in order to leave them free to entangle with the patient's dominant projected object or object of the moment" (de Paola, 1990, p. 328). In fact, the clinician's empathic reception of and resonance with changes in the patient's inner states is a major focus of the initial stage of treatment (one that may last for a long period of time with some patients), and it literally determines whether or not a therapeutic alliance may form.

The therapeutic alliance has classically been defined by Zetzel (1956) as the patient's attachment to the therapist. The therapist's facilitating behaviors combine with the patient's capacities for attachment to permit the development of the alliance. Importantly, it emerges from the positive aspects of the mother–child relationship. In Muir's (1995) terms, the "psychobiological connection" that mediates attachment bond formation is embedded within a system of adaptive interactive projective identification, and this allows for the communication of positive states by the patient and the elicitation of relationship behavior in the therapist. The clinician's receptive orientation allows for a condition of resonance within the intersubjective field, that is the crescendos and decrescendos of the empathic clinician's psychobiological state is in resonance with similar crescendos and decrescendos of the patient's state.

In physics, a property of resonance is harmonic sympathetic vibration, which is the tendency of one resonance system to enlarge and amplify through matching the resonance frequency pattern of another resonance system. The therapist's empathic ability to receive, resonate with, and amplify the patient's often "shimmering," transient states of positive affect facilitates the interactive generation of higher and more enduring levels of positively valenced states than the patient can autogenerate (Schore, 2000e). Reciprocal transactions within a dyadic system of adaptive projective identification thus interactively generate amplified levels of dynamic "vitality" affects (Stern, 1985), the positive states that drive an attachment bond, facilitate the coconstruction of the positive transfer-

ence, and fuel hope. These moments of intersubjective resonance also facilitate dyadically expanded states of consciousness in both the mother–infant and
patient–therapist intersubjective fields (Tronick et al., 1998). Loewald (1986)
described "resonances between the patient's and the analyst's unconscious,"
and Sander (1992) stated that "moments of meeting" between patient and therapist occur when there are "matched specificities between two systems in resonance, attuned to each other."

Empathy, defined as "the ability to sample other's affects . . . and to be able
to respond in resonance to them" (Easser, 1974), has long been considered to
be a critical element of an effective therapeutic alliance (Bohart & Greenberg,
1997). The cocreation of the alliance is a central task of the early treatment,
and in this work:

> The empathic character of a therapeutic interaction is determined by
> letting the empathic-resonance process develop within the therapist and
> then by tuning into the client's experience to check for an ultimate test
> of accuracy to see how close the therapist is. The criterion of accuracy of
> the therapist's responses is the . . . degree to which the response carries
> the client's experiencing a little forward. (Vanaerschot, 1997, p. 148)

According to Kantrowitz, when the patient and analyst are able to overcome
resistance to engagement, an "intense affective engagement takes place" (1999,
p. 70). She further stated that "When patient and analyst are affectively engaged, when the patient has come to trust in the analyst's basic benevolence,
and when in this context the patient feels safe enough to lessen defences, the
modification of intrapsychic organization becomes possible" (p. 69).

As a result, the patient establishes what Kohut (1984) called an "archaic
bond" with the therapist, and thereby facilitates the revival of the early phases
at which his psychological development has been arrested. The emotional bond
between the patient and therapist, manifested in the working alliance, promotes the exploration of the individual's internal experiences and affective
states (Bordin, 1979). This strongly felt bond enables the patient to confront
inner states associated with frightening aspects of the self (Jaenicke, 1987). This
safe interpersonal context sets up a condition in which trauma and the coping
mechanism to deal with trauma, defensive projective identification, can be
openly expressed, and therefore amenable to change.

A cardinal tenet of developmental projective identification is that the infant
projects parts or the whole of its emerging self "into the mother's body," and like
the empathic mother who aligns with her infant's in order to regulate and be
regulated by his/her internal state, the clinician's body is a primary instrument
for psychobiological attunement and the reception of the transmission of nonconscious affect. Aron (1998) described the process as follows:

> Gradually, patient and analyst mutually regulate each other's behaviors,
> enactments, and states of consciousness such that each gets under the

other's skin, each reaches into the other's guts, each is breathed in and absorbed by the other. . . . Where the patient is not capable of using symbolic or metaphoric thought, the analyst may receive communications only nonverbally often in the form of bodily communications, a change in the climate, the air (mediated by the breath), a change in the feel of things (mediated by the skin). . . . [T]he analyst must be attuned to the nonverbal, the affective . . . to his or her bodily responses. (p. 26)

Bromberg (1991) wrote of the patient's unarticulated wish that the therapist know him/her "from the inside out."

In a similar vein, Wrye (1998) concluded that the therapist's use of projective identification increases the permeability of his/her ego boundaries so that he/she can attain a closer state of attunement to the patient. And Sands offered the clinical observation that via projective identification: "The patient and I succeeded in co-creating in me a state in which I could 'get' something viscerally about the pathogenic interactions of his childhood that he unconsciously needed me to understand" (1997a, p. 653).

Because affects are psychobiological phenomena and the self is bodily based, projective identification represents not linguistic but *mind-body communications*. According to Basch, "The language of mother and infant consist of signals produced by the autonomic, involuntary nervous system in both parties" (1976, p. 766). Basch also pointed out the direct parallel of this to projective identification, which is manifest in "a situation in which the patient subtly causes the therapist to resonate *autonomically* with the patient's unconscious affect-laden fantasies" (1992, p. 179; italics added).

The ensuing amplification of the patient's autonomic state is subjectively experienced by the clinician as what Damasio (1994) called a "somatic marker," "gut" feelings that are experienced in response to both real and imagined events, including threatening stimuli. Somatic markers have been described in the psychotherapy literature as the felt sense (Gendlin, 1970), a bodily based perception of meaning (Bohart, 1993). In recent psychoneurobiological models the felt sense is defined as "the sum total of all sensations from all sense organs, both conscious and subliminal at any given moment" (Scaer, 2001). Sensations from the internal environment — viscero-sensation — are thought to be acquired via a "sixth sense," a faculty of perception that does not depend upon any outward sense that is used to describe "heightened sensitivity, 'gut-feeling' or 'psychic' ability" (Zagon, 2001, p. 671). Neuroscience conceptions which postulate that sensory inputs originating from the internal environment act to alter (heighten or dull) the perception of the outside world and elicit a behavioral response (Zagon, 2001) mirror Freud's (1915/1957a) concept of drive, "the psychical representative of the stimuli originating from the organism and reaching the mind."

In order to read the implicit output of the patient's unconscious brain/mind/body system, the intuitive clinician's reflective function appraises not only exteroceptive visual and prosodic information emanating from the patient but also interoceptive information that is triggered by these supra- and subliminal interpersonal signals. This psychobiological attunement is performed by a preconscious monitoring of the moment-to-moment dynamic changes of the sympathetic and parasympathetic components of the therapist's ANS, the "physiological bottom of the mind." In other words, the empathically resonating therapist's matching of the rhythmic crescendos and decresendos of his/her psychobiological state with the patient's represents the psychobiological attunement of his/her felt sense to the patient's felt sense. The key to working with dissociated affect is the cocreation of a stronger signal of the felt sense — the therapist serves as a source of autonomic feedback of the patient's dissociated affect, thereby allowing the therapeutic alliance to amplify the intensity and duration of an unconscious affect long enough for it to enter into consciousness. In *Affect Regulation and the Origin of the Self* (Schore, 1994) I extensively described how the psychobiologically attuned caregiver serves as an arousal amplifier of the infant's bodily-based affective autonomic states.

The therapist's detection of his/her countertransferential interoceptive responses that resonate with the patient's autonomic responses to threatening stimuli is especially important to the reception of defensive projective identifications. These are registered in the therapist's right brain, especially in its limbic-autonomic circuits. It is established that "a primary role for the right ventral medial prefrontal cortex may be the integration of internal physiological states with salient environmental cues, to guide behavior in an optimally cautious or adaptive manner in situations of perceived threat or conflict" (Sullivan & Gratton, 2002a, p. 77). With regard to the patient's state, this same right-lateralized structure is where the emotional trace of a conditioned fear is formed and stored (Fischer, Anderrson, Furmark, Wik, & Fredrikson, 2002). Other key structures activated in the heightened therapeutic moment are the right amygdala, an area involved in "unseen fear" (Morris et al., 1999), the right insula, which generates a cortical image of the interoceptive condition of the body (Craig, 2002), and the vagus nerve which delivers viscero-sensation from the stomach, bowels, heart, lung, pancreas, and liver to awareness (Zagon, 2002).

The clinician's implicit countertransferential reactions to the patient's communicating self system are thus registered in his/her right brain, because this hemisphere, dominant for the corporeal self (Devinsky, 2000), contains the most comprehensive and integrated map of the body state available to the brain (Damasio, 1994), processes the autonomic correlates of emotional arousal (Witting & Roschmann, 1993), plays a special role in the perception of the affective qualities of somatic signals coming from the body (Galin, 1974), decodes emotional stimuli by "actual felt [somatic] emotional reactions to the stimuli, that is, by a form of empathic responding" (Day & Wong, 1996, p. 651), and is dominant for attentional processes (Heilman et al., 1977; Coule et al., 1996). Indeed it is the repository of the therapist's autobiographical memory (Fink et al., (1996). According to Gabbard (2001) countertransference "is determined by the fit between what the patient projects into the therapist and what preexisting structures are present in the therapist's intrapsychic world" (2001, p. 990). These intrapsychic structures are located in the therapist's right brain.

Isakower (in Balter et al., 1980) described the therapist's state of "evenly hovering attention," which shifts between what comes from the outside (from the patient) and what is emerging from inside (visual, auditory, and bodily images within the therapist). This bears upon the matter of "somatic counter-transference" (Dosamentes-Beaudry, 1997). Clinical observers have noted that "perhaps the most striking evidence of successful empathy is the occurrence in our bodies of sensations that the patient has described in his or hers" (Havens, 1979, p. 42), and that psychotherapeutic resonance is expressed in "specific sensations and/or feelings kinesthetically perceived by the therapist" (Larson, 1987, p. 322). In fact, Parker Lewis (1992) pointed out that the therapist's use of his/her body is especially involved in the reception of right-brain-to-right-brain transferential projections of split-off parts of the self, and asserted that this mechanism specifically mediates defensive projective identification. Feldman described an example of the awareness of his bodily sense and the patient's emotional state at the moment of the reception of the projection: "There was a tense and expectant silence and I felt aware of a *pressure* to respond quickly to what she had brought. When I did not do so, she commented that the silence seemed rather *ominous*" (1997, p. 236; italics added).

Alvarez articulated the clinical principle that "patients have the right to bring us the bad objects in their emotional baggage and explore them and experience them with us" (1999, p. 214). The clinician's task of receiving and containing defensive projective identifications is obviously more difficult than adaptive projective identifications. This is because resonating with the dissociated, negatively affectively charged chaotic bodily states of personalities manifesting "primitive emotional disorders" is, indeed, no easy matter. Boyer (1990) pointed out that:

> The range of experiences the analyst must be able to tolerate, understand, and interpret meaningfully extends from feeling like an excluded object whose interventions, if acknowledged, are treated by the patient as evidence of the analyst's madness, to reacting to the patient's fusional regression and dependence as though the analyst is an extension of his mind and/body, and to his sometimes startling somatic displays. (p. 306)

As Feldman observed, "If the analyst is receptive to the patient's projections, the impact of the patient's disturbing unconscious fantasies that concern the nature of the relationship with the patient inevitably touch on the analyst's own anxieties" (1997, p. 235). Grinberg (1995) stated that:

> With regressive cases and borderline patients . . . it would be necessary to be more disposed to receive and contain the patient's projections for as long as required. The receptive attitude of the analyst reveals itself by

consenting to be invaded by the projections of the analysand's psychotic anxieties and fantasies and contain them so as to feel, think, and share the emotions contained in such projections with him, as they were part of his own self, whatever their nature may be (murderous hate, fear of death, catastrophic terror, etc.). (p. 104)

In other words, resonating with and then internally amplifying the patient's negatively valenced primitive affective state triggers a disequilibrium within the therapist's right brain, the hemisphere that is specialized for generating physiological responses to emotional stimuli (Spence et al., 1996). There is convincing evidence in the neurobiological literature to show that the right hemisphere is specialized for coping with stress (Wittling & Schweiger, 1993) and for processing negative affect (Davidson, 1998; Gainotti, 2001; Otto et al., 1987; Schore, 1997b). Furthermore, the experience of strong sustained negative emotion causes interference with normal right hemisphere functioning (Hartikainen, Ogawa, & Knight, 2000; Ladavas et al., 1984), and this aversive subjective emotional experience would accompany the reception of a defensive projective identification. In a striking metaphor of projective identification, Rosenfeld (1971) described the patient's fantasy of "worming his way into the analyst's brain." Clinical studies show that the therapist's technical competence may specifically deteriorate when the patient attempts to transform the therapist into someone "bad" (Gorney, 1979).

THE THERAPIST'S DEFLECTION OF PROJECTED
NEGATIVE STATES AND THE INTENSIFICATION
OF INTERACTIVE DYSREGULATION

How the therapist, who is now also experiencing a stress state, responds to the patient's defensive projective identification becomes an essential factor in the treatment. In writing on the therapeutic process, Binder and Strupp concluded that "negative process is a major obstacle to successful treatment, and . . . its pervasiveness has been underestimated" (1997, p. 121). The clinician's ability to recognize and regulate the negative affect within himself/herself has been described as the most difficult part of treatment (Ellman, 1991).

This task is difficult because the experience of traumatic pain is stored in bodily based implicit-procedural memory in the right brain (Schore, 2001d), and therefore communicated at a nonverbal, psychophysiological level, not in the verbal articulation of a discrete subjective state. As Sands pointed out: "The material [embedded in projective identification] may remain unsymbolized because it was encoded under traumatic conditions or because it pertains to a preverbal period of life. Whatever the reason, because such experience remains in somatosensory or iconic form, it must be communicated in like manner" (1997b, p. 702).

Bion (1977) suggested that therapeutic "containing" is required because the mother's capacity to contain the child's distressing emotions was insufficient, and they were therefore returned to the child little changed and difficult to integrate. Importantly, the mother herself could not provide a model for the child's containment of its own feelings; this the therapist must do. It should be emphasized, however, that "the task of receiving, containing, and processing the patient's dissociated early experience and returning its content to him in a more benign form is not an easy one because emotionally intense resistances against the containment of patient's toxic material are mobilized within the therapist" (Dosamantes, 1992, p. 361). As Gill pointed out, "An analyst who is ever alert to his (or her) participation in the process may be under as much, if not more, stress than the patient" (1994, p. 103).

The key here is whether the therapist can autoregulate the negative state enough to act as an interactive affective regulator for the patient. If he/she blocks his/her own negatively valenced somatic markers, for example by defensively shifting out of the right brain state into a left brain state, he/she cuts off his/her empathic connection to his/her own pain and therefore to the patient's pain. Frequently, because the clinician is now in a left-hemispheric dominant state, he/she will quickly present a verbal interpretation (Brenman Pick, 1985), typically a communication of a resistance analysis that "paradoxically" intensifies into an enactment. Ryle (1994) noted that:

> When projective identification is conceived of as an expression of innate destructive forces or as a motivated defence against them, and when it is interpreted as such, the interpretation is often sensed as critical, and coming from the powerful position of the analyst, can easily be subsumed as an aspect of an existing critical or persecutory role in the patient's system, serving to reinforce that system. (p. 111)

Furthermore, Spezzano (1993) described:

> The analyst is . . . limited in her ability to make use of the unconscious affective communications of the patient by her ability to hold them in herself—to hold especially those particular blends of disturbing affects that the patient is forced to project, enact, or crumble under and to hold them long enough to be able to identify them, think about them, and say something useful on the basis of them—rather than simply projecting them back between the lines of a resistance interpretation or warding them off through a prolonged blindness to or enactment of them. (p. 212)

Plakun (1999) observed that the therapist's "refusal of the transference," particularly the negative transference, is an early manifestation of an enactment. It is important to note that the clinician's "refusal" or "deflection" of the patient's projected negative state is a spontaneous behavior that is perceived by the patient, albeit through a negatively biased subjective lens. The therapist's verbal interpretation is often accompanied by spontaneous disgusted-contemptuous facial expression and/or a sarcastic tone of voice. Although this negative affective expression is brief and unconscious to the clinician, it is detected by the patient's right hemisphere.

Psychophysiological studies of emotion communication demonstrate that human vocal affect expressions of anger elicit electromyographically detectable changes in the receiver's facial affect expressions (Hietanen, Surakka, & Linnankoski, 1998), and hence the therapist's face briefly mimics the state changes induced by the patient's negative communication. Thus, the patient in a face-to-face context implicitly detects the therapist's countertransferential visually expressed aversive response, and even in nonface-to-face contexts, perceives alterations in the clinician's tone of voice to his/her negatively valenced affective communications. But, in addition, neurobiological research demonstrates that aberrant early social experiences alter the ability to efficiently process facial expessions of emotion, and that such individuals overinterpret signals as threatening and overidentify anger (Pollak & Kistler, 2002). This may mediate the transference process, defined as a selective bias in dealing with others that is based on previous early experiences and that shapes current expectancies (McLaughlin, 1981).

The interaction of these two nonconscious mechanisms may account for the synergistic effects of the therapist's transient countertransferential "mindblindness" and the patient's negatively biased transferential expectation—the co-creation of an enactment. Furthermore, Feldman noted that the fulminating negative state "may evoke forms of projection and enactment by the analyst, in an attempt at restoring an internal equilibrium, of which the analyst may initially be unaware" (1997, p. 235). This maneuver of the stressed therapist is, however, expressed in gestures and body language, behaviors that play a prominent role in the unconscious interpersonal communications embedded within the enactment (Frayn, 1996). It is now well established that enactments are fundamentally mediated by nonverbal unconscious relational behaviors within the therapeutic dyad (McLaughlin, 1991; Schore, 1997c).

The therapist who misattunes and is subsequently unable to recorrect will thus project the unregulated state back, further stressing the working alliance. The patient who rereceives an unmodulated stressful communication now becomes, as a repetition of his/her early history, further psychophysiologically dysregulated by the misattuning object. According to Bach, "Difficult patients continue to respond at the sensorimotor-physiological level, precisely because that is where the earliest mutual regulation went awry" (1998, p. 188). As a result of this increasing stress level, a pathological internal representation is activated, a negatively valenced representation of a dysregulated-self-in-interaction-with-a-misattuning-object, one that triggers an expectation of imminent self-disorganization (Schore, 1994, 1997c). In other words, there is now an overt expression of an intense, unregulated negative transference reaction. The emotions evoked in the transference "hinge on the range and extent of expectations for different situations that are already a part of the patient's repertory" (Singer, 1985, p. 198).

This rapidly amplifying perturbation instantly disorganizes the intersubjective field, and an interactively intensified physiological stress response now propels the patient's immature self-system into accelerating levels of arousal that are beyond his/her fragile, limited, and inefficient affect-regulating coping capacities. The patient thus will instantly access an internal working model of an insecure attachment that encodes a primitive defense for coping with interactive stress—the right-brain strategies of dissociation and projective identification. It is now thought that "it is the person's specific experiences that will determine the cues that trigger the breakdown of regulatory processes as well as the dominant responses that will be released when regulatory processes fail" (Newman & Wallace, 1993, p. 717).

The essential defensive nature of this primitive regulatory mechanism is echoed in the term *defensive* projective identification. The patient's sympathetically driven hyperarousal reaches a point of such intensity that a massive parasympathetic counterregulatory strategy must be activated. In other words, projective identification occurs in the context of a "malignant transference reaction" that reflects hyperarousal and hypoarousal-associated alterations of limbic regions (McKenna, 1994). Specifically, this mechanism represents a sudden shift from energy-expending hyperarousal into dissociation and energy-conserving hypoarousal. The fact that this stress-regulating mechanism represents a sudden transition from a hyperaroused into a hyperinhibited state indicates that the accelerating negative affect is not "emptied" or "discharged." The hyperarousal still remains and thus the pain endures, but is now instantly dissociated, and thereby "anesthetized" or "numbed."

This bears upon some controversial aspects of the concept of projective identification. It is often written that projective identification is an attempt to intentionally control the therapist, but it should be noted that beneath the initial forceful explosive expression is intense disorganization and insecurity, and not intentionality but hopelessness, helplessness, and a total lack of an organized coping mechanism. Alvarez held that the interpretation of projective identification is harmful, in that it triggers defenses that are "desperate attempts to overcome and recover from states of despair and terror," yet these defences are "inadequate to manage . . . powerful feelings" (1997, p. 754).

Furthermore, this primitive coping mechanism does represent an affective communication, and it does allow the precarious personality organization to disown parts of the self, that is to "rid" the individual contact with his/her own mind—and body(!)—but it does not represent a literal evacuation or expelling out into an other, so that the negative state no longer exists within. The tension is not relieved, because the state of hyperarousal remains. And the pain still exists within, but is instantly dissociated by increased endogenous opioid release, and experienced as an enduring "dead spot" in the patient's subjectivity.

Thus, at the moment of an adaptive projective identification the patient's affect is subjectively deepened and communicated, while in the instance of a defensive projective identification affect is not just diminished but totally blocked from consciousness (dissociated) and its interpersonal communication suddenly ceases. As a result of the sudden shift from a state of active coping into an inhibited state of passive coping, the patient will "implode" under stress, and further dissociate from the state, so that it appears as if only the therapist holds it. In other words, in the moments after the defensive projective identification, the dissociating patient, now in a state of dense emotional inhibition, is no longer overtly expressing a dysregulating emotion, but the nondissociating, resonating therapist is still subjectively experiencing the amplified negative state. In this case it may seem to the therapist that the state originates endogenously within himself/herself and is not an emotional response to the patient's communication. This state now frequently becomes amplified into a lingering dysphoric mood.

Defensive Projective Identification as Early Events in Dyadic Enactments

Despite the fact that the patient's conscious experience of pain is dissociated by his/her numbing and mindblinding defensive autoregulatory strategy, the still-dysregulated patient will often soon exert increasing amounts of "pressure" on the therapist for interactive regulation. This may seem paradoxical, but actually it reflects the patient's communications of an unconscious attachment need for interactive regulation to help him/her cope with the dysregulation. Bion (1959) vividly described how the infant, confronted with what seems like an impenetrable object, is driven to project into such an object with more and more force. The means by which the patient applies this "controlling" pressure "may be explicit, through direct appeals and provocations, or may be indirect and subtle, relying on non-verbal cues and on discrepancies between what is said and the emotion conveyed" (Ryle, 1994, p. 111). Indeed, according to Strupp, "The greatest challenge facing the therapist is the skillful management of enactments that often put the therapist on the defensive, evoke boredom, irritation, anger, and hostility and in other respects 'put pressure' on the therapist to behave in ways that are incompatible with his or her stance as an empathic listener and clarifier" (1989, p. 719). And yet it is important to be aware of the fact that "the patient's use of more forceful projection may be driven by his experience of the analyst as a non-understanding, non-receptive figure, which the analyst may not perceive" (Feldman, 1997, p. 233).

Although the therapist is in a state of "prolonged blindness" (Spezzano, 1993) and therefore no longer externally scanning for implicit external signals of the patient's internal disorganization, the patient continues to send out signals of intensifying stress. According to Putnam (1997), dissociative switches are manifest in changes in facial expression, scanning of the environment, and marked postural shifts. Such expressions may be very subtle, and not recognized even at a preconscious level by the defended therapist, who now is "switched-off" (Spezzano, 1993).

Loewald offered a clinical example of this process, and pointed out that this defensive countertransferential strategy, if not recognized and processed by the clinician, can cause gross interference with the therapeutic process. Loewald (1986) noted:

> Less spectacular, but more insidious and often more damaging, are behaviors of the analyst that are the results of inner defense against his countertransference reactions, such as rigid silences, unbending attitudes, repression or isolation of troublesome impulses, fantasies, or memories. . . . The analyst . . . in his effort to stay sane and rational is often apt to repress the very transference-countertransference resonances and responses induced by the patient that would give him the deepest but also the most unsettling understanding of himself and the patient. (p. 283)

I would add that this unconscious maneuver may not represent repression, but a partial dissociation that matches the patient's state.

Embedded in the patient's projected transmissions are nonverbal communications of pain, but "the therapist because of intense countertransference pain, flees from the patient's experience of chaos and the intensity of affects that accompany an experience of dissolution" (Mordecai, 1995, p. 492). This maneuver, the therapist's precipitous "retreat from the patient's vantage point" (Schwaber, 1992), however, disrupts the functioning of the "analyzing instrument" (Balter et al., 1980). The evolving mutual projective identification becomes "a slippery slope on which the therapist is in danger of sliding away from the . . . therapeutic role," which "can lead a therapist to become lost in the dyad with the patient, becoming unmoored from the larger task" (Plakun, 1999, p. 287).

According to Plakun (1999), the dyadic enactment is triggered when the therapist:

> participates unwittingly by projecting back into the patient reciprocal and complementary unconscious conflicted countertransference material from the therapist's own life history. The therapist unwittingly colludes with the patient in a process of mutual and complementary projective identification organized around significant past events from the lives of *both* participants. Within such an enactment, the therapist is as much an active participant as the patient. (p. 286)

This dysregulating interactive context is a direct analog of an earlier developmental scenario that was common in the patient's attachment history of the first two years of life. In developmental writings, Murray (1991) concluded that:

> If . . . the infant's state is experienced by the mother as threatening or overwhelming, she may feel the need to switch off from the infant, and may likely be drawn instead to focus on her own experience. If, however, she is unable to switch off, for example in the face of the infant's persistent demands, the mother may find it hard to distinguish the infant's perspective from the impact his state makes on her, in which case she may experience the infant as trying to tyrannize her and may regard with hostility. (p. 223)

It is within this stressful context that the mother unconsciously yet forcefully (re)projects into the infant certain disavowed, yet highly invested negative attributions (Lieberman, 1997). Notice the similarity of the mother's (mis)attribution of tyranny to the infant, and the classical (mis)conception of intentional control to the patient manifesting a projective identification. This developmental context of a dysregulating interaction with first a "switched off" caregiver and then an intrusive and hyperarousing caregiver is a primary source of the repetition compulsion enacted by the mutually projecting therapist and patient.

The enactment, now driven on both sides by a dyadic system that mutually amplifies intense negative affect, can rapidly escalate. Borderline patients, who are extremely sensitive to humiliation, can often persuade even experienced therapists to become enmeshed in distressing affects, and "even to feel overwhelmed by feelings of passionate attachments to patients . . . at times such patients accurately perceive subtle or hidden feelings of the therapist and then facilitate intensification of such feelings until the therapist behaves in some fashion that can even be irrational, all usually occurring without the therapist (or the patient) aware of the coercive dynamics" (Park & Park, 1997, p. 144).

Feldman (1997) wrote on "projective identification: the *analyst's* involvement" (italics added). This clearly implies that an area of self analysis is:

> the analyst's superego, for example; the patient will expect, and often get, criticism, usually unintentional and unwitting, from the analyst . . . problems obstructing the understanding of what is happening in the intrapsychic world of the patient arise from the psychoanalyst's mind becoming overrun with disturbance; the psychoanalyst's own disturbance mating with the patients. (Hinshelwood, 1994, p. 169)

The rapid-onset, dynamic events of the "negative therapeutic reaction" are thus an overt manifestation of the interaction of the patient's covert deep unconscious defensive transference patterns with the clinician's covert deep unconscious defensive countertransference patterns (Schore, 1997c). The patient does not project an internal critic into the therapist, but rather the therapist's internal critic, stimulated by the patient's negative affective communications, resonates with the patient's and is thereby amplified. The receptivity of both members of the dyad breaks down and seals over, leading to a long-enduring therapeutic impasse when it comes to intense affective states, or even a precipitous termination. A poor therapeutic outcome is thereby "the result of the linkage of the therapist's affective relationship regulation to the unconscious signals of the patient which leads to a stabilization of the patient's conflictive structure" (Merten, Anstadt, Ullrich, Krause, & Buchheim, 1996, p. 210).

The nontherapeutic effects of the therapist's defensiveness in response to the patient's defensive projective identification are due to the fact that these events prevent "reinternalization": "If it does not occur, there is no change in the patient's psychological functioning and consequently he still needs to use the projective identification" (Migone, 1995, p. 628). Feldman wrote, "It is as if the patient has such doubts about the possibility either of symbolic communication or the object's subjectivity to any form of projection that he cannot relent until he has evidence of the impact on the analyst's mind and body. If this consistently fails, confirming an early experience of an unavailable, hateful object, he may give up in despair" (1997, p. 232).

According to Perna, "The absence of receptivity on the part of the therapist, that is, the resistance to live with the therapist in harmonious interpenetrating mix-up, may lead to the inability of the patient to evolve through the chaos-regression and achieve a higher level of structural integration" (1997, p. 266). The untoward, iatrogenic effects of the therapist's deflection of the patient's defensive projective identification is also described by Sands: "If the analyst cannot make herself available . . . and cannot receive the patient's indirect, visceral communications, then these dissociated, not me aspects of self that are being communicated will be unconsciously experienced as intolerable to the analyst as well, and the patient will not be able to bring these aspects into the analytic relationship" (1997a, p. 665).

More so, the therapist's use of defensive projective identification to evacuate unwanted "toxic" aspects of the self back into the patient has significant consequences:

> The projected affects often involve the therapist's hidden feeling of shame, envy, vulnerabilty, and impotence. The hidden shame is signalled by the therapist's use of "attack other" defenses such as sarcasm, teasing, ridicule, and efforts to control the patient in some way. Later on, the tragic projection comes full circle when the patient feels humiliated, exploited, betrayed, abandoned, and isolated (Epstein, 1994, p. 100).

With borderline patients the clinician's lack of recognition of his/her refusal to "take the negative transference" is a central factor in boundary violations and enactments involving both sexual misconduct and self-destructive behaviors (Plakun, 1999, 2001).

THE THERAPIST'S AUTOREGULATION
OF PROJECTED NEGATIVE STATES
AND COPARTICIPATION IN INTERACTIVE REPAIR

It is important to note that the rapid, mutually disorganizing stressful events occurring within episodes of defensive projective identification and clinical enactments offer important possibilities for not only "grasping the patient's inner world as it intersects with the therapist's own" (Plakun, 1999), but also for structural growth of right-lateralized internal psychic systems that unconsciously process emotional communications and regulate stressful emotional states. The right hemisphere, which is dominant for processing stress and negative emotions, especially for monitoring "failure-linked emotions," shows a strong response to error and negative emotional feedback (Koshkarov, Pokrovskaja, Lovota, & Mordvintsev, 1996; Sobotka et al., 1992), yet is centrally involved in the potential utilization of negative feedback from the external environment for error compensation (Kaplan & Zaidel, 2001).

In an earlier writing I contended that the therapist's misattunement often triggers the enactment, that involvement of both members of the dyad is necessary for interactive repair, and that this regulatory process must be initiated by the therapist *while he or she is under interactive stress* (Schore, 1997a). Writing in the trauma literature on "dramatic reenactments" that occur well into the treatment, Lindy asked, "Is there some aspect of the here-and-now situation with the therapist that is unwillingly precipitating the configuration of the traumatic event, and which, if understood, would aid in the working through of the trauma?" (1996, pp. 534–535). Bach asserted that "disruptions of the therapeutic alliance may result from the patient's impulses or our own ineptness, expressed in a mutual enactment or a projective identification, but they demand immediate understanding and rectification" (1998, p. 186).

It has been pointed out that it is the therapist's "emotional containment" that breaks the "vicious cycle" of the defensive projection within the therapeutic dyad (Migone, 1995). The stressful context in which this is accomplished is heightened by the simultaneous activation and communication of different motivations by the patient: The analyst will experience powerful transferential pulls that emanate both from the patient's repetitious, pathological relational configurations and from the patient's strivings for the needed vitalizing (self object) experiences" (Fosshage, 1994, p. 277).

In other words, embedded within the patient's often vociferous communication of the dysregulated state is also a definite, yet seemingly inaudible, urgent appeal for interactive regulation. Sands wrote "In projective identification, the individual unconsciously puts pressure on the other to experience what he cannot experience in order to vicariously explore and become known to himself" (1997b, p. 697). Joseph pointed out, "I could see . . . the way in which I was being pushed and carried along to feel and react . . . [the patient] was invading me with despair and, at the same time, attempting unconsciously to force me to calm myself" (1988, p. 73).

This same mechanism has been described by developmental workers. In the essential regulatory pattern of "disruption and repair" (Beebe & Lachmann, 1994; Lewis, 2000; Schore, 1994) the "good-enough" caregiver who induces a stress response in his/her infant through a misattunement, reinvokes in a timely fashion his/her psychobiologically attuned regulation of the infant's negative affect state *that he/she has triggered*. Tronick (1989) described "interactive repair," a process in which the mother who induces interactive stress and negative emotion in the infant is instrumental to the transformation of negative back into positive emotion.

In the developmental literature Murray observed that the mother must both be open to how the infant feels and also have an affective response that complements the infant process. Murray (1991) observed:

> This may well be unproblematic in periods of infant quiet alertness and containment, but, in the inevitable times of infant distress and agitation, emotions may be provoked in the mother that will be disturbing to her if she does not have available the resources to accommodate or contain them. To the extent that the mother is able to both identify with her infant and contain difficult feelings that the infant's behavior provokes in her, she will be able to respond in an appropriate fashion that meets, or complements, the infant's requirements; and the infant will, in turn, develop the capacity to tolerate and manage his own distress. (p. 223)

This maternal sensitivity to and modulation of the infant's states was also described by Krystal: "Possibly the most crucial and difficult aspect of mothering consists in permitting the child to bear increasingly intense affective tension, but stepping in and comforting the child before his emotions overwhelm him" (1978, p. 96).

In order to perform this parental regulatory function, the adult must not only mirror the infant's distress state, but then "go beyond mirroring" to "deal with distress" rather than being overwhelmed by it (Fonagy et al., 1995). To do this he/she needs to sense and then regulate his/her own as well as the child's affective state, a particularly emotionally demanding task. According to Carpy, "The normal infant needs to be able to sense that her mother is struggling to tolerate her projected distress without major disruption of her maternal function. [The mother] will be unable to avoid giving the infant slight indications of the way she is affected by [her infant], and it is these indications which allow the infant to see that the projected aspects of herself can indeed be tolerated" (1989, p. 293).

This affect-regulating mechanism is identical to Winnicott's (1975) "holding functions," defined as a complex of emotional and physical maternal functions, expressed especially through eye and voice, which the available "good-enough mother" utilizes in the face of her infant's emotional/impulsive expressions. Recall that the maternal comforting substrate resides in the mother's right brain (Horton, 1995), the hemisphere that is dominant for nonverbal behavior and for responding to stress (Wittling, 1997). More so than the clinician's verbalizations, it is his/her nonverbal activity (Davis & Hadiks, 1994) that creates the safe holding environment. Muir concluded that "the holding situation includes both physiologic and psychological holding. The transpersonal process is the medium for this necessary psychobiologic connection" (1995, p. 252).

In order to maintain a holding environment during moments when an intersubjective field is dynamically generating an increasing density of negative affect, the clinician needs to resist, at an implicit level, a homeostatic impulse to counterregulate a state of right brain psychobiological disequilibrium by shifting into a left hemispheric dominant state. As opposed to the left, the right hemisphere has a "wait and see" mode of processing (Federmeier & Kutas, 2002, p. 730). And so the therapist must "attempt to refrain from doing something until she has lived with the evoked feelings for some time" (Stark, 1999, p. 276). If he/she fails to "hold" long enough it will be overtly manifest in an expression of left brain activity, the sudden onset of verbal behavior; that is, a premature interpretation. It has been pointed out that the clinician must hold the projective identification and not return it prematurely (Joseph, 1978). Premature interpretations thus reflect a therapeutic misattunement in which the clinician shifts back into a left hemispheric, secondary process, linear mode in order to extricate himself/herself from falling more deeply into an interactively rapidly amplifying right dominant primary-process psychobiological state that is inherently nonlinear and chaotic.

It is important to again stress that early relational trauma, attachment psychopathology, and the defenses of dissociation are stored in the right hemisphere. The emergence of strong affect during psychotherapy sessions is known to be accompanied by increased right hemispheric activation in the patient (Hoffman & Goldstein, 1981). And thus in these central moments of the treatment of developmentally disordered patients, holding the right brain-to-right brain context of emotional communication is essential. This holding occurs in implicit processing, and involves "being able to prolong one's experiential process at the level of implicit experiencing" (Vanaerschot, 1997, p. 148); that is, staying in the right brain mode of "implicit learning" (Hugdahl, 1995).

The right hemisphere is dominant not only for emotional communication (Blonder et al., 1991), empathy (Perry et al., 2001), and affect regulation (Schore, 1994), but also for nonlinear (Schore, 1997b) and primary-process cognition (Galin, 1974; Joseph, 1996). Rotenberg pointed out that in contrast to linear left hemispheric, formal logical thinking that builds up "a pragmatically convenient, but simplified model of reality," right cortical image thinking is adaptive when information is "complex, internally contradictory and basically irreducible to an unambiguous context" (1995, p. 57).

Thus, in the heightened affective moment of an enactment, the key to sustaining a cocreated right brain-to-right brain holding environment is the clinician's capacity of "avoiding closure" and tolerating ambiguity, uncertainty, and lack of differentiation in order "to wonder." This means holding the felt-sense component of an affective state in working memory over a longer duration of time, an adaptive function because "the longer the period during which a person is influenced by physiological and cognitive processes activated by the emotion the higher the probability that this experience will be subjectively perceived as important and meaningful" (Gilboa & Revelle, 1994, p. 135). This mechanism is critical to the clinician's deep intersubjective perception of the operations of the patient's meaning systems. Recall that the felt sense acts as a bodily based perception of meaning (Bohart, 1993).

Furthermore, a dynamic systems theory perspective of the psychotherapy process holds that both the therapist and the patient need to understand that destabilization and the tolerance of uncertainty may be fundamental to a healthy growth process, and that such experiences are important opportunities for change. Perna described, "This point of reorganization in the therapeutic process can be quite difficult as many therapists, not to mention patients, may find the uncertainty anxiety producing. A traditional view rooted in linear thinking may lead the therapist to impose at this juncture a reality constraint that forces a specific construction of the therapist's making onto the patient's psyche" (1997, p. 266). This mistimed, intrusive interpretation inevitably destroys for the patient the possibility of creating something out of himself (Balint, 1968).

Because the holding environment is organized by preverbal communications (Rubin & Niemeier, 1992), the continuously attuned clinician must instantiate a right brain regulatory strategy that allows him/her to remain in a state of "regressive openness and receptivity." The essential step in creating a holding environment in which an affect-communicating reconnection can be forged is the therapist's ability, initially at a nonverbal level, to detect, recognize, monitor, and autoregulate the countertransferential stressful alterations in his/her bodily state that are evoked by the patient's transferential communication. Thus, the clinician simultaneously monitors the information coming from the patient as well as his/her own psychobiological response to this emotional communication.

Holmes wrote of the therapist's essential capacity for "binocular vision" that enables him/her to both engage with the patient and be aware of the nature of this engagement (1998), and suggested "focusing on the totality of the patient, and the totality of my response to the patient, I am aware that I am focusing on the patient and my response to her" (1996, p. 86). The ability to act as a holding container (interactive psychobiological regulator) for the patient's "affective energy" "may require the therapist to live in dual modes of existence. . . . The therapist must attend to his or her own self-regulatory functioning and at the same time participate fully with the patient in mutual exploration, development, and affective exchange" (Perna, 1997, p. 260). Notice the similarity of this process to the developmental dual processes described by Murray (1991). These two modes represent shifting up and down between the higher and lower levels of the right brain (see Schore, 2001b).

In order to accomplish this, the resonating therapist must flexibly shift, in a timely manner, into a state of "reparative withdrawal," a self-regulating maneuver that allows continued access to a state in which a symbolizing process can take place, thereby enabling him/her to create a parallel affective and imagistic scenario that resonates with the patient's (Friedman & Lavender, 1997). This "symbolizing process" involves being open to the patient's communication and holding onto the state long enough to allow internal sensoriaffective images to emerge into consciousness. Recall, countertransferential processes are manifest in the capacity to recognize and utilize the sensory (visual, auditory, tactile, kinesthetic, and olfactory) and affective qualities of imagery that the patient generates in the therapist.

To do this, the therapist must reestablish equilibrium enough to access "potential space," a right hemispheric organization (Weinberg, 2000), which, according to Ogden (1990), lies between "the symbol and the symbolized" where the self distinguishes one's feelings from what one is responding to. Winnicott (1971a) described this space as an intermediate zone of experience that lies between outer external reality and inner psychic fantasy. As described by Gendlin (1981), the ability to develop an internal imaginal "working space" allows the self to attend to one's felt sense and thereby a symbolic expression in the form of an image or a metaphor. One of the prominent characteristics of the processing of metaphors, which is a right hemispheric activity (Anaki, Faust, & Kravetz, 1998; Cox & Theilgaard, 1997; Winner & Gardner, 1977), is its image-generating picturing function, in which inner states are "set before the eye." This hemisphere is dominant for "image thinking," a holistic, synthetic strategy that allows individual facets of images to interact with each other on many planes simultaneously (Rotenberg, 1995).

In this "state-dependent recall" (Bower, 1981), images may arise from the clinician's unconscious bodily based, implicit-procedural affective memory, specifically those regulatory strategies associated with his/her own experiences with, and perhaps regulation of, this particular negative state. The clinician's monitoring and autoregulation of the negative state is performed at preconscious levels, and this allows for recovery of his/her "evenly hovering attention" to not only the patient's externally expressed distress state, but also to his/her state-dependent perceptual-somatic-affective internal images. Reiser (1997) described that in this state:

> The analyst's inner thoughts and images draw upon his or her memory networks, which encode not only personal life experiences, but also the patient's memory networks as these have developed in the analyst's mind as the analysis has been unfolding. This means that the analyst . . . will be able to identify elements encoded there from the patient's history that

are relevant to the analytic situation and the patient's problems in the here and now, including the transference. (p. 903)

But even more than this, Stark noted that in an optimal therapeutic intervention to a projective identification the therapist may "use her self" to share something about the impact of the patient's transferential activity on her own experience: "the therapist may well need to bring some aspect of her internal experience of the patient into the picture—[namely] the therapist's judicious disclosure of selective aspects of her countertransferential response . . . (to) the impact on her of the patient's activity in the transference" (1999, pp. 265, 267). In line with a dyadic view of therapeutic communication, Renik observed, "A willingness to self-disclosure on the analyst's part facilitates self-disclosure by the patient, and therefore productive dialectical interchange between analyst and patient is maximized" (1999, p. 529).

This disclosure is centered in not so much the therapist's countertransferential content-oriented cognitive responses as in his/her process-oriented experiential countertransferential bodily responses. Loewald (1986) pointed out that countertransference dynamics are appraised by the therapist's observations of his/her own visceral reactions to the patient's material. Similarly, Jacobs (1991) asserted that the therapist's own posture, gesture, and movement can be valuable cues to transference analysis. Jacobs further noted that the therapist's visual imagery often "stimulates in the analyst kinesic behavior and autonomic responses that are reactions on an unconscious level to nonverbal messages" (1994, p. 749).

In a clinical study, Friedman and Lavender (1997) concluded that the presence or absence of the therapist's recognition of his/her countertransferential discomforting bodily signals (the somatic markers triggered by his/her perception of the projective identification), and the capacity to then autoregulate the painful disruption in state triggered by his/her empathic resonance with the patient, may literally determine whether or not the countertransference is destructive or constructive, "desymbolizing" or "symbolizing," "reactive" or "reflective." These ideas were supported in a study by Beard (1992), who reported that analysts understood their physical responses to patients to be projective identifications. Clinicians manifested two types of responses to bodily experienced content—an "interpretive" style that frequently evolved into mutual reprojections, or an "empathic developmental stance" that involved the analysts holding these physical sensations and thereby modeling the capacity for self-regulation for the patient.

This autoregulatory maneuver may allow for restoration of the clinician's "analyzing instrument" (Balter et al., 1980). Feldman noted that "the analyst's temporary and partial recovery of his capacity for reflective thought rather than action is crucial for the survival of his analytical role" (1997, p. 239). The key to the analysis of the countertransference may be a self-reflective function by which the clinician determines whether he/she is internally sensing his/her counterregulatory reactions to the patient's dysregulation, or is psychobiologically resonating with the patient's chaotic state. According to Fonagy and Target (1996), the reflective function is a mental operation that enables the perception of another's state, "including apparently irrational unconscious motives."

An essential element of the treatment was articulated by Vanaerschot: "For the therapist to be able to contain painful (patient) experiences, the therapist must be able to be congruent with his or her painful experiences" (1997, p. 146). The attuned therapist's contingent responsivity to the subtle changes in the patient's state (Sander, 1992) and vocal rhythm matching (Beebe et al., 2000) had earlier conveyed that his/her right brain was attuned to the patient's state long enough to resonate with the patient's pain. The right hemisphere is dominant not only for processing negative primary emotions (Ross et al., 1994), but also for mediating pain and pain endurance (Cubelli et al., 1984; Hari et al., 1997; Hsieh et al., 1995) and modulating distress states via a right-brain circuit of inhibition and emotion regulation (Porges et al., 1994). This right-lateralized regulatory maneuver facilitates the therapist's countertransferential modulation of sensed negative affect; that is, it allows for the countertransference to be not "grossly" but only "partially" acted out.

But this "partial acting out" is critical to the patient's implicit learning of a corrective emotional experience. Pick (1985) suggested that it represents an important opportunity for the patient to perceive (in real time) that the therapist is affected by the patient's projected communication, that he/she struggles to tolerate the negative affect, but, ultimately, he/she manages to contain it without grossly acting it out. I would add that as a result of the therapist's largely nonconscious regulation of his/her own stress state, his/her rate of speech spontaneously slows, his/her voice becomes calmer and his/her facial expression less tense—an overt expression of a "metabolized" negative affect. As in an optimal developmental context, the clinician's regulatory strategy, observed even at levels beneath the patient's awareness, allows for the creation of a *nonconsciously* sensed "safe" interpersonal environment.

Adaptive Relational Processing of Defensive Projective Identifications and Therapeutic Progression

More specifically, the therapist's state change from dysregulated negative to regulated positive affect is communicated prosodically, and if the dyad is face to face, visually. Neurobiological research indicates that the detection and complex processing of the smallest change within a human face occurs within 100 milliseconds (Lehky, 2000), and that such facially expressed state changes are mirrored (Dimberg & Ohman, 1996) and synchronously matched by an observer's right hemisphere within 300–400 milliseconds, at levels beneath awareness (Stenberg, Wiking, & Dahl, 1998). It has been established that unconsciously perceived positive and negative emotional facial expressions elicit expessions of unconscious facial expressions, and that the right hemisphere is dominant for the control of spontaneously evoked emotional reactions (Dimberg & Petterson, 2000; Dimberg, Thunberg, & Elmehed, 2000). Recall that the right hemisphere recognizes an emotion from a visually presented facial expression and then generates a somatosensory, bodily based representation of how another feels when displaying that certain facial expression (Adolphs et al., 2000). In addition, this hemisphere is dominant for affect regulation.

The adaptive aspect of this mechanism, which onsets in early mother–infant mirroring transactions (Schore, 1994), was described by Bruner: "[A] quick-triggered mimetic reaction might not only facilitate affective bonding with a putative partner, but could also send reafferent signals back into the systems to assure arousal-appropriate perceptual processing of that partner" (1994, p. 278). Applying this to the current clinical context, the rapid dyadic state matching allows the interactively regulated patient to begin to transition out of the negative and into a more positively valenced state. Sands stated, "If I allow myself to be taken over by (the patient's) experience, successfully contain it (and wait until later to interpret it), she becomes calmer and more organized, and her need to communicate through me decreases in intensity" (1997, p. 700).

The dyad's state-regulating, stress-reducing maneuvers, occurring at mostly preconscious levels, allows the therapist to remain connected to the patient's state at the point of an "attuned" intervention, and for the patient to now switch out of a dissociated state into one in which he/she can internalize the therapist's spontaneous expression of his/her empathic recognition of the patient's pain. On the part of the therapist, the most effective interpretations are based on the clinician's "awareness of his own physical, emotional, and ideational responses to the patient's veiled messages" (Boyer, 1990, p. 304). On the part of the patient, the most "correct understandings" can be used by the patient "only if the analyst is attuned to the patient's state at the time the interpretation is offered" (Friedman & Moskowitz, 1997, p. xxi).

In light of the observation that "physical containment by the therapist of the patient's disavowed experience needs to precede its verbal processing" (Dosamantes, 1992, p. 362), the interactive regulation of the patient's state enables him/her to now begin to verbally label the affective experience. In a "genuine dialogue," the therapist accesses a "focusing attitude" of waiting patiently in the presence of "the not yet speakable, being receptive to the not yet formed" (Leisjssen, 1990), an intersubjective context that facilitates the patient's capacity to raise to an inner word and then into a spoken word what he/she needs to say at a particular moment but does not yet possess as speech (Buber, 1957). But the patient must experience that this verbal description of an internal affective state is heard and felt, "witnessed" by an empathic other.

Stern (1989) suggested that the "narrative" model is the verbal rendition of the nonverbal internal working models of regulation as told to oneself or to another. These models are encoded in implicit relational knowledge (Stern, Bruschweiler-Stern, et al., 1998). The transfer of self-information from the nonverbal to the verbal level (and back) reflects a bidirectional transfer of information between implicit and explicit processing, an adaptive advance. According to Bornstein, "When an implicit memory is made explicit, the origin of that memory is also made explicit, and the patient can better understand the causal chain of events that led from past experience to present functioning. Simply put, the translation of implicit memories allows the patient to gain insight regarding the relationship between past and present experience" (1993a, p. 341).

The therapeutic process thus allows for a critical interactive linkage of the two levels of experiencing processes. Vanaerschot (1997) contended that:

> The first level refers to the bodily implicitly felt whole concerning a situation and originates in the interaction between person and situation or environment. . . . The interaction between body and situation gives rise to an implicit, bodily felt sense, which is preconceptual and undifferentiated. It is a knowing without words: a knowing that precedes words and from which words emerge. . . . The bodily feeling is implicit . . . in the sense of . . . implying something that presses for expression.
>
> This leads us to the second level of interaction, which is the one between bodily sensing and symbols (such as words) through which explicit meanings are formed from preconceptual, implicit, and incomplete meanings. . . . The explicit meaning is not a previously hidden or repressed one that now becomes clear, but one that is formed in the interaction between felt sense and symbols. . . . Following a correct symbolization, a new sense forms, a new implicit feeling of oneself in the situation. . . . This is a step towards change. . . . Healthy mental functioning implies a constant and flexible interaction at both these levels, by which experience is continuously carried further. An adequate way of experiencing is characterized by reflective attention to the felt sense about a situation. (pp. 142–143)

As Bucci (1993) described, the patient's "referential structures" can now link the nonverbal and verbal representational domains. This structural alteration allows for the development of linguistic symbols to represent the meaning of an experience, *while one is feeling and perceiving the emotion generated by the experience.* Ultimately, such therapeutic experiences allow for an "evolution of affects from their early form, in which they are experienced as bodily sensations, into subjective states that can gradually be verbally articulated" (Stolorow & Atwood, 1992, p. 42). This process is a central component of therapeutic narrative organization, of turning "raw feelings into symbols" (Holmes, 1993, p. 150). Near the end of the 1930s Klein wrote of "preverbal emotions . . . revived in the transference situation . . . appear[ing] . . . as memories in feelings . . . which are reconstructed and put into words with the help of the analyst" (1937/1981, p. 316).

This same therapeutic sequence for processing defensive projective identification, of dyadic bodily physiological regulation followed by a new level of interactive dialogue, was described by Ogden's (2001) use of two spontaneous interventions at a critical point in the treatment of an early traumatized patient:

> The first of these interventions . . . involved speaking from a form of "I-ness" (reflected in the voice in which I spoke) which was new to me. It was a parental voice that took on the responsibility of protectively "minding" the patient while he was in a state of imminent psychotic fragmentation. The second intervention involved my spontaneously inviting the patient to imagine himself (with me) as two adults into a story of molestation) based on his history and the history of the analysis) in which I was a third presence bearing witness, bearing language and bearing compassion. Both interventions seemed to have had important consequences for the progress of the analysis. My responding to the patient's psychotic-level anxiety and feelings of impending psychic disintegration in the spontaneous ways described seems to have contributed to the process of his developing a greater sense of being alive in the experience of a coextensive minded body and bodied mind. (p. 103)

In a similar vein, Lichtenberg and colleagues (1996) described the importance of an analytic communication that deviates from the more customary therapeutic interventions, what they termed "disciplined spontaneous engagements." These events occur "at a critical juncture in analysis" and they are usually prompted by some breach or miscommunication that requires "a human response." Although there is a danger of "exchanges degenerating into mutually traumatizing disruptions" that "recreate pathogenic expectations," the clinician's communications signal a readiness to participate authentically in the immediacy of an enactment. This is spontaneously expressed in the clinician's facial expressions, gestures, and unexpected comments that result from an "unsuppressed emotional upsurge," and they provide "intense moments that opened the way for examination of the role enactments into which the analyst had fallen unconsciously." The authors stated that if the analyst can "self-right," these engagements can facilitate changes in symbolic representations.

The changes that result from optimal relational processing of the patient's projective identifications have been described by a number of authors. According to Ogden, "The recipient who successfully manages the feelings engendered in him makes available to the projector (through the interaction) a modified, more integrable version of the set of meanings that had been previously impossible to manage" (1990b, p. 470). Bach asserted that "through projective identifications that are contained and metabolized . . . a transitional space develops in which confusion, ambiguity, and separation can be tolerated and explored" (1998, p. 194). And Stark concluded that the net result of successful clinical work with projective identification "is the patient's development of capacity (to tolerate previously unmanageable aspects of herself), where before she had need (to deny their existence by disowning them)" (1999, p. 267). Recall Boyer's (1990) description that the patients who excessively access defensive projective identification attempt to rid themselves immediately of tension because the discomfort is intolerable.

The developmental progression that results from the growth-promoting environment embedded in the therapeutic relationship allows not only for a more stable and constant sense of self, but also for the emergence of a "reflective self" that is capable of in-sight, a visuoperceptual metaphor of internal sight—that is, access to the mind's eye that can see not just hidden thoughts but also the rhythms and flows of one's inner psychobiological self-states, and hold these affective experiences in mind long enough to tolerate, recognize, label, and introspect upon them. This advance allows the patient's increasingly complex self-system to access not only a more fully developed subjective nonverbal affective "support-experience" factor, but also an objective "insight" factor that is activated by adequate interpretation (de Jonghe et al., 1992).

Over the course of the treatment, the therapist's role as a psychobiological regulator and coparticipation in the "dyadic regulation of emotion" (Sroufe, 1996), especially during clinical heightened affective moments and episodes of projective identification, can facilitate the emergence of a reflective capacity and an "earned secure" attachment (Schore, 2000a). In writings on "the clinical body and the reflexive mind," Aron (1998) concluded that the clinician:

> must be attuned to the nonverbal, the affective, the spirit (breath) of the session, the feel of the material, to his or her own bodily responses, so that these may be gradually utilized to construct metaphors and symbols that may be verbally exchanged by the analytic pair, gradually permitting the differentiation of the more primitive shared skin-ego and the construction of a more developed, articulated, and differentiated personal attachment and interpersonal connection. (p. 26)

Aron was describing the recontinuation of the experience-dependent development of the right hemisphere, known to be dominant for the ability to tolerate and integrate a multiplicity of perspectives, affects and self- and object-representations into a meaningful whole (Rotenberg & Weinberg, 1999).

The right brain, the biological substrate of the human unconscious (Schore, 2002e), is the generator of not only intense affective states, but also of the early-developing defenses associated with these states. And so effective treatment of severe disorders of the self also induces an expansion of the adaptive capacity to utilize adaptive (realistic) rather than defensive projective identification. This developmental advance allows for the elevation of emotions from a primitive presymbolic sensorimotor representational level to a mature symbolic representational level, and it reflects an expansion of the patient's capacity for affect regulation. The patient, in the course of the interaction with the therapist who tolerates the countertransference and regulates the intense distress states that have been projected into himself/herself, "learns how the analyst does it, learns new skills or adaptive behaviors useful to cope with emotional stressors . . . the therapist may show the patient, often through his own behavior rather than through verbal interpretation, that it is indeed possible to tolerate stressful feelings and to survive" (Migone, 1995, p. 628).

In summarizing the critical role of the therapist in the difficult work with patient's who extensively utilize projective identification, Stark (1999) suggested:

> The therapist's handling of the feelings the patient projects requires considerable effort, skill, and strain on the therapist's part, because the feelings with which the patient struggles are highly charged, painful areas of human experience that are probably as conflictual for the therapist as they are for the patient. But it is hoped that because of the therapist's greater psychological integration resulting from both her own developmental experience and the work she has done in her own treatment, the therapist (in contradistinction to the patient) will be less frightened of, and less prone to run from, these feelings. (p. 276)

The dyadic mechanisms within the attuning-misattuning-reattuning therapeutic alliance allow for a shared struggle within the negatively valenced intersubjective field. But there are also shared rewards—in line with an interactive view of treatment, as a result of coparticipation in the dyadic process of interactive repair, not only the patient's but also the therapist's capacities for repairing dysregulated affective states are expanded (de Paola, 1990). Giovacchini asserted that successful therapeutic use of transference-countertransference interactions "is a shared experience that enhances both participants—an act of mutual discovery. Though revealing hidden facets of the patient is its aim, often enough, especially with severely disturbed patients, the analyst digs up certain aspects of his own character, aspects not always pleasant to face. Patient and therapist expand the dimensions of their personalities" (1986, p. 13). A psychotherapeutic focus on interactively regulated projective identifications allows both members of the emotion-transacting therapeutic relationship to become, both subjectively and objectively, more knowledgeable coexplorers of the primitive mind.

INTERACTIVELY REGULATED PROJECTIVE IDENTIFICATION, INTERNALIZATION, AND THE GENESIS OF RIGHT-BRAIN SYSTEMS INVOLVED IN SELF-REGULATION

The developmental structural growth that results from adaptive projective identification and containment was described by Hamilton (1992):

> When children have strong affects that threaten to overwhelm them, they externalize their distress. The parent takes in the projected feeling and self object state, contains it, modulates it, gives it meaning, and returns the transformed affect in the form of holding, a meaningful comment, or some other communication. The child can now accept the metabolized affect and self object state as his own. He eventually takes in the contain-

ing process itself along with the transformed projections, identifies with it, and learns to contain his own affects to a large degree. (p. xiii)

This internal transformation was described by Bion (1962b). During the depressive position the infant uses the object as a "container" to "metabolize" projective identifications, the beta element precursors of mind, into alpha elements that comprise integrated and differentiated symbolic thought. Robbins noted, "The therapist's role is to identify the beta elements of enactment forced on him by the patient, metabolize them into alpha elements of thought, and assist the patient to do likewise" (1996, p. 773). This "alpha function" or "dream work alpha" describes primary process function, and it operates in waking and sleeping and orders and transforms events into personal experiences as "alpha elements" that can be mentally processed.

I suggest that Bion was describing developmental progressions in regulatory structures, particularly in the right hemisphere, the locus of primary process functions and a right brain circuit of emotion regulation. This ontogenetic maturation is identical to Kohut's (1977) "transmuting internalization," the developmental process by which the mother's selfobject function that regulates the child's homeostatic state is internalized by the infant and psychological self regulatory structures are formed. Muir (1995) contended that the adaptive aspect of projective identification is associated with attachment and represents "the cradle of the emergent potential self." And so, "The therapeutic action of heightened affective moments is mediated through state transformations that potentially usher in opportunities for expanded self-regulatory range and altered patterns of mutual regulation" (Lachmann & Beebe, 1996, p. 7).

Current neurobiological studies now identify the location and functional properties of the intrapsychic structural systems that are involved in self-regulation, an interest of psychoanalysis that traces back to Freud's seminal ideas in his *Project for a Scientific Psychology* (Schore, 1997b, 1999b). In previous works directed toward updating Freud's structural model, I have discussed, in some detail, how the orbitofrontal (ventromedial) regions of the right hemisphere, come to act in the capacity of an executive control system for entire right brain (Schore, 1994, 1996, 1997a, 1997b, 1998a, 1998b, 1999i, 2000a, 2000d, 2000e, 2001b, 2001c, 2001d, 2001f, 2002e). A growing body of experimental and clinical evidence in neuroscience indicates that "the orbitofrontal cortex is involved in critical human functions, such as social adjustment and the control of mood, drive and responsibility, traits that are crucial in defining the 'personality' of an individual" (Cavada & Schultz, 2000, p. 205). Current neuroimaging studies demonstrate that the processing of self (Keenan et al., 2000) and self-regulation (Levine et al., 1998, 1999) occurs within the right prefrontal cortices, and that the self-concept is represented in right frontal areas (Craik et al., 1999).

This prefrontal system, the hierarchical apex of the limbic system, acts as the "senior executive of the emotional brain" (Joseph, 1996), and plays a major role in attachment functions as well as in the processing visual and auditory information associated with emotionally expressive faces and voices, the self-regulation of bodily states, and the correction of emotional responses (i.e., affect regulation). The ventral and medial regions of the prefrontal cortex act in "the highest level of control of behavior, especially in relation to emotion" (Price et al., 1996).

But, in addition this prefrontal system detects "somatic markers"—"gut" feelings that are experienced in response to both real and imagined events, including threatening stimuli (Damasio, 1994). This is due to the involvement of the orbitofrontal areas in the regulation of autonomic responses to social stimuli (Craig, 2002; Papousek & Schulter, 2001; Zald & Kim, 1996). Recent studies demonstrate that the right ventral medial prefrontal cortex plays a primary role in "optimizing cautious and adaptive behavior in potentially threatening situations" (Sullivan & Gratton, 2002a, p. 69). Even more specifically, the orbitofrontal regions modulate the processing of pain and coping with a painful stimulus (Petrovic et al., 2000). These functional capacities allow the clinician to process the emotionally painful somatic components of projective identifications during moments in which "the patient subtly causes the therapist to resonate autonomically with the patient's unconscious affect-laden fantasies" (Basch, 1992, p. 179).

This same system is critically and directly involved in evaluating facial expressions, in the processing of emotion-evoking stimuli without conscious awareness, and in controlling the allocation of attention to possible contents of consciousness (Schore, 1994, 1997a, 1998b). In addition, orbitofrontal activity is essential to the capacities of empathizing with the feeling states of others (Eslinger, 1998; Mega & Cummings, 1994). These functions underlie the fundamental mechanism of projective identification as first described by Klein—the processing of unconscious information projected from the sender to the recipient (1946). In addition, the orbital prefrontal cortex plays a critical role in mediating between the internal environment and the external milieu (Schore, 1994), thereby enabling this right prefrontal system to operate at "the intrapsychic edge of the object world, the perceptual edge of the transference" (Smith, 1990, p. 225).

The orbitofrontal regulatory system is intimately involved in the generation of an "emotional hunch" (Adolphs, 2001), but also in "cognitive-emotional interactions" (Barbas, 1995) and in "the processing of affect-related meanings" (Teasdale et al., 1999). It can thus "integrate and assign emotional-motivational significance to cognitive impressions; the association of emotion with ideas and thoughts" (Joseph, 1996, p. 427). A maturational advance of this system allows for the "unthought known" (Bollas, 1987), earlier only expressed as projective identifications, to become symbolized and thereby communicated as coherent subjective affect states. Alvarez (1997) proposed that "extreme" projective identification is associated with a "developmental delay." I suggest that an early history of "ambient trauma" is responsible for the maturational delay of, specifically, this "senior executive" prefrontal system (Schore, 1997b, 1998e, 1998i, 1999f, 1999g, 2001c).

Orbital activity is also associated with a lower threshold for awareness of sensations of both external and internal origin (Goldenberg et al., 1989) and "self-reflective awareness" (Stuss et al., 1992). The central involvement of this psychic system in preconscious functions (Frank, 1950) and in directed attention allows it to act as an "internal reflecting and organizing agency" (Kaplan-Solms & Solms, 1996) with which one can reflect on one's own internal emotional states, as well as others (Povinelli & Preuss, 1995). Neurobiological studies reveal that the orbitofrontal system is critically involved in detecting "changes of emotional state" and "breaches of expectation" (Nobre et al., 1999), and in "processing feedback information" (Elliott, Frith, & Dolan, 1997) and "hypothesis selection" (Goel & Dolan, 2000). Indeed, this coping system is specialized to act in contexts of "uncertainty or unpredictability" (Elliott, Dolan, & Frith, 2000), an operational definition of stress.

These and the previously described functional properties are thus essential to the clinician's capacity for evenly hovering attention, which shifts between what comes from the outside and what is emerging from inside—that is, to the operations of "the analyzing instrument" (Balter et al., 1980). An appreciation of the neurobiological mechanisms by which the clinician's right prefrontolimbic system is involved in "oscillating attentiveness" (Schwaber, 1995) to "barely perceptible cues that signal a change in state" in both patient and therapist (Sander, 1992), and to "nonverbal behaviors and shifts in affects" (McLaughlin, 1996), is thus directly relevant to a deeper understanding of "the metapsychology of the analyst's mental processes during analysis" (Ferenczi, 1928/1980).

Within the intersubjective field coconstructed by the resonating therapist and patient bodily based experiences and preconscious images are automatic and fleeting, but when such "nonconscious affect" (Murphy et al., 1995), which shapes the subsequent conscious emotional processing of a stimulus (Dimberg & Ohman, 1996), is interactively regulated, amplified, and held in short-term memory long enough to be felt and recognized, the patient's affectively charged but now regulated right brain experiences can then be communicated to the left brain for further conscious processing. The clinician's role in this was further described by Basch: "In analysis our patient's show us in the transference where the right and left brain have failed to synchronize; we act the part of the corpus callosum, so to speak, until that structure can take over and the patient can do for himself what he needed us to do with and for him" (1985, p. 11).

As opposed to orbitofrontal areas of the right cerebral cortex that are associated with affective shifts, those in the left verbal-linguistic hemisphere are specifically involved in "semantic implicit retrieval that does not depend upon intentional recollection" (Demb et al., 1995). An increase of connections between the right and left orbital areas may thus allow for left hemispheric retrieval from implicit-procedural memory and semantic encoding of right-hemispheric emotional states. In light of the facts that the orbiotofrontal areas are "critical to the experience of emotion" (Baker, Frith, & Dolan, 1997, p. 565) and fundamentally involved in "emotion-related learning" (Rolls, Hornak, Wade, & McGrath, 1994) and "cognitive-emotional interactions" (Barbas, 1995), the therapeutic relationship can act as a growth-facilitating environment for this self-regulatory system.

A functional magnetic resonance imaging study conducted by Hariri, Book-heimer, and Mazziotta provided evidence that higher regions of specifically the right prefrontal cortex attenuate emotional responses at the most basic levels in the brain, that such modulating processes are "fundamental to most modern psychotherapeutic methods," (2000, p. 43), that this lateralized neocortical network is active in "modulating emotional experience through interpreting and labeling emotional expressions" (p. 47), and that "this form of modulation may be impaired in various emotional disorders and may provide the basis for therapies of these same disorders" (p. 48).

Because the structural maturation of the infant's right hemisphere ("right mind") is directly influenced by its interactions with the primary caregiver, a knowledge of its development is relevant to a deeper understanding of the early ontogeny of the primitive human brain-mind-body. The operations of the early-maturing hemisphere mediates the empathic perception of the emotional states of other humans. It is important to note that the right hemisphere cycles back into growth phases throughout the lifespan (Schore, 2001b; Thatcher, 1994) and that the orbitofrontal cortex retains a capacity for plasticity in later life (Barbas, 1995), thereby allowing for the continuing experience-dependent maturation of the right-frontal regulatory system within the growth-facilitating environment of an affect-regulating therapeutic relationship. This structural organization, in turn, is reflected in a progression in the complexity of the patient's coping mechanisms—specifically, a developmental advance in the form of a mature personality organization that accesses adaptive over defensive projective identification. A deeper apprehension of the developmental and therapeutic changes in this right-brain system that is centrally involved in the regulation of emotional states is therefore directly relevant to Klein's pioneering explorations that are fundamentally concerned with the "regulation of feelings."

2002

CHAPTER 4

Advances in Neuropsychoanalysis, Attachment Theory, and Trauma Research: Implications for Self Psychology

I N 1971, HEINZ KOHUT, TRAINED in neurology and then psychoanalysis, published *The Analysis of the Self*, a detailed exposition of the central role of the self in human existence. This classic volume of both 20th-century psychoanalysis and psychology was more than a collection of various clinical observations — rather, it represented an overarching integrated theory of the *development, structuralization, psychopathogenesis*, and *psychotherapy of disorders of the self*. Although some of these ideas were elaborations of previous psychoanalytic principles, a large number of his concepts, including an emphasis on self rather than ego, signified an innovative departure from mainstream psychoanalysis and yet a truly creative addition to Freud's theory.

Kohut expanded the theoretical and clinical conceptions of self psychology in his second volume, *The Restoration of the Self* (1977), and finally in *How Does Analysis Cure?* (1984). Over the course of his career he continually attempted to deepen his understanding of the four basic problems he initially addressed in his seminal volume: How do early relational affective transactions with the social environment facilitate the emergence of self (*development of the self*)? How are these experiences internalized into maturing self-regulating structures (*structuralization of the self*)? How do early-forming deficits of self-structure lead to later self pathologies (*psychopathogenesis*)? How can the therapeutic relationship lead to a restoration of self (*the mechanism of psychotherapeutic change*)?

In this chapter I want to suggest that although Kohut's ideas represent perhaps the most significant revision of classical psychoanalysis in the last 50 years, despite the fact that he was originally trained as a neurologist, he, like his contemporaries, was highly ambivalent about the incorporation of scientific data into the core of psychoanalysis and into the core of self psychology. Although there have been certain notable exceptions, this ambivalence still exists within current self psychology, even now when an interdisciplinary perspective is rapidly emerging in a number of other clinical and scientific disciplines that border psychoanalysis.

In an earlier work I suggested that the time is right for a rapprochement between psychoanalysis, the study of the unconscious mind, and the biological sciences (Schore, 1997a). Developmental psychoanalysis is currently generating a complex model of the early ontogeny of the biological substrate of the human unconscious (Schore, 2002e), one that can potentially bridge the relational and intrapsychic realms of the unconscious mind. And neuropsychoanalysis is also contributing to this effort, by identifying the brain systems involved in the development of the dynamic unconscious (Schore, 2002e). Writing in the neuropsychoanalytic literature, Watt (2000) described the critical importance of recent work on "(neuro) development": "In many ways, this is the great frontier in neuroscience where all of our theories will be subject to the most acid of acid tests. And many of them I suspect will be found wanting. . . . Clearly, affective processes, and specifically the vicissitudes of attachment, are primary drivers in neural development (the very milieu in which development takes place, without which the system cannot develop)" (p. 191).

In the following I first present a brief overview of Kohut's concepts that represent the core of self psychology. In subsequent sections I integrate interdisciplinary data in order to construct a psychoneurobiological conception of the *development* and *structuralization* of the self, focusing on the experience-dependent maturation of the early-developing right brain. Then, in a major focus of this work, I apply this developmental neuropsychoanalytic perspective to the *psychopathogenesis* of severe deficits in the self-system. In particular, I articulate a model of the self psychology and neurobiology of infant trauma and the etiology of posttraumatic stress disorder and borderline states. And finally I offer thoughts on the neurobiology of regulatory structures that result from *psychotherapeutic change*.

INTRODUCTION: CORE CONCEPTS OF KOHUT'S MODEL

Development of the Self

Perhaps Kohut's most original and outstanding intellectual contribution was his developmental construct of selfobject. Indeed, self psychology is built upon a fundamental developmental principle—that parents with mature psychological organizations serve as selfobjects that perform critical regulatory functions for the infant who possesses an immature, incomplete psychological organization. The child is thus provided, at nonverbal levels beneath conscious awareness, with selfobject experiences that directly effect the vitalization and structural cohesion of the self. According to Wolf: "The most fundamental finding of self psychology is that the emergence of the self requires more than the inborn tendency to organize experience. Also required is the presence of others, technically described as objects, which provide certain types of experiences that will evoke the emergence and maintenance of the self" (1988, p. 11).

The selfobject construct contains two important theoretical components. First, the concept of the mother–infant pair as a self–selfobject unit emphasizes that early development is essentially characterized as interdependence between self and objects in a system. This core concept of Kohut's theory was a major intellectual impetus for the expansion of the relational perspective in psychoanalysis. Indeed, his emphasis on the dyadic aspects of unconscious communications shifted psychoanalysis from a solely intrapsychic to a more balanced intrapsychic-relational perspective. This challenged psychoanalysis to explore mechanisms that could integrate both the realms of a one-person psychology and a two-person psychology.

The second component of the selfobject construct is the concept of regulation. In his developmental speculations Kohut (1971, 1977) stated that the infant's dyadic reciprocal regulatory transactions with selfobjects allows for the maintenance of his/her internal homeostatic equilibrium. These regulating self–selfobject experiences provide the particular intersubjective affective experiences that evoke the emergence and maintenance of the self (Kohut, 1984). Kohut's idea that regulatory processes and structures are fundamentally involved with affect is supported in current interdisciplinary studies that are highlighting not just the centrality of affect, but also affect regulation. Regulation thus occupies the intellectual core of Kohut's model, just as it does in the works of Freud (Schore, 1997a), Bowlby (Schore, 2000a, 2000c, 2001d), and Klein (Schore, 2002b).

Despite his intense interest in the early ontogeny of the self, over the course of his career Kohut never spelled out the precise developmental details of his model, nor did he attend to the significant advances in developmental psychoanalysis that were occurring simultaneously to his own theorizing. There is now agreement that current psychoanalysis is "anchored in its scientific base in developmental psychology and in the biology of attachment and affects" (Cooper, 1987, p. 83). And yet it is only recently that self psychology has begun to incorporate the broad range of developmental research into its theoretical model. The integration of current attachment theory in volumes of *Psychoanalytic Inquiry* is an example of that effort (Diamond & Blatt, 1999).

Structuralization of the Self

A cardinal principle of Kohut's model dictates that as a result of self–selfobject experiences the infant becomes able to perform the drive-regulating, integrating, and adaptive functions that had previously been performed by the external object. Specifically, he posits that phase-appropriate maternal optimal frustrations of the infant elicit "transmuting internalization," the developmental process by which selfobject function is internalized by the infant and psychological regulatory structures are formed. Indeed, the essential experience and definition of the self are built out of internalized selfobject functions that allow for the emergence of more complex psychological regulatory structures.

These ideas on psychic structure, in addition to the aforementioned effects of regulation on the maintenance of homeostatic equilibrium, clearly direct the theory toward not a psychology but a psychobiology of the self. However, Kohut, like Freud before him (Schore, 1997a), eschewed his earlier neurological knowledge, and attempted to create a purely psychological model of the unconscious systems that underly human functioning. Three days before his death Kohut declared, "I do not believe, however hard as it was tried, that there is a possibility to create such a misalliance as psychobiology, or biopsychology or something of that order" (1981, p. 529).

When self psychology, like psychoanalysis in general, discards the biological realm of the body—when it overemphasizes the cognitive and verbal realms—it commits Descartes's error, "the separation of the most refined operations of mind from the structure and operation of a biological organism" (Damasio, 1994, p. 250). Damasio described the essential adaptive function of the brain: "The overall function of the brain is to be well informed about what goes on in the rest of the body, the body proper; about what goes on in itself; and about the environment surrounding the organism, so that suitable survivable accommodations can be achieved between the organism and the environment" (1994, p. 90). Indeed, according to Damasio, the self is a "repeatedly reconstructed biological state" that "endows our experience with subjectivity."

This same critique has been leveled against the heavy emphasis on cognition in developmental psychoanalysis. Lieberman asserted, "In the last two decades . . . efforts at understanding the subjective world of the infant have focused primarily on mental representations as the building blocks of inner experience. The baby's body, with its pleasures and struggles, has largely been missing from this picture" (1996, p. 289).

In upcoming sections of this chapter I suggest that information on the developmental neurobiology of the selfobject relationship (Schore, 1994, Mollon, 2001) and the early-developing right hemisphere, which is more deeply connected into the body than the left, can deepen Kohut's concept of self. Indeed, it is thought that the function of the right hemisphere is to "maintain a coherent, continuous, and unified sense of self" (Devinsky, 2000). Current neuroscience is now intensely interested in "the synaptic self," especially the nonconscious "implicit self" (LeDoux, 2002), and in "self-representation in neural systems," representations that "coordinate inner body signals to generate survival-appropriate inner regulation" that allow the organism "to act as a coherent whole" (Churchland, 2002, p. 310). *The biological organism, the body, must be brought into the core of self psychology.*

Psychopathogenesis

Kohut proposed that a defective self and an impaired regulatory structure lie at the foundation of early-forming psychopathologies. Kohut described "the role of specific environmental factors [the personality of the parents, for example; certain traumatic external events] in the genesis of the developmental arrest" (1971, p. 11), and speculated that when "the mother's response are grossly unempathic and unreliable . . . no transmuting internalization can take place, and the psyche . . . does not develop the various internal functions which re-establish narcissistic equilibrium" (p. 65). In a continuation of this principle, other, more current writers in self psychology have affirmed that affect dysregulation is a central principle of psychopathogenesis. According to Lichtenberg and his colleagues, "Self psychologists have demonstrated that disturbed regulation of physiological requirements in patients result from primary disturbances or deficiencies in [selfobject] experiences" (1996, p. 143).

Self psychology has recently become very interested in the problem of trauma, an area of controversy since the dawn of psychoanalysis. In his earliest writings, Freud accepted Janet's (1889) idea that dissociation is the central force in psychopathology, but he later rejected this for his repression theory. In classic writings, Janet postulated that "all [traumatized] patients seem to have the evolution of their lives checked; they are attached to an insurmountable object" (in van der Kolk, 1996, p. 53), and that the major psychological consequence of trauma is "the breakdown of the adaptive mental processes leading to the maintenance of an integrated sense of *self*" (in Liotti, 1999, p. 293; italics added).

In later sections on psychopathogenesis, I suggest that recent studies in developmental traumatology indicate that experiences with a traumatizing caregiver negatively impact the child's attachment security, right brain maturation, and sense of self. I also propose that relational trauma and dissociation are common elements of the histories of borderline personality disorders, a clinical population of increasing interest to self psychology.

Psychotherapy

The selfobject and regulatory concepts embedded in Kohut's developmental model clearly suggest that affect and affect regulation are a primary focus of the treatment of early-forming personality disorders. Indeed, Kohut's major contribution to clinical psychoanalysis is the expansion of its techniques to include the treatment of the deficits of affect regulation of early-forming personality disorders, especially narcissistic personality disorders. In therapeutic models of such patients, all schools of contemporary psychoanalysis are now emphasizing the centrality of affect. Self psychology has been at the forefront of this trend, and it has been asserted that "Kohut makes major contributions to the understanding of emotional life, and his conceptualizations have far-reaching implications for the understanding and treatment of emotional states" (A. M. Siegel, 1996, p. 1).

Furthermore, Kohut prescribed that "psychoanalysis cures by the laying down of psychological structure" (1984, p. 98). In upcoming sections I argue that neuropsychoanalysis is now in a position to offer important information about the precise nature of the affect-regulating structures described by self psychology, and can elaborate the critical mechanisms by which the self–selfobject transactions embedded in the infant–mother and patient–therapist dyads create a growth-facilitating environment for the experience-dependent maturation of these same structures.

With this introduction, throughout the following integration of interdisciplinary data into self psychology, keep in mind the words of Kohut's colleague, Michael Basch: "The more I know about how we are designed to function — what neurophysiology, infant research, affect theory, cognitive psychology, semantics, information theory, evolutionary biology, and other pertinent disciplines can tell me about human development — the better I am prepared to be empathic with a patient's communication at a particular time in his or her treatment" (1995, p. 372).

DEVELOPMENT: REGULATED AFFECTIVE COMMUNICATIONS, SELF–SELFOBJECT INTERACTIONS, AND THE DYADIC GENESIS OF A SECURE ATTACHMENT

In a review of Kohut's work, A. M. Siegel (1996) concluded:

> Although developmental concepts sit at the heart of Kohut's theory, the microscopic elements of early development are not available for study . . . The infant's critical early states are unavailable to psychoanalysis. . . . The field of infant research, however, with its ingenious methods of investigation, does have access to the information we seek. Its observations are rich and can provide psychoanalysis with valuable information and explanations. (pp. 197, 198)

Toward that end, in *Affect Regulation and the Origin of the Self* and subsequent works, I suggested that very recent research from developmental neuropsychoanalysis and affective neuroscience can make important contributions to a deeper understanding of how early attachment experiences indelibly affect the trajectory of the self over the course of the lifespan.

The essential task of the first year of human life is the creation of a secure attachment bond of emotional communication between the infant and primary caregiver. Indeed, research now suggests that "learning how to communicate represents perhaps the most important developmental process to take place during infancy" (Papousek & Papousek, 1997, p. 42). Developmental researchers of infant–mother mutual gaze transactions have observed: "Face-to-face interactions, emerging at approximately 2 months of age, are highly arousing, affect-laden, short interpersonal events that expose infants to high levels of cognitive and social information. To regulate the high positive arousal, mothers and infants . . . synchronize the intensity of their affective behavior within lags of split seconds" (Feldman, Greenbaum, & Yirmiya, 1999, p. 223).

These dyadic experiences of "affect synchrony" (Kohutian "mirroring") occur in the first expression of positively charged social play, what Trevarthen (1993) termed "primary intersubjectivity," and at this time they are patterned by an infant-leads-mother-follows sequence. In this communicational matrix, both parties match psychobiological states and then simultaneously adjust their social attention, stimulation, and accelerating arousal to each other's responses. In such synchronized contexts of "mutually attuned selective cueing," the infant learns to send specific social cues to which the mother has responded, thereby reflecting "an anticipatory sense of response of the other to the self, concomitant with an accommodation of the self to the other" (Bergman, 1999, p. 96).

According to Lester, Hoffman, and Brazelton, "synchrony develops as a consequence of each partner's learning the rhythmic structure of the other and modifying his or her behavior to fit that structure" (1985, p. 24). In order to enter into this synchronized communication, the mother must be psychobiologically attuned not so much to the child's overt behavior as to the reflections of the rhythms of his/her internal state. These are critical events, because they represent a fundamental opportunity to practice the interpersonal synchronization of biological rhythms (Nishihara, Horiuchi, Eto, & Uchida, 2002). And so, in these exchanges of affect synchrony, as the mother and infant match each other's temporal and affective patterns, each recreates an inner psychophysiological state similar to the partner's.

In such positively charged heightened affective moments, not only the tempo of their engagement but also of their disengagement and reengagement is coordinated. The more the psychobiologically attuned mother tunes her activity level to the infant during periods of social engagement, the more she allows him/her to recover quietly in periods of disengagement, and the more she attends to the child's reinitiating cues for reengagement, the more synchronized their interaction. These mutually attuned synchronized interactions are fundamental to the healthy affective development of the infant (J. R. Schore, 2003).

The context of a specifically fitted interaction between the infant and mother has been described as a resonance between two systems attuned to each other by corresponding properties (Sander, 1991). When synchronously vibrating with a neighboring object, a resonant system produces the largest and most prolonged possible response to the object. *Resonance* refers to the condition in which an object or system is subjected to an oscillating signal having a frequency at or close to that of a natural vibration of the object or system and the resulting amplification of the natural vibration. In other words, an amplification of state especially occurs when external sensory stimulation frequency coincides with the organism's genetically encoded endogenous rhythms. The transfer of emotional information is thus intensified in resonant contexts. This means that the resonating caregiver does more than reflect back the infant's state. Rather, in cocreating a context of intersubjective resonance, her role as a "biological mirror" (Papousek & Papousek, 1979) is more precisely described as an "amplifying mirror" (Schore, 1994).

It is well established that the primary caregiver is not always attuned and optimally mirroring—there are frequent moments of misattunement in the dyad, ruptures of the attachment bond. The disruption of attachment bonds in infancy leads to a regulatory failure and an "impaired autonomic homeostasis" (Reite & Capitanio, 1985). Studies of interactive attunement following dyadic misattunement, of "interactive repair" (Tronick, 1989), support Kohut's (1977) assertion that the parental selfobject acts to "remedy the child's homeostatic imbalance." In this pattern of "disruption and repair" (Beebe & Lachmann, 1994), the good-enough caregiver who induces a stress response in his/her infant through a misattunement, reinvokes in a timely fashion a reattunment, a regulation of the infant's negatively charged affective state. Kohut (1971) speculated that phase-appropriate maternal optimal frustration elicits the developmental process by which selfobject function is internalized. Current developmental data are consonant with this, although interdisciplinary research emphasizes that not just optimal stressful frustration but also interactive repair are essential to the internalization of a structural system that can regulate stressful negative affect.

The dual regulatory processes of affect synchrony that creates states of positive arousal and interactive repair that modulates states of negative arousal are the fundamental building blocks of attachment and its associated emotions. They also allow for the maximization of the communication of emotional states within an intimate dyad, and represents the psychobiological underpinning of empathy, a phenomenon of intense interest to self psychology. Kohut (1977) described that as a result of the empathic merger of the child's rudimentary psyche with the maternal selfobject's highly developed psychic organization, the child experiences the feeling states of the selfobject as if they were his/her own.

Selfobjects are thus external psychobiological regulators that facilitate the regulation of affective experiences, and they act at nonverbal levels beneath conscious awareness to cocreate states of maximal cohesion (Mollon, 2001; Palombo, 1992; Schore, 1994; Wolf, 1988). Lichtenberg, Lachmann, and Fosshage (1996) pointed out that there are two classes of selfobject regulatory experiences, vitalization and soothing. If the former refers to the interactive regulation of positive affect, the latter refers to the interactive regulation of negative affect. These same processes are highlighted in current psychobiological models of attachment, now defined as the interactive regulation of states of biological synchronicity between organisms (Schore, 2000a, 2000c, 2001b,

2002a). Through the mechanism of the dyadic regulation of emotion, the baby becomes attached to the regulating caregiver who expands opportunities for positive and minimizes negative affective states.

Lichtenberg's group also asserted that: "Regulation of state lies at the heart of our theory. In infancy . . . success in regulating smoothness of transitions between states is a principal indicator of the organization and stability of the emergent and core self as well as caregiver success" (Lichtenberg, Lachmann, & Fosshage 1992, p. 162). Emde (1983) identified the primordial central integrating structure of the nascent self to be the emerging "affective core" that functions to maintain positive mood and to regulate the infant's interactive behavior, and Weil stated that "the infant's initial endowment in interaction with earliest maternal attunement leads to a basic core which contains directional trends for all later functioning" (1985, p. 337)

STRUCTURALIZATION: SELFOBJECT AND ATTACHMENT DYNAMICS AND THE DEVELOPMENT OF THE RIGHT BRAIN

Kohut described a core or "nuclear self," an early-developing structure that is the basis for "our experience that *our body and mind form a unit in space and a continuum in time*" and that "forms *the central sector of the personality*" (1977, p. 178; italics added). Indeed, Kohut's colleague Basch contended that the formation of self-organization is "the supraordinate ordering principle of human life" (1983, p. 41). What do we now know about the process of self-organization? How are early selfobject regulatory experiences internalized into the developing self, and why do intersubjective emotional communications play such a central role in the evolution of the brain-based core self?

In studies of "primary and secondary intersubjectivity," Trevarthen asserted that "the intrinsic regulators of human brain growth in a child are specifically adapted to be coupled, by emotional communication, to the regulators of adult brains" (1990, p. 357). Even more specifically, researchers concluded, "The emotional experience of the infant develops through the sounds, images, and pictures that constitute much of an infant's early learning experience, and are disproportionately stored or processed in the right hemisphere during the formative stages of brain ontogeny" (Semrud-Clikeman & Hynd, 1990, p. 198).

Indeed, the early-maturing emotion processing right brain is dominant in human infants and for the first 3 years of life (Chiron et al., 1997; Schore, 1994). A magnetic resonance image (MRI) study of infants reports that the volume of the brain increases rapidly during the first 2 years, that normal adult appearance is seen at 2 years and all major fiber tracts can be identified by age 3, and that infants under 2 years show higher right than left hemispheric volumes (Matsuzawa et al., 2001). The human brain growth spurt spans the last trimester of pregnancy through the middle of the second year (Dobbing & Sands, 1973). This exact interval represents a period of accelerated growth of the right hemisphere: "The right hemisphere is more advanced than the left in surface features from about the 25th (gestational) week and this advance persists until the left hemisphere shows a post-natal growth spurt starting in the second year" (Trevarthen, 1996, p. 582). The maturation of the socioemotional right hemisphere is experience dependent, and these experiences are provided in the attachment transactions that occur in the first 2 years of life (Schore, 1994, 1996, 1998b, 1998f, 2000d, 2000e, 2000h).

Over the course of a number of works I have suggested that attachment represents synchronized dyadic bioenergetic transmissions (1994), that resonant emotional transactions involve synchronized and ordered directed flows of energy in the infant's and mother's brains (2000e), that the attachment dynamic involves the right brain regulation of biological synchronicity between organisms (2000a), and that the developing self-system is located in the early-maturing right hemisphere (1994, 2001b). This conception confirms Wolf's (1988) assertion that early selfobject experiences provided to the child directly effect the energic vigor and structural cohesion of the self.

Furthermore, in *Affect Regulation and the Origin of the Self* (Schore, 1994), I asserted that early emotional development and self-development are inextricably intertwined. In the neuroscience literature, the central role of emotions is also highlighted in the work of Damasio (1994), Panksepp (1998), Siegel (1999), and in the current work of LeDoux (2000), who concluded:

> Because emotion systems coordinate learning, the broader the range of emotions that a child experiences the broader will be the emotional range of the self that develops. . . . And because more brain systems are typically active during emotional than during nonemotional states, and the intensity of arousal is greater, the opportunity for coordinated learning across brain systems is greater during emotional states. By coordinating parallel plasticity throughout the brain, emotional states promote the development and unification of the self. (p. 322)

Kohut's hypothesis of the central role of early dyadic affective experience in the emergence of self was furthered by Basch, who proposed, "from the beginning of life, affective reactions are the basis for the ordering function of the brain" (1985, p. 34). In 1994 I translated self psychological developmental principles into neurobiological terms, offering a detailed interdisciplinary model of the early organization of the self, in which dyadic emotional attachment communications regulated the experience-dependent maturation of the emotion processing limbic system (Schore, 1994). In continuing work, I have asserted that this theoretical regulation model suggests a program of developmental psychoneurobiological research, and have cited such work as it has appeared. There is now a growing body of studies documenting, in detail, how the functional maturation of limbic circuits is significantly influenced by the social-emotional experiences embedded in the attachment relationship.

To cite but one notable example of this line of research, Braun and her colleagues reported a number of studies on the impact of the presence or absence of maternal visual, vocal, and tactile emotional stimuli on the infant's limbic brain development, and thereby its psychosocial and cognitive capacities or deficits in later life (Braun, Lange, Metzger, & Poeggel, 2000; Braun & Poeggel, 2001; Helmeke, Ovtscharoff, Poeggel, & Braun, 2001; Helmke, Poeggel, & Braun, 2001; Ovtscharoff & Braun, 2001; Poeggel & Braun, 1996; Poeggel et al., 1999). This work is guided by a perspective that dictates,

> The dyadic interaction between the newborn and the mother constantly controls and modulates the newborn's exposure to environmental stimuli and thereby serves as a regulator of the developing individual's internal homeostasis. The regulatory function of the newborn-mother interaction may be an essential promoter to ensure the normal development and maintenance of synaptic connections during the establishment of functional brain circuits. (Ovtscharoff & Braun, 2001, p. 33)

This program of research clearly echoes Kohut's psychoanalytic description of the effects of the maternal selfobject's regulatory function on the maintenance of the infant's internal homeostatic equilibrium, and the critical aspect of these reciprocal regulatory transactions on the development of self. But it also describes current attachment theory, which is emphasizing the critical nature of the mutual regulation of affective homeostasis (Amini et al., 1996). In my own work I have argued that attachment theory is fundamentally a regulatory theory (Schore, 1994, 2000a). In their most recent writings Fonagy and Target also concluded that the whole of child development can be considered to be "the enhancement of self-regulation" (2002, p. 313), and that "attachment relationships are formative because they facilitate the development of the brain's major self-regulatory mechanisms" (p. 328). Both clinical and research models are thus stressing the importance of not only affect but affect regulation in psychological and biological development (Schore, 1994).

In a number of continuing contributions on this theme, I have suggested that the development of affect regulation is an essential organizing principle of emotional development and brain maturation, especially the early-developing right brain. This knowledge is directly relevant to self psychology. In my 1994 book, I postulated that the regulatory "mirroring" transactions embedded in infant–mother self–selfobject transactions, equated with face-to-face emotional communications embedded in the attachment relationship, represent right-brain-to-right-brain communications.

These proposals are confirmed in research. A recent neuroimaging study demonstrated that infants as young as 2 months show right hemispheric activation when exposed to a woman's face (Tzourio-Mazoyer et al., 2002). Modelling of face processing by the right hemisphere of 4-month-old infants (Acerra, Burnod, & de Schonen, 2002) suggests that the eyes play a special role, in line with research showing a right hemisphere dominance for processing information in mutual gaze (Ricciardelli, Ro, & Driver, 2002; Watanabe, Miki, & Kakigi, 2002; Wicker, Michel, Henaff, & Decety, 1998). Such early experience is associated with the development of enduring visual representations of facial expressions of emotion (Pollak & Kistler, 2002). High speed video analysis of mouth asymmetry reveals that the right hemisphere controls the emotional expression of a spontaneous smile at 5 months (Holowka & Petitto, 2002). These early right-lateralized events also impact the auditory realm—a functional magnetic resonance image (fMRI) study showed that the human maternal response to an infant's cry is accompanied by activation of the mother's right brain (Lorberbaum et al., 2002).

The right hemisphere, more so than the left, forms extensive connections with the emotion-processing limbic system. The limbic system derives subjective information in terms of emotional feelings that guide behavior (MacLean, 1985), and functions to allow the brain to adapt to a rapidly changing environment and organize new learning (Mesulam, 1998). A large number of studies indicate that this hemisphere is dominant not only for the nonconscious reception (Adolphs et al., 1996; Borod et al., 1998; George et al., 1996; Gur et al., 2002; Karow, Marquardt, & Marshall, 2001; Keil et al., 2002; Nakamura et al., 1999; Pizzagalli et al., 2001), expression (Borod, Haywood, & Koff, 1997; Dimberg & Peterson, 2000; Nicholls, Wolfgang, Clode, & Lindell, 2002), and communication (Blonder, Bowers, & Heilman, 1991; Bryan & Hale, 2001; Caplan & Dapretto, 2001) of emotion, but also for the physiological and cognitive components of emotional processing (Spence, Shapiro, & Zaidel, 1996; Stoll, Hamann, Mangold, Huf, & Winterhoff-Spurk, 1999), the critical function of distinguishing internal emotional states (Cicone, Wapner, & Gardner, 1980), the control of spontaneously evoked emotional reactions (Dimberg & Petterson, 2000), the modulation of "primary emotions" (Ross, Hohman, & Buck, 1994), and the adaptive capacity for the regulation of affect (Schore, 1994, 1999a, 1999d, 1999e, 2000b, 2000c, 2001a).

Current findings in neuroscience further suggest that "while the left hemisphere mediates most linguistic behaviors, the right hemisphere is important for broader aspects of communication" (van Lancker & Cummings, 1999, p. 95). The activity of this hemisphere, the "right mind" (Ornstein, 1997), is thus instrumental to the perception of the emotional states of other selves, that is, for empathy (Perry et al., 2001; Schore, 1996). A study by Damasio's group reported that "recognizing emotions from visually presented facial expressions requires right somatosensory cortices," and in this manner "we recognize another individual's emotional state by internally generating somatosensory representations that simulate how the individual would feel when displaying a certain facial expression" (Adolphs, Damasio, Tranel, Cooper, & Damasio, 2000, p. 2683). This hemisphere is also dominant for evaluating the trustworthiness of faces (Winston, Strange, O'Doherty, & Dolan, 2002).

But the right hemisphere is specialized for another essential function of the self-system. It is centrally involved in "the analysis of direct information received by the subject from his own body and which, it can easily be understood, is much more closely connected with direct sensation than with verbally logical codes" (Luria, 1973, p. 165). This is due to the fact that this hemisphere, more so than the left, contains extensive reciprocal connections with the autonomic nervous system (ANS), which regulates the functions of every organ in the body (Wittling, Block, Schweiger, & Genzel, 1998; Ahern et al., 2001). The energy-expending sympathetic and energy-conserving parasympathetic circuits of the ANS generate the involuntary bodily functions that represent the somatic components of all emotional states (Schore, 1994, 2001b, 2002d). An autonomic mode of reciprocal sympathetic-parasympathetic control is behaviorally expressed in an organism that responds alertly and adaptively to a personally meaningful (especially social) stressor, yet as soon as the context is appraised as safe, immediately returns to the relaxed state of autonomic balance. (For a more extensive characterization of the ANS, see Schore, 2002c.)

Information about the operations of the ANS is directly relevant to self psychology's intense interest in regulation of state (Lichtenberg et al., 1992) and affective experience (Lichtenberg et al., 1996). In fact, Kohut's (1971, 1977) characterization of the infant's continuous dyadic reciprocal interactions with selfobjects describes the rapid, spontaneous, involuntary, nonconscious communications between the mother's and infant's autonomic nervous systems (Basch, 1976; Schore, 1994, 2002b). Kohut's observation of the selfobject's facilitation and maintenance of the infant's homeostatic balance in essence describes the external psychobiological regulation of the infant's organization of a state of sympathetic-parasympathetic autonomic balance (Schore, 1994).

According to A. M. Siegel, Kohut described "the drives" as "an intruding biological principle, not available to empathy or introspection, therefore not a part of psychology," and concluded that the drive concept had significant deleterious consequences for psychoanalysis (A.M. Siegel, 1996, p. 197). However, the deep connections of the right brain, the biological substrate of the human unconscious into both the sympathetic and parasympathetic components of the ANS (Schore, 1996, 1997b, 1999c, 2001b), "the physiological bottom of the mind" (Jackson, 1931), supports Freud's idea about the central role of drive in the system unconscious.

The fact that the right hemisphere contains "the most comprehensive and integrated map of the body state available to the brain" (Damasio, 1994, p. 66) indicates that Freud's (1915/1957a) definition of "drive" as "the psychical representative of the stimuli originating from the organism and reaching the mind" may be more properly characterized as reaching the "right mind" (Ornstein, 1997). For the rest of the lifespan the nonverbal right brain, more so than the later maturing verbal left, plays a superior role in the regulation of physiological, endocrinological, neuroendocrine, cardiovascular, and immune functions (Hugdahl, 1995; Sullivan & Gratton, 1999). Its operations are essential to the vital coping functions that support self-survival, and therefore to the human stress response (Wittling, 1997). This information about the ANS and the right brain, the locus of the corporeal self, again indicates that self psychology must incorporate current biological data into its models of self and subjectivity.

In an important review of the literature on the neurology of self, Devinsky (2000) delineated the known functions of the right hemisphere: identify a corporeal image of self and its relation to the environment; distinguish self from nonself; recognize familiar members of the species, emotionally understand and react to bodily and environment stimuli; recall autobiographical information; relate self to environmental reality and to the social group; and maintain a coherent, continuous, and unified sense of self. Indeed, neurobiological studies indicate that *the right hemisphere is specialized for generating self-awareness and self-recognition, and for the processing of "self-related material"* (Keenan et al., 2000, 2001; Kircher et al., 2001; Miller et al., 2001; Ruby & Decety, 2001; Schore, 1994). These and the above data clearly indicate that self psychology is in essence a psychology of the unique functions of the right brain.

The highest level of the right brain that processes affective information, the orbitofrontal cortex (Schore, 1994, 1996, 1997b, 1998b, 2000a, 2001b), acts as the "senior executive of the emotional brain" (Joseph, 1996). The maturation of this prefrontal system overlaps and mediates what Stern (1985) termed the developmental achievement of "the subjective self." This cortex functions to refine emotions in keeping with current sensory input, and allows for the adaptive switching of internal bodily states in response to changes in the external environment that are appraised to be personally meaningful (Schore, 1998b). Due to its direct links into stress-regulating systems this right prefrontal cortex represents the highest level of self-regulation (Levine et al., 1999; Schore, 1994; Sullivan & Gratton, 2002b). The orbitofrontal system acts as a recovery mechanism that efficiently monitors and autoregulates the duration, frequency, and intensity of not only positive but also negative affect states.

The functioning of the "self-correcting" right hemispheric system is thus central to self-regulation, the ability to flexibly regulate emotional states through interactions with other humans in interconnected contexts via a two-person psychology, or autoregulation in independent, autonomous contexts via a one-person psychology. The adaptive capacity to shift between these dual regulatory modes, depending upon the social context, emerges out of a history of secure attachment interactions of a maturing biological organism and a psychobiologically attuned social environment. Furthermore, this "thinking part of the emotional brain" is centrally involved in integrating and assigning emotional-motivational significance to cognitive impressions, the association of emotion with ideas and thoughts (Joseph, 1996), in empathy (Eslinger, 1998), and in "critical human functions, such as social adjustment and the control of mood, drive and responsibility, traits that are crucial in defining the *'personality'* of an individual" (Cavada & Schultz, 2000, p. 205; italics added).

Neurobiological research indicates that the orbitofrontal system critically contributes to "the integration of past, present, and future experiences, enabling adequate performance in behavioral tasks, social situation, or situations involving survival" (Lipton, Alvarez, & Eichenbaum, 1999, p. 356). But perhaps the most complex of all functions of the right prefrontal cortex is what the neuroscientists Wheeler, Stuss, and Tulving (1997) called "the ability to mentally travel through time"—the capacity to mentally represent and become aware of subjective experiences in the past, present, and future. This unique capacity to self reflect comes on line at 18 months (the time of orbitofrontal maturation):

> The [right] prefrontal cortex, in conjunction with its reciprocal connections with other cortical and subcortical structures, empowers healthy human adults with the capacity to consider the *self's extended existence throughout time*. The most complete expression of this capacity, autonoetic awareness, occurs whenever one consciously recollects or reexperiences a happening from a specific time in the past, attends directly to one's present or on-line experience, or contemplates one's existence and conduct at a time in the future. (Wheeler et al., 1997, p. 350; italics added)

PSYCHOPATHOGENESIS: THE NEUROBIOLOGY AND SELF PSYCHOLOGY OF EARLY RELATIONAL TRAUMA

It is important to stress that the developmental attainment of an efficient self-system that can adaptively regulate various forms of arousal and psychobiological states—and thereby affect, cognition, and behavior—only evolves in a growth-facilitating emotional environment. The good-enough mother of the securely attached infant permits access to the child after a separation and shows a tendency to respond appropriately and promptly to his/her emotional expressions. She also allows for the interactive generation of high levels of positive affect in shared play states. These regulated events promote an expansion of the child's coping capacities, and thus security of the attachment bond is the primary defense against trauma-induced psychopathology.

In contrast to this scenario, the abusive mother not only shows less play with her infant, she also induces long-lasting traumatic states of negative affect in the child. Because her attachment is weak, she provides little protection against other potential abusers of the infant, such as the father. Affective communications, so central to the attachment dynamic, are distorted in the abused/ neglected caregiver-infant relationship (Gaensbauer & Sands, 1979). This caregiver is inaccessible and reacts to her infant's expressions of emotions and stress inappropriately and/or rejectingly, and therefore shows minimal or unpredictable participation in the various types of arousal-regulating processes. Instead of modulating she induces extreme levels of stimulation and arousal, very high in abuse, and very low in neglect. The enduring detrimental effects of parent-inflicted traumatic abuse and neglect on the attachment bond is now well established: "The continued survival of the child is felt to be at risk, because the actuality of the abuse jeopardizes [the] primary object bond and challenges the child's capacity to trust and, therefore, to securely depend (Davies & Frawley, 1994, p. 62). Thus, "the essential experience of trauma [is] an unraveling of the relationship between self and nuturing other, the very fabric of psychic life" (Laub & Auerhahn, 1993, p. 287). In contexts of relational trauma the caregiver(s), in addition to dysregulating the infant, withdraw any selfobject interactive repair functions, leaving the infant for long periods in an intensely disruptive psychobiological state that is beyond her immature coping strategies. According to McDougall, "It must . . . be emphasized that the long-range traumatic impact of a catastrophic event depends to a large degree on the parental reactions to the trauma in question" (1989, p. 208).

Lachmann and Beebe (1997) pointed out that an event becomes traumatic when it ruptures the individual's selfobject tie, without opportunity for repair, thereby dramatically altering his/her self-state. Similarly, Mollon emphasized, "It is the non-availability of caregivers who can provide empathy and soothing which means the child abused within the family must resort to pathological forms of internal escape. . . . [W]ithout this soothing by reliable and consistent caregivers, the traumatized child is unable to regulate his or her mental state and restore emotional equilibrium" (2001, p. 212).

In studies of a neglect paradigm, Tronick and Weinberg described: "When infants are not in homeostatic balance or are emotionally dysregulated (e.g., they are distressed), they are at the mercy of these states. Until these states are brought under control, infants must devote all their regulatory resources to reorganizing them. While infants are doing that, they can do nothing else" (1997, p. 56). The "nothing else" these authors referred to is a failure to continue to develop. Traumatized infants forfeit potential opportunities for socioemotional learning during critical periods of right brain development (Schore, 2001b, 2002c).

It should be noted that recent National Child Abuse and Neglect statistics (2000) reported that the highest victimization rate occurs in children aged 0–3, and that over half of fatalities due to maltreatment occur in this age group. Early experiences with a traumatizing caregiver are well known to negatively impact the child's attachment security, stress-coping strategies, and sense of self (Crittenden & Ainsworth, 1989; Erickson, Egeland, & Pianta, 1989). It is here that attachment theory can offer self psychology important information about the origins of severe self-psychological deficits.

Indeed in classic research, Main and Solomon (1986) studied the attachment patterns of infants who had suffered trauma in the first year of life. This lead to the discovery of a new attachment category, "type D," an insecure-disorganized/disoriented pattern, one found in 80% of maltreated infants (Carlson, Cicchetti, Barnett, & Braunwald, 1989). These authors contended that such infants are experiencing low stress tolerance and that their disorganization and disorientation reflect the fact that the infant, instead of finding a haven of safety in the relationship, is alarmed by the parent. They noted that because the infant inevitably seeks the parent when alarmed, any parental behavior that directly alarms an infant should place it in an irresolvable paradox in which it can neither approach, shift its attention, nor flee. At the most basic level, these infants are unable to generate a coherent behavioral coping strategy to deal with this emotional challenge (see Schore, 2001c, 2002c, 2003 for a detailed description of the developmental and neuro-psychoanalysis of the disorganized/disoriented attachment).

Neurobiological studies in developmental traumatology indicate that the infant's psychobiological response to trauma is comprised of two separate response patterns, hyperarousal and dissociation (Perry, Pollard, Blakely, Baker, & Vigilante, 1995; Schore, 1998i, 1999f, 1999g, 2001c, 2001e, 2001g, 2002c). In the initial stage of threat, an alarm reaction is initiated, in which the sympathetic component of the ANS is suddenly and significantly activated, resulting in increased heart rate, blood pressure, and respiration. Distress is expressed in crying and then screaming. Beebe described an episode of "mutually escalating overarousal" of a disorganized attachment pair: "Each one escalates the ante, as the infant builds to a frantic distress, may scream, and, in this example, finally throws up. In an escalating overarousal pattern, even after extreme distress signals from the infant, such as ninety-degree head aversion, arching away . . . or screaming, the mother keeps going" (2000, p. 436). This state of fear-terror is mediated by sympathetic hyperarousal, and it reflects increased levels of the major stress hormone corticotropin releasing factor, which in turn regulates noradrenaline and adrenaline activity (see Schore, 1997b, 2001c, 2002c).

But a second, later-forming, longer-lasting traumatic reaction is seen in dissociation, in which the child disengages from stimuli in the external world and attends to an "internal" world. The child's dissociation in the midst of terror involves numbing, avoidance, compliance, and restricted affect. Traumatized infants are observed to be staring off into space with a glazed look. This parasympathetic dominant state of conservation-withdrawal occurs in helpless and hopeless stressful situations in which the individual becomes inhibited and strives to avoid attention in order to become "unseen" (Kaufman & Rosenblum, 1967; Schore, 1994).

This primary regulatory process for maintaining organismic homeostasis (Engel & Schmale, 1972) is characterized by a metabolic shutdown (Schore, 2001c, 2002c) and low levels of activity (McCabe & Schneiderman, 1985). It is used throughout the lifespan, when the stressed individual passively disengages in order "to conserve energies . . . to foster survival by the risky posture of feigning death, to allow healing of wounds and restitution of depleted resources by immobility" (Powles, 1992, p. 213). Beebe and Lachmann (1988b), described a stressed-induced "inhibition of responsivity" in which a sudden total cessation of infant movement accompanies a limp, motionless headhang.

Tronick and Weinberg (1997) observed:

> When infants' attempts to fail to repair the interaction infants often lose postural control, withdraw, and self-comfort. The disengagement is pro-

found even with this short disruption of the mutual regulatory process and break in intersubjectivity. The infant's reaction is reminiscent of the withdrawal of Harlow's isolated monkey or of the infants in institutions observed by Bowlby and Spitz. (p. 75)

It is this parasympathetic mechanism that mediates the "profound detachment" (Barach, 1991) of dissociation. If early trauma is experienced as "psychic catastrophe" (Bion, 1962a), dissociation represents "detachment from an unbearable situation" (Mollon, 1996), "the escape when there is no escape" (Putnam, 1997), and "a last resort defensive strategy" (Dixon, 1998).

The neurobiology of the later forming dissociative reaction is different than the initial hyperarousal response (for models of the neurobiology of dissociation (see Scaer, 2001; Schore, 2001c). In this passive state, pain-numbing and blunting endogenous opiates and behavior-inhibiting stress hormones, such as cortisol, are elevated. Furthermore, activity of the dorsal vagal complex in the brainstem medulla increases dramatically, decreasing heart rate, blood pressure, and metabolic activity, despite increases in circulating noradrenaline and adrenaline. This intensified parasympathetic arousal allows the infant to maintain homeostasis in the face of the internal state of sympathetic hyperarousal. This same sequential defensive operation was observed in the psychophysiological literature by Porges, who described, "the sudden and rapid transition from an unsuccessful strategy of struggling requiring massive sympathetic activation to the metabolically conservative immobilized state mimicking death associated with the dorsal vagal complex" (1997, p. 75). Notice that in the traumatic state, and this may be of long duration, both the sympathetic energy-expending and parasympathetic energy-conserving components of the infant's developing ANS are hyperactivated.

THE DEVELOPMENTAL PSYCHOANALYSIS AND SELF PSYCHOLOGY OF RELATIONAL TRAUMA

As episodes of relational trauma commence, the infant is processing information from the external and internal environment. The mother's face is the most potent visual stimulus in the child's world, and it is well known that direct gaze can mediate not only loving but powerful aggressive messages. In coding the mother's frightening behavior, Hesse and Main described "in non-play contexts, stiff-legged 'stalking' of infant on all fours in a hunting posture; exposure of canine tooth accompanied by hissing; deep growls directed at infant" (1999, p. 511). The image of the mother's aggressive face, as well as the chaotic alterations in the infant's bodily state that are associated with it, are indelibly imprinted into the infant's developing limbic circuits as a "flashbulb memory" and thereby stored in imagistic implicit-procedural memory in the visuospatial right hemisphere.

But within the traumatic interaction the infant is presented with another affectively overwhelming facial expression, a maternal expression of fear-terror. Main and Solomon (1986) noted that this occurs when the mother withdraws from the infant as though the infant were the source of the alarm, and they reported that dissociated, trancelike, and fearful behavior is observed in parents of type D infants. Studies show a specific link between frightening, intrusive maternal behavior and disorganized infant attachment (Schuengel, Bakersmans-Kranenburg, & van IJzendoorn, 1999).

During these episodes the infant is matching the rhythmic structures of these states, and this synchronization is registered in the firing patterns of the right corticolimbic brain regions that are in a critical period of growth. And thus not just the trauma but the infant's defensive response to the trauma, the regulatory strategy of dissociation, is inscribed into the infant's right-brain implict-procedural memory system. In light of the fact that many of these mothers have suffered from unresolved trauma themselves (Famularo, Kinscherff, & Fenton, 1992), this spatiotemporal imprinting of terror and dissociation is a primary mechanism for the intergenerational transmission of trauma (see Schore, 2001c, 2003 for a detailed discussion of the neurobiology of the dissociative defense and body-mind psychopathology).

Even more specifically, in certain critical moments the caregiver's entrance into a dissociative state represents the real-time manifestation of neglect. Such a context of an emotionally unavailble, dissociating mother and a disorganized infant was evocatively captured by Selma Fraiberg (cited in Barach, 1991):

> The mother had been grudgingly parented by relatives after her mother's postpartum attempted suicide and had been sexually abused by her father and cousin. During a testing session, her baby begins to cry. It is a hoarse, eerie cry. . . . On tape, we see the baby in the mother's arms *screaming hopelessly; she does not turn to her mother for comfort.* The mother looks distant, self-absorbed. She makes an absent gesture to comfort the baby, then gives up. She looks away. The sceaming continues for five dreadful minutes. In the background we hear Mrs. Adelson's voice, gently encoraging the mother. "What do you do to comfort Mary when she cries like this?" (The mother) murmurs something inaudible. . . . As we watched this tape later . . . we said to each other incredulously, "It's as if this mother doesn't hear her baby's cries." (p. 119; italics added)

Ultimately, the child will transition out of heightened protest into detachment, and with the termination of the intensely energy-expending extreme protest, he/she will become silent. He/she will shift out of the hyperarousal, and dissociate and match the mother's state. This state switch from a regulatory strategy of intense struggling into the dissociative immobilized state mimicking death is ultimately experienced as a "dead spot" in this child's subjective experience (Kestenberg, 1985).

Notice that this traumatic context is totally devoid of any mutually regulating interactions. Rather, both mother and infant, although in physical proximity, are simultaneousy autoregulating their stress, in a very primtive manner, in parallel but nonintersecting dissociative states. There is a void of subjectivity within each, and there is a void in the communications within the intersubjective field. There's no dyadic attachment mechanism to convey or sense signals from the other. What stands out between them, both verbally and nonverbally, is this silent void, this vacuum, this black hole of nothingness. In fact, in this dissociated context there is no intersubjective field. This is a context in which a two-person psychology does not exist and does not apply.

The extreme alteration of subjectivity within the traumatically dissociated infant was described by Winnicott (1958a) as an episode of discontinuity in the child's need for going on being. Dissociation has classically been characterized as a constrictcd state of primary consciousness, a void therefore of subjectivity. This is the context of a one-person psychology, but a trauma-induced, radically altered, survival-focused one-person psychology. Thus, in infancy, as at all later points of the lifespan, in the profound detachment of dissociative moments both the subjective self and the intersubjective field instantly switch off and do not exist. Due to the metabolic shutdown, higher-brain activity, including the capacities of processing external social stimuli and generating internal images, ceases. During dissociative episodes the complex processing of both external and internal objects ceases.

In classical developmental research, Ribble (1944) observed:

> The infant is, by its very incompleteness of brain and nervous system, continuously in danger of functional disorganisation. Outwardly the danger is of sudden separation from the mother who either intuitively or knowingly must sustain this functional balance. . . . Inwardly the danger appears to be the mounting of tension from biological needs and *the inability of the organism to maintain its inner energy or metabolic equilibrium* and reflex excitability. (p. 630; italics added)

In neuroscience, Damasio (1994) wrote, the self is a "repeatedly reconstructed biological state" that "endows our experience with subjectivity." Psychoanalytic models support this neurobiological concept, and expand upon it. Indeed, the central tenet of self psychology prescribes that regulatory self–selfobject experiences provide the particular intersubjective affective experiences that evoke the emergence and maintenance of the self (Kohut, 1984). But in the case of relational trauma-induced dissociation, under conditions of massive default in metabolic energy production for basic brain/mind/body functions, there is not sufficient energy to reconstruct the biological state that sustains cohesion of self-function and thereby subjectivity.

Mollon (2001) referred to the devastating effects of early "selfobject catastrophes." I suggest that in contrast to the optimal continuous dyadic reciprocal interactions with regulating selfobjects that maintain the infant's homeostatic balance and thereby the energic vigor and structural cohesion and integration of the self, the selfobject catastrophes and defensive dissociative responses embedded in relational trauma induce a severe failure of the infant's capacity to maintain metabolic-energetic equilibrium in both its central and autonomic nervous systems, and thereby a dis-integration of the self. How long the infant remains in this state is an essential factor in psychopathogenesis.

Recall that Kohut referred to two types of disintegration, differentiating a "fragmented self" from a "depleted self" (1977). According to Mollon, "fragmentation arises in the baby and child whose mental and physiological state is not regulated adequately by the caregiving environment" (2001, p. 13). I suggest that at all points in the lifespan a fragmented self describes the context of a self-system that is in intense, dysregulated sympathetic hyperarousal, a condition of excessive energy expenditure, an explosive disaggregation of the core, or nuclear self. This hyperenergetic state would be subjectively experienced as "organismic panic," which Pao described as "a shock-like reaction in which the ego's integrative function is temporarily paralyzed" (1979, p. 221). I would amend this to say that it is more than the ego that is paralyzed, it is the right-brain core self.

But in addition, Kohut's "depleted" self characterizes an organismic state of dysregulated parasympathetic hypoarousal, dissociation, and excessive energy conservation, subjectively experienced as an implosion of the self, wherein there is not enough energy in the brain/mind/body system to form the interconnections responsible for coherence. This would be clinically manifest as an anaclitic depression that accompanies a state of conservation-withdrawal marked by high levels of dissociation (see Weinberg, 2000, on right-hemisphere deficiency and suicide). In this condition there is a simultaneous loss of both modes of self-regulation, interactive regulation and autoregulation. The former would be subjectively experienced as a lingering state of intense hopelessness, the latter of helplessness. These self survival states and their accompanying self-cognitions are obviously relevant to Kohutian, intersubjective, relational, as well as classical psychoanalytic perspectives. Self psychology, like psychoanalysis in general, must now revise its theoretical and clinical models of early trauma and reincorporate the concept of dissociation into its models of psychopathogeneis.

CLINICAL PSYCHOANALYTIC CONCEPTIONS OF TRAUMA AND DISSOCIATION

Indeed, the problem of trauma has been one of great controversy for psychoanalysis. In 1893, Breuer and Freud, citing the contemporary work of Janet (1889), described dissociation as the major mechanism for "strangulations of affect." By 1900 and *The Interpretation of Dreams*, however, Freud discarded this notion and favored repression as the major mechanism of psychopathogenesis. Despite this, there has been a long tradition in the classical psychoanalytic literature of the traumatic effects of a sudden and unexpected influx of massive external stimulation (sympathetic hyperexcitation) that breaches the infant's stimulus barrier and precludes successful self-regulation (Freud, 1920/1955, 1926/1959). This has led to an emphasis of the role of overstimulation and annihilation anxieties in classical, object relational, and self psychological models of trauma. Kohut also suggested that the experience of fragmentation of the mind-body self represents "the deepest anxiety man can experience" (1984, p. 16). I suggest that Fraiberg's description of "screaming hopelessly" is the vocal expression of the earliest manifestation of annihilation anxiety, the threat to one's bodily wholeness and survival, the annihilation of one's core being.

However, Freud additionally described the psychic helplessness associated with the ego's immaturity in the first years of childhood, and postulated that the passively experienced reemergence of the trauma is "a recognized, remembered, expected situation of helplessness" (1926/1959, p. 166). In writings on psychic trauma and "emotional surrender" Anna Freud (1951/1968, 1964/1969) also referred to helplessness, defined as a state of "disorientation and powerlessness" that the organism experiences in the traumatic moment. Although almost all psychoanalytic theoreticians have overlooked or undervalued this, Krystal (1988) and Hurvich (1989) emphasized that at the level of psychic survival helplessness constitutes the first basic danger. This helplessness is a component of the survival strategy of conservation-withdrawal, the early-appearing primitive organismic defense against the growth-inhibiting effects of maternal over- or understimulation.

These issues also bear upon another area of long-standing controversy. Winnicott offered the observation that, "In certain cases, the mother's central internal object is dead at the critical time in her child's early infancy, and her mood is one of depression. Here the infant has to fit in with a role of dead object. . . . Here the opposite to the liveliness of the infant is an antilife factor derived from the mother's depression" (1965, p. 181). This scenario was described in the previously cited observation of Fraiberg. Instead of interactively generating vitality affects, each member of the traumatized dyad experiences "an antilife factor" and "dead spots" in their subjective experience. Very recent basic research indicates that maternal deprivation increases cell death in the infant brain (Zhang et al., 2002). Is this the death instinct and is the traumatizing caregiver enhancing it? Recall that the state of conservation-withdrawal, a primary regulatory process of decreased metabolic energy, is accessed when active coping (flight or fight) is not possible, occurs in hopeless and helpless contexts, and is behaviorally manifest as feigning death (Engel & Schmale, 1972; Powles, 1992). Dissociation is defined as "a submission and resignation to the inevitability of overwhelming, even psychically deadening danger" (Davies & Frawley, 1994).

Furthermore, Kohut (1977) speculated that in optimal contexts the parental selfobject acts to "remedy the child's homeostatic imbalance," and thus the relational context of a selfobject catastrophe is characterized by not only

the induction of abuse but also a lack of interactive repair of the infant's dissociative reactions. Because these events are occurring in a critical period of development they have long-enduring effects. McDougall asserted, "The way in
which the potential trauma is handled by the environment is therefore a critical
factor in determining the extent to which the child will suffer future pathological consequences" (1989, p. 208).

This context of psychopathogenesis was, again, characterized by Winnicott:
"If maternal care is not good enough, then the infant does not really come into
existence, since there is no continuity in being; instead, the personality becomes built on the basis of reactions to environmental impingement" (1960,
p. 54). Tustin (1981) referred to this impingement as a "psychological catastrophe," which is responded to by "autistic withdrawal" or "encapsulation," an
innate defensive measure against bodily hurt that involves a "shutting out of
mind" what can not be handled at the moment. This is an operational definition of the growth-inhibiting defense of dissociation.

Mollon (2001) described the outcome of the selfobject failures embedded
in ambient and cumulative relational trauma:

> Dissociation and related forms of detachment, including depersonaliza-
> tion and derealization, are among the most fundamental reactions to
> trauma. If childhood trauma or abuse is repeated, and if the abuser is a
> caregiver, so that the child has *nowhere to run and no one to turn to*, then
> internal escape is resorted to—the child learns to dissociate more easily
> and in a more organized way. In this way, the personality system preserves
> at least parts of itself from the impinging trauma or violation, by seques-
> tering, or sealing off, the area of damage. (p. 218; italics added)

Although Kohut never used the term *dissociation*, in his last book (1984) he
characterized an early interaction that could describe a type D attachment, and
spoke of the dire long-term consequences of a tendency of an individual to
characterologically "wall himself off" from traumatizing experiences:

> If the mother's empathic ability has remained infantile, that is, if she
> tends to respond with panic to the baby's anxiety, then a deleterious
> chain will be set into motion. She may chronically wall herself off from
> the baby, thus depriving him of the benefical effect of merging with her
> as she returns from experiencing mild anxiety to calmness. Alternatively,
> she may continue to respond with panic, in which case two negative
> consequences may ensue: the mother may lay the groundwork in the
> child for a lifelong propensity toward the uncurbed spreading of anxiety
> or other emotions, or by forcing the child to wall himself off from such
> an overly intense and thus traumatizing [experience, she] may foster in
> the child an impoverished psychic organization, the psychic organization

of a person who will later be unable to be empathic himself, to experience human experiences, in essence, to be fully human. (p. 83)

The pathological walling off or dissociation from stress and pain has devastating effects on self, and therefore psychobiological functions. According to Putnam (1997) dissociation is a lack of the normal integration of thoughts, feelings, and experiences into the stream of consciousness and memory. Bromberg described how dissociated traumatic experience "tends to remain unsymbolized by thought and language, exists as a separate reality outside of self-expression and is cut off from authentic human relatedness and deadened to full participants in the life of the rest of the personality" (1991, p. 405). Dissociation represents a disruption of the monitoring and controlling functions of consciousness. Fonagy and colleagues (1996) described:

victims of childhood abuse who coped by refusing to conceive of the contents of their caregiver's mind and thus successfully avoided having to think about their caregiver's wish to harm them. The initially defensive disruption of the capacity to depict feelings and thoughts in themselves and others becomes a characteristic response to all subsequent intimate relationships. It also drastically limits their capacity to come to terms with these abusive experiences in later life and creates a vulnerability to interpersonal stress. (p. 384)

These conceptions reflect the negative impact of *psychological dissociation* (alterations in cognition, attention, and memory-amnesia) on personality development.

However, echoing the developmental traumatology findings, there is currently a shift from the cognitive to the affective-somatic aspects of dissociation in the neuropsychiatric literature. In neurological studies of trauma Scaer referred to *somatic dissociation*, and concludes, "Perhaps the least appreciated manifestations of dissociation in trauma are in the area of perceptual alterations and somatic symptoms" (2001, p. 104). He further pointed out that distortion of proprioceptive awareness of the trauma patient's body is a most common dissociative phenomena. Similarly, in clinical psychiatric studies Nijenhuis (2000) described not just psychological (e.g., amnesia) but *somatoform dissociation* associated specifically with early onset traumatization, often involving physical abuse and threat to life by another person. This pattern of psychophysiologic responses to trauma is thus associated with coping in contexts where there is a threat to inescapable physical injury. Somatoform dissociation is expressed as a lack of integration of sensorimotor experiences, reactions, and functions of the individual and his/her self-representation.

Clinical research suggests a link between childhood traumatic experiences and somatoform dissociation in chronic posttraumatic stress disorder (PTSD), borderline, and somatoform disorders (Waller et al., 2000). This dissociation is manifest as a suppression of autonomic physiological responses (e.g., heart rate and skin conductance), especially when recalling traumatic experiences (Carrey, Butter, Persinger, & Bialek, 1995; Griffin, Resick, & Mechanic, 1997). A study of psychophysiological reactivity in adults with childhood abuse demonstrated a significant decline in heart rate and diastolic blood pressure in a PTSD patient, while she was dissociating (Schmahl, Elzinga, & Bremner, 2002). Recall that in the previous description of early relational trauma, the infant's dissociative response is mediated by heightened dorsal vagal activity that dramatically decreases heart rate and blood pressure.

In previous work (Schore, 2001c, 2002c), I have proposed that the massive inhibition of the dorsal motor vegetative vagal system mediates dissociation, a primitive defensive mechanism which has long been implicated in trauma-induced psychopathogenesis (Janet, 1889; Chu & Dill, 1990). Basic research has indicated that the dorsal motor nucleus of the vagus acts to shut down metabolic activity during immobilization, death feigning, and hiding behaviors (Porges, 1997, 2001). These hiding behaviors, components of dissociation, "the escape when there is no escape," are elicited in the therapeutic context, especially when the patient is attempting to escape from the physiological aspects of an intense emotional experience. It is important to emphasize that in traumatic abuse the individual dissociates not only from the external world, from processing external stimuli that signal imminent dysregulation, but also from the internal world, that is chaotic and painful stimuli originating within the body.

In the psychoanalytic literature, Davies (1996), Aron and Anderson (1998), and Bromberg (1994) have made important efforts to reincorporate the concept of dissociation into psychodynamic treatment models. This latter author proposed that the concept of personality disorder can be defined as the characterological outcome of the inordinate use of dissociation, and that in all forms (borderline, schizoid, narcissistic, paranoid), it constitutes a personality structure organized as a proactive, defensive response to the potential repetition of childhood trauma (Bromberg, 1995). Dissociation, the last resort defensive strategy, may represent the greatest counterforce to effective psychotherapeutic treatment of personality disorders.

TRAUMATIC ATTACHMENT
AND RIGHT BRAIN PATHOMORPHOGENESIS

The "psychically deadening danger" of excessive unregulated dissociation that accompanies early relational traumatic attachments and creates a context for an "impoverished psychic organization" is the major mechanism that engenders what Balint called the "basic fault," a deep and pervasive sense that there exists within a fault that extends widely to include "the whole psychobiological structure of the individual" (1968, p. 22), and that is experienced as "a feeling of emptiness, being lost, deadness, and futility" (p. 19). This structural defect is due, according to Balint, to a severe discrepancy between the needs of the person as an infant and the capacity of people in his/her early environment to provide them.

What has been undetermined to date in the psychoanalytic literature is, as Mahler (1958) stated almost 50 years ago, precisely how trauma interferes with psychic structure formation. Freud (1940/1964) observed that trauma in early life effects all vulnerable humans because "the ego . . . is feeble, immature and incapable of resistance." Bowlby postulated that the major negative impact of early traumatic attachments is an alteration of the organism's normal developmental trajectory. Over 30 years ago Bowlby wrote: "Since much of the development and organization of [attachment] behavioral systems takes place whilst the individual is immature, there are plenty of occasions when an atypical environment can divert them from developing on an adaptive course" (1969b, p. 130). Specifically how this developmental deflection takes place can only be answered with reference to current neurobiological models of how detrimental early socioaffective experiences provide a growth-inhibiting environment for the developing brain. Indeed, research on maltreatment-related (pediatric) PTSD is under way (Beers & De Bellis, 2002; Carrion et al., 2001, 2002).

Studies in developmental traumatology have concluded that "the overwhelming stress of maltreatment in childhood is associated with adverse influences on brain development" (De Bellis et al., 1999, p. 1281). And so it is thought that specifically a dysfunctional and traumatized early relationship is the stressor that leads to PTSD, that severe trauma of interpersonal origin may override any genetic, constitutional, social, or psychological resilience factor, and that the ensuing adverse effects on brain development and alterations of the biological stress systems may be regarded as "an environmentally induced complex developmental disorder" (De Bellis, 2001).

Advances in the 1990s, the "decade of the brain" are therefore allowing us to more deeply understand the underlying mechanisms by which dysregulating traumatic attachments embedded in abuse and neglect interfere with the organization of particularly, the right brain (Schore, 2001c, in 2002c). During the first 2 years of life, chronic and cumulative states of overwhelming, hyperaroused affective states, as well as hypoaroused dissociation, have devastating effects on the growth of psychic structure. The survival mode of conservation-withdrawal induces an extreme alteration of the bioenergetics of the developing brain. In critical periods of regional synaptogenesis this would have growth-inhibiting effects, especially in the right brain, which specializes in withdrawal. This is because the biosynthetic processes that mediate the proliferation of synaptic connections in the postnatally developing brain demand, in addition to sufficient quantities of essential nutrients, massive amounts of energy. An infant brain that is chronically shifting into hypometabolic survival modes has little energy available for growth (see Schore, 1994, 1997b, 2001c).

Furthermore, during the brain growth spurt, when psychic structure is organizing at a rapid rate, the severe and prolonged states of physiological dysregulation that results from relational trauma abuse, neglect, or both are routinely accompanied by deficiencies in the provision of selfobject experiences of affect synchrony and interactive repair. Instead of optimal dyadic contexts of right-brain-to-right-brain intersubjectivity, the infant is exposed to severe "breaks in intersubjectivity" (Tronick & Weinberg, 1997) that engender "dead spots" in this child's subjective experience (Kestenberg, 1985). These experiences negatively impact the experience-dependent maturation of the right hemisphere, which is dominant for "subjective emotional experiences" and affect regulation (Schore, 1994, 1999a, 1999c, 2001a, 2001b, 2002e, in press b).

Grotstein (1983) referred to "a failure in the development of self-regulatory functions under the sponsorship of the selfobject." This failure to evolve an efficient regulatory system would cause the personality to have a deficient and decreased capacity for autoregulation, which is partially compensated for by an increased need for external regulators at later stages. In fact, this very deficit, a direct parallel to Kohut's increased need for pathological selfobjects in developmental disorders, is now considered to be a risk factor of insecure attachments (Maunder & Hunter, 2001).

Laub and Auerhahn (1993) proposed that the essential experience of trauma is a disruption of the link between the "self" and the mothering "empathic other," and therefore the maternal introject, or mothering (selfobject regulatory) function, is "damaged" or "deficient." This deficiency is expressed in a poorly evolved right frontolimbic system, the locus of the brain's major regulatory functions. Relational traumatic attachment experiences are "affectively burnt in" (Stuss & Alexander, 1999) this right frontal structure and its cortical and subcortical connections during its critical period of growth. In this manner, "early adverse developmental experiences may leave behind a permanent physiological reactivity in limbic areas of the brain" (Post, Weiss, & Leverich, 1994, p. 800). Basic research in affective neuroscience demonstrated that emotional and social deprivation interferes with the normal development of the synaptic architecture of cortical and subcortical limbic areas, and leads to "neurological scars" that underlie subsequent behavioral and cognitive deficits (Poeggel & Braun, 1996; Poeggel et al., 1999). The deficits described by self psychology are thus, specifically, functional deficits that reflect structural defects of cortical-subcortical circuits of the right brain, the locus of the corporeal-emotional self.

RIGHT BRAIN DYSFUNCTION
AND SELF PSYCHOLOGICAL DEFICITS

What would be the functional indicators of this structural impairment of the right brain? Due to the altered development of the right cortical system that nonconsciously decodes emotional stimuli by actual felt emotional responses to stimuli, individuals with poor attachment histories display empathy disorders, the limited capacity to perceive the emotional states of others. An inability to read subtle facial expressions leads to a misattribution of emotional states and a misinterpretation of the intentions of others. In addition to this deficit in social cognition in appraising external social cues, such individuals also exhibit a poor ability to appraise the internal cues of their bodily states, and what Krystal (1997) termed *desomatization*. Impairments of these right brain functions preclude an adaptive capacity to evaluate external-social and internal-physiological signals of safety and danger.

The coping deficits in right hemispheric self-regulation are manifest in a limited capacity to modulate the intensity and duration of affects, especially biologically primitive affects like shame, rage, excitement, elation, disgust, panic-terror, and hopeless despair. Under stress such individuals experience not discrete and differentiated affects, but diffuse, undifferentiated, chaotic states accompanied by overwhelming somatic and visceral sensations. The poor capacity for what Fonagy and Target (1997) called *mentalization* leads to a restricted ability to reflect upon their emotional states. Solms described a mechanism by which disorganization of a damaged or developmentally deficient right hemisphere is associated with a "collapse of internalized representations of the external world" in which "the patient regresses from whole to part object relationships" (1996, p. 347), a hallmark of early-forming personality disorders. This regression is equated with Kohut's "disintegration" into a "fragmented" or "depleted" self.

Traumatic attachment experiences negatively affect the early organization of the right brain, and thereby produce deficits in its adaptive functions of emotionally understanding and reacting to bodily and environmental stimuli, identifying a corporeal image of self and its relation to the environment, distinguishing the self from the other, and generating self-awareness. Optimal attachment experiences allow for the emergence of self-awareness, the adaptive a capacity to sense, attend to, and reflect upon the dynamic changes of one's subjective self-states, but traumatic attachments in childhood lead to self-modulation of painful affect by directing attention away from internal emotional states. Pain integration, a determinant factor in species survival, is preferentially dependent on the right hemisphere (Ostrowsky et al., 2002).

Indeed, there is now evidence to show that early relational trauma is particularly expressed in right hemisphere deficits. Very recent studies reveal that maltreated children diagnosed with PTSD manifest right-lateralized metabolic limbic abnormalities (De Bellis, Keshaven, Spencer, & Hall, 2000; De Bellis et al., 2002), and that right brain impairments associated with severe anxiety disorders are expressed in childhood (De Bellis, Casey, et al., 2000). Adults severely abused in childhood (Raine et al., 2001) and diagnosed with PTSD (Galletly, Clark, McFarlane, & Weber, 2001) show reduced right hemisphere activation during a working memory task. Neurological studies of adults confirm that dysfunction of the right frontal lobe is involved in PTSD symptomatology (Freeman & Kimbrell, 2001) and dissociative flashbacks (Berthier, Posada, & Puentes, 2001). Current neuropsychiatric research indicates that right-sided prefrontal activation occurs during the acquisition of conditioned fear (Fischer,

Anderson, Furmark, & Fredrikson, 2000; Fischer, Andersson, Furmark, Wik, & Fredrikson, 2002; Hugdahl et al., 1995; Pizzagalli, Greischar, & Davidson, 2003), that the paralimbic areas of the right hemisphere are preferentially involved in the storage of traumatic memories (Schiffer, Teicher, & Papanicolaou, 1995), and that altered right-sided activity occurs in panic and social phobic anxiety states (Davidson, Marshall, Tomarken, & Henriques, 2000; Galderisi et al., 2001; Massana et al., 2002; Wiedemann et al., 1999).

The neuroscience literature also indicates that dissociation is associated with a deficiency of the right brain (Weinberg, 2000). Crucian and colleagues described "a dissociation between the emotional evaluation of an event and the physiological reaction to that event, with the process being dependent on intact right hemisphere function" (2000, p. 643). A failure of orbitofrontal function is seen in the hypometabolic state of pathological dissociation, and this dysfunction would interfere with its normal role in processing motivational information and modulating the motivational control of goal-directed behavior, and therefore manifest as a deficit in organizing the expression of a regulated emotional response and an appropriate motivational state for a particular social environmental context.

As a result, during times of traumatic dissociation, the major motivational systems that are programmed to actively cope with the external social environment are switched off. This would lead to a deactivation of every component of Panksepp's (1998) system of prototypic affective states, including those associated with "attachment to conspecifics," such as nurturance/maternal care, play/joy/social affection, and sexuality, as well as the "organismic defence system" of rage/anger and fear. Similarly, the active coping strategies of Lichtenberg's (1989) attachment-affiliation, exploratory-assertive, aversive, and sensual-sexual motivational systems all collapse in subcortically programmed survival states of passive disengagement, conservation-withdrawal, energy depletion, and dissociation, the escape when there is no escape, the last-resort defensive strategy.

In psychoanalytic work, Mollon (2001) described the similarities of the enduring pathological effects of both early psychological and neurological damage. In the developmental neuropsychological literature, Anderson, Damasio, Tranel, and Damasio delineated the sequelae of early versus late neurological damage to the prefrontal cortex and concluded that these "impairments largely reflect a failure to ever develop specific cognitive and behavioral competencies, whereas in the adult-onset cases the defects arose through deterioration or loss of normally developed abilities" (2000, p. 291).

The deficits described by self psychology thus represent enduring developmental failures of specifically the higher regulatory prefrontal areas of the early-developing right brain. This hemisphere is dominant for attachment functions (Henry, 1993, Schore, 1994; Siegel, 1999), and for the adaptive capacity to "maintain a coherent, continuous, and unifed sense of self" (Devinsky, 2000). The maladaptive deficits of affect regulation that accompany pathological dissociation, a primitive defense against overwhelming affects, are expressed in a spectrum of severe self-pathologies, from reactive attachment disorder of infants (Hinshaw-Fuselier, Boris, & Zeanah, 1999), to psychotic experiences (Allen & Coyne, 1995), dissociative identity disorders (Putnam, 1989), posttraumatic stress disorders (van der Kolk, McFarlane, & Weisaeth, 1996), and borderline personality disorders (Golynkina & Ryle, 1999). *Early traumatic attachments are therefore a powerful source generator of the most severe deficits described by self psychology.*

CONTINUITY BETWEEN EARLY TRAUMATIC ATTACHMENTS AND LATER SEVERE SELF PATHOLOGY

Integrating physiology, neurobiology, and attachment theory, James Henry concluded,

> The ability to maintain personally relevant bonds is vital for our evolutionary survival. The infant's tie to the mother's voice and odor is recognized even by the newborn, yet this personal relevance and recognition of the familiar can be impaired by anxious insecurity resulting from difficult early experiences or traumatic stress. The vital task of establishing a personally relevant universe and the solace derived from it depend on right hemispheric functioning. If this function is indeed lost in the insecurely attached, much has been lost. (Henry, cited in Wang, 1997)

The insecurely attached infant's all-to-common stressful experiences with a caregiver who chronically initiates but poorly repairs intense and long-lasting dysregulated states are incorporated into right-brain long-term autobiographical memory as a pathological internal object relation, an interactive representation of a dysregulated-self-in-interaction-with-a-misattuning-object (Schore, 1997c). This internal working model of a disorganized/disoriented insecure attachment stores critical exteroceptive information about the social source of relational trauma as well as the infant's interoceptive physiological responses to the stress. It encodes both an expectation of imminent "mutually escalating overarousal" and the autoregulatory strategy for coping with overwhelming interactive stress—the primitive coping strategy of dissociation. Kiersky and Beebe (1994) described "nonverbal presymbolic forms of relating" that protected the infant from trauma and continue to be used by the adult to avoid retraumatization. Indeed, it is now accepted that, "the clinical data, reinforced by research findings, indicate that preverbal children, even in the first year of life, can establish and retain some form of internal representation of a traumatic event over significant periods of time" (Gaensbauer, 2002, p. 259).

A central principle of this psychoneurobiological perspective dictates that there is a continuity between early early traumatic attachment and later severe disorders of personality development (Schore, 1994, 1996, 1997b, 1998i, 1999f,

1999g, 2001c, 2001e, 2002c, in press a). Clinical researchers have described a continuity in infant and adult coping strategies:

> The stress responses exhibited by infants are the product of an immature brain processing threat stimuli and producing appropriate responses, while the adult who exhibits infantile responses has a mature brain that . . . is capable of exhibiting adult response patterns. However, there is evidence that the adult brain may regress to an infantile state when it is confronted with severe stress. (Nijenhuis, Vanderlinden, & Spinhoven, 1998, p. 253)

This "infantile state" is a disorganized-disoriented state of insecure attachment. As in infancy, children, adolescents, and adults with posttraumatic stress disorders and severe self-pathologies cannot generate an active coherent behavioral coping strategy to confront subjectively perceived overwhelming, dysregulating events, and thus they quickly access the passive survival strategy of disengagement and dissociation.

Indeed, clinical studies affirm that the type D attachment classification is observed to utilize dissociative behaviors in later stages of life (van Ijzendoorn, Schuengel, & Bakermans-Kranenburg, 1999), and that the occurrence of dissociation at the time of a stressful trauma is a strong predictor of PTSD (Koopman, Classen, & Spiegel, 1994; Shalev, Peri, Canetti, & Schreiber, 1996). In developmental psychopathological research, Sroufe and his colleagues concluded that early trauma moreso than later trauma has a greater impact on the development of dissociative behaviors. They wrote, "The vulnerable self will be more likely to adopt dissociation as a coping mechanism because it does not have either the belief in worthiness gained from a loving and responsive early relationship or the normal level of defenses and integration that such a belief affords" (Ogawa, Sroufe, Weinfield, Carlson, & Egeland, 1997, p. 875). The characterological use of dissociation over the developmental stages was described by Allen and Coyne: "Although initially they may have used dissociation to cope with traumatic events, they subsequently dissociate to defend against a broad range of daily stressors, including their own posttraumatic symptoms, pervasively undermining the continuity of their experience" (1995, p. 620).

These "initial traumatic events" are embedded in the abuse and neglect experienced by type D infants, the first relational context in which dissociation is used to autoregulate massive stress. The ultimate endpoint of chronically experiencing catastrophic states of relational-induced trauma in early life is a progressive impairment of the ability to adjust, take defensive action, or act on one's own behalf, and a blocking of the capacity to register affect and pain, adaptive functions that are all critical to survival.

LeDoux described the legacy of childhood abuse: "If a significant proportion of the early emotional experiences one has are due to activation of the fear system rather than the positive systems, then the characteristic personality that begins to build up from the parallel learning processes coordinated by the emotional state is one characterized by negativity and hopelessness rather than affection and optimism" (2002, p. 322). Ultimately these individuals perceive themselves as different from other people and outside of, as well as unworthy of, meaningful attachments (Lansky, 1995). These personalities clearly manifest the self-pathology of a developmental disorder. But can we be more specific about the type of severe personality disorder associated with early relational trauma?

TRAUMATIC ATTACHMENT
AND THE PSYCHONEUROBIOLOGICAL ETIOLOGY
OF BORDERLINE PERSONALITY DISORDERS

Kohut's speculations on development and psychopathogenesis mainly centered on the etiology of the deficits of narcissistic personality disorders. In his last work, Kohut stated that his analytic experience with borderline states was "very limited." And yet he offered a developmental speculation that, in borderline states, "a nuclear self has not been shaped in early development" (1984, p. 8). In my own work I have suggested that the developmental psychoneurobiological origins of earlier-forming borderline personality disorders can be differentiated from later-forming narcissistic personality disorders (Schore, 1991, 1994). In contrast to the narcissistic infant–mother dyad that derails their attachment communications in the last quarter of the first through the second year, the borderline dyad derails much earlier in the first year. As opposed to disorganized insecure attachments discussed here, narcissistic personality disorder is the outcome of an organized insecure pattern, specifically an avoidant (adult dismissive) attachment pattern (Pistole, 1995). This suggests a qualitatively different developmental history in these groups of personality disorders. Recall that insecure disorganized/disoriented and not organized insecures are associated with abuse and neglect.

At about the same time that Kohut was offering his conceptions of early-forming personality disorders, two other pioneers were also putting forth new models of these disorders. In 1975, Masterson and Rinsley, influenced by the developmental models of Mahler, highlighted the role of the mother in the genesis of altered intrapsychic structure of borderline personality disorders. More recently, Masterson (2000) incorporated contemporary developmental psychoanalysis and developmental neurobiology to update this model. The other major theoretician of severe personality pathologhies was Kernberg, who emphasized the role of excess (unregulated) endogenous aggression. He asserted a conception of psychopathogenesis that is similar to the psychoneurobiological ambient relational trauma model described above: "The most important cause of severe personality disorders is severe chronic traumatic experiences, such as physical or sexual abuse, severe deprivation of love, severe neglect, unavailable parental objects as familial dispositions that can lead to the development of personality disorders" (Kernberg, 1988a).

Indeed, a large body of studies indicates disrupted attachments and early trauma and abuse in the histories of children and adults diagnosed as specifically, borderline personality disorder (Lyons-Ruth & Jacobvitz, 1999), and thus there is a high correlation of PTSD and borderline diagnoses (Famularo, Kinscherff, & Kenton, 1992; Herman, Perry, & van der Kolk, 1989; van der Kolk, Hostetler, Heron, & Fisler, 1994). It has been observed that although sexual abuse is a weak predictor (Fossati, Maddeddu, & Maffei, 1999), a history of neglectful and traumatic experiences co-occurs in these patients (Zanarini et al., 1997). These latter researchers report that 91% of borderline patients report childhood abuse, and 92% report some type of childhood neglect. In an overview of the literature, Paris summarized the developmental data and asserts "the weight of the research evidence supports the hypothesis that abuse during childhood is an important risk factor for borderline personality disorder" (1995, p. 15).

A number of researchers in child psychiatry confirm the presence of early abuse and neglect and neuropsychological deficits in this clinical population. The etiology of borderline pathology in childhood is currently understood to depend upon diatheses (constitutional predisposition) and stressors. Diatheses are now identified through neurobiological and neuropsychological markers, including deficits in frontal lobe functions, and stressors are childhood trauma and parental psychopathology (Ad-Dab'Bagh & Greenfield, 2001). The latter environmental stressors are thought to combine with neurobiological vulnera- bilities to shape the clinical syndrome (Zelkowitz, Paris, Guzder, & Feldman, 2001). In the latest models it has been suggested that the neuropsychological abnormalities of borderline children are the *result* of environmental stressors, specifically reflecting the effects of neonatal stress on brain development (Gra- ham, Heim, Goodman, Miller, & Nemeroff, 1999).

Subsequent neuropsychological vulnerabilities account for the cognitive limitations that negatively affect the child's ability to integrate the traumatic experience, and interfere with the resilience mechanism that can cope with the traumatic environment. These neurobiological impairments endure. In clinical studies of adults Stone observed, "the red thread running through . . . border- line personality disorder is irritability: specifically, a special sort of nervous sys- tem irritability, heterogeneous in etiology, that conduces to impulsive, often chaotic behavior" (1992, p. 9). In fact throughout the lifespan borderline per- sonality disorders, like PTSD, exhibit massive disturbances in affect regulation, impulse control, interpersonal difficulties, self-integration, and a bias to use dissociation when under stress (Herman & van der Kolk, 1987). These func- tions are subserved by the right hemisphere, and so early abuse and neglect produce an inefficient right brain, which is centrally involved in affect regula- tion, dissociation, and survival functions. The neuropsychiatrist Vadim Roten- berg (1995) concluded:

> [The] functional deficiency of the right hemisphere . . . may be caused by
> the lack of emotional relationships between the child and the parents. Such
> emotional relationships . . . stimulate the development of the right hemi-

sphere functions and correspond to these functions as a key to the lock. If these emotional relationships are insufficient, the right hemisphere will become inefficient, its contribution in psychological defense mechanisms and emotional stabilization will be lost, and there will be a general predisposition to subsequent mental and psychosomatic disorders. (p. 59)

A defining symptom of psychosomatic disorders, PTSD, and borderline personality disorders, alexithymia, reflects right hemispheric dysfunction (Dewarja & Sasaki, 1990; Jessimer & Markham, 1997; Parker, Taylor, & Bagby, 1992; Schore, 2001c; Sifneos, 1988).

The neuroscience literature has described "early emotional learning occuring in the right hemisphere unbeknownst to the left; learning and associated emotional responding may later be completely unaccessible to the language centers of the brain" (Joseph, 1982, p. 243). In the trauma literature, McFarlane and Yehuda observed, "Essentially, the core of traumatic syndromes is the capacity of current environmental triggers (real or symbolic), to provoke the intense recall of affectively charged traumatic memory structures, which come to drive current behaviour and perception" (2000, p. 900). According to Valent (1998), early handling and misattunements may be deeply remembered in later life not in verbal explicit memory but in the form of disconnected physiological responses, emotions, and acting out.

The most significant consequence of early relational trauma is the loss of the ability to regulate the intensity and duration of affects. Clinical research has revealed that borderline personalitites, when stressed, attribute high levels of primitive, negative ("all bad") evaluations to others (splitting), exhibit poor empathy and psychological understanding, manifest more intense negative responses to everyday life events, and show an increased sensitivity to even low-level emotional stimuli (Arntz & Veen, 2001; Herpetz, Kunert, Schwenger, & Sass, 1999; Levine, Marziali, & Hood, 1997). These severe deficits in socioemotional functions are paralleled by structural defects in limbic areas involved in the processing of socioemotional information. A growing body of neurobiological research has demonstrated dysfunctions of the amygdala and the orbitofrontal cortex, the "Senior Executive" of the social-emotional brain, in both PTSD and borderline personality disorders (Berthier et al., 2001; Galletly et al., 2001; Goyer, Konicki, & Schulz, 1994; Herpetz et al., 2001; Koenen et al., 2001; Shin et al., 1999). This work has implied a similarity in the developmental precursors, the functional deficits, and the structural defects of these early-forming self-psychopathologies.

PSYCHOTHERAPY: CHANGES IN RIGHT BRAIN REGULATORY STRUCTURES

In *The Restoration of the Self*, Kohut (1977) referred to borderline states only once, concluding these "are in principle not analyzable." The severe right-brain deficits that result from traumatic attachments characterize much more than the self-esteem regulation of narcissistic personality disorders; rather, they are descriptive of the deficts in bodily based survival functions that characterize severe borderline personality disorders. These deficits are a focus of current updated treatment models (see appendix for an outline of psychotherapy principles).

Rotenberg described, "The importance of the emotional relationships between psychotherapist and client can be explained by the restoration, in the process of such relationships, of . . . right hemispheric activity. In this way the emotional relationships in the process of psychotherapy are covering the deficiency caused by the lack of emotional relations in early childhood" (1995, p. 59). The deficiency of the right hemisphere, the locus of emotional self and the human stress response, echoes the deficits in psychic structure described by Kohut's self psychology.

Affect dysregulation, a central feature of borderline personality disorders, is specifically manifest when "highs and lows are too extreme, too prolonged, or too rapidly cycled and unpredictable" (Bach, 1998, p. 188). Such rapid state shifts are expressed in moments of interpersonal stress within a close interpersonal relationship, including the therapeutic relationship. The ambient relational trauma of disorganized-disoriented insecure attachments, imprinted in implicit-procedural memory, is reexperienced in the arousal and autonomic dysregulation of severe self-pathologies. Liotti (1992) described that patients using dissociation:

> often oscillate quickly between clinging to the therapist, emotionally withdrawing from him or her, and becoming frightened as if expecting to be assaulted by the therapist. Sometimes the display by these incompatible types of interpersonal behavior is almost simultaneous, taking place within a single session: in this case, the patient may show a trance-like or dazed expression while shifting from one attitude to another. This is of course, strongly reminiscent of . . . disorganized/disoriented behavior observed in infants. (p. 202)

Furthermore, Valent contended that "transference and countertransference may be the only way infants or severely traumatized persons can communicate their stories of distress, and are therefore central tools for discerning unprocessed or defended events" (1999, p. 73). This frequently occurs in the form of projective identifications, especially in highly charged, negatively affectively-valenced intersubjective enactments (Schore, 2002b, 2002d, 2002g). Howell noted, "The power of projective identification . . . to blindside one in interpersonal situations such as the psychotherapeutic dyad is a significant part of the 'difficulty' of working with 'borderline' persons" (2002, p. 941). Towards understanding this "blindside," Sands (1997) offered the clinical observation that,

> [P]atients will use projective identification because they are seeking to bring into the [therapeutic] relationship affective experiences that have

not been symbolically encoded and cannot yet be verbally communicated. The material may remain unsymbolized because it was encoded under traumatic conditions or because it pertains to a preverbal period of life. . . . [B]ecause such experience remains in somatosensory or iconic form it must be communicated in like manner (p. 703).

In order to receive these transferential communications of traumatically dissociated affect, the therapist must shift from a left to right hemispheric dominant state of evenly hovering attention (Schore, 1994, 1997c, 2000b, 2001d, 2002b, 2002d), an empathic state in which, according to Kohut, "the deeper layers of the analyst's psyche are open to the stimuli which emanate from the patient's communications while the intellectual activities of the higher levels of cognition are temporarily largely but selectively suspended" (1971, p. 274). Fosshage (1994) noted that when the selfobject seeking dimension is in the foreground, the analyst must resonate at the deepest layers of his/her personality to be sufficiently available to the patient's developmental and self-regulatory needs.

The clinical exploration of empathic (mirroring) processes has been a central theme of self psychology, but the mechanisms underlying them has been elusive. It is important to emphasize that empathic communications within the therapeutic alliance are not voluntary. The therapist is not "doing something" as much as "learning to be with the patient," not matching or imitating overt behavior but resonating with the external expressions of the patient's inner states. Clinical studies have indicated that this nonverbal exchange represents a major factor in the therapeutic process. These nonverbal communications are expressed in tone of voice, body posture, and facial expression outside the realm of awareness of both, yet transference and countertransference reactions occur in response to these cues (Eisenstein, Levy, & Marmor, 1994).

As previously mentioned, the right hemisphere, which specializes in nonverbal communication and nonconscious operations, mediates empathy (Schore, 1994; Perry et al., 2001). Neuropsychological and developmental studies of fast-acting nonverbal interpersonal processes that occur at levels beneath conscious awareness indicated that empathic phenomena involve more than receptive functions. Rather, the nonconscious face-to-face communication of affective states is dyadic, bidirectional, reciprocal, dynamic, and mutually amplifying, a facial feedback loop with both sensory receptive and motor expressive components. Social psychological and psychophysiological researchers are thus investigating not only empathy, the capacity to recognize the emotional states of another, but also emotional contagion, the ability to organize an affective state that matches the other's emotional display (Cappella, 1999; Hatfield, Cacioppo, & Rapson, 1992; Lundqvist & Dimberg, 1995).

Converging neurobiological investigations revealed that the detection and complex processing of the smallest change within a human face occurs within 100 milliseconds (Lehky, 2000), and such facially expressed state changes are mirrored (Dimberg & Ohman, 1996) and synchronously matched by an observer's right hemisphere within 300–400 milliseconds, at levels beneath awareness (Stenberg, Wiking, & Dahl, 1998). These studies show that unconsciously perceived positive and negative emotional facial expressions elicit reactions to expressions of unconscious facial expressions, and that the right hemisphere is dominant for the control of spontaneously evoked emotional reactions (Dimberg & Petterson, 2000; Dimberg et al., 2000). Recall, the right hemisphere recognizes an emotion from a visually presented facial expression and then generates a somatosensory, bodily-based representation of how another feels when displaying that certain facial expression (Adolphs et al., 2000).

This psychoneurobiological mechanism is activated particularly in the psychotherapeutic context during stressful disruption and repair transactions (Beebe & Lachmann, 1994, 2002; Lewis, 2000; Schore, 1994). In these moments of primitive communication of intense negative yet nonconscious dissociated affects, the therapist detects changes in the patient's vocal tone, facial expression, and posture and resonates with the patient's dysregulated negatively valenced psychobiological state. In a cocreated intersubjective field the clinician accesses autoregulatory capacities to modulate and contain the stressful negative state induced in him by the patient's communications of dysregulated negative affect. The self-reflective, empathic therapist has an opportunity to act as an interactive affect regulator of the patient's dysregulated states (see Schore, 1994, 1997c, 2002b). This clinical mechanism is a central component of the treatment of traumatically attached patients who are not psychologically minded, lack a reflective capacity, and are alexithymic ("no words for feelings"). Over time it facilitates the "evolution of affects from their early form, in which they are experienced as bodily sensations, into subjective states that can gradually be verbally articulated" (Stolorow & Atwood, 1992, p. 42).

The borderline's impairment in the recognition and communication of overwhelming and therefore dissociated subjective states reflects the fact that due to the ambient early trauma of a growth-inhibiting relational environment, the higher right brain corticolimbic regulatory systems have never optimally evolved. In a number of works I have presented interdisciplinary data suggesting that the co-constructed therapeutic alliance can act as a growth-facilitating environment for the experience-dependent maturation of these same regulatory systems (1994, 1997c, 1999h, 2000b, 2001d, 2002c, in press b). Recall Kohut's description of "missing psychic structure" and his assertion that "psychoanalysis cures by the laying down of psychological structure" (1984, p. 98). Writing in the psychoanalytic literature, Spezzano (1993) asserted:

> The analytic relationship heals by drawing into itself those methods of processing and regulating affect relied on by the patient for psychological survival and then transforming them. The mechanism of these transformations is the regulation of affect in a better way within the analysis than it was previously managed by the patient and the subsequent modification of what, in the classical language of structural change, might be called the patient's unconscious affect-regulating structures. (pp. 215–216)

In parallel writings, Andreasen, the editor of the *American Journal of Psychiatry*, concluded that psychoanalytic intensive therapy "may be viewed as a long-term rebuilding and restructuring of the memories and emotional responses that have been embedded in the limbic system" (2001, p. 314).

I suggest that these authors were describing developmental advances in complexity of the orbitofrontal system and its cortical and subcortical connections. This hierarchical apex of the limbic system represents the most plastic areas in the cortex (Barbas, 1995). In support of this, a functional magnetic resonance imaging study provides evidence that higher regions of specifically the right prefrontal cortex attenuate emotional responses at the most basic levels in the brain, that such modulating processes are "fundamental to most modern psychotherapeutic methods," that this lateralized neocortical network is active in "modulating emotional experience through interpreting and labeling emotional expressions," and that "this form of modulation may be impaired in various emotional disorders and may provide the basis for therapies of these same disorders" (Hariri, Bookheimer, & Mazziotta, 2000, p. 48).

In more recent neuroimaging research, Furmack and his colleagues (2002) reported that symptomatic improvement of social phobic patients with psychotherapy is accompanied by significantly reduced blood flow in amygdala-limbic circuits, particularly in the right hemisphere. According to the authors, this right laterlized change reflects "an alteration of the emotional experience" (2002, p. 431). These results confirm an earlier positron emission tomography (PET) imaging study which demonstrated that patients showed significant changes in metabolic activity in the right orbitofrontal cortex and its subcortical connections as a result of successful psychological treatment (Schwartz et al., 1996). In 1994 I proposed that "the patient-therapist relationship acts as a growth promoting environment that supports the experience-dependent maturation of the right brain, especially those areas that have connections with the subcortical limbic structures that mediate emotional arousal" (1994, p. 473).

In longer term treatment, the experience-dependent organization of more complex vertical circuits within the right brain and horizontal circuits with the left brain allow for the emergence of more complex functions. The dyadic therapeutic context acts as a growth-facilitating environment for the patient's more densely interconnected right brain-left brain systems that can access not only a more fully developed subjective nonverbal affective "support-experience" factor, but also an objective "insight" factor that is activated by adequate interpretation (de Jonghe et al., 1992). In light of the well-documented principle that creative thinking and insight derive from unconscious processes, it now thought that the right hemispheric coarse processing mode that activates "distantly related information or unusual interpretation of words" activates solution of insight problems (Bowden & Beeman, 1998, p. 435).

The inceptive capacity to use a support factor (cocreate a system of interactive regulation with the therapist) as well as access insight enhances the patient's reflective function. This emergent function, the product of a structural reorganization of the "integrative" right hemisphere (Federmeier & Kutas,

1999) and its connections with the left's verbal reasoning capacity (Langdon & Warrington, 2000), is facilitated by the empathic-regulatory aspects of the therapeutic relationship. The patient's developmental advance, in turn, underlies the onset of a higher level integrative capacity that allows "free access to affective memories of alternate states, a kind of superordinate reflective awareness that permits multiple perspectives of the self" (Bach, 1985, p. 179).

The prominent role of the right hemisphere in social emotional, moral, and empathic functions also reflects it's important contributions to high level cognitive functions. It is dominant over the left in maintaining larger stores of information, with greater specificity, over longer periods of time (Kirsner & Brown, 1981; Marsolek, Kosslyn, & Nicholas, 1996). I suggest that this description also pertains to this hemisphere's central involvement in social cognition. Therapeutic advances in what Stern and his colleagues called "implicit relational knowledge" (Lyons-Ruth et al., 1998) thus are due to more complex operations of the right brain, a central locus of "implicit learning" (Hugdahl, 1995). Changes in nonverbal implicit relational knowledge are at the core of therapeutic change (Stern et al., 1998). Towards that end, affectively-focused interpretations are directed towards a deeper understanding of the patient's emotion-enhancing and emotion-distancing coping mechanisms, and at the conflicts and tensions between autoregulation (autonomy) and interactive regulation (interconnectedness). In this work, as Sander pointed out, "it is not the past we seek but the logic of the patient's own state regulating strategies" (in Schwaber, 1990, p. 238).

It is commonly assumed that left hemispheric language and abstraction capacities represent the highest human capacities. If the left hemisphere has an adaptive advantage over the right in reasoning involving abstract content, work on "the neurology of reasoning" suggested that the right is better suited for analogical reasoning and reasoning involving familiar situations (Shuren & Grafman, 2002). In a conceptualization consonant with psychodynamic models, Shuren and Grafman concluded:

> [T]he right hemisphere holds representations of the emotional states associated with events experienced by the individual. When that individual encounters a familiar scenario, representations of related past emotional experiences are retrieved by the right hemisphere and are incorporated into the reasoning process. In the absence of or failure to activate such representations, the left hemisphere applies learned rules of logic. (p. 918)

Other imaging research revealed the existence of a logic-specific network in the right hemisphere that supports deductive reasoning. In summarizing this work Parsons and Osherson (2001) stated that their findings

> . . . contradict the belief often expressed in the cognitive sciences and philosophy that deductive reasoning is derivative to linguistic processing.

. . . Deduction (as well as other forms of reasoning) might rather be pre-formed in a format that is antecedent to natural language, the latter being acquired for the purpose of expressing meanings that exist prior to their linguistic expression. (p. 963)

This work clearly implies that a preconscious yet fundamental meaning system can operate before a conscious language meaning system.

Earlier I cited Van Lancker and Cummings's assertion that "while the left hemisphere mediates most linguistic behaviors, the right hemisphere is impor-tant for broader aspects of communication" (1999, p. 95). Buck has character-ized right brain-driven "spontaneous emotional communication," that "employs species-specific expressive displays in the sender that, given attention, activate emotional preattunements and are directly perceived by the receiver . . . *The 'meaning' of the display is known directly by the receiver*. . . . This spon-taneous emotional communication constitutes a *conversation between limbic systems*" (1994, p. 266; italics added). This right brain-to-right brain process allows for affects to be communicated and interactively regulated within the therapeutic alliance, and thereby facilitates a social environmental enrichment of both nonconscious and conscious emotion-cognition, meaning-processing structures.

The treatment of "developmental arrests" (Stolorow & Lachmann, 1980) of early self pathologies is currently conceptualized as being directed toward the mobilization of fundamental modes of development (Emde, 1990) and the com-pletion of interrupted developmental processes (Gedo, 1979). Recall that cur-rent developmental models emphasize that "learning how to communicate represents perhaps the most important developmental process to take place dur-ing infancy" (Papousek & Papousek, 1997, p. 42). In total, the incorporation of interdisciplinary data into the clinical theory of psychoanalysis indicates that psychoanalysis is not "the talking cure," but more precisely "the communicat-ing cure."

Note that the system that underlies psychotherapeutic change is in the nonverbal right as opposed to the verbal left hemisphere. The right hemi-sphere, the biological substrate of the human unconscious (Schore, in press b), is also the locus of the emotional self. Kohut's emphasis on the central role of nonconscious selfobject dynamics, which act at nonverbal levels beneath conscious awareness, also points to the right brain, the locus of the dynamic unconscious (Schore, 2002e). In an earlier work (Schore, 1999c) I contended that recent advances in developmental psychoanalysis and neuropsychoanalysis clearly suggest that the center of psychic life shifts from Freud's ego, which he located in the "speech-area on the left-hand side" (1923/1961b) and the poste-rior areas of the verbal left hemisphere, to the highest levels of the nonverbal right hemisphere, the locus of the bodily based self-system (Schore, 1994). In a recent overview, Stuss and Levine concluded, "It is in the frontal lobes, with perhaps a preeminent role of the right frontal lobe, that the complete integration of subjective experience in a fully self-aware person is achieved" (2002, p. 417).

The clinical theory of psychoanalysis rests upon conceptions of psychopathogenesis and change. One of Kohut's major contributions was the expansion of the clinical theory beyond neurosis and into personality disorders, especially narcissistic personality disorders. In light of the documented finding that almost half of the patients seen by psychoanalysts have a personality disorder, with borderline personality disorder the most common and severe (Doidge, Simon, Gillies, & Ruskin, 1994; Friedman, Bucci, Christian, Drucker, & Garrison, 1998), self psychological, relational, and intersubjective psychoanalytic clinicians now need to integrate updated developmental and neurobiological information into their conceptions of psychopathogenesis. Self psychology must move beyond narcissistic disorders, into trauma and borderline personality organizations. An incorporation of current neuropsychoanalytic data, developmental psychoanalytic findings, and trauma research into the theoretical base of self pathologies could allow for a significant expansion of its clinical model, both in terms of deepening its therapeutic efficacy and broadening its application to a wider array of severe self-pathologies.

2002

PART II

DEVELOPMENTAL
NEUROPSYCHOANALYSIS

CHAPTER 5

Early Superego Development:
The Emergence of Shame and Narcissistic
Affect Regulation in the Practicing Period

A N UNDERSTANDING OF SUPEREGO processes and particularly the role of the mal-functioning superego in symptom formation is an essential part of the treatment process. Historically, the focus has been on the role of undischarged guilt in the etiology of neurotic disorders, with the role of shame, the "keystone affect" of narcissistic pathologies (Broucek, 1982), given much less attention and less clearly traced. Furthermore, the clinical and theoretical distinctions between shame and guilt are still not precisely characterized. One approach at attempting to elucidate the singular nature of each of these superego affects is to study their differential ontogeny in early development. Advances in clinical technique that focus on shame (Basch, 1988; Miller, 1985; Morrison, 1989; Nathanson, 1987) underscore the critical import of "returning internalized shame to its interpersonal origin" (Kaufman, 1985) in effective psychotherapeutic treatment. The specification and delineation of the genesis and functional role of shame in socioaffective development has direct clinical relevance to the understanding of normal and abnormal early superego development, and to the etiology of early-forming self-pathology (Kohut, 1971).

A central tenet of the developmental approach of this chapter is that critical early object relations involving attuned and misattuned affect transactions, reflected in the internalization of early interactive representations, are required for the maturation of effective superego autoregulatory systems. Furthermore, it is postulated that two separate superego affect systems arise in different early stages. Miller (1989) pointed out that the exact ontogenetic course of shame is controversial and still uncharted, and Emde (1988) suggested that the "early moral emotion" of shame that appears in the second year is in need of systematic research. The major purpose of this work is to present a developmental object relations model of the emergence of shame during Mahler's practicing period of separation-individuation and to examine the critical functional role of shame in successive stages of socioemotional developement. The shame regulatory system that has its onset during the practicing phase will be shown to be instrumental to the effective resolution of the later rapprochement crisis, specifically in terms of the modulation of narcissistic rage and the developmental progression of psychological and gender identification processes. Finally, the relevance of the model to the etiology of the fundamental pathology of narcissistic disorders and to the functional characterization of the ego ideal component of the superego as a mood regulator will be presented.

The methodology of this theoretical research involves the integration of current observations from various fields that are studying the problem of socioemotional development—psychoanalysis, infant research, developmental psychology, and neurobiology. Thus, in the course of this pursuit, a sizeable number of studies will be presented, not as a literature review, but as a multidisciplinary source pool of clinical observations, theoretical concepts, and experimental data from which to generate an overarching conceptual model that attempts to elucidate the common underlying functional mechanism of shame, "the primary social emotion" (Scheff, 1988).

A more general objective is an inquiry into the relationship between the dynamics of early interactional development and the ontogeny of the emergent function of self-regulation, particularly the "process of self-regulation of affect" (Krystal, 1988). "Self-regulatory mechanisms are organized . . . in relation both to endogenous activity and to the surrounding life support system" (Sander, 1977, p. 29). Demos and Kaplan framed the central question as "how organized systems retain continuity while changing in response to developmental and environmental pressures" (1986, p. 156). A guiding principle in this investigation is embodied in the assertion that "any comprehensive theory of affects needs to include the physiologic segment as well as the psychoanalytic" (Panel, 1974, p. 612).

The investigation and characterization of a unique affect, emerging in a specific time and with a particular developmental function, thus utilizes various contributions of clinical and experimental work on the development of emotion from within and without psychoanalysis. Basch (1976) argued that the earliest forms of affective behavior are general physiologic reactions such as response to stimulation (autonomic reactivity) mediated by the autonomic nervous system (ANS). In ensuing developmental stages they provide the substrate for all emotional experience. Krystal (1978) proposed that all later-developing affects evolve out of a neonatal state of contentment and a state of distress that differentiate into two developmental lines, an infantile nonverbal affect system and an adult verbalized, desomatisized system. He asserted "The development and maturation of affects is seen as the key event in infancy" (Krystal 1988, p. 211), and wrote of nodal points in affect development that allow for the maturation of particular affects. Spitz (1965) concluded that significant organizational shifts occur regularly in development that are signalled by the emergence of new affective behaviors. Buechler and Izard, in a paper on the emergence and regulation of the expression of emotions in infancy, stated that "the age at which the infant is able to regulate expression may differ for each of the discrete emotions" (1983, p. 301), whereas Pine (1980) emphasized that the earliest expressions of affect are automatic responses described as varying along a singular pleasure-unpleasure continuum, but later this is followed by an "expansion in the affect array." As development proceeds, "[S]ome affects represent alterations, transformations, specifications of earlier affect states, whereas others are first born at later stages in the developmental process when the psychological conditions for their emergence are met. These psychological conditions involve new learnings, new acquisition of mental life, that have consequences for affective experiences" (Pine, 1980, p. 232).

More specifically to the ontogenesis of the later-appearing superego affects, a review of the clinical literature reveals a common observation that shame has an earlier developmental origin than guilt. This conceptualization was first proposed by Freud (1923/1961b), who distinguished shame associated with early narcissistic conflicts from guilt associated with later moral conflicts. Erikson (1950) asserted the psychosocial stage of "autonomy versus shame and self doubt" takes place in the second year, while "initiative versus guilt" occurs at a later age. Lewis (1980) argued that shame is a more regressed and primitive mode of superego functioning than guilt, in agreement with Wallace (1963) and Jacobson (1964). Levin (1967) and Anthony (1981) also concluded that shame is preoedipal and originates before guilt. Miller (1989) differentiated early-appearing affects on a developmental line with shame from a later-emerging affect developmental line that culminates in guilt.

Despite continuing controversy in the adult psychoanalytic literature (Garza Guerrero, 1981), developmental infant research has tended to support these clinical deductions. Indeed, it pinpoints the specific period of the onset of the shame response. Darwin (1873/1965) noted that early infants do not show the physiological hallmark of shame, blushing. Confirming this, Tomkins (1963) found no facial expressions expressive of shame in earliest infancy and characterized "shame-humiliation" as an auxillary affect which appears later, and Field (1982) encountered no "ashamed" responses in 4-month-old infants. Self-consciousness, a behavior reflecting embarrassment (a component of shame), was earliest observed at 12 months by Dixon (1957). In the most extensive research on this topic, Amsterdam (1972; Amsterdam & Leavitt, 1980) noted that embarassment and affective self-consciousness first appear at 14 months, coinciding with the acquisition of upright, free locomotion. These responses are completely absent before 12 months. In a more recent series of developmental studies, M. Lewis (1982) first observed the self-conscious emotion of shame in the period of 12 to 18 months. Plutchik, citing the work of Piaget, concluded, "in stage 5 (12–18 months) with the development of the cognitive ability to represent the self and external causation, affects such as shame, defiance, and negativism appear" (1983, p. 243). There is thus consistent evidence for the onset of shame in the junior toddler; that is, Mahler's practicing subphase of the separation-individuation stage of development (10–12 to 16–18 months).

It should be kept in mind that the effective vocabulary of the average 12-month-old is 3 words; at 15 months, it is 19 words (Mussen, Conger, & Kagan, 1969). Kaufman noted shame, "a total experience that forbids communication with words" (1974, p. 565), arises prior to language development and is therefore preverbal. In contrast, Pine argued that guilt "comes into being somewhere from age 3 to 6" (1980, p. 222). Izard (1978) and Sroufe (1979) also found guilt appearing at 36 months. Importantly, notice that the shame system emerges in the preverbal toddler, guilt in the neoverbal child. Their separate origins is one factor indicating that these two superego affect systems are dissociable and independent.

THE PSYCHOPHYSIOLOGICAL FUNCTION OF SHAME

In preparation for the exploration of the ontogeny of shame, it is necessary to present a more detailed description of this unique affect, which perhaps more than any other emotion is so intimately tied to the physiological expression of a stress response. This hyperactive physiological state (Darwin, 1873/1965) is associated with ANS reactions like sweating, greater body awareness, intensification of perceptual functions, uncoordinated motor activity, cognitive impairment, and gaze aversion, thus implying "the more primitive, biologically based nature of shame" (Broucek, 1982, p. 375). The deep physiological substrate of shame is perhaps best reflected in blushing (Wurmser, 1981), which represents the end result of a preceeding intense "affective spell"; that is, the end product of the physiological discharge of shame (Miller, 1965). MacCurdy (1930) proposed that the shock-like onset of blushing reflects a shift of balance from sympathetic to parasympathetic components of the ANS, the system that determines the physiological expression of all emotions. Supporting this, Knapp (1967) explained that activity of the parasympathetic branch of the ANS accounts for blushing. Thus the activity of the ANS, which is an effector channel of the emotion-mediating limbic system, is the basis of the acute phenomenology of shame. In a heightened state of affect, one is overwhelmed by intense internal physiological sensations over which there is no conscious control; notice the similarity of this to a classic acute "stress state" (Seyle, 1956). Indeed, in social-psychological experiments, shame, specifically used as a psychosocial stressor (Buck, Parke, & Buck, 1970), induced a psychophysiologic stress reaction.

Furthermore, Freud's (1905/1953c) original conceptualization of shame was that it acted as a superego counterforce or counterreaction formation against exhibitionistic excitement and overstimulation that have potential ego-disruptive effects. This underscores the requisite preexisting state of hyperarousal for shame induction, and the function of shame as an arousal blocker, a regulator of hyperstimulated (elated, excited, grandiose, manic, euphoric) states. Tomkins (1963), who identified the function of this "affect auxillary" as a specific inhibitor of the activated, ongoing affects of interest-excitement and enjoyment-joy, pointed out that shame reduces self-exposure or self-exploration powered by these positive affects. Shame signals the self-system to terminate interest in whatever has come to its attention (Nathanson, 1987). Thus, the "superego-mediated flight from positively experienced exhibitionism to negatively experienced shame" (Miller, 1985) changes the affective valence and diminishes the arousal level of the organism, thereby blocking the further escalation and intensification of stimulation. The end result is a painfully stimulated state of shame. Kohut (1971) presented a similar model: At a moment of exhibitionism of the self, the sudden unexpected impact of shame is to ground the person who is overstimulated by omnipotent, grandiose affective states.

A model of shame is proposed here in which the neo-individuating self, in a hyperstimulated, elated, grandiose, narcissistically charged state of heightened arousal, exhibits itself during a reunion with the caregiver. Despite an excited anticipation of a shared affect state, the self unexpectedly experiences an affective misattunement, thereby triggering a sudden stress, shock-induced deflation. It is proposed that this first occurs in the preverbal practicing subphase of the separation-individuation period, and that this specific object relation and its internalization is the prototype of the shame experience.

THE ASCENDANCY OF NARCISSISM, ELATION, AND HEIGHTENED AROUSAL DURING THE PRACTICING PERIOD

The onset of the practicing period is usually marked by rapid changes in motor behavior (i.e., of upright posture and locomotion supporting the child's first independent steps), but it is its affective characteristics that are unique and definitional. Bowlby (1969) pointed out important affective changes occur when locomotion emerges; Bertenthal, Campos, and Barrett (1984) found that mobile infants show different types of emotional reactions than prelocomotor infants; and Fox and Davidson noticed "tight linkages exist between the onset of locomotion and the occurrence of important changes in affective behavior" (1984, p. 370). Mahler described the practicing junior toddler as "intoxicated with his own faculties and with the greatness of his world. . . . He is exhilarated by his own capacities" (1980, p. 7). Mahler wrote of the stage-specific omnipotent exhilaration and elation of this period (high arousal affects), and noted that at this time more than any other in development, "narcissism is at its peak" (1975, p. 71), while Johnson affirmed, "The practicing period offers a release into manic excitement and involvement in a world far more reinforcing than that of the unreliable nurturance offered earlier" (1987, p. 26).

The 1-year-old's frequent mood of elation has also been described by other psychoanalytic (Emde, 1989) and developmental (Sroufe, 1979) researchers. Confirming this, in a neuropsychological study of infant emotional expression, Rothbart, Taylor, and Tucker (1989) found a statistically significant increase in positive emotion and decrease in negative emotion over the developmental period of 10 to 13½ months.

In an important paper tracing the development of narcissistic systems and their affects, Parkin referred to the omnipotence, grandiosity, and elation of the emergent "ideal ego," a precursor of the superego ego ideal component and the embodiment of the "narcississtic perfection of childhood." The illusion of omnipotence central to the ideal ego normally arises out of the experience of being merged with the attuned, powerful mother. During the practicing period, the child "has reached the highest point in the development of his primary narcissism and in the over-estimation of his powers. His ideal ego is at its full" (1985, p. 146). Parkin (in agreement with the developmental studies reported earlier) noted that it is at this time when shame, self-consciousness, and embarassment first appear and that the toddler first becomes aware of himself/herself as an object for observation and evaluation by another. Broucek, also studying shame and its relationship to early narcissistic development, similarly concluded, "Significant shame experiences may occur in the first one and a half years of life" (1982, p. 372).

In addition to the developmental affective changes at practicing onset, major maturational behavioral (Plooij & van de Plooij, 1989) and cognitive (Zelazo, 1982) reorganizations are known to occur at 12 months. Lester (1983) pointed out that the practicing period represents Piaget's fifth stage of sensorimotor intelligence, a time of the first appearance of tertiary circular reactions that enable the toddler to actively and spontaneously explore for newness in the environment (curiosity onset?). By 1 year of age, stimulation-seeking exploratory play time may amount to as much as 6 hours of the child's day. Pine asserted that elated affect (excitement and joy) is "coupled with boundless energy in the constantly moving toddler" (1980, p. 229), and cited White's (1963) discussion of "pleasure in function" associated with the elation of the period. Indeed, it could be speculated that White's concepts of competence and effectance have their roots in the practicing phase. He defined *effectance* as the infant's sense of what can and cannot be accomplished; it is an emotional mood that characterizes the infant's mastery experiences. Interestingly, White (1960) asserted that shame is always associated with incompetence. Along the same lines, Broucek (1982) suggested that inefficacy experiences may be the earliest releasers of shame.

Two important points should be made at this juncture. It is proposed that shame modulates high-arousal affective states; these states first appear during the practicing period (a developmental period of hyperarousal), and the onset of shame at this time acts as a regulator of hyperstimulated states. Second, hyperaroused narcissistic states developmentally occur at this critical period only if the infant–caregiver dyad has successfully negotiated the preceding stages, allowing the child to tolerate much higher arousal states than earlier. Under optimal conditions, thresholds of stimulation decrease and the ability to tolerate higher levels of stimulation increases during infancy (Field, 1985a). Fogel (1982) referred to a major developmental task of the first year as the evolution of increasing affective tolerance for high arousal. This occurs in attachment transactions in which the psychobiologically attuned (Field, 1985a) caregiver amplifies the infant's highly stimulated state of excitement and joy, one that fuels his/her grandiosity.

On the other hand, Parkin (1985) asserted that certain forms of inadequate mothering in the third quarter of the first year of life inhibit identification of the child with the fantasied omnipotence of the mother and lead to a hypocathected, dormant, and impoverished ideal ego. The ability to experience the practicing high arousal states of elation and interest-excitement depends upon precedent successful experiences of merger with the omnipotent mother. If this does not occur earlier in the symbiotic phase there will be a drastic reduction in primary narcissism. In support of this, the expression of interest, which Piaget (1967) pointed out underlies the process of assimilation and is essential for the development of sensorimotor intelligence, was shown by Bell (1970) to be predicated upon a "harmonious relationship" between mother and infant.

Interestingly, it is known that the practicing characteristic hedonic tone of elation (Lipsitt, 1976), high levels of arousal (Field, 1985b), and elevated activity level (boundless energy; Breese et al., 1973) are all associated with heightened activation of the sympathetic component of the ANS. Furthermore, in various animal models, it has been found that young mammals typically pass through a hyperactive period of mid-infancy in which they display a state of organismic hyperarousal and increased energy metabolism (Reite, Kaufman, Pauley, & Stynes, 1974), especially when apart from the mother, reflecting unmodulated excitatory activity of early maturing, reticular formation brain stem systems responsible for arousal (Campbell & Mabry, 1972; Moorcroft, 1971). In late infancy this activity is decreased due to the later onset of forebrain inhibitory systems. The high level of behavioral arousal that reflects unchecked subcortical reticular excitability is proposed to be identical to the excitement component of Tomkins's "interest-excitement," and to underlie Kohut's (1971) "age-appropriate exhibitionism."

Sympathetic and parasympathetic components are known to have different timetables of development, resulting in unique physiological organizations at different stages of postnatal life. Hofer (1984a) consistently observed high levels of energy-expending sympathetic activity and high resting heart rates in mid-infancy, followed by a reduction in late infancy due to the neural maturation of energy-conserving parasympathetic (vagal) restraint.

Parasympathetic inhibitory function, associated with heart rate deceleration, is expressed by two distinct brain stem systems. A primitive dorsal motor vagal system responsible for metabolic shut-down and immobilization ontogenetically precedes a later maturing more flexible nucleus ambiguus vagal system (Schwaber, Wray, & Higgins, 1979; Geis & Wurster, 1980; Daly, 1991). Over 100 years ago, the British neurologist Hughlings Jackson (1931) postulated that the infant will pass through an excitable stage in ontogenesis that is diminished by the later functional onset of cortical inhibitory centers, reflecting the sequential caudal to rostral development of the brain. Furthermore, it is known that essential subcortical limbic system substrates involved in emotional and cognitive behavior postnatally mature earlier than corresponding systems in the cerebral cortex (Meyersburg & Post, 1979). It could be speculated that the affective, behavioral, and cognitive aspects unique to the practicing period reflect a biologically timed period of sympathetic dominant limbic hyperarousal and behavioral overexcitation, and that the shame system that emerges in this period represents an evolving cortical inhibitory control mechanism of excessive, hyperstimulated states.

SHAME STRESS AND THE NEUROPHYSIOLOGY OF AROUSAL DYSREGULATION DURING PRACTICING REUNION EPISODES

An even closer inspection of the practicing terrain reveals the unique and specific nature of "practicing" object relations that engender shame and elucidates the more general process of the socialization of emotion during infancy. Parens (1980) described the typical practicing behavior in which the child brings the things he/she is exploring and attempting to master to the mother's vicinity. Mahler (1979) noted:

> The functions, during the practicing period, attract so much libido that the junior toddler is emotionally relatively independent of the love object and absorbed in his own narcissistic pleasures. Upon the attainment of mastery of some autonomous ego functions, however, he becomes increasingly aware of his separateness and *pari passu* very much aware of his need for his mother's acceptance and renewed participation. (p. 63)

It is this moment of reunion of the "returning," highly aroused, elated, practicing toddler, in a state of excited expectation, reconnecting with the mother, that is the prototypical object relation in the emergence of shame. The "attachment emotion" of shame (Lewis, 1980) occurs at the point of reattachment. Infant socioemotional research specifically reveals that separation does not activate shame (Izard, Hembree, & Huebner, 1987). Notice the self-exhibiting nature of this practicing transaction, keeping in mind Freud's emphasis on exhibitionistic excitement and overstimulation in shame dynamics. Research utilizing a behavioral microanalysis of reunion episodes has produced rich material concerning stage-specific object relations. This methodology derives from Ainsworth's (Ainsworth, Blehar, Waters, & Wall, 1978) studies of infant attachment patterns after periods of separation, and the work of Mahler, Pine, and Bergman (1975) on "emotional refueling," which is conceptualized as an exchange of energy between the partners in the caregiver–infant dyad. "Reunion between baby and mother serves to regulate either high or low lovels of arousal, to a more organized affective and attentional state" (Brent & Resch, 1987, p. 16). It is during these moments of caregiver–infant interaction that the mother acts to maintain the child's arousal within a moderate range that is high enough to foster interactions, yet not so intense as to cause distress and avoidance (Brazelton, Koslowski, & Main, 1974; Stern, 1977).

Reunion microinteractions are therefore critical moments of early object relations involving emotional reconnection after separations, specifically reentering into patterned affective transactions with the object. This moment of initial interface in a dyadic affectively communicating system has been shown to be critical to the infant's modulation of arousal, affect, and attention. Optimal reunion experiences, lasting only 30 seconds to 3 minutes, have been shown not only to "enable the infant to differentiate internal needs but . . . allow for increasingly active regulation of both separation and individuation of the self" (Brent & Resch, 1987, p. 25). Practicing reunions represent affectively significant "central moments" of the growing child's daily experience that are associated with high intensity object relations (Pine, 1985).

Germinative memories and percepts are organized around these moments of highly narcissistically charged affect transactions common in this developmental period. Stern noted that "important experiences (and their memory and representation) are affect state-dependent . . . the affect state acts as the cardinal organizing element" (1985, p. 245). Importantly, early reunion transactions act as a developmental matrix for the evolution of affects and affect tolerance: "In the further course of development, repeated experiences of separation and reunion are remembered and anticipated, providing the structural basis for progressively more varied and modulated affective responses, whether basically painful or basically pleasurable" (Pao, 1971 p. 788).

But these reunion episodes can also be moments engendering arousal dysregulation and psychosocial stress. Mahler specifically noted that the practicing infant's burgeoning narcissism is "particularly vulnerable to the danger of delation" (Mahler, Pine, & Bergman, 1975, p. 228). The neo-toddler's first ambulatory, exploratory forays away from the mother and into the world represent critical initial attempts to separate himself/herself from his/her mother (Rheingold & Eckerman, 1970) and define the onset of the separation individuation period. The ambulatory infant, now able to physically separate himself/herself from the mother for longer periods of time, is able to explore realms of the physical and social environment that are beyond her watchful eye. However, upon return from these forays, the nature of their face-to-face reunions is altered in that they now more than any time previously can engender intense interactive stress.

More specifically, the grandiose practicing toddler, highly aroused by what he/she (but not necessarily the caregiver) appraises to be a mastery experience, returns to the mother after a brief separation. The nascent self, in a state of accelerating positive arousal, exhibits itself in a reunion transaction. Despite an excited expectation of a psychobiologically attuned shared positive affect state with the mother and a dyadic amplification of the positive affects of excitement and joy, the infant unexpectedly encounters a facially expressed affective misattunement. The ensuing break in an anticipated visual-affective communication triggers a sudden shock-induced deflation of positive affect, and the infant is thus propelled into a state that he/she cannot yet autoregulate. Shame represents this rapid state transition from a preexisting positive state to a negative state.

Translating this into self-psychology terms, the returning toddler, eagerly looking forward to the maternal smile of recognition and the expected satisfaction of "the need of the budding self for the joyful response of the mirroring selfobject" (mutually attuned elation; Kohut, 1977, p. 788) is suddenly and unpreparedly confronted with the "unexpected noncooperation of the mirroring object" (Kohut, 1972, p. 655). This is specifically communicated visually not only in the "absence of the smile of contact" (Basch, 1976, p. 765), but in the presense of the mother's "strange face," a physical expression denoting her negative emotional state. Basch stated, "The shame-humiliation response . . . represents the failure or absence of the smile of contact, a reaction to the loss of feedback from others" (p. 765).

Broucek (1982) noted that shame arises

> in the infant's contacts with mother at those moments when mother becomes a stranger to her infant. This happens when the infant is disappointed in his excited expectation that certain communicative and interactional behavior will be forthcoming in response to his communicative readiness. . . . Shame arises from a disturbance of recognition, producing familiar responses to an unfamiliar person, as long as we understand the "different" mother to be the unfamiliar person. That a mother (even a "good enough" mother) can be a stranger to her own infant at times is not really surprising since the mother's moods, preoccupations, conlicts and defences will disturb her physiognomy and at times alter her established communication patterns. (p. 370)

It is the sudden and rapid processing of this dissonant visuoaffective information that underlies the "unexpected" quality of shame (Lynd, 1958). Research on face scanning indicates that infants are most sensitive to affective expressions in which specifically the eyes vary the most (Haith, Bergman, & Moore, 1979). The instant state of shame distress derives not so much from the perception of the mother's face or smile as much as from the infant's recognition of the mother's break in participation from anticipated communicative visuoaffective eye-to-eye contact. The induction of a stress state at this point is understandable in that "stress is defined as a change or a threat of change demanding adaptation by an organism" (Schneiderman & McCabe, 1985, p. 13). The experience of shame has been associated with unfulfilled expectations (Wurmser, 1981). The shock of shame results from the violation of the infant's expectation of affective attunement based on a memory of the last contact with the mother that was energizing, facilitating, and rewarding for the grandiose self.

McDevitt (1975) argued that the practicing infant maintains an illusion (holds a memory) that the mother is with him/her whenever he/she chooses to move away from her. Sherwood furthered this idea in postulating a "practicing illusion" of maintaining oneness while at a distance from the mother, which reflects the grandiose cognition "that the mother is constantly available in her mirroring function" (1989, p. 15). Shame-stress experiences puncture this illusion at reunion as the emerging self encounters a discrepancy between the memory of an ideal symbiotic attunement and the current perceptual input of dyadic affective misattunement. The mother's mirroring function suddenly vanishes, and there is a rapid deenergizing affective experience, a deactivation of the attachment system, a reduction of interest-excitement, and a "sudden decrement in mounting pleasure" (enjoyment-joy; Tomkins, 1963) in the precipitous fall from positively experienced pleasurable exhibitionism to negatively experienced painful shame. The infant switches from an affectively elated externally focused state to an affectively deflated internally focused state, and active expressive affective communication is suddenly displaced by passive receptive emotional surveillance. Interest, curiosity, focused attention, and positive hedonic tone are instantly transformed into diffuse distress, unfocused attention, and negative hedonic tone.

This deflated, "toned-down" state of low arousal, negative emotion, and unfocused attention has been described in practicing infants under ongoing separation stress. Mahler noted that, in opposition to periods of elation, when separated from mother for a period of time "they become low-keyed.... At such times, their gestural and performance motility slowed down; their interest in their surroundings diminished; and they appeared to be preoccupied . . . with inwardly concentrated attention" (1979, p. 127). The low-keyed state, isomorphic to the shame state in which interest and attention to the external environment is suddenly terminated, is a defensive and adaptive phenomenon that comes to the foreground and is most visible under situations of extended separation stress. It has been suggested to represent a narcissistic regressive defense (McDevitt, 1980); as such it reflects a passive rather than an active coping mechanism.

Mahler likened this state to Kaufman and Rosenblum's (1969) separation state of "conservation-withdrawal," which occurs in "helpless" stressful situations where active coping responses are unavailable, and which "may be adaptive for the "exhausted' organism in replenishing energy stores and restoring physiological equilibrium" (Field, 1985b, p. 215). This state is driven by dorsal motor vagal activity associated with immobilization and hiding behaviors. Recall Erikson's (1950) assertion that the defensive reaction of shame is expressed as hiding or concealment. Furthermore, it is similar to Bowlby's (1969b) "profound detachment" phase of infant separations in which metabolic conservation and inhibition (e.g., a dorsal motor vagal induced heart rate deceleration) is maintained until reunion with the mother becomes possible (during the high-arousal, agitated "protest" stage heart rate acceleration occurs). Also note that in the shame transaction the break in the attachment bond is not caused by the highly aroused child's movement away from the mother, or even the mother's movement away from the child, but instead by the active blockade of the child's return to and emotional reconnection with the mother; *a separation-induced stress response is triggered in the presence of and by the mother.*

The shame-induced failure in the modulation of affect, attention, cognition, and motor activity is produced by the sudden plummeting mood shift and propulsion of the toddler into a disorganized deflation state of sensory under-load-induced low arousal. Since this low-keyed state below the limits of the infant's "optimal activation band" (Field, 1981) or "optimal range of stimulation" (Stern, 1985), it produces a shame state of "narcissistic distress" (Miller, 1988) which he/she cannot at this age actively self-regulate. It is known that moderate levels of arousal are associated with positive affect and focused attention, while extreme levels of arousal (high or low) are related to negative emotion and distracted attention (Malmo, 1959). Brent and Resch (1987) specifically observed this with practicing infants. Activation theorists have shown that extremely low levels of arousal, like high levels, are associated with uncomfortable negative emotional states and behavioral inefficiency (Cofer & Appley, 1964); both understimulation stress and overstimulation stress are known to be aversive (Goldberger, 1982). Phenomenologically, the toddler experiences a hyperactive physiological state, as reflected in suddenly increased dorsal motor vagal parasympathetic ANS activity (i.e., a stress state). Interestingly, the heightened autonomic reactions in shame, blushing, sweating, and so on, have been likened to the infantile preverbal psychosomatic state (Anthony, 1981). Broucek (1982) also equated an infant "distress state" with a primitive shame experience.

It is proposed that in the toddler, as well as the adult, the brake of incrementing arousal seen in shame (e.g., reflected in cardiac deceleration, switch in mood, gaze aversion, and blushing) reflects a sudden dynamic switch from sympathetic dominant to parasympathetic dominant ANS activity (drive reduction). The diminution of sympathetic activity in shame underlies the hedonic mood change and the disruption of motor (behavioral) and cognitive activities, and the replacement of parasympathetic passive for sympathetic active coping processes is reflected in the common shame experience of helplessness and passivity accompanying the exquisitely painful sensitivity to critical reactions of others (Morrison, 1985); that is, the loss of a mechanism to actively cope with narcissistic pain. (I suggest that as opposed to the elevated dorsal motor vagal parasympathetic autonomic component that always accompanies shame, humiliation involves an elevated parasympathetic plus a heightened sympathetic reactivity.)

The two components of the centrally, brain-stem-regulated ANS are known to be antagonistic, reciprocally integrated circuits (Hess, 1954) that control arousal, with the catabolic sympathetic branch responsible for energy-mobilizing excitatory activity and heart rate acceleration and the anabolic parasympathetic branch involved in energy-conserving inhibitory activity and heart rate deceleration (Porges, 1976). Broverman, Klaiber, Kobayashi, and Vogel noted that "the sympathetic and parasympathetic autonomic nervous systems are frequently in competition and the final effect then depends upon the relationship between the momentary activity of the two systems" (1968, p. 29).

It has long been acknowledged that "the physiological expression of emotion is dependent, in part, upon both sympathetic and parasympathetic components of the autonomic nervous system" (Truex & Carpenter, 1964, p. 431). It is posited that predominant sympathetic activity underlies high-intensity, narcissistically cathected affect states, and dominant dorsal motor vagal parasympathetic function is reflected in low-keyed emotional states. Hofer's work (1983) indicated that attachment and separation responses reflect the activity of not a single but multiple emotional systems. Again, it should be remembered that the practicing period represents a developmental phase of imbalance, of unregulated sympathetic overexcitation.

The idea that the prototypical shame transaction involves a break in attachment, a barrier to a reconnection after a separation, an expectation of seeing the gleam in the mother's eye in a reunion, but suddenly encounters frustration and experiences instead a bodily-based autonomic stress response may seem unfamiliar. And yet in *The Interpretation of Dreams* (1900/1953b), Freud, in his longest exposition on shame, described:

> If you are wandering about in a foreign land, far from your home and from all that you hold dear, if you have seen and heard many things, have known sorrow and care, and are wretched and forlorn, then without fail you will dream one night that you are coming near to your home; you will see it gleaming and shining in fairest colors, and the sweetest, dearest and most beloved forms will move towards you. Then suddenly you will become aware that you are in rags, naked and dusty. You will be seized with a nameless shame and dread, you will seek to find covering and to hide yourself, and you will awake bathed in sweat. This, so long as men breathe, is the dream of the unhappy wanderer.

MATERNAL RESPONSE AND THE REGULATION
OF SHAME-DEFLATED NARCISSISTIC AFFECT

Shame induction triggers an assault on the burgeoning narcissism of the practicing infant, on the ideal ego (primary narcissism), and represents the first experience of narcissistic injury and narcissistic depletion associated with all later shame experiences. It is at the point of this painful type of rupture in the infant–mother bond that the neoevolving, emotionally fragile, differentiating nascent self collapses, triggering physiological upheaval (the infantile psychosomatic state). Schneider (1977) noted that in shame a break occurs in the self's relationship to others and to itself; the self is no longer whole but divided. In Kohutian terminology, shame is related to an empathic break between the mirroring self object and the grandiose self (Josephs, 1989). In an attachment theory conception, Lewis (1980) noted that the "attachment emotion" of shame is an "implosion" or transient destruction of the self (while the self is intact in guilt). And in Mahlerian terms, Broucek pointed out that early experiences of large toxic doses of shame may impair ongoing development by "undermining separation-individuation processes and promoting regressive efforts to reestablish a symbiotic type of relationship" (1982, p. 37).

As maturation proceeds, this object relations sequence and its associated shame affect is internalized; ultimately shame is associated with the self's vicarious experience of the other's negative evaluation (Lewis, 1979). What once took place within the caregiver–infant unit is subsequently performed intrapsychically. As Parkin noted, the "awareness of the discrepancy or conflict between the self-admiring ideal ego and the reality ego's perception of the absence or contradiction of the admiration in the outside world constitutes the experience of shame" (1985, p. 150). As Basch maintained, "Later in life this same reaction occurs under similar circumstances, i.e. when we think we have failed to achieve or have broken a desired bond with another. The exquisite painfulness of that reaction in later life harks back to the earliest period when such a condition is not simply uncomfortable but threatens life itself" (1976, p. 767).

In the shame transaction there is thus a state of dysynchrony, a break of attachment, of "misattunement" between the toddler and caregiver, a "mismatch of need and anticipation in the caregiver–infant pairing" (Lichtenberg, 1983). However, the object-relation sequence within the dyad is not quite completed—the pair may attempt to resynchronize. In fact, an adaptation by the infant to the psychosocial stress can only be established with the mother's cooperation at reunion. Indeed, stress has been defined as the occurrence of an asynchrony in an interactional sequence. Further, "a period of synchrony, following the period of stress, provides a 'recovery' period" (Chapple, 1970, p. 631).

The frustrative state in shame has been conceptualized as arising from "an inability to effectively arouse the other person's positive reactions to one's communication" (Basch, 1976, p. 767). The overt behavior of the toddler, his/her facial expression of shock, his/her motionless headhang and body posture due to a reduction in tonus of the neck, body, and facial muscles causing a loss of the social smile, his/her averting the eyes, and the hallmark of shame, blushing, act as a signal to the attuned mother of the toddler's internal state of distress. Indeed, the preverbal infant communicates to her the dysregulation of his/her ANS, because "the language of mother and infant consists of signals produced by the autonomic, involuntary nervous system in both parties" (Basch, 1976, p. 766), and the mother is the regulator of the infant's developing ANS (Hofer, 1984b).

The infant's averted gaze, which reflects the attenuation of an object-relating interactional mode, has been shown to be a potent elicitor of attention from mothers of securely attached infants, but not from those of insecurely attached infants (Leavitt & Donovan, 1979). Darwin (1873/1965) originally pointed out that the function of emotional facial gestures is to communicate the individual's internal state to another. Sroufe (1979) suggested that infant affects have three functions: the amplification and exaggeration of behavior, the communication of information about internal states, and the elicitation of helpful reactions from the mother. Stern (1985) emphasized that the infant uses facial behaviors to invite higher levels of stimulation from the caregiver when the level of excitation has fallen too low. The child's face thus powerfully signals the caregiver of his/her internal shame-dominated affective state, isolation, and experience that the object-relation link has been severed. Basch noted, "The shame-humiliation reaction in infancy of hanging the head and averting the eyes . . . indicates that affective contact with another person has been broken" (1976, p. 765). Yet there is a need to repair the sundered attachment bond: "In shame the individual wishes to resume his or her commerce with the exciting state of affairs, to reconnect with the other, to recapture the relationship that existed before the situation turned problematic" (Tomkins, 1987, p. 144).

The nature of the caregiver's response (or lack of it) at this point is critical to the regulation of the shame affect, that is, shame recovery and the subsequent evolution of an internalized mechanism to regulate shame stress states. An important principle of attachment theory is that parental sensitivity and responsiveness to the child's affective communications is critical to the child's organization and regulation of his/her emotional experiences (Sroufe & Waters, 1977). Sensitive mothers offer stimulation contingent upon the infant's facial orientation: "At the most basic, 'security of attachment' relates to a physiological coding that the universe is benign and need-satisfying, that is, homeostatic disruptions will be set right" (Pipp & Harmon, 1987, p. 650). Demos and Kaplan pointed out that the caregiver's response to the infant's affective states is fundamental to the attachment phenomenon: "[T]he baby will become attached to the caregiver who can help to modulate and to minimize the experience of negative and who maximizes and expands opportunities for positive affect" (1986, p. 169).

Mothers of securely attached infants show a tendency to respond appropriately and promptly to their infants' emotional expressions (Ainsworth et al., 1978). This faciltates the creation of a system of reciprocal regulation, and fosters an expectation that during times of stress the attachment object will remain available and accessible. It also engenders a precursor of self-confidence, a sense in the infant that his/her own activity can control the effect that his/her environment will have on the infant (Ainsworth & Bell, 1974). This sense of "control" could underly the emergence of "active" (as opposed to passive) coping responses to emotional stress, and the ontogeny of early intrapsychic psychological defenses, which have been characterized as a subset of coping mechanisms (Rutter, 1987). Notice the critical role of early object relations in the ontogeny of stress coping systems, mechanisms to cope with mismatches in the social environment. Indeed, Levine (1983) argued that the development of coping responses is dependent upon early experience.

The work of Tronick (1989) with 2- to 9-month-old infants demonstrated that interactive stress is a ubiquitous component of maternal–infant transactions and that it is the caregiver who is reponsible for the reparation of dyadic misattunements and the transformation of the infant's negative emotion to this stress into a positive emotion. Tronick argued that mismatches allow for the development of interactive, coping, and self-regulatory skills, and enable the child to maintain engagement with the social environment in the face of stress. He also noted that the capacity for interactive repair will later contribute to the security of attachment. Infants of mothers who were responsive during early dyadic affect transfer interactions show, at 12 months, persisitent efforts to overcome an interactive stress. Furthermore, under the aegis of a sensitive and cooperative caregiver, the infant develops an internal representation of himself/herself as effective, of his/her interactions as positive and reparable, and of the caregiver as reliable. Although Tronick's studies include symbiotic and not practicing-phase toddlers, he noted that the process of interactive repair is central to the regulation of later-emerging affects, specifically mentioning shame and guilt.

It is important to distinguish among shame stress, the narcissistic affect shame, and the process which regulates this affect, shame regulation. As outlined earlier, practicing caregiver-induced shame stress produces a state of dyadic mismatch and misattunement, triggering rapid offset of narcissistic, positive hedonic affect and onset of negative affective shame distress, propelling the previously hyperaroused child into an internally focused, passive, hypoaroused shame state. The maternal response to the reengaging toddler at reunion after an attachment break is critical to the reparative process of affect regulation. If she is responsive and approachable, the object relations link is reconnected, the infant's attachment system is reactivated, the arousal deceleration is inhibited, and shame is metabolized. As a result, the child recovers from the injury to narcissism and recovers from shame.

This active recovery mechanism develops in the context of effective early object relations in an "average, expectable environment" (Plutchik, 1983) in order to regulate affective perturbations associated with disruptions in self- and object relationships. The prototype for the evolution of this mechanism lies in the mother's response to the child's shame distress. Kaufman asserted that the shame state that "originates from an interpersonal severing process" may be ameliorated by the process of "restoring the interpersonal bridge" (1985, p. 143).

This practicing onset-shame modulation is identical to the maternal response and regulation of the practicing child's low-keyed states (earlier shown to be isomorphic to shame states) that represent a drop in the child's level of arousal and is reminiscent of a miniature anaclitic depression (Mahler, 1979). Previously, a description was given of the practicing toddler's venturing away from the mother and becoming exhilarated during exploratory forays into the novel physical environment. At reunion, he/she may return in an excited state and attempt to emotionally share the elation resulting from his/her mastery experiences with the caregiver, or in a depleted low-keyed state, triggered by inefficacy, in which he/she is less inclined to reengage the physical surroundings. Mahler noted that this toned-down state is visibly terminated at reunion with the briefly absent mother: "The wilting and fatigued infant 'perks up' in the shortest time, following such contact, after which he quickly goes on with his explorations, once again absorbed in pleasures in his own functioning" (1980, p. 6). In this transaction the underaroused practicing baby is energized by the mother. Consequently, unfocused attention and negative hedonic tone is transformed within ten seconds into focused attention and positive hedonic tone.

In the dyadic shame transaction the infant's low-keyed state was triggered by the caregiver's misattunement, and so, subsequent to her induction of the infant's stressful low arousal state she now acts to interactively regulate the shame state. In doing so, the shame-modulating caregiver and the infant again co-create a psychobiological bond of interactive regulation, which switches off the infant's dorsal motor vagal parasympathetic-mediated low arousal that fuels the child's anhedonic depressive state, thereby allowing for a reignition of sympathetic activity which supports higher levels of arousal. The stress regulating caregiver thus facilitates a transition from the primitive dorsal motor vagal to the later maturing and flexible nucleus ambiguus vagal system in the infant's developing brain. Recall, as opposed to the "vegetative" or "reptillian" parasympathetic system in the dorsal motor nucleus that shuts down metabolic activity during immobilization, death feigning, and hiding behaviors, the "smart" or "mammalian" vagal system in the nucleus ambiguus allows for the ability to communicate via facial expressions (mutual gaze), vocalizations, and gestures in contingent social interactions. This interactive regulation produces a shift from passive to active coping, and negative/passive to postive/active mood.

It should be pointed out that these shame regulating transactions are carried out repeatedly throughout the practicing period, and that a characteristic and prototypical pattern of dealing with misattuned states and distressing affects develops between the primary attachment figure and the child; Waters (1978) found stable reunion patterns of affect regulation at 12 and 18 months (practicing and rapprochement).

It is the child's experiencing of an affect and the caregiver's response to this particular affect that is internalized as an affect-regulating interactive representation during reunion episodes. The internalization of affective and cognitive components of relationships operationally defines the construction of internal working models (Pipp & Harmon, 1987) that organize the individual's construction of subsequent relationships. These practicing-imprinted models are equated with Stern's (1985) "generalized episodes of interactions that are mentally represented," and with Kernberg's (1984) internalized representations of the self affectively transacting with objects in the social environment. According to Bowlby (1973), these models of attachment relationships contain internalized representations of early parental attributes, particularly conceptions of the caregiver's accessibility and responsiveness. Bretherton (1985) stressed the involvement of internal working models in superego formation.

Kobak and Sceery noted that these internal models that define "styles of affect regulation" provide "rules for regulating distress-related affect . . . in the context of parental responsiveness to the child's signals of distress" (1988, p. 142). This principle also refers to distress that is maternally induced (i.e., shame distress) and the caregiver's responsiveness to the infant's narcissistic stress *that she has triggered*. Importantly, practicing shame transactions and the maternal regulation of shame stress act as a developmental matrix for the evolution of the capacity to experience, tolerate, and regulate shame, and represent an interpersonal source of the emergence of adaptive coping strategies for dealing with subsequent narcissistic stress. These practicing-internalized models involving the attachment emotion of shame are imprinted into the earliest episodic memory, which stores events that have meaning for the concept of self (Tulving, 1972), and are the source of early, preverbal (and therefore later unconscious), deep transference patterns. Bowlby (1988) posited that the uncovering and reassessment of early internalized working models is the essential task of psychothetrapy.

It is in this particular interpersonal context late in the practicing period that the developmental transition of external to internal regulation via increasing levels of internalization occurs (McDevitt, 1980). Hofer (1984b) proposed that internal representations of human relationships serve as "biologic regulators"; the physiological regulatory function of the infant's ANS is initially performed by the mother, and subsequently internalized by the infant. Greenspan (1981) argued that in the ontogeny of homeostatic regulation of the infant's arousal or excitation, the function is first performed by the responsive mother, and then gradually acquired by the infant. Thus, interactive regulation of the infant's external emotional expression that is observable and exogenous in the symbiotic phase (Tronick's interactive repair) is a precursor to self-regulation of internal emotional states that is unobservable, endogenous, and subjective at the end of the practicing phase.

Similarly, Kohut noted that "there may be some internalization of the actual functions carried out by the mother and the 'transmuting' into regulatory mental structures to deal with uncomfortable emotions, in much the same way as the mother provided relief" (1971, p. 13). These maternal "selfobject" functions are specifically affect regulatory functions, of both arousal reduction and arousal induction. Stolorow, Brandchaft, and Atwood (1987) argued that the caregiver's attuned responsiveness to the child's intense, shifting affective states allows for the evolution of an internalized structure that can modulate and contain strong affect. Such opportunities for internalization determine the structural development of an affect regulator allowing for later emotional self-regulation that provides for constancy of internal affective states, that is, mood autoregulation.

Furthermore, this affect regulator is critical to the maintenance of recurrent positive mood and the establishment of Emde's (1983) "affective core" that regulates the infant's interactive behavior. In securely attached infants, distress does not endure for long periods beyond the conditions that elicit them; rapid recovery to positively toned emotions is typical (Gaensbauer & Mrazek, 1981). In contrast, infants who are insecurely attached show "a greater tendency for negative emotional states to endure beyond the precipitating stimulus events" (Gaensbauer, 1982, p. 169)

SHAME AND AFFECT REGULATION
THROUGH THE RAPPROCHEMENT CRISIS

Within the major developmental transition from practicing to rapprochement, important affective, cognitive, and behavioral changes occur. The emergence of new function and structure during this boundary period rests upon successful passage through preceeding stages. Mahler and colleagues asserted: "Normal autism and normal symbiosis are prerequisite to the onset of the normal separation and individuation process" (1975, p. 47). Similarly, adequate development in the practicing subphase is a prerequisite for rapprochement success. More specifically, it is required for successful passage from one stage into the next; that is, through the portal of the rapprochement crisis.

Mahler and colleagues described that at practicing offset/rapprochment onset "the toddler's elated preoccupation with locomotion and exploration *per se* [is] beginning to wane" (1975, p. 90). Pine referred to the "rapprochement crisis" involving the collapse of the illusion of omnipotence: "Now he is small and alone in a big world, rather than sharing in the (imagined) omnipotence of the mother–child unit" (1980, p. 226). (This omnipotence, supported by the tolerance of high arousal affect, reflects a fairly successful transition through all stages up to and including the practicing phase; a poor symbiotic experience would obviate this.) Parkin (1985) desribed the transition from the exhilarated practicing state, which represents the highest point in the development of primary narcissism and in the overestimation of the child's powers, into rapprochement. Parkin defined the "narcissistic crisis" (Mahler's rapprochement crisis) as "the necessity of yielding up to reality the child's illusory claims to omnipotence" (1985, p. 146). Freud wrote of the reluctant "departure from primary narcissism" (1914a/1957b, p. 100), and Fast (1984) pointed out that the child's emergence from this early state of infantile narcissism is marked by considerable resistance, evasion, and a sense of injury.

This critical developmental transition emotionally tests the mother–child dyad and their ability to remain connected during the stage-specific narcissistic distress that unfolds. The crucial import of the continued libidinal availability of the mother to a healthy resolution of the crisis has been stressed (Settlage,

1977). More specifically, although during the crisis the ambitendent toddler moves away from the mother, he/she returns during periods of distress. The mother's "quiet availability" in these reunions for regulation of distressing affects (arousal modulation) is an essential caregiver function. During this period of developmental crisis, separation anxiety is intensified due to fear of loss of the mother as a newly discovered separate object, and narcissistic rages and tantrums are used by the child to regain control. As mentioned earlier, the response of attachment figures to this behavior is critical.

The markers of a successful developmental passage through this stage transition are well known. Kohut (1971) underscored the principle that a true sense of self is a product of the accomodation or neutralization of the individual's grandiosity and idealization. Parkin emphasized that "with this resolution there is a subsidence of the child's rages and of his external struggles with his mother for power" (1985, p. 147), and Settlage (1977) asserted that one of the major developmental tasks of the rapprochement phase is the modulation of infantile rage.

What fundamental internal transformations are being reflected in these changes? Kagan (1979) found the period of 17 to 21 months (the practicing-rapprochement border) to be a critical developmental point, noting a shift from spatial-perceptual to a more symbolic-linguistic cognitive mode of problem solving. Lester (1983) noted that rapprochement onset parallels the transition from Piaget's fifth stage to the sixth and final stage of sensorimotor development, "invention of new means through mental combinations." Focusing on the emergent cognitive functions at this time, Lester stated, "The child can now perform true mental operations with ever-increasing speed, and he can deal with a large segment of reality at once. This level of maturation of the mental apparatus correlates with and possibly explains the phenomenon of the rapprochement crisis" (1983, p. 151). It should be pointed out, however, that the child at this point in development is still essentially "preverbal." The effective vocabulary (words spoken or understood) of the average 18-month-old is only 22 words (Mussen, Conger, & Kagan, 1969), and emotion-descriptive language does not first emerge until 20 months of age (Bretherton, McNew, & Beeghly, 1981).

Notice the focus solely on the appearance of new cognitive abilities, presumably reflecting the ongoing postnatal maturation of the cerebral cortex (Yakovlev & LeCours, 1967), especially the early-maturing right cerebral hemisphere (Geschwind & Galaburda, 1987). This could explain the more efficient ability to process and internally store symbolic representations of the external world, but, to my mind, does not reveal the essential transformation in affect and affect regulation that marks the rapprochement crisis—the deflation of practicing "elation" and "exhilaration" that supports the illusion of omnipotence. Mahler emphasized that during the rapprochement crisis, which is essentially an emotional crisis, the toddler shows "an increasing differentiation of his emotional life" (1980, p. 9). Krystal, also stressing the importance of affect at this developmental phase, noted, "Separation-individuation is a process of growth and development regulated by the intensity of the feelings that can be tolerated during . . . separation. This process provides an opportunity to develop the affect and increase this tolerance" (1988, p. 35).

It is posited here that the shame system, the regulator of hyperstimulated (excited, elated, grandiose, manic) states, critical to the modulation of high-arousal narcissistic affects characteristic of the practicing period, is required for deflation of omnipotence and resolution of the rapprochement (narcissistic) crisis. McDevitt (1980) asserted that the formation of superego structure is instrumental to the resolution of the rapprochement crisis. Johnson (1987) pointed out that from the practicing phase onward, the parents must supply repeated but supportive and not humiliating frustration of the child's illusion of grandiosity. In optimal situations this deflation should be gradual and not precipitous and overwhelming; the nascent self is plastic, yet fragile.

These early-frustrative socializing events may serve as stress immunization experiences that allow for tolerance, coping, and recovery from later attachment stresses; Greenspan (1981) pointed out that the ultimate indicator of attachment capacity is resilience in the face of stress. Hunt (1965) suggested that regularly sheltering children from stressors is counterproductive for optimal emotional development. Moreover, Kohut proposed, "Small (subliminal) shame signals play a role in maintaining a homeostatic narcissistic equilibrium" (1971, p. 181). These may represent the mechanism of modulated phase-appropriate empathic failures that allow for transmuting internalizations. Kohut stipulated, "Tolerable disappointments in the pre-existing (and externally sustained) primary narcissistic equilibrium lead to the establishment of internal structures which provide the ability for self-soothing and the acquisition of basic tension tolerance in the narcissistic realm" (1971, p. 64).

Broucek asserted, "In small, unavoidable 'doses,' shame may enhance self and object differentiation and assist the individuation process because it involves acute awareness of one's separateness from the important other" (1982, p. 37). Similarly, Nathanson (1987) pointed out that shame experiences producing lapses in the smooth physiological functioning of the organism act as a major force in shaping the infantile self. Basch (1988) maintained that shame acts to protect the self-system by modifying patterns of expectations in the interest of social maturation. The positive aspect of this unique affect "which in contrast to all other affects . . . is an experience of the self by the self" (Schneider, 1977, p. 25), and which reflects "heightened self-consciousness" (Tomkins, 1963), can be seen in its role in protecting individuation, the growth process of delimiting the boundaries and nature of the self. Spero (1984) argued that the constructive function of shame can be seen in the process of differentiation of the self in the presence of danger of self-other merger; and Severino, McNutt, and Feder (1986), using clinical case material, concluded that the capacity to experience shame is crucial for the achievement of autonomy.

The importance of experienced, regulated (as opposed to bypassed, unregulated) shame to ongoing development (Shane, 1980; Ward, 1972) may lie in its role as a socializing agent. Measured, repeated exposures to limitation may dilute primary infantile narcissism and neutralize primitive aggressive drives, especially during the narcissistic crisis. Mahler (1979) noted that a surplus of unneutralized aggression thwarts favorable development. Parens (1980) described the upsurge in aggressive drive that occurs specifically in the practicing phase, and Kagan (1976) characterized "separation protest" that peaks at 12 months and diminishes between 15 to 24 months (rapprochement). In a study of 13-month-old infants, Izard found that the dominant, typical negative emotional response to brief separation at this age is anger, not sadness, and not "separation anxiety" (Shiller, Izard, & Hembree, 1986). Bowlby (1969b) observed a "bitter" separation protest as a response to a broken attachment tie, which Lewis (1985) specifically equated with "shame-rage" (humiliated fury). Willock (1986) observed the phenomenon of narcissistic vulnerability in hyperaggressive children.

It is proposed that these phenomena commonly reflect "narcissistic rage," the unmodulated, overexcited sympathetic arousal triggered by object loss, which is characteristic of this period. The activation of high levels of sympathetic arousal is known to facilitate aggressive behavior (Zillman & Bryant, 1974). At this age, the infant can not yet autoregulate this state, as it propels him/her into extremely high levels of arousal in excess of his/her optimal activation band, and is therefore beyond his/her active coping capacities. It is known that "negative emotional responses occur in high-arousal situations in which active coping methods are not available" (Dienstbier, 1989, p. 93). This unregulated hyperstimulated condition consequently precipitates an explosive (as opposed to shame-induced implosive) self-fragmentation.

Fox and Davidson (1984) asserted that a major developmental milestone occurs in the middle of the second year (practicing offset/rapprochement onset). At this time a system of affect regulation emerges with the capacity for inhibition of distress and other negative affects. Pine (1980) suggested that "control/delay/inhibition processes" (affect regulatory processes) are involved in the expansion of the affect array. This principle may be demonstrated in the transformation of diffuse, explosive rage of the infant into focused and modulated anger. In a classic study of the early expressions of aggression within the first 2 years of life, Goodenough (1931) reported a developmental transition from frustration-induced anger manifested as tantrums, undirected energy, and outbursts of motor activity into directed motor and language responses. The initiation of the modulation of this negative/active affect during the late-practicing/early-rapprochement period (Settlage, 1977) reflects the onset of functional activity of the shame regulator's control of sympathetic, hyperaroused limbic aggressive states and may underly "the transformation of narcissistic rage into mature aggression" (Kohut, 1978b, p. 649).

Furthermore, the emergence of evocative memory (Fraiberg, 1969) at the practicing rapprochement border can only be maintained if preexisting forms of infantlie rage can be regulated (Adler & Buie, 1979). During this developmental period the child's anger "interferes with the capability to maintain a sense of the good internal object image during the mother's absence, so that the serene state of mind implied in the capacity to be alone (Winnicott, 1958)

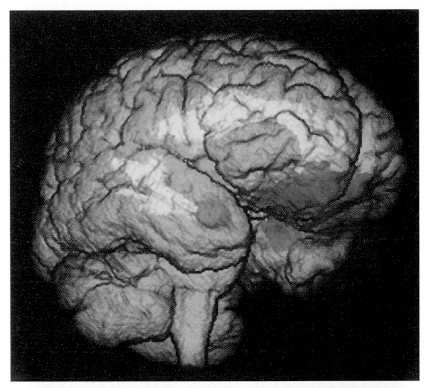

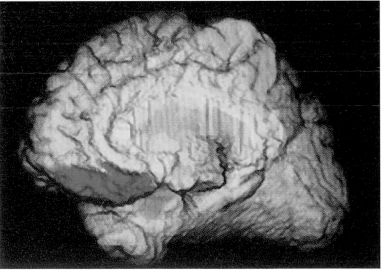

FIGURE A-1 Neuroanatomy of human social cognition represented in a partially transparent brain (right lateral view of whole brain at top, medial view of the right hemisphere at bottom). Some of the most central structures are shown: the amygdala (blue), the ventromedial (orbital) prefrontal cortex (red), the cingulate cortex (yellow), and somatosensory-related cortices in the right hemisphere (green).

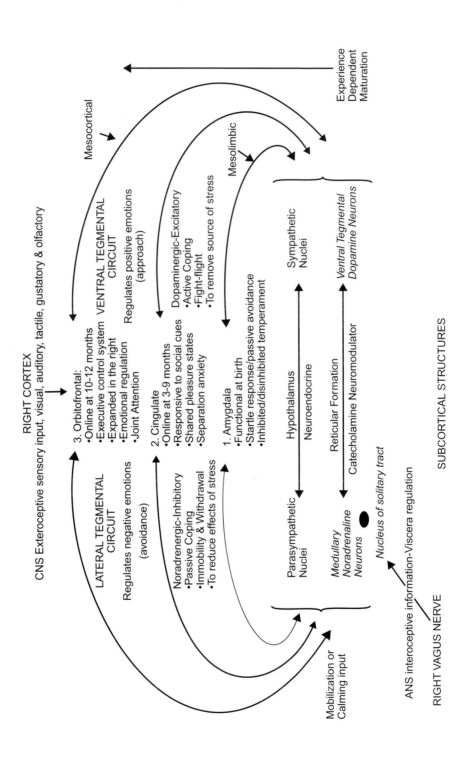

FIGURE A-2 The right brain dual cortical-limbic circuits.

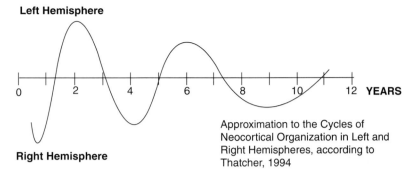

Left Hemisphere

0   2   4   6   8   10   12 **YEARS**

Right Hemisphere

Approximation to the Cycles of
Neocortical Organization in Left and
Right Hemispheres, according to
Thatcher, 1994

FIGURE A-3   Note the right hemisphere is in a growth cycle in the first year. According to the author of the report, the right hemisphere is more advanced in surface features from the 25th week and this persists until the left hemisphere shows a growth spurt starting in the second year. These brain growth cycles continue asymmetrically throughout childhood, correlated with changes in the balance of functions in the two hemispheres. See Chapters 1, 4, and 8.

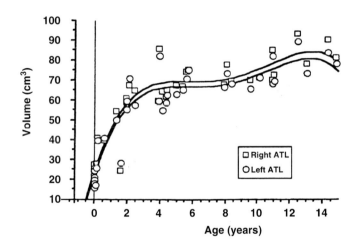

FIGURE A-4   The volume of the anterior temporal lobes increases sharply until the age of 2 years, and continues to increase slowly thereafter. The right anterior temporal lobe (which contains the limbic hippocampus and amygdala) is larger than the left from early infancy onward. The authors of the report noted that these limbic connections regulate emotional behavior and are integral to learning and memory. This representation may thus reflect the growth of the early "core self." See Chapter 4.

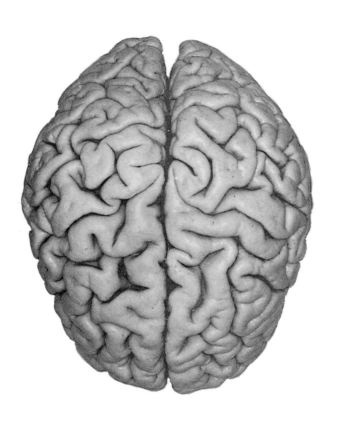

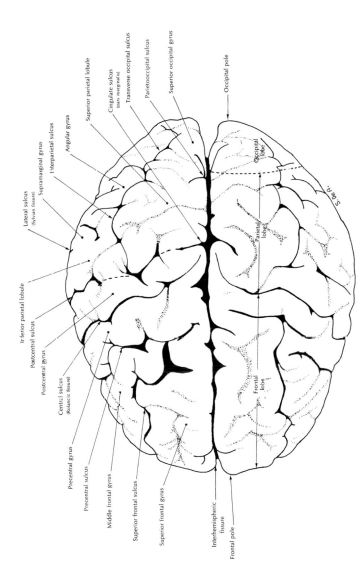

Lateral sulcus
(Sylvian fissure)

Supramarginal gyrus

Interparietal sulcus

Angular gyrus

Superior parietal lobule

Cingulate sulcus
(pars marginalis)

Transverse occipital sulcus

Parietooccipital sulcus

Superior occipital gyrus

Occipital pole

Occipital lobe

Parietal lobe

Frontal lobe

Inferior parietal lobule

Postcentral sulcus

Postcentral gyrus

Central sulcus
(Rolandic fissure)

Precentral gyrus

Precentral sulcus

Middle frontal gyrus

Superior frontal sulcus

Superior frontal gyrus

Interhemispheric fissure

Frontal pole

FIGURE A-5A   Photograph and neuroanatomy of the superior surface of the brain. From this perspective it is obvious that there are two brains, and that the brain is a dual system.

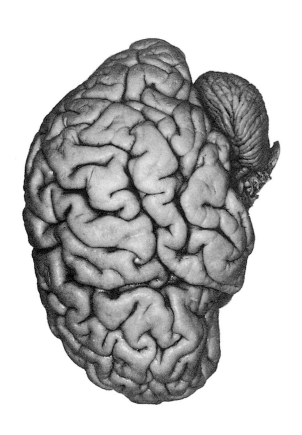

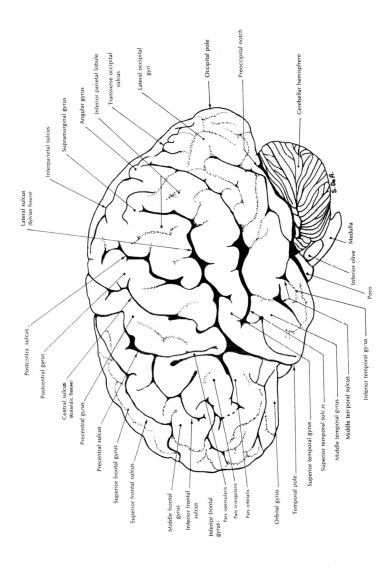

Postcentral sulcus

Postcentral gyrus

Central sulcus
(Rolandic fissure)

Precentral gyrus

Precentral sulcus

Superior frontal gyrus

Superior frontal sulcus

Middle frontal
gyrus

Inferior frontal
sulcus

Inferior frontal
gyrus:
　Pars opercularis
　Pars triangularis
　Pars orbitalis

Orbital gyrus

Temporal pole

Superior temporal gyrus

Superior temporal sulcus

Middle temporal gyrus

Middle temporal sulcus

Inferior temporal gyrus

Lateral sulcus
(Sylvian fissure)

Interparietal sulcus

Supramarginal gyrus

Angular gyrus

Inferior parietal lobule

Transverse occipital
sulcus

Lateral occipital
gyri

Occipital pole

Preoccipital notch

Cerebellar hemisphere

Medulla

Inferior olive

Pons

S. De A.

FIGURE A-5B   Photograph and neuroanatomy of the lateral surface of the left hemisphere. This common depiction visually suggests a single brain.

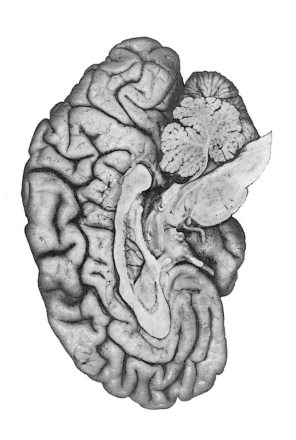

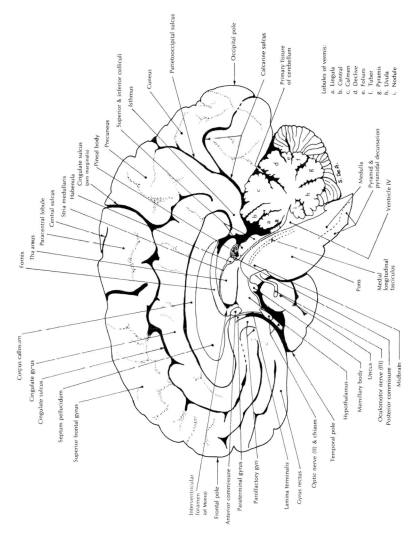

Corpus callosum
Cingulate gyrus
Cingulate sulcus
Septum pellucidum
Superior frontal gyrus

Fornix
Thalamus
Paracentral lobule
Central sulcus
Stria medullaris
Habenula
Cingulate sulcus
(pars marginalis)
Pineal body
Precuneus
Superior & inferior colliculi
Isthmus
Cuneus
Parietooccipital sulcus
Occipital pole
Calcarine sulcus
Primary fissure
of cerebellum

Lobules of vermis:
a. Lingula
b. Central
c. Culmen
d. Declive
e. Folium
f. Tuber
g. Pyramis
h. Uvula
i. Nodule

S. De A.

Medulla
Pyramid &
pyramidal decussation
Ventricle IV

Medial
longitudinal
fasciculus

Pons

Hypothalamus
Mamillary body
Uncus
Oculomotor nerve (III)
Posterior commissure
Midbrain

Temporal pole
Optic nerve (II) & chiasm
Gyrus rectus
Lamina terminalis
Parolfactory gyri
Paraterminal gyrus
Anterior commissure
Frontal pole
Interventricular
foramen
(of Monro)

FIGURE A-5C   Photograph and neuroanatomy of the medial surface of the brain.

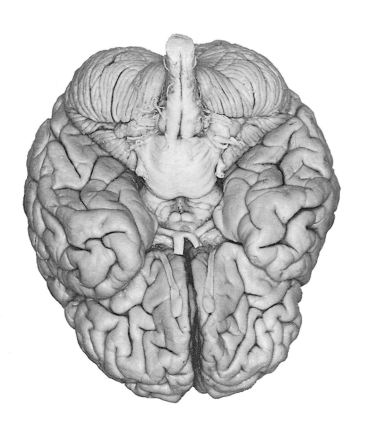

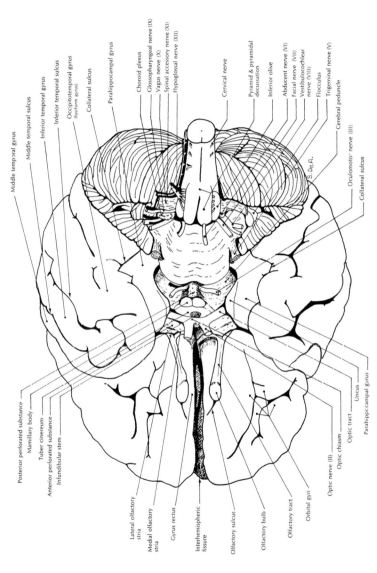

Middle temporal gyrus
Middle temporal sulcus
Inferior temporal gyrus
Inferior temporal sulcus
Occipitotemporal gyrus (fusiform gyrus)
Collateral sulcus
Parahippocampal gyrus
Choroid plexus
Glossopharyngeal nerve (IX)
Vagus nerve (X)
Spinal accessory nerve (XI)
Hypoglossal nerve (XII)
Cervical nerve
Pyramid & pyramidal decussation
Inferior olive
Abducent nerve (VI)
Facial nerve (VII)
Vestibulocochlear nerve (VIII)
Flocculus
Trigeminal nerve (V)
Cerebral peduncle
S. De A.
Oculomotor nerve (III)
Collateral sulcus

Posterior perforated substance
Mamillary body
Tuber cinereum
Anterior perforated substance
Infundibular stem
Lateral olfactory stria
Medial olfactory stria
Gyrus rectus
Interhemispheric fissure
Olfactory sulcus
Olfactory bulb
Olfactory tract
Orbital gyri
Optic nerve (II)
Optic chiasm
Optic tract
Uncus
Parahippocampal gyrus

FIGURE A-5D   Photograph and neuroanatomy of the inferior, ventral surface of the brain. The right hemisphere is on the bottom half of the photo and figure.

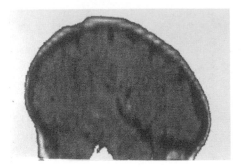

FIGURE A-6   Positron emission tomographic (PET) scan of a 2-month-old infant looking at the image of a woman's face. Activation is shown in the right fusiform gyrus, the visual associative cortex specialized for processing human faces. At this age, infants first recognize their mother's face and distinguish it from among others.

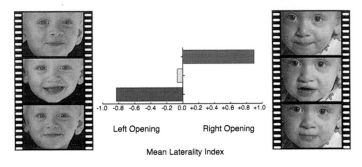

FIGURE A-7   Consecutive frames from video recordings show a baby's left mouth opening (reflecting right hemisphere activation) while smiling (left) and right mouth opening (reflecting left hemisphere activation) while babbling (right). A standard Laterality Index was calculated for infants 5 to 12 months. These data suggest that, like adults, the emotional expression of 5-month-old infants might be more controlled by the right hemisphere.

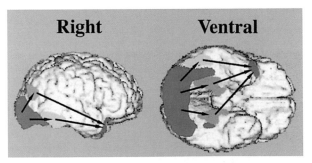

FIGURE A-8   Schematic diagram of possible information streams in the human brain for the recognition of faces and scenes. Four functionally distinct areas are illustrated on the right and ventral views of 3D brain: 1) the occipital and posterior fusiform regions (blue) extract physical features of complex visual stimuli; 2) the right inferior temporal/fusiform gyri (yellow) process faces; 3) the parahippocampal and parieto-occipital regions (green) process scenes; and 4) the right temporal pole (red) is used for the recognition of familiar faces and scenes. Each arrow represents a stream of information. See Chapters 3 and 8.

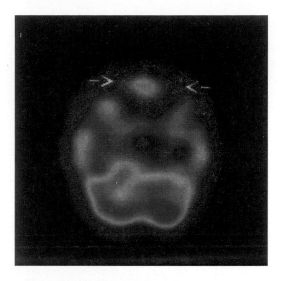

FIGURE A-9   Orbitofrontal perfusion defect in a patient with dissociative identity disorder (transverse section). The patient reported a history of childhood trauma. See Chapter 4 for a discussion of the neurobiology of dissociation.

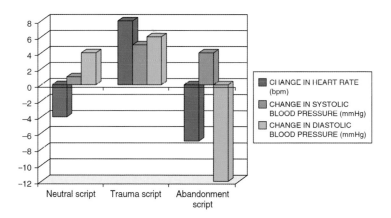

FIGURE A-10   Heart rate and blood pressure reactivity in a patient with posttraumatic stress disorder (PTSD) and borderline personality disorder, manifest in suicide attempts, self-injurious behavior, and severe emotional instability. This 36-year-old woman, with a history of childhood abuse, listened to a personalized script of childhood abuse and abandonment situations. When the trauma script was read to her, she displayed an intense emotional reaction and her heart rate increased 7bpm. While listening to the abandonment script she dissociated. During this period her heart rate fell by 7bpm and her diastolic blood pressure decreased by 12mmHg. See Chapters 3 and 4 for the same shift from hyperarousal and heart rate increase to dissociation, hypoarousal, and heart rate decrease in infant relational trauma.

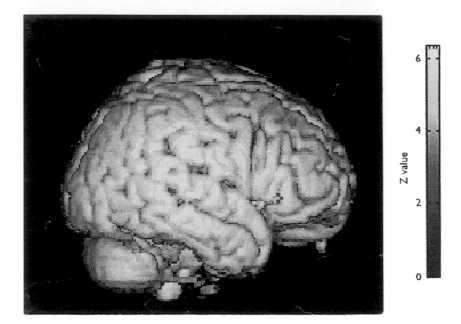

FIGURE A-11   Functional magnetic resonance image (fMRI) of affect regulation. When subjects watched a fearful or angry face, increased blood flow is seen in the right and left amygdala, the brain's major fear center. When these facial expressions are linguistically labeled, blood flow is decreased in the amygdalae, but increased in the right prefrontal cortex (above), a cortical area implicated in regulating emotional responses. Notice that when a verbal label is provided to the emotional stimulus, the higher regions of the right—not left—hemisphere are activated. These data suggest a neural basis for modulating emotional experiences through labeling and interpreting emotional expressions. It further suggests that this form of affect regulation might be impaired in various emotional disorders and may provide the basis for therapies of these same disorders. See Chapters 2 and 3 for a discussion.

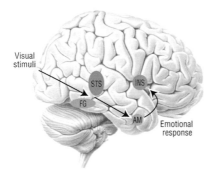

FIGURE A-12   A neurological basis for judging trustworthiness from facial features. The major routes of processing socially relevant information about trust are shown. The right fusiform gyrus (FG, green) and right superior temporal sulcus (STS, red) process features of the face stimulus. The amygdala (AM, blue) associates perception of the face with an emotional response to the face. The insula (INS, purple) participates in representing this emotional response as a feeling about the person whose face is viewed. Activation of the STS can also be modulated by the task, demonstrating top-down influences and suggesting that most information flows in both directions along this circuit. I suggest that this circuit mediates Eriksonian "basic trust," and that it organizes in the first year of life and is influenced by attachment transactions. Furthermore, this mechanism operates within the positive transference of the therapeutic alliance (see Chapters 1, 2, and 3).

FIGURE A-13 Hierarchical organization of interoception, the sense of the physiological condition of the body. Autonomic information from bodily tissues is relayed to the brain via parallel sympathetic and parasympathetic afferents. The latter are delivered to the nucleus of the solitary tract in the medulla. Interoceptive information then travels to the parabrachial nucleus (the main brainstem homeostatic integration site) then to the ventromedial thalamic nucleus and the dorsal insula. It then is re-represented in the right anterior insula, and finally forwarded to the hierarchical apex—the right orbitofrontal cortex—where hedonic valence is represented, allowing for approach/avoidance in relation to the body's needs. The author of the report concluded that cortical representations of feelings from the body are the basis for human awareness of the physical self as a feeling entity. In Chapters 3 and 4, I propose that in the therapeutic context the processing of the patient's felt experience by this right lateralized system allows for the evolution of affects from bodily sensations into subjective emotional states.

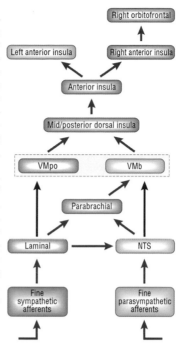

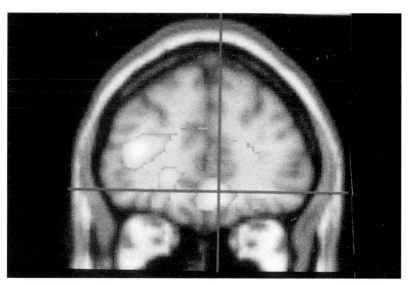

FIGURE A-14 A functional magnetic resonance image (fMRI), showing activation of the medial area of the orbitofrontal cortex while guessing in an unpredictable context. This adaptive strategy is used in the face of uncertainty, where a feeling of "rightness" or familiarity rather than a rational analysis of semantic features is used to comprehend meaning. This form of cognition describes the therapist's generation of intuitive hypotheses about the moment-to-moment processes in the patient's internal world (see Chapters 2 and 3). Notice the lateralization to the right side of the brain.

FIGURE A-15 (Left side of the figure is the right side of the brain.) Transverse positron emission tomographic (PET) image, superimposed on a magnetic resonance reference image (MRI), showing significant decreases of regional blood flow in the temporal lobe of the right hemisphere (right amygdala and hippocampus) of social phobic patients treated with psychotherapy. PET scans were performed during an anxiogenic public speaking task, and a greater reduction in neural response to public speaking is shown in psychotherapy relative to waiting-list group. The degree of subcortical amygdalar-limbic attenuation was associated with clinical improvement a year later. See Chapter 7 for further discussion.

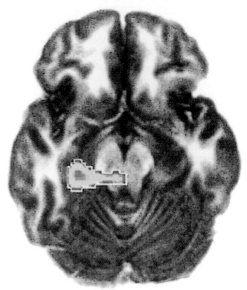

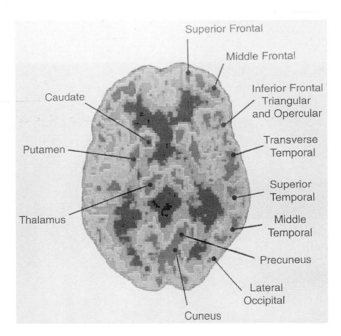

FIGURE A-16 A positron emission tomographic (PET) scan during a two- to three-hour period of relaxed awareness. Cortical gyri are identified on the subject's—and viewer's—right side. In sections farther down, the middle temporal gyrus and the fusiform gyrus also revealed greater metabolic activity on the right side. The author of the report noted a right-sided preponderance of cortical activity in this nonverbal state of mental and physical relaxation. Frontal lobes are at the top; red indicates regions of highest metabolic activity.

is frequently not attainable. This ability to be alone includes the sense of being alone with an ego supportive other, and this image is not available at times of anger or frustration" (Wagner & Fine, 1981, p. 11).

A further fundamental consequence of the importance of shame downregulation of the practicing infant's hyperstimulated, high-arousal states is found in its critical effect on ongoing internalization and subsequent identification processes. Wallace (1963) noted that, in adults there is an association between shame predominance (unregulated shame) and a "deficiency of introjects," Morrison (1989) highlighted the relationship of shame to "faulty identity-formation," and Spero (1984) observed that shame-prone personalities manifest "deficits in capacity for internalization." Freud postulated that anaclitic identification occurs when the mother, to whom the child has developed an attachment, frustrates the child by withholding rewards she had previously freely dispensed; this motivates the child to "introject" her. Thus, the stress of frustration (as outlined earlier in shame) is requisite to the child's internalization of dyadic object relations sequences and the construction of internalized working models of attachment in episodic memory.

Unmodulated hyperaroused manic affect is known to interfere with learning and memory processes (Johnson & Magaro, 1987), and to specifically disrupt long-term memory processes, particularly retrieval (Henry, Weingartner, & Murphy, 1971). Bandura and Walters's (1963) studies of social learning phenomena indicate that "imitation," which they equate with "identification," is facilitated by moderate arousal, but becomes more and more limited and fragmentary as the level of arousal increases. It follows that the extremely high arousal levels of unregulated, self-fragmenting narcissistic rage disrupt identification processes critical to the resolution of the rapprochement crisis. This phenomenon is reflected in McDevitt's (1975) demonstration of prolonged states of unmetabolized aggression producing "interferences with identification" in this critical period.

The critical import of shame regulation of hyperaroused, grandiose practicing affect to identification processes also applies to emerging gender identification that is actively occuring at 18 months (Money & Ehrhardt, 1968), rapprochement onset. Nathanson (1987) pointed out that "the earliest manifestations of genitality and gender identity are exactly contemporaneous with the period during which shame takes on its deepest significance in terms of the self" (p. 39), and Amsterdam and Leavitt (1980) noted that parental response to the rapprochement onset upsurge in genital sexuality is critical to developing shame affect. Fast (1979) asserted that early gender development in girls involves the transition from an early undifferentiated, grandiose, omnipotent, narcissistic state to a more differentiated state of feminine identification in which earlier illusory claims of omnipotence are yielded up to reality. If this does not occur, an "incompletely differentiated feminine gender" results.

Furthermore, the narcissistic mother either overstimulates or does not modulate her infant's high-arousal grandiose affect. Mahler and Kaplan (1977) described the developmental history of a very aggressive narcissistic girl who manifested a predominance of shame and a "poor feminine identification." In an unpublished study (J. Schore, 1983), shame-prone women with inefficient shame-regulatory systems were shown to have weak feminine identifications, presumably reflecting poor early maternal internalizations and attachment. It is posited that this occurred because the narcissistic mother did not downregulate the practicing toddler's hyperarousal, a state detrimental to the learning and memory processes underlying identification. If the mother does not shame-regulate phase-typical hyperarousal, the maternal introjection and gender identification will be "weak." Also, in psychotherapeutic work with adults, Kaufman (1985) noted a strong connection between "failures in identification" due to intense early shame histories and homosexual manifestations.

As pointed out earlier, in addition to the shame experience and its consequent affective misattunement, the caregiver's response of deactivating and subsequently reactivating sympathetic arousal is critical to the organization of a system to regulate the negative effect of shame (i.e., the shame regulator). Thus, at the critical period of the practicing/rapprochement boundary, a favorable resolution of the narcissistic (rapprochement) crisis and the emergence of a system to regulate narcissistic affects depends on the emergence, by the end of the practicing phase, of an internalized, efficient, affect-autoregulatory system that can bidirectionally modulate the high-arousal affects intrinsic to the grandiose, narcissistically charged practicing stage, even in the caregiver's absence. This mechanism underlies Freud's (1923/1961b) observation that by both frustrating and satisfying the infant in the correct proportion, the mother facilitates the transformation of the pleasure into the reality principle.

IMPLICATIONS FOR THE ETIOLOGY
OF NARCISSISTIC DISORDERS

The developmentally impaired narcissistic disorders, which manifest shame-sensitivity (DSM-III-R, 1987; Kohut, 1971; Lewis, 1980), defective superego formation, vulnerability to narcissistic injuries, low self-esteem, and unmodulated narcissistic rage do not effectively negotiate the rapprochement crisis. In support of this, Mahler and Kaplan (1977) speculated that the early etiology of the narcissistic disorder of a 13-year-old girl involved the absence of practicing phase refueling and the irresolution of the rapprochement crisis. Masterson correctly pointed out, "The narcissistic personality disorder must be fixated or arrested before the development of the rapprochement crisis, since one of the important tasks of that crisis is not performed, i.e., the deflation of infantile grandiosity and omnipotence" (1981, p. 29). Spitz (1964) decribed a type of "psychotoxic" maternal care, manifest in an overdose of affective stimulation, that is dispensed by the narcissistic mother who is concerned more with her own emotional needs than her infant's.

When the child is in a grandiose state, mirroring of her narcissism, the primary caregiver is emotionally accessible. However, because the infant's hyperaroused state mirrors the mother's heightened narcissism, the mother may do little to modulate it. On the other hand, when the infant is in a negative hyperaroused state, such as aggressive separation protest, she either fails to modulate it (in herself or in her child) or even hyperstimulates the infant into a state of dyscontrol. She also may be ineffective in regulating the infant up out of hypoaroused states that she herself triggers, such as occurs in maternal shame-stress depletion of narcissistic affect. Kohut described this inconsistent attunement of the mother as an important element in the etiology of narcissistic disorders: "On innumerable occasions she appeared to have been totally absorbed in the child—overcaressing him, completely in tune with every nuance of his needs and wishes—only to withdraw from him suddenly, either by turning her attention totally to other interests or by grossly and grotesquely misunderstanding his needs and wishes" (1977, p. 52).

Thus, after a shame-induced infant–caregiver misattunement, at reunion, a moment of emotional reconnection, the infant encounters a narcissistically injured, aggressively teasing, and humiliating mother who rather than decreasing shame distress hyperstimulates the child into an agitated state of narcissistic rage. The caregiver does not act to modulate shame and allow for the internalization and organization of a shame-regulatory system in the child that can reduce hyperstimulated states and enable recovery from hypostimulated states. Repeated early failures of attunement create "a belief that one's affective needs generally are somehow unacceptable and shameful" (Basch, 1985, p. 35). The inner experience of the affect of shame therefore becomes associated with an expectation of a painful, self-disorganizing internal state that cannot be regulated, and therefore is consciously avoided or "bypassed" (Lewis, 1971). The developmental arrest of narcissism regulation thus occurs specifically at rapprochement onset, and is due to the failure to evolve a practicing affect regulatory system that can neutralize grandiosity, regulate practicing excitement, or modulate narcissistic distress.

Kohut noted that the specific pathological affective experiences of narcissistic disorders "fall into a spectrum ranging from anxious grandiosity and excitement on the one hand to mild embarassment and self-consciousness or severe shame, hypochondria, and depression on the other" (1971, p. 200). Broucek (1982) described:

> With the advent of objective self-awareness, the child becomes more acutely conscious of his comparative smallness, weakness and his relative incompetence in the larger scheme of things. The shame evoked by this self-consciousness is more intense and more threatening for the child with a grandiose self than for the child with a less fantastic, more "normal" ideal self, due to the greater discrepancy between objectively derived self-observation and the defensively exalted grandiose self. (p. 375)

This phenomenon is due to a failure to downregulate the high arousal affects that fuel the "fantastic" grandiose self. As a result, "the ideal ego may remain sequestered from the developing reality ego as a persisting structure ready for grandiose revival" (Parkin, 1985, p. 146). The hypercathected archaic ideal ego (Kohut's archaic grandiose self), as an unintegrated persisting remnant, moves forward in development, and may be activated and expressed in "the appearance of affects similar to those associated with the earlier system such as grandiosity, omnipotence and euphoria or even elation" (Parkin, 1985, p. 152). Kohut decribed a personality structure "with a poorly integrated grandiose self concept and intense exhibitionistic-narcissistic tensions who is most prone to experience shame" (1978a, p. 441). Shame-prone narcissistic personalities (Lewis, 1980) defend "against feelings of unworthiness and self-contempt by assuming an attitude of grandiosity and entitlement, which is often accompanied by feelings of elation and contempt for others" (Hartocollis, 1980, p. 137).

Referring to selfobject (preoedipal) transferences in narcissistic personality disorders, Dorpat pointed out, "The narcissistic transference object (or selfobject) serves as a substitute for the patient's missing or defective psychic structures. In analysis and in their everyday life, such patients seek selfobjects to carry out functions (guiding, controlling, comforting) that persons with more differentiated ego and superego structures are capable of doing for themselves" (1981, p. 162).

In early development, preoedipal caregivers serve as selfobjects, specifically to perform psychological functions "such as tension management and self-esteem regulation that the infant is unable to perform for himself" (Glassman, 1988, p. 601). This developmental principle underlies the clinical transferential phenomenon of the uneasy dependence of the narcissistic patient on the psychotherapist for self-esteem regulation and the stabilization of narcissistic equilibrium (Bleiberg, 1987), thus promoting the clinician's critical role as an "auxilliary superego" (Strachey, 1934). Self object functions are specifically and exclusively unconscious, nonverbal affect regulatory functions that stabilize self-structure against the hyperstimulated-explosive fragmenting or hypostimulated-implosive depleting potential of stressful levels of stimulation and affect. An effective structural superego system to autoregulate mood and narcissistic affects, which is required for self-esteem homeostasis and for restoration and recovery of narcissistic equilibrium subsequent to affective stress and narcissistic injury, never ontogenetically evolves. Kernberg (1984) and Tyson and Tyson (1984) emphasized the clinical observation that superego pathology plays a central role in narcissistic disturbances.

The essential psychological lesion in these individuals (as well as in borderline personalities who also manifest a heightened vulnerability to shame and a failure to self regulate emotional experience; Grotstein, 1990) is that they do not have the capacity to tolerate or recover from narcissistic injuries that expose distressing negative affect, especially hyperaroused affects like narcissistic rage and hypoaroused shame, while maintaining constructive engagement with others. The coping ability to affectively reconnect with an emotionally significant other after a shame-stress separation, and indeed to use the other to recover from shame associated narcissistic injury and object loss, has never effectively developed in this personality structure due to its early practicing experiences. Narcissistic disorders are thus disorders of the regulation of narcissistic affect, especially shame, the central affective experience of narcissism (Broucek, 1982; Kinston, 1983; Morrison, 1989), and their pathology is most observable during times of stress of narcissistic affect. Self-regulatory failure has recently been proposed to be responsible for the "affectomotor lability" of narcissistic disorders (Rinsley, 1989).

Despite this inefficient capacity to autoregulate distress, during periods of stress, when it may be more adaptive to communicate one's disorganized affective state to a significant other, such individuals emotionally withdraw from object relations in order to protect against the unconsciously anticipated painful exposure of shame-humiliation. Shame-prone narcissistic personalities are known to suffer from narcissistic injury-triggered, overwhelming, internal self-shaming tendencies (Morrison, 1984) and repetitive oscillations of self-esteem, which necessitate "endless attempts at repair" (Reich, 1960). Bursten noted "The task of the narcissistic repair mechanism is to be rid of shame" (1973, p. 294), an affect state that "tends to linger for quite a long time until the subject recovers" (Nathanson, 1987, p. 26), and which "spreads out from one specific content . . . to all of inner reality and hence to the entire function of expressing oneself" (Wurmser, 1981, p. 272). When a narcissistically undesirable trait is suddenly exposed (to the self and/or the other), an uncontrolled escalating shame reaction occurs, and there is no adequate affect-regulating mechanism for the personality to use to modulate or recover from this painful affective state. Without a system to actively cope with and thereby tolerate this potent affect, the immature, undeveloped, archaic superego avoids risk experiences that are potential points of shameful self-exposure, thereby diminishing the expansion and the province of the ego ideal.

THE EMERGENCE OF EGO IDEAL REGULATION OF NARCISSISTIC AFFECT

Under optimal growth conditions a developmental transformation of narcissism occurs: The omnipotence and grandiosity of the psychic system of primary narcissism, the ideal ego, is diminished in the narcissistic crisis, giving way to the dominant emergence of the system of secondary narcissism, the nascent ego ideal. The ego ideal has been conceptualized to have its origins in the early introjection of the idealized loved and loving omnipotent mother (if the child has had such an experience). As a result of this internalization, "internal regulation of self-esteem becomes possible for the first time" (Parkin, 1985, p. 147). The function of the ego ideal, a system by which the self measures itself, is in general similar to other self-regulatory systems that modulate the internal milieu and stabilize the relationship between the organism and the internal enviornment. However, in particular it acts to autoregulate narcissistic affects that underlie self-esteem, thereby sustaining autonomous emotional control, especially in response to social-environmental induced affective stress.

Blos (1974) characterized the ego ideal as a controlling agency that regulates maintenance of self-esteem and narcissistic balance. "Fulfillment of the ideal results in an increase of self-esteem, while a failure to meet the standards of the ideal [shame] results in a decrease in self-esteem" (Turiell, 1967). Self-esteem has been conceptualized as an "affective picture of the self," with high self-esteem connoting a predominance of positive affects and low self-esteem connoting a predominance of negative ones (Pulver, 1970). Stolorow and Lachmann defined *narcissism* functionally: "Mental activity is narcissistic to the degree that its function is to maintain the structural cohesion, temporal stability and positive affective coloring of the self representation" (1980, p. 10). The maintainence of narcissistic equilibrium, a functional role of the superego (Tyson & Tyson, 1984), is manifest in the ego ideal regulation of narcissistic affect that underlies self-esteem. Self-esteem regulation has been identified as a function of the superego system (Josephs, 1989; Kernberg, 1984), and Nathanson (1987) described the superego as functionally capable of processing "minute gradations of self esteem." Pulver (1970) noted that the maintainance of self-esteem is the personality's best protection against narcissistic vulnerability and shame propensity. The functioning of the ego ideal is thus intimately tied into the ego mechanism of episodic memory, which stores events that have meaning for the concept of self and are significant for the maintenance of self-esteem (Tulving, 1972).

The ego ideal, which originates at the end of the practicing period, allows for a successful transition through the rapprochement crisis via its mediation in the efficient regulation of high and low arousal states. Brickman noted, "The evolution of a properly functioning superego system may be seen to be contingent on the successful resolution of developmental . . . issues" (1983, p. 90), and Grotstein (1983) referred to the critical importance of the establishment of a particular internal object to the function of the superego/ego ideal. The work presented here specifically outlines the importance of shame in the genesis of the evolving superego. Notice a psychological function (affect regulation) that is externally regulated in one phase is internalized and autoregulated in the succeeding phase. The ego ideal, a narcissistic component of the superego along with the conscience (Hartmann & Lowenstein, 1962), contains grandiose fantasies and ideals and a "core of narcissistic omnipotence (which) . . . represents the sum of the positive identifications with the parental images" (Piers & Singer, 1953, p. 14). These latter authors also theorized that it contains the goals of striving for mastery, or a "maturation drive," which "would signify a psychic representation of all the growth, maturation, and individuation processes in the human being" (p. 15).

Shame, which is associated with a "narcissistic depletion within the self-structure" (Spero, 1984, p. 264), and is an affective component of low self-esteem (Josephs, 1989), has been commonly conceptualized in the psychoanalytic literature as the affect that arises when a self-monitoring and self-evaluating process concludes that there has been a failure to live up to ego ideal images (Piers & Singer, 1953). From a sociological viewpoint, Scheff (1988) pointed out that this affect, the primary social emotion, though it is usually almost invisible, is generated by the virtually constant monitoring of the self in relation to others. Shame is typically triggered by incompetence (White, 1960) and the concomitant threat of abandonment or rejection by the "significant object" (Levin, 1967), and is thus the affective response to the self's failure to approximate its ideal state of maximized positive and minimized negative narcissistic affect when contrasted to the current level of the actual state.

The ontogenetic origin of shame similarly involves an appraisal process in which a discrepancy exists between the memory of the caregiver in an ideal, attuned, positive affective state and the perception of the reality of a misattuned mother in a negative affective state. Though the developmental origin of the negative evaluation of the self that produces shame arises from the interpersonal failure of expectation (excited anticipation), shame later occurs when certain intrapersonal self-expectations (goals), the predominantly unconscious standards of the ego ideal, are not fulfilled. The central role of the self-monitoring ego ideal to the understanding of shame has been stressed by Morrison (1989).

Due to its intrinsically nonverbal nature, the subjective experience of shame is ineffable. Despite this various authors have attempted to describe the phenomology of the moment of shame. This ubiquitous primary social emotion in which one is visible and not ready to be visible (Erikson, 1950) operates subtly in even the healthiest of human interactions (Kaufman, 1974). This misattuned relational transaction triggers gaze aversion (Tomkins, 1963), a response of hiding the face "to escape from this being seen or from the one who sees" (Wright, 1991, p. 30), and a state of withdrawal (Lichtenberg, 1989). Under the lens of a "shame microscope" which amplifies and expands this negative affect (Malatesta-Magai, 1991), visible defects, narcissistically charged undesirable aspects of the self, are exposed (Jacobson, 1964). "It is as though something we were hiding from everyone is suddenly under a burning light in public view" (Izard, 1991, p. 332). Shame throws a "flooding light" upon the individual (Lynd, 1958), who then experiences "a sense of displeasure plus the compelling desire to disappear from view" (Frijda, 1988, p. 351), and "an impulse to bury one's face, or to sink, right then and there, into the ground" (Erikson, 1950, p. 223) which impels him to "crawl through a hole" and culminates in feeling as if he "could die" (H. B. Lewis, 1971, p. 198).

The sudden shock-induced deflation of positive affect which supports grandiose omnipotence has been phenomenologically characterized as a whirlpool — a visual representation of a spiral (Potter-Effron, 1989) and as a "flowing off" or "leakage" through a drain hole in the middle of one's being (Sarte, 1957, p. 256). The individual's subjective conscious experience of this affect is thus a sudden, unexpected, and rapid transition from what Freud (1914/1957b) called "primary narcissism" — a sense of being "the center and core of the universe," to what Sarte (1957) described as a shame triggered "crack in my universe."

Furthermore, the unique potency of this bodily-based negative affect has been described by Tomkins (1963):

> Though terror speaks of life and death and distress makes of the world a vale of tears, yet shame strikes deepest into the heart of man. While terror and distress hurt, they are wounds inflicted from outside which penetrate the smooth surface of the ego; but shame is felt as an inner torment, a sickness of the soul. It does not matter whether the humiliated one has been shamed by derisive laughter or whether he mocks himself. In either event he feels himself naked, defeated, alienated, lacking in dignity or worth. (p. 118)

Broucek (1982) argued that shame is the basic affective experience of mental unpleasure and pain associated with disturbances of narcissism, and Amsterdam and Leavitt (1980) equated it with painful, heightened self-consciousness. Campos and his colleagues (1983) posited that it results from injury to any salient aspect of one's self-concept, Kohut (1977) spoke of "narcissistic injury," and Lynd described this affect as "a peculiarly painful feeling of being in a situation that incurs the scorn or contempt of others" (1958, p. 24). Shame stress, a social "microstressor" of daily living, like physical injury and pain, activates a classical stress response; the physiological expression of physical and mental pain is thus identical. Work on brain opioids and social emotions suggests that visceral pain and the affective response to social isolation share common evolutionary histories and neurochemical substrates (Panksepp, Siviy, & Normansell, 1985). Affect tolerance, which allows for the conscious experience of emotions, was proposed by Krystal (1988) to be analogous to the capacity to bear pain. Parkin (1985) equated the mental pain of disorders of narcissism with shame. Blos (1974) characterized a major function of the ego ideal to be repair of narcissistic injuries produced by comparison with or slights by others, thus underscoring the recovery function of this autoregulatory agency.

Notice that the earliest-evolving component of the internal-monitoring superego system is the autoregulatory ego ideal. This dovetails nicely with Brickman's formulation that "the origins of the superego may be traced to the earliest attempts of the child to differentiate himself from his environment" (1983, p. 83). The earlier origin of the ego ideal component before the conscience component of the superego has been posited by others as well (e.g., Anthony, 1981; Parkin, 1985). Further support for this was seen in Kagan's developmental study of preverbal 2-year-olds in which he concluded, "The appearance of internal standards is not a late development that occurs after the child learns to fear adult punishment, but is present early in ontogeny. These first standards are concerned with task competence" (1979, p. 1053). Note that these internal standards are preverbal, supporting the concept that the preverbal ego ideal forms before the verbal conscience. Early superego function is first manifested at 18 months (the practicing/rapprochement boundary), when toddlers begin to exhibit "moral" prosocial behavior in the form of approaching persons in distress and initiating positive, other-oriented, affective, and instrumental activities in order to comfort the other (Radke-Yarrow & Zahn-Waxler, 1984).

Although the content of the ego ideal is modified throughout development (aspirations are altered and what triggers shame changes), its homeostatic function of narcissistic affect regulation in infancy, childhood, adolescence, and adulthood is not. Related to this is the problem of the distinction between a system's functional onset as a "primitive ego ideal" and its attainment of a "definitive structure" as a "mature ego ideal" (Blos, 1974). Although ego ideal content (i.e., self-representations and images in episodic memory) may not reflect complex identifications and "definitive organization" until adolescence (Blos, 1974), the basic mechanism underlying its functional onset and therefore its origin traces directly back to the early separation individuation period. Indeed, Blos dated the origin of the infantile ego ideal at the age of attainment of object constancy, 18 months; this coincides with the rapprochement crisis genesis outlined earlier. Spiegel (1966) pointed out that the function of the primordial ego ideal is the "dampening of extreme affects" and is associated with "the early appearance of shame." The necessity for a psychic structural system to autoregulate affect, shame, and self-esteem is required from toddlerhood through adulthood, and its existence and availability depends on early object-relations experiences in the practicing-critical period.

The self-regulatory ego ideal, a stress-sensitive coping system involved in the modulation of affects by "toning down" intense "all good" (positive hedonic tone) or "all bad" (negative hedonic tone) affective dispositions (Garza-Guerrero, 1981), (modulates "splitting defenses") is here proposed to be an affect-regulatory system that monitors, adjusts, and corrects emotional responses, thereby providing flexibility and unity in socioemotional function. The superego system here described is equivalent to Fox and Davidson's (1984) negative affect regulating system that first appears in the middle of the second year. The ego ideal shame regulator is composed of two components that control the biphasic process of narcissistic affect regulation. The functional operation of this structural system is relevant to the process by which shame plays a central role in maintaining narcissistic equilibrium (Kohut, 1971). The shame stimulator component acutely reduces hyperaroused and hyperstimulated states; diminishes positive narcissisitic affective coloring of self-representations; contracts the self; lowers expectations; decreases self-esteem, active coping, interest, and curiosity; interferes with cognition; and increases overt consciously experienced shame, parasympathetic supported passive coping, blushing, gaze aversion, and depressive affect-toned mood.

The second component, the shame modulator, reduces consciously experienced shame (narcissistic pain), negative affective self-representations, low-keyed depressive states, and passive coping, and initiates recovery of sympathetic-supported positive hedonic-toned mood and narcissistic affect, facilitation of the cathexis of the self-representation, expansion of the self, increased self-esteem, and active stress-coping capacities. This dual-component, dual-process system thus homeostatically reestablishes an optimal sympathetic-parasympathetic limbic balance of autonomic-affective functioning, (autonomic balance underlying an optimal level of emotionality), thereby maintaining self-identity and self-continuity in the face of continuously changing external environmental conditions.

The bulk of contemporary psychoanalytic developmental theory (Emde, 1989; Loewald, 1978; Pine, 1985; Stern, 1985) and research (Lichtenberg, 1983) strongly suggests that the infant's early object relations with the mother are indispensable to the development and organization of psychic structure responsible for self-regulation and adaptation. Studies in developmental neuroscience reveal that the stupendous accelerated growth of brain structure in infancy is critically influenced by "social forces" (Lecours, 1982), and it has been suggested that the neurodevlopmental processes that are responsible for postnatal structural brain growth are influenced by events at the interpersonal and intrapersonal levels (Scheflen, 1981). The critical nature of early socioemotional experiences may lie in their effects of enhancing or inhibiting the maturation of adaptive self-regulating systems, especially limbic and cortical structures that anatomically and physiologically mature during particular periods of infancy, and the subsequent socioemotional functions that these structures will subserve.

Utilizing a neuropsychoanalytic perspective, it is suggested that the psychoanalytic ego ideal can be identified as an affect-regulatory structure with the orbital prefrontal cortex. This cortical inhibitory system is expanded in the right hemisphere and has extensive limbic connections; regulates emotion (Jouandet & Gazzaniga, 1979), attachment behavior (Steklis & Kling, 1985), and aggression (DeBruin, van Oyen, & VandePoll, 1983); and influences parasympathetic and sympathetic autonomic function (Fuster, 1980). The rapid growth and development of this prefrontal system during the first 18 months of is critically influenced by early "social contact" (Luria, 1980), and its maturation enables the self-modulation of arousal in late infancy (Bowden, Goldman, Rosvold, & Greenstreet, 1971). During the practicing critical period, shame experiences associated with the socialization process specifically influence the maturation of this superego affect-regulatory system.

SUPEREGO FUNCTION IN MOOD REGULATION
AND FURTHER THEORETICAL CONSIDERATIONS

Pine stated, "The awareness of separateness . . . culminates in the rapprochement stage, in sadness or depressive mood" (1980, p. 227). Noting the transition from the "good mood" of the practicing period to the lingering depressive mood of rapprochement, McDevitt asserted, "Thoughts and feelings persist beyond the situation in which they had their origin. Conflicts with the mother no longer simply flare up and disappear; they appear to continue in the child's mind for longer periods of time" (1975, p. 728). Mahler observed, "A basic mood is established during the separation-individuation process. . . . The characteristic baseline of the child's emotional responsiveness seems to derive from the preponderance and perpetuation of one or the other of the subphases of the separation-individuation process" (1979, p. 156).

The onset of superego (ego ideal) autoregulatory functions at the end of the practicing period that enables the successful resolution of the rapprochement crisis in which there is a transformation of mood states fits well with Jacobson's (1964) conceptualization of the superego as an affect-regulatory system, a mood (defined as a general enduring highly persistent state of affect) regulator:

> I have stated that the centralised, regulating power of the superego can modify the course of the self- and object-directed discharge processes in a generalized way. But generalized modifications of all discharge patterns lend our thoughts, actions, and above all our feelings a characteristic color which finds expression in what we call our mood. Thus the superego also becomes a governing force for our moods and keeps them at a comparatively even level. This is why any pathology and deficiency of the superego functions will manifest itself in conspicuous disturbances of the mood level. (p. 133)

Kernberg (1984) postulated that the mature superego exerts functional control by modulating mood swings. The function of the internal monitoring superego system, originally proposed by Freud to regulate drive (hyperstimulated aggression and sexuality), later described by Jacobson (1964) as an autonomous central system for the regulation of libidinal and aggressive cathexes of self-representations, is fundamentally to regulate affect.

The hallmark of a developmentally and functionally evolved superego, which is often too narrowly defined in terms of cognitive and verbal aspects of conscience, is reflected in mood stability and a relatively rapid recovery from disruptive emotional distress states to positively toned emotional states. On the other hand, a developmentally and functionally immature superego, especially under narcissistic stress, would manifest a tendency to easily slip from a positive or neutral state into a negative emotional state. These negative emotional states endure well beyond the precipitating stimulus event as a lingering dysphoric mood.

This conceptualization fits well with Wallace's (1963) clinical observation that shame-prone individuals have undeveloped or partially developed superegos, and Freud's concept, presented in the *Ego and the Id* (1923/1961b), that psychiatric disturbances reflect a malfunctioning superego. Structural defects in the undeveloped superego are particularly exposed under high pressure. Superego lacunae (Aldrich, 1987) and the failure of internal controls to regulate internal aggressive impulses will form in response to intense, unmodulated stress states. Superego dysfunction is thus manifest in impaired affect regulation as found, for example, in affective disturbances (Giovacchini, 1979) and mood disorders, as well as in self-esteem pathology as found in narcissistic and border-line patients. Eisnitz noted, "Rapid shifts in self-esteem may be an indicator of superego function dominated by highly aggressivized and libidinized energy" (1988, p. 156).

I suggest that this symptomatology reflects an unevolved, inefficient ego ideal shame regulator that is unable to modulate these hyperenergetic states. Furthermore, I agree with Kernberg's assertion that a lack of superego integration is diagnostic of narcissistic and borderline personality organizations, and with his clinical postulate that as a "criterion for the indication or contraindication of long-term, intensive psychotherapy . . . the quality of object relations and the quality of superego functioning are probably the two most important prognostic criteria" (1984, p. 21). However, the focus should be shifted from the later-forming conscience component and guilt to the developmentally earlier ego ideal and its associated superego affect, shame.

The essential psychological (and biochemical) lesions of disorders of affective functioning are found in structurally unevolved, physiologically altered, inefficient prefrontal regulatory systems that impair active recovery processes. Self-regulatory failure has been proposed to be responsible for the pathological "affectomotor lability" of narcissistic disorders (Rinsley, 1989), and to be the proximal cause of depressive disorders (Morris, 1989; Pyszcznski & Greenberg, 1987). Patients with cyclothymic and dysthymic affective pathology recover more slowly from negative life events than do normals (Goplerud & Depue, 1985). These regulatory impairments are manifest very early in specific vulnerable critical periods. For example, a generalized disturbance in affect regulation, as reflected in long-enduring negative affective states, which is identifiable at 12 months and increases to prominence by 18 months (the span of the practicing period), has been found in infants of manic-depressive parents (Gaensbauer Harmon, Cytryn, & McKnew, 1984).

With the practicing-rapprochement transition, a period in which attachment ties with the mother are loosened (Galenson & Roiphe, 1976) yet attachment intensity to the father is significantly increased (Abelin, 1971), the practicing subphase-specific, obligatory, and dominant mood of elation is supplanted by the subphase-specific mood of rapprochement, soberness, and even temporary depression. Notice the typical high-arousal affect of the "elated" practicing subphase versus the low-arousal, "depressed" affect of the rapprochement phase. At reunion, the practicing caregiver is predominantly regulating an elated junior toddler; the rapprochement caregivers are generally regulating a senior toddler who is in a very different mood state, low energy, and deflated. Again, it should be remembered that emotional distress can take the form of hyperaroused or hypoaroused affects. The "affective climate" of the two subphases is qualitatively very different, both in terms of the predominant affective valence and in terms of the tempo (arousal level) of the predominant emotional state. Practicing elation, characterized as positive/active, is supplanted by rapprochement depression, which is negative/passive.

"Nameless shame" (Kohut, 1977), which originates in the sensorimotor nonverbal practicing period, and the ego ideal component of the superego are both operative at this transitional point in development. However, guilt, which first emerges in the verbal child, and the conscience component, which relies on the internalization of verbal, moral values and parental standards, do not first appear until the end of rapprochement/beginning of the phallic stage (i.e., Mahler's fourth subphase and Piaget's first stage of preoperational representations; Izard, 1978; Pine, 1980; Sroufe, 1979). This dual model of superego onset and function fits well with Miller's (1989) division of an early-appearing developmental line associated with shame from a later-emerging affect line associated with guilt, and with Krystal's (1978) differentiation of two lines of emotional development, an infantile nonverbal affect system and a verbal adult system; he specifically cited guilt as an "adult type of affect."

Similarly, in the neuroscience literature, Gazzaniga (1985) postulated the existence of two affect-mediating systems, a basic primitive system and a verbal-conceptual system, that are localized in separate hemispheres. Neuropsychological research with very young children has indicated early autonomous affective as well as cognitive functioning of the two hemispheres. I propose that the earlier development of nonverbal shame and the ego ideal before verbal guilt and conscience reflects the known biologically determined earlier differentiation and functional onset of the nonverbal visuospatial-holistic right hemisphere (Geschwind & Galaburda, 1987; Giannitrapani, 1967; Whitaker, 1978) and the later maturation of the linguistic-rational capacity of the verbal analytic left hemisphere (Miller, 1986; Taylor, 1969). Indeed, a developmental neuropsychological study (Rothbart, Taylor, & Tucker, 1989) of practicing infants has revealed that right, but not left, hemispheric specialization for emotions begins at the end of the first year, with greater right hemispheric cortical inhibition of subcortical emotional processes. In contrast, Thatcher, Walker, and Giudice (1987) showed that the left hemisphere growth spurt does not begin until age 2.

In addition, an impressive volume of research on hemispheric lateralization of emotions reveals the existence of dual affective systems, a right hemisphere system dominant for nonverbal mood and affect, and a left hemisphere system involved in verbally mediated affective and mood states (Silberman & Weingartner, 1986). The function of these two systems may be reflected in the processing of unconscious and conscious affective information, respectively. In adults, the right hemisphere is known to be "predominant in the experience, expression and discrimination of emotion and . . . differentially important for the regulation of arousal" (Levy, Heller, Banich, & Burton, 1983, p. 332), preferentially activated under stress conditions (Tucker, Roth, Arneson, & Buckingman, 1977), responsible for maintaining important controls over autonomic activities (Heilman, Schwartz, & Watson, 1977), and to be particularly well connected with subcortical processes (Tucker, 1981). Joseph concluded, "Right hemispheric involvement with emotional functioning is due to greater abundance of reciprocal interconnections with the limbic system" (1982, p. 16).

The emergent ego ideal is here conceptualized to be the right hemispheric, dual-component, narcissistic affect-shame regulator that manifests structural organization and functional onset at the end of the practicing period. Ego ideal shame regulation may be pertinent to the dynamic mechanism by which the right hemisphere, which is responsible for primary process functions ascribed to the unconscious (Galin, 1974) and transference phenomena (Watt, 1986), regulates emotional information. The superego components of ego ideal and conscience may thus respectively represent systems of right and left hemispheric affect regulation.

1991

CHAPTER 6

A Century After Freud's Project:
Is a Rapprochement Between
Psychoanalysis and Neurobiology at Hand?

O N APRIL 27, 1895, SIGMUND FREUD wrote his friend Wilhelm Fliess that he was rapidly becoming preoccupied, indeed obsessed, with a problem that had seized his mind. In what would turn out to be a creative spell he was attempting to integrate his extensive knowledge of brain anatomy and physiology with his current experiences in psychology and psychopathology in order to construct a systematic model of the functioning of the human mind in terms of its underlying neurobiological mechanisms. In the preceding month he had completed the final chapter on psychotherapy for *Studies on Hysteria*, and at this point in time, 20 years into his professional career, he had produced over 100 scientific works. Yet in his letter to Fliess he openly admitted that "I am so deeply immersed in the 'Psychology for Neurologists' as to be entirely absorbed until I have to break off, really exhausted by overwork. I have never experienced such intense preoccupation. I wonder if anything will come of it?" (in Jones, 1953, p. 380).

Throughout the summer Freud continued to relay to Fliess messages of both his progress and frustration on the Project, describing his mood as alternately "proud and happy" or "ashamed and miserable." Breuer wrote to Fliess in July 1895, "Freud's intellect is soaring at its highest" (in Sulloway, 1979, p. 114). In September he feverishly began to write it out, and within one month he had filled two notebooks totalling 100 manuscript sheets that he sent to Fliess in early October. In a letter of October 20, commenting on his ambitious attempt to work out the direct links between the operations of the brain and the functions of the mind, he wrote:

> One evening last week when I was hard at work, tormented with just that amount of pain that seems to be the best state to make my brain function, the barriers were suddenly lifted, the veil drawn aside, and I had a clear vision from the details of the neuroses to the conditions that make con-

sciousness possible. Everything seemed to connect up, the whole worked well together, and one had the impression that the Thing was now really a machine and would soon go by itself. . . . Naturally I don't know how to contain myself for pleasure. (in Jones, 1953, p. 382)

The state of elation and excitement would not last. A month later he admitted to Fleiss, "I no longer understand the state of mind in which I hatched out the 'Psychology', and I can't understand how I came to inflict it on you" (in Jones, 1953, p. 383). In fact, he never asked for the return of the manuscript and never wanted to see it again. Fleiss kept it, however, and after Freud's death it was finally published in 1950 under a title devised by Strachey, "Project for a Scientific Psychology."

Despite Freud's repudiation of and disappointment with this work, Strachey characterized the essay as an "extraordinarily ingenious working model of the mind and a piece of neurological machinery" (Freud, 1895/1966, p. xvii). Jones called it "a magnificent tour de force," and concluded that the experience released in Freud, "something vital in him that was soon to become his scientific imagination" (1953, p. 384). Yet Jones also wrote that the Project "imposes more exacting demands on the reader than any of his published work; there must be very few who can apprehend its full meaning with several perusals" (p. 383). More recently, Sulloway asserted that "No other document in the history of psychoanalysis has provoked such a large body of discussion with such a minimum of agreement as Freud's Project" (1976, p. 118). And Gay offered the observation that "the Project, or rather its invisible ghost, haunts the whole series of Freud's theoretical writings to the very end" (1989, p. 87).

What was Freud attempting to accomplish, and why did the seeming possibility of achieving this goal create in him an exhilaration that he was hardly able to contain, yet his failure trigger a quick and apparently irreversible repudiation? What are the contents of this controversial document that appeared at the dawn of psychoanalysis, and how did they influence Freud's subsequent thinking? How did Freud later view the possibility of a rapprochement between neurobiology and psychoanalysis, and why do the issues first broached in the Project critically relate to the current status of psychoanalysis as it enters it second centennium?

At the very outset of this short essay, Freud proclaimed that the essential aim of the Project is to *"furnish a psychology that shall be a natural science"* (in Jones, 1953, p. 295). He then presented, for the first time, a number of new elemental constructs that literally serve as the foundation, the very bedrock of psychoanalytic theory. In this remarkable document Freud introduced the concepts of primary and secondary processes (which Jones called Freud's most fundamental contribution to psychology); the principles of pleasure-unpleasure, constancy, and reality testing; the concepts of cathexis and identification; the theories of psychical regression and hallucination; the systems of perception, memory, and unconscious and preconscious psychic activity; and the wish-fulfillment theory of dreams.

These ideas are very familiar to us, but it should be mentioned that this seminal work also contained Freud's earliest thoughts about the essential nature of two problems that Freud struggled with for the rest of his career, affect and motivation. In Freud's neuropsychological model of a living organism interacting with its environment, energies from the external world impinge on sensory neurons, thereby filling them with a "sum of excitation" or "quota of affect" that is proportional to the impinging energy. It is the fundamental property of each neuron, and therefore of the organism, to rid itself of excitation through a process of discharge. The organism also receives stimulation from within, the primary needs, and these stimuli also give rise to excitations that must be discharged through a motor apparatus. Affect is brought about by a sudden discharge of previously stored excitation. Freud speculated that although affect is initiated by environmental stimulation, it is supported and augmented by the resulting endogenous excitation. An affect can also be precipitated suddenly by the environmental activation of a memory that is charged with an endogenously originating load.

Freud's special interest in the problem of regulation also first appeared in this monograph. The Project, in essence, suggested "a model whereby excitation from various sources arising both from within and from outside the individual might be regulated by processes essentially within the individual" (Sander, 1977, p. 14). Freud posited a close connection between affect and primary process, and asserted that memories capable of generating affect are "tamed" until the affect provides only a "signal." In his later writings Freud never strayed too far from (nor really expanded upon) these basic principles of affect and it regulation. To this date, psychoanalysis has a great need of a comprehensive theory of affect.

The Project also contained the seeds of Freud's "developmental point of view in psychoanalysis" (Sulloway, 1979). Indeed, here Freud gave us his conception of early infancy, one that never changed throughout the rest of his writings. It is the helplessness and distress of the infant, expressed in his/her cries, that causes a change in the outer world—it brings the mother to the child. The fundamental purpose of this is, also, the discharge of inner tension. Furthermore, "This path of discharge thus acquires the highly important secondary function of establishing human contact. . . . " As we are well aware, contemporary developmental research and attachment theory has supplanted Freud's model of a monadic, exclusively drive-reducing infant in favor of a dyadic, object-related, stimulation-seeking infant.

Most importantly, each of these phenomena was described by Freud in a language that was familiar to him, a scientific language of cerebral physiology and physics. And each individual psychic function is presented in the context of an overall attempt to build a comprehensive neuropsychology of brain functioning. In order to construct this model of the brain mechanisms corresponding to processes central to his psychodynamic approach (Segalowitz, 1994), Freud, the skilled scientist and neurologist, had to deduce the existence of certain neurobiological phenomena that were not yet discovered. For example, though he spoke of the essential function of "contact barriers," Sherrington was not to introduce the term *synapse* until 2 years after the Project was finished! And he referred to the critical activity of "secretory neurons" in the brainstem, yet the biogenic amines of the reticular core of the brain were not discovered until well into the 20th century.

If it is true that Freud disavowed the Project, why are we so familiar with the concepts it introduced? Jones provided us with the answer—it is contained in the seventh chapter of Freud's masterwork, *The Interpretation of Dreams*. On February 13, 1896, Freud wrote Fleiss that he had revised the Project and formally renamed it "metapsychology." This was the same year that he would use the term *psychoanalysis* for the first time. In his essay "On the history of the psycho-analytic movement," Freud stated that *The Interpretation of Dreams*, though published in 1900, "was finished in all essentials at the beginning of 1896" (1914/1957c, p. 22). Here, in the work that Freud publicly declared to be "the starting point of a new and deeper science of the mind," Jones noted that "Freud employed a working model of the mind very similar to the one he had in the Project and also a good many of the same fundamental conceptions, *but the physiological terminology has almost entirely disappeared*" (1953, p. 395; italics added).

In other words, every major psychoanalytic concept introduced by Freud in the Project was originally accompanied by a model of its underlying mechanism. He initially formulated these mechanisms on the basis of his biological and neurological knowledge. He then chose to keep the mechanisms intact, but leave their neurobiological foundations implicit: "But deprived of their roots and explicitness, the mechanisms became isolated from contemporary developments in science" (Pribram & Gill, 1976, p. 10).

Freud's disavowal of the Project occurred at the moment of birth of psychoanalysis. It should be remembered that "At the turn of the century neuroscience had very little to offer dynamic psychology as it was attempting to localize psychological processes in discrete cortical regions" (Solms & Saling, 1986, p. 411), a position Freud had earlier rejected in *On Aphasia*. His ambivalence about the importance of achieving an overarching integration among psychoanalysis, psychology, and neurobiology was echoed throughout his later writings. In *The Interpretation of Dreams*, he proclaimed: "I shall entirely disregard the fact that the mental apparatus with which we are here concerned is also known to us in the form of an anatomical preparation, and I shall carefully avoid the temptation to determine the psychological locality in any anatomical fashion. I shall remain on psychological ground" (1900/1953, p. 536).

In 1916, in *Introductory Lectures on Psychoanalysis*, he asserted, "Psychoanalysis must keep itself free from any hypothesis that is alien to it, whether of an anatomical, chemical or physiological kind, and must operate entirely with purely psychological auxilliary ideas; and for that very reason, I fear, it will seem strange to you to begin with" (1917/1961 & 1963, p. 21).

Yet at about this same time, in *The Claims of Psycho-Analysis to Scientific Interest*, Freud (1913/1958c) stated:

> We have found it necessary to hold aloof from biological considerations during our psycho-analytic work and to refrain from using them for heuristic purposes, so that we may not be misled in our impartial judgement of the psycho-analytic facts before us. But after we have completed our psycho-analytic work *we shall have to find a point of contact with biology*; and we may rightly feel glad if that contact is already assured at one important point or another. (pp. 181–182; italics added)

How has the Project been viewed more recently? McCarley and Hobson (1977) argued that this work represents the source pool from which Freud developed the major concepts of his psychoanalytic model, and Gay declared that it "contains within itself the nucleus of a great part of Freud's later theories" (1989, p. 87). In the opinion of Solomon, "What Freud attempted in the 'Project' was monumental effort, an attempt to overcome the dualism that plagued and still plagues psychology and neurology" (1974, p. 39). According to Sulloway, author of *Freud, Biologist of the Mind*, Freud "never abandoned the assumption that psychoanalysis would someday come to terms with the neurophysiological side of mental activity" (1979, p. 131). Sulloway pointed out that the Project is rather modern in its interdisciplinary approach—it is not reductionistic, but rather "combines clinical insights and data, Freud's most fundamental psychophysicalistic assumptions, certain undeniably mechanical and neuroanatomical constructs, and a number of organic, evolutionary, and biological ideas—into one remarkably well-integrated psychobiological system" (1979, p. 123). More recently, Hofer, whose work has integrated psychobiology with psychoanalysis, concluded that the Project "anticipated the development of new scientific fields to a degree that gives it an air of uncanny prescience when read today" (1990, p. 56).

In perhaps the most comprehensive analysis of the Project, the psychoanalyst Gill, in collaboration in collaboration with the neuroscientist Pribram, suggested in *Freud's Project Reassessed* that "its importance lies in the fact that it contains explicit formulations and definitions of many central concepts and terms of psychoanalytic theory known as metapsychology, concepts and terms that Freud continued to use throughout his life but never again defined as explicitly and comprehensively" (1976, p. 5). These authors argued that the concrete neurobiological hypotheses in the Project are subject to testing and modification in light of new findings and alternate conceptualizations. In other words, the obscure concepts of psychoanalytic metapsychology, especially Freud's germinal hypotheses concerning the regulatory structures and dynamics that underlie the mechanisms of affect, motivation, attention, and consciousness, may be illuminated by modern neurobiology. Furthermore, they contended that Freud felt "that ultimately this psychoanalytic science could be rejoined to its biochemical and neurological origins, but that a) *the time was not right* and b) this rejoining would not be a simplistic 'taking over' or 'reductive explanation' of psychoanalytic knowledge in biochemical or neurophysiological terms" (p. 168; italics added).

THE CURRENT SITUATION

Can a rapprochement between psychoanalysis and neurobiology be at hand? Let me state straight out that to my mind, *the time is right*. Psychoanalysis, described as being in a state of "vibrant ferment" (Wilson, 1995), is perhaps more than ever ready for this rapprochement, the possibility of which poses it an essential challenge. The central core of its model of the mind, almost unchanged for most of its first century, is now undergoing a period of rapid transformation. The scaffolding of clinical psychoanalysis is supported by underlying theoretical conceptions of psychic development and structure, and it is these basic concepts that are now being reformulated, largely as a result of the vital contributions made by contemporary developmental psychoanalysis.

I will argue that the "point of contact with biology" that Freud referred to is be found specifically in the central role of right brain psychobiological processes in the organization and regulation of affect, motivation, and unconscious cognition. Although psychoanalysis has reworked many of Freud's initial conceptualizations, it is only now beginning to reevaluate Freud's original model of emotion. Moreover, an ever-increasing number of theoreticians and clinicians are now converging on the fundamental significance of affect regulation to both intrapsychic and interpersonal functioning. Indeed, "Affect theory is increasingly recognized as the most likely candidate to bridge the gap between clinical theory and general theory in psychoanalysis" (Spezzano, 1993, p. 39).

Even as psychoanalytic theory undergoes profound changes, a host of borderling disciplines, now freed from the narrow behavioral model that dominated psychology in much of this century, are actively probing questions about the internal processes of mind, questions that for too long were deemed to be outside the realm of "scientific" analysis and were addressed only by psychoanalysis. In *Affect Regulation and the Origin of the Self* (Schore, 1994), I documented how researchers from a spectrum of sciences—from developmental, cognitive, physiological, and social psychology to sociobiology and behavioral neurology—are studying the covert yet essential mechanisms (especially those involving the role of emotional states) that underlie overt behaviors.

More specifically, psychobiologists are detailing the neurochemical mechanisms that mediate affective functions, while psychophysiologists are now systematically investigating the bidirectional transduction of psychological and physiological processes that underlie mind-body relations. And neurobiologists are elucidating the operations of the brain systems involved in the processing of emotional information, especially the limbic and cortical circuits that mediate affect and its regulation. Advances in the new fields of "affective neuroscience" (Panksepp, 1991) and "social neuroscience" (Cacioppo & Berntson, 1992), in conjunction with data from the more established area of "cognitive neuroscience" (Gazzaniga, 1995), are giving us a more detailed picture of the brain structural systems that mediate the psychological and especially the emotional phenomena that Freud began to describe in the Project.

This work is providing important clues to the identification of psychic structure—psychoanalytic models of internal structural systems should not be reduced to neurobiology, but they should be compatible with current knowledge of brain structure. This means that "psychic structure" needs to be defined in terms of what is currently known about biological structure as it exists in nature. Workers pioneering at the interface of psychoanalysis and neuroscience are offering valuable contributions to this revitalization (Hadley, 1989; Levin, 1991; Miller, 1991; Reiser, 1985; Schwartz, 1992). Further, Cooper argued that "neurobiology can help us to understand which of our concepts are unlikely and which are congruent with biologic experimentation" (1985, p. 1402). This brings psychology and along with it psychoanalysis back to biology, and emphasizes the importance of neuroscience. The integration of neurobiological with psychological perspectives, of structure-function relationships, Freud's starting point in the Project, is absolutely essential to future advances in contemporary psychoanalysis, whose focus of primary study was described by Langs and Badalamenti (1992) as "human emotional development and functioning." Indeed, Modell (1993), Gedo (1991), Lichtenberg (1989), and others are turning to neuroscience to identify the components and dynamic properties of psychic structures.

Let me return now to where we began, to the issues first raised in the Project. In their book, Pribram and Gill contended that "The 'Project' is specific in detail as to how the neural structures that *regulate* behavior—i.e. the organism's motivational structures—come to be" (1976, p. 48). If Freud's metapsychological theories of psychic structure are inadequate or elementary, then what can modern neurobiology tell us about the anatomical nature and functional properties of the brain systems that regulate the intrapsychic mechanisms that mediate adaptive psychological—especially emotional, motivational, and social—functioning?

It has been known for some time that the sides of the frontal lobes between the hemispheres and the pathways between and just under the hemispheres that connect the cortex with the subcortical drive and affective integrative centers subserve unique roles in emotional processes. The work of Aleksandr Luria, perhaps the most important clinical neuropsychologist of the 20th century, clearly demonstrated that the orbital prefrontal cortex acts as the essential cortical system that adaptively modulates lower structures, inhibits drive, and regulates arousal and activity states. Luria extensively documented neurological disturbances of the orbital frontal regions that elicit gross changes in affective processes in the form of lack of self control, emotional outbursts, generalized disinhibition, and disorganization of personality. (It is interesting to note that Luria was influenced by Freud in his youth. During the 1920s, he established a Russian psychoanalytic society and translated Freud's work into Russian.)

In fact, due to the link between impaired prefrontal activity and dysregulated states, at mid-20th century the ablation of the orbital regions was utilized by psychiatry to treat untractable severe psychiatric disorders. Indeed, the sectioning of the pathways between this cortex and the subcortex defines the lobotomy procedure (Hofstatter, Smolik, & Busch, 1945). The disciplined study of lobotomized patients represented an opportunity to learn which functions are associated with this system and, in fact, a small number of psychoanalytic studies of these patients were performed. Ostow (1954) reported that these individuals lacked a depth of personality, and presented with a loss of the ability to create derivatives of instinctual drives, to fantasize and process unconscious wish fantasies, and to maintain a fully affective consciousness of self. Earlier, Frank (1950) observed that patients with sectioned orbital cortices showed impairments in the preconscious functions of internalization and symbolic elaboration, and concluded that a loss of orbitofrontal activity leads to an "emotional asymbolia." It is important to point out during the time period of these studies, the 1950s, the first extensive anatomical studies of the orbitofrontal regions were reported. (Much of this early work was done by Pribram, who wrote works not only with Gill but also with Luria, a fellow pioneer of modern neuroscience.)

It is only within the 1990s that experimental studies began to provide more detailed anatomical and functional information about this relatively unexplored area of the brain. The orbital frontal cortex (so called because of its relation to the orbit of the eye) is "hidden" in the ventral and medial surfaces of the prefrontal lobe (Price, Carmichael, & Drevets, 1996). In addition to receiving multimodal input from the limbic thalamus and all sensory areas of the posterior cortex and relaying to the motor areas in the anterior cortex, this cortical system uniquely projects extensive pathways to other limbic structures in the temporal pole and amygdala, to subcortical drive centers in the hypothalamus, to arousal and reward centers in the midbrain, and to vagal nuclei and autonomic centers in the medulla oblongata. These connections with both the cortex and subcortex allow it to act as a "convergence zone," one of the few brain regions that is "privy to signals about virtually any activity taking place in our beings' mind or body at any given time" (Damasio, 1994, p. 181). But the system is also is responsive to events in the external environment, especially the social environment. Studies demonstrate that orbitofrontal neurons fire in response to the emotional expressions of the human face (Thorpe, Rolls, & Maddison, 1983), and that this structure is functionally involved in attachment processes and in the pleasurable qualities of social interaction (Steklis & Kling, 1985).

The orbital prefrontal area is situated at the hierarchical apex of the limbic system, the brain system responsible for the rewarding-excitatory and aversive-inhibitory aspects of emotion. It also functions as a major center of central nervous system (CNS) control over the energy-mobilizing sympathetic and energy-conserving parasympathetic components of the autonomic nervous system (ANS) that are involved in emotional behavior. In addition to eliciting alterations in biogenic amines in the reticular formation, its stimulation brings about changes in neurohormonal levels in the hypothalamus, pituitary, and adrenals. The brain and body state changes produced by these biochemical activities are phenomenologically experienced as the onset of an emotion. Most significantly, in the cortex, *the orbitofrontal region is uniquely involved in social and emotional behaviors, and in the homeostatic regulation of body and motivational states* (Schore, 1994, 1996).

Its position at the interface of higher and lower brain structures enables the orbital system to play an essential adaptive role. At the orbitofrontal level cortically processed information concerning the external environment (e.g., visual and auditory stimuli emanating from the emotional face of the object) is integrated with subcortically processed information regarding the internal visceral environment (e.g., concurrent changes in the emotional or bodily self state), thereby enabling incoming information about the environment to be associated with motivational and emotional states. Neuroanatomists have described that the function of this system is involved with the internal state of the organism and is "closely tied to the synthesis of object-emotion relationships in a behavioral context" (Pandya & Yeterian, 1990, p. 89).

Orbitofrontal areas also subserve memory and cognitive-emotional interactions and are activated during the mental generation of images of faces. These areas are specialized to participate in the encoding of high-level, psychological representations of other individuals (Brothers & Ring, 1992). This system thus contains the operational capacity to generate an internalized object relation; that is, a self-representation, an object representation, and a linking affect state (Kernberg, 1976), or a representation of interactions that have been generalized (RIGS; Stern, 1985). Similarly, Edelman (1987) described the brain's creation of models of environment, images of a context, that consist of the internal state of the brain as it responds to certain objects and events in the world.

The orbital prefrontal region is especially expanded in the right cortex, the hemisphere that is responsible for regulating homeostasis and modulating physiological state in response to both internal (i.e., visceral) and external (i.e., environmental) feedback. Because the early-maturing (Chiron et al., 1997) and "primitive" right cortical hemisphere (more so than the left) has extensive reciprocal connections with limbic and subcortical regions, it is dominant for the processing, expression, and regulation of emotional information (Joseph, 1988; Porges, Doussard-Roosevelt, & Maiti, 1994). This prefrontal region comes to act in the capacity of an executive control function for the entire right cortex, the hemisphere that modulates affect, nonverbal communication, and unconscious processes.

Most intriguingly, the activity of this "nondominant" hemisphere, and not the later-maturing "dominant" verbal-linguistic left, is instrumental to the capacity of empathic cognition and the perception of the emotional states of other human beings (Voeller, 1986). It contains an affective-configurational representational system, one that encodes self-and-object images unique from the lexical-semantic mode of the left (Watt, 1990). According to Hofer (1984), internal representations of external human interpersonal relationships serve an important intrapsychic role as "biological regulators" that control physiological processes.

The orbitofrontal system, "the thinking part of the emotional brain," (Goleman, 1995) is an essential component of what Langs called "the emotion-processing mind"—"the cognitive mental module that is responsible for human adaptations in the emotional realm" (1996, p. 106). It plays a major role in the internal state of the organism (Mega & Cummings, 1994), the temporal organization of behavior (Fuster, 1985), and in the appraisal (Pribram, 1987; Schore, 1997d) and adjustment or correction of emotional responses (Rolls, 1986)—that is, affect regulation. This system acts as a recovery mechanism that efficiently monitors and autoregulates the duration, frequency, and intensity of not only positive but negative affect states. This allows both for the ability to use affects as signals and for a self-comforting capacity that can modulate distressing psychobiological states and reestablish positively toned states.

The essential activity of this psychic system is the adaptive switching of internal bodily states in response to changes in the external environment that are appraised to be personally meaningful. This orbitofrontal function mediates "the ability to alter behavior in response to fluctuations in the emotional significance of stimuli" (Dias, Robbins, & Roberts, 1996). In its unique position at the convergence point of right cortical and subcortical systems, it critically influences the superior role that the nonverbal right brain plays in the control of vital functions supporting survival and enabling the organism to cope actively and passively with stress and external challenge. Recall that Freud's (1923/1961b) structural model theorized a system that regulates the individual's adaptation to the environment.

Further, this neurobiological system is identical to the internalized structure described by Stolorow, Brandchaft, and Atwood (1987) that modulates and contains strong affect, and is a central component of a brain system that generates the complex symbolic representations of evocative memory, detailed by Fraiberg (1969), that allows the individual who is experiencing a negative state to evoke an image of a comforting other. The system thus enables the individual to recover from disruptions of state and to integrate a sense of self across transitions of state, thereby allowing for a continuity of experience in various environmental contexts. These capacities are critical to the operation of a self-system that is both stable and adaptable. The prominent neurological researcher

Damasio (1994) also concluded that the orbital prefrontal cortex plays an essential adaptive role in the bioregulatory and social domains. His neurological studies have revealed that this homeostatic system is an essential component of what he termed "the neural self" that generates "somatic markers" expressed as emotions. In convergent findings in the psychoanalytic literature, Modell concluded that "the continuity and coherence of the self is a homeostatic requirement of the psyche-soma," a finding that suggested to him "the frontier between psychoanalysis and biology" (1993, p. 48).

IMPLICATIONS OF INTERDISCIPLINARY RESEARCH
FOR PSYCHOANALYSIS

This returns us again to our starting point, the interface of psychoanalysis with the other sciences. To my mind, the borderland between disciplines gives us entry to domains of science yet to be explored, including the conscious and unconscious realms of the human mind that is engaged in this exploration. An important benefit of using interdisciplinary approaches to study internal processes is that we can now reframe metapsychological questions and hypotheses about affect, motivation, consciousness, and psychic structure in a manner that renders them heuristic and "falsifiable" (Popper, 1962). Grunbaum asserted that "If there exists empirical evidence for the principal psychoanalytic doctrines, it cannot be obtained without well-designed extra-clinical studies of a kind that have for the most part yet to be attempted" (1986, p. 217). This endeavor is now underway.

With reference to the hundredth anniversary of Freud's attempt to create a biological psychology, Krystal concluded that "The more we learn and the more we check our views against the new developments in other sciences, the more we can solve our hitherto insoluble problems, and we are more able to refine our views and approaches" (1992, p. 409). In that spirit, let me cite some examples of how interdisciplinary integrations can help clarify a number of long-unresolved psychoanalytic metapsychological conundrums. First I will focus on theoretical psychoanalysis, and present findings from other sciences that relate to the concepts of drive, internal representations, consciousness, the awareness of emotional states, and dreaming. Then I will briefly discuss the relevance of current and recent research for clinical psychoanalytic conceptions of psychopathology and treatment.

Theoretical Implications

DRIVE

Neurobiological studies show that the orbitofrontal cortex and its cortical and subcortical connections critically participates in the adaptive functions of mediating between the external environment and the internal milieu, in balancing internal desires with external reality, and in modulating drive excitation and drive restraint. This system is therefore uniquely and centrally relevant to psychoanalysis, since its operational capacities define Freud's internal mechanism, first outlined in the Project, that regulates excitation from sources within and outside of the individual. This system is also identical to a controlling structure, described by Rapaport (1960), that maintains constancy by delaying press for discharge of aroused drives, states of psychic excitation that impel the individual to activity geared at alleviating it (Freud, 1920/1955). In Freud's most widely used definition, noted Greenberg and Mitchell, "Drive is a concept at the frontier between the psychic and the somatic, an endogenous source of stimulation which impinges on the mind by virtue of the mind's connection with the body" (1983, p. 21). As Holzman and Aronson wrote, "In acknowledging the powerful role of anticipations and planning in the emerging reality principle, [Freud] might have had some interest in contemporary neuropsychological studies of the frontal lobes in providing the organic infrastructure for channeling drives" (1992, p. 72).

In *Descartes' Error*, Damasio argued that emotions are "a powerful manifestation of drives and instincts," and emphasized their motivational role: "In general, drives and instincts operate either by generating a particular behavior directly or by inducing physiological states that lead individuals to behavior in a particular way" (1994, p. 115). Descartes's error, carried forward into present-day psychological and medical sciences, was specifically the separation of the operations of the mind from the structure and operation of a biological organism, the body. In the psychoanalytic literature, Deri reminded us that the ego functions within the context of a total psychobiological organism, and warned of "the danger of a purely psychological model that disregards the unavoidable psychosomatic oneness of a functioning human being" (1990, p. 518). Psychobiological and neurobiological studies from the last decade or so thus strongly indicate that *the concept of drive, devalued over the last 20 years, must be reintroduced as a central construct of psychoanalytic theory.*

INTERNAL REPRESENTATIONS

Multidisciplinary findings can also clarify another metapsychological construct that is central to clinical psychoanalysis, the concept of internal representation. Freud introduced the term *object representation* in his neurological treatise of 1891, *On Aphasia*. His first discussions included not only ideas about the nature and formation of representations but also speculations on the underlying brain mechanisms. He specifically noted that the physiological correlate of a representation is "something in the nature of a *process*" (1891/1953a, p. 55). Freud thus concluded that neither the psychological representation nor its physiological correlate can be localized in a structure, and yet later theorists have confused structure with function and have erroneously asserted that representations *are* structures. In 1991, exactly 100 years after *On Aphasia*, Pribram, in his book *Brain and Perception*, concluded that a representation is not "an immutable structure" but rather "a process."

After Freud, our understanding of the concept of internal representations was, of course, greatly advanced by Hartmann, who argued that the concept of "self-representation" was a logical extension of Freud's "object representation," and Jacobson and Kernberg, who emphasized the affective linkages between object representations and self representations. Loewald (1970) stressed the important principle that what becomes internalized are not objects but relationships and interactions. In developmental work, Beebe and Lachmann (1988b) showed that affective experiences with the early social environment are mentally stored in the form of interactive representations of the self emotionally transacting with significant objects. There is now evidence that the development of parental representations and the development of self-representations occur in synchrony (Bornstein, 1993) and that internal representations of self and other evolve in hierarchical stages and encode templates that influence the child's expectations, perceptions, and behavior toward the interpersonal environment (Horner, 1991). Most importantly, the current interdisciplinary research on affect regulation strongly supports Schafer's (1968) assertion, made more than 30 years ago, that internalization is fundamentally a transformation of external regulations into internal ones.

Meanwhile, the concept of mental representations has been accepted and absorbed into developmental, social, and cognitive psychology as well as into neurobiology. The neuroscientist Kandel (1983, p. 1281) wrote that "By emphasizing mental structure and internal representation, psychoanalysis served as a source of modern cognitive psychology." As I mentioned, studies in these fields now indicate that internalized representations of relationships act as "biological regulators." My integrative work suggests that the same interactive representations are distributed in the orbital cortex and its cortical and subcortical connections, and that they act as templates that guide interpersonal behaviors. They contain information about psychobiological state transitions and encode strategies of affect regulation that are accessed in order to switch internal bodily states in response to changes in the external environment that are appraised to be emotionally meaningful.

Thus, a century after Freud outlined his concept of representation, science is now able to use it heuristically. Interdisciplinary research has validated and expanded upon the concept, as now the fundamental function of representations is best described as not "mental" but "psychobiological." Current neurological thinking holds that the brain represents the outside world in terms of the modifications it causes in the body proper (Damasio, 1994). This appears to be a significant departure from Freud's original conception, but is it? In *On Aphasia*, Freud clearly stated that what is represented in the cortex is "the periphery of the body" (1891/1953a, p. 51), and that all object representations are related to bodily representations!

CONSCIOUSNESS, AWARENESS OF EMOTIONAL STATES, AND DREAMING

Studies have shown that the orbitofrontal system plays a fundamental role in preconscious functions (Frank, 1950), in the processing of emotion-evoking stimuli without conscious awareness (Wexler, Warrenburg, Schwartz, & Janer, 1992), and in controlling the allocation of attention to possible contents of consciousness (Goldenberg et al., 1989). These covert processes are now being studied by modern imaging techniques that allow us to image function as well as anatomy, to literally visualize "images of mind" (Raichle, 1994). These techniques offer valuable data to psychoanalysis, which essentially is a theory of mind. For example, a recent positron emission tomography (PET) study demonstrates the important role of the orbitofrontal cortex in emotional-cognitive processes (Pardo, Pardo, & Raichle, 1993). When normal subjects silently fantasize dysphoric affect-laden images of object loss such as imagining the death of a loved one, increased blood flow and activation is recorded in specifically the orbital prefrontal areas. Interestingly, the PET scans of females showed orbitofrontal activity in both hemispheres, while males displayed only unilateral activation, and more of the females than males experienced tearfulness. An additional PET study also shows that women display significantly greater activity in this affect-regulating structure than do men, especially in the right hemisphere (Andreason, Zametkin, Guo, Baldwin, & Cohen, 1994). These data indicate gender differences in the wiring of the limbic system, and relate to differences in empathic styles or capacities of processing nonverbal affect between the sexes.

In a functional neuroimaging study of introspective and self-reflective capacities, when subjects are asked to relax and listen to words that specifically describe what goes on in the mind (mental state terms such as *wish*, *hope*, *imagine*, *desire*, *dream*, and *fantasy*), a specifically increased activation of the right orbitofrontal cortex occurs (Baron-Cohen et al., 1994). Andreasen and colleagues (1995) reported that during focused episodic memory (the recalling and relating of a personal experience to another), an increase of blood flow occurs in the orbitofrontal areas. Right frontal activity specifically occurs when the brain is actively retrieving this personal event from the past. Even more intriguingly, this same inferior frontal region is activated when the subject is told to allow the mind to rest. In this condition of uncensored and silently unexpressed private thoughts, the individual's mental activity consists of loosely linked and freely wandering past recollections and future plans. The authors concluded that this orbitofrontal activity reflects "free association" that taps into psychoanalytic primary process.

With regard to yet another aspect of primary process activity, Solms, whose work is at the interface of neurology and psychoanalysis, has presented neurological data indicating that the control mechanism of dreaming is critically mediated by anterior limbic orbitofrontal structures. He concluded, "These regions are essential for affect regulation, impulse control, and reality testing;

they act as a form of 'censorship' " (1994, pp. 60–61). Normal activity in this brain system during sleep allows for the processing of information by symbolic representational mechanisms during dreaming, while failures in regulatory functioning caused by overwhelming experiences causes a breakdown in dreaming, disturbed sleep, and nightmares. These findings support Frank's (1950) earlier observations that patient's with ablated orbital cortices show a reduction in the frequency and complexity of dreams, and a dream content reflecting (like children's dreams) direct wish fulfillment. The problem of identifying the mechanisms of dream formation and primary process was, of course, first addressed by Freud in the Project.

CLINICAL IMPLICATIONS

Psychoanalytic Models of Structural Psychopathology

In groundbreaking interdisciplinary work, Grotstein (1986) asserted that all psychopathology constitutes primary or secondary disorders of bonding or attachment and manifests itself as disorders of self and/or interactional regulation. This clearly implies that the orbitofrontal system, with its essential role in attachment and regulatory processes, is involved in psychiatric disturbances. My own theoretical research has indicated that the orbital prefrontal areas undergo a critical period of growth at the end of the first and into the second year of infancy, and that extensive experiences with an affectively misattuned primary caregiver represent a growth-inhibiting environment for a maturing corticolimbic system (Schore, 1994, 1996, 1997b). Interactively generated dysregulating psychobiological events, in conjunction with genetic factors, can result in a predisposition to later psychiatric and psychosomatic psychopathologies. Indeed, there is now extensive evidence indicating that impaired function of this frontolimbic system is accompanied by affective symptomatology.

The functional indicators of impaired affect regulatory systems that are the products of developmental psychopathology are specifically manifest in recovery deficits of internal reparative mechanisms. These deficits in coping with intense affect are most obvious under challenging conditions that call for behavioral flexibility and adaptive responses to socioemotional stress. In other words, affect pathology reflects a regulatory dysfunction in the orbitofrontal structure that is centrally involved in the adjustment or correction of emotional responses. Indeed, recent imaging studies demonstrate impaired orbitofrontal functioning in an array of disorders with an early developmental etiology: autism (Baron-Cohen,1995), mania (Starkstein, Boston, & Robinson, 1990), phobic states (Rauch et al., 1995), alcoholism (Adams et al., 1995), and drug addiction (Volkow et al., 1991). Of particular interest to clinical psychoanalysis are PET studies showing orbital prefrontal deficits in depression (Mayberg,

Lewis, Regenold, & Wagner, 1994), posttraumatic stress disorder (Semple et al., 1992), and character and borderline personality disorders (Goyer, Konicki, & Schulz, 1994).

Psychoanalytic Treatment

Many of these very same developmental primitive emotional disorders are targets of contemporary models of psychoanalytic treatment. The next question is: Can the psychoanalytic therapeutic relationship alter these psychoneurobiological deficits? An answer to this comes from current brain research, which indicates that the capacity for experience-dependent plastic changes in the nervous system remains throughout the lifespan. In fact, there is very specific evidence that the prefrontal limbic cortex, more than any other part of the cerebral cortex, retains the plastic capacities of early development (Barbas, 1995). The orbitofrontal cortex, even in adulthood, continues to express anatomical and biochemical features observed in early ontogeny, and this property allows for structural changes that can result from psychotherapeutic treatment. (For a more detailed account of the implications of developmental and neurobiological data for psychotherapy, see discussions of the nonverbal transference-countertransference in Schore [1994, 1997c].)

There is now convincing evidence that the orbitofrontal cortex functionally mediates the capacity to empathize with the feelings of others (Mega & Cummings, 1994) and to reflect on one's own internal emotional states as well as those of others (Povinelli & Preuss, 1995). These results are relevant to both the interpersonal and intrapsychic processes that are activated in the psychotherapeutic relationship. Most intriguingly, a PET study published in 1996 demonstrated that patients show significant changes in metabolic activity in the right orbitofrontal cortex and its subcortical connections as a result of successful psychological treatment (Schwartz, Stoessel, Baxter, Martin, & Phelps, 1996). These data support a growing literature that indicate changes in "mind and brain" in psychotherapeutic treatment (Gabbard, 1994).

Indeed, Spezzano (1993) argued that the analytic relationship specifically produces changes in the patient's "unconscious affect regulating structures." Gedo contended that working through involves "the actual reorganization of the relevant aspects of brain function," in which "cortex and midbrain collaborate to provide better control" (1995b, pp. 352–353). He regarded working through as being directed toward "the completion of development" (p. 341). This process, the core of therapy, is accomplished by "the mastery of affective intensities" and it facilitates the emergence of "new channels of intrapsychic communication" (p. 353). As a result, the patient who formerly was unable to read his/her affective-somatic signals becomes able to interpret the meanings of personal experience. Gedo further concluded that "working through must refer to the difficult transitional process whereby reliance on former modes of behavioral regulation is gradually superseded by more effective adaptive measures" (p. 344). Although he did not identify the regulatory system that is involved in such activities, this characterization is clearly descriptive of orbito-frontal functions (Schore, 1994). In the final portion of his paper, Gedo confi-dently stated that his ideas are "congruent with Freud's usage in the 1895 Project" as well as with "the view of contemporary brain science" (p. 385).

CONCLUSION

Let me end where we began, with this question: Is a rapprochement between psychoanalyis and neurobiology now at hand? I suggest that this could not occur until psychoanalysis, which Langs (1995) redefined as "a science of emo-tional cognition," as well as the other human sciences, earnestly commit them-selves to the investigation of emotional processes. The neuroscientist Damasio (1995) addressed this issue:

> By the end of the nineteenth century, Charles Darwin had made incisive observations on the expression of emotions in animals and humans and had placed emotion in the perspective of biological evolution; William James had produced a scientific description of the phenomenon of emo-tion, thus opening the way to its experimental study; and Sigmund Freud was writing about the means by which emotion might play a role in psychopathology. Somebody freshly arrived on earth in 1994 and inter-ested in the topic of emotion would have good cause to wonder why such groundbreaking developments did not lead an assault on the neurobiol-ogy of emotion. What could possibly have gone wrong in the intervening century? The simplest answer . . . is that emotion has received benign neglect from neuroscience and has been passed over in favor of the study of attention, perception, memory, and language. (p. 19)

In a paper in the journal *Brain and Cognition* entitled "Personal Relevance and the Human Right Hemisphere," van Lancker cited neuropsychological evi-dence to show that "the ability to establish, maintain, and recognize personally relevant objects in the environment" is an important attribute of human behav-ior (1991, p. 66). This phenomenon "involves an affective interaction between subject and object" (p. 72), and the recognition of familiar objects requires a relationship and is accompanied by a "cognitive/affective inner state" (p. 65). Neurobiology is now moving toward embracing the concept of object relations, just as cognitive psychology has coopted the psychoanalytic concept of internal representations.

Is the time right? I suggest that the answer to this fundamental question involves much more than an objective appraisal of the match or mismatch of different current bodies of knowledge, although this is certainly a part of the process. But in addition to this, response of psychoanalysis will have to involve a reintegration of its own internal theoretical divisions, a reassessment of its educational priorities, a reevaluation of its current predominant emphasis on cognition, especially verbal mechanisms, as well as a reworking of its Cartesian mind-body dichotomies. This redefinition involves the identity of psychoanalysis itself, in terms of its self-reference and its relations with the other sciences. In principle, whether or not a rapprochement after a disconnection takes place between two parties depends upon not only the information they share in common, but also on their individual willingness to enter into a communicative system.

In the final paragraph of Pribram and Gill's book on the Project (1976), the latter suggested that psychoanalysis must go its own way and that meant purging it of its natural science metapsychology; Pribram disagreed, welcoming psychoanalysis back into the natural sciences. Approximately 10 years later, Reiser (1985) noted a disturbing trend in which neurobiological data was being increasingly ignored by psychoanalysts, and contemporary psychoanalytic data dismissed by neurobiologists. At about the same time, Sabshin wrote, "For a field stimulated by the author of the 'Project' to separate itself from important new developments a century later would be tragic" (1984, p. 489). Five years after that, Holt, in his book *Freud Reappraised*, concluded, "[W]e must go to a nonbehavioral realm, such as neurophysiology, to test a great deal of the most distinctive parts of the clinical theory: Psychoanalysis is not autonomous, existing in self-sufficient isolation on an island remote from other sciences. No science can do that, and it was a great mistake for psychoanalysis to have cut its ties to the rest of the scientific world" (1989, p. 340).

In the December 1994 through March 1997 issues of *Psychoanalytic Abstracts*, which covers articles published in 40 different psychoanalytic journals as well as books and chapters in books, the annual subject index contained not a single title referring to affect, emotion, or motivation, nor to psychoanalytic research or to the brain. Analysts might do well to heed the words of Modell: "All sciences are autonomous, yet must share concepts that lie across their frontiers" (1993, p. 198).

1997

CHAPTER 7

The Right Brain, the Right Mind, and Psychoanalysis

O NE OF THE CENTRAL ORGANIZING PRINCIPLES of my ongoing work is that the fundamental problems of the human condition can best be studied by an interdisciplinary perspective. In my book *Affect Regulation and the Origin of the Self* (1994), I argued that the frontiers of science lie in the borderland between its separate fields, and in the last chapter I offered a proposal for a rapprochement between psychoanalysis (the study of the mind) and neurobiology (the study of the brain). Following this, in an article in the *Journal of the American Psychoanalytic Association* (Schore, 1997), I suggested that the time was right for this reconnection. I continued this theme in a keynote address in 1998 at the Georgetown University conference "Freud at the Millennium," which coincided with the opening of the exhibit of the Freud Archives at the Library of Congress. And in 1999 I contributed to the inaugural issue of the interdisciplinary journal *Neuro-Psychoanalysis*, which contains an editorial board of both neuroscientists and psychoanalysts.

The first issue, entitled "Freud's Theory of Affect: Questions for Neuroscience," contained articles by Panksepp, Damasio, LeDoux, myself, and others. It represented an important step forward toward an active interdisciplinary dialogue between neuroscience and psychoanalysis, and suggested that this mutual exchange can act as an enriched environment that can intellectually energize both realms. The existence of the journal indicates that there is now enough common ground between these two perspectives to open an ongoing communication. Furthermore, the problem of affect is an important convergence point. A consensus is now building that the deeper mechanisms that underlie affective processes, which play an essential role in adaptive functions, can be elucidated by a neuropsychoanalytic perspective that attends to both psychic structure and function. This common focus on the centrality of affective states clearly suggests that both neuroscience and psychoanalysis must pay more attention to the links of the brain-mind into the body.

Freud's monumental contribution to science was his discovery of the critical role of the dynamic unconscious in everyday life (1901/1960), and in his works he created a theoretical perspective that could bring into focus the unconscious subjective internal world that is instrumental in guiding the individual's moment-to-moment interactions with the external environment. Drawing upon his early experience as a scientist and neurologist, over the course of his prolific later career as a psychoanalyst all of his investigations represented attempts to elucidate the realms of the mind beneath conscious awareness.

Freud also proposed a developmental model of psychopathogensis, and an applied scientific model—clinical psychoanalysis—a treatment approach that was based upon his understanding of the intrapsychic mechanisms that underlie both normal and abnormal functioning. These interventions, derived from his theoretical base, represented an aggregate of experimental methods that could most effectively access this inner realm, and thereby maximize the possibility of change in the patient's unconscious internal structural systems. Over the course of his early career as a theoretical and clinical neurologist of the brain and later career as a theoretical and clinical psychologist of the mind, Freud increasingly emphasized the central role of unconscious motivational and affective systems in understanding the human experience (Schore, 1997a, 1998g).

In my contribution to the first issue of *Neuro-Psychoanalysis* (Schore, 1999b), I suggested that Freud's remarkably perceptive observations of the unconscious mechanisms that mediate the affective and motivational expressions of intrapsychic structural systems describe the operations of the right brain, or "right mind" (Ornstein, 1997). In this offering, I want to expand upon the problem of affect and its regulation, first raised by Freud and now becoming a major focus of both the experimental and clinical sciences. A central proposal of this work is that the problems of affect and motivation can only be addressed by moving down from the cortex and describing cortico-subcortical systems, especially those in the right brain that connect into the body.

Emotion theorists outside of psychoanalysis stress that emotions involve rapid appraisals of events that are important to the individual (Frijda, 1988) and represent reactions to fundamental relational meanings that have adaptive significance (Lazarus, 1991). This adaptive aspect of the nonverbal communication of emotions was first introduced by Darwin in *The Expression of Emotion in Man and Animals* (1872/1965), and must now be integrated with Freud's models of affect, motivation, and the unconscious, first presented in his *Project for a Scientific Psychology* (1895/1966). These respective interpersonal and intrapsychic conceptions of emotion can be brought together in a psychoneurobiological model of the nonconscious processing of socioemotional information by the right brain.

In this continuation of my earlier contribution to *Neuro-Psychoanalysis*, I shall present additional multidisciplinary evidence indicating that a deeper understanding of affective phenomena cannot be attained without also attending to the problem of affect regulation. The essential aspect of this function was highlighted by Westen, who asserted that "The attempt to regulate affect—to minimize unpleasant feelings and to maximize pleasant ones—is the driving force in human motivation" (1997, p. 542). And so I shall focus upon the vertical organization of the right brain, especially the "higher" orbitofrontal areas, which are structurally expanded in the right hemisphere (Falk et al., 1990) and functionally involved in a number of adaptive self-regulatory processes.

At the orbitofrontal level, complex cortically processed exteroceptive information concerning the external environment (e.g., visual and prosodic information emanating from an emotional face) is integrated with subcortically processed interoceptive information regarding the internal visceral environment (e.g., concurrent changes in bodily states). This cortex thus functions to refine emotions in keeping with current sensory input, and allows for the adaptive switching of internal bodily states in response to changes in the external environment that are appraised to be personally meaningful (Schore, 1998b).

The orbitofrontal system sits at the hierarchical apex of the limbic system, which is more developed in the right rather than the left brain. Due to this fact, this higher cortical system, when acting efficiently, can regulate lower-level subcortical structures that are involved in the earlier processing stages of socioemotional information. This prefrontolimbic regulatory system therefore acts as an "internal reflecting and organizing agency" (Kaplan-Solms & Solms, 1996). In an attempt to forge deeper links between the right brain and the right mind, I propose that the orbitofrontal system's organization of lower levels of the vertically arranged, right-lateralized limbic system represents the structural intrapsychic mechanism by which higher levels of Freud's system preconscious regulate lower levels of the system unconscious. In other words, the orbitofrontal system acts as a higher preconscious system that organizes lower-level unconscious states of mind-body.

In the following, I will further develop my contention that "the emotion-processing right mind is the neurobiological substrate of Freud's dynamic unconscious" (Schore, 1999a, p. 53). I will suggest that current knowledge of the development and organization of the orbitofrontal system, which has been called the "senior executive of the emotional brain" (Joseph, 1996), can be used to evaluate Freud's topographical, structural, and affect theories. And I will then show how this psychoneurobiological perspective can elucidate the roles of right-lateralized unconscious-preconscious systems in a spectrum of affectively driven adaptive functions.

JACKSON AND FREUD: THE SHARED ORIGIN OF NEUROPSYCHOLOGY AND PSYCHOANALYSIS

More than any other discipline, psychoanalysis, the scientific study of the unconscious mind (Brenner, 1980), can offer the other sciences its century-old body of knowledge that describes the unique qualities of the essential processes that continuously operate at levels beneath conscious awareness. To this date, psychoanalysis has preferentially looked to "cognitive neuroscience" (Gazzaniga,

1995) to generate models of psychoanalytic phenomena, a field whose studies are mostly targeted to the left hemisphere's explicit functions in consciously processing verbal materials. And yet the paralimbic networks that underlie the rapid nonconscious processing of affect are known to be more expressed in the right hemisphere (Joseph, 1996; Tucker, 1992). I therefore suggest that the currently expanding fields of "affective neuroscience" (Panksepp, 1998) and "social neuroscience" (Cacioppo & Berntson, 1992) may generate more comprehensive models of the unconscious mind-body mechanisms by which right-lateralized nonverbal systems implicitly guide the individual's adaptive and maladaptive emotional reactions and motivational states.

The central nervous system (CNS) circuits that process social and emotional information at unconscious levels are deeply connected into the sympathetic and parasympathetic circuits of the autonomic nervous system (ANS) that regulate the functions of every organ in the body, and these are highly lateralized in the right brain (Schore, 1994, 1996, 1997b, 1998b). Porges (1997) described this ANS-CNS interaction in a contribution entitled "Emotion: an evolutionary by-product of the neural regulation of the autonomic nervous system":

> Emotion depends on the communication between the autonomic nervous system and the brain; visceral afferents convey information on physiological state to the brain and are critical to the sensory or psychological experience of emotion, and cranial nerves and the sympathetic nervous system are outputs from the brain that provide somatomotor and visceromotor control of the expression of emotion. (p. 65)

Freud recognized the critical role of the ANS in his assertion that the brain fundamentally acts as a "sympathetic ganglion" (1895/1966, p. 303), although, as I pointed out in an earlier work (Schore, 1994), he overlooked the essential role of the parasympathetic nervous system.

Emotional receptive and expressive functions are thus mediated by the co-activation of limbic circuits of the central nervous system and energy-mobilizing sympathetic and energy-conserving parasympathetic components of the autonomic nervous system. The meaning of this neuroanatomical structure-function relation is that any theoretical model of affective phenomena must take into account not just the "higher" central but also the "lower" autonomic nervous system. John Hughlings Jackson (1931), the great 19th-century neurologist who most profoundly influenced Freud (Goldstein, 1995; Sulloway, 1979), described the autonomic nervous system as "the physiological bottom of the mind." Citing Jackson, Neafsey concluded, "The key to understanding the cerebral cortex, then, appears to be the body" (1990, p. 147). In other words, affect directs both neuroscience's right brain and psychoanalysis's right mind into the body.

Although Jackson is unknown to most psychoanalysts (and many neuroscientists), the concepts that he first proposed and that Freud later developed are very familiar to clinicians. The essential contributions of Jackson's groundbreaking neurological theories to Freud's major concepts has been underscored within the psychoanalytic literature by a number of authors. Solms and Saling (1986) described Freud's siding with Jackson against the reigning localizationist tradition of 19th-century neurology, and Sulloway referred to Freud's contention that "what is really important . . . is an appreciation of how a hypothetical lesion might affect *the whole system, dynamically understood*" (1979, p. 271; italics added). In my own work, which incorporates a dynamic systems approach (Schore, 1994, 1997b, 2000e), I have continued to expand upon Jackson's hierarchical model by delineating the development of an unconscious regulatory system that was described by Freud.

In depicting Jackson's hierarchical-developmental model, Sulloway (1979) stated:

> Jackson conceived the human mind in terms of a hierarchical series of functional levels, with "higher," voluntary functions overlaying and "keeping down" the more involuntary, "lower" ones. The lower functional capacities of mind, he maintained, had been superseded in the course of human evolution by the higher ones, which now serve to integrate and observe the whole; and *a similar evolutionary sequence was to be observed in individual mental development.* . . . He also taught that the lower functional levels of mind—dynamically and subconsciously present in all healthy individuals—are temporarily unleashed during states of sleeping and dreaming. (p. 270; italics added)

These lower-level functions represent the earliest stage of cognition, characterized by Jackson as preverbal and closely tied to visceral functions. The similarity of Jackson's lower-level functions to Freud's primary process functions has been pointed out by a number of authors, including Goldstein (1995).

Jackson further suggested that pathology involves a "dissolution," a loss of inhibitory capacities of the most recently evolved layers of the nervous system that support higher functions (negative symptoms) as well as the release of lower, more automatic functions (positive symptoms). Freud incorporated Jackson's stratified model, which he specifically praised, into *On Aphasia*, (1891/1953a). Here, Freud wrote of a pathological condition as a retrogression to an earlier state of functional development, a conceptualization he used for the rest of his career. In other words, regression, the essential psychoanalytic mechanism of psychopathology for Freud, derives directly from the neurological hierarchical model of Jackson. Indeed, Sulloway referred to "the Jackson–Freud theory of psychical regression" (1979, p. 272). Additionally, at later dates Freud incorporated Jackson's hierarchical concept of higher levels inhibiting lower levels of function into both his topographic (1900/1953) model of stratified conscious, preconscious, and unconscious systems, and his structural model (1923/1961b) of a superego and ego that sit astride the id.

Jackson's ideas, far ahead of his time, are directly relevant to contemporary neuroscience and psychoanalysis, especially as both are now intensely focusing upon the problems of affect and motivation. Goldstein (1995) described:

> Jackson's observation of aphasics led him to postulate lateralization of two main aspects of mentation—emotive and intellectual. The emotive functions are described as essentially preverbal and automatic, and as residing in the right hemisphere. There all mentation arises, according to nonexperiential functions, and only thereafter are ideas arranged in words in the left hemisphere, where they achieve propositional form. (p. 498)

Jackson's work deeply influenced not only Freud, but also the ensuing neurological work of Head, Goldstein, and, most significantly, Luria, who in his youth corresponded with Freud. Luria noted that as opposed to the "narrow localization" of Broca and other 19th-century neurologists, "Jackson argued that . . . the cerebral organization of complex mental processes must be approached from the standpoint of the level of their construction rather than that of their localization in particular areas of the brain" (1973, p. 25). Luria continued, "That is why mental functions, as complex functional systems, cannot be localized in narrow zones of the cortex, but must be organized in systems of concertedly working zones, each of which performs its role in a complex functional system, and which may be located in completely different and often far distant areas of the brain" (p. 31).

But perhaps even more specifically to the topic at hand, emotional functions, 3 decades ago Luria (1973) wrote,

> Nearly a century ago, Hughlings Jackson postulated that the right hemisphere . . . participates directly in perceptual processes and is responsible for more direct, visual forms of relationships with the outside world. This hypothesis failed to attract due attention for many decades, and it is only recently that it has been begun to be appreciated. First of all it was noticed that the right hemisphere is directly concerned with the analysis of direct information received by the subject *from his own body* and which, it can easily be understood, is much more closely connected with direct sensation than with verbally logical codes. (p. 165; italics added)

Since Luria's writings, an explosion of studies has confirmed the essential role of the right hemisphere in the processing of emotional information, validating Jackson's insights. But the primary reason I am presenting Jackson's view of how the brain operates is to emphasize the fact that the problem of emotion can not be understood with a localizationist perspective, one that still dominates neuroscience. Attempts to localize explicit learning in the hippocampus, drive in the hypothalamus, fear processing in the amygdala, or indeed executive functions in the frontal lobe all represent such a perspective. This principle was echoed by Bigler and colleagues: "seeking out a single structure will never be effective in answering the role of that structure without somehow accounting for the interrelationship of that structure with other systems in its network. Along these lines, in the context of cognitive neuroscience, Goldberg argues convincingly for a paradigmatic shift from modular to interactive brain systems" (1995, p. 34). A localizationist approach can never offer us a complex model of what Damasio described as the essential adaptive role of brain systems: "The overall function of the brain is to be well informed about what goes on in the rest of the body, the body proper; about what goes on in itself; and about the environment surrounding the organism, so that suitable survivable accommodations can be achieved between the organism and the environment" (1994, p. 90).

The fact that most localization studies, whether utilizing a neuropathological-experimental lesion analysis, electroencephalogram (EEG), or neuroimaging methodology, are looking at only the cortical level presents a particular problem for the deeper study of affective, bodily based processes. Rather, we must move down from the cortex, and look into the vertical dimension of cortical-subcortical systems. The brain is organized as a complex dynamic system (Lewis & Granic, 2000; Siegel, 1999) and any theoretical model of affects, or brain development, or psychopathogenesis, or of the unconscious must also use a dynamic systems approach (Schore, 1997b, 2000e). This clearly suggests that any rapprochement between psychoanalysis and neurobiology must involve a joining of current psychoanalytic conceptions and specifically a Jacksonian and not localizationalist neurobiology. I am suggesting that, at their inception, neurology and psychoanalysis were interlinked in a Jacksonian–Freudian co-constructed conception, and thus the rapprochement between these disciplines will result in a more complex integrated model of a Jacksonian hierarchical brain and a Freudian unconscious mind.

Continuing a central theme of my ongoing work, in this contribution I will expand my thesis that psychoanalysis' large and growing body of clinical and theoretical functional descriptions of the structural unconscious describes the functional properties of neuroscience's structural systems located in the right brain. Clinical neuropsychological studies of adults have linked the right brain and the unconscious (Joseph, 1992) and have been used as a model for generating an "anatomy of the unconscious" (Solms, 1996). But I suggest that only a developmental perspective can trace both how the earliest socioemotional experiences are registered in the deep unconscious, and how they influence the development of the systems that dynamically process unconscious information for the rest of the lifespan. Knowledge of these developmental events offers us a chance to more deeply understand not just the contents of the dynamic unconscious, but its origin, structure, and dynamics.

The fundamental problems of affect, motivation, development, psychopathology, consciousness, and regulation were first presented by Freud in the *Project for a Scientific Psychology* his attempt to create "a psychology which shall be a natural science" (1895/1966, p. 295). I suggest that a deeper understanding of the psychoneurobiological mechanisms of these essential processes may do more than forge deeper links *between* psychoanalysis and neuroscience. Rather, a common theoretical conception of affect, motivation, and the unconscious mind, and a common clinical conception of the transference-countertransference relationship, could allow for an integration of the different theoretical currents *within* psychoanalysis. This could move us closer to what Rangell described as a "total composite theory," one that should not "equate disparate [theoretical] systems but [should] fuse the valid and enduring elements of all into one" (1997, p. 585).

THE ISOLATED BRAIN AND A ONE-PERSON PSYCHOLOGY; THE INTERACTING BRAIN AND A TWO-PERSON PSYCHOLOGY

On the whole, the major orientation of most neuroscientists traces back to the one Freud used in both *On Aphasia* (1891/1953a) and *The Project* (1895/1966); that is, an approach grounded in clinical neurology, neuroanatomy, and neuropsychology. This classical methodological approach explores brain-behavior relationships within the context of neurological patient populations and animal lesion studies, and it attempts to model both abnormal and normal processes. Its application to affective phenomena is a rather late development, but as Damasio, Ledoux, and others have repeatedly shown, this clinico-anatomical perspective within neuroscience continues to make major contributions to our understanding of not only brain diseases but of the human experience.

I will not describe, as others have done, the limitations of this approach, except to mention that just as psychoanalysis has been criticized for developing models of normal development from the study of neurotic patients, the observations of abnormal brain systems as a model of normal brain function suffers from the same methodological weakness. Modern imaging studies that can noninvasively observe and measure brain states in normal populations can, of course, bypass this limitation. But I would argue, as Brothers did, that another bias intrinsic to this classical methodology is that it emphasizes a model of an isolated brain: "The brain has been implicitly seen as a knower of the world, as a socially isolated organ whose purpose is to grasp the inanimate world outside it" (1997, p. 66).

This paradigm, with its almost restrictive focus on cognition (the action or faculty of knowing), has been automatically applied as the major if not exclusive experimental methodology for studying affective phenomena. In these studies, "context," especially the potential interpersonal influences of the experimenter on the brain activity of the subject, is seen as a confounding factor that must be controlled. In animal studies, an isolated, passive animal is stressed by intensifying or reducing parameters in the physical environment, and not through exposure to species-specific organismic stressors; then coping responses are measured. In human studies, the subject is usually presented with supra-liminal verbal stimuli, aspects of the inanimate world, and not nonverbal facial stimuli of the animate world; verbal self-report or questionnaires are used as response measures. This research focuses on the capacity of an isolated brain to *autoregulate* homeostatic alterations to stressors in the physical environment. Neuroscience is beginning to focus upon a deeper understanding of affect within brain circuitries and on internal brain systems that efficiently or ineffi-ciently autoregulate dysregulated psychobiological states and negative affect.

It is no coincidence that this objective "intra-brain" neurological perspective is paralleled by psychoanalytic models that emphasize an almost exclusive "in-trapsychic" perspective. In this model of an "isolated mind," motivation is es-sentially activated by drives, biological forces that originate within the organism, and the unconscious mind operates by the principles of a "one-person psychol-ogy" that is elaborated by "classical" or "structural" psychoanalytic theoretical models. During the decades when psychoanalysis was almost totally dis-connected from the other sciences, "drive-dominated" models of the psyche were strongly devalued, seen as irrelevant, and almost totally discarded from psychoanalysis.

And, yet, neurobiological studies that highlight the essential role of the adap-tive functions of right hemispheric control centers in regulating drive centers in the hypothalamus (Schore, 1994), and of the right brain in the metacontrol of fundamental physiological and endocrinological functions (Wittling & Pfluger, 1990), support the notion of an unconscious mind operating in a "one-person" autoregulatory strategy. This mode does represent one organizational configuration of an unconscious mind, a mode that is accessed when one is processing emotion but not transacting with external social objects.

Clinical psychotherapeutic interventions that are exclusively theoretically grounded in "drive-centered" models of the mind are directed toward a thera-peutic goal of increased autoregulation of conscious systems over unconscious systems, of "making the unconscious conscious." "Consciousness," a mental state of "cold cognition," is thus seen as the critical manifestation of the human experience, and autonomy and autoregulation the desired end-state. Since intense negative affect interferes with this state of consciousness, it must be autoregulated.

This scenario seems to be uniquely psychoanalytic, and yet psychopharma-cological treatments that target negative affective states are also based on at-tempts to improve the efficiency of autoregulating brain systems. Although these forms of treatment have been seen as antithetical to each other, both share the commonality of being based on a perspective that is biased toward an "isolated brain" and a "one-person psychology" model of mind. In addition, I propose that models that exclusively focus on intra-brain events also lead to etiological conceptions of psychopathology that heavily emphasize the role of genetic and constitutional factors in psychopathogenesis.

As opposed to this intra-brain focus, now extensively used in cognitive neuroscience, the newer fields of affective neuroscience and especially social neuroscience are exploring inter-brain interactions. These disciplines are focusing on not only the perceptual, cognitive, and motoric mechanisms within individual brains, but also on how these internal processes are interactively regulated and dysregulated by affective transactions with other brains. In this paradigm, the individual is exposed to species-specific signals that trigger changes in brain organization associated with the subjective responses that accompany interpersonally induced stress. In such animal studies, the presence or absence of other organisms are presented as stressors. In human studies, visual representations of emotionally expressive faces, often presented at subliminal levels, are used as experimental stimuli, and then coping responses, usually at a nonverbal, physiological level, are measured.

The idea that facial expressions of emotion have an adaptive value in social communication because they reveal one's inner state to another was first proposed in 1872 by Darwin, a work well known to Freud (Sulloway, 1979). This paradigm has lead to an immense literature on "basic emotions" (e.g., Ekman, 1992; Izard, 1992). But it has also been adopted within the developmental sciences in order to explore the dyadic affective communications within the emotion-transacting attachment relationship. Animal and human psychobiological investigations are now tracing how visual and auditory affective transmissions between the mother's and infant's emotionally expressive faces can acts as signals that coregulate their internal states. These early interactive events are encoded within an internal working model of attachment that guides the individual's behavior in interpersonal interactions, and this model of the earliest intersubjective experiences is stored in limbic areas of the right brain (Schore, 1994, 1996, 1997b, 1998b, 1998d, 1999d). MacLean defined the adaptive role of the limbic system as the brain network that "derives subjective information in terms of emotional feelings that guide behavior" (1985, p. 220).

A primary focus of this perspective is on not only subjective affective phenomena but also on the reception and expression of affective communications and "hot cognitions" between the brains of different individuals. Brothers argued that emotion occurs "in the context of evolved systems for the mutual regulation of behavior, often involving bodily changes that act as signals" (1997, p. 123). Trevarthen asserted that "The emotions constitute a time-space field of intrinsic brain states of mental and behavioral vitality that are signaled for communication to other subjects and that are open to immediate influence from the signals of these others" (1993, p. 155). This brain-brain interactive perspective explores the neurobiology of intersubjectivity; that is, the mechanisms by which interpersonal interactions coregulate psychobiological states in an intersubjective field created by two interacting brains. Such an area of inquiry seeks the mechanisms described by Freud (1937/1961) at the end of his career: "For the psychical field, the biological field does in fact play the part of the underlying bedrock."

An inter-brain paradigm thus supports current "relational" models that operate under the principles of a "two-person psychology." Empathy is thus seen as the critical manifestation of the human experience, and relatedness and interactive regulation the desired end-state. Furthermore, these "intersubjective" conceptualizations "construe the fundamental operation of mind as based in its striving for relational connection and communication, rather than discharge and gratification of endogenous instinctual pressures" (Dunn, 1995, p. 724). "Relational" psychoanalytic models thus emphasize the potent intersubjective influences that flow between two affectively communicating minds (Natterson, 1991; Stolorow & Atwood, 1996). These communications are occurring on both conscious, and more importantly, unconscious levels (Schore, 1994, 1997c, 1998c). In this perspective, affectively charged transference-countertransference interactions between patient and therapist represent the mechanisms by which the unconscious mind of one communicates with the unconscious mind of another.

This model of brain-brain interactions is strongly supported by studies of the critical role of the right hemisphere in the processing of social and emotional information (Schore, 1997a, 1997c) and by research that highlights the role of right-brain-to-right-brain affective communications, at levels beneath awareness in both mother–infant and therapist–patient dyads (Schore, 1994, 1997c, 2002b). The dominance of the right cortex for organizing "subjective emotional experiences" (Wittling & Roschmann, 1993) implies that the fast-acting affective communications within these dyads can be characterized as "intersubjectivity." Inter-brain models more so than intra-brain models are thus a more fertile source of hypotheses for understanding how the therapist perceives the unconscious states of the patient, and how emotional communications are transacted within the therapeutic relationship. In addition, an interactive brain perspective emphasizes social environmental factors in psychopathology, and models how affectively dysregulating early experiences with misattuned objects mediates the transmission of psychopathologies.

These ideas lead to the suggestion that the next generation of brain research should simultaneously measure the different activation patterns of two brains as they are interacting with each other during different classes of affectively charged interpersonal interactions. The stress-inducing and stress-regulating transactions of mother–infant and therapist–patient dyads are obvious candidates for such research. Such studies could offer us more detailed information about the subtle socioaffective signals that trigger changes in different patterns of psychobiological state in both brains. These transitions may represent switch points between right-brain interactive and autoregulatory modes.

Ultimately, the most powerful theoretical and clinical models of both psychoanalysis and neuroscience must incorporate both aspects of the one-person psychology of an autoregulating isolated brain and the two-person psychology of an interactively regulating brain. In psychoanalysis, both the "classical" and "relational" models share the fundamental assumptions, first promulgated by Freud, of the centrality of early experiences and of the primacy of the dynamic unconscious. Wallerstein wrote that theoretically "psychoanalysis is inevitably and necessarily both a one-person and a two-person psychology" (1998, p. 1031), and that clinically "the analyst's receptive role is to discern as best as possible which psychology the patient is offering at any given moment, and then to react accordingly" (p. 1033).

I suggest that the adaptive self-regulating processes of the "right mind" that occur at levels beneath awareness do so in two modes: autoregulation, via the processes of a "one-person psychology," or interactive regulation, under the operations of a "two-person psychology." The capacity of the unconscious right mind to shift between these two modes, depending upon context, reflects different organizational modes of the right brain, and this adaptive function allows the individual to self-regulate either with or without objects.

DEVELOPMENTAL PSYCHOANALYTIC
AND DEVELOPMENTAL NEUROPSYCHOANALYTIC
CONTRIBUTIONS TO AFFECT THEORY

An exploration of the fundamental processes that mediate self-regulation is a central theme of my ongoing attempts to integrate neuroscience and psychoanalysis. In my book *Affect Regulation and the Origin of the Self: The Neurobiology of Emotional Development* (1994), I presented a model of affective ontogeny that is compatible with Jackson's triadic concepts of an "evolutionary sequence in mental development," of higher functions superseding and overlying lower functions, and of the preeminent role of the right hemisphere in emotional functions. When applied to affective phenomena, Jackson's hierarchical principle directs us to look for later-developing higher-cortical affect-regulatory systems that modulate earlier-developing lower-subcortical centers involved in affective processes.

In that volume, I presented a psychoneurobiological model holding that the affective events that occur in the early postnatal stages of maturation of the emotional brain are critical to the development of systems that process socioemotional information at levels beneath awareness and regulate affective and motivational states for the rest of the lifespan (Schore, 1994). Over the course of the first 2 years, the child's regulatory capacities expand from an initial position where the primary caregiver externally regulates the child's affective states, to one where the child internalizes this function. This transformation has been described in the developmental psychoanalytic literature as "the processes whereby the primary object relations become internalized and transformed into psychic structure" (Stechler & Halton, 1987, p. 823). Thus, I contend that the experiences required for the experience-dependent maturation of the emotion-processing right brain are the attachment experiences described by developmental psychoanalysis.

Over the last 3 decades, developmental psychoanalysis has emerged as a central force in the field, so much so that all current theoretical and clinical models now incorporate models of early emotional development. The covers of the two most influential books in the field, Bowlby's *Attachment and Loss* (1969b) and Stern's *The Interpersonal World of the Infant* (1985), as well as my book, featured the visual image of a mother and baby, thus iconically highlighting the centrality of the early events of life to personality formation. These groundbreaking volumes not only offered detailed models of early-appearing affective processes, but also emphasized the preeminent role of the affectively attuned mother in shaping the individual's emotional capacities. Through their considerable influence, as well as a growing body of work of a number of developmental psychoanalytic researchers and theoreticians, this discipline is now a major contributor of updated and clinically relevant affective concepts into psychoanalysis.

The cover of Panksepp's remarkable book, *Affective Neuroscience: The Foundations of Human and Animal Emotions* (1998), also featured the image of a mother and baby, but in this case a primate mother and baby. This is more than a coincidence or mere analogy to the similar covers of the above-mentioned volumes—it derived from the fact that Panksepp has extensively investigated the psychobiology of Bowlby's attachment processes. This perspective underscores the essential contributions of affective neuroscience to a deeper understanding of the fundamental trans-species psychobiological processes that mediate that critical mechanisms of emotional development.

But in addition to developmental psychoanalysis and affective neuroscience, developmental neuroscience—the current derivative of Jackson–Freud's hierarchical-developmental model—can also offer us essential information for theories of affect and the early development of the unconscious mind. It should be remembered that one of the major findings of neuroscience is that the developing brain, whether animal or human, is qualitatively different from an adult brain (Noebels, 1989; Schore, 1994; Thatcher, Lyon, Rumsey, & Krasnegor, 1996). I point out this obvious fact because it is directly relevant to not only psychoanalytic models of affect, but also to one of the fundamental problems of science—how and why a primitive organism first develops, and then continues to become more complex. The central question is: How can development be both discontinuous and continuous?

If it is clear that an adequate model of early development cannot be drawn from psychoanalytic reconstructions of an adult mind, it is also true that a comprehensive neuropsychological model of brain self-organization and reorganization, of plasticity, of how the brain changes with experience, cannot be gained by studying only adult normal or abnormal brains. However, neuroscience, which is still much more concerned with "cognitive" rather than "affective" neuroscience, has paid little attention to developing brains.

And yet explorations in specifically developmental neuroscience can offer us more detailed information about a spectrum of essential human problems that include constructing more accurate models of the development of the primitive mind, elucidating the gene-environment events that underlie the development of brain systems that process affect, modeling the emergence of various forms of consciousness, describing the experience-dependent maturation of brain systems that foster resilience or high risk to psychopathologies, understanding the ontogenetic progression of primitive into more complex brain-mind-body psychobiological states, and ultimately offering more powerful models of how human relationships can alter, for better or worse, internal affective systems. This overarching perspective necessitates an integration of developmental neuroscience, developmental psychology, and developmental psychoanalysis into models of how and why early experiences are so critical to the evolution of adaptive and maladaptive mechanisms.

The centrality of Freud's developmental perspective is expressed in his statement, "From the very first, psychoanalysis was directed towards tracing developmental processes. It . . . was led . . . to construct a genetic psychology" (1913/1958c, pp. 182–183). Freud's developmental perspective included an ontogenetic stage theory, a model he incorporated from Jackson (Goldstein, 1995). Although his oral, anal, and phallic model may be somewhat imprecise, the idea that development occurs in stages is supported by current neurobiological research indicating that the brain matures in stages (Martin et al., 1988; Schore, 1994; Thatcher, 1991).

Indeed, Freud's conviction that the elaboration of what Sulloway (1979) called his "genetic psychobiology" can be a fertile and essential area of scientific inquiry has been confirmed. His thesis that early stressful experiences in the developmental environment have long-lasting effects is now being explored in a growing body of developmental psychobiological research (e.g., Cabib, Puglisi-Allegra, & D'Amato, 1993; Champoux, Byrne, DeLizio, & Suomi, 1992; Clarke et al., 1996; Kehoe et al., 1996; Ladd, Owens, & Nemeroff, 1996; Liu et al., 1997; Poeggel et al., 1999; Rosenblum et al., 1994; Suomi, 1995). In such work, Coplan and colleagues concluded, "These data . . . neurobiologically substantiate the view proposed by Freud . . . stressing the importance of early life experience on the development of psychopathology in adulthood" (1996, p. 1622).

Freud's ontogenetic perspective was subsequently taken up by other psychoanalysts, so much so that developmental models are now a rich point of contact with the other developmental sciences and a central force in psychoanalytic theory and practice (Schore, 1994, 1996, 1997b, 1997c). Interestingly, Freud downplayed the role of the mother in early development, and advanced a model in which the father and later-forming oedipal dynamics were the primary early influence. It was thus Ferenczi who was responsible for advocating formal recognition of the mother's significance (and an intersubjective approach) into psychoanalysis, a position that lead to Freud's disavowal of his work (Vida, 1997).

But Freud's developmental concepts were especially elaborated upon by a number of psychoanalysts who began to explore development not in the reconstructions of adult patients, but in the psychoanalytic observation of infants and children. This rich tradition includes the writings of Freud's daughter Anna, as well as Klein, Winnicott, Bowlby, and Mahler, and continues in the current work of Stern, Emde, Beebe, Fonagy, and other developmentally oriented theoreticians and clinicians. My own contributions to this literature have been directed toward demonstrating the direct relevance of developmental psychoanalysis to such theoretical issues as the determination of the early origins of the primitive mind and the processes by which the dynamic unconscious self-organizes and continues to evolve over the course of the lifespan, and such clinical matters as what are the interpersonal and intrapsychic mechanisms that allow for growth in psychoanalytic treatment. A central tenet of all developmental psychoanalytic models has been the primacy of affect in the first 2 years of life. As Krystal (1988) noted, the maturation of affects represents the key event in infancy, and the developmental emergence of the self-regulation of affect is an ontogenetic attainment that is an essential adaptive capacity.

Indeed, the three most significant advances in psychoanalytic theory since Freud are grounded in developmental affect-transacting phenomena. Object relations theory (Greenberg & Mitchell, 1983; Horner, 1991; Scharff & Scharff, 1998) models how early affect-laden experiences with the primary caregiver indelibly influences internal psychic structural ("representational") systems. Self psychology theory (Kohut, 1971, 1977) details how early affectively charged interactions between the infant's emerging self and the mother's psychobiologically regulating ("selfobject") functions are critical to the organization of the self. And Bowlby's (1969b, 1973, 1980) attachment theory, which to this date represents the most successful integration of psychoanalysis and the biological sciences, highlights the importance of the infant's emotional attachment to the mother to the individual's capacity to enter into all later interpersonal relationships. His concepts now lie at the heart of developmental psychology, which is also currently intensively studying the long-enduring effects of early emotional development (e.g., Cassidy & Shaver, 1999; Sroufe, 1996).

It is important to point out that the affective transactions described by psychoanalytic self psychology, object relations, and attachment theory are occurring during a critical period of neurobiological maturation of the developing limbic system. Anders and Zeanah (1984) put forth the argument that the emotion-generating limbic system is the most obvious site of developmental changes associated with the ascendence of attachment behaviors. Indeed, the specific period from 7 to 15 months (roughly Bowlby's period for the establishment of attachment patterns) has been shown to be critical for the myelination and therefore the maturation of particular rapidly developing limbic and cortical association areas (Kinney, Brody, Kloman, & Gilles, 1988; Yakovlev & Lecours, 1967). Psychoanalysis and neuroscience thus strongly fertilize each other in cocreating interdisciplinary models of emotional development (Schore, 1994, 1998b).

If psychoanalysis has been actively incorporating developmental data over the last few decades, contemporary neuroscience has been much slower in the process. It should be pointed out however, that MacLean, one of the pioneer explorers of the limbic system, concluded that: "One wonders whether the limbic system would ever have become such a 'solar plexus' with respect to emotional feelings if it had not been for the development in mammals of the family unit dependent upon the nursing mother" (1985, p. 220). And yet neuroscientific studies of affect continue to heavily focus on adult brains, despite neurology's long-standing interest in the effects of early experience on brain development. In 1891, the year of Freud's *On Aphasia*, Dareste, using neuroembryological data, formulated the critical period hypothesis, which stated that in the maturing organism developmental processes in different areas proceed at different rates. During these periods of intensified growth and differentiation, the organism is subject to environmental conditions, and if these are outside the normal range a permanent arrest of development occurs. This conception modeled how detrimental early experiences could *negatively* impact the maturation of the brain, and Freud (1895) incorporated it into his ideas about how early stressful "pathological" environments play a role in adult psychopathology.

In 1894, one year before Freud's "Project," Ramon y Cajal (1899/1995) began to describe how enriched epigenetic experiences *positively* affect neural expression with beneficial psychological outcomes. This line of research continued in studies demonstrating how early "enriched" environments promote brain growth (Rosenzweig, Bennet, & Diamond, 1972), and how the expansion of dendritic growth and synaptogenesis of the postnatally developing brain is "experience-sensitive" (Greenough, 1986) and "experience-dependent" (Aoki & Siekevitz, 1988). In the case of the growth of the emotion-processing limbic system, these "experiences" are contained in early maternal–infant contingently responsive and synchronized psychobiological interactions. And so the most recent expression of this type of work is in research on the neurobiology of mother–infant relationships. For example, Fleming, O'Day and Kraemer (1999) described:

> The optimal coordination between the new mammalian mother and her young involves a sequence of behaviors on the part of each that ensures that the young will be adequately cared for and show healthy physical, emotional, and social development. This coordination is accomplished by each member of the relationship having the appropriate sensitivities and responses to cues that characterize the other. [This developmental model] . . . emphasizes the importance of learning and plasticity in the

formation and maintenance of the mother–young relationship and mediation of the experience effects by the brain and its neurochemistry. (p. 673)

The next question is: At this point in time can we tell what specific parts
of the brain does this early interactive experience impacting? There is a body of
animal and human studies showing that the infant's early-maturing (Best, 1988;
Geschwind & Galaburda, 1987; Hellige, 1993; Ornstein, 1997; Schore, 1994;
Taylor, 1969) right hemisphere is specifically impacted by early social experiences
(Denenberg, Garbanti, Sherman, Yutzey, & Kaplan, 1978; Schore, 1994). This
body of studies is supported in a single photon emission computed tomographic
(SPECT) study by Chiron and colleagues (1997), which indicated that the
right brain hemisphere is dominant in human infants.

This suggests that the infant's developing right brain may require specific
forms of experiences that are provided by the mother's right brain (Rotenberg,
1994; Schore, 1994). In fact, there is now evidence for early right-hemisphere-
to-right-hemisphere communications in very early infancy. Studies show that
most human females show a tendency to cradle infants on the left side of their
body (Manning et al., 1997). This behavior is well developed in women but
not men, and is independent of handedness. Manning and colleagues contended that the left-cradling tendency "facilitates the flow of affective information from the infant via the left ear and eye to the center of emotional decoding,
that is, the right hemisphere of the mother" (1997, p. 327). Visual cues of affect
are important to the maintenance of left cradling, since an image of the baby
transmitted to the left side of the mother's visual field (right hemisphere) is a
necessary stimulus for the preference (Manning & Chamberlain, 1991).

The right cerebral cortex shows a hemispheric advantage in the infant's processing of individual faces (Deruelle & de Schonen, 1998), in the infant's recognition of arousal-inducing maternal facial affective expressions (Nelson, 1987),
in the infant's response to the prosody of motherese (Fernald, 1989), and in
early language development (Locke, 1997; Schumann, 1997). In describing the
greater involvement of the right hemisphere in infancy, Semrud-Clikeman and
Hynd stated, "The emotional experience of the infant develops through the
sounds, images, and pictures that constitute much of an infant's early learning
experience, and are disproportionately stored or processed in the right hemisphere during the formative stages of brain ontogeny" (1990, p. 198).

Indeed, the right hemisphere is centrally involved in human attachment and
in the development of reciprocal interactions within the mother–infant regulatory system (Henry, 1993; Schore, 1994, 1996, 1997b, 1998a; Siegel, 1999).
In a series of contributions I have offered evidence that face-to-face interactions
that generate high levels of positive arousal between the psychobiologically
attuned mother and her infant represent an essential mechanism in the development of affect regulation. The interpersonal contexts created in mutual
gaze transactions allow for the establishment of "affect synchrony" (Feldman,
Greenbaum, & Yirmiya, 1999). In this process of "contingent responsivity," the

more the mother tunes her activity level to the infant during periods of social engagement, the more she allows him/her to recover quietly in periods of disengagement, and the more she attends to the child's reinitiating cues for re-engagement, the more synchronized their interaction.

This mutual regulation of affect occurs in maternal–infant play experiences. In such positively charged transactions, the infant's right hemisphere, which is dominant for the infant's recognition of the maternal face—and for the perception of arousal-inducing maternal facial affective expressions, visual emotional information, and the prosody of the mother's voice—is appraising the output of the mother's right hemisphere, which is dominant for nonverbal communication and the processing and expression of emotional information (see Schore, 1994). The maternal comforting substrate is also located in the mother's right brain (Horton, 1995). The fact that connections into the autonomic nervous system are highly lateralized to the right brain (Schore, 1994, 1997b) may explain Basch's (1976, p. 766) contention that "the language of mother and infant consist of signals produced by the autonomic, involuntary nervous system in both parties."

Trevarthen noted, "The intrinsic regulators of human brain growth in a child are specifically adapted to be coupled, by emotional communication, to the regulators of adult brains" (1990, p. 357). In these affective interchanges, the mother maximizes positive and minimizes negative affect states in the infant, and they culminate in the development of an attachment system, the function of which is the dyadic regulation of emotion (Sroufe, 1996). The mother is thus a regulator of arousal (van der Kolk & Fisler, 1994), and the transfer of affect between mother and infant are thus mediated by right-hemisphere-to-right-hemisphere arousal-regulating transactions. Confirming this model, Ryan, Kuhl, and Deci using EEG and neuroimaging data, proposed that "The positive emotional exchange resulting from autonomy-supportive parenting involves participation of right hemispheric cortical and subcortical systems that participate in global, tonic emotional modulation" (1997, p. 719).

These events are inscribed in implicit-procedural memory in the early-developing right hemisphere that is specialized for the processing of visuospatial information (Galin, 1974). This model fits nicely with the clinical psychoanalytic observations that early mental representations are specifically visually oriented (Giovacchini, 1981), and that historical visual imagery may be derivative of events of early phases of development (Anthi, 1983). But the right cerebral cortex is also dominant for "implicit" learning (Hugdahl, 1995), an adaptive process that underlies all emotional phenomena, including those at the core of the psychotherapeutic relationship. According to Siegel, "When implicit memory is retrieved, the neural net profiles that are reactivated involve circuits in the brain that are a fundamental part of our everyday experience of life: behaviors, emotions, and images. These implicit elements form part of the foundation for our subjective sense of ourselves: We act, feel, and imagine without recognition of the influence of past experience on our present reality" (1999, p. 29).

The early face-to-face attachment experiences that are encoded in implicit memory continue to be expressed in ongoing emotional development, and the right cortex plays a crucial role in the processing of affectively salient visual and auditory information emanating from the human face throughout the life-span. In optimal early environments the right hemisphere—the lateralized substrate of early socioemotional learning and attachment processes—ends its growth phase in the second year, when the linear left hemisphere begins one, but it cycles back into growth phases at later periods of the life cycle (Thatcher, 1994). This allows for the continuity of attachment mechanisms in subsequent functioning, and yet also for the potential continuing reorganization of the emotion-processing right brain throughout life.

RIGHT BRAIN PROCESSING OF SOCIOEMOTIONAL INFORMATION AND RIGHT MIND-BODY CONNECTIONS

Although most neuroscientists would define the experimental activity of their discipline as "brain research," a term that implies investigations of a singular natural system, there is a long tradition in the neurological sciences of the concept of dual-lateralized brain systems (Harrington, 1985). In the 19th century, the golden age of neurology, Broca's (1861) discovery that left hemisphere lesions often result in linguistic loss was later matched by Jackson's (1931) findings that the right hemisphere supports emotional speech and mediates preverbal mentation and automatic emotional functions that are subsequently arranged in words in the left hemisphere into a propositional form.

The resulting asymmetries of the hemispheres was then translated into models of dominance, and "around 1900 . . . there arose the view that the left cerebral hemisphere was dominant for all higher functions" (Bogen, 1997, p. 12). Freud's contention that the ego is located in cortex in the "speech-area on the left-hand side" (1923/1961b, p. 26) was undoubtedly influenced by these trends on lateralization within neurological science. But in addition, it may reflect the hemispheric bias of Freud's own brain. It has been pointed out that his development of "an uncompromising oral and auditory psychotherapy" may reflect the fact that, within Freud, "the subtle cortical organization of the minor cerebral hemisphere (his 'right brain') was less highly developed than that of the major" (Cheshire, 1996, p. 1160).

Over the course of the 20th century the body of evidence for lateralization of the human hemispheres became massive, and it is currently accepted that the right hemisphere is specialized for more nonlinear, holistic, analogical processing while the left is specialized for linear, analytic processing (van Kleek, 1989); that the right uses an expansive attention mechanism that focuses on global features while the left uses a restricted mode that focuses on local detail (Derryberry & Tucker, 1994); and that the hemispheres use two types of image generation (Kosslyn, Maljkovic, Hamilton, Horowitz, & Thompson, 1995). The laterality research from the split-brain studies of the 1970s has been cited

by both psychoanalytic (Galin, 1974) and neuroscience (Joseph, 1996) authors
to demonstrate the similarities of right hemispheric cognition with Freud's
primary process and left with secondary process cognition.

But recent advances in laterality research may be even more relevant to
psychoanalysis. These studies have been going beyond investigating the hemispheric processing of cognitive information to the right hemispheric processing
of affective information (Silberman & Weingartner, 1986) at unconscious levels
(Wexler, Warrenburg, Schwartz, & Janer, 1992). This hemisphere is dominant
both for the perception of nonverbal emotional expressions embedded in facial
and prosodic stimuli (Blonder, Bowers, & Heilman, 1991) and for implicit
learning (Hugdahl, 1995). In experimental studies there has been intense interest in the implicit perception of affective information transmitted by faces (Niedenthal, 1990), and in the distinct dynamic properties of "nonconscious" affect,
which is relatively diffuse, more readily displaced, and yields stronger or less
adulterated effect (Murphy, Monahan, & Zajonc, 1995).

This "automatic emotion" operates in infancy and beyond at nonconscious
levels (Hansen & Hansen, 1994), and such early automatic reactions shape the
subsequent conscious emotional processing of a stimulus (Dimberg & Ohman,
1996). Because the unconscious processing of emotional information is extremely rapid, the dynamic operations of the "transmission of nonconscious
affect" (Murphy et al., 1995, p. 600) and the spontaneous communication of
"automatic emotion" cannot be consciously perceived. These processes are fast
acting, since the implicit appraisal of facially expressed emotional cues is initiated in as little as 2 milliseconds (Niedenthal, 1990), far beneath levels of
awareness (Schore, 2002e).

The right hemisphere is also centrally involved in not just the reception but
the expression of affective states. Right cortical functions mediate the expression
of facial displays of emotion (Borod, Haywood, & Koff, 1997), thereby facilitating "spontaneous emotional communication" (Buck, 1994) and "spontaneous"
gestural communication (Blonder, Burns, Bowers, Moore, & Heilman 1995).
These rapid communications are not only sensed by another face, they trigger
motor responses in the facial musculature of the recipient. Such studies describe
the lateralized neurobiological substrate of "primitive emotional contagion"
(Hatfield, Cacioppo, & Rapson, 1992). This process describes the unconscious,
automatic, and uncontrollable tendency to mimic and synchronize another
person's facial expression, postures, movements, and vocalizations, thereby allowing for the interpersonal modulation of emotions.

For example, studies of emotion communication demonstrate that human
vocal affect expressions elicit electromyographically detectable changes in the
receiver's facial affect expressions (Hietanen, Surakka, & Linnankoski, 1998).
Even more than this, the perceiver mimics the perceived expression within 300
to 400 milliseconds, at levels beneath awareness (Stenberg, Wiking, & Dahl,
1998). In discussing how a perceiver rapidly mimics the facial gestures of faces

Bruner concluded, "A quick-triggered mimetic reaction might not only facilitate *affective bonding* with a putative partner, but could also send reafferent signals back into the systems to assure arousal-appropriate perceptual processing of that partner" (1994, p. 278; italics added). Note that this description mirrors my earlier characterization of the right brain-to-right brain affective bonding mechanism embedded within the infant–maternal attachment relationship. It also fits well with the documented role of the right hemisphere in mediating facial expressivity during spontaneous social interactions that take place in the "natural conversation" of "interpersonal family communication" (Blonder, Burns, Bowers, Moore, & Heilman, 1993).

Right brain-to-right brain psychophysiological processes also explicate Dimberg and Ohman's assertion that "long sequences of interactions between people may be partly determined by nonconscious perceptions and automatic responses on the part of both the sender and receiver. Their conscious understanding of what is going on in the interaction that they can formulate verbally, on the other hand, may be quite independent of this basic level of interaction" (1996, p. 177). Indeed, these authors specifically implicated right hemispheric processes in these events. Note how this characterization also describes the nonverbal unconscious right brain-to-right brain communications within the psychotherapeutic transference-countertransference relationship (see Schore, 1994, 1997c, 2002e).

In addition, very current neuroscience data indicates that hemispheric asymmetry is not just a human characteristic, but also extends down to mammals (Adamec, 1997), fish, reptiles, amphibians (Bisazza, Rogers, & Vallortigara, 1998), and birds (Vallortigara, 1992). Furthermore, although earlier thinking considered only lateralization at the cortical hemispheric level, there is now considerable support for right versus left lateralization of the human subcortical structures that mediate affective phenomena. Right-lateralized components of emotional and facial processing are seen in, for example, the human right amygdala (Cahill et al., 1996; Morris, Ohman, & Dolan, 1999), right insula (Berthier, Starkstein, & Leiguarda, 1987); right basal ganglia (Cohen, Riccio, & Flannery, 1994), and right thalamus (Woodman & Tabatabai, 1998).

One of the most important aspects of the relationship between asymmetrical subcortical structures and affective functions is the lateralization of right-brain connections into the reticular formation that supports the fundamental brain arousal mechanisms (see Schore, 1994). According to Solms (1996), arousal processes, which have their epicenter in the ascending reticular activating system, represent the physiological correlates of those mental processes conceptualized by Freud as "psychical energy." This has been confirmed in studies showing that arousal levels are associated with changes in metabolic energy (Gonzalez-Lima & Scheich, 1985), and that the biogenic amines that mediate arousal also regulate blood flow, an indicator of oxidative energy metabolism (Krimer, Mully, Williams, & Goldman-Rakic, 1998; Schore, 1994). In addition to mediating the arousal dimension of emotional and motivational states, these bioamines also have growth-promoting, trophic effects on developing neuronal systems (see Schore, 1994).

Importantly, there is evidence indicating that the right hemisphere is involved in the bilateral regulation of arousal (Heilman & Van Den Abell, 1979), and that the phasic arousal system is right lateralized, thereby supporting this hemisphere's global perceptual and cognitive processes (Derrybery & Tucker, 1994). In line with these findings, I have proposed a preferential reciprocal interconnectivity of higher right-corticolimbic structures into the dopamine neurons of the ventral tegmental area of the rostral reticular formation and the noradrenaline neurons in the nucleus of the solitary tract in the caudal reticular formation (Schore, 1994, 1996, 1997b). In Chapter 22 of *Affect Regulation and the Origin of the Self* (1994), I offered a detailed model of how right cortically processed visual and auditory information emanating from the face of a meaningful other can trigger both top-down and bottom-up alterations in subcortical arousal systems.

Another equally important subcortical structure intimately associated with affective processes is the neuroendocrine neuronal system in the hypothalamus. These neuropeptide-producing neurons also impact arousal levels, especially peripheral arousal. It is well established that the diencephalic hypothalamus is critical to the expression of emotional behavior (Thatcher & John, 1977) and is the hub of the motivational systems (Hadley, 1989). In a groundbreaking study, Kalogeras and colleagues (1996) demonstrated that the right side of the human hypothalamus is dominant for the corticotropin-releasing factor-induced neurosecretion of ACTH, vasopressin, and oxytocin (all of which are involved in the developmental psychobiology of attachment). Citing studies indicating that "the right hemisphere predominates in spatial abilities, expression of affect, and control of vital functions supporting survival," they concluded, "Such a dominant side of the hypothalamus could result from increased stimulatory input from higher centers in the limbic system and/or the cortex" (Kalogeras et al., 1996, p. 2049).

The right-cerebral hemisphere shows, more so than the left, preferential interconnections with the limbic system (Joseph, 1996; Tucker, 1992). Hugdahl asserted that "Although traditionally restricted to cortical function, laterality . . . (implies) . . . not only subcortical functions but also peripheral, autonomic, endocrine, and immune functions. Thus . . . laterality goes beyond the more traditional meaning of specialization only for higher cognitive functions, like language and visuo-spatial processing" (1995, p. 238). This general principle is supported not only by the above-mentioned hypothalamic neuropeptides, but also in work showing that cortical regulation of the adrenal stress hormone cortisol is under primary control of the right hemisphere (Wittling & Pfluger, 1990; Wittling & Schweiger, 1993).

The hypothalamus, the head ganglion of the autonomic nervous system, acts as the major subcortical center that regulates both sympathetic and parasympathetic autonomic activities (Truex & Carpenter, 1964). For example, hypothalamic corticotropin-releasing factor activates the sympathetic nervous system by raising plasma noradrenaline, which in turn increases energy metabolism and generates a state of emotional excitement (Brown et al., 1982). A growing body of work has revealed the preeminent role of the right hemisphere in the control of both the sympathetic and parasympathetic components of the autonomic nervous system (e.g., Lane & Jennings, 1995; Porges, Doussard-Roosevelt, & Maiti, 1994; Spence, Shapiro, & Zaidel, 1996; Yoon, Morrillo, Cechetto, & Hachinski, 1997). Wittling, Block, Schweiger, and Genzel (1998) reported that when subjects viewed "depressing, appalling, piteous, deeply moving" negative affectively charged scenes from the film *Schindler's List*, the sympathetically driven pump capacity of the heart was increased only when the film was presented to the right and not left hemisphere.

A right lateralization is also found in the brain stem medullary systems involved in autonomic regulation of the parasympathetic nervous system, specifically through the action of the right vagus. Porges and colleagues (1994, p. 176) stated that "the right vagus and, thus, cardiac vagal tone are associated with processes involving the expression and regulation of motion, emotion, and communication." In this manner "the right hemisphere—including the right cortical and subcortical structures—would promote the efficient regulation of autonomic function via the source nuclei of the brain stem" (p. 175).

I would add to this conceptualization the idea that affectively charged, facially mediated, right brain-to-right brain communications, at levels beneath awareness, can instigate the regulation (or dysregulation) of autonomic function. Despite earlier controversies, it is well established that the autonomic nervous system reacts to perceptual stimuli that may never enter consciousness (Lazarus & McCleary, 1951) and that it is involved in the generation of nonconscious affect that is triggered by the visual perception of an emotionally expressive face. This unconscious process may initiate early in infancy as the "implicit mere exposure effect" (Gordon & Holyoak, 1983) of attachment imprinting (Lickliter & Gottlieb, 1986), and may be expressed at later points as "primitive emotional contagion" (Hatfield, Cacioppo, & Rapson, 1992). I also suggest that this transfer of nonconscious affect is mediated by a right amygdala-to-right amygdala communication, since this lateralized structure is activated in eye contact tasks (Kawashima et al., 1999).

Both neuroscientists (Joseph, 1992) and psychoanalysts (Galin, 1974; Hoppe, 1977; McLaughlin, 1978; Miller, 1991; Stone, 1977) have contended that Freud's unconscious systems are lateralized in the right hemisphere. The lateralization of the hypothalamus, the anatomical locus of drive centers (Stellar, 1954), supports Freud's idea about the central role of drive in the system unconscious. The fact that the right hemisphere contains "the most comprehensive and integrated map of the body state available to the brain" (Damasio, 1994, p. 66) indicates that Freud's (1915/1957a) definition of "drive" as "the psychical representative of the stimuli originating from the organism and reaching the mind" may be more properly characterized as reaching the "right mind" (Ornstein, 1997). It may also elucidate Freud's remark to Groddeck (from a letter dated June 5, 1917): "The unconscious is the proper mediator between the somatic and the mental, perhaps the long-sought 'missing link'" (in Groddeck, 1977, p. 38).

The above-mentioned neurobiological studies of right-corticosubcortical systems also bear upon the proposals that the left half of the body (regulated by the contralateral right brain) is more accessible to unconscious impulses (Ferenczi, 1926/1952b), that the early development of right-limbic interconnections into the immune system influence the etiology of a vulnerability to psychosomatic disorders (Schore, 1994, 1997b), that the right hemisphere is more involved than the left with somatization symptom formation related to emotional disturbances (Min & Lee, 1997), that an underactivation of the right brain is associated with a high degree of physical health complaints (Wittling & Schweiger, 1993), and that strategies of the right hemisphere are underutilized by coronary heart disease patients (Soufer et al., 1998). Indeed, an integration of neuroscience and psychoanalysis may lead to a deeper understanding of mind-body connections (Pally, 1998) and treatment models of psychosomatic illness, a focus of recent clinical writings (Aron & Anderson, 1998).

A HIERARCHICAL MODEL OF THE ONTOGENY
OF THE LIMBIC SYSTEM

The importance of vertical corticosubcortical functional systems was described by Hecaen and Albert: "Cortical neural mechanisms of one hemisphere would be responsible for a particular performance, and subcortical structures connected to these cortical zones would participate in the realization of the performance, creating a complex, corticosubcortical functional system specific to each hemisphere" (1978, p. 414). The clinical utility of the concept of the vertical organization of the brain is now being applied over a spectrum of neurobiological domains, from functional studies of the emergence of self-regulation in the developing brain (Luu & Tucker, 1996), to research on the "deep and early cerebral asymmetry" in the infant brain (Trevarthen & Aitken, 1994), to studies of dysfunction in the neural circuitry of emotion dysregulation (Davidson, 1998b; Davidson, Putnam, & Larson, 2000). This trend derives directly from, once again, the far-sighted work of Jackson (1931).

As mentioned earlier, Jackson proposed that the evolution of the brain is an ascending process, in which ontogenetically early-maturing structures are progressively superseded by later-maturing structures. Over discrete stages of development, each higher level rerepresents and expands at a more complex level of organization those functions present in the previous, more primitive level of organization. In this hierarchical model of brain maturation in the vertical dimension, later-developing higher cortical levels thus come to regulate earlier developing lower subcortical levels. These illuminating insights have been further advanced by Pribram (1960), who established that situated at the top of the corticosubcortical hierarchy is the frontal lobe, which acts a regulator of internal functions, Nauta (1971) and Fuster (1980), who argued that the frontal lobe is the cortical representative of the subcortical brain stem reticular arousal activating systems, and Luria (1973), who posited that the development of the ventral and medial prefrontal areas that regulate arousal occurs postnatally and is influenced by the social environment.

This neurobiological perspective has been advocated by Luu and Tucker: "Consistent with the Jacksonian principle of vertical organization, the prefrontal areas, mainly the medial and ventral surfaces, have been suggested to play a regulatory role, *through inhibition and facilitation*, over the ascending system, so that it can indirectly regulate the arousal state for the rest of the brain" (1996, p. 299; italics added). Because the orbitofrontal cortex is positioned as an association area for the limbic endbrain (Pribram, 1960), this ventromedial prefrontal system acts as the "senior executive" of limbic arousal (Joseph, 1996). But a critical question arises: What specific "lower" limbic structures and arousal mechanisms does this "higher" cortical system regulate? And what kinds of alterations within cortical-subcortical circuitries would be associated with normal and pathological brain-mind-body systems?

In line with Jackson's and Freud's ontogenetic perspectives, I suggest that only a developmental psychoneurobiological perspective, a model of the experience-dependent ontogenesis of the limbic system, can answer this question. Furthermore, I propose that this information bears directly upon psychoanalysis' question of how and why the primitive mind first develops, and then continues to become more complex (Schore, 2000e), and psychiatry's interest in the brain mechanisms that mediate psychopathogenesis (Schore, 1997b, 1997e). This work also directly speaks to the valuable contributions of John Gedo's (1991) explorations of hierarchical concepts in psychoanalysis.

Toward that end I would like to offer some thoughts on the early ontogeny of the limbic system, on what Luu and Tucker (1996) described as the developmental process of "cerebral maturation in the vertical dimension." If the orbitofrontal areas, the hierarchical apex of the limbic system (Schore, 1994), are in a critical period of maturation from 10–12 to 16–18 months, then what limbic structures are operating in the earlier months of the first year of life? Recall that the right hemisphere is in a growth spurt in the first year and a half of life, and that this hemisphere is deeply connected into the limbic system.

A clue to an answer comes from a number of researchers who have simultaneously described a "rostral limbic system," a hierarchical sequence of interconnected limbic areas in orbitofrontal, insular cortex, anterior cingulate, and amygdala (Devinsky, Morrell, & Vogt, 1995); an "anterior limbic system" composed of orbitofrontal cortex, basal forebrain, amygdala, and hypothalamus (Schnider & Ptak, 1999); a "paralimbic circuit" containing orbitofrontal, insular, and temporopolar cortices (Mesulam & Mufson, 1982); and an "anterior limbic prefrontal network" interconnecting the orbital and medial prefrontal cortex with the temporal pole, cingulate, and amygdala, which "is involved in affective responses to events and in the mnemonic processing and storage of these responses" (Carmichael & Price, 1995, p. 639).

There is a body of anatomical evidence to show that the orbitofrontal-insula, medial frontal anterior cingulate, and amygdala systems all interconnect with each other and with brain stem monoaminergic and hypothalamic neuroendo-crine nuclei (Schore, 2001b, 2003). Because they are all components of the limbic system, each processes current exteroceptive information about changes in the external social environment with interoceptive information about con-current alterations in internal bodily states. And because they all directly inter-connect with the autonomic nervous system (Neafsey, 1990), they all are influenced by and in turn regulate the events that occur at "the physiological bottom of the mind" (Jackson, 1931). Thus, they are each involved in the regulation of bodily driven affective states.

A model of limbic ontogeny can be generated on the basis of the Jacksonian ontogenetic concept of vertical brain organization and the principle of caudal to rostral brain development. Reversing the sequence of the rostral limbic sys-tem (amygdala, anterior cingulate, insula, orbitofrontal) could offer specific ideas about how a number of discrete limbic components could come on line in a defined sequence in the first year. Again, I point out that these adaptive systems are vertically organized from the simplest to the most complex, and that they onset in a fixed progression of critical periods over the first year, with the later-maturing cortical structures hierarchically regulating the earlier-maturing systems. This principle is articulated in the psychoanalytic literature, where Hartmann (1939) proposed that adaptation is primarily a reciprocal rela-tionship of the organism and its environment, and that development is a differ-entiation in which primitive regulatory systems are increasingly replaced or supplemented by more effective regulatory systems.

At birth, only the amygdala, a primitive limbic regulatory system that ap-praises crude information about external stimuli and modulates autonomic and arousal systems, is on line (Chugani, 1996). The right amygdala is known to be involved in processing of olfactory stimuli (Zald, Lee, Fluegel, & Pardo, 1998) within the mother and the perinatal infant relationship (van Toller & Kendal-Reed, 1995). This suggests that right amygdala-driven olfactory pro-cesses may underlie the proto-attachment mechanisms that are driven by the unique salience of maternal breast odors for newborn infants (Porter & Win-berg, 1999), and may account for the organization of the earliest representations of the infant maternal relationship that allow 6-day-old infants to be able to reliably discriminate the scent of their mother's breast pad from that of another woman (MacFarlane, 1977).

I propose that areas of the amygdala in the medial temporal lobe, especially the central and medial nuclei, are continuing in a critical period of maturation that onsets in the last trimester of pregnancy and continues through the first 2 months of human life, the earliest period of bonding. In growth-facilitating perinatal environments, the experience-dependent maturation of interconnections between the infant's right amygdala and right paraventricular hypothalamic nuclei could allow for coregulation of oxytocin and vasopressin release in early maternal–infant interactions (Panksepp, 1998). Alternatively, early growth-inhibiting environments containing frightening maternal behavior (Schuengel, Bakersmans-Kranenburg, & van IJzendoorn, 1999) would also be registered in the infant's right amygdala, a structure that is known to be involved in visuoaffective interactions that are maintained by eye contact (Kawashima et al., 1999) and to be activated by threatening faces (Phillips et al., 1997). Early abuse would more than disorganize the infant—severe maternal stressors would also shape and be stored in lateralized amygdalar circuits. In the psychoanalytic literature, the importance of the amygdala in the infant's very earliest (especially stressful) affective and memorial processes has been described by Share (1994).

Beginning at 8 weeks, as demonstrated in recent functional magnetic resonance imaging studies by Yamada and colleagues (1997, 2000), a dramatic rise in metabolic rate occurs in the cerebral cortex, heralding a significant advance in brain maturation. Visual stimulation specifically induces a rapid change in energy metabolism in the occipital cortex, and the authors concluded that this reflects the onset of a critical period during which synaptic connections in the primary visual cortex are modified by visual experience. It is at this very time that the earlier-described face-to-face interactions, occurring within the primordial experiences of human play, first appear (Cohn & Tronick, 1987).

This very interval represents a critical period for the development of the anterior cingulate areas of the medial frontal cortex, an area involved in play and separation behaviors, laughing and crying vocalizations, face representations, and modulation of autonomic activity (MacLean, 1988, 1993; Paus, Petrides, Evans, & Meyer, 1993). Recall the previous depiction of mutually regulated states of high arousal that occur in play experiences that emerge at this time. This is also the onset of the positive resonances that occur within the mother–infant "protoconversations" that induce what Trevarthen called primary intersubjectivity (Trevarthen, Aitken, Papoudi, & Roberts, 1998). In these highly positively affectively charged interactions, the mother and infant are coregulating their opiate systems (Kalin, Shelton, & Lynn, 1995), thereby jointly cogenerating high states of positive arousal and pleasurable affect. These data underscore an essential principle overlooked by many emotion theorists—affect regulation is not just the dampening of emotion, the reduction of negative affective intensity. It also involves an amplification, an intensification of positive emotion.

Furthermore, in light of the known role of the cingulate in consciousness (Kennard, 1955), it is tempting to speculate that the experience-dependent maturation of this limbic structure may be activated in moments of dyadically expanded states of consciousness that onset in the middle of the first year. Tronick and colleagues (1998) described how microregulatory social-emotional processes of communication literally expand intersubjective states of consciousness in the infant–mother (and patient–therapist) dyad. Tronick argued that the baby's self-organizing system, when coupled with the mother's, allows for a brain organization that can be expanded into more coherent and complex states of consciousness. This developmental work supports the idea that consciousness is a product of that part of the brain that handles human relations, and is a property of a brain that is and has been in communication with other brains (Barlow, 1980; Schore, 1994). In psychoanalytic writings, Davies (1996) spoke of a "relational unconscious."

I suggest that Tronick was describing an expansion of what Edelman (1989) called primary consciousness. Edelman stated that primary consciousness relates visceral and emotional information pertaining to the biological self to stored information pertaining to outside reality, and that it is lateralized to the right brain. This right limbic-driven state is equated with Jackson's (1931) "subject consciousness," a preverbal mode that organizes perceptions and memories automatically and nonconsciously, according to similarity and affective valence. Primary process cognition is thus well under way, indeed expanding by the middle of the first year. According to Neisser, "Primary-process thinking is based on overall shapes, simple movements, and gross sound patterns, just the properties to which the preattentive process of vision and hearing are sensitive" (1967, p. 302).

In the last quarter of the first year, the quality of the infant's social relatedness changes dramatically (see Schore, 1994) due to the concurrent rapid myelination and maturation of developing limbic and cortical association areas (Kinney et al., 1988). If earlier face-to-face interactions involve only spontaneous communication processes, after 9 months the infant can engage in "joint attention," the ability to shift attention between an object and a person. In this form of nonverbal communication the infant coordinates his/her visual attention with that of the caregiver, and is now not only aware of an object but simultaneously aware of the mother's attention to the object. In such instances of what Trevarthen and colleagues (1998) called "secondary intersubjectivity," each member of the dyad coaligns separable, yet related forms of consciousness.

Joint attention occurs within highly affectively charged social referencing transactions, an attachment process that mediates a resonance of positive affect. This dyadic mechanism allows the infant to appreciate that "the other person is a locus of psychological attitudes toward the world, that the other is attending in such a way that shared experiences are possible" (Hobson, 1993, p. 267), a critical advance in the child's adaptive capacities. This advance represents a further maturation of the right hemisphere, since research suggests "a special role for the right frontal lobe in sustaining attention over time" (Rueckert & Grafman, 1996, p. 952). In developmental neurobiological research, Caplan and colleagues hypothesized that "the development of joint attention might reflect maturation of the prefrontal cortex" (1993, p. 589).

In my continuing work I offer evidence to show that the frontolimbic areas of the orbital prefrontal cortex enter into a critical period of growth that spans from the last quarter of the first through the middle of the second year, an interval that corresponds with the beginnings of human socialization (Schore, 1994). The experience-dependent postnatal growth of interconnections within this frontolimbic system and the insula (Augustine, 1996), anterior cingulate (Devinsky, Morrell, & Vogt, 1995), and amygdala (Barbas & de Olmos, 1990) represents the anatomical construction of the "rostral limbic system." I have also suggested that the orbitofrontal cortex is positioned at the hierarchical apex of two limbic circuits, an excitatory dopaminergic ventral tegmental limbic forebrain-midbrain circuit and an inhibitory noradrenergic lateral tegmental limbic forebrain-midbrain circuit (Schore, 1994, 1996, 1998b).

Due to the fact that it contains neurons that fire in response to faces (Scalaidhe, Wilson, & Goldman-Rakic, 1997) and that it processes face and voice information (Hornak, Rolls, & Wade, 1996), this system is capable of appraising changes in the external environment, especially the social, object-related environment. The orbital prefrontal system, (Joseph's previously mentioned "senior executive of the emotional brain"), which receives sensory input processed in the limbic thalamus, is activated in contexts of uncertainty (Elliott, Rees, & Dolan, 1999), and it computes, on a moment-to-moment basis, the affective salience of external stimuli (Schore, 1998b). The principle that these appraisals operate by Freud's pleasure-unpleasure principle is reflected in studies demonstrating orbitofrontal processing of responses to pleasant touch, taste, smell (Francis et al., 1999), and music (Blood, Zatorre, Bermudez, & Evans, 1999), as well as to unpleasant images of angry and sad faces (Blair, Morris, Frith, Perrett, & Dolan, 1999).

But in addition to this evaluative, affect receptive function, this system also supports the expression of affective states. Due to its projections into the ventral striatum (basal ganglia), the interface between the limbic cortex and motor systems, as well as autonomic areas (Neafsey, 1990), it impacts both emotional and motivational responses (Haber, Kunishio, Mizobuchi, & Lynd-Balta, 1995; Mogenson, Jones, & Yim, 1980). Orbitofrontal areas are involved in the regulation of autonomic responses to social stimuli (Zald & Kim, 1996), and in the processing of feedback information (Elliott, Frith, & Dolan, 1997). So after a rapid subcortical evaluation of the regulatory significance of an environmental stimulus, the right orbitofrontal coping system monitors feedback about the current internal state in order to make assessments of coping resources, and it adaptively updates appropriate autonomic response outputs in order to make adaptive adjustments to particular environmental perturbations (Schore, 1998b). These operations organize the expression of a regulated emotional state that is adaptive to a particular social environmental context.

In previous publications (Schore, 1991, 1994), I argued that this right-hemispheric prefrontal affect regulator that performs an appraisal function is isomorphic to the ego ideal, a controlling agency of the superego (Hartmann & Loewenstein, 1962) that originates at 18 months, the same time as orbitofrontal maturation. This structural system is involved in temporal and delay functions (Chasseguet-Smirgel, 1985) and acts as a "pilot and guide for the ego" (Jacobson, 1954). According to Freud, the function of the internal monitoring superego is to regulate drive (i.e., hyperstimulated aggression and sexuality), but current revisions of psychoanalytic theory hold that the superego (and not the ego) modulates emotional expression and mood states (Jacobson, 1971; Kernberg, 1984; Schore, 1991, 1994). In agreement with this model, Solms also suggested that "the functions of the superego are especially closely bound up with the mediobasal regions of the prefrontal lobe" (1996, p. 359).

In addition, Vitz (1990) stressed the importance of right hemispheric emotional-imagistic processes in moral development. Current models of moral development also emphasize an important superego function overlooked by Freud in his structural model, the emergence of a capacity for empathy, also known to be a right-hemispheric process (Voeller, 1986). This neurobiological-psychoanalytic conceptualization of the central involvement of right orbitofrontal regulatory activity in superego functions represents an updating of Jackson's hierarchical principle and Freud's structural model (1923/1961b) of a superego that sits astride the id.

Furthermore, this hierarchical-developmental model of the ontogeny of the lower and higher levels of the limbic system is similar to Freud's ideas about the early "archeology" of the primitive mind. In his last work he wrote, "The id contains everything that is inherited, that is present at birth, that is laid down in the constitution" (1940/1964, p. 145). This is confirmed by current neuroscience, where Luu and Tucker described that "the brain is mutable, such that its structural organization reflects the history of the organism. Moreover, this structure reflects both what is most important to the organism and what the organism is capable of at that particular time" (1996, p. 297).

An ontogenetic conception posits that the limbic system is a three-tiered hierarchical system, with each level (amygdala, anterior cingulate, and insula-orbitofrontal) containing separable state-dependent affective, cognitive, and behavioral functions. Each level contains an imprinted and thus stored representations of an early sensoriaffectively charged mode of engaging the social environment. This implies that there can be different levels of implicit memory, each associated with a unique cluster of psychobiological self-states. Each of the three levels also manifests itself in different states of consciousness, with the amygdala being the deepest unconscious level, and the orbitofrontal the highest. The primitive amygdala level, furthest from higher cortical operations yet closely adjacent to hypothalamic and autonomic structures, would contain the realm of Freud's (1923/1961) "bodily ego" and Bollas's (1987) "unthought known."

As this vertically organized system ontogentically matures, affects can become more complex, moving from the expression of what Stern (1985) called early-appearing, lower-level "vitality affects" that are expressed in forms and contours of feelings, to later-appearing, higher-level "categorical affects," expressed in discrete, content-associated emotions. This developmental progression thus allows for an evolution of affects from their early form, where they are experienced as bodily sensations, into a later, more complex form, where they are experienced as discrete subjective states.

Anatomical points of synaptic connections between these three right-lateralized, vertically organized systems represent dissociable yet interlocking juncture points of Freud's unconscious-preconscious. Luu and Tucker (1996, p. 302) articulated the principle, "From a vertical perspective, information must pass up and down the vertical hierarchy to achieve coherence, a form of reentrant processing (Edelman, 1989)." When these three limbic levels are resonantly intercommunicating, the right brain acts as an efficient, cohesive system that can rapidly and relatively flexibly cope with the changing demands of the inner and outer worlds, and thereby adaptively maintain a coherent subjective experience.

This ontogenetic model of the hierarchical organization of the dynamic unconscious thus posits that unconscious-preconscious systems develop in stages as separate, dissociable, yet interconnected levels. When, however, early ambient trauma interferes with the experience-dependent maturation of the interconnections within these right limbic subsystems of the "rostral limbic system," they will, under future interactive stress, too easily lose coherence and become dissociated from each other. This would result in amygdala-processed intensely dysregulating somatic states being unable to pass up the vertical hierarchy for more organized and complex processing, and therefore never reaching the highest orbitofrontal level, which is known to be central for not only affect regulation but for the processing of cognitive-emotional interactions (Barbas, 1995) and affect-related meanings (Teasdale et al., 1999).

In other words, trauma-related dissociated affects cannot evolve to discrete, subjectively experienced categorical affects, but are rather "unconscious affects," just as Freud described. He wrote: "Unconscious ideas continue to exist after repression as actual structures in the system Ucs, whereas all that corresponds in that system to unconscious affects is a potential beginning which is prevented from developing" (1915/1957d, p. 178). This psychoneurobiological conception directly bears upon the current clinical interest in primitive mental states, trauma, pathological dissociation, and the multiplicity of self-states (e.g., Bromberg, 1994; Davies; 1999).

There is now a call for an integration of neuroscience and not only psychoanalysis (Kandel, 1999) but also psychiatry (Sacks, 1998), with a contact point being new discoveries of "the emotional brain." In line with this, over a series of contributions, I have continued to outline a psychoneurobiological model of how interactive stress-induced excessive pruning of cortical-subcortical right-brain circuits is responsible for various patterns of insecure attachments that are associated with an increased risk for a spectrum of later-forming psychopathologies (see Schore, 1994, 1997b, 1997e, 1998h). I also have described the relevance of recent research on the infant brain to clinical psychiatry (Schore, 1997b, 1997e, 1998h). Additionally, I have proposed that early trauma, either in the form of neglect or abuse, impairs the development of the right brain and leads to a predisposition to posttraumatic stress disorders (PTSD; Schore, 1998i, 1999f) and/or violence (Schore, 1999d, 2001c).

For example, an experientially driven developmental overpruning (see Schore, 1994, 1997b) of orbital-amygdala synaptic connections would result in right amygdala activity that is unmodulated by higher corticolimbic systems. Neuroimaging studies have been demonstrating a subcortical pathway to the right amygdala mediating "unseen fear" (Morris, Ohman, & Dolan, 1999), and a dysfunction of the anterior limbic circuit in PTSD patient's experiencing traumatic emotional reactions (Rauch et al., 1996; Shin et al., 1997). The methodology of this research involves measuring not just the basal state of an individual patient, but evaluating stress-induced alterations that accompany symptom provocation. This experimental paradigm should be adopted for studying the efficiency or inefficiency of affect regulation. These findings also underscore the fact that any updated theory of affect must also address the problem of affect dysregulation, a cardinal feature of all psychopathologies (Schore, 1994, 1996, 1997b).

THE VERTICAL ORGANIZATION OF THE RIGHT BRAIN MEDIATES ADAPTIVE AFFECTIVE FUNCTIONING

An optimal early environment facilitates the experience-dependent maturation of a right-lateralized hierarchical system, and it allows later-evolving higher-corticolimbic centers to efficiently regulate the psychobiological states expressed by early-evolving lower subcortical limbic centers. This developmental attainment represents an ontogenetic advance in the individual's capacity to adaptively auto-regulate and interactively regulate bodily driven affective states. More specifically, although the early-maturing amygdala acts as a sensory gateway to the limbic system, amygdala processing, although very rapid, is crude compared to the more complex processing of affectively salient stimuli by later-maturing corticolimbic areas. In a demonstration of this Jacksonian principle, Morgan and Le Doux (1995) stated that:

> while the amygdala determines the emotional significance of threatening stimuli, the ventromedial prefrontal cortex uses this information to monitor and give feedback about the internal state of the [organism] and to update response outputs dependent on this internal state. Without the internal feedback as to the level of threat posed by the stimulus at any given time, the [organism] might, for adaptive purposes, remain in the defensive response state longer than necessary. (p. 687)

Furthermore, as described by Tucker, Luu, and Pribram, "the ventral limbic pathway from the amygdala to orbitofrontal cortex may impliment a tight, restricted mode of motor control that reflects adaptive constraints of self-preservation" (1995, pp. 233–234).

A functional magnetic resonance image (fMRI) study (Teasdale et al., 1999) demonstrated that while the subcortical amygdala responds to emotional stimuli at a direct perceptual level, its operations are less relevant to cognitively elicited emotions. In contrast, the ventromedial cortex, "the thinking part of the emotional brain" (Goleman, 1995), is centrally involved in "emotion-related learning" (Rolls, Hornak, Wade, & McGrath, 1994). The orbitofrontal cortex thus takes over amygdala functions (Rolls, 1996), and "provides a higher level coding that more flexibly coordinates exteroceptive and interoceptive domains and functions to correct responses as conditions change" (Derryberry & Tucker, 1992, p. 335). On the other hand, "In the absence of the contribution from orbitofrontal cortex the original encoding is more difficult to alter and exerts a stronger control over behavior. In other words, behavior becomes more rigid and less amenable to control by changing contingencies and more subtle contextual features of the environment" (Schoenbaum, Chiba, & Gallagher, 2000, p. 5188).

According to Rolls, "Although the amygdala is concerned with some of the same functions as the orbitofrontal cortex, and receives similar inputs, there is evidence that it may function less effectively in the very rapid learning and reversal of stimulus-reinforcement associations" (1996, p. 1443). This model is also explicated in a current positron emission tomography (PET) study by Morris, Ohman, and Dolan, who concluded: "Although subcortical sensory pathways appear sufficient for rapid and unconscious processing of behaviorally important stimuli, the engagement of specialized neocortical areas seems to be required for high-level processes, including object identification and conscious perception" (1999, p. 1684). As previously mentioned, Teasdale and colleagues (1999) recently provided experimental evidence showing that the orbitofrontal function is central to the processing of *affect-related meanings*.

The involvement of the orbitofrontal system in cognitive-emotional interactions (Barbas, 1995) describes what Rolls (1996) called "the executive functions of the orbitofrontal cortex." These executive functions include more than just regulating right anterior and posterior cortical activities—this "senior executive" of limbic arousal (Joseph, 1996)—hierarchically regulates the activity of the entire right brain. Studies have shown the central involvement of this cortico-limbic system in the modulation of hunger states (Tataranni et al., 1999), energy balance (McGregor & Atrens, 1991) and slow wave sleep (Maquet et al., 1997), the regulation of body (Luria, 1980) and motivational states (Pandya & Yeterian, 1985), and the motivational control of goal-directed behavior (Tremblay & Schultz, 1999).

These functional capacities are due to the fact that "The orbitofrontal cortex is the only cortical structure with direct . . . connections to the hypothalamus, the amygdala, and brainstem biogenic amine nuclei, and through these connections it (can) modulate *instinctual* behavior" (Starkstein & Robinson, 1997, p. 113, italics added). Because of its connections into the cervical, thoracic, lumbar, and sacral divisions of the spinal cord (Burstein & Potrebic, 1993), and into the vagal nerve that delivers autonomic information (Schore, 1994), and due to its sensitivity to hormones and energy substrates traveling in the circulatory system (Schore, 1994), it receives (like the amygdala and cingulate) moment-to-moment interoceptive information from the entire body, especially ("drive") information concerning changes in the bodily state. Orbitofrontal activation is thus associated with a lower threshold for awareness of sensations of both internal and external origin (Goldenberg et al., 1989).

Jackson (1931) concluded that "the highest nervous processes are potentially the whole organism." From its unique position at the convergence point of the highest processing centers of the central and autonomic nervous systems, this frontolimbic system processes exteroceptive information concerning the external environment and integrates it with subcortically processed interoceptive information regarding the visceroendocrine environment (Nauta, 1971), thereby generating a complex representation of highly integrated information on the current organismic state (Tucker, 1992). In recent work Craig (2002) provides evidence to show that the right orbitofrontal cortex, the hierarchical apex of the right limbic system, generates the most complex subjective evaluation of interoceptive state, the highest representation of the sense of physiological condition of the body (Craig, 2002).

THE ESSENTIAL RELEVANCE
OF NEUROPSYCHOANALYSIS
TO CLINICAL PSYCHOANALYSIS

This hierarchical model of the ontogeny of the right limbic system is an elaboration of Jackson's hierarchical-developmental model, which, as I mentioned earlier, significantly influenced Freud's primordial conceptions of the unconscious mind. A deeper neuropsychoanalytic understanding of the dynamic operations of the right mind may thus deepen our understanding of psychoanalytic "metapsychology" that lies beneath theoretical and clinical psychoanalysis (see Chapter 37 of Schore, 1994). The central involvement of the orbitofrontal system in differentiating an affect associated with a bodily feeling, according to the body's homeostatic needs (Craig, 2002), in modulating instinctual behavior (Starkstein & Robinson, 1997), and in the control of drive (Cavada & Schultz, 2000), bear directly upon Freud's concept of *Trieb*, translated as *instinct* but better expressed as *drive*. In *Instincts and Their Vicissitudes* (1915/1957a), he defines instinct as a borderline concept, on the frontier between the somatic and the psychic — a psychic representation of stimuli originating from inner organic sources.

These findings clearly suggest that in order for psychoanalytic theory to be truly psychobiological, as Freud intended, his concepts of drive and instinct need to be retained, albeit in an updated form. The psychodynamic concept of drive, more than any other, directly refers to motivation. Neither the problem of motivation nor the problem of emotion, both of which are basically defined in terms of *processes* of physiological activation or deactivation, can be understood solely in terms of the *content* of cognitions. In the neurobiological literature, Damasio argued that emotions are "a powerful manifestation of drives and instincts," and emphasized their motivational role: "In general, drives and instincts operate either by generating a particular behavior directly or by inducing physiological states that lead individuals to behavior in a particular way" (1994, p. 115). When psychoanalysis discards drive, it commits Descartes's error, "the separation of the most refined operations of mind from the structure and operation of a biological organism" (p. 250).

Furthermore, the anatomical finding that the early-maturing orbital prefrontal area is expanded in the visuospatial right hemisphere (in contrast to the later-maturing nonlimbic dorsolateral prefrontal area, which is larger in the left; White, Lucas, Richards, & Purves, 1994) has been suggested to account for the dominance of this hemisphere in the processing of emotional information (Falk et al., 1990). The fact that the orbital prefrontal system receives information from the ventral or object-processing visual stream (Ungerleider & Haxby, 1994) while the nonlimbic dorsolateral receives information from the dorsal processing stream accounts for the finding that face processing neurons are only found in the ventromedial areas (Scalaidhe, Wilson, & Goldman-Rakic, 1997).

Because the prefrontal areas can be viewed as the end points of the dorsal and visual streams (Kolb & Whishaw, 1996), and since each hemisphere has unique cortical-subcortical connections, I have suggested (Schore, 1994) that the expansion of the orbital prefrontal cortex in the right cerebral hemisphere allows it to perform a functionally distinct executive function for the "nonlinear" right brain, and the expansion of the dorsolateral prefrontal cortex in the left cerebral hemisphere allows it to perform an executive function for the "linear" left brain. The facts that the orbital prefrontal surfaces develop in more primitive stages and precede dorsolateral maturation (Pandya & Barnes, 1987) and that this sequence parallels the early development of the right, followed by the left hemisphere, also supports this suggestion.

This model, which explains the lateralized specializations of the verbal left and emotion-processing right hemispheres, is supported by the findings that the left dorsolateral prefrontal cortex is dominant for processing semantic information (Binder et al., 1995), while the right orbital prefrontal cortex is dominant for processing socioemotional information (Schore, 1994). This translates into the specialization of the ventromedial prefrontal areas for primary process and the dorsolateral prefrontal areas for secondary process cognition, a conception also proposed by Solms (1996). In earlier work I updated Freud's structural theory in proposing a dual component superego system, with an early-developing right orbital prefrontal ego ideal and a later-developing left dorsolateral prefrontal conscience (Schore, 1991).

In addition, the expansion of the ventral stream in the right hemisphere may account for its role in "implicit" (Hugdahl, 1995) or "procedural" (Grigsby & Hartlaub, 1994) learning, while the predominance of the dorsal stream in the left may underlie its emphasis in "explicit" or "declarative" functions. Zaidel, Esiri, and Beardsworth's proposal that "human memory systems in the two sides are wired up differently to support separate but complementary functional specialization in the hemispheres" (1998, p. 1050) suggests that the storage of right hemispheric implicit-procedural learning of affective information may be mediated by very different operations than explicit learning mechanisms of the left. Psychoanalytic authors are very interested in the implicit and explicit realms (Cooper, 1994) and in the power of implicit memories (Bornstein, 1999).

It is also now clear that just as the right hemisphere matures before the left, the implicit-procedural memory system operates ontogenetically before the explicit, a matter that bears upon the problem of "infantile amnesia." Kandel's observation that "the infant relies primarily on its procedural memory systems" during "the first 2–3 years of life" (1999, p. 513) may shed light upon Joseph's description of "early emotional learning occurring in the right hemisphere unbeknownst to the left; learning and associated emotional responding may later be completely unaccessible to the language centers of the brain" (1982, p. 243). Clinical psychoanalysis has long been interested in the mechanisms that can access preverbal memories, and these findings suggest that they are stored in what Stern and his colleagues called "implicit relational knowledge" (Lyons-Ruth et al., 1998; Stern et al., 1998).

The orbital prefrontal system, the central mechanism of affect regulation in the dual-hemispheric brain, is known to access memory functions (Frey & Petridas, 2000; Schnider, Treyer, & Buck, 2000; Stuss et al., 1982) and operate by implicit processing (Rolls, 1996). As described by Westen, Muderrisoglu, Fowler, Shedler, and Koren, "From a cognitive perspective, affect regulation mechanisms constitute a form of procedural knowledge; that is, they are triggered when situations match a prototype of past experiences in which they have proven useful" (1997, p. 430). When efficiently functioning, rapid-acting orbitofrontal appraisals of the social environment are accomplished at levels beneath awareness by a visual and auditory scanning of information emanating from an emotionally expressive face, and they act as nonconscious biases that guide behavior before conscious knowledge does (Bechara, Damasio, Tranel, & Damasio, 1997).

In other words, they act as transferential biases but, in highly stressful transference-countertransference ruptures, frontolimbic systems will be unable to perform a higher regulatory function over lower levels, and thereby manifest a transient Jacksonian dissolution (Schore, 1994, 1997c, 2002e). It is at this moment when a release of lower-level right limbic activity and its associated, more deeply unconscious psychobiological states are expressed in the transference. A study by Schnider and Ptak suggested that orbitofrontal dysfunction is associated with "a failure to distinguish between currently relevant and previously encountered information; that is between 'now' and the past" (1999, p. 680). This characterization is strikingly similar to a transference distortion, which I have previously characterized as a right brain phenomenon (Schore, 1994, 1997c). Solms has also described a mechanism by which disorganization of a damaged or developmentally deficient right hemisphere is associated with a "collapse of internalized representations of the external world" in which "the patient regresses from whole to part object relationships" (Solms, 1996, p. 347).

These disorganizing, affectively charged events occur during enacted transference-countertransference sequences, which represent an intersubjective matrix that potentially allows the patient to achieve "higher levels of psychic organization" (Katz, 1998). Bornstein wrote, "the transference reaction, in and of itself, actually represents an expression of the patient's implicit perceptions and implicit memories" (1999, p. 170). He also contended, "When an implicit memory is made explicit, the origin of that memory is also made explicit, and the patient can better understand the causal chain of events that led from past experience to present functioning. Simply put, the translation of implicit memories allows the patient to gain insight regarding the relationship between past and present experience" (1993, p. 341).

Interestingly, Freeman (2000) asserted that the ventromedial prefrontal regions are concerned with "social skills and the capacity for deep interpersonal relationships" and contribute to "insight." This suggests that the essential mechanism for insight is located in the upper levels of the "nonverbal" right hemisphere and not in the verbal left, and that insight refers to a right prefrontal preconscious scanning of the bodily states represented in lower levels of the right mind-brain-body system. But insight also refers to insight into the unconscious mind of an other. On this matter, Stone, Baron-Cohen, and Knight (1998) reported that "theory of mind" is a property of orbital and not left-dorsolateral prefrontal systems.

These ideas highlight the important principle that any updated psychoanalytic theory of affect must also be clinically relevant, and offer heuristic and more comprehensive models of the mechanism of treatment, the transference-countertransference relationship. Toward that end I have offered contributions on such topics as a psychoneurobiological model of therapeutic empathy, the affect-communicating mechanisms embedded in the therapeutic alliance, the importance of bodily based countertransference responses to the patient's affective communications, the psychobiological mechanism underlying early-forming primitive affective defenses such as projective identification and dissociation, and a model of how psychoanalytic treatment acts as a growth-facilitating environment for inducing structural alterations in the patient's preconscious regulatory systems, thereby expanding the patient's tolerance of a broader array of positive and negative affects and the emergence of a self-reflective position that can appraise the significance and meaning of affects (Schore, 1994, 1997c, 1998c, 1998d, 1999e, 2000b, 2000i).

The current validation of Jackson's (1931) original speculations about the automatic, preverbal functions of the right hemisphere, as well as the demonstration of the central involvement of the orbitofrontal system in preconscious functions (Frank, 1950) and in controlling the allocation of attention to possible contents of consciousness (Goldenberg et al., 1989), are thus directly relevant to an updating of Freud's topographic model. Recall that the hallmark of preconscious material, according to Freud, is that it can be brought to conscious awareness by an act of intention. This conception is supported by neuropsychological studies showing a superiority of the right hemisphere for mediating intention (Verfaellie, Bowers, & Heilman, 1988) and is echoed in cognitive theories asserting that "automatic evaluations are a form of preconscious filtering that serves the purpose of guiding conscious attention to some stimuli more than others" (Pratto, 1994, p. 134).

In the psychoanalytic literature there is an increased interest in preconscious functions of both the patient (Ross, 1999) and analyst (Hamilton, 1996). Kantrowitz referred to "preconscious resonance between patient and analyst" (1999, p. 65). But 2 decades ago Epstein described, in some depth, the salience of "the preconscious level of awareness," where preconscious cognitions play an essential role in structuring experience, particularly, "emotions and moods": "Freud believed that unconscious motivation is the most significant source of human behavior. I submit that the preconscious level of functioning deserves the honor because it is here that the implicit beliefs and values reside, which automatically organize and direct out everyday experience and behavior" (1983, p. 235). Epstein was thus describing the adaptive functions of the right orbitofrontal cortex, a system that mediates what has been alternatively termed preconscious (Erdelyi, 1985), or nonconscious (Lewicki, 1986), or implicit (Bornstein, 1999) perception. As mentioned earlier, this system cannot only receive but express and communicate psychobiological states. And so Kantrowitz (1999) was describing resonant right hemisphere-to-right hemisphere nonconscious communications between the patient's and therapist's right orbitofrontal systems.

This frontolimbic system sits at the apex of the rostral limbic system, described as "a mental control system that is essential for adjusting thinking and behavior to ongoing reality" (Schnider & Ptak, 1999, p. 680). The object-related ontogeny of this preconscious "internal reflecting and organizing agency" (Kaplan-Solms & Solms, 1996), which functions "to balance internal desires with external reality" (Jouandet & Gazzaniga, 1979), is posited to be critical to the emergence of Freud's reality principle, a developmental achievement that is accompanied by the control and restriction of affect (Suler, 1989). According to Bronson, "The ability to control motivational orientation in light of factors not present in the immediate environment, a capacity basic to the development of the reality principle, must depend in part on maturation of the prefrontal lobes" (1963, p. 59).

The demonstration of the development of the frontal lobe in stages by the neuropsychologist Thatcher (1991) may thus underly the description of the development of the sense of reality in stages by the psychoanalyst Ferenczi (1916/1952s) some 80 years ago. A logical corollary of this developmental model suggests that "reality testing," especially the adaptive capacity to accurately process the socioemotional information that derives from other humans, is mediated by preconscious activities of the "right mind" of the nonverbal right hemisphere, and not the conscious mind of the verbal-analytic left. Rotenberg also came to this conclusion in contrasting the organizing modes of the two hemispheres. He noted that the advantages of a right hemispheric strategy "manifest themselves only when the information is itself complex, internally contradictory and basically irreducible to an unambiguous context" while the left hemispheric strategy "makes it possible to build a pragmatically convenient but simplified model of reality" (1994, p. 489).

But perhaps the most complex of all functions of the right-prefrontal cortex is what the neuroscientists Wheeler, Stuss, and Tulving called *autonoetic consciousness*—"the capacity to mentally represent and become aware of subjective experiences in the past, present, and future" (1997, p. 331). This unique capacity to "mentally travel through time" and self-reflect comes on line at 18 months (the time of orbitofrontal maturation). These authors proposed that the individual must be in a right-prefrontal state to retrieve personal experiences from the past. I suggest that the description of this capacity by Wheeler, Stuss, and Tulving (1997) describes the context of the psychoanalytic experience:

> the prefrontal cortex, in conjunction with its reciprocal connections with other cortical and subcortical structures, empowers healthy human adults with the capacity to consider the self's extended existence throughout time. The most complete expression of this capacity, autonoetic awareness, occurs whenever one consciously recollects or re-experiences a happening from a specific time in the past, attends directly to one's present or on-line experience, or contemplates one's existence and conduct at a time in the future. (p. 350)

Daniel Brown (1993) concluded that the process of development, as it continues in adulthood, brings the potential to observe and understand the processes of our own minds:

> Adult affective development is the potential for self-observation and reflection on the very processes of mental functioning . . . not simply of the affective content of experience but of the very processes by which affect comes into experience—how it is experienced by the self and what informs the self about its relationship to internal and external reality. . . .

> Psychotherapy is one medium of adult affective development in the sense
> that it serves the purpose of disciplined conscious reflection on affective
> processes. (p. 56)

The right hemisphere, the substrate of the emotional brain, ends its growth
phase in the second year, when the left hemisphere begins one. Using EEG
coherence data, Thatcher (1994) demonstrated that this left-hemisphere growth
spurt continues to 3 years, when the right cycles back. But during this time the
right is still dominant—Chiron and colleagues reported that between 1 and 3
years resting cerebral blood flow shows a right hemisphere predominance,
which then shifts to the left in the fourth year. They concluded "The right-to-
left asymmetry seems to be related to the consecutive emergence of functions
dedicated first to the right (visuospatial abilities), and then to the left posterior
associative cortex (language abilities)" (1997, p. 1064).

I suggest that the onset of left hemispheric dominance, the usual organizational pattern of most brains, results from the growth of prefrontal callosal axons
over to the right. Levin (1991) pointed out that callosal transmission begins at
3½ years, a period of intense interest to Freud:

> Thus, the beginning of the oedipal phase, a psychological and neuroana-
> tomical watershed in development, coincides with the onset of the ability
> (or inability) of the hemispheres to integrate their activities. . . . The de-
> velopment of this defensive function, which Freud called the repression
> barrier, is accomplished by the increasing and reversible dominance of
> the left over the right hemisphere, which is known to occur during brain
> maturation. (pp. 21, 194)

Basch also proposed that "in repression it is the path from episodic to semantic
memory, from right to left [brain], that is blocked" (1983, p. 151).

Previously, I referred to the earlier maturation of the orbital prefrontal system, which is expanded in the right hemisphere, and the later maturation of
the dorsolateral prefrontal system, which is expanded in the left hemisphere. I
contend that these two systems are first operating together between the third
and fourth year, the onset of Freud's oedipal period. Davidson (1994) proposed
that the inhibition of negative affect is an expression of dorsolateral activity,
suggesting that this inhibition represents the left hemisphere's dampening-
down right brain affect.

This means that at this point in development each hemisphere is capable of
forming independent self-representations, one stored in explicit memory and
accessible to language functions in the left, and another stored in implicit
memory in the right. Such a dual-hemispheric system allows for cooperation
but competition between the right and left brain (right mind-left mind) systems,
and the presence of *conflict*, especially, as Brenner (1982) suggested, involving
sexual and aggressive forces that are active at this time. But this condition also

represents a developmental advance, where somatic signals can be processed into more complex subjective affective states by the right orbitofrontal system, then communicated to the left for further semantic processing, and then returned to the right hemisphere.

If, however, the developing individual is exposed to an early growth-inhibiting environment that deprives the child of nutritional and/or emotional supplies, this ontogenetic level of maturation will not be achieved. As a result, the right-brain vertical cortical-subcortical system is inefficient (Hinshaw-Fuselier, Boris, & Zeanah, 1999; Schore, 1994, 1997b), and the resulting right-to-left orbitofrontal communication is therefore poor. In order for conflict or competition to occur between the two hemispheric processors, the late-acting verbal left must have access to the emotional appraisals and outputs of the nonverbal early-right processor, which it can then in turn inhibit. But due to the nonoptimal experience-dependent maturation of the higher levels of the right-prefrontal areas, the subgenual (Drevets et al., 1997) interhemispheric transfer of affective information is inefficient, and this results in "a right to left hemisphere callosal transfer deficit" and alexithymia, "no words for feelings" (Dewarja & Sasaki, 1990). Alexithymia is known to reflect a right-hemispheric dysfunction (Jessimer & Markham, 1997).

In groundbreaking work, Krystal (1988, 1997) has shown that alexithymia, a lack of a reflective capacity, and affect regulatory disturbances are primary manifestations of "preoedipal" psychopathologies, all of which are in essence an "arrest" of affective development. In other words, early self-pathologies show a poor developmental organization and therefore a *deficit* within the vertical dimension of the emotion-processing right brain. This developmental neurobiological ("structural") conceptualization bears directly upon the current interest in integrating deficit and conflict models (Druck, 1998) and on treating the early-dysregulated "difficult" patient (Bach, 1998). The psychotherapy of "developmental arrests" (Stolorow & Lachmann, 1980) is currently conceptualized as being directed toward the mobilization of fundamental modes of development (Emde, 1990) and the completion of interrupted developmental processes (Gedo, 1979), specifically in the patient's deficient right hemisphere (Schore, 1994, 1997c, 2002e). Rotenberg described "the importance of the emotional relationships between psychotherapist and client can be explained by the restoration, in the process of such relationships, of . . . right hemispheric activity. In this way the emotional relationships in the process of psychotherapy are covering the deficiency caused by the lack of emotional relations in early childhood" (1995, p. 59).

The problem of the long-term sequelae of early affective deficiencies was, of course, investigated by Freud in his changing models of early trauma. Recall that in 1893, Breuer and Freud, citing the recent work of Janet (1889), described dissociation as the major mechanism for "strangulations of affect," but by 1900 and *The Interpretation of Dreams*, Freud discarded this notion and favored repression as the sole mechanism by which material in the preconscious becomes unconscious. Ellman (1991) pointed out that Freud struggled with his "pathogenic memory model" and the idea of an unconscious defense throughout his writings. Current neurobiology suggests that repression is a developmentally more advanced left brain defense against affects like anxiety that are represented at the cortical level of the right brain, but the earlier-appearing and more primitive dissociation is a defense against traumatic affects like terror that are stored subcortically in the right brain.

This neurobiological conceptualization indicates that Freud's ideas about trauma must be reassessed (van der Kolk, Weisaeth, & van der Hart, 1996) and that the concept of dissociation must be reincorporated into theoretical and clinical psychoanalysis. It is now clear that dissociation represents the most primitive defense against traumatic affective states and that it must be addressed in the treatment of severe psychopathologies (Putnam, 1997; Schore, 1994, 1997c; van der Kolk, van der Hart, & Marmar, 1996). A psychoneurobiological updating of trauma theory leads to very different therapeutic approaches that are consonant with current clinical models in which the primary mechanism of the treatment revolves around relational "noninterpretative" interventions rather than verbal interpretations (e.g., Bromberg, 1994; Davies, 1996; Stern et al., 1998; Schore, 2000e). A cardinal tenet of clinical psychoanalytic models is that the treatment must match the developmental level of the patient (Gedo, 1991; Holinger, 1999). With early-forming severe right brain pathologies, the clinician's primary function is as an affect regulator for the patient's primitive, traumatic states, including those affective states that are walled off by dissociation.

THE DYNAMIC UNCONSCIOUS: A REFORMULATION

Freud's concept of the dynamic unconscious is usually interpreted to refer to the self-regulatory capacities of an unconscious system that operates via the process of repression in order to bar access of sexual and aggressive wishes into consciousness. This characterization describes the left-hemispheric horizontal inhibition of right-hemispheric cognitive-emotional representations. The current expanding body of knowledge of the right hemisphere suggests a major alteration in the conceptualization of the Freudian unconscious. It is now established that "operation of the right prefrontal cortex is integral to autonomous regulation" (Ryan, Kuhl, & Deci, 1997, p. 718). Freud's seminal model of a dynamic, continuously active unconscious mind describes the moment-to-moment operations of a hierarchical, self-organizing regulatory system that is located in the right brain. The orbitofrontal executive regulatory centers of the right hemisphere have direct contact with both the lower levels of the right and the higher areas of the left brain. The center of psychic life thus shifts from Freud's *ego*, which he located in the "speech-area on the left-hand side" (1923/

1961b) and the posterior areas of the verbal left hemisphere, to the highest levels of the nonverbal right hemisphere, the locus of the bodily based *self-system* (Devinsky, 2000; Mesulam & Geschwind, 1978; Schore, 1994) and the unconscious mind (Joseph, 1992).

The current findings of neuroscience imaging research that study the brain in real time suggest that the adaptive operations of the dynamic unconscious in everyday life is best described not in terms of ongoing repressive functions, but rather in terms of nonconsciously mediated processes that are essential components of normal and abnormal cognition. Such dynamic operations are nonconscious because they occur so rapidly, and therefore at levels beneath conscious awareness. These early automatic appraisal processes which allocate attention and inattention to salient, valued aspects of the external environment shape the subsequent conscious processing of a stimulus. Current data support Jackson's speculation that right lateralized early, automatic, preverbal, emotional mentation precedes a later organization of ideas in words in the left hemisphere, where they achieve propositional form. The cognitive-emotional processes that underlie the representation of a theory of mind and an unconscious dynamic internal working model that guides the individual in his transactions with the world are distributed in the subcortical and cortical areas of the right brain.

Thus, I conclude that "the emotion processing right mind is the neurobiological substrate of Freud's dynamic unconscious" (Schore, 1999b, pp. 125). Winson has asserted that "the unconscious is a cohesive, continually active mental structure that takes note of life's experiences and reacts according to its scheme of interpretation" (1990, p. 96). It is heartening to note that this conception is now being incorporated into mainstream psychology. In a recent issue of the journal *American Psychologist*, Bargh and Chartrand asserted that: "most of moment-to-moment psychological life must occur through nonconscious means if it is to occur at all . . . various nonconscious mental systems perform the lion's share of the self-regulatory burden, beneficiently keeping the individual grounded in his or her current environment" (1999, p. 462).

But in an even more complex characterization, one consonant with the dynamic operations of the vertical dimension of the right brain/mind, Davies (1996) described a "relational unconscious," one that:

> evolves out of an ever present, yet constantly changing, system of affective, cognitive, and physiologically based self-experiences in ongoing interactive and dialogic discourse with a host of significant internally and externally derived objects. . . . Not one unconscious, not *the* unconscious, but multiple levels of consciousness and unconsciousness, in an ongoing state of interactive articulation as past experiences infuses the present and present experience evokes state-dependent memories of formative interactive representations. (p. 197)

Furthermore, Thatcher's (1996) neurobiological finding of continual right brain growth spurts throughout the lifespan, and Tronick and colleagues' (1998) developmental work on the dyadic expansion of consciousness clearly suggest that the dynamic unconscious is capable of becoming more complex as a result of effective, affectively focused psychoanalytic treatment. That is to say, the continuing development of this somatopsychic self-system is dependent upon ongoing external and internal affectively charged relational experiences, and its ontogenetic progression allows for a wider range of auto- and interactive regulatory activities and thereby the generation of more complex psychobiological states and higher levels of self-reflective consciousness. Jung described the "collective unconscious" as an "image of the world" that is the source of self-sufficiency, as it contains "all those elements that are necessary for the self-regulation of the psyche as a whole" (1928/1943, p. 187).

Science's quest into the nature of the human brain began in earnest a century ago, and at its very onset, it became obvious that beneath the skull there are two structurally segregated, yet intercommunicating brains. The early observation that the left is specialized for linguistic functions and the right with affective processing—that there were dual brains—said something so fundamental about the human experience that it could not be ignored. And thus an attempt was made then, and continues now, to understand the meaning of the unique structure-function relationships of the anatomically distinct right and left brains. This continues today in studies that attempt to understand how each acts as an independent entity, yet to also understand how their structure-functions relationships are altered when they organize to become a single system, "a brain," "a mind."

This, in turn, bears upon a continuing interest in the neuropsychological concept of "dominance," a concept that also touches upon the question of what, in essence, makes us "human." To this date, "science" continues to speak of the left hemisphere's specialization for the sequential, linear processing of verbal-linguistic information as the explanation for the "dominance" of the left brain. The left hemisphere, the conscious mind, is thus seen as the essence of the human experience. In sharp contrast to this position, Freud's body of work brings to light another realm of human experience, beneath conscious awareness, yet one that expresses itself in everyday life and contributes, fundamentally, to human motivation. Freud's work continues to say, "Look beneath the words," and on this basis I suggest that his early contributions to the scientific study of the brain plus his later contributions to the study of the mind are now reconverging to tell neuroscience *"Look to the right brain."*

Over the last years of the 20th century, neuroscience firmly established that the right brain plays a central role in organizing the psychobiological processes that underlie a number of vital functions that occur beneath levels of awareness: the regulation of fundamental physiological and endocrinological functions located in subcortical regions of the brain (Wittling & Pfluger, 1990), the control of vital functions that support survival and enable the organism to cope with stressors (Wittling & Schweiger, 1993), the storage of early attachment experiences and internal working models that encode strategies of affect regulation and guide the individual in his interactions with others (Schore, 1994), the processing of socioemotional information that is meaningful to the individual (Schore, 1998b), the ability to empathize with the emotional states of other humans beings (Schore, 1996; Voeller, 1986), the mediation of important emotional-imagistic processes in moral development (Vitz, 1990), the cerebral representation of one's own past and the activation of autobiographical memory (Fink et al., 1996), the establishment of a "personally relevant universe" (van Lancker, 1991), and the capacity to self-reflect and "mentally travel through time" (Wheeler et al., 1997). These basic coping mechanisms reflect the right mind's essential role in primary process cognition and affective and motivational phenomena. It is undoubtedly true that adaptive internal and external functioning involves the activation of both right and left brain processes. But I interpret Freud's dictum of the centrality of dynamic unconscious processes in everyday life to mean that *the right brain is "dominant" in humans*, and that the most fundamental problems of human existence, studied by both psychoanalysis and neuroscience, cannot be understood without addressing this primal realm.

1999

The Right Brain as the Neurobiological Substratum of Freud's Dynamic Unconscious

O VER THE LAST 3 DECADES, Sigmund Freud's seminal model of a dynamic, continuously active unconscious mind has undergone a major transformation. This reformulation has been driven by not only clinical advances, but also by modifications of the theoretical underpinnings of the theory, especially updated concepts of development and structure. In a comprehensive overview of the field in this period Gedo concluded that the substantial progression of the theory is in great part due to "the rapid expansion of the field of infant observation (started within psychoanalysis but now spread beyond its boundaries)," and perhaps most importantly to "the explosion of new knowledge about the early development of the central nervous system" (1999, p. xv).

It is therefore understandable that during the same time frame, more so than any other in its one hundred year history, the field has returned to its origins, first outlined in Freud's interdisciplinary opus, *Project for a Scientific Psychology* (1985/1966). In this seminal work that appeared at the dawn of psychoanalysis, the science of unconscious processes, Freud attempted to create a systematic model of the functioning of the human mind in terms of its underlying neurobiological mechanisms. In this remarkable document he articulated every one of the major theoretical concepts that he would continue to explore in all later work. At the core, however, were two fundamental problems — the basic nature of the human unconscious mind and the central role of affect and its development in human behavior. The current reformulations within psychoanalysis, accompanied by the return of an interdisciplinary perspective, have specifically focused upon these dual essential themes.

During this same time period, a host of other scientific disciplines, liberated from the narrow behavioral model that dominated psychology for much of the 20th century, began to actively probe questions about the internal processes of mind that were for so long only addressed by psychoanalysis and deemed to be outside the realm of "scientific" analysis. In my ongoing work I document how a spectrum of sciences that border psychoanalysis are now researching the covert yet essential mechanisms that underlie overt behaviors, especially the role of emotional states. In a paper in the *Journal of the American Psychoanalytic Association* ("A century after Freud's Project: Is a rapprochement between psychoanalysis and neurobiology at hand?") I suggested that affect and its regulation are a potential point of convergence of psychoanalysis and neuroscience, and that the time is now right for the rapprochement Freud predicted (Schore, 1997a).

Thus I, along with others who are calling for this integration, am quite pleased with the appearance of the new journal *Neuro-Psychoanalysis*. I am particularly honored to be part of an editorial board of distinguished psychoanalysts including Otto Kernberg and Arnold Modell, and neuroscientists like Oliver Sacks, Eric Kandel, Karl Pribram, Joseph LeDoux, and Antonio Damasio. The first issue of the journal was devoted to Freud's theory of affect in the light of contemporary neuroscience, and in the following I want to expand upon some thoughts that are outlined in a paper I contributed to the premier issue (Schore, 1999a).

In the journal I suggested that a common ground of both psychoanalysis and neuroscience lies in a more detailed charting of the unique structure-function relationships of the emotion-processing right brain, which Ornstein (1997) called "the right mind." Psychoanalysis has been interested in the right hemisphere since the split-brain studies of the 1970s, when a number of psychoanalytic investigators began to map out its preeminent role in unconscious processes (Galin, 1974; Hoppe, 1977; McLaughlin, 1978). I propose that Freud's affect theory describes a structural system, associated with unconscious primary-process affect-laden cognition and regulated by the pleasure-unpleasure principle, which is organized in the right brain. Knowledge of this right brain system can offer us a chance to more deeply understand not just the contents of the unconscious, but its origin, structure, and dynamics.

In the following, I will briefly evaluate Freud's affect theory in light of contemporary neuroscience. This neuropsychoanalytic perspective integrates current neuroscience research on the brain, especially as it is dynamically processing environmental and self-related information, with the rich observational data, documented by the major psychoanalytic theorists over the course of the first psychoanalytic century, on the subtle functional processes of the dynamic unconscious mind. Then I will offer a developmental perspective of affective phenomena, and finally outline a dynamic systems theory perspective of emotional processes.

FREUD'S AFFECT THEORY IN LIGHT
OF CONTEMPORARY NEUROSCIENCE

Freud's Conception of Affects

Freud's ideas on affect were formulated at the point where his career as a neurologist was transforming into a new discipline, psychoanalysis. They first appeared in *The Project for a Scientific Psychology* (1895/1966), and remained essentially unchanged over the course of his writings (Schore, 1999a; for a summary, see Solms & Nersessian, 1999). In his *Introductory Lectures on Psychoanalysis*, Freud concluded (1916–1917/1961 & 1963),

> And what is an affect in the dynamic sense? It is in any case something highly composite. An affect includes in the first place particular motor innervations or discharges and secondly certain feelings; the latter are of two kinds — perceptions of the motor actions that have occurred and the direct feelings of pleasure and unpleasure which, as we say, give the affect its keynote. (p. 395)

As mentioned previously, Freud suggested that although affect is initiated by environmental stimulation, it is supported and augmented by the resulting endogenous excitation. An affect can also be precipitated suddenly by the environmental activation of a memory that is charged with an endogenously originating load. Current experimental data on imagery of emotional stimuli confirm this latter conception (e.g, Kreiman, Koch, & Fried, 2000). In a review of the neural foundations of imagery, Kosslyn, Ganis, and Thompson concluded, "visualizing an object has much the same effect as seeing the object . . . imagery can engage neural structures that are also engaged in perception, and these neural structures can, in turn, affect events in the body itself" (2001, p. 641).

Basic Emotions

Throughout Freud's subsequent writings he held that affects are "for the most part innately pre-wired, although some basic emotions are apparently forged during early development by momentous biological events of universal significance," and that in later life they represent "reproductions of very early experiences of vital importance" (Freud, 1926/1959). There is now an intense interest in "biologically primitive emotions" which are evolutionarily very old, appear early in development, and are facially expressed (Johnson & Multhaup, 1992). The early-maturing right hemisphere (Saugstad, 1998; Schore, 1994) is dominant for the first 3 years of life (Chiron et al., 1997), and it contains a basic primitive affect system (Gazzaniga, 1985) that is involved in the modulation of "primary emotions" (Ross, Hohman, & Buck, 1994).

The Perceptual Aspect of Affects

Although Freud repudiated the Project, its central ideas appear in the seventh chapter of *The Interpretation of Dreams*. Here, Freud (1900/1953b) proposed that the psychical apparatus is "turned towards the external world with its sense-organ of the Pcpt. [perceptual] systems," and through the regulatory mechanism of the "pleasure principle" value is assigned to mental performance. Freud thus highlighted the importance of affective appraisals of the personal significance of external stimuli to the generation of value and meaning.

Current emotion researchers are emphasizing the importance of the appraisal of facial expressions and the evaluative function of affects. The right hemisphere is dominant for the processing of facial information from infancy (Acerra, Burnod, & de Schonen, 2002; Deruelle & de Schonen, 1998) to adulthood (Gur et al., 2002; Kim et al., 1999; Nakamura et al., 1999, 2000), and is faster than the left in performing valence-dependent, automatic, preattentive appraisals of emotional facial expressions (Pizzagalli, Regard, & Lehmann, 1999). There is now agreement that early experience is associated with the development of representations for facial expressions of emotion (Pollak & Kistler, 2002), and that emotions involve rapid appraisals of events that are important to the individual (Frijda, 1988) and reactions to fundamental relational meanings that have adaptive significance (Lazarus, 1991).

From a neurobiological perspective, LeDoux (1989) asserted that "the core of the emotional system" is a mechanism for computing the affective significance of stimuli. In earlier work, I offered a chapter on the maturation of an evaluative system in the right cortex (Schore, 1998b). This lateralized system performs a "valence tagging" function (Watt, 1998), in which perceptions receive a positive or negative affective charge, in accord with a calibration of degrees of pleasure-unpleasure. The essential roles of the right hemisphere in emotional perception (Adolphs, Damasio, Tranel, & Damasio, 1996; Borod et al., 1998; Keil et al., 2001) and in the allocation of attention (Casey et al., 1997; Gainotti, 1996; Mesulam, 1990; Sturm & Wilmes, 2001) are well documented.

The Expressive Aspect of Affects

In addition to a perceptual dimension, Freud (1915/1957a) also intuited the "expressive" aspect of emotions, that the expression of emotions represented reflexive patterns of motor discharge. Current interdisciplinary research is demonstrating the dominance of the right hemisphere for facial displays of emotion (Borod, Haywood, & Koff, 1997; Nicholls, Wolfgang, Clode, & Lindell, 2002), spontaneous gestures (Blonder, Burns, Bowers, Moore, & Heilman, 1995), and the control of spontaneously evoked emotional reactions (Dimberg & Petterson, 2000). In regard to Freud's ideas on the communication functions of affects, neuropsychological studies now report the preeminent role of the right hemisphere in emotional (Blonder, Bowers, & Heilman, 1991), spontaneous (Buck, 1994), and nonverbal (Benowitz et al., 1983) communication. Studies demonstrating that emotional words are processed in the right hemisphere (Borod et al., 1992; Neininger & Pullvermuller, 2003) confirm Freud's (1891) proposal that the brain's correlates of words are not restricted to the left hemisphere language centers but are distributed over cortical areas of both hemispheres. And with respect to his speculations on the memorial aspects of affect, there is now evidence for a right cerebral dominance for the representation of affect-laden autobiographical information (Fink et al., 1996) and for the retrieval of episodic memory (Henson, Shallice, & Dolan, 1999; Nolde, Johnson, & Raye, 1998).

The Adaptive Aspect of Affects

Solms and Nersessian have emphasized Freud's characterization of the adaptive function of affects: "According to Freud, the mental apparatus as a whole serves the biological purpose of meeting the imperative internal needs of the subject in a changing . . . environment" (1999, p. 5). This essential psychobiological function was echoed by Damasio who concluded, "The overall function of the brain is to be well informed about what goes on in the rest of the body, the body proper; about what goes on in itself; and about the environment surrounding the organism, so that suitable survivable accommodations can be achieved between the organism and the environment" (1994, p. 90). But the two brain hemispheres have different patterns of cortical-subcortical connections, and therefore do not play an equal role in this function. The right hemisphere contains the most comprehensive and integrated map of the body state available to the brain (Damasio, 1994) and is central to the control of vital functions supporting survival and enabling the organism to cope with stresses and challenges (Wittling & Schweiger, 1993), and thus its adaptive functions mediate the human stress response (Wittling, 1997).

Furthermore, it is now established that the right hemisphere plays a central role in higher cognitive function, such as deductive reasoning (Parsons & Osherson, 2001; Shuren & Grafman, 2002). According to these latter authors:

> [The] right hemisphere holds representations of the emotional states associated with events experienced by the individual, when that individual encounters a familiar scenario, representations of past emotional experiences are retrieved by the right hemisphere and are incorporated into the reasoning process. (p. 918)

The characterization, in the neuroscience literature, of these adaptive right brain functions, performed at levels beneath awareness, is consonant with Winson's description, in current psychoanalytic writings, of revised models of the unconscious. Winson concluded, "Rather than being a cauldron of untamed passions and destructive wishes, I propose that the unconscious is a cohesive, continually active mental structure that takes note of life's experiences and reacts according to its scheme of interpretation" (1990, p. 96).

Mind-Body Connections

From the beginning, Freud posited that affective stimuli also arise "from within the organism and reaching the mind, as a measure of the demand made upon the mind in consequence of its connection with the body" (1915/1957a,

p. 122). According to Greenberg and Mitchell, "Drive is a concept at the frontier between the psychic and the somatic, an endogenous source of stimulation which impinges on the mind by virtue of the mind's connection with the body" (1983, p. 21). Damasio (1994) argued that emotions are "a powerful manifestation of drives and instincts." Although some psychoanalysts are now becoming interested in the body, much of the field is still mired in "Descartes's Error"—the separation of the operations of the mind from the structure and operation of a biological organism, the body (Damasio, 1994). Neuroscientists are now stressing that "The brain is but one component of the complex system that is the body. We take in information and interact with the world through our bodies, and our bodies change with—and in some cases change—cognitive and emotional processing" (Kutas & Federmeier, 1998, p. 135).

Current "cognitive" neuroscience is less interested in the body that in the verbal and conscious capacities of the left hemisphere. But it is the right hemisphere that is more deeply connected into both the sympathetic and parasympathetic branches of the peripheral autonomic nervous system than the left (Spence, Shapiro, & Zaidel, 1996), and thus dominant for "the metacontrol of fundamental physiological and endocrinological functions whose primary control centers are located in subcortical regions of the brain" (Wittling & Pfluger, 1990, p. 260). Solms noted that the right hemisphere encodes representations "on the basis of perception derived initially from the bodily ego" (1996, p. 347), clearly implying its dominant role in drive-related functions. In a number of recent contributions I have described how the therapist's and patient's bodily reactions and autonomic responses can be incorporated into clinical work (Schore, 2002b, 2002d, 2002f).

Affect Regulation

Freud's special interest in the problem of regulation also first appears in the Project, a document that suggests "a model whereby excitation from various sources arising both from within and from outside the individual might be *regulated* by processes essentially within the individual" (Sander, 1977, p. 14; italics added). And in this same farsighted opus Freud went on to say that there is a close connection between affect and primary process, and that memories capable of generating affect are "tamed" (regulated) until the affect provides only a "signal."

In my ongoing work I have detailed the development and unique functional capacities of the orbital prefrontal area of the cortex that regulates emotional and motivational states (Schore, 1994, 1998b, 1999a, 1999c, 2001b, 2001c, 2002c). Due to its extensive reciprocal connections with energy-controlling bioaminergic nuclei in the reticular formation and drive-inducing and drive-inhibiting systems in the hypothalamus, the orbitofrontal cortex is critical to the modulation of instinctual behavior (Starkstein & Robinson, 1997), the experience of emotion (Baker, Frith, & Dolan, 1997), and the motivational control of goal-directed activities (Tremblay & Schultz, 1999). This prefrontal cortex, situated at the apogee of the "rostral limbic system"—a hierarchical sequence of interconnected limbic areas in orbitofrontal cortex, insular cortex, anterior cingulate, and amygdala (Schore, 1997b, 2000e, 2001b)—is expanded in the right hemisphere (Falk et al., 1990). This hemisphere, more so than the left, is densely reciprocally interconnected with limbic regions (Borod, 2000; Gainotti, 2000; Tucker, 1992), and therefore contains the major circuitry of emotion regulation (Porges, Doussard-Roosevelt, & Maiti, 1994). Furthermore, the orbitofrontal system matures at the end of a right hemisphere growth spurt in late infancy, and is centrally involved in attachment representations that encode strategies of affect regulation (Schore, 1994, 1996, 2000a, 2000c, 2001a, 2001b, 2001c).

A PSYCHONEUROBIOLOGICAL PERSPECTIVE OF AFFECTIVE DEVELOPMENT

In a continuation of Freud's principle of the primacy of early experience, recent developmental studies on the centrality of the attachment relationship have been a major contributor to the current emphasis on affect within psychoanalysis. Early attachment is the "momentous biological event of universal significance" that Freud alluded to, and although for much of his career he seemed ambivalent about the role of maternal influences in earliest development, in his very last work he stated, in a definitive fashion, that the mother–infant relationship "is unique, without parallel, established unalterably for a whole lifetime as the first and strongest love-object and the prototype of all later love-relations" (Freud, 1940/1964).

This fundamental ontogenetic principle was subsequently explored by a number of developmental psychoanalysts, most importantly in Bowlby's attachment theory, a point of convergence of psychoanalysis and behavioral biology. In a departure from the classical Freudian developmental model, contemporary psychoanalysis now views these "vital" attachment experiences of the first 2 years as more central to personality formation than the later occurring oedipal events of the 3rd and 4th years.

My own work in this area (Schore, 1994, 1996, 1997b, 1998b, 2001a, 2001b, in press c) has focused on the reciprocal affective transactions within the mother–infant dyadic system—in these face-to-face (Feldman, Greenbaum, & Yirmiya, 1999) emotional communications the mother is essentially regulating the infant's psychobiological states. The attachment relationship is thus a regulator of arousal, and attachment is, in essence, the dyadic regulation of emotion (Sroufe, 1996). But even more, these interactive affect regulating events act as a mechanism for the "social construction of the human brain" (Eisenberg, 1995). Trevarthen (1993) concluded that "the affective regulations of brain growth" are embedded in the context of an intimate relationship, and that they promote the development of cerebral circuits. This interactive mechanism requires older brains to engage with mental states of awareness, emotion, and interest in younger brains, and involves a coordination between the motivations of the infant and the subjective feelings of adults. Thus, "the intrinsic regulators of human brain growth in a child are specifically adapted to be coupled, by emotional communication, to the regulators of adult brains" (Trevarthen 1990, p. 357). In this manner, "attachment relationships are formative because they facilitate the development of the brain's major self-regulatory mechanisms" (Fonagy & Target, 2002, p. 328).

In a number of works I have offered evidence which suggests that attachment communications represent right hemisphere-to-right hemisphere affective transactions between mother and infant (Schore, 1994; 1996; 1997b; 2000b). Recent neuroimaging studies demonstrate that infants as young as two months show right hemispheric activation when exposed to a woman's face (Tzourio-Mazoyer et al., 2002), and that the human maternal response to an infant's cry, a fundamental behavior of the attachment dynamic, is accompanied by an activation of the mother's right brain (Lorberbaum et al., 2002). Other studies confirm that this hemisphere is specialized for processing mutual gaze (Ricciardelli, Ro, & Driver, 2002; Watanabe, Miki, & Kakigi, 2002), a primary mechanism of the attachment dynamic. And basic research indicates that the right hemisphere is centrally involved in imprinting, the learning mechanism that underlies attachment (Johnston & Rogers, 1998).

More specifically, affective communications of facial expressions, prosody, and gestures with the social environment are central to the experience-dependent maturation of the infant's early developing right brain. Authors are now emphasizing the critical role of the right hemisphere in the infant's emerging capacity to establish "certainty about the environment" (Burnand, 2002). Ryan, Kuhl, and Deci (1997, p. 719), using electroencephalogram (EEG) and neuroimaging data, proposed that "The positive emotional exchange resulting from autonomy-supportive parenting involves participation of right hemispheric cortical and subcortical systems that participate in global tonic emotional modulation."

The emotional interactions of early life thus directly influence the organization of brain systems that process affect and cognition. In modelling the developmental neurobiology of attachment I have proposed that the attachment experiences of infancy are stored in implicit memory in the early maturing right hemisphere. Implicit memory is a regulatory memory (Fogel, 2003), and so unconscious working models of the attachment relationship encode strategies of affect regulation for coping with stress, especially interpersonal stress (Schore, 1994, 1997, 2000b, 2001a, 2001b). For the rest of the lifespan these internal representations are accessed as guides for future interactions, and the term "working" refers to the individual's unconscious use of them to interpret and act on new experiences.

This psychoneurobiological mechanism mediates the internalization of the attachment relationship and the mother's regulatory functions. A secure attachment relationship facilitates the emergence, at the end of the second year, of what Bowlby (1969) termed a control system in the cortex. I identify this as the orbitofrontal system, which, via its control of the autonomic nervous system (Neafsey, 1990), mediates the highest level of control of emotional behavior (Price, Carmichael, & Drevets, 1996) that is, affect regulation. This frontolimbic system is specialized for "inhibitory control" (Garavan, Ross, & Stein, 1999).

The observations that the right orbitofrontal region is centrally involved in self-regulation (Schore, 1994; Stuss & Levine, 2002), in the recognition of a pleasant facial expression associated with social reward (Gorno-Tempini et al., 2001), and in the short-term storage of icon-like representations of visual objects (Szatkowska, Grabowska, & Szymanska, 2001), and that the human orbitofrontal cortex encodes "a primary reinforcer than can produce affectively positive emotional responses" (Rolls, 2000), support the idea that the visual image of the loving mother's positive emotional face as well as the imprint of the mother's regulatory capacities are inscribed into the circuits of this lateralized prefrontal system.

As the "senior executive of the emotional brain" (Joseph, 1996), the operations of this ventromedial prefrontal cortex are essential to a number of adaptive intrapsychic and interpersonal functions — it appraises facial information (Scalaidhe et al., 1997), operates by implicit processing (Rolls, 1996), generates nonconscious biases that guide behavior before conscious knowledge does (Bechara, Damasio, Tranel, & Damasio, 1997); functions to correct responses as conditions change (Derryberry & Tucker, 1992); processes feedback information (Elliott et al., 1997), and thereby monitors, adjusts, and corrects emotional responses (Rolls, 1986) and modulates the motivational control of goal-directed behavior (Tremblay & Schultz, 1999).

In an object relational transaction, after a rapid evaluation of an environmental stimulus, the orbitofrontal system monitors feedback about the current internal state in order to make assessments of coping resources, and it updates appropriate response outputs in order to make adaptive adjustments to particular environmental perturbations (Schore, 1998; 2000a). In this manner, "the integrity of the orbitofrontal cortex is necessary for acquiring very specific forms of knowledge for regulating interpersonal and social behavior" (Dolan, 1999, p. 928). Most significantly, this prefrontal system sits atop of an implicit processing system located in specific cortical-subcortical circuits. These processes, which track moment-to-moment events in the external and internal environment, are extremely fast acting and therefore beneath levels of conscious awareness. The end product of these right-lateralized operations is a conscious emotional state.

The frontolimbic cortex is situated at the hierarchical apex of the "rostral limbic system," a hierarchical sequence of interconnected limbic areas in orbitofrontal, insular cortex, anterior cingulate, and amygdala (Devinsky, Morrell, & Vogt, 1995). Interactions between cortical orbitofrontal areas and subcortial amygdala areas enable inviduals "to avoid making choices associated with adverse outcomes, without their first having to experience those adverse outcomes," and therefore, this circuit of "immense biological significance" (Baxter, Parker, Lindner, Izquierdo, & Murray, 2000, p. 4317). In total, "the orbitofrontal cortex is involved in critical human functions, such as social adjustment and the control of mood, drive and responsibility, traits that are crucial in defining the 'personality' of an individual" (Cavada & Schultz, 2000, p. 205).

The functioning of the "self-correcting" orbitofrontal system is central to self-regulation, the ability to flexibly regulate emotional states through interactions with other humans—interactive regulation in interconnected contexts via a two-person psychology, and without other humans—autoregulation in autonomous contexts via a one-person psychology. The adaptive capacity to shift between these dual regulatory modes, depending upon the social context, emerges out of a history of secure attachment interactions of a maturing biological organism and an early attuned social environment.

THE RIGHT BRAIN, BODILY PROCESSES, AND SYMBIOSIS

The current intense interest on affect in psychoanalysis and the related sciences emphasizes the critical role of somatic, bodily-based activities in adaptive self-functions during all stages of development. In an important article, Lieberman wrote that current models of development are almost exclusively focusing on cognition. She stated, "The baby's body, with its pleasures and struggles, has been largely missing from this picture" (1996, p. 289). Once again, information about the development and dynamic operations of the right hemisphere is critical to a deeper understanding of the evolution of the organismic substrate of the corporeal/social/emotional self (Devinsky, 2000; Schore, 1994).

This hemisphere is preeminently concerned with the analysis of direct information received from the body. Somatosensory processing and the representation of visceral and somatic states, body sense, and painful sensation are all under primary control of the "non-dominant" hemisphere (Coghill, Gilron, & Iadorola, 2001; Damasio, 1994; Devinsky, 2000; Hsieh, Hannerz, & Ingvar, 1996; Ostrowsky et al., 2002). Neuroimaging research reveal that two other bodily-based drives of intense interest to Freud, sex and aggression, are also under right hemispheric control (Arnow et al., 2002; Janszky et al., 2002; Raine et al., 2001; Schore, 2003). Other studies on conversion seizures and conversion hysteria (hysterical paralysis), an area of great interest to Freud (1893), implicate right hemisphere structures in what are now termed somatization disorders (Devinsky, Mesad, & Alper, 2001; Halligan, Athwal, Oakley, & Frackowiak, 2000; Marshall, Halligan, Fink, Wade, & Frackowiak, 1997). Right hemispheric operations are thus centrally involved in allowing the individual to emotionally react to and understand bodily stimuli, to identify a corporeal image of self and its relation to the environment, and to distinguish self from nonself (Devinsky, 2000).

These adaptive functions and the structures that underlie them are specifically influenced by the attachment relationship. Thus emotion-regulating attachment transactions, in addition to producing neurobiological consequences, are also generating important events in the infant's bodily state; that is, at the psychobiological level (Henry, 1993; Schore, 1994; Siegel, 1999; Wang, 1997). Winnicott proposed that "The main thing is a communication between the baby and mother in terms of the anatomy and physiology of live bodies" (1986, p. 258).

These body-to-body communications also involve right-brain-to-right-brain interactions. Indeed, most human females cradle their infants on the left side of the body (controlled by the right hemisphere). This tendency is well developed in women but not in men, is independent of handedness, and is widespread in all cultures (Manning et al., 1997). It has been suggested by Manning and colleagues that this left-cradling tendency "facilitates the flow of affective information from the infant via the left ear and eye to the center for emotional decoding, that is, the right hemisphere of the mother" (1997, p. 327). As the neurologist Damasio (1994) indicated, this hemisphere contains the most comprehensive and integrated map of the body state available to the brain.

Even more specifically, psychobiological studies of attachment indicate that the intimate contact between the mother and her infant is regulated by the reciprocal activation of their opiate systems—elevated levels of opiates (beta endorphins) increase pleasure in both (Kalin, Shelton, & Lynn, 1995). In these mutual gaze transactions, the mother's face is also inducing the production of not only endogenous opiates but also regulated levels of dopamine in the infant's brain, which generates high levels of arousal and elation. The expanding attachment mechanism thus sustains increased regulated synchronized positive arousal in play episodes, and in them the mother, in a state of excitement, is also stimulating regulated levels of corticotropin releasing factor in the infant brain, which in turn increases ACTH and noradrenaline and adrenaline activity in the child's sympathetic nervous system (Schore, 1994, 1996, 2001b).

In her soothing and calming functions, the mother is also regulating the child's oxytocin levels. It has been suggested that oxytocin, a vagally controlled hormone with antistress effects, is released by "sensory stimuli such as tone of voice and facial expression conveying warmth and familiarity" (Uvnas-Moberg, 1997, p. 42). Oxytocin induces a sustained decrease of the stress hormone cortisol (Petersson, Hulting, & Uvnas-Moberg, 1999). In regulating the infant's vagal tone and cortisol level—activities regulated by the right brain (Schore, 2001b)—the mother also influences the ongoing development of the infant's postnatally maturing parasympathetic nervous system. The sympathetic and parasympathetic components of the autonomic nervous system, important elements of the affect-transacting attachment mechanism, are centrally involved in the child's developing coping capacities. Neurobiological and psychobiological studies thus support the concept of attachment as, fundamentally, the interactive regulation of biological synchronicity between organisms (Schore, 2000a; Wang, 1997).

Basch speculated that "the language of mother and infant consist of signals produced by the autonomic, involuntary nervous system in both parties" (1976, p. 766). This conception is consonant with a large body of developmental psychobiological research that describes the attachment relationship in terms of the mutual regulation of vital endocrine, autonomic, and central nervous systems of both mother and infant by elements of their interaction with each other. Hofer (1990) emphasized the importance of "hidden" regulatory processes by which the caregiver's more mature and differentiated nervous system regulates the infant's "open," immature, internal homeostatic systems. Buck's (1994) neuropsychological description of attachment as a conversation between limbic systems is thus isomorphic to Hofer's psychobiological characterization of the adult's and infant's individual homeostatic systems that are linked together in a superordinate organization.

Importantly, Hofer described the latter relational context as a mutually regulating "symbiotic" state. These matters bear upon the concept of symbiosis, which has had a controversial history in developmental psychoanalytic writings. This debate centers around Mahler, Pine, and Bergman's reference to a normal symbiotic phase during which the infant "behaves and functions as though he and his mother were a single omnipotent system—a dual unity within one common boundary" (1975, p. 8). Although the symbiotic infant is dimly aware that the mother is the source of his pleasurable experiences, he/she is in a "state of undifferentiation, a state of fusion with the mother, in which the 'I' is not differentiated from the 'not-I'" (p. 9).

This latter defintion of symbiosis departs from the classical biological concept and is unique to psychoanalytic metapsychology. Current evidence may not directly support any inferences about the limits of the infant's awareness, nor about an entire stage that describes the infant's behavior only with this characterization. However, moments of face-to-face affective synchrony do begin at 2–3 months (the advent of Mahler's symbiotic phase), they do generate high levels of positive arousal, and such mutually attuned sequences can be portrayed as what Mahler and colleagues (1975) called instances of "optimal mutual cueing." Indeed, in her earliest writings Mahler (1968) did emphasize the affective nature of these interactions, describing "the emotional rapport of the mother's nurturant care, a kind of social symbiosis."

But even more importantly, Hofer's work as well as recent brain research calls for a return of the definition of symbiosis to its biological origins. The Oxford dictionary offers the derivation from the Greek, "living together," and defines *symbiosis* as an interaction between two dissimilar organisms living in close physical association, especially *one in which each benefits the other*. An even more basic definition from biological chemistry suggests that "symbiosis is an association between different organisms that leads to a reciprocal enhancement of their ability to survive" (Lee, Severin, Yokobayashi, & Reza Ghadiri,

1997, p. 591). Recall Buck's (1994) description of an emotionally communicating dyad as "literally a biological unit," a conception that echoes Polan and Hofer's (1999) description of the dyad as a self-organizing regulatory system composed of mother and infant as a unit. These conceptions suggest that instances of positively charged, psychobiologically attuned attachment transactions of affect synchrony are an example of biological symbiosis.

The construct of symbiosis is thus reflected in the conception of attachment as the interactive regulation of biological synchronicity between organisms. In discussing the central role of facial signalling in attachment, Cole asserted, "It is through the sharing of facial expressions that mother and child become as one. It is crucial, in a more Darwinian biological context, for the infant to bond her mother to ensure her own survival" (1998, p. 11). Recall Bowlby's (1969a) assertion that the development of attachment has consequences that are vital to survival and that the infant's capacity to cope with stress is correlated with certain maternal behaviors. The early-developing right hemisphere is dominant for both attachment and the control of vital functions that support survival and enable the organism to cope with stressors (Schore, 1994, 2001b, 2001c, 2002c, 2002f, in press a; Wittling & Schweiger, 1993).

THE RELEVANCE OF NEUROBIOLOGICAL AND PSYCHOBIOLOGICAL RESEARCH ON EMOTION FOR CLINICAL PSYCHOANALYSIS

These neurobiological data on affective structure-function relationships have implications for clinical psychoanalysis. In treatment models, affects, including unconscious affects, are both "the center of empathic communication" and the "primary data," and "the regulation of conscious and unconscious feelings is placed in the center of the clinical stage" (Sandler & Sandler, 1978). In this work, as Sander stated, "It is not the past we seek but the logic of the patient's own state regulating strategies" (in Schwaber, 1990, p. 238).

The direct relevance of studies of emotional development to the psychotherapeutic process derives from the commonality of interactive emotion-transacting mechanisms in the caregiver–infant relationship and in the therapist–patient relationship (Schore, 1994, 1997c, 2000a, 2001d, 2002b, in press a). In the current neurobiological literature, the right hemisphere is dominant for "subjective emotional experiences" (Gainotti, 2001; Wittling & Roschmann, 1993). The interactive "transfer of affect" between the right brains of the members of the mother–infant and therapeutic dyads is thus best described as "intersubjectivity," a finding consonant with recent psychoanalytic "intersubjective" models of the mind (Natterson, 1991; Stolorow & Atwood, 1992). Emotions, by definition, involve subjective states, and studies of the right hemisphere are thus detailing the neurobiology of subjectivity and intersubjectivity.

The contribution of neurobiology to psychoanalysis is much more than just the discovery of new pharmacological agents to treat "disorders of the mind." In "A clinician's view of attachment theory," Chused concluded, "Attachment research can help us understand how intersubjective experience (an aspect of psychoanalysis as well as development) becomes transformed into intrapsychic structure" (2000, p. 1187). Toward that specific end, in a series of publications I have offered interdisciplinary research indicating that both mother–infant attachment transactions and therapist–patient transference-countertransference communications, occurring at levels beneath awareness, represent rapid right hemisphere-to-right hemisphere nonverbal affective transactions (Schore, 1994, 1997c, 2001d, 2002b).

These rapid expressions of the emotional right brain suggest that the small movements of facial muscles, spontaneous gestures, gaze aversions, and emotional tone of voice may be a better reflection of a person's affective state than his/her verbalizations (Panksepp, 1999; Schore, 1994, 2001d, 2002b). In non-face-to-face contexts (e.g., the couch), the emotional tone of voice of therapist and patient also reflect the output of the right hemisphere. Right-lateralized communications have been well described by those working in the "nonverbal realm of psychoanalysis" (i.e., Jacobs, 1994; Schwaber, 1995).

I suggest that just as the left brain communicates its states to other left brains via conscious linguistic behaviors, so the right nonverbally communicates its unconscious states to other right brains that are tuned to receive these communications (Schore, 2001d, 2002b). Marcus observed "The analyst, by means of reverie and intuition, listens with the right brain directly to the analysand's right brain" (1997, p. 238). This neurobiological perspective is consonant with Kantrowitz's emphasis of the centrality of "intense affective engagements" and conclusion that "It is in the realm of preconscious communication that the interwovenness of intrapsychic and interpersonal phenomena become most apparent" (1999, p. 72).

Current psychobiological studies indicate that affects are not merely by-products of cognition—they have unique temporal and physiological characteristics that, more than thoughts, define our internal experience of self. Although facial emotions can be appraised by the right brain within 30 milliseconds, spontaneously expressed within seconds, and continue to amplify within less than a half-minute, it can take hours, or days, or even weeks or longer for certain personalities experiencing extremely intense negative emotion to get back to a "normal" state again. Working with very rapid affective phenomena in real time involves attention to a different time dimension than usual, a focus on interpersonal attachment and separations on a microtemporal scale. This moment-to-moment tracking attends to the internal mechanism by which the patient regulates emotional distance. The emphasis is less on enduring traits and more on transient states, less on temporally distant and more on short-term immediate motivational factors.

Furthermore, neurobiological studies demonstrate the involvement of the right hemisphere in "implicit learning" (Hugdahl, 1995) and "nonverbal processes" (Schore, 1994). Such structure-function relationships may elucidate how alterations in what Stern, Nahum, Sander, and Tronick (1998) called nonverbal "implicit relational knowledge are at the core of therapeutic change." In light of the central role of the limbic system in both attachment functions and in "the organization of new learning" (Mesulam, 1998), the corrective emotional experience of psychotherapy, which can alter attachment patterns, must involve unconscious right-brain limbic learning.

Integrated psychoanalytic-neurobiological conceptualizations of emotional development can thus generate clinically relevant, heuristic models of treatment. Drawing upon findings in psychoanalytic research Westen suggested that "The attempt to regulate affect — to minimize unpleasant feelings and to maximize pleasant ones — is the driving force in human motivation" (1997, p. 542). In parallel neuroscience research, Beauregard, Levesque, and Bourgouin argued that "the ability to modulate emotions is at the heart of the human experience" (2001, p. RC165). They also stated that "the use of emotional self-regulatory processes constitutes the core of several modern psychotherapeutic approaches," (p. RC165), a conclusion echoed by Posner and Rothbart's assertion that the development of self-regulation "may be open to change in adult life, providing a basis for what is attempted in therapy" (1998, p. 1925).

Indeed, affect dysregulation, a fundamental mechanism of the right hemispheric (Cutting, 1992) dysfunctions of all psychiatric disorders (Schore, 1997b; Taylor, Bagby, & Parker, 1997), is now a primary focus of updated clinical psychoanalytic models. Interdisciplinary models clearly suggest that an essential function of psychoanalytic treatment is to complete interrupted developmental processes (Gedo, 1979), and that a critical role of the psychotherapist is to act as an affect regulator of the patient's dysregulated states and to provide a growth-facilitating environment for the patient's immature affect regulating structures (see Schore, 1994; 1997c, 2002a).

In other words, dyadic affective transactions within the working alliance co-create an intersubjective context that allows for the structural expansion of the patient's orbitofrontal system and its cortical and subcortical connections. Orbitofrontal function is essential to not only affect regulation but also to the processing of cognitive-emotional interactions (Barbas, 1995) and affect-related meanings (Teasdale et al., 1999). This "thinking part of the emotional brain" (Goleman, 1995) functions as an "internal reflecting and organizing agency" (Kaplan-Solms & Solms, 1996) involved in "emotion-related learning" (Rolls, Hornak, Wade, & McGrath, 1994). It acts to "integrate and assign emotional-motivational significance to cognitive impressions; the association of emotion with ideas and thoughts" (Joseph, 1996, p. 427), and "presents an important site of contact between emotional or affective information and mechanisms of action selection" (Rogers et al., 1999). All of these functions are essential components of the therapeutic process.

A functional magnetic resonance imaging (fMRI) study conducted by Hariri, Bookheimer, and Mazziotta provided evidence that higher regions of specifi- cally the right prefrontal cortex attenuate emotional responses at the most basic levels in the brain, that such modulating processes are "fundamental to most modern psychotherapeutic methods," (2000, p. 43), that this lateralized neo- cortical network is active in "modulating emotional experience through inter- preting and labeling emotional expressions" (p. 47), and that "this form of modulation may be impaired in various emotional disorders and may provide the basis for therapies of these same disorders" (p. 48). More recently, Furmark and his colleagues (2000) reported that social phobic patients who underwent psychotherapy showed significantly reduced blood flow in amygdala-limbic cir- cuits, particularly in the right hemisphere, a change they interpreted to reflect "an alteration of an emotional experience." These data support Andreasen's assertion, "we are steadily recognizing that the effectiveness of psychotherapy is a consequence of the ability to affect 'mind functions' such as emotion and memory by affecting 'brain functions' such as the connections and communica- tions between nerve cells" (2001, p. 31).

According to Emde (1990), the therapeutic context mobilizes in the patient a biologically prepared positive developmental thrust. The findings that the prefrontal limbic cortex, more than any other part of the cerebral cortex, retains the plastic capacities of early development (Barbas, 1995) and that the right hemisphere cycles into growth phases throughout the lifespan (Thatcher, 1994) allows for the possibility of changes in "mind and brain" (Gabbard, 1994) in psychotherapy. Updated, psychobiologically oriented psychoanalytic treatment models may potentiate what Kandel (1998), in a clarion call for a paradigm shift in psychiatry, described as "biology and the possibility of a renaissance of psychoanalytic thought."

A DYNAMIC SYSTEMS THEORY PERSPECTIVE OF EMOTIONAL PROCESSES

The psychobiological realm of affective phenomena represents not only a con- vergence point of psychoanalysis with neuroscience, but also with the trans- scientific perspective of nonlinear dynamic systems theory (e.g., Gleik, 1987; Kaufmann, 1993; Prigogine & Stengers, 1984). The causal variables involved in affect and its regulation are notoriously dynamic; they may change rapidly over time in intensity and frequency in a nonlinear pattern. Taylor, Bagby, and Parker asserted that "linear models may be inappropriate for the study of affect regulation and state transitions. . . . [T]he study of affect regulation may be im- proved by utilizing concepts and ideas from chaos theory and non-linear dy- namical modelling" (1997, p. 270).

Nonlinear dynamic systems theory, which Scharff and Scharff (1998) and others are now delivering into psychoanalysis, models the mechanism of self- organization, of how complex systems that undergo discontinuous changes come to produce both emergent new forms yet retain continuity. A central assumption of this theory is that energy flows are required for self-organizing processes. In an article on the self-organization of developmental paths, Lewis (1995) asked, "What is the best analogy for energy in psychological systems?" He pointed out that the energy flowthrough for self-organization has been conceived of as "information," an idea that fits well with Harold's (1986) formulation that information is a special kind of energy required for the work of establishing biological order. He then went on to argue that information can be defined subjectively as what is relevant to an individual's goals or needs, an idea that echoes recent concepts of emotion as adaptive functions that guide attention to the most relevant aspects of the environment, and of emotional appraisals that monitor and interpret events in order to determine their significance to the self. Lewis concluded that there is no better marker of such information than the emotion that accompanies it, that emotions amplify fluctuations to act in self-organization, and that the processing of relevant information in the presence of emotion may be analogous to the flowthrough of energy in a state of disequilibrium. Stability is a property of interpersonal attractors that maintain their organization by perpetuating equilibrium as well as resolving emotional disequilibrium.

A central tenet of dynamic systems theory holds that at particular critical moments, a flow of energy allows the components of a self-organizing system to become increasingly interconnected, and in this manner organismic form is constructed in developmental processes. As the patterns of relations among the components of a self-organizing system become increasingly interconnected and well ordered, it is more capable of maintaining a coherence of organization in relation to variations in the environment. In previous work I have proposed that emotional transactions involving synchronized ordered patterns of energy transmissions (directed flows of energy) represent the fundamental core of the attachment dynamic (Schore, 1994, 2000e).

More specifically, in right brain-to-right brain emotion-transacting attachment communications, patterns of information emanating from the caregiver's face, especially of low visual and auditory frequencies (Ornstein, 1997), trigger metabolic energy shifts in the infant. The caregiver is thus modulating changes in the child's energetic state, since arousal levels are known to be associated with changes in metabolic energy. Such regulated increases in energy metabolism are available for biosynthetic processes in the baby's brain, which is in the brain growth spurt. An article in *Science* indicated that "mothers invest extra energy in their young to promote larger brains" (Gibbons, 1998, p. 1347). Furthermore, these regulated emotional exchanges trigger synchronized energy shifts in the infant's developing right brain, and these allow for a coherence of activity within its cortical and subcortical levels and the organization of the emotion-processing right brain into a self-regulating "integrated whole." In this manner, "the self-organization of the developing brain occurs in the context of a relationship with another self, another brain" (Schore, 1997b, 2000e).

This description of how early affective experience creates energy that, in turn, facilitates the organization of developing internal structure directly applies to psychoanalytic energetic metapsychological constructs, a body of knowledge that has been ignored or devalued since the 1960s. In psychoanalytic writings, Schulman (1999) argued that energic "binding" is viewed as energy tied up in structures, and is therefore needed for "the transformation and structuralization of the ego [and superego]." Energic concepts, he stated, become the means for "new psychological developments" such as "ordered thoughts, goal-directed behavior, and controlled affect" (p. 480). Freud's energy models, long considered obsolete, need to be modernized and reintegrated into psychoanalysis (Schore, 1994, 1997a; Shevrin, 1997; Solms, 1996).

Indeed, throughout the lifespan, energy shifts are the most basic and fundamental features of emotion, discontinuous states are experienced as affect responses, and nonlinear psychic bifurcations are manifest as rapid affective shifts. Such state transitions result from the activation of synchronized bioenergetic processes in central nervous system limbic circuits that are associated with concomitant homeostatic adjustments in the autonomic nervous system's energy-expending sympathetic and energy-conserving parasympathetic branches. Emotional mind-body states thus reflect the nonlinear pulsing of energy flows between the components of a self-organizing, dynamic, right-lateralized mind-body system. Furthermore, the fact that affectively charged psychobiological states are known to be a product of the balance between energy-expending and energy-conserving components of the autonomic nervous system may be specifically relevant to Freud's emphasis on a *dynamic conception* of forces in the mind that work together or against one another in order to strive toward a goal.

A cardinal tenet of dynamic theory is that the nonlinear self acts iteratively, so that minor changes, occurring at the right moment, can be amplified in the system, launching it into a qualitatively different state. An example of this principle is found within the intersubjective field co-constructed by the patient and therapist. According to Kohut (1971) the empathically immersed clinician is attuned to the continuous flow and shifts in the patient's feelings and experiences. This attunement involves both subcortical and cortical processing in the clinician's right brain ("right mind"). The therapists's right amygdala acts as a sensor of unconscious affective communications, since this structure is known to act as "a dynamic emotional stimulus detection system" (Wright et al., 2001).

But in addition, the empathic clinician's right orbitofrontal cortex, a preconscious (Frank, 1950) intrapsychic system activated by affective shifts and responsive to fluctuations in the emotional significance of stimuli (Dias, Robbins, & Roberts, 1996), is responsible for his or her "oscillating attentiveness" (Schwaber, 1995) to "barely perceptible cues that signal a change in state" in both patient and therapist (Sander, 1992), and to "nonverbal behaviors and shifts in affects" (McLaughlin, 1996). It generates an "emotional hunch" (Adolphs, 2002). In line with the principle that affect acts as an "analog amplifier" that extends the duration of whatever activates it (Tomkins, 1984), the clinician's resonance with the patient's psychobiological states allows for an amplification of affect within the intersubjective field.

This interactive regulation of the patient's state enables him/her to begin to verbally label the affective experience. In a "genuine dialogue" with the therapist, the patient raises to an inner word and then into a spoken word what he/she needs to say at a particular moment but does not yet possess as speech. But the patient must experience this verbal description of an internal state is heard and felt by an empathic other. This, in turn, facilitates the "evolution of affects from their early form, in which they are experienced as bodily sensations, into subjective states that can gradually be verbally articulated" (Stolorow & Atwood, 1992, p. 42).

The patient's affectively charged but now-regulated right brain experience can then be communicated to the left brain for further processing. This effect, which must follow a right-brain-then-left-brain temporal sequence, allows for the development of linguistic symbols to represent the meaning of an experience, while one is feeling and perceiving the emotion generated by the experience. The objective left hemisphere can now coprocess subjective right-brain communications, and this allows for a linkage of the nonverbal and verbal representational domains.

In addition, I have argued that as opposed to the verbal left hemisphere's "linear" consecutive analysis of information, the processing style of the visuospatial right hemisphere is best described as "nonlinear," based on multiple converging determinants rather than on a single causal chain (Schore, 1997b, 2000e). According to Ramachandran and colleagues (1996), the cognitive style of the right hemisphere shows a highly sensitive dependence to initial conditions and perturbations, a fundamental property of chaotic systems. This minor (!) hemisphere utilizes image thinking, a holistic, synthetic strategy that is adaptive when information is "complex, internally contradictory and basically irreducible to an unambiguous context" (Rotenberg, 1994, p. 489). These characterizations also apply to primary process cognition, a right hemispheric function (Dorpat & Miller, 1992; Galin, 1974; Joseph, 1996; Schore, 1994) of the unconscious mind.

Neurobiological studies reveal greater right hemispheric involvement in the unconscious processing of emotion-evoking stimuli (Wexler, Warrenburg, Schwartz, & Janer, 1992) and conditioned autonomic responses after subliminal presentations of faces to the right and not left cortex (Johnsen & Hugdahl, 1991). A positron emission tomographic (PET) study demonstrates that unconscious processing of emotional stimuli is specifically associated with activation of the right and not left hemisphere (Morris, Ohman, & Dolan, 1998), supporting the idea that "the left side is involved with conscious response and the right with the unconscious mind" (Mlot, 1998, p. 1006). These and the aforementioned studies strongly suggest that the emotion-processing right mind (Ornstein, 1997) is the neurobiological substrate of Freud's unconscious.

NEUROPSYCHOANALYTIC REVISIONS OF CLASSICAL
MODELS OF INTRAPSYCHIC STRUCTURE

Freud's concept of the dynamic unconscious is usually defined in terms of self-regulatory capacities of an unconscious system that operates via the process of repression in order to bar access of sexual and aggressive wishes into consciousness. This characterization describes the left hemispheric verbal horizontal (callosal) inhibition of right hemispheric cognitive-emotional representations (recall the earlier cited right lateralization of bodily based expressions of sexual and aggressive behavior). The current expanding body of knowledge of the right hemisphere suggests a major alteration in the conceptualization of the Freudian unconscious, the internal structural system that processes information at nonconscious levels.

In the last two decades of the twentieth century, the two theoretical engines within psychoanalysis that have substantially modified and expanded Freud's classical concepts have been self psychology and attachment theory. Both of these models focus on early developmental events, the first two years of life. Preoedipal experiences occur well before the oedipal experiences of the third and the fourth year. This developmental perspective also emphasizes the indelible influence of relational factors on the early development of psychic structure. Attachment theory has significantly impacted conceptions of normal development and psychopathogenesis. Self psychology has been a major force in the emergence of relational, intersubjective treatment models. Yet both retain the central Freudian concept of the unconscious. Both still use Freud's concept of repression, and not dissociation, as the major force in psychopathogenesis, and both still rely upon Freud's original definition of the dynamic unconscious as the central mechanism of adaptive human functioning in every day life. In my own work, I have argued that both attachment theory (Schore, 2000a, 2000c) and self psychology (Schore, 2002f) are describing the social experience-dependent maturation of the early developing right brain. The right hemisphere processes exteroceptive and interoceptive information rapidly, at levels beneath conscious awareness.

Another central reformulation of psychoanalysis in the last few decades has been a shift from ego functions to an increasing emphasis on the dynamic operations of the bodily-based self system (Kohut, 1971, 1977; Schore, 1994, 2002f). Neuropsychological research has indicated clearly that the right hemisphere is specialized for generating self-awareness and self-recognition, and for the processing of "self-related material" (Keenan, et al., 2000, 2001; Kircher et al., 2001; Miller et al., 2001; Ruby & Decety, 2001; Schore, 1994). Neuropsychoanalytic models are also moving away from verbal, conscious, explicit left hemispheric to nonverbal, nonconscious, implicit right hemispheric operations.

In a description of Freud's traditional definition, Opatow (1997) stated that as the secondary process comes to overlay and inhibit primary process functioning the dynamic unconscious is established. As mentioned previously, this conceptualization characterizes left hemisphere explicit inhibition of right hemisphere implicit functioning, that is, repression. It fits well with findings that the left uses conscious verbal operations while the right uses nonconscious nonverbal operations and that the left hemisphere dampens down right brain affect. It is also consonant with developmental neuropsychological data indicating that the left hemisphere's callosal inhibition of the right brain onsets between the third and fourth year. However, it overlooks the fact that there are other mechanisms of inhibition, more primitive ones associated with not only primary process cognition but organismic survival that are on-line much earlier.

In fact, well before the left hemisphere matures, the critical nonconscious processing functions of the right brain are well established and indeed, central to the child's adaptive affect regulation, cognition, and memorial capacities. These functions are critical to the earliest formation of the unconscious mind, an area of intense interest to clinical psychoanalysis. Nonconscious internal working models of attachment stored in the right brain are used by the developing psyche to dynamically interact, on a moment-to-moment basis, with the internal world of other humans. In turn, these interactive representations guide the child in its interactions with the external social world. Deficits in this function and consequent adaptive failures are not due to left brain repression, which has not even formed yet, but to dissociative deficits within the right brain itself.

The classical definitions of the dynamic unconscious and repression can not explicate the earliest operations of the human psyche, nor the seemingly chaotic operations of a mind that has been traumatically shattered and prevented from developing in its earliest stages of development. In such cases the later-forming left hemisphere does ultimately form compensatory defensive operations, but the essential motive forces that seal off overwhelmingly painful early experience in infantile trauma are located in an immature, poorly developed right brain and its primitive defenses of dissociation and projective identification.

These data lead me to propose that Freud's seminal model of a dynamic, continuously active unconscious mind describes the moment-to-moment operations of a hierarchical, self-organizing regulatory system that is located in the right brain, "the right mind." The center of psychic life thus shifts from Freud's *ego*, which he located in the "speech-area on the left-hand side" (1923/1961b) and the posterior areas of the verbal left hemisphere, to the highest levels of the nonverbal right hemisphere, the locus of the bodily-based *self* system (Mesulam & Geschwind, 1978; Schore, 1994) and the unconscious mind (Joseph, 1992; Schore, 1994). The system unconscious is more than a frozen memorial function hidden deep within a static intrapsychic structure. Rather, in stable contexts, it acts as an actively communicating relational unconscious (Zeddies, 2000) one that rapidly expresses and receives nonverbal, bodily-based, imagistic, and prosodic information. In unstable contexts, under stress, this dynamic right brain system, and not the left, becomes the dominant hemisphere.

Within the other sciences the term dynamics refers to motive forces or changes. In human beings these forces for growth and development, for movement towards more complexity, are primarily located in the right brain. The fundamental change in the central concept of the dynamic unconscious thus reflects the significant expansions of psychoanalytic models of development and structure. These advances are directly due to the invaluable contributions of self psychology and attachment theory, as well as developmental psychoanalysis and neuropsychoanalysis, to Freud's groundbreaking explorations of the unconscious mind.

Furthermore, the right brain, the locus of the corporeal and emotional self, is also dominant for the ability to understand the emotional states of other human beings, that is, empathy (Devinsky, 2000; Perry et al., 2001; Schore, 1994, 1996). Empathy, an orbitofrontal function (Eslinger, 1998; Moll, Oliveira-Souza, Bramati, & Grafman, 2002), is a moral emotion associated with attachment function (Mikulincer et al., 2001), and so attachment experiences thus directly impact the neurobiological substrate of moral development (Schore, 1994, 2002a). The importance of right hemispheric emotional-imagistic processes in moral development has been stressed by Vitz (1990). A model of the intrapsychic structures that unfluence moral functions was outlined by Freud in his topographic model of a hierarchical supergo regulating lower id centers.

In 1991, I suggested that the superego component, the ego ideal (Hartmann & Lowenstein, 1962), can be identified as an affect regulatory structure within the right orbital prefrontal cortex (Schore, 1991), and cited Piers and Singer's (1953) speculation that the ego ideal contains "a psychic representation of all the growth, maturation, and individuation processes in the human being" (p. 15). In my 1994 book (Schore, 1994), I referred to the classical neurological work of Kleist (1931, cited in Starkstein, Boston, & Robinson, 1988), who considered the orbitofrontal cortex to be the center of emotional life and critically involved in ethical and moral behaviors, and the later observations of Pribram (1981), who concluded that frontolimbic function, manifest in increased internal control, is activated when the human turns inward to process the ethical considerations of his or her behavior. These ideas are supported in the recent neuroscience literature, which describes a "frontal moral guidance system" (Bigler, 2001) and an orbitofrontal system implicated in "the neurology of morals" (Anderson, Bechara, Damasio, Tranel, & Damasio, 1999; Dolan, 1999). In total, this data suggests that the right-lateralized self-system, more so than the left-lateralized ego, is responsible for the nonconscious yet essential functions of Freud's superego.

Recall that the hierarchical concept is fundamental to not only Freud's structural model (1923/1961) of a superego and ego that sit astride the id, but also his topographic model (1900/1953) of stratified conscious, preconscious, and unconscious systems. In earlier contributions (Schore, 1997a, 1999c) I suggested that the hierarchical position of the orbitofrontal regions in the vertically arranged, right-lateralized limbic system represents the structural intrapsychic mechanism by which higher levels of Freud's preconscious system regulate lower levels of the unconscious system. In other words, the orbitofrontal system acts as a higher preconscious system that adaptively organizes lower-level unconscious states of mind-body. In classical neuropsychoanalytic research, Frank (1950) observed that patients with sectioned orbital cortices showed impairments in the preconscious functions of internalization and symbolic elaboration.

Very recent research reveals that the orbitofrontal cortex plays a fundamental role in another preconscious function — the ability to refer thinking and behavior to ongoing reality. This work shows that the human orbitofrontal cortex "sorts out mental associations that pertain to ongoing reality . . . this mechanism allows the free flow of mental associations but ensures that thinking and behavior can always be referred back to true ongoing reality" (Schnider, Treyer, & Buck, 2000, p. 5884). This essential process occurs rapidly, at levels beneath conscious awareness. Researchers report that "by the time the content of a mental association is recognized and consolidated, its cortical representation has already been adjusted to whether it relates to ongoing reality or not" (Schnider, Valenza, Morand, & Michel, 2002, p. 54), and that "the suppression of memories that do not pertain to reality is a pre-conscious process" (p. 59). In light of the expanded role of the orbitofrontal cortex in right brain functions, these data support the idea that "reality testing," especially the adaptive capacity to match interoceptive bodily state with exteroceptive socioemotional information provided by different interpersonal contexts, is mediated by preconscious activities of the "right mind" of the nonverbal right hemisphere, and not the conscious mind of the verbal-analytic left.

The right brain plays a fundamental role in the maintenance of "a coherent, continuous, and unified sense of self" (Devinsky, 2000). But it is important to stress that the self is hierarchically organized. The right brain contains a three-tiered vertically organized hierarchical limbic system, with the higher right orbital prefrontal cortex acting in an executive regulatory function for the right cortical hemisphere and its subcortical connections, that is for the entire right brain (see Schore, 2001b). The most recent conceptualization of corticolimbic architecture visualizes a core-and-shell model (Tucker, 2001), where the shell interfaces with the environment via sensory and motor cortical networks, while the "limbic regulatory core" connects directly into drive centers in the hypothalamus and arousal centers in the reticular formation (Tucker, 2001). I would amend this model and add that there are three limbic levels, each appearing in a caudal to rostral sequence in postnatal critical periods, each being influenced by attachment transactions with the early social environment (Schore, 2001b).

These data suggest that the right-lateralized self system represents a nested system, with an outer later-developing orbitofrontal-limbic regulated core, an inner earlier-developing cingulate-limbic regulating core, and an earliest-evolving amygdala-limbic regulated core that lies deepest within, like nested Russian dolls. These three levels of organization of the right brain represent three levels of the system unconscious: the preconscious, unconscious, and deep unconscious. The unconscious systems of the limbic core thus reflect the early developmental history of the self.

Emde (1983) identified the primordial central integrating structure of the nascent self to be the emerging "affective core" that functions to maintain positive mood and to regulate the infant's interactive behavior, and Weil stated that "the infant's initial endowment in interaction with earliest maternal attunement leads to a basic core which contains directional trends for all later functioning" (1983, p. 337). In 1996, referring to this "basic core," I wrote:

> I equate this with LeDoux's (1989) "core of the emotional system" that computes the affective significance of environmental stimuli, Tucker's (1992) "paralimbic core" that functions in the evaluation of information for adaptive significance and in corticolimbic self-regulation, and Joseph's (1992) "childlike central core," localized in the right brain and limbic system that maintains the self image and all associated emotions, cognitions, and memories that are formed during childhood. I suggest that the orbitofrontal system is an essential component of the affective core. (p. 73)

Authors are describing the developmental process of "cerebral maturation in the vertical dimension" (Luu & Tucker, 1996), and a "rostral limbic system," a hierarchical sequence of interconnected limbic areas in orbitofrontal cortex, insular cortex, anterior cingulate, and amygdala (Schore, 1997b, 2000e, 2001b). There is a considerable amount of experimental, clinical, and theoretical evidence to show that the operation of the higher right prefrontal cortex is integral to autonomous regulation (Ryan, Kuhl, & Deci, 1997; Schore, 1994, 2001b).

It is important to stress that recent models are emphasizing the adaptive nature of both "top-down" and "bottom-up" processing. This conception supports Loewald's description (1949/1980), in the middle of the last century, of the necessity of a flexible bidirectional transfer of information between the unconscious and conscious domains for adaptive self-functioning:

> It is not merely a question of survival of former stages of ego-reality integration, but that people shift considerably, from day to day, at different periods in their lives, in different moods and situations, from one such level to other levels. In fact, it would seem that the more alive people are (though not necessarily more stable), the broader the range of their ego-reality levels is. Perhaps the so-called fully developed, mature ego is not one that has become fixated at the presumably highest or latest stage of development, having left the others behind it, but is an ego that integrates its reality in such a way that the earlier and deeper levels of ego-reality integration become alive as dynamic sources of higher organization. (p. 20)

I suggest that Loewald was describing the dynamic operations of not the ego, but the three tiered right brain self system, which developmentally evolves in a stage-dependent manner.

The critical role of the hierarchical apex of the right-lateralized self system, the "right mind" (Ornstein, 1997), has been described by Alexander and Stuss: "[One] major role of the right frontal lobe is "affectively burning in" information, that is, giving experience a personal quality, essential for humor, awareness, and episodic memory. This brain region, once considered to be functionally "silent," appears to be critical for the highest human behaviors" (2000, p. 434). This process of "affectively burning in" information is heightened during the critical period of maturation of the right frontal lobe, the first two years of human life. The information that is burnt into this neurobiological regulatory structure, as it is first organizing, is specifically social emotional and bodily-based information imprinted in attachment bond communciations. The term "imprinting," the learning mechanism of the attachment process, is derived from the German word *Prägung* which literally means forging or stamping, a clear analog of "burning in." Attachment experiences indelibly imprint developing limbic circuits that lie at the core of the evolving unconscious mind.

EPILOGUE AND IMPLICATIONS FOR EARLY INTERVENTION AND FURTHER RESEARCH

Attachment theory, the dominant model of human social and emotional development currently available to science, was an outgrowth of psychoanalysis. Throughout his career, Freud's believed that his model of a dynamic, continuously active unconscious mind had applications to not only the human individual but to human societies. He, like Darwin before him, also emphasized the fundamental importance of the events at the beginning of human life for all later emotional and personality development. Furthering this line of thought, at the very beginning of my 1994 book, I asserted that "the beginnings of living systems set the stage for every aspect of an organism's internal and external functioning throughout the lifespan" (Schore, 1994, p. 30). This perspective is now strongly supported by current advances in not only developmental psychoanalysis and neuropsychoanalysis, but also in developmental neuropsychiatry and developmental affective neuroscience (Schore, 2003).

Researchers in this latter field are now concluding that "positive (formation of emotional attachment) or negative (e.g., maternal separation or loss) emotional experience may carve a permanent trace into a still developing neuronal network of immature synaptic connections, and thereby can extend or limit the functional capacity of the brain during later stages of life" (Helmeke, Ovtscharoff, Poegel, & Braun, 2001, p. 717). These networks are in the early developing right hemisphere. Developmental neurobiological studies show that this hemisphere is "more advanced thatn the left in surface features from about the 25th (gestatational) week and this advance persists until the left hemisphere shows a post-natal growth spurt starting in the second year" (Trevarthen, 1996, p. 582), and that the volume of the brain increases rapidly during the first two years, normal adult appearance is seen at two years and all major fiber tracts can be identified by age three, and infants under two years show higher right than left hemispheric volumes (Matsuzawa et al., 2001).

These new data strongly suggest that the developmental trajectory of the right brain, the biological substrate of the human unconscious, is indelibly shaped by the pre- and postnatal interpersonal events that occur during the brain growth spurt that ends in the second year of human life. The attachment outcome is the product of the child's genetically encoded biological (temperamental) predisposition and the particular caregiver environment. In recent years the nature of the caregiver environment has been dramatically reshaped within western culture. At the end of my 1994 book I offered some disquieting thoughts about the implications of a psychoneurobiological model of right brain emotional development for the practice of day care, as it practiced in industrialized western societies.

These disturbing trends continue. Sagi, Koren-Karie, Ziv, and Joels recently published a study (2002) of early child care that reported the poor quality of center-care and a high infant-caregiver ratio adversely increased the likelihood of infants developing insecure attachments. These researchers also noted that "being cared for by a relative on a one-to-one basis yielded the most favorable outcome" (2002, p. 1183). Another, the National Institute of Child Health and Human Development Study of Early Child Care in this country found that even when controlling for child-care quality, the quality of the home environment, and maternal sensitivity, maternal employment of 30 hours of more of work per week during the infant's first 9 months of life negatively impacted the child's cognitive development at 36 months (Brooks-Gunn, Han, & Waldfogel, 2002). In a summary overview of the developmental risks associated with early child care, Belsky (2001) concluded that early, extensive, and continuous non-maternal care is associated with subsequent less harmonious parent-child relations and elevated levels of aggression and noncompliance.

The advances in developmental psychoanalytic and neuropsychoanalytic regulation theory clearly suggest that early nonoptimal social environments and insecure attachments impact not just later behavior, cognition, and affect but more fundamentally, the evolution of the brain structural systems that will come to regulate these functions (Schore, 1994, 1996, 1997b, 1998b, 2000a, 2000d, 2000e, 2001b, 2001c, 2002c). Current conceptions of attachment, as articulated by Fonagy and Target assert that the whole of child development can be considered to be "the enhancement of self-regulation" (2002, p. 313), and that "attachment relationships are formative because they facilitate the development of the brain's major self-regulatory mechanisms" (p. 328).

In a series of works I have offered a rather large body of interdisciplinary evidence which strongly suggests that the capacity for affect and therefore self-regulation is fundamentally shaped in the child's early attachments, and that it is primarily nonconscious, nonverbal, and involuntary (Schore, 1994, 1998a, 1998b, 2000a, 2000e, 2002a). This latter conclusion is echoed in psychology in general, where it is now held that most of moment-to-moment psychological life occurs through nonconscious means (Bargh & Chartrand, 1999), and that the autoregulation of aggression involves the operation of a self-regulatory mechanism operating at a preconscious level (Berkowitz, 1990). These are right brain functions, and their development is dependent upon an early interpersonal environment that can be growth-facilitating or growth-inhibiting. These first interactions with the primary caregiver directly impact the experience-dependent maturation of a right brain-driven resilience to stress or a predisposition to psychopathology (Schore, 1994, Schore, 2001b, c).

The psychoneurobiological perspective, outlined in this and the companion volume (Schore, 2003), clearly implies that early brain-based prevention programs, applied on societal scales, can have far-reaching effects on not only individuals but also on cultures (Schore, 2001a). Citing a considerable body of research, Raine concluded that "a biological risk factor (initial right hemisphere dysfunction), when combined with a psychosocial risk factor (severe early physical abuse) predisposes to serious violence" (2002, p. 319). Indeed, EEG measures diagnostic of right brain dysfunction in newborns are now available (Field, Diego, Hernandez-Reif, Schanberg, & Kuhn, 2002). These authors contended that this right lateralized marker for nonoptimal biochemical and behavioral profiles can serve as a risk index for targeting newborns needing early intervention.

Attachment researchers and clinicians have devised psychological (e.g., Cohen et al., 2000, 2002; Duyvesteyn, 1995; van IJzendoorn, Juffer, & Lieberman & Zeanah, 1999) and psychobiological (Field, 1998) treatment protocols for high risk infant-mother dyads. These treatments, especially if they are neurobiologically informed, would impact the right brain growth spurt at a point of maximal plasticity, and thus have enduring effects on the future evolution of the dynamic unconscious and the development of the self over the ensuing lifespan. These efforts to move the mental health professions into early prevention would implement Bowlby's (1988) proposal that fostering psychological security is an important aspect of public health.

In his recent work, the neuroscientist LeDoux differentiated an implicit from an explicit "synaptic self," and asserted, "That explicit and implicit aspects of the self exists is not a particularly novel idea. It is closely related to Freud's partition of the mind into conscious, preconscious (accessible but not currently accessed), and unconscious (inaccessible) levels" (2002, p. p. 28). In a review of this work Davidson, a major figure in affective neuroscience, argued that the self and personality, rather than consciousness, is the outstanding issue in contemporary neuroscience. Davidson, concluded, "Who we are is not synonymous with who we consciously believe ourselves to be. And the former is the much more fundamental because it often allows for a better prediction of behavior than the latter" (2002, p. 268).

Freud's major contribution to science was his discovery of the unique operations of an unconscious mind, one that underlied yet critically effected all functions of another more accessible conscious mind. The sum of his work indicates that a deeper understanding of the fundamental problems of human emotion, motivation, behavior, and cognition can only be achieved by further investigations of this nonconscious realm. At present, there is now, perhaps more than any previous time, a rather pressing need to more deeply comprehend the essential forces that organize and disorganize human nature.

At the beginning of the last century, 2 decades after the *Project*, Freud (1917/1963) proclaimed that "the unconscious is the infantile mental life" and described the unconscious as "a special realm, with its own desires and modes of expression and peculiar mental mechanisms not elsewhere operative." Further clinical and experimental studies of the early developing dynamic, right brain mind-body self system are now called for.

2001

Appendix: Principles of the Psychotherapeutic Treatment of Early-Forming Right Hemispheric Self Pathologies Based Upon the Developmental Models of Schore's Regulation Theory

1. A conceptualization of self psychopathology as deficits of affect regulation that result from an arrest of emotional development, and a formulation of a treatment model that is matched to the developmental level of the patient.
2. A model of right brain interactive affect regulation as a fundamental process of both psychobiological development and psychotherapeutic treatment.
3. A focus on the identification and integration not of conscious mental states but of nonconscious psychobiological states of mind/body that underlie state-dependent affective, bodily, behavioral, and cognitive-memorial functions.
4. An understanding of therapeutic empathy, a major mechanism of the treatment, as not so much a match of left brain verbal cognitions but as a right brain nonverbal psychobiological attunement, and the use of affect synchronizing transactions for interactively generating and amplifying positive affect that forges the patient's attachment to the therapist.
5. An operational definition of the therapeutic alliance in terms of nonconscious yet mutually reciprocal influences, whereby the patient's capacity for attachment combines with the therapist's contingently-responsive facilitating behaviors to permit development of the working relationship.
6. A requirement that the therapist must be experienced as being in a state of vitalizing attunement to the patient, i.e., the dynamic crescendos and

decrescendos of the therapist's right brain-driven autonomic states must be in resonance with similar states of crescendos and decresendos, cross-modally, of the patient's right brain.

7. A stress on dysregulated right brain "primitive affects" — such as shame, disgust, elation, excitement, terror, rage, and hopeless despair — and the identification of unconscious dissociated affects that were never developmentally interactively regulated, rather than the analysis of unconscious resistance and disavowal of repressed affect.

8. An approach that accesses an awareness of the clinician's right hemispheric countertransferential visceral-somatic responses to the patient's transferential, automatic, facially, prosodically, and somatically expressed affects, as well as an attention to the intensity, duration, frequency, and lability of the patient's internal state.

9. A moment-to-moment tracking of content-associated subtle and dramatic shifts in arousal and state in patient narratives, and the identification of nonconscious "hot" cognitions that trigger nonlinear discontinuities of right brain and therefore dysregulate self function.

10. An awareness of dyadically-triggered nonverbal shame dynamics, and the cocreation of an interpersonal context within the therapeutic alliance that can be nonconsciously sensed by the patient as safe enough to allow deeper self-revelation.

11. A conception of defense mechanisms as nonconscious strategies of emotional regulation for avoiding, minimizing, or converting affects that are too difficult to tolerate, with an emphasis on dissociation and projective identification; these right brain defenses prevent the entrance into "dreaded states" charged with intense affects that can potentially traumatically disorganize the self system.

12. An uncovering of insecure attachment histories imprinted in implicit-procedural memory and stored as right hemispheric internal working models that encode strategies of affect regulation and guide the individual's behavior in interpersonal interactions.

13. An identification of early-forming, rapid-acting, and, thereby, nonconscious right brain perceptual biases for covertly detecting threatening social stimuli (transferential biases); these stress coping strategies that program motivational expectations of misattunement-induced self dysregulation are overtly expressed during stressful transference-countertransference ruptures that occur in "enactments."

14. An appreciation of the centrality of interactive repair as a therapeutic mechanism that facilitates the mutual regulation of affective homeostasis, which in the short-term disconfirms the patient's transferential expectations that underlie defensive avoidance, and in the long-term allows for the emergence of a right brain system that more effectively regulates the intensity, frequency, and duration of negative and postive affect.

15. An understanding that the therapist's affect tolerance is a critical factor determining the range, types, and intensities of emotions that are explored or disavowed in the transference-countertransference relationship and the therapeutic alliance.

16. An emphasis on process rather than genetic interpretations, and an attention to the right hemispheric prosodic (emotion communicating) form as well as the left hemispheric linguistic content of interpretations.

17. A directing of therapeutic technique towards the elevation of emotions from a primitive presymbolic sensorimotor level of experience to a mature symbolic representational level, and a creation of a self-reflective position that can appraise the significance and meanings of these affects.

18. The self-organization, in an interactive growth-facilitating therapeutic environment, of an implicit self system capable of efficiently modulating a broader range of affects, integrating these discrete emotions into a variety of adaptive motivational states, utilizing affects as signals, and linking coherent behavioral states to appropriate social contexts.

19. A primary objective of the treatment is the restoration or expansion of the patient's capacity for self-regulation: the ability to flexibly regulate emotional states through interactions with other humans (interactive regulation in interconnected contexts) and without other humans (autoregulation in autonomous contexts) as well as the resilient capacity to adaptively shift between these dual regulatory modes.

20. A long-term goal of reorganizing insecure internal working models into earned secure models that allow for more complex modes of intrapsychic organizations and interpersonal behaviors, and a developmental progression of the ability, in a variety of familiar and novel contexts, to maintain a coherent, continuous, and unified sense of self, a function of the right brain, the biological substrate of the human unconscious mind.

Permissions

Schore, A. N. "The Right Brain As the Neurobiological Substratum of Freud's Dynamic Unconscious," copyright © 2001 by Other Press. This excerpt originally appeared in *The Psychoanalytic Century: Freud's Legacy for the Future*, edited by David E. Scharff.

FIGURES

Figure 1.1

Himwich (1975), Forging a Link Between Basic and Clinical Research: Developing Brain, *Biological Psychiatry* 10:130. Plenum.

Figures 1.2 and 1.3

Schore, A. N. (1997), Interdisciplinary developmental research as a source of clinical models, *Neurobiological and Developmental Basis for Psychotherapeutic Intervention*: Jason Aronson.

Figure 1.4

Beebe, B. and Lachmann F. (1988), Mother-infant mutual influence and precursors of psychic structure, *Frontiers in Self Psychology: Progress in Self Psychology* 3. Copyright The Analytic Press, 1988.

Figure 1.5

Field, T. and Fogel, A. (Eds.) (1982), Affective displays of high-risk infants during early interactions, *Emotion and Early Interaction*, 101–125: Lawrence Erlbaum.

Figure 1.6

Aitken, K. J. and Trevarthen, C. (1997), Self/other organization in human psychological development, *Development and Psychopathology* 9: 653–677. Reprinted with permission of Cambridge University Press.

Figure 1.7

Human Neuropsychology by Bryan Kolb and Ian Q. Whishaw © 1980, 1985, 1990, 1996 by Worth Publishers. Used with permission.

Figure 1.8

From *Human Brain Anatomy in Computerized Images* by Hanna Damasio, copyright © 1995 by Oxford University Press, Inc. Used by permission of Oxford Universtiy Press, Inc.

Figure 1.9

Nieuwenhuys, Voogd, and van Huijzen (1981), *The Human Central Nervous System, Second Revised Edition*: Springer-Verlag.

Figure 1.10   Watson (1977), *Basic Human Neuroanatomy, An Intro-
                              ductory Atlas, Second Edition*: Little, Brown & Company.

Figure 1.11   Smith, C. G. (1981), *Serial Dissections of the Human
                              Brain*: Urban & Schwarzenberg.

Figure 1.12   Martin, J. (1989), *Neuroanatomy: Text and Atlas*: Mc-
                              Graw-Hill Education.

Figure 2.2   Trevarthen, Aitken, Papoudia, and Robarts (1998),
                              *Children with Autism, Second Edition: Diagnosis and
                              Interventions to Meet Their Needs*: Jessica Kingsley Pub-
                              lishers.

                              COLOR INSERT

Figure A-1   Reprinted from *Current Opinion in Neurobiology 11*,
                              by R. Adolphs, "The neurobiology of social cognition,"
                              231–239, copyright 2001, with permission from Elsevier
                              Science.

Figure A-2   Schore, A. N. (2001), Effects of a secure attachment
                              relationship on right brain development, affect regula-
                              tion, and infant mental health. *Infant Mental Health
                              Journal 22*, 7–77: Wiley Interscience.

Figure A-3   Reprinted from *Neuroscience and Biobehavioral Reviews
                              20*, C. Trevarthen, Lateral asymmetries in infancy: Im-
                              plications for the development of the hemisperes, 571–
                              586, copyright 1996, with permission from Elsevier
                              Science.

Figure A-4   Utsunomiya, H. et al., "Development of the temporal
                              lobe in infants and children: Analysis by MR-based
                              volumetry," *American Journal of Neuroradiology 20*:
                              717–723. Copyright by the American Society of Neuro-
                              radiology (www.ajnr.org).

Figure A-5a–d   From *Structure of the Human Brain: A Photographic
                              Atlas*, 3rd Edition, by S. J. De Armond and M. M.
                              Fusco and M. M. Dewey, copyright 1974, 1976, 1989
                              by Oxford University Press, Inc. Used by permission of
                              Oxford University Press, Inc.

Figure A-6   Tzourio-Mazoyer, N. et al. (2002), "Neural correlates of
                     woman's face processing by 2-month-old infants." *Neu-
                     roImage 15*: 454–461. New York: Elsevier.

Figure A-7   Holowka, S. and L. A. Petitto (2002), "Left Hemisphere
                     cerebral specialization for babies while babbling," *Sci-
                     ence 297*: 1515, copyright 2002 by the American Associ-
                     ation for the Advancement of Science.

Figure A-8   Nakamura, K. et al. (2000), "Functional delineation of
                     the human occipito-temporal areas related to face and
                     scene processing: A PET study," *Brain 123*: 1903–1912,
                     by permission of Oxford University Press.

Figure A-9   Sar, V. et al., "HMPAO SPECT study of regional cere-
                     bral blood flow in dissociative identity disorder," *Journal
                     of Trauma and Dissociation 2*: 5–25, copyright 2001,
                     The Haworth Press.

Figure A-10   Schmahl, C. G., B. E. Elzinga, and J. D. Bremner
                     (2002), "Individual differences in psychophysiological
                     reactivity in adults with childhood abuse," *Clinical Psy-
                     chology and Psychotherapy 9*: 271–276. Copyright 2002
                     © John Wiley & Sons Limited. Reproduced with per-
                     mission.

Figure A-11   Hariri, A. R. et al., (2002), "Modulating emotional re-
                     sponses: Effects of a neocortical network on the limbic
                     system," *NeuroReport 11*: 43–48, by permission of Lip-
                     pincott Williams & Wilkins.

Figure A-12   Adolphs, R. (2002), "Trust in the brain," *Nature Neuro-
                     science 5*: 192–193, by permission of Nature Publishing
                     Group.

Figure A-13   Reprinted by permission from Nature Reviews Neuro-
                     science. A. D. Craig (2002), "How do you feel? Intero-
                     ception: The sense of the physiological condition of the
                     body," *Nature Reviews Neuroscience 3*: 655–666. Figure
                     3. Copyright 2002 Macmillan Magazines Ltd.

Figure A-14   Elliott, R. et al. (2000), "Dissociable function in the
                     medial and lateral orbiotfrontal cortex: Evidence from

human neuroimaging studies," *Cerebral Cortex* 10: 308–317, by permission of Oxford University Press.

Figure A-15   Furmack, T. et al., "Common changes in cerebral blood flow in patients with social phobia treated with citalopram or cognitive-behavioral therapy," *Archives of General Psychiatry* 59: 425–433. Copyrighted 2002, American Medical Association.

Figure A-16   Austin, James H., *Zen and the Brain*. Frontispiece, PET scan of relaxed awareness, by permission of The MIT Press.

References

Abelin, E. (1971). The role of the father in the separation-individuation process. In J. B. McDevitt & C. F. Settlage (Eds.), *Separation-individuation* (pp. 229–252). New York: International University Press.

Acerra, F., Burnod, Y., & de Schonen, S. (2002). Modelling aspects of face processing in early infancy. *Developmental Science, 5,* 98–117.

Adamec, R. (1997). Transmitter systems involved in neural plasticity underlying increased anxiety and defense—implications for understanding anxiety following traumatic stress. *Neuroscience and Biobehavioral Reviews, 21,* 755–765.

Adams, K. M., Gilman, S., Koeppe, R., Kluin, K., Junck, L., Lohman, M., Johnson-Greene, D., Berent, S., Dede, D., & Kroll, P. (1995). Correlation of neuropsychological function with cerebral metabolic rate in subdivisions of the frontal lobes of older alcoholic patients measured with [^{18}F] fluorodeoxyglucose and positron emission tomography. *Neuropsychology, 9,* 275–280.

Ad-Dab'Bagh, Y., & Greenfield, B. (2001). Multiple complex developmental disorder: the "multiple and complex" evolution of the "childhood borderline syndome" construct. *Journal of the Academy of Child and Adolescent Psychiatry, 40,* 951–964.

Adler, G., & Buie, D. H. J. (1979). Aloneness and borderline psychopathology: The possible relevance of child development issues. *International Journal of Psycho-Analysis, 60,* 83–96.

Adler, G., & Rhine, M. W. (1992). The selfobject function of projective identification. In N. G. Hamilton (Ed.), *From inner sources: New directions in object relations psychotherapy* (pp. 139–162). Northvale, NJ: Jason Aronson.

Adolphs, R. (2001). The neurobiology of social cognition. *Current Opinion in Neurobiology, 11,* 231–239.

Adolphs, R., Damasio, H., Tranel, D., Cooper, G., & Damasio, A. R. (2000). A role for somatosensory cortices in the visual recognition of emotion as revealed by three-dimensional lesion mapping. *Journal of Neuroscience, 20,* 2683–2690.

Adolphs, R., Damasio, H., Tranel, D., & Damasio, A. R. (1996). Cortical systems for the recognition of emotion in facial expressions. *Journal of Neuroscience, 23,* 7678–7687.

Aftanas, L. I., Koshkarov, V. I., Pokrovskaja, V. L., Lotova, N. V., & Mordvintsev, Y. N. (1996). Event-related desynchronization (ERD) patterns to emotion-related feedback stimuli. *International Journal of Neuroscience, 87,* 151–173.

Ahern, G. L., Sollers, J. J., Lane, R. D., Labiner, D. M., Herring, A. M., Weinand, M. E., Hutzler, R., & Thayer, J. F. (2001). Heart rate and heart rate variability changes in the intracarotid sodium amobarbital test. *Epilepsia, 42,* 912–921.

Ainsworth, M. D. S. (1967). *Infancy in Uganda: Infant care and the growth of love.* Baltimore: Johns Hopkins University Press.

Ainsworth, M. D. S. (1969). Object relations, dependency and attachment: A theoretical review of the infant-mother relationship. *Child Development, 40,* 969–1025.

Ainsworth, M. D. S., & Bell, S. M. (1974). Mother–infant interaction and the development of competence. In K. Connolly & J. Bruner (Eds.), *The growth of confidence* (pp. 97–118). New York: Academic Press.

Ainsworth, M. D. S., Blehar, M. C., Waters, E., & Wall, S. (1978). *Patterns of attachment.* Hillsdale, NJ: Erlbaum.

Aldrich, C. K. (1987). Acting out and acting up: The superego lacuna revisited. *American Journal of Orthopsychiatry, 57,* 402–406.

Alexander, M. P., & Stuss, D. T. (2000). Disorders of frontal lobe functioning. *Seminars in Neurology, 20,* 427–437.

Allen, J. G., & Coyne, L. (1995). Dissociation and vulnerability to psychotic experience. The Dissociative Experiences Scale and the MMPI-2. *Journal of Nervous & Mental Disease, 183,* 615–622.

Alpert, M., Cohen, N. L., Martz, M., & Robinson, C. (1980). Electorencephalographic analysis: A methodology for evaluating psychotherapeutic process. *Psychiatry Research, 2,* 323–329.

Alvarez, A. (1997). Projective identification as a communication: Its grammer in borderline psychotic children. *Psychoanalytic Dialogues, 7,* 753–768.

Alvarez, A. (1999). Widening the bridge. Commentary on papers by Stephen Seligman, Robin C. Silverman, and Alicia F. Lieberman. *Psychoanalytic Dialogues, 9,* 205–217.

American Psychiatric Association. (1987). *The diagnostic and statistical manual of mental disorders* (DSM-III-R; 3rd ed. rev.). Washington, DC: Author.

Amini, F., Lewis, T., Lannon, R., et al. (1996). Affect, attachment, memory: Contributions toward pscychobiologic integration. *Psychiatry, 59,* 213–239.

Amsterdam, B. (1972). Mirror self-image reactions before age two. *Developmental Psychobiology, 5,* 297–305.

Amsterdam, B., & Levitt, M. (1980). Consciousness of self and painful self-consciousness. *Psychoanalytic Study of the Child, 35,* 67–83.

Anaki, D., Faust, M., & Kravetz, S. (1998). Cerebral hemispheric asymmetries in processing lexical metaphors. *Neuropsychologia, 36,* 691–700.

Anders, T. F., & Zeanah, C. H. (1984). Early infant development from a biological point of view. In J. D. Call, E. Galenson, & R. L. Tyson (Eds.), *Frontiers of infant psychiatry* (vol. 2) (pp. 55–69). New York: Basic Books.

Andersen, S. M., Reznik, I., & Manzella, L. M. (1996). Eliciting facial affect, motivation, and expectancies in transference: Significant-other representations in social relations. *Journal of Personality and Social Psychology, 71,* 1108–1129.

Anderson, S. W., Bechara, A., Damasio, H., Tranel, D., & Damasio, A. R. (1999). Impairment of social and moral behavior related to early damage in human prefrontal cortex. *Nature Neuroscience, 2,* 1032–1037.

Anderson, S. W., Damasio, H., Tranel, D., & Damasio, A. R. (2000). Long-term sequelae of prefrontal cortex damage acquired in early childhood. *Developmental Neuropsychology, 18,* 281–296.

Andreasen, N. C. (2001). *Brave new brain.* New York: Oxford University Press.

Andreason, P. J., O'Leary, D. S., Cizadlo, T., Arndt, S., Rezai, K., Watkins, G. L., Boles Ponto, L. L., & Hichwa, R. D. (1995). Remembering the past: Two facets of episodic memory explored with positron emission tomography. *American Journal of Psychiatry, 152,* 1576–1585.

Andreason, P. J., Zametkin, A. J., Guo, A. C., Baldwin, P., & Cohen, R. M. (1994). Gender-related differences in regional cerebral glucose metabolism in normal volunteers. *Psychiatry Research, 51,* 175–183.

Anthi, P. R. (1983). Reconstruction of preverbal experience. *Journal of the American Psychoanalytic Association, 31,* 33–58.

Anthony, E. J. (1981). Shame, guilt, and the feminine self in psychoanalysis. In S. Tuttman (Ed.), *Object and self: A developmental approach* (pp. 191–234). New York: International Universities Press.

Aoki, C., & Stekevitz, P. (1988). Plasticity and brain development. *Scientific American, 259,* 56–68.

Arnow, B. A., Desmond, J. E., Banner, L. L., Glover, G. H., Solomon, A., Polan, M. L., Lue, T. F., & Atlas, S. W. (2002). Brain activation and sexual arousal in healthy, heterosexual males. *Brain, 125,* 1014–1023.

Arntz, A., & Veen, G. (2001). Evaluations of others by borderline patients. *Journal of Nervous & Mental Disease, 189,* 513–521.

Aron, L. (1998). The clinical body and the reflexive mind. In L. Aron & F. Sommer Anderson (Eds.), *Relational perspectives on the body* (pp. 3–37). Hillsdale, NJ: Analytic Press.

Aron, L., & Anderson, F. S. (1998). *Relational perspectives on the body.* Hillsdale, NJ: Analytic Press.

Atchley, R. A., & Atchley, P. (1998). Hemispheric specialization in the detection of subjective objects. *Neuropsychologia, 36,* 1373–1386.

Auerbach, J. S. (1990). Narcissism: Reflections on others' images of an elusive concept. *Psychoanalytic Psychology, 7,* 545–564.

Augustine, J. R. (1996). Circuitry and functional aspects of the insular lobe in primates including humans. *Brain Research Reviews, 22,* 229–244.

Austin, J. H., *Zen and the brain.* Cambridge, MA: MIT Press.

Bach, S. (1985). *Narcissistic states and the therapeutic process.* New York: Jason Aronson.

Bach, S. (1998). On treating the difficult patient. In C. S. Ellman, S. Grand, M. Silvan, & S. J. Ellman (Eds.), *The modern Freudians: Contemporary psychoanalytic technique* (pp. 185–195). Northvale, NJ: Jason Aronson.

Baker, S. C., Frith, C. D., & Dolan, R. J. (1997). The interaction between mood and cognitive function studied with PET. *Psychological Medicine, 27,* 565–578.

Balint, M. (1968). *The basic fault.* London: Tavistock.

Balter, L., Lothane, Z., & Spencer, J. H., Jr. (1980). On the analyzing instrument. *Psychoanalytic Quarterly, 49,* 474–504.

Bandura, A., & Walters, R. H. (1963). *Social learning and personality development.* New York: Holt, Rinehart & Winston.

Barach, P. M. M. (1991). Multiple personality disorder as an attachment disorder. *Dissociation, IV,* 117–123.

Barbas, H. (1995). Anatomic basis of cognitive-emotional interactions in the primate prefrontal cortex. *Neuroscience and Biobehavioral Reviews, 19,* 499–510.

Barbas, H., & De Olmos, J. (1990). Projections from the amygdala to basoventral and mediodorsal prefrontal regions in the rhesus monkey. *Journal of Comparative Neurology, 301,* 1–23.

Bargh, J. A., & Chartrand, T. L. (1999). The unbearable automaticity of being. *American Psychologist, 54,* 462–479.

Barlow, H. B. (1980). Nature's joke: A conjecture on the biological role of consciousness. In B. D. Josephson & V. S. Ramachandran (Eds.), *Consciousness and the physical world* (pp. 81–94). Oxford, UK: Pergamon Press.

Baron-Cohen, S. (1995). *Mindblindness: An essay on autism and theory of mind.* Cambridge, MA: MIT Press.

Baron-Cohen, S., Ring, H., Moriarty, J., Schmitz, B., Costa, D., & Ell, P. (1994). Recognition of mental state terms: Clinical findings in children with autism and a functional neuroimaging study of normal adults. *British Journal of Psychiatry, 165,* 640–649.

Basch, M. F. (1976). The concept of affect: A re-examination. *Journal of the American Psychoanalytic Association, 24,* 759–777.

Basch, M. F. (1983). The perception of reality and the disavowal of meaning. *Annual of Psychoanalysis, 11,* 125–154.

Basch, M. F. (1985). Interpretation: Toward a developmental model. In A. Goldberg (Ed.), *Progress in self psychology* (vol. 1, pp. 33–42). New York: Guilford Press.

Basch, M. F. (1985). New directions in psychoanalysis. *Psychoanalytic Psychology, 2,* 1–19.

Basch, M. F. (1988). *Understanding psychotherapy.* New York: Basic Books.

Basch, M. F. (1992). *Practicing psychotherapy: A casebook.* New York: Basic Books.

Basch, M. F. (1995). Kohut's contribution. *Psychoanalytic Dialogues, 5,* 367–373.

Baxter, M. G., Parker, A., Lindner, C. C. G., Izquierdo, A. D., & Murray, E. A. (2000). Control of response selection by reinforcer value requires interaction of amygdala and orbital prefrontal cortex. *Journal of Neuroscience, 20,* 4311–4319.

Beard, D. K. (1992). *Somatic knowing with the psychosomatic patient: An answer in kind.* Unpublished doctoral dissertation, California School of Professional Psychology, Los Angeles.

Beauregard, M., Levesque, J., & Bourgouin, P. (2001). Neural correlates of conscious self-regulation of emotion. *Journal of Neuroscience, 21,* R165.

Bechara, A., Damasio, A. R., Damasio, H., & Anderson, S. W. (1994). Insensitivity to future consequences following damage to human prefrontal cortex. *Cognition, 50,* 7–15.

Bechara, A., Damasio, H., Tranel, D., & Damasio, A. R. (1997). Deciding advantageously before knowing the advantageous strategy. *Science, 275,* 1293–1295.

Beebe, B. (2000). Coconstructing mother–infant distress: The microsychrony of maternal impingement and infant avoidance in the face-to-face encounter. *Psychoanalytic Inquiry, 20,* 412–440.

Beebe, B., Jaffe, J., Lachmann, F., Feldstein, S., Crown, C., & Jasnow, J. (2000). Systems models in development and psychoanalysis: The case of vocal rhythm coordination and attachment. *Infant Mental Health Journal, 21,* 99–122.

Beebe, B., & Lachman, F. M. (1988a). Mother–infant mutual influence and precursors of psychic structure. In A. Goldberg (Ed.), *Progress in self psychology* (vol. 3, pp. 3–25). Hillsdale, NJ: Analytic Press.

Beebe, B., & Lachmann, F. M. (1988b). The contribution of mother–infant mutual influence to the origins of self- and object relationships. *Psychoanalytic Psychology, 5,* 305–337.

Beebe, B., & Lachmann, F. M. (1994). Representations and internalization in infancy: Three principles of salience. *Psychoanalytic Psychology, 11,* 127–165.

Beebe, B., & Lachmann, F. M. (2002). *Infant research and adult treatment.* Hillsdale, NJ: Analytic Press.

Beeman, M. (1998). Coarse semantic coding and discourse comprehension. In M. Beeman & C. Chiarello (Eds.), *Right hemisphere language comprehension* (pp. 255–284). Mahwah, NJ: Erlbaum.

Beers, S. R., & De Bellis, M. D. (2002). Neuropsychological function in children with maltreatment-related posttraumatic stress disorder. *American Journal of Psychiatry, 159,* 483–486.

Bell, S. M. (1970). The development of the concept of object as related to infant–mother attachment. *Child Development, 41,* 291–311.

Belsky, J. (2001). Emanuel Miller lecture: developmental risks (still) associated with early child care. *Journal of Child Psychology and Psychiatry, 42,* 845–859.

Benowitz, L. I., Bear, D. M., Rosenthal, R., Mesulam, M.-M., Zaidel, E., & Sperry, R. W. (1983). Hemispheric specialization in nonverbal communication. *Cortex, 19*, 5–11.

Bergman, A. (1999). *Ours, yours, mine: Mutuality and the emergence of the separate self.* Northvale, NJ: Analytic Press.

Berkowitz, L. (1990). On the formation and regulation of anger and aggression. *American Psychologist, 45*, 494–503.

Bertenthal, B., Campos, J., & Barrett, K. (1984). Self-produced locomotion: An organizer of emotional, cognitive, and social development in infancy. In R. Emde & R. J. Harmon (Eds.), *Continuities and discontinuities in development* (pp. 175–210). New York: Plenum.

Berthier, M. L., Posada, A., & Puentes, C. (2001). Dissociative flashbacks after right frontal injury in a Vietnam veteran with combat-related posttraumatic stress disorder. *Journal of Neuropsychiatry and Clinical Neuroscience, 13*, 101–105.

Berthier, M., Starkstein, S., & Leiguarda, R. (1987). Behavioral effects of damage to the right insula and surrounding regions. *Cortex, 23*, 673–678.

Best, C. T. (1988). The emergence of cerebral asymmetries in early human development: A literature review and a neuroembryological model. In S. Segalowitz & D. L. Molfese (Eds.), *Developmental implications of brain lateralization* (pp. 5–34). New York: Guilford Press.

Bigler, E. D., Johnson, S. C., Anderson, C. V., Blatter, D. D., Gale, S. D., Russo, A. A., Ryser, D. K., MacNamara, S. E., Bailey, B. J., Hopkins, R. O., & Abildskov, T. J. (1996). Traumatic brain injury and memory: The role of hippocampal atrophy. *Neuropsychology, 10*, 333–342.

Bigler, E. D., Raine, A., LaCasse, L., & Colletti, P. (2001). Frontal lobe pathology and antisocial personality disorder. *Archives of General Psychiatry, 58*, 609–611.

Binder, J. R., Rao, S. M., Hammeke, T. A., Frost, J. A., Bandettini, P. A., Jesmanowicz, A., & Hyde, J. S. (1995). Lateralized human brain language systems demonstrated by task subtraction functional magnetic resonance imaging. *Archives of Neurology, 52*, 593–601.

Binder, J., & Strupp, H. H. (1997). "Negative process": A recurrently discovered and underestimated facet of therapeutic process and outcome in the individual psychotherapy of adults. *Clinical Psychology Science & Practice, 4*, 121–139.

Bion, W. R. (1959). Attacks on linking. *International Journal of Psycho-Analysis, 4*, 308–315.

Bion, W. R. (1962a). *Learning from experience.* London: Heinemann.

Bion, W. R. (1962b). The psychoanalytic study of thinking: II. A theory of thinking. *International Journal of Psycho-Analysis, 43*, 306–310.

Bion, W. R. (1967). *Second thoughts.* New York: Jason Aronson.

Bion, W. R. (1977). *Seven servants.* New York: Jason Aronson.

BisazzaI, A., Rodgers, L. J., & Vallortigara, G. (1998). The origins of cerebral asymmetry: A review of evidence of behavioural and brain lateralization in fishes, reptiles and amphibians. *Neuroscience and Biobehavioral Reviews, 22*, 411–426.

Blair, R. J. R., Morris, J. S., Frith, C. D., Perrett, D. I., & Dolan, R. J. (1999). Dissociable neural responses to facial expressions of sadness and anger. *Brain, 122*, 883–893.

Blank, H. R. (1975). Reflection on the special senses in relation to the development of affect with special emphasis on blindness. *Journal of the American Psychoanalytic Association, 23*, 32–50.

Blatt, S. J., Quinlan, D. M., & Chevron, E. (1990). Empirical investigations of a psychoanalytic theory of depression. In J. Masling (Ed.), *Empirical studies of psychoanalytic theories* (vol. 3, pp. 89–147). Hillsdale, NJ: Analytic Press.

Bleiberg, E. (1987). Stages in the treatment of narcissistic children and adolescents. *Bulletin of the Menninger Clinic, 51,* 296–313.

Blonder, L. X., Bowers, D., & Heilman, K. M. (1991). The role of the right hemisphere in emotional communication. *Brain, 114,* 1115–1127.

Blonder, L. X., Burns, A. F., Bowers, D., Moore, R. W., & Heilman, K. M. (1993). Right hemisphere facial expressivity during natural conversation. *Brain and Cognition, 21,* 44–56.

Blonder, L. X., Burns, A. F., Bowers, D., Moore, R. W., & Heilman, K. M. (1995). Spontaneous gestures following right hemisphere infarct. *Neuropsychologia, 33,* 203–213.

Blood, A. J., Zatorre, R. J., Bermudez, P., & Evans, A. C. (1999). Emotional responses to pleasant and unpleasant music correlate with activity in paralimbic brain regions. *Nature Neuroscience, 2,* 382–387.

Blos, P. (1974). The genealogy of the ego ideal. *Psychoanalytic Study of the Child, 29,* 43–88.

Bogen, J. E. (1997). Does cognition in the disconnected right hemisphere require right hemisphere possession of language? *Brain and Language, 57,* 12–21.

Bohart, A. C. (1993). Experiencing: The basis of psychotherapy. *Journal of Psychotherapy Integration, 3,* 51–68.

Bohart, A. C., & Greenberg, L. (1997). *Empathy reconsidered: New directions in psychotherapy.* Washington, DC: American Psychological Association.

Bollas, C. (1987). *The shadow of the object: Psychoanalysis and the unthought known.* London: Free Association.

Bordin, E. (1979). The generalizability of the psychoanalytic concept of the working alliance. *Psychotherapy: Theory, Research and Practice, 16,* 252–260.

Bornstein, R. F. (1993a). Implicit perception, implicit memory, and the recovery of unconscious material in psychotherapy. *Journal of Nervous and Mental Disease, 181,* 337–344.

Bornstein, R. F. (1993b). Parental representations and psychopathology: A critical review of the empirical literature. In J. M. Masling & R. F. Bornstein (Eds.), *Psychoanalytic perspectives on psychopathology* (pp. 1–41). Washington, DC: American Psychological Association.

Bornstein, R. F. (1999). Source amnesia, misattribution, and the power of unconscious perceptions and memories. *Psychoanalytic Psychology, 16,* 155–178.

Borod, J. (2000). *The neuropsychology of emotion.* New York: Oxford University Press.

Borod, J. C., Andelman, F., Obler, L. K., Tweedy, J. R., & Welkowitz, J. (1992). Right hemisphere specialization for the identification of emotional words and sentences: Evidence from stroke patients. *Neuropsychologia, 30,* 827–844.

Borod, J., Cicero, B. A., Obler, L. K., Welkowitz, J., Erhan, H. M., Santschi, C., Grunwald, I. S., Agosti, R. M., & Whalen, J. R. (1998). Right hemisphere emotional perception: Evidence across multiple channels. *Neuropsychology, 12,* 446–458.

Borod, J. C., Haywood, C. S., & Koff, E. (1997). Neuropsychological aspects of facial asymmetry during emotional expression: A review of the adult literature. *Neuropsychology Review, 7,* 41–60.

Bowden, D. M., Goldman, P. S., Rosvold, H. E., & Greenstreet, R. L. (1971). Free behavior of rhesus monkeys following lesions of the dorsolateral and orbital prefrontal cortex in infancy. *Experimental Brain Research, 12,* 265–274.

Bowden, E. M., & Beeman, M. J. (1998). Getting the right idea: Semantic activation in the right hemisphere may help solve insight problems. *Psychological Science, 9,* 435–440.

Bower, G. H. (1981). Mood and memory. *American Psychologist, 36,* 129–148.

Bowers, D., Bauer, R. M., & Heilman, K. M. (1993). The nonverbal affect lexicon: Theoretical perspectives from neuropsychological studies of affect perception. *Neuropsychology, 7*, 433–444.

Bowlby, J. (1969). *Attachment and loss. Vol. 1: Attachment.* New York: Basic Books.

Bowlby, J. (1973). *Attachment and loss. Vol. 2, separation, anxiety and anger.* New York: Basic Books.

Bowlby, J. (1978). Attachment theory and its therapeutic implications. In S. C. Feinstein & P. L. Giovacchini (Eds.), *Adolescent psychiatry: Developmental and clinical studies.* Chicago: University of Chicago Press.

Bowlby, J. (1981). *Attachment and loss. Vol. 3: Loss, sadness, and depression.* New York: Basic Books.

Bowlby, J. (1988). Attachment, communication, and the therapeutic process. In J. Bowlby (Ed.), *A secure base: Clinical applications of attachment theory* (pp. 137–157). London: Routledge.

Bowlby, J. (1991a). *Charles Darwin.* New York: Norton.

Bowlby, J. (1991b, Autumn). The role of the psychotherapist's personal resources in the therapeutic situation. *Tavistock Gazette.*

Boyer, L. B. (1990). Countertransference and technique. In L. B. Boyer & P. L. Giovacchini (Eds.), *Master clinicians on treating the regressed patient* (pp. 303–324). Northvale, NJ: Jason Aronson.

Bradley, S. (2000). *Affect regulation and the development of psychopathology.* New York: Guilford Press.

Braun, K., Lange, E., Metzger, M., & Poeggel, G. (2000). Maternal separation followed by early social deprivation affects the development of monoaminergic fiber systems in the medial prefrontal cortex of *octodon degus. Neuroscience, 95*, 309–318.

Braun, K., & Poeggel, G. (2001). Recognition of mother's voice evokes metabolic activation in the medial prefrontal cortex and lateral thalamus of *octodon degus* pups. *Neuroscience, 103*, 861–864.

Brazelton, T. B., Koslowski, B., & Main, M. (1974). The origins of reciprocity: The early mother–infant interaction. In M. Lewis & L. Rosenblum (Eds.), *The effect of the infant on its caregiver.* New York: Wiley.

Breese, G. R., Smith, R. D., Mueller, R. A., Howard, J. L., Prange, A. J., Lipton, M. A., Young, L. D., McKinney, W. T., & Lewis, J. K. (1973). Induction of adrenal catecholamine synthesizing enzymes following mother–infant separation. *Nature New Biology, 246*, 94–96.

Brende, J. O. (1982). Electrodermal responses in post-traumatic syndromes: A pilot study of cerebral hemisphere functioning in Vietnam veterans. *Journal of Nervous and Mental Disorders, 170*, 353–361.

Brenner, C. (1980). A psychoanalytic theory of affects. In R. Plutchik & H. Kellerman (Eds.), *Emotion: Theory, research, and experience* (vol. 1). New York: Academic Press.

Brenner, C. (1982). *The mind in conflict.* Madison, CT: International Universities Press.

Brent, L., & Resch, R. C. (1987). A paradigm of infant–mother reciprocity: A re-examination of "emotional refueling." *Psychoanalytic Psychology, 4*, 15–31.

Bretherton, I. (1985). Attachment theory: Retrospect and prospect. *Monographs of the Society for Research in Child Development, 50*, 3–35.

Bretherton, I., McNew, S., & Beeghly, M. (1981). Early person knowledge in gestural and verbal communication: When do infants acquire a "theory of mind"? In M. Lamb & L. Sherrod (Eds.), *Infant social sognition* (pp. 335–373). Hillsdale, NJ: Erlbaum.

Breuer, J., & Freud, S. (1955). Studies on hysteria. In J. Strachey (Ed. & Trans.), *Standard edition of the Complete Psychological Works of Sigmund Freud.* (Vol. 2, pp. 3–305). London: Hogarth Press. (Original work published 1893)

Brickman, A. S. (1983). Pre-oedipal development of the superego. *International Journal of Psycho-Analysis, 64,* 83–92.

Broca, P. (1861). *Sur le siège de la faculté du langage articulé avec deux observations d'aphémie (perte de la parole).* Paris: Victor Masson et fils.

Brody, S. (1982). Psychoanalytic theories of infant development and disturbances: A critical evaluation. *Psychoanalytic Quarterly, 51,* 526–597.

Bromberg, P. (1991). On knowing one's patient inside out: The aesthetics of unconscious communication. *Psychoanalytic Dialogues, 1,* 399–422.

Bromberg, P. (1994). "Speak! That I may see you"; Some reflections on dissociation, reality, and psychoanalytic listening. *Psychoanalytic Dialogues, 4,* 517–547.

Bromberg, P. (1996). Standing in the spaces: The multiplicity of self and the psychoanalytic relationship. *Contemporary Psychoanalysis, 32,* 509–535.

Bromberg, P. M. (1995). Psychoanalysis dissociation and personality organization. In *Standing in the spaces: Essays on clinical process, trauma, and dissociation* (pp. 189–204). Hillsdale, NJ: The Analytic Press.

Bronson, G. (1963). A neurological perspective on ego development in infancy. *Journal of the American Psychoanalytic Association, 11,* 55–65.

Brooks-Gunn, J., Han, W-J., & Waldfogel, J. (2002). Maternal employment and child cognitive outcomes in the first three years of life: the NICHD study of early child care. *Child Development, 73,* 1052–1072.

Brothers, L. (1990). The social brain: A project for integrating primate behavior and neurophysiology in a new domain. *Concepts in Neuroscience, 1,* 27–51.

Brothers, L. (1995). Neurophysiology of the perception of intentions by primates. In M. S. Gazzaniga (Ed.), *The cognitive neurosciences* (pp. 1107–1115). Cambridge, MA: MIT Press.

Brothers, L. (1997). *Friday's footprint.* New York: Oxford University Press.

Brothers, L., & Ring, B. (1992). A neuroethological framework for the representation of minds. *Journal of Cognitive Neuroscience, 4,* 107–118.

Broucek, F. J. (1982). Shame and its relationship to early narcissistic developments. *International Journal of Psycho-Analysis, 63,* 369–378.

Broverman, D. M., Klaiber, E. L., Kobayashi, Y., & Vogel, W. (1968). Roles of activation and inhibition in sex differences in cognitive abilities. *Psychological Review, 75,* 23–50.

Brown, D. (1993). Affective development, psychopathology, and adaptation. In S. L. Ablon, D. Brown, E. J. Khantzian, & J. E. Mack (Eds.), *Human feelings: Explorations in affect development and meaning* (pp. 5–66). Hillsdale, NJ: Analytic Press.

Brown, M. R., Fisher, L. A., Rivier, J., Spiess, J., Rivier, C., & Vale, W. (1982). Corticotropin-releasing factor: Effects on the sympathetic nervous system and oxygen consumption. *Life Sciences, 30,* 207–219.

Bruner, J. (1994). The view from the heart's eye: A commentary. In P. M. Niedentahl & S. Kiyayama (Eds.), *The heart's eye: Emotional influences in perception and attention* (pp. 269–286). San Diego: Academic Press.

Bryan, K. L., & Hale, J. B. (2001). Differential affects of left and right cerebral vascular accidents on language competency. *Journal of the International Neuropsychological Society, 7,* 655–664.

Buber, M. (1957). Elements of the interhuman. *Psychiatry, 20,* 105–113.

Bucci, W. (1993). The development of emotional meaning in free association: A multiple code theory. In A. Wilson & J. E. Gedo (Eds.), *Hierarchical concepts in psychoanalysis* (pp. 3–47). New York: Guilford Press.

Buck, R. (1993). Spontaneous communication and the foundation of the interpersonal self. In U. Neisser (Ed.), *The perceived self: Ecological and interpersonal sources of self-knowledge* (pp. 216–236). New York: Cambridge University Press.

Buck, R. (1994). The neuropsychology of communication: Spontaneous and symbolic aspects. *Journal of Pragmatics, 22,* 265–278.

Buck, R. W., Parke, R. D., & Buck, M. (1970). Skin conductance, heart rate, and attention to the environment in two stressful situations. *Psychonomic Science, 18,* 95–96.

Buechler, S., & Izard, C. E. (1983). On the emergence, functions, and regulation of some emotion expressions in infancy. In R. Plutchik & H. Kellerman (Eds.), *Emotion, theory, research, and experience* (vol. 3, pp. 292–313). New York: Academic Press.

Burnand, G. (2002). Hemisphere specializtion as an aid in early infancy. *Neuropsychology Review, 12,* 233–251.

Bursten, B. (1973). Some narcissistic personality types. *International Journal of Psycho-Analysis, 54,* 287–300.

Burstein, R., & Potrebic, S. (1993). Retrograde labeling of neurons in the spinal cord that project directly to the amygdala or the orbital cortex in the rat. *Journal of Comparative Neurology, 335,* 469–485.

Cabib, S., Puglisi-Allegra, S., & D'Amato, F. R. (1993). Effects of postnatal stress on dopamine mesolimbic responses to aversive experiences in adult life. *Brain Research, 604,* 232–239.

Cacioppo, J. T., & Berntson, G. G. (1992). Social psychological contributions to the decade of the brain: Doctrine of multilevel analysis. *American Psychologist, 47,* 1019–1028.

Cahill, L., Haier, R. J., Fallon, J., Alkire, M. T., Tang, C., Keator, D., Wu, J., & McGaugh, J. L. (1996). Amygdala activity at encoding correlated with long-term, free recall of emotional information. *Proceedings of the National Academy of Sciences of the United States of America, 93,* 8016–8021.

Campbell, B. A., & Mabry, P. D. (1972). Ontogeny of behavioral arousal: A comparative study. *Journal of Comparative and Physiological Psychology, 81,* 371–379.

Campos, J. J., Barrett, K. C., Lamb, M. G., Goldsmith, H. H. & Stenberg, C. (1983). Socioemotional development. In P. H. Mussen (Ed.), *Handbook of child psychology* (4th ed., pp. 783–915). New York: Wiley.

Caplan, R., Chugani, H. T., Messa, C., Guthrie, D., Sigman, M., De Traversay, J., & Mundy, P. (1993). Hemispherectomy for intractible seizures: Presurgical cerebral glucose metabolism and post-surgical non-verbal communication. *Developmental Medicine and Child Neurology, 35,* 582–592.

Caplan, R., & Dapretto, M. (2001). Making sense during conversation: An FMRI study. *NeuroReport, 12,* 3625–3632.

Cappella, J. N. (1993). The facial feedback process in human interaction: review and speculation. Special issue: emotional communication, culture, and power. *Journal of Language and Social Psychology, 12,* 13–29.

Carlson, V., Cicchetti, D., Barnett, D., & Braunwald, K. (1989). Disorganized/disoriented attachment relationships in maltreated infants. *Developmental Psychology, 25,* 525–531.

Carmichael, S. T., & Price, J. L. (1995). Limbic connections of the orbital and medial prefrontal cortex in macaque monkeys. *Journal of Comparative Neurology, 363,* 615–641.

Carmon, A., Harishanu, Y., Lowinger, E., & Lavy, S. (1972). Asymmetries in hemispheric blood volume and cerebral dominance. *Behavioral Biology, 7,* 853–859.

Carpy, D. V. (1989). Tolerating the countertransference: A mutative process. *International Journal of Psycho-Analysis, 70,* 287–294.

Carrey, N. J., Butter, H. J., Persinger, M. A., & Bialek, R. J. (1995). Physiological and cognitive correlates of child abuse. *Journal of the Academy of Child and Adolescent Psychiatry, 34*, 1067–1075.

Carrion, V. G., Weems, C. F., Eliez, S., Patwardhan, A., Brown, W., & Ray, R. D. (2001). Attenuation of frontal asymmetry in pediatric posttraumatic stress disorder. *Biological Psychiatry, 50*, 943–951.

Carrion, V. G., Weems, C. F., Ray, R. D., Glaser, B., Hessl, D., & Reiss, A. L. (2002). Diurnal salivary cortisol in pediatric posttraumatic stress disorder. *Biological Psychiatry, 51*, 575–582.

Casey, B. J., Trainor, R., Giedd, J., Vauss, Y., Vaituzis, C. K., Hamburger, S., Kozuch, P., & Rapoport, J. L. (1997). The role of the anterior cingulate in the automatic and controlled processes: A developmental neuroanatomical study. *Developmental Psychobiology, 30*, 61–69.

Cassidy, J., & Shaver, P. R. (Eds.) (1999). *Handbook of attachment: Theory, research, and clinical applications.* New York: Guilford Press.

Castelnuovo-Tedesco, P. (1974). Toward a theory of affects (panel discussion). *Journal of the American Psychoanalytic Association, 22*, 612–625.

Cavada, C., Company, T., Tejedor, J., Cruz-Rizzolo, R. N., & Reinoso-Suarez, F. (2000). The anatomical connections of the macaque monkey orbitofrontal cortex. A review. *Cerebral Cortex, 10*, 220–242.

Cavada, C., & Schultz, W. (2000). The mysterious orbitofrontal cortex. Foreword. *Cerebral Cortex, 10*, 205.

Champoux, M., Byrne, E., Delizio, R., & Suomi, S. J. (1992). Motherless mothers revisited: Rhesus maternal behavior and rearing history. *Primates, 33*, 251–255.

Chapple, E. D. (1970). Experimental production of transients in human interaction. *Nature, 228*, 630–633.

Chasseguet-Smirgel, J. (1985). *The ego ideal.* London: Free Association Books.

Cheshire, N. M. (1996). The empire of the ear: Freud's problem with music. *International Journal of Psycho-Analysis, 77*, 1127–1168.

Chiron, C., Jambaque, I., Nabbout, R., Lounes, R., Syrota, A., & Dulac, O. (1997). The right brain hemisphere is dominant in human infants. *Brain, 120*, 1057–1065.

Chu, J. E., & Dill, D. L. (1990). Dissociative symptoms in relation to childhood physical and sexual abuse. *American Journal of Psychiatry, 147*, 887–892.

Chugani, H. T. (1996). Neuroimaging of developmental nonlinearity and developmental pathologies. In R. W. Thatcher, G. Reid Lyon, J. Rumsey, & N. Krasnegor (Eds.), *Developmental neuroimaging: Mapping the development of brain and behavior* (pp. 187–195). San Diego: Academic Press.

Churchland, P. S. (2002). Self-representation in nervous systems. *Science, 296*, 308–310.

Chused, J. F. (2000). Discussion: A clinician's view of attachment theory. *Journal of the American Psychoanalytic Association, 48*, 1175–1187.

Cicone, M., Wapner, W., & Gardner, H. (1980). Sensitivity to emotional expressions and situation in organic patients. *Cortex, 16*, 145–158.

Cimino, C. R., Verfaellie, M., Bowers, D., & Heilman, K. M. (1991). Autobiographical memory: Influence of right hemisphere damage on emotionality and specificity. *Brain and Cognition, 15*, 106–118.

Clarke, A. S., Hedecker, D. R., Ebert, M. H., Schmidt, D. E., McKinney, W. T., & Kraemer, G. W. (1996). Rearing experience and biogenic amine activity in infant rhesus monkeys. *Biological Psychiatry, 40*, 338–352.

Cofer, C. N., & Appley, M. H. (1964). *Motivation: Theory and research.* New York: Wiley.

Coghill, R. C., Gilron, I., & Iadorola, M. J. (2001). Hemispheric lateralization of somatosensory processing. *Journal of Neurophysiology, 85*, 2602–2612.

Cohen, M. J., Riccio, C. A., & Flannery, A. M. (1994). Expressive aprosodia following stroke to the right basal ganglia: A case report. *Neuropsychology, 8,* 242–245.

Cohen, N. J., Lojkasek, M., Muir, E., Muir, R., & Parker, C. J. (2002). Six-month follow-up of two mother–infant psychotherapies: Convergence of therapeutic outcomes. *Infant Mental Health Journal, 23,* 361–380.

Cohen, N. J., Muir, E., Lojkasek, M., Muir, R., Parker, C. J., Barwick, M., & Brown, M. (1999). Watch, wait, and wonder: Testing the effectiveness of a new approach to mother–infant psychotherapy. *Infant Mental Health Journal, 20,* 429–451.

Cohn, J. F., & Tronick, E. Z. (1987). Mother–infant face-to-face interaction: The sequence of dyadic states at 3, 6, and 9 months. *Developmental Psychology, 23,* 68–87.

Cole, J. (1998). *About face.* Cambridge, MA: MIT Press.

Cole, P. M., Michel, M. K., & O'Donnell Teti, L. (1994). The development of emotion regulation and dysregulation: A clinical perspective. *Monographs of the Society for Research in Child Development, 59,* 73–100.

Cooper, A. M. (1985). Will neurobiology influence psychoanalysis? *American Journal of Psychiatry, 142,* 1395–1402.

Cooper, A. M. (1987). Changes in psychoanalytic ideas: Transference interpretation. *Journal of the American Psychoanalytic Association, 35,* 77–98.

Cooper, A. M. (1994). Formulations to the patient: Explicit and implicit. *International Journal of Psycho-Analysis, 75,* 1107–1120.

Coplan, J. D., Andrews, M. W., Rosenblum, L. A., Owens, M. J., Friedman, S., Gorman, J. M., & Nemeroff, C. B. (1996). Persistent elevations of cerebrospinal fluid concentrations of corticotropin-releasing factor in adult nonhuman primates exposed to early-life stressors: Implications for the pathophysiology of mood and anxiety disorders. *Proceedings of the National Academy of Sciences of the United States of America, 93,* 1619–1623.

Coule, J. T., Frith, C. D., Frackowiak, R. S. J., & Grasby, P. M. (1996). A fronto-parietal network for rapid visual information processing: A PET study of sustained attention and working memory. *Neuropsychologia, 34,* 1085–1095.

Cox, M., & Theilgaard, A. (1997). *Mutative metaphors in psychotherapy: The aeolian mode.* London: Jessica Kingsley.

Craig, A. D. (2002). How do you feel? Interoception: the sense of the physiological condition of the body. *Nature Reviews Neuroscience, 3,* 655–666.

Craik, F. I. M., Moroz, T. M., Moscovitch, M., Stuss, D. T., Winocur, G., Tulving, E., & Kapur, S. (1999). In search of self: A positron emission tomography study. *Psychological Science, 10,* 26–34.

Critchley, H., Daly, E., Philips, M., Brammer, M., Bullmore, E., Williams, S., Van Amelsvoort, T., Robertson, D., David, A., & Murphy, D. (2000). Explicit and implicit neural mechanisms for processing of social information from facial expressions: A functional magnetic resonance imaging study. *Human Brain Mapping, 9,* 93–105.

Critchley, H., Elliott, R., Mathias, C. J., & Dolan, R. J. (2000). Neural activity relating to generation and representation of galvanic skin conductance responses: A functional magnetic resonance imaging study. *Journal of Neuroscience, 20,* 3033–3040.

Crittenden, P. M., & Ainsworth, M. D. S. (1989). Child maltreatment and attachment theory. In D. Cicchetti & V. Carlson (Eds.), *Child maltreatment: Theory and research on the causes and consequences of child abuse and neglect* (pp. 432–463). New York: Cambridge University Press.

Crucian, G. P., Hughes, J. D., Barrett, A. M., Williamson, D. J. G., Bauer, R. M., Bowres, D., & Heilman, K. M. (2000). Emotional and physiological responses to false feedback. *Cortex, 36,* 623–647.

Cubelli, R., Caselli, M., & Neri, M. (1984). Pain endurance in unilateral cerebral lesions. *Cortex, 20,* 369–375.

Cutting, J. (1992). The role of right hemisphere dysfunction in psychiatric disorders. *British Journal of Psychiatry, 160,* 583–588.

Daly, M. de Burgh. (1991). Some reflex cardioinhibitory responses in the cat and their modulaton by central inspiratory activity. *Journal of Physiology, 422,* 463–480.

Damasio, A. R. (1994). *Descartes' error.* New York: Grosset/Putnam.

Damasio, A. R. (1995). Toward a neurobiology of emotion and feeling: Operational concepts and hypotheses. *The Neuroscientist, 1,* 19–25.

Damasio, H. (1995). *Human brain anatomy in computerized images.* New York: Oxford University Press.

Dareste, M. C. (1891). *Recherches sur la production artificielle des monstruosités.* Paris: C. Reinwald.

Darwin, C. (1965). *The expression of emotion in man and animals.* Chicago: University of Chicago Press. (Originally published 1872)

Darwin, C. B. (1965). Blushing. In *The expression of emotions in man and animals* (pp. 309–346). Chicago: University of Chicago Press. (Originally published 1873.)

Davidson, R. J. (1994). Asymmetric brain function, affective style, and psychopathology: The role of early experience and plasticity. *Development and Psychopathology, 6,* 741–758.

Davidson, R. J. (1998a). Affective style and affective disorders: Perspectives from affective neuroscience. *Cognition and Emotion, 12,* 307–330.

Davidson, R. J. (1998b). Anterior electrophysiological asymmetries, emotion, and depression: Conceptual and methodological conundrums. *Psychophysiology, 35,* 607–614.

Davidson, R. J. (2002). Synaptic substrates of the implicit and explicit self (book review of *Synaptic Self* by J. LeDoux). *Science, 296,* 268.

Davidson, R. J., Marshall, J. R., Tomarken, A. J., & Henriques, J. B. (2000). While a phobic waits: Regional brain electical and autonomic activity in social phobics during anticipation of public speaking. *Biological Psychiatry, 47,* 85–95.

Davidson, R. J., Putnam, K. M., & Larson, C. L. (2000). Dysfunction in the neural circuitry of emotion regulation—a possible prelude to violence. *Science, 289,* 591–594.

Davies, J. M. (1996). Dissociation, repression and reality: Testing in the countertransference. The controversey over memory and false memory in the psychoanalytic treatment of adult survivors of childhood sexual abuse. *Psychoanalytic Dialogues, 6,* 189–218.

Davies, J. M. (1999). Getting cold feet, defining "safe-enough" borders: Dissociation, multiplicity, and integration in the analyst's experience. *Psychoanalytic Quarterly, 68,* 184–208.

Davies, J. M., & Frawley, M. G. (1994). *Treating the adult survivor of childhood sexual abuse: A psychoanalytic perspective.* New York: Basic Books.

Davis, M., & Hadiks, D. (1994). Nonverbal aspects of therapist attunement. *Journal of Clinical Psychology, 50,* 393–405.

Dawson, G. (1994). Development of emotional expression and emotion regulation in infancy. In G. Dawson & K. W. Fischer (Eds.), *Human behavior and the developing brain* (pp. 346–379). New York: Guilford Press.

Dawson, G., Panagiotides, H., Klinger, L. G., & Hill, D. (1992). The role of frontal lobe functioning in the development of infant self-regulatory behavior. *Brain and Cognition, 20,* 152–175.

Day, R., & Wong, S. (1996). Anomalous perceptual asymmetries for negative emotional stimuli in the psychopath. *Journal of Abnormal Psychology, 105,* 648–652.

De Armond, S. J., Fusco, M. M., & Dewey, M. M. (1989). *Structure of the human brain. A photographic atlas, 3rd Edition.* New York: Oxford University Press.

De Bellis, M. D. (2001). Developmental traumatology: The psychobiological development of maltreated children and its implications for research, treatment, and policy. *Development and Psychopathology, 13,* 539–564.

De Bellis, M. D., Baum, A. S., Birmaher, B., Keshavan, M. S., Eccard, C. H., Boring, A. M., Jenkins, F. J., & Ryan, N. D. (1999). Developmental traumatology, Part I: Biological stress systems. *Biological Psychiatry, 45,* 1259–1270.

De Bellis, M. D., Casey, B. J., Dahl, R. E., Birmaher, B., Williamson, D. E., Thomas, K. M., Axelson, D. A., Frustaci, K., Boring, A. M., Hall, J., & Ryan, N. D. (2000). A pilot study of amygdala volume in pediatric generalized anxiety disorder. *Biological Psychiatry, 48,* 51–57.

De Bellis, M. D., Keshaven, M. S., Spencer, S., & Hall, J. (2000). N-acetylaspartate concentration in anterior cingulate with PTSD. *American Journal of Psychiatry, 157,* 1175–1177.

De Bellis, M. D., Keshavan, M. S., Shifflett, H., Iyengar, S., Beers, S. R., Hall, J., & Moritz, G. (2002). Brain structures in pediatric maltreatment-related posttraumatic stress disorder: A sociodemographically matched study. *Biological Psychiatry, 52,* 1066–1078.

DeBruin, J. P. C., Van Oyen, H. G. M., & Vande Poll, N. E. (1983). Behavioral changes following lesions of the orbital prefrontal cortex in male rats. *Behavioral and Brain Research, 10,* 209–232.

De Jonghe, F., Rijnierse, P., & Janssen, R. (1992). The role of support in psychoanalysis. *Journal of the American Psychoanalytic Association, 40,* 475–499.

Demb, J. B., Desmond, J. E., Wagner, A. D., Vaidya, C. J., Glover, G. H., & Gabrieli, J. D. E. (1995). Semantic encoding and retrieval in the left inferior prefrontal cortex: A functional MRI study of task difficulty and process specificity. *Journal of Neuroscience, 15,* 5870–5878.

Demos, V. (1991). Resiliency in infancy. In T. F. Dugan & R. Coles (Eds.), *The child in our times: Studies in the development of resiliency* (pp. 3–22). New York: Brunner/Mazel.

Demos, V. (1992). The early organization of the psyche. In J. W. Barron, M. N. Eagle, & D. L. Wolitsky (Eds.), *Interface of psychoanalysis and psychology* (pp. 200–232). Washington, DC: American Psychological Association.

Demos, V., & Kaplan, S. (1986). Motivation and affect reconsidered: Affect biographies of two infants. *Psychoanalysis and Contemporary Thought, 9,* 147–221.

Denenberg, V. H., Garbanti, J., Sherman, G., Yutzey, D. A., & Kaplan, R. (1978). Infantile stimulation induces brain lateralization in rats. *Science, 201,* 1150–1152.

de Paola, H. F. B. (1990). Countertransference and reparative processes within the analyst. In L. B. Boyer & P. L. Giovacchini (Eds.), *Master clinicians on treating the regressed patient* (pp. 325–337). Northvale, NJ: Jason Aronson.

Deri, S. (1990). Changing concepts of the ego in psychoanalytic theory. *Psychoanalytic Review, 77,* 512–518.

Derryberry, D., & Tucker, D. M. (1992). Neural mechanisms of emotion. *Journal of Clinical and Consulting Psychology, 60,* 329–338.

Derryberry, D., & Tucker, D. M. (1994). Motivating the focus of attention. In P. M. Niedentahl & S. Kiyayama (Eds.), *The heart's eye: Emotional influences in perception and attention.* San Diego: Academic Press.

Deruelle, C., & De Schonen, S. (1998). Do the right and left hemispheres attend to the same visuospatial information within a face in infancy? *Developmental Neuropsychology, 14,* 535–554.

Devinsky, O. (2000). Right cerebral hemisphere dominance for a sense of corporeal and emotional self. *Epilepsy & Behavior, 1,* 60–73.

Devinsky, O., Mesad, S., & Alper, K. (2001). Nondominant hemisphere lesions and conversion nonepileptic seizures. *Journal of Neuropsychiatry and Clinical Neuroscience, 13,* 367–373.

Devinsky, O., Morrell, M. J., & Vogt, B. A. (1995). Contributions of anterior cingulate cortex to behaviour. *Brain, 118,* 279–306.

Dewaraja, R., & Sasaki, Y. (1990). A right to left callosal transfer deficit of nonlinguistic information in alexithymia. *Psychotherapy and Psychosomatics, 54,* 201–207.

Diamond, A., & Doar, B. (1989). The performance of human infants on a measure of frontal cortex function, the delayed response task. *Developmental Psychobiology, 22,* 271–294.

Diamond, D., & Blatt, S. J. (1999). Attachment research and psychoanalysis. 1. Research considerations. *Psychoanalytic Inquiry, 19,* 423–667.

Diamond, M. C., Krech, D., & Rosenzweig, M. R. (1963). The effects of an enriched environment on the histology of the rat cerebral cortex. *Journal of Comparative Neurology, 123,* 111–120.

Dias, R., Robbins, T. W., & Roberts, A. C. (1996). Dissociation in prefrontal cortex of affective and attentional shifts. *Nature, 380,* 69–72.

Dienstbier, R. A. (1989). Arousal and physiological toughness: Implications for mental and physical health. *Psychological Review, 96,* 84–100.

Dimberg, U., & Ohman, A. (1996). Behold the wrath: Psychophysiological responses to facial stimuli. *Motivation and Emotion, 20,* 149–182.

Dimberg, U., & Petterson, M. (2000). Facial reactions to happy and angry facial expressions: Evidence for right hemispheric dominance. *Psychophysiology, 37,* 693–696.

Dimberg, U., Thunberg, M., & Elmehed, K. (2000). Unconscious facial reactions to emotional facial expressions. *Psychological Science, 11,* 86–89.

Dixon, A. K. (1998). Ethological strategies for defense in animals and humans: Their role in some psychiatric disorders. *British Journal of Medical Psychology, 71,* 417–445.

Dixon, J. C. (1957). Development of self-recognition. *Journal of Genetic Psychology, 91,* 251–256.

Dobbing, J., & Sands, J. (1973). Quantitative growth and development of human brain. *Archives of Disease in Childhood, 48,* 757–767.

Doidge, N., Simon, B. Gillies, L. A., & Ruskin, R. (1994). Characteristics of psychoanalytic patients under a nationalized health plan: DSM-III-R diagnoses, previous treament, and childhood trauma. *American Journal of Psychiatry, 151,* 586–590.

Dolan, R. J. (1999). On the neurology of morals. *Nature Neuroscience, 2,* 927–929.

Dorpat, T. L. (1981). Basic concepts and terms in object relations theories. In S. Tuttman, C. Kaye, & M. Zimmerman (Eds.), *Object and self: A developmental approach* (pp. 149–178). New York: International Universities Press.

Dorpat, T., & Miller, M. (1992). *Clinical interaction and the analysis of meaning.* NJ: Analytic Press.

Dosamantes, I. (1992). The intersubjective relationship between therapist and patient: A key to understanding denied and denigrated aspects of the patient's self. *The Arts & Psychotherapy, 19,* 359–365.

Dosamantes-Beaudry, I. (1997). Somatic experience in psychoanalysis. *Psychoanalytic Psychology, 14,* 517–530.

Doucet, P. (1992). The analyst's transference imagery. *International Journal of Psycho-Analysis, 73,* 647–659.

Dozier, M., Cue, K. L., & Barnett, L. (1994). Clinicians as caregivers: Role of attachment organization in treatment. *Journal of Consulting and Clinical Psychology, 62,* 793–800.

Drevets, W. C., Price, J. L., Simpson, J. R., Jr., Todd, R. B., Reich, T., Vannier, M., & Raichle, M. E. (1997). Subgenual prefrontal cortex abnormalities in mood disorders. *Nature, 386,* 824–826.

Druck, A. B. (1998). Deficit and conflict: An attempt at integration. In C. S. Ellman, S. Grand, M. Silvan, & S. J. Ellman (Eds.), *The modern Freudians: Contemporary psychoanalytic technique* (pp. 209–233). New York: Jason Aronson.

Dunn, J. (1995). Intersubjectivty in psychoanalysis: A critical review. *International Journal of Psycho-Analysis, 76,* 723–738.

Easser, R. (1974). Empathic inhibition and psychoanalytic technique. *Psychoanalytic Quarterly, 43,* 557–580.

Edelman, G. (1987). *Neural Darwinism.* New York: Basic Books.

Edelman, G. (1989). *The remembered present: A biological theory of consciousness.* New York: Basic Books.

Eisenberg, L. (1995). The social construction of the human brain. *American Journal of Psychiatry, 152,* 1563–1575.

Eisenstein, S., Levy, N. A., & Marmor, J. (1994). *The dyadic transaction: An investigation into the nature of the psychotherapeutic process.* New Brunswick, NJ: Transaction Publishers.

Eisnitz, A. J. (1988). Some superego issues. *Journal of the American Psychoanalytic Association, 36,* 137–163.

Ekman, P. (1992). Are there basic emotions? *Psychological Review, 99,* 550–553.

Elliott, R., Dolan, R. J., & Frith, C. D. (2000). Dissociable functions in the medial and lateral orbitofrontal cortex: Evidence from human neuroimaging studies. *Cerebral Cortex, 10,* 308–317.

Elliott, R., Frith, C. D., & Dolan, R. J. (1997). Differential neural response to positive and negative feedback in planning and guessing tasks. *Neuropsychologia, 35,* 1395–1404.

Elliott, R., Rees, G., & Dolan, R. J. (1999). Ventromedial prefrontal cortex mediates guessing. *Neuropsychologia, 37,* 403–411.

Ellman, S. J. (1991). *Freud's technique papers: A contemporary perspective.* New York: Jason Aronson.

Emde, R. (1983). The pre-representational self and its affective core. *Psychoanalytic Study of the Child, 38,* 165–192.

Emde, R. N. (1988). Development terminable and interminable. I. Innate and motivational factors from infancy. *International Journal of Psycho-Analysis, 69,* 23–42.

Emde, R. (1989). The infant's relationship experience: Developmental and affective aspects. In A. J. Sameroff & R. N. Emde (Eds.), *Relationship disturbances in early childhood* (pp. 33–51). New York: Basic Books.

Emde, R. N. (1990). Mobilizing fundamental modes of development: Empathic availability and therapeutic action. *Journal of the American Psychoanalytic Association, 38,* 881–913.

Engel, G. L., & Schmale, A. H. (1972). Conservation-withdrawal: A primary regulatory process for organismic homeostasis. In Ciba Foundation, *Physiology, emotion, and psychosomatic illness* (pp. 57–85). Amsterdam: Elsevier.

Epstein, R. S. (1994). *Keeping boundaries: Maintaining safety and integrity in the psychotherapeutic process.* Washington, DC: American Psychiatric Press.

Epstein, S. (1983). The unconscious, the preconscious, and the self concept. In J. Suls & A. G. Greenwald (Eds.), *Psychological perspectives on the self* (vol. 2, pp. 219–247). Mahwah, NJ: Lawrence Erlbaum Associates.

Erdelyi, M. H. (1985). *Psychoanalysis: Freud's cognitive psychology.* New York: Freeman.

Erickson, M. F., Egeland, B., & Pianta, R. (1989). The effects of maltreatment on the development of young children. In D. Cicchetti & V. Carlson (Eds.), *Child maltreatment: Theory and research on the causes and consequences of child abuse and neglect* (pp. 647–684). New York: Cambridge University Press.

Erikson, E. (1950). *Childhood and society.* New York: Norton.

Eslinger, P. J. (1998). Neurobiological and neuropsychological bases of empathy. *European Neurology, 39,* 193–199.

Falk, D., Hildebolt, C., Cheverud, J., Vannier, M., Helmkamp, R. C., & Konigsberg, L. (1990). Cortical asymmetries in frontal lobes of Rhesus monkeys *(Macaca mulatta)*. *Brain Research, 512*, 40–45.

Famularo, R., Kinscherff, R., & Fenton, T. (1992). Posttraumatic stress disorder among children clinically diagnosed as borderline personality disorder. *Journal of Nervous & Mental Disease, 179*, 428–431.

Fast, I. (1979). Developments in gender identity: Gender differentiation in girls. *International Journal of Psycho-Analysis, 60*, 443–453.

Fast, I. (1984). *Gender identity: A differentiation model*. Hillsdale, NJ: Analytic Press.

Federmeier, K. D., & Kutas, M. (1999). Right words and left words: Electrophysiological evidence for hemispheric differences in meaning processes. *Cognitive Brain Research, 8*, 373–392.

Federmeier, K. D., & Kutas, M. (2002). Picture the difference: Electrophysiological investigations of picture processing in the two cerebral hemispheres. *Neuropsychologica, 40*, 730–747.

Feldman, M. (1997). Projective identification: The analyst's involvement. *International Journal of Psycho-Analysis, 78*, 227–241.

Feldman, R., & Greenbaum, C. W. (1997). Affect regulation and synchrony in mother–infant play as precursors to the development of symbolic competence. *Infant Mental Health Journal, 18*, 4–23.

Feldman, R., Greenbaum, C. W., & Yirmiya, N. (1999). Mother–infant affect synchrony as an antecedent of the emergence of self-control. *Developmental Psychology, 35*, 223–231.

Feldman, R., Greenbaum, C. W., Yirmiya, N., & Mayes, L. C. (1996). Relations between cyclicity and regulation in mother-infant interaction at 3 and 9 months and cognition at two years. *Journal of Applied Developmental Psychology, 17*, 347–365.

Ferenczi, S. (1952a). *First contributions to psycho-analysis*. E. Jones (Trans.). London: Hogarth Press. (Originally published in 1916)

Ferenczi, S. (1952b). *Further contributions to the theory and technique of psychoanalysis*. J. Richman (Ed.). New York: Basic Books. (Originally published 1926)

Ferenczi, S. (1980). *Final contributions to the problems and methods of psycho-analysis*. M. Balint (Ed.). New York: Brunner/Mazel. (Originally published 1928)

Fernald, A. (1989). Intonation and communicative interest in mother's speech to infants: Is the melody the message? *Child Development, 60*, 1497–1510.

Field, T. (1981). Infant arousal, attention and affect during early interactions. *Advances in Infancy Research, 1*, 58–96.

Field, T. (1982). Affective displays of high-risk infants during early interactions. In T. Field & A. Fogel (Eds.), *Emotion and early interaction* (pp. 101–125). Hillsdale, NJ: Erlbaum.

Field, T. (1985a). Attachment as psychobiological attunement: Being on the same wavelength. In M. Reite & T. Field (Eds.), *The psychobiology of attachment and separation* (pp. 415–454). Orlando: Academic Press.

Field, T. (1985b). Coping with separation stress by infants and young children. In T. Field, P. M. McCabe, & N. Schneiderman (Eds.), *Stress and coping* (pp. 197–219). Hillsdale, NJ: Erlbaum.

Field, T. (1998). Maternal depression effects on infants and early interventions. *Preventive Medicine, 27*, 200–203.

Field, T., Diego, M., Hernandez-Reif, M., Schanberg, S., & Kuhn, C. (2002). Relative right versus left frontal EEG in neonates. *Developmental Psychobiology, 41*, 147–155.

Field, T., & Fogel, A. (1982). *Emotion and early interaction*. Hillsdale, NJ: Erlbaum.

Fink, G. R., Markowitsch, H. J., Reinkemeier, M., Bruckbauer, T., Kessler, J., & Heiss, W.-D. (1996). Cerebral representation of one's own past: Neural networks involved in autobiographical memory. *Journal of Neuroscience, 16,* 4275–4282.

Fischer, H., Andersson, J.L., Furmark, T., & Fredrikson, M. (2000). Fear conditioning and brain activity: A positron emission tomography study in humans. *Behavioral Neuroscience, 114,* 671–680.

Fischer, H., Andersson, J. L. R., Furmark, T., Wik, G., & Fredrikson, M. (2002). Right-sided human prefrontal brain activation during activation of conditioned fear. *Emotion, 2,* 233–241.

Fischer, K. W., & Pipp, S. L. (1984). Development of the structures of unconscious thought. In K. S. Bowers & D. Meichenbaum (Eds.), *The unconscious reconsidered* (pp. 88–148). New York: Wiley.

Fleming, A. S., O'Day, D. H., & Kraemer, G. W. (1999). Neurobiology of mother–infant interactions: Experience and central nervous system plasticity across development and generations. *Neuroscience and Biobehavioral Reviews, 23,* 673–685.

Fogel, A. (1982). Affect dynamics in early infancy: affective tolerance. In T. Field & A. Fogel (Eds.), *Emotion and early interaction.* Hillsdale, NJ: Erlbaum.

Fogel, A. (2003). Remembering infancy: Accessing our earliest experiences. In G. Bremner & A. Slater (Eds.), *Theories of infant development.* Cambridge, England: Blackwell.

Fonagy, P., Leigh, T., Kennedy, R., Matoon, G., Steele, H., Target, M., Steele, M., & Higgitt, A. (1995). Attachment, borderline states and the representation of the emotions and cognitions in self and other. In D. Cicchetti & S. L. Toth (Eds.), *Emotion, cognition, and representation* (pp. 371–414). Rochester, NY: University of Rochester Press.

Fonagy, P., Leigh, T., Steele, M., Steele, H., Kennedy, R., Matoon, G., Target, M., & Garber, A. (1996). The relation of attachment status, psychiatric classification, and response to psychotherapy. *Journal of Consulting and Clinical Psychology, 64,* 22–31.

Fonagy, P., Steele, M., Steele, H., Moran, G. S., & Higgitt, A. C. (1991). The capacity for understanding mental states: The reflective self in parent and child and its significance for security of attachment. *Infant Mental Health Journal, 12,* 201–218.

Fonagy, P., & Target, M. (1996). Playing with reality. I. Theory of mind and the normal development of psychic reality. *International Journal of Psycho-Analysis, 77,* 217–233.

Fonagy, P., & Target, M. (1997). Attachment and reflective function: Their role in self-organization. *Development and Psychopathology, 9,* 679–700.

Fonagy, P., & Target, M. (2002). Early intervention and the development of self-regulation. *Psychoanalytic Inquiry, 22,* 307–335.

Fossati, A., Maddeddu, F., & Maffei, C. (1999). Childhood sexual abuse and BPD: A meta-analysis. *Journal of Personality Disorders, 13,* 268–280.

Fosshage, J. L. (1994). Toward reconceptualising transference: Theoretical and clinical considerations. *International Journal of Psycho-Analysis, 75,* 265–280.

Fox, N. A., & Davidson, R. J. (1984). Hemispheric substrates of affect: A developmental model. In N. A. Fox & R. J. Davidson (Eds.), *The psychobiology of affective development* (pp. 353–381). Hillsdale, NJ: Erlbaum.

Fraiberg, S. (1969). Libidinal object constancy and mental representation. *Psychoanalytic Study of the Child, 24,* 9–47.

Fraiberg, S., & Freedman, D. A. (1964). Studies in the ego development of the congenitally blind. *Psychoanalytic Study of the Child, 19,* 113–169.

Francis, S., Rolls, E. T., Bowtell, R., McGlone, F., O'Doherty, J., Browning, A., Clare, S., & Smith, E. (1999). The representation of pleasant touch in the brain and its relationship with taste and olfactory areas. *Cognitive Neuroscience, 10,* 453–459.

Frank, J. (1950). Some aspects of lobotomy (prefrontal leucotomy) under psychoanalytic scrutiny. *Psychiatry*, *13*, 35–42.

Frayn, D. H. (1996). Enactments: An evolving dyadic concept of acting out. *American Journal of Psychotherapy*, *50*, 194–207.

Freeman, T. W., & Kimbrell, T. (2001). A "cure" for chronic combat-related posttraumatic stress disorder secondary to a right frontal lobe infarct: A case report. *Journal of Neuropsychiatry and Clinical Neuroscience*, *13*, 106–109.

Freeman, W. J. (2000). Emotion is essential to all intentional behaviors. In M. D. Lewis & I. Granic (Eds.), *Emotion, development, and self-organization* (pp. 209–235). New York: Cambridge University Press.

Freud, A. (1968). Notes on the connection between the states of negativism and psychic surrender. In *The writings of Anna Freud* (vol. 4, pp. 256–259). New York: International Universities Press. (Original work published 1951)

Freud, A. (1969). Comments on psychic trauma. In *The writings of Anna Freud* (vol. 4, pp. 221–241). New York: International Universities Press. (Original work published 1964)

Freud, S. (1891). *Zur Auffassung der Aphasien. eine Kritische Studie* [On aphasia]. Leipzig: F. Deuticke.

Freud, S. (1893). Quelques considérations pour une étude comparative des paralysies motrices organiques et hystériques. *Archives de Neurologie*, *26*, 29–43.

Freud, S. (1953a). *On aphasia*. E. Stengel (Trans.). New York: International Universities Press. (Original work published 1891)

Freud, S. (1953b). The interpretation of dreams. In J. Strachey (Ed. & Trans.), *Standard edition of the complete psychological works of Sigmund Freud*: (Vols. 4 & 5, pp. 1–627). London: Hogarth Press. (Original work published 1900)

Freud, S. (1953c). Three essays on the theory of sexuality. In J. Strachey (Ed. & Trans.), *Standard edition of the complete psychological works of Sigmund Freud*: (Vol. 7, pp. 135–243). London: Hogarth Press. (Original work published 1905)

Freud, S. (1955). Beyond the pleasure principle. In J. Strachey (Ed. & Trans.), *Standard edition of the complete psychological works of Sigmund Freud*: (Vol. 18, pp. 7–64). London: Hogarth Press. (Original work published 1920)

Freud, S. (1957a). Instincts and their vicissitudes. In J. Strachey (Ed. & Trans.), *Standard edition of the complete psychological works of Sigmund Freud*: (Vol. 14, pp. 117–140). London: Hogarth Press. (Original work published 1915)

Freud, S. (1957b). On narcissism: An introduction. In J. Strachey (Ed. & Trans.), *Standard edition of the complete psychological works of Sigmund Freud*: (Vol. 14, pp. 67–102). London: Hogarth Press. (Original work published 1914)

Freud, S. (1957c). On the history of the psycho-analytic movement. In J. Strachey (Ed. & Trans.), *Standard edition of the complete psychological works of Sigmund Freud*: (Vol. 14, pp. 7–66). London: Hogarth Press. (Originally published 1914)

Freud, S. (1957d). Repression. In J. Strachey (Ed. & Trans.), *Standard edition of the complete psychological works of Sigmund Freud*: (Vol. 14, pp. 146–158). London: Hogarth Press. (Original work published 1915)

Freud, S. (1957e). The unconscious. In J. Strachey (Ed. & Trans.), *Standard edition of the complete psychological works of Sigmund Freud*: (Vol. 14, pp. 166–204). London: Hogarth Press. (Original work published 1915)

Freud, S. (1958a). On beginning the treatment. In J. Strachey (Ed. & Trans.), *Standard edition of the complete psychological works of Sigmund Freud*: (Vol. 12, pp. 23–144). London: Hogarth Press. (Original work published 1913)

Freud, S. (1958b). Recommendations to physicians practicing psycho-analysis. In J. Strachey (Ed. & Trans.), *Standard edition of the complete psychological works of Sigmund Freud*: (Vol. 12, pp. 111–120). London: Hogarth Press. (Original work published 1912)

Freud, S. (1958c). The claims of psycho-analysis to scientific interest. In J. Strachey (Ed. & Trans.), *Standard edition of the complete psychological works of Sigmund Freud*: (Vol. 13, pp. 165–190). London: Hogarth Press. (Original work published 1913)

Freud, S. (1959). Inhibition, symptoms, and anxiety. In J. Strachey (Ed. & Trans.), *Standard edition of the complete psychological works of Sigmund Freud*: (Vol. 20, pp. 87–174). London: Hogarth Press. (Original work published 1926)

Freud, S. (1960). The psychopathology of everyday life. In J. Strachey (Ed. & Trans.), *Standard edition of the complete psychological works of Sigmund Freud*: (Vol. 6, pp. 1–279). London: Hogarth Press. (Original work published 1901)

Freud, S. (1961a). Analysis terminable and interminable. In J. Strachey (Ed. & Trans.), *Standard edition of the complete psychological works of Sigmund Freud*: (Vol. 23, pp. 211–253). London: Hogarth Press. (Original work published 1937)

Freud, S. (1961b). The ego and the id. In J. Strachey (Ed. & Trans.), *Standard edition of the complete psychological works of Sigmund Freud*: (Vol. 19, pp. 12–63). London: Hogarth Press. (Original work published 1923)

Freud, S. (1961 & 1963). Introductory lectures on psycho-analysis. In J. Strachey (Ed. & Trans.), *Standard edition of the complete psychological works of Sigmund Freud*: (Vols. 15 & 16, pp. 15–463). London: Hogarth Press. (Original work published 1916–1917)

Freud, S. (1964). An outline of psychoanalysis. In J. Strachey (Ed. & Trans.), *Standard edition of the complete psychological works of Sigmund Freud*: (Vol. 23, pp. 144–207). London: Hogarth Press. (Original work published 1940)

Freud, S. (1966). Project for a scientific psychology. In J. Strachey (Ed. & Trans.), *Standard edition of the complete psychological works of Sigmund Freud*: (Vol. 1, pp. 295–397). London: Hogarth Press. (Original work published 1895)

Frey, S., & Petrides, M. (2000). Orbitofrontal cortex: A key prefrontal region for encoding information. *Proceedings of the National Academy of Sciences of the United States of America, 97*, 8723–8727.

Freyd, J. J. (1987). Dynamic mental representations. *Psychological Reviews, 94*, 427–438.

Fridlund, A. (1991). Evolution and facial action in reflex, social motive, and paralanguage. *Biological Psychology, 32*, 3–100.

Friedman, N., & Lavender, J. (1997). On receiving the patient's transference: The symbolizing and desymbolizing countertransference. *Journal of the American Psychoanalytic Association, 45*, 79–103.

Friedman, N., & Moskowitz, M. (1997). Introduction. In M. Moskowitz, C. Monk, C. Kaye, & S. Ellman (Eds.), *The neurobiological and developmental basis for psychotherapeutic intervention* (pp. XIII–XXVI). Northvale, NJ: Jason Aronson.

Friedman, R. C., Bucci, W., Christian, C., Drucker, P., & Garrison, W. B. (1998). Private psychotherapy patients of psychiatrist psychoanalysts. *American Journal of Psychiatry, 155*, 1772–1774.

Frijda, N. H. (1988). The laws of emotion. *Amerian Psychologist, 43*, 349–358.

Furmark, T., Tillfors, M., Marteindottir, I., Fischer, H., Pissiota, A., Långstrom, B., & Fredrikson, M. (2002). Common change in cerebral blood flow in patients with social phobia treated with citalopram or cognitive-behavioral therapy. *Archives of General Psychiatry, 59*, 425–433.

Fuster, J. M. (1980). *The prefrontal cortex: Anatomy, physiology, and neurophysiology of the frontal lobe*. New York: Raven Press.

Fuster, J. M. (1985). The prefrontal cortex and temporal integration. In A. Peters & E. G. Jones (Eds.), *Cerebral cortex. Vol. 4. Association and auditory cortices* (pp. 151–171). New York: Plenum Press.

Gabbard, G. O. (1994). Mind and brain in psychiatric treatment. *Bulletin of the Menninger Clinic, 58*, 427–446.

Gabbard, G. O. (1995). Countertransference: The emerging common ground. *International Journal of Psycho-Analysis, 76,* 475–485.

Gabbard, G. O. (2001). A contemporary psychoanalytic model of countertransference. *In Session: Psychotherapy in Practice, 57,* 983–991.

Gaensbauer, T. (1982). Regulation of emotional expression in infants from two contrasting caretaking environments. *Journal of the American Academy of Child Psychiatry, 21,* 163–171.

Gaensbauer, T. J. (2002). Representations of trauma in infancy: Clinical and theoretical implications for the understanding of early memory. *Infant Mental Health Journal, 23,* 259–277.

Gaensbauer, T., Connell, J. P., & Schultz, L. A. (1983). Emotion and attachment: Interrelationships in a structural laboratory paradigm. *Developmental Psychobiology, 19,* 815–831.

Gaensbauer, T., Harmon, R. J., Cytryn, L., & McKnew, D. H. (1984). Social and affective development in infants with a manic-depressive parent. *American Journal of Psychiatry, 141,* 223–229.

Gaensbauer, T., & Mrazek, D. (1981). Differences in the patterning of affective expression in infants. *Journal of the American Academy of Child Psychiatry, 20,* 673–691.

Gaensbauer, T. J., & Sands, K. (1979). Distorted affective communications in abused/neglected infants and their potential impact on caretakers. *Journal of the American Academy of Child Psychiatry, 18,* 238–250.

Gainotti, G. (1996). Lateralization of brain mechanisms underlying automatic and controlled forms of spatial orienting and attention. *Neuroscience and Biobehavioral Reviews, 20,* 617–622.

Gainotti, G. (2000). Neuropsychological theories of emotion. In J. Borod (Ed.), *The neuropsychology of emotion* (pp. 214–236). New York: Oxford University Press.

Gainotti, G. (2001). Disorders of emotional behavior. *Journal of Neurology, 248,* 743–749.

Galderisi, S., Bucci, P., Mucci, A., Bernardo, A., Koenig, T., & Maj, M. (2001). Brain electrical microstates in subjects with panic disorder. *Psychophysiology, 54,* 427–435.

Galenson, E., & Roiphe, H. (1976). Some suggested revisions concerning early female development. *Journal of the American Psychoanalytic Association, 24*(Suppl.), 29–57.

Galin, D. (1974). Implications for psychiatry of left and right cerebral specialization: A neurophysiological context for unconscious processes. *Archives of General Psychiatry, 31,* 572–583.

Galletly, C., Clark, C. R., McFarlane, A. C., & Weber, D. L. (2001). Working memory in posttraumatic stress disorder—an event-related potential study. *Journal of Traumatic Stress, 14,* 295–309.

Gans, J. S. (1994). Indirect communication as a therapeutic technique: A novel use of countertransference. *American Journal of Psychotherapy, 48,* 120–140.

Garavan, H., Ross, T. J., & Stein, E. A. (1999). Right hemisphere dominance of inhibitory control: An event-related functional MRI study. *Proceedings of the National Academy of Sciences of the United States of America, 96,* 8301–8306.

Garza-Guerrero, A. C. (1981). The superego concept: Part I: Historical review; object relations approach. *Psychoanalytic Review, 68,* 321–342.

Gay, P. (Ed.). (1989). *The Freud reader.* New York: Norton.

Gazzaniga, M. S. (1985). *The social brain: Discovering the networks of the mind.* New York: Basic Books.

Gazzaniga, M. S. (1995). *The cognitive neurosciences.* Cambridge, MA: MIT Press.

Gedo, J. (1979). *Beyond interpretation.* New York: International Universities Press.

Gedo, J. (1991). *The biology of clinical encounters: Psychoanalysis as a science of the mind.* Hillsdale, NJ: Analytic Press.

Gedo, J. (1995a). Encore. *Journal of the American Psychoanalytic Association, 43,* 384–392.

Gedo, J. (1995b). Working through as metaphor and as a modality of treatment. *Journal of the American Psychoanalytic Association, 43,* 339–356.

Gedo, J. (1999). *The evolution of psychoanalysis: Contemporary theory and practice.* New York: Other Press.

Geis, G. S., & Wurster, R. D. (1980). Cardiac responses during stimulation of the dorsal motor nucleus and nucleus ambiguus in the cat. *Circulation Research, 46,* 606–611.

Gendlin, E. T. (1970). A theory of personality change. In J. T. Hart & T. H. Tomlinson (Eds.), *New directions in client-centered therapy* (pp. 129–174). Boston: Houghton Mifflin.

Gendlin, E. T. (1981). *Focusing* (2nd ed.). New York: Bantam Books.

George, M. S., Parekh, P. I., Rosinsky, N., Ketter, T. A., Kimbrell, T. A., Heilman, K. M., Herscovitch, P., & Post, R. M. (1996). Understanding emotional prosody activates right hemispheric regions. *Archives of Neurology, 53,* 665–670.

Geschwind, N., & Galaburda, A. M. (1987). *Cerebral lateralization: Biological mechanisms, associations, and pathology.* Boston: MIT Press.

Giannitrapani, D. (1967). Developing concepts of lateralization of cerebral functions. *Cortex, 3,* 353–370.

Gibbons, A. (1998). Solving the brain's energy crisis. *Science, 280,* 1345–1347.

Gilboa, E., & Revelle, W. (1994). Personality and the structure of affective responses. In S. H. M. Van Goozen, N. E. Van de Poll, & J. A. Sergeant (Eds.), *Emotions: Essays on emotion theory* (pp. 135–159). Hillsdale, NJ: Erlbaum.

Gill, M. M. (1982). *Analysis of transference.* New York: International Universities Press.

Gill, M. M. (1994). Transference: A change in conception or only in emphasis? *Psychoanalytic Inquiry, 4,* 489–523.

Giovacchini, P. (1979). *Treatment of primitive mental states.* New York: Jason Aronson.

Giovacchini, P. (1981). Object relations, deficiency states, and the acquisition of psychic structure. In S. Tutman, C. Kaye, & M. Zimmerman (Eds.), *Object and self: A developmental approach* (pp. 397–427). New York: International Universities Press.

Giovacchini, P. (1986). *Developmental disorders. The transitional space in mental breakdown and creative integration.* Northvale, NJ: Jason Aronson.

Glassman, M. (1988). A test of competing psychoanalytic models of narcissism. *Journal of the American Psychoanalytic Association, 36,* 597–625.

Gleik, J. (1987). *Chaos, making a new science.* New York: Viking Penguin.

Goel, V., & Dolan, R. J. (2000). Anatomical segregation of component processes in an inductive inference task. *Journal of Cognitive Neuroscience, 12,* 110–119.

Goldberg, E. (1995). Rise and fall of modular orthodoxy. *Journal of Clinical and Experimental Neuropsychology, 17,* 193–208.

Goldberger, L. (1982). Sensory deprivation and overload. In L. Goldberger & S. Breznitz (Eds.), *Handbook of stress: Theoretical and clinical aspects* (pp. 410–418). New York: Free Press.

Goldenberg, G., Podreka, I., Uhl, F., Steiner, M., Willmes, K., & Deecke, L. (1989). Cerebral correlates of imagining colours, faces and a map—I. SPECT of regional cerebral blood flow. *Neuropsychologia, 27,* 1315–1328.

Goldstein, R. G. (1995). The higher and lower in mental life: An essay on J. Hughlings Jackson and Freud. *Journal of the American Psychoanalytic Association, 43,* 495–515.

Goleman, D. (1995). *Emotional intelligence.* New York: Bantam Books.

Golynkina, K., & Ryle, A. (1999). The identification and characteristics of the partially dissociated states of patients with borderline personality disorder. *British Journal of Medical Psychology, 72,* 429–435.

Gonzalez-Lima, F., & Scheich, H. (1985). Ascending reticular activating system in the rat: A 2-deoxyglucose study. *Brain Research, 344,* 70–88.

Goodenough, F. L. (1931). *Anger in young children.* Institute of Child Welfare Monographs. Minneapolis: University of Minnesota Press.

Goplerud, E., & Depue, R. A. (1985). Behavioral response to naturally occurring stress in cyclothymia and dysthymia. *Journal of Abnormal Psychology, 94,* 128–139.

Gordon, P. C., & Holyoak, K. J. (1983). Implicit learning and generalization of the mere exposure effect. *Journal of Personality and Social Psychology, 45,* 492–500.

Gorney, J. E. (1979). The negative therapeutic reaction. *Contemporary Psychoanalysis, 15,* 288–337.

Gorno-Tempini, M. L., Pradelli, S., Serafini, M., Pagnoni, G., Baraldi, P., Porro, C., Nicoletti, R., Umita, C., & Nichelli, P. (2001). Explicit and incidental facial expression processing: An fMRI study. *NeuroImage, 14,* 465–473.

Goyer, P. F., Konicki, P. E., & Schulz, S. C. (1994). Brain imaging in personality disorders. In K. R. Silk (Ed.), *Biological and neurobehavioral studies of borderline personality disorders* (pp. 109–125). Washington, DC: American Psychiatric Press.

Graham, Y. P., Heim, C., Goodman, S. H., Miller, A. H., & Nemeroff, C. B. (1999). The effects of neonatal stress on brain development: Implications for psychopathology. *Development and Psychopathology, 11,* 545–565.

Greenberg, J. R., & Mitchell, S. A. (1983). *Object relations in psychoanalytic theory.* Cambridge, MA: Harvard University Press.

Greenberg, L. S., & Safran, J. D. (1984). Hot cognition: Emotion coming in from the cold. A reply to Rachman and Mahooney. *American Psychologist, 44,* 19.

Greenough, W. T. (1986). What's special about development? Thoughts on the bases of experience-sensitive synaptic plasticity. In W. T. Greenough & J. M. Juraska (Eds.), *Developmental neuropsychology* (pp. 195–221). Orlando: Academic Press.

Greenspan, S. I. (1981). *Psychopathology and adaptation in infancy and early childhood.* New York: International Universities Press.

Griffin, M. G., Resick, P. A., & Mechanic, M. B. (1997). Objective assessment of peritraumatic dissociation: Psychophysiological indicators. *American Journal of Psychiatry, 154,* 1081–1088.

Grigsby, J., & Hartlaub, G. (1994). Procedural learning and the development and stability of character. *Perceptual and Motor Skills, 79,* 355–370.

Grinberg, L. (1995). Nonverbal communication in the clinic with borderline patients. *Contemporary Psychoanalysis, 31,* 92–105.

Groddeck, G. (1977). *The meaning of illness.* London: The Institute of Psychoanalysis/Hogarth Press.

Grotstein, J. S. (1981). *Splitting and projective identification.* New York: Jason Aronson.

Grotstein, J. S. (1983). Some perspectives on self psychology. In A. Goldberg (Ed.), *The future of psychoanalysis* (pp. 165–203). New York: International Universities Press.

Grotstein, J. S. (1986). The psychology of powerlessness: Disorders of self-regulation and interactional regulation as a newer paradigm for psychopathology. *Psychoanalytic Inquiry, 6,* 93–118.

Grotstein, J. S. (1987). The borderline as a disorder of self-regulation. In J. S. Grotstein, J. Lang, & M. Solomon (Eds.), *The borderline patient: Emerging concepts in diagnosis* (pp. 347–383). London: Analytic Press.

Grotstein, J. S. (1990). Invariants in primitive emotional disorders. In L. B. Boyer & P. L. Giovacchini (Eds.), *Master clinicians on treating the regressed patient* (pp. 139–163). Northvale, NJ: Jason Aronson.

Grunbaum, A. (1986). Precis of *The foundations of psychoanalysis: A philosophical critique*. *Behavioral and Brain Sciences, 9,* 217–284.

Gunnar-Vongnechten, M. R. (1978). Changing a frightening toy into a pleasant toy by allowing the infant to control its actions. *Developmental Psychology, 14,* 157–162.

Gur, R. C., Schroeder, L., Turner, T., McGrath, C., Chan, R. M., Turetsky, B. I., Alsop, D., Maldjian, J., & Gur. R. E. (2002). Brain activation during facial emotion processing. *NeuroImage, 16,* 651–662.

Haber, S. N., Kunishio, K., Mizobuchi, M., & Lynd-Balta, E. (1995). The orbital and medial prefrontal circuit through the primate basal ganglia. *Journal of Neuroscience, 15,* 4851–4867.

Hadley, J. (1989). The neurobiology of motivational systems. In J. L. Lichtenberg (Ed.), *Psychoanalysis and motivation* (pp. 337–372). Hillsdale, NJ: Analytic Press.

Haith, M. M., Bergman, T., & Moore, M. (1979). Eye contact and face scanning in early infancy. *Science, 218,* 179–181.

Halligan, P. W., Athwal, B. S., Oakley, D. A., Frackowiak, R. S. J. (2000). Imaging hypnotic paralysis: Implications for conversion hysteria. *Lancet, 355,* 986–987.

Hamilton, N. G. (1992). Introduction. In N. G. Hamilton (Ed.), *From inner sources: New directions in object relations psychotherapy* (pp. xi–xxi). Northvale, NJ: Jason Aronson.

Hamilton, V. (1996). *The analyst's preconscious*. Hillsdale, NJ: Analytic Press.

Hammer, E. (1990). *Reaching the affect: Style in the psychodynamic therapies*. Northvale, NJ: Jason Aronson.

Hansen, C. H., & Hansen, R. D. (1994). Automatic emotion: Attention and facial efference. In P. M. Niedenthal & S. Kitayama (Eds.), *The heart's eye: Emotional influences in perception and attention* (pp. 217–243). San Diego: Academic Press.

Hari, R., Portin, K., Kettenmann, B., Jousmaki, V., & Kobal, G. (1997). Right hemisphere preponderance of responses to painful CO_2 stimulation of the human nasal mucosa. *Pain, 72,* 145–151.

Hariri, A. R., Bookheimer, S. Y., & Mazziotta, J. C. (2000). Modulating emotional responses: Effects of a neocortical network on the limbic system. *NeuroReport, 11,* 43–48.

Harold, F. M. (1986). *The vital force. A study of bioenergetics*. New York: W.H. Freeman.

Harrington, A. (1985). Nineteenth-century ideas on hemisphere differences and "duality of mind." *Behavioral and Brain Sciences, 8,* 617–634.

Hartikainen, K. M., Ogawa, K. H., & Knight, R. T. (2000). Transient interference of right hemispheric function due to automatic emotional processing. *Neuropsychologia, 38,* 1576–1580.

Hartmann, H. (1939). *Ego psychology and the problem of adaptation*. New York: International Universities Press.

Hartmann, H., & Loewenstein, R. M. (1962). Notes on the superego. *Psychoanalytic Study of the Child, 17,* 42–81.

Hartocollis, P. (1980). Affective disturbances in borderline and narcissistic patients. *Bulletin of the Menninger Clinic, 44,* 135–146.

Hatfield, E., Cacioppo, J. T., & Rapson, R. L. (1992). Primitive emotional contagion. In M. S. Clark (Ed.), *Emotion and social behavior* (pp. 151–171). Newbury Park, CA: Sage.

Havens, L. (1979). Explorations in the uses of language in psychotherapy: Complex empathic statements. *Psychiatry, 42,* 40–48.

Hecaen, H., & Albert, M. L. (1978). *Human neuropsychology*. New York: Wiley.

Heilman, K. M., Schwartz, H., & Watson, R. T. (1977). Hypoarousal in patients with the neglect syndrome and emotional indifference. *Neurology*, *38*, 229–232.

Heilman, K. M., & van den Abell, T. (1979). Right hemispheric dominance for mediating cerebral activation. *Neuropsychologia*, *17*, 315–321.

Heimann, P. (1950). On counter-transference. *International Journal of Psycho-Analysis*, *31*, 60–76.

Hellige, J. B. (1993). *Hemispheric asymmetry: What's right and what's left*. Cambridge, MA: Harvard University Press.

Helmeke, C., Ovtscharoff, W. Jr., Poeggel, G., & Braun, K. (2001). Juvenile emotional experience alters synaptic inputs on pyramidal neurons in the anterior cingulate cortex. *Cerebral Cortex*, *11*, 717–727.

Helmeke, C., Poeggel, G., & Braun, K. (2001). Differential emotional experience induces elevated spine densities on basal dendrites of pyramidal neurons in the anterior cingulate cortex of *octodon degus*. *Neuroscience*, *104*, 927–931.

Henry, G. M., Weingartner, H., & Murphy, D. L. (1971). Idiosyncratic patterns of learning and word association during mania. *American Journal of Psychiatry*, *128*, 564–574.

Henry, J. P. (1993). Psychological and physiological responses to stress: The right hemisphere and the hypothalamo-pituitary-adrenal axis, an inquiry into problems of human bonding. *Integrative Physiological and Behavioral Science*, *28*, 369–387.

Henry, J. P., & Wang, S. (1998). Effects of early stress on adult affiliative behavior. *Psychoneuroendocrinology*, *23*, 863–875.

Henson, R. N. A., Shallice, T., & Dolan, R. J. (1999). Right prefrontal cortex and episodic memory retrieval: A functional MRI test of the monitoring hypothesis. *Brain*, *122*, 1367–1381.

Herman, J. L., Perry, J., & van der Kolk, B. A. (1989). Childhood trauma in borderline personality disorder. *American Journal of Psychiatry*, *146*, 490–495.

Herman, J. L., & van der Kolk, B. A. (1987). Traumatic antecedents of borderline personality disorder. In B. A. van der Kolk (Ed.), *Psychological trauma* (pp. 111–126). Washington, DC: American Psychiatric Press.

Herpetz, S., Dietrich, T. M., Wenning, B., Krings, T., Erberich, S. G., Wilmes, K., Thron, A., & Sass, H. (2001). Evidence of abnormal amygdala functioning in borderline personality disorder: A functional MRI study. *Biological Psychiatry*, *50*, 292–298.

Herpetz, S., Kunert, H. J., Schwenger, U. B., & Sass, H. (1999). Affective response in borderline personality disorder—a psychophysiological approach. *American Journal of Psychiatry*, *156*, 1550–1556.

Hess, E. H. (1975a). The role of pupil size in communication. *Scientific American*, *233*, 110–119.

Hess, E. H. (1975b). *The tell-tale eye*. New York: Van Nostrand Reinhold.

Hess, W. R. (1954). *Diencephalon, autonomic and extrapyramidal functions*. New York: Grune & Stratton.

Hesse, E., & Main, M. M. (1999). Second-generation effects of unresolved trauma in nonmaltreating parents: Dissociated, frightened, and threatening parental behavior. *Psychoanalytic Inquiry*, *19*, 481–540.

Hietanen, J. K., Surrakka, V., & Linnankoski, I. (1998). Facial electromyographic responses to vocal affect expressions. *Psychophysiology*, *35*, 530–536.

Himwich, W. A. (1975). Forging a link between basic and clinical research: Developing brain. *Biological Psychiatry*, *10*, 125–139.

Hinshaw-Fuselier, S., Boris, N. W., & Zeanah, C. H. (1999). Reactive attachment disorder in maltreated twins. *Infant Mental Health Journal*, *20*, 42–59.

Hinshelwood, R. D. (1994). *Clinical Klein: From theory to practice*. New York: Basic Books.

Hobson, R. P. (1993). Through feeling and site through self and symbol. In U. Neisser (Ed.), *The perceived self: Ecological and interpersonal sources of self-knowledge* (pp. 254–279). New York: Cambridge University Press.

Hofer, M. (1983). On the relationship between attachment and separation processes in infancy. In R. Plutchik & H. Kellerman (Eds.), *Emotion: Theory, research and experience* (vol. 2, pp. 199–219). New York: Academic Press.

Hofer, M. A. (1984a). Early stages in the organization of cardiovascular control. *Proceedings of the Society of Experimental and Biological Medicine, 175*, 147–157.

Hofer, M. A. (1984b). Relationships as regulators: A psychobiologic perspective on bereavement. *Psychosomatic Medicine, 46*, 183–197.

Hofer, M. A. (1990). Early symbiotic processes: Hard evidence from a soft place. In R. A. Glick & S. Bone (Eds.), *Pleasure beyond the pleasure principle* (pp. 55–78). New Haven, CT: Yale University Press.

Hofer, M. A. (1994). Hidden regulators in attachment, separation, and loss. *Monographs of the Society for Research in Child Development, 59*, 192–207.

Hoffman, E., & Goldstein, L. (1981). Hemispheric quantitative EEG changes following emotional reactions in neurotic patients. *Acta Psychiatrica Scandinavica, 63*, 153–164.

Hoffman, H. S. (1987). Imprinting and the critical period for social attachments: Some laboratory investigations. In M. H. Bornstein (Ed.), *Sensitive periods in development: Interdisciplinary studies* (pp. 99–121). Hillsdale, NJ: Erlbaum.

Hofstatter, L., Smolik, E. A., & Busch, A. K. (1945). Prefrontal lobotomy in treatment of chronic psychoses with special reference to section of the orbital areas only. *Archives of Neurology Psychiatry, 53*, 125–130.

Hollinger, P. C. (1999). Noninterpretive interventions in psychoanalysis and psychotherapy. A developmental perspective. *Psychoanalytic Psychology, 16*, 233–253.

Holmes, J. (1993a). Attachment theory: A biological basis for psychotherapy? *British Journal of Psychiatry, 163*, 430–438.

Holmes, J. (1993b). *John Bowlby and attachment theory.* London: Routledge.

Holmes, J. (1996). *Attachment, intimacy, autonomy. Using attachment theory in adult psychotherapy.* Northvale, NJ: Jason Aronson.

Holmes, J. (1998). The changing aims of psychoanalytic psychotherapy. An integrative perspective. *International Journal of Psycho-Analysis, 79*, 227–240.

Holowka, S., & Petitto, L. A. (2002). Left hemisphere cerebral specialization for babies while babbling. *Science, 297*, 1515.

Holt, R. R. (1989). *Freud reappraised. A fresh look at psychoanalytic theory.* New York: Guilford Press.

Holzman, P., & Aronson, G. (1992). Psychoanalysis and its neighboring sciences: Paradigms and opportunities. *Journal of the American Psychoanalytic Association, 40*, 63–88.

Hoppe, K. D. (1977). Split brains and psychoanalysis. *Psychoanalytic Quarterly, 46*, 220–244.

Hornak, J., Rolls, E. T., & Wade, D. (1996). Face and voice expression identification in patients with emotional and behavioural changes following ventral frontal lobe damage. *Neuropsychologia, 34*, 247–261.

Horner, A. J. (1991). *Psychoanalytic object relations therapy.* Northvale, NJ: Jason Aronson.

Horowitz, M. J. (1983). *Image formation and psychotherapy.* New York: Jason Aronson.

Horowitz, M. J. (1987). *States of mind: Configurational analysis of individual psychology.* New York: Plenum Medical Book Company.

Horton, P. C. (1995). The comforting substrate and the right brain. *Bulletin of the Menninger Clinic, 59*, 480–486.

Horvath, A. O., & Greenberg, L. S. (1994). *The working alliance: Theory, research, and practice*. New York: Wiley.

Howell, E. F. (2002). Back to the "states." Victim and abuser states in borderline personality disorder. *Psychoanalytic Dialogues, 12*, 921–957.

Hsieh, J. C., Hannerz, J., & Ingvar, M. (1996). Right lateralised central processing for pain of nitroglycerin-induced cluster headache. *Pain, 67*, 59–68.

Hsieh, J.-C., Belfrage, M., Stone-Elander, S., Hannson, P., & Ingvar, M. (1995). Central representation of chronic ongoing neuropathic pain studied by positron emission tomography. *Pain, 64*, 303–314.

Hugdahl, K. (1995). Classical conditioning and implicit learning: The right hemisphere hypothesis. In R. J. Davidson & K. Hugdahl (Eds.), *Brain asymmetry* (pp. 235–267). Cambridge, MA: MIT Press.

Hugdahl, K., Berardi, A., Thompson, W. L, Kosslyn, S. M., Macy, R., Baker, D. P., Alpert, N. M., & LeDoux, J. E. (1995). Brain mechanisms in human classical conditioning: A PET blood flow study. *NeuroReport, 6*, 1723–1728.

Hunt, J. M. (1965). Traditional personality theory in light of recent evidence. *American Scientist, 53*, 80–96.

Hurvich, M. (1989). Traumatic moment, basic dangers and annihilation anxiety. *Psychoanalytic Review, 6*, 309–323.

Izard, C. E. (1978). On the ontogenesis of emotions and emotion-cognition relationships in infancy. In M. Lewis & L. Rosenblum (Eds.), *The development of affect* (pp. 389–413). New York: Plenum.

Izard, C. E. (1991). *The psychology of emotions*. New York: Plenum Press.

Izard, C. E. (1992). Basic emotions, relations amongst emotions, and emotion-cognition relations. *Psychological Review, 99*, 561–565.

Izard, C. E., Hembree, E. A., & Huebner, R. R. (1987). Infants' emotion expressions to acute pain: Developmental change and stability of individual differences. *Developmental Psychology, 23*, 105–113.

Jackson, J. H. (1931). *Selected writings of John Hughlings Jackson, volumes I and II*. London: Hodder & Stoughton.

Jacobs, T. J. (1991). *The use of the self: Countertransference and communication in the analytic situation*. Madison, CT: International Universities Press.

Jacobs, T. J. (1994). Nonverbal communications: Some reflections on their role in the psychoanalytic process and psychoanalytic education. *Journal of the American Psychoanalytic Association, 42*, 741–762.

Jacobson, E. (1971). *Depression*. New York: International Universities Press.

Jacobson, E. (1964). *The self and the object world*. New York: International Universities Press.

Jaenicke, C. (1987). Kohut's concept of cure. *Psychoanalytic Review, 74*, 537–548.

Janet, P. (1889). *L'Automatisme psychologique*. Paris: Alcan.

Janszky, J., Szües, A., Halász, P., Borbély, C., Holló, A., Barsi, P., & Mirnics, Z. (2002). Orgasmic aura originates from the right hemisphere. *Neurology, 58*, 302–304.

Jessimer, M., & Markham, R. (1997). Alexithymia: A right hemisphere dysfunction specific to recognition of certain facial expressions. *Brain and Cognition, 34*, 246–258.

Johnsen, B. H., & Hugdahl, K. (1991). Hemispheric asymmetry in conditioning to facial emotional expressions. *Psychophysiology, 28*, 154–162.

Johnson, M. H., & Magaro, P. A. (1987). Effects of mood and severity on memory processes in depression and mania. *Psychological Bulletin, 101*, 28–40.

Johnson, M. K., & Multhaup, K. S. (1992). Emotion and MEM. In S.-A. Christianson (Ed.), *The handbook of emotion and memory: Research and theory* (pp. 33–66). Mahwah, NJ: Lawrence Erlbaum Associates.

Johnson, S. M. (1987). *Humanizing the narcissistic style*. New York: Norton.

Johnston, A. N. B., & Rogers, L. J. (1998). Right hemisphere involvement in imprinting memory revealed by glutamate treatment. *Pharmacology, Biochemistry, and Behavior, 60,* 863–871.

Jones, E. (1953). *The life and work of Sigmund Freud. Volume 1. The formative years and the great discoveries, 1856–1900.* New York: Basic Books.

Jones-Gottman, M., & Zatorre, R. J. (1993). Odor recognition memory in humans: Role of right temporal and orbitofrontal regions. *Brain and Cognition, 22,* 182–198.

Joseph, B. (1988). Projective identification. Some clinical aspects. In J. Sandler (Ed.), *Projection, identification, projective identification* (pp. 65–76). London: Karnac.

Joseph, B. (1997). Projective identification. In R. Schafer (Ed.), *The contemporary Kleinians of London* (pp. 100–116). Madison, CT: International Universities Press.

Joseph, R. (1982). The neuropsychology of development: Hemispheric laterality, limbic language, and the origin of thought. *Journal of Clinical Psychology, 38,* 4–33.

Joseph, R. (1988). The right cerebral hemisphere: Emotion, music, visual-spatial skills, body-image, dreams, and awareness. *Journal of Clinical Psychology, 44,* 630–673.

Joseph, R. (1992). *The right brain and the unconscious: Discovering the stranger within.* New York: Plenum Press.

Joseph, R. (1996). *Neuropsychiatry, neuropsychology, and clinical neuroscience* (2nd ed.). Baltimore: Williams & Wilkins.

Josephs, L. (1989). Self psychology and the analysis of the superego. *Psychoanalytic Psychology, 6,* 73–86.

Jouandet, M., & Gazzaniga, M. S. (1979). The frontal lobes. In M. S. Gazzaniga (Ed.), *Handbook of behavioral neurobiology* (vol. 2, pp. 25–59). New York: Plenum Press.

Jung, C. G. (1943). *Two essays on analytical psychology.* Cleveland: Meridian Books. (Original work published 1928)

Kagan, J. (1976). Emergent themes in human development. *American Scientist, 64,* 186–196.

Kagan, J. (1979). The form of early development. *Archives of General Psychiatry, 36,* 1047–1054.

Kalin, N. H., Shelton, S. E., & Lynn, D. E. (1995). Opiate systems in mother and infant primates coordinate intimate contact during reunion. *Psychoneuroendocrinology, 20,* 735–742.

Kalogeras, K. T., Nieman, L. K., Friedman, T. C., Doppman, J. L., Cutler, G. B., Chrousos, G. P., Wilder, R. L., Gold, P. W., & Yanovski, J. A. (1996). Inferior petrosal sinus sampling in healthy human subjects reveals a unilateral corticotropin-releasing hormone-induced arginine vasopressin release associated with ipsilateral adrenocorticotropin secretion. *Journal of Clinical Investigation, 97,* 2045–2050.

Kandel, E. (1983). From metapsychology to molecular biology: Explorations into the nature of anxiety. *American Journal of Psychiatry, 140,* 1277–1293.

Kandel, E. R. (1998). A new intellectual framework for psychiatry. *American Journal of Psychiatry, 155,* 457–469.

Kandel, E. R. (1999). Biology and the future of psychoanalysis: A new intellectual framework for psychiatry revisited. *American Journal of Psychiatry, 156,* 505–524.

Kantrowitz, J. L. (1999). The role of the preconscious in psychoanalysis. *Journal of the American Psychoanalytic Association, 47,* 65–89.

Kaplan, J. T., & Zaidel. E. (2001). Errors monitoring in the hemispheres: The effect of lateralized feedback on lexical decision. *Cognition, 82,* 157–178.

Kaplan-Solms, K., & Solms, M. (1996). Psychoanalytic observations on a case of frontal-limbic disease. *Journal of Clinical Psychoanalysis, 5,* 405–438.

Karow, C. M., Marquardt, T. P., & Marshall, R. C. (2001). Affective processing in left and right hemisphere brain-damaged subjects with and without subcortical involvement. *Aphasiology, 15,* 715–729.

Karr-Morse, R., & Wiley, M. S. (1997). *Ghosts from the nursery*. New York: Atlantic Monthly Press.

Katz, G. A. (1998). Where the action is: The enacted dimension of analytic process. *Journal of the American Psychoanalytic Association, 46*, 1129–1167.

Kaufman, G. (1974). The meaning of shame: Toward a self-affirming identity. *Journal of Counseling Psychology, 21*, 568–574.

Kaufman, G. (1985). *Shame: The power of caring*. Boston: Schenkman.

Kaufman, I. C., & Rosenblum, L. A. (1967). The reaction to separation in infant monkeys: Anaclitic depression and conservation-withdrawal. *Psychosomatic Medicine, 40*, 649–675.

Kaufman, I. C., & Rosenblum, L. A. (1969). Effects of separation from mother on the emotional behavior of infant monkeys. *Annals of the New York Academy of Science, 159*, 681–695.

Kaufmann, S. A. (1993). *The origins of order: Self-organization and selection in evolution*. New York: Oxford University Press.

Kawashima, R., O'Sullivan, B. T., & Roland, P. E. (1995). Positron-emission tomography studies of cross-modality inhibition in selective attentional tasks: Closing the "mind's eye." *Proceedings of the National Academy of Sciences of the United States of America, 92*, 5969–5972.

Kawashima, R., Sugiura, M., Kato, T., Nakamura, A., Hatano, K., Ito, K., Fukuda, H., Kojima, S., & Nakamura, K. (1999). The human amygdala plays an important role in gaze monitoring: A PET study. *Brain, 122*, 779–783.

Keeler, W. R. (1958). Autistic patients and defective communication in blind children with retrolental fibroplasia. In P. H. Hoch & J. Zubin (Eds.), *Psychopathology of communication* (pp. 64–83). New York: Grune & Stratton.

Keenan, J. P., McCutcheon, B., Freund, S., Gallup, G. C., Jr., Sanders, G., & Pascual-Leone, A. (1999). Left hand advantage in a self-face recognition task. *Neuropsychologia, 37*, 1421–1425.

Keenan, J. P., Nelson, A., O'Connor, M., & Pascual-Leone, A. (2001). Self-recognition and the right hemisphere. *Nature, 409*, 305.

Keenan, J. P., Wheeler, M. A., Gallup, G. G., Jr., & Pascual-Leone, A. (2000). Self-recognition and the right prefrontal cortex. *Trends in Cognitive Science, 4*, 338–344.

Kehoe, P., Shoemaker, M. J., Triano, L., Hoffman, J., & Arons, C. (1996). Repeated isolation in the neonatal rat produces alterations in behavior and ventral striatal dopamine release in the juvenile after amphetamine challenge. *Behavioral Neuroscience, 110*, 1435–1444.

Keil, A., Bradley, M. M., Hauk, O., Rockstroh, B., Elbert, T., & Lang, P. J. (2002). Large-scale neural correlates of affective picture processing. *Psychophysiology, 39*, 641–649.

Keil, A., Müller, M. M., Gruber, T., Wienbruch, C., Stolarova, M., & Elbert, T. (2001). Effects of emotional arousal in the cerebral hemispheres: A study of oscillatory brain activity and event-related potentials. *Clinical Neurophysiology, 112*, 2057–2068.

Kennard, M. A. (1955). The cingulate gyrus in relation to consciousness. *Journal of Nervous and Mental Disease, 121*, 34–39.

Kernberg, O. (1976). *Object relations and clinical psychoanalysis*. New York: Jason Aronson.

Kernberg, O. (1980). *Internal world and external reality*. New York: Jason Aronson.

Kernberg, O. (1984). *Severe personality disorders: Psychotherapeutic strategies*. New Haven: Yale University Press.

Kernberg, O. (1988a). Interview with the developer of an object relations psychoanalytic therapy for borderline personality disorder. *American Journal of Psychotherapy, 52* (2) Spring.

Kernberg, O. (1988b). Object relations theory in clinical practice. *Psychoanalytic Quarterly, 57*, 481–504.

Kestenberg, J. (1985). The flow of empathy and trust between mother and child. In E. J. Anthony & G. H. Pollack (Eds.), *Parental influences in health and disease* (pp. 137–163). Boston: Little, Brown.

Khan, M. M. R. (1974). Ego-distortion, cumulative trauma and the role of reconstruction in the analytic situation. In M. M. R. Khan, *The privacy of the self: Papers on psychoanalytic theory and technique* (pp. 59–68). New York: International Universities Press.

Kiersky, S., & Beebe, B. (1994). The reconstruction of early nonverbal relatedness in the treatment of difficult patients. A special form of empathy. *Psychoanalytic Dialogues, 4*, 389–408.

Kim, J. J., Andreasen, N. C., O'Leary, D. S., Wiser, A. K., Boles Ponto, L. L., Watkins, G. L., & Hichwa, R. D. (1999). Direct comparison of the neural substrates of recognition memory for words and faces. *Brain, 122*, 1069–1083.

Kinney, H. C., Brody, B. A., Kloman, A. S., & Gilles, F. H. (1988). Sequence of central nervous system myelination in human infancy. II. Patterns of myelination in autopsied infants. *Journal of Neuropathology and Experimental Neurology, 47*, 217–234.

Kinston, W. (1983). A theoretical context for shame. *International Journal of Psycho-Analysis, 64*, 213–226.

Kircher, T. T. J., Senior, C., Phillips, M. L., Rabe-Hesketh, S., Benson, P. J., Bullmore, E. T., Brammer, M., Simmons, A., Bartels, M., & David, A. S. (2001). Recognizing one's own face. *Cognition, 78*, B1–B5.

Kirsner, K., & Brown, H. (1981). Laterality and recency effects in working memory. *Neuropsychologia, 19*, 249–261.

Klauber, J. (1987). *Illusion and spontaneity*. London: Free Association Books.

Klein, M. (1981). Love, guilt, and reparation. In R. E. Money-Kyrle (Ed.), *The writings of Melanie Klein* (vol. 1, pp. 306–343). London: Hogath Press. (Original work published 1937)

Klein, M. (1952a). On observing the behaviour of young infants. In J. Riviere (Ed.), *Developments in psycho-analysis* (pp. 237 230). London: Hogarth Press. (Original work published 1943–1944)

Klein, M. (1952b). Some theoretical conclusions regarding the emotional life of the infant. In J. Riviere (Ed.), *Developments in psycho-analysis* (pp. 198–236). London: Hogarth Press. (Original work published 1943–1944)

Klein, M. (1946). Notes on some schizoid mechanisms. *International Journal of Psycho-Analysis, 27*, 99–110.

Klein, M. (1975). On identification. In *Envy and gratitude and other works 1946–1963* (pp. 141–175). London: Hogarth Press. (Original work published 1955)

Knapp, P. H. (1967). Purging and curbing: An inquiry into disgust, satiety and shame. *Journal of Nervous & Mental Disease, 144*, 514–544.

Knapp, P. H. (1992). Emotion and the psychoanalytic encounter. In T. Shapiro & R. N. Emde (Eds.), *Affect: Psychoanalytic perspectives* (pp. 239–264). Madison, CT: International Universities Press.

Kobak, R. R., & Sceery, A. (1988). Attachment in late adolescence: Working models, affect regulation, and representations of self and others. *Child Development, 59*, 135–146.

Koenen, K. C., Driver, K. L., Oscar-Berman, M., Wolfe, J., Folsom, S., Huang, M. T., & Schlessinger, L. (2001). Measures of prefrontal system dysfunction in posttraumatic stress disorder. *Brain and Cognition, 45*, 64–78.

Kohut, H. (1971). *The analysis of the self*. New York: International Universities Press.

Kohut, H. (1977). *The restoration of the self*. New York: International Universities Press.

Kohut, H. (1978a). Forms and transformations of narcissism. In P. Ornstein (Ed.), *The search for the self* (pp. 427–460). New York: International Universities Press.

Kohut, H. (1978b). Thoughts on narcissism and narcissistic rage. In P. Ornstein (Ed.), *The search for the self* (pp. 615–658). New York: International Universities Press.

Kohut, H. (1981). On empathy. In P. Ornstein (Ed.), *The search for the self* (vol. 4, pp. 525–535). New York: International Universities Press.

Kohut, H. (1984). *How does analysis cure?* Chicago: University of Chicago Press.

Kolb, B., & Whishaw, I. Q. (1996). *Fundamentals of human neuropsychology* (4th ed.). New York: W.H. Freeman.

Koopman, C., Classen, C., & Spiegel, D. (1994). Predictors of posttraumatic stress symptoms among survivors of the Oakland/Berkeley, Calif, firestorm. *American Journal of Psychiatry, 151*, 888–894.

Kosslyn, M., Ganis, G., & Thompson, W. L. (2001). Neural foundations of imagery. *Nature Reviews Neuroscience, 2*, 635–642.

Kosslyn, S. M., Maljkovic, V., Hamilton, S. E., Horowitz, G., & Thompson, W. L. (1995). Two types of image generation: Evidence for left and right hemisphere processes. *Neuropsychologia, 33*, 1485–1510.

Krause, R., & Lutolf, P. (1988). Facial indicators of transference processes within psychoanalytic treatment. In H. Dahl & H. Kachele (Eds.), *Psychoanalytic process research strategies* (pp. 258–272). New York: Springer-Verlag.

Kreiman, G., Koch, C., & Fried, C. (2000). Imagery neurons in the human brain. *Nature, 408*, 357–361.

Krimer, L. S., Mully, C. III, Williams, G. V., & Goldman-Rakic, P. S. (1998). Dopaminergic regulation of cortical microcirculation. *Nature Neuroscience, 1*, 286–289.

Krystal, H. (1978). Trauma and affects. *Psychoanalytic Study of the Child, 33*, 81–116.

Krystal, H. (1988). *Integration and self-healing: affect-trauma-alexithymia*. Hillsdale, NJ: Analytic Press.

Krystal, H. (1992). Psychoanalysis as a "normal science." *Journal of the American Academy of Psychoanalysis, 20*, 395–412.

Krystal, H. (1997). Desomatization and the consequences of infantile psychic trauma. *Psychoanalytic Inquiry, 17*, 126–150.

Kutas, M., & Federmeirer, K. D. (1998). Minding the body. *Psychophysiology, 35*, 135–150.

Lachmann, F., & Beebe, B. (1996). Three principles of salience in the organization of the patient–analyst interaction. *Psychoanalytic Psychology, 13*, 1–22.

Lachmann, F., & Beebe, B. (1997). Trauma, interpretation, and self-state transformation. *Psychoanalysis & Contemporary Thought, 20*, 269–291.

Ladavas, E., Nicoletti, R., Umilta, C., & Rizzolatti, G. (1984). Right hemisphere interference during negative affect: A reaction time study. *Neuropsychologia, 22*, 479–485.

Ladd, C. O., Owens, M. J., & Nemeroff, C. B. (1996). Persistent changes in corticotropin-releasing factor neuronal systems induced by maternal deprivation. *Endocrinology, 137*, 1212–1218.

Lane, R. D., Chua, P. M.-L., & Dolan, R.J. (1999). Common effects of emotional valence, arousal and attention on neural activation during visual processing of pictures. *Neuropsychologia, 37*, 989–997.

Lane, R. D., & Jennings, J. R. (1995). Hemispheric asymmetry, autonomic asymmetry, and the problem of sudden cardiac death. In R. J. Davidson & K. Hugdahl (Eds.), *Brain asymmetry* (pp. 271–304). Cambridge, MA: MIT Press.

Langdon, D., & Warrington, E. K. (2000). The role of the left hemisphere in verbal and spatial reasoning tasks. *Cortex, 36*, 691–702.

Langs, R. (1976). *The bipersonal field*. New York: Jason Aronson.

Langs, R. (1995). Psychoanalysis and the science of evolution. *American Journal of Psychotherapy, 49,* 47–58.

Langs, R. (1996). Mental Darwinism and the evolution of the emotion-processing mind. *American Journal of Psychotherapy, 50,* 103–124.

Langs, R., & Badalamenti, A. (1992). The three modes of the science of psychoanalysis. *American Journal of Psychotherapy, 46,* 163–182.

Lansky, M. R. (1995). *Posttraumatic nightmares: Psychodynamic explorations.* New York: Analytic Press.

Lapierre, D., Braun, C. M. J., & Hodgins, S. (1995). Ventral frontal deficits in psychopathy: Neuropsychological test findings. *Neuropsychologia, 33,* 139–151.

Larson, V. A. (1987). An exploration of psychotherapeutic resonance. *Psychotherapy, 24,* 321–324.

Laub, D., & Auerhahn, N. (1993). Knowing and not knowing massive psychic trauma: Forms of traumatic memory. *International Journal of Psycho-Analysis, 74,* 287–302.

Lazarus, R. S. (1991). Progress on a cognitive-motivational-relational theory of emotion. *American Psychologist, 46,* 819–834.

Lazarus, R. S., & McCleary, R. A. (1951). Autonomic discrimination without awareness: A study of subception. *Psychological Review, 58,* 113–122.

Leavitt, L. A., & Donovan, W. L. (1979). Perceived infant temperament, locus of control, and maternal physiological response to infant gaze. *Journal of Research in Personality, 13,* 267–278.

Lecours, A. R. (1982). Correlates of developmental behavior in brain maturation. In T. G. Bever (Ed.), *Regressions in mental development: Basic phenomena and theories* (pp. 267–298). Hillsdale, NJ: Erlbaum.

LeDoux, J. (1989). Cognitive-emotional interactions in the brain. *Cognition and Emotion, 3,* 267–289.

LeDoux, J. (2002). *Synaptic self: How our brains become who we are.* New York: Viking.

Lee, D. H., Severin, K., Yokobayashi, Y., & Reza Ghadiri, M. (1997). Emergence of symbiosis in peptide self-replication through a hypercyclic network. *Nature, 390,* 591–594.

Lehky, S. R. (2000). Fine discrimination of faces can be performed rapidly. *Journal of Cognitive Neuroscience, 12,* 848–855.

Leiman, M. (1994). Projective identification as early joint action sequences: A Vygotskian addendum to the procedural sequence object relations model. *British Journal of Medical Psychology, 67,* 97–106.

Leisjssen, M. (1990). On focusing and the necessary conditions of therapeutic personality change. In G. Lietar, J. Rombauts, & R. Van Balen (Eds.), *Client-centered and experiential psychotherapy in the Nineties* (pp. 225–250). Leuven, Belgium: Leuven University Press.

Lester, B. M., Hoffman, J., & Brazelton, T. B. (1985). The rhythmic structure of mother–infant interaction in term and preterm infants. *Child Development, 56,* 15–27.

Lester, E. P. (1983). Separation-individuation and cognition. *Journal of the American Psychoanalytic Association, 31,* 127–156.

Levin, F. (1991). *Mapping the mind.* Mahwah, NJ: Analytic Press.

Levin, S. (1967). Some metapsychological considerations on the differentiation between shame and guilt. *International Journal of Psycho-Analysis, 48,* 267–276.

Levine, B., Black, S. E., Cabeza, R., Sinden, M., Mcintosh, A. R., Toth, J. P., Tulving, E., & Stuss, D. T. (1998). Episodic memory and the self in a case of isolated retrograde amnesia. *Brain, 121,* 1951–1973.

Levine, B., Freedman, M., Dawson, D., Black, S., & Stuss, D. T. (1999). Ventral frontal contribution to self-regulation: Convergence of episodic memory and inhibition. *Neurocase, 5,* 263–275.

Levine, D., Marziali, E., & Hood, J. (1997). Emotion processsing in borderline personality disorders. *Journal of Nervous & Mental Disease, 185,* 240–246.

Levine, S. (1983). A psychobiological approach to the ontogeny of coping. In N. Garmezy & M. Rutter (Eds.), *Stress, coping, and development in children* (pp. 107–131). New York: McGraw-Hill.

Levy, J., Heller, W., Banich, M. T., & Burton, L. A. (1983). Are variations among right-handed individuals in perceptual asymmetries caused by characteristic arousal differences between hemispheres? *Journal of Experimental Psychology: Human Perception and Performance, 9,* 329–359.

Lewicki, P. (1986). *Nonconscious social information processing.* San Diego: Academic Press.

Lewis, H. B. (1971). *Shame and guilt in neurosis.* New York: International Universities Press.

Lewis, H. B. (1978). Sex differences in superego mode as related to sex differences in psychiatric illness. *Social Science and Medicine, 12B,* 199–205.

Lewis, H. B. (1979). Shame in depression and hysteria. In C. E. Izard (Ed.), *Emotions in personality and psychopathology* (pp. 399–414). New York: Plenum Press.

Lewis, H. B. (1980). "Narcissistic personality" or "Shame-prone superego mode." *Comprehensive Psychotherapy, 1,* 59–80.

Lewis, H. B. (1985). Depression vs. paranoia: Why are there sex differences in mental illness? *Journal of Personality and Social Psychology, 53,* 150–178.

Lewis, J. M. (2000). Repairing the bond in important relationships: A dynamic for personality maturation. *American Journal of Psychiatry, 157,* 1375–1378.

Lewis, M. (1982). Origins of self-knowledge and individual differences in early self-recognition. In J. Suls (Ed.), *Psychological perspectives on the self* (vol. 1, pp. 55–78). Hillsdale, NJ: Erlbaum.

Lewis, M. (1995). Cognition-emotion feedback and the self-organization of developmental paths. *Human Development, 38,* 71–102.

Lewis, M., & Granic, I. (2000). *Emotion, development, and self-organization.* New York: Cambridge University Press.

Lichtenberg, J. D. (1983). *Psychoanalysis and infant research.* Hillsdale, NJ: Analytic Press.

Lichtenberg, J. D. (1989). *Psychoanalysis and motivation.* Hillsdale, NJ: Analytic Press.

Lichtenberg, J. D., Lachmann, F. M., & Fosshage, J. L. (1992). *Self and motivational systems: Toward a theory of psychoanalytic technique.* Mahwah, NJ: Analytic Press.

Lichtenberg, J. D., Lachmann, F. M., & Fosshage, J. L. (1996). *The clinical exchange.* Mahwah, NJ: Analytic Press.

Lickliterl, R., & Gottlieb, G. (1986). Visually imprinted maternal preference in ducklings is redirected by social interaction with siblings. *Developmental Psychobiology, 19,* 265–277.

Lieberman, A. (1996). Aggression and sexuality in relation to toddler attachment: Implications for the caregiving system. *Infant Mental Health Journal, 17,* 276–292.

Lieberman, A. (1997). Toddler's internalization of maternal attributions as a factor in quality of attachment. In L. Atkinson & K. J. Zucker (Eds.), *Attachment and psychopathology* (pp. 277–291). New York: Guilford Press.

Lieberman, A. F., & Zeanah, G. H. (1999). Contributions of attachment theory to infant-parent psychotherapy and other interventions with infants and young children. In J. Cassidy & P. Shaver (Eds.), *Handbook of attachment theory and research* (pp. 555–574). New York: Guilford.

Lieberman, M. D. (2000). Intuition: A social neuroscience approach. *Psychological Bulletin, 126,* 109–137.

Likierman, M. (1988). Maternal love and positive projective identification. *Journal of Child Psychotherapy, 14,* 29–46.

Lindy, J. D. (1996). Psychoanalytic psychotherapy of posttraumatic stress disorder. The nature of the therapeutic relationship. In B. A. van der Kolk, A. C. McFarlane, & L. Weisaeth (Eds.), *Traumatic stress: The effects of overwhelming experience on mind, body, and society* (pp. 525–536). New York: Guilford Press.

Liotti, G. (1992). Disorganized / disoriented attachment in the etiology of the dissociative disorders. *Dissociation, 5,* 196–204.

Liotti, G. (1999). Understanding the dissociative processs: The contribution of attachment theory. *Psychoanalytic Inquiry, 19,* 757–783.

Lipsitt, L. P. (1976). Developmental psychology comes of age: A discussion. In L. P. Lipsitt (Ed.), *Developmental psychology: The significance of infancy* (pp. 109–127). Hillsdale, NJ: Erlbaum.

Lipton, P. A., Alvarez, P., & Eichenbaum, H. (1999). Crossmodal associative memory representations in rodent orbitofrontal cortex. *Neuron, 22,* 349–359.

Liu, D., Diorio, J., Tannenbaum, B., Caldji, C., Francis, D., Freedman, A., Sharma, S., Pearson, D., Plotsky, P. M., & Meaney, M. J. (1997). Maternal care, hippocampal glucocorticoid receptors, and hypothalamic-pituitary-adrenal responses to stress. *Science, 277,* 1659–1662.

Locke, J. L. (1997). A theory of language development. *Brain and Language, 58,* 265–326.

Loewald, H. (1980). The ego and reality. In *Papers on psychoanalysis* (pp. 3–20). New Haven, CT: Yale University Press. (Original work published 1949)

Loewald, H. (1970). Psychoanalytic theory and psychoanalytic process. *Psychoanalytic Study of the Child, 25,* 45–68.

Loewald, H. (1978). Instinct theory, object relations, and psychic structure formation. *Journal of the American Psychoanalytic Association, 26,* 493–506.

Loewald, H. (1986). Transference-countertransference. *Journal of the American Psychoanalytic Association, 34,* 275–287.

Lorberbaum, J. P., Newman, J. D., Horwitz, A. R., Dubno, J. R., Lydiard, R. B., Hamner, M. B., Bohning, D. E., & George, M. S. (2002). A potential role for thalamo-cingulate circuitry in human maternal behavior. *Biological Psychiatry, 51,* 431–445.

Lundqvist, L.-O. (1995). Facial EMG reactions to facial expressions: A case of facial emotional contagion? *Scandanavian Journal of Psychology, 36,* 130–141.

Lundquist, L. O., & Dimberg, U. (1995). Facial expressions are contagious. *Journal of Psychophysiology, 9,* 203–211.

Luria, A. R. (1973). *The working brain.* New York: Basic Books.

Luria, A. R. (1980). *Higher cortical functions in man* (2nd ed.). New York: Basic Books.

Luu, P., & Tucker, D. M. (1996). Self-regulation and cortical development: Implications for functional studies of the brain. In R. W. Thatcher, G. Reid Lyon, J. Rumsey, & N. Krasnegor (Eds.), *Developmental neuroimaging: Mapping the development of brain and behavior* (pp. 297–305). San Diego, CA: Academic Press.

Lynd, H. M. (1958). *On shame and the search for identity.* New York: Harcourt, Brace & Company.

Lyons-Ruth, K. (2000). "I sense that you sense that I sense . . . ": Sander's recognition process and the specificity of relational moves in the psychotherapeutic setting. *Infant Mental Health Journal, 21,* 85–98.

Lyons-Ruth, K., Bruschweiler-Stern, N., Harrison, A. M., Morgan, A. C., Nahum, J. P., Sander, L., Stern, D. N., & Tronick, E. Z. (1998). Implicit relational knowing: Its role in development and psychoanalytic treatment. *Infant Mental Health Journal, 19,* 282–289.

Lyons-Ruth, K., & Jacobvitz, D. (1999). Attachment disorganization. Unresolved loss, relational violence, and lapses in behavioral and attentional strategies. In J. Cassidy & P. R. Shaver (Eds.), *Handbook of attachment: Theory, research, and clinical applications* (pp. 520–554). New York: Guilford Press.

MacCurdy, J. T. (1930). The biological significance of blushing and shame. *British Journal of Psychology, 21,* 174–182.

MacFarlane, A. (1977). *The psychology of childbirth.* Cambridge, MA: Harvard University Press.

MacLean, P. (1985). Evolutionary psychiatry and the triune brain. *Psychological Medicine, 15,* 219–221.

MacLean, P. D. (1993). Perspectives on cingulate cortex in the limbic system. In B. A. Vogt & M. Gabriel (Eds.), *Neurobiology of cingulate cortex and limbic thalamus.* Boston: Birkhauser.

MacLean, P. D., & Newman, J. D. (1988). Role of midline frontolimbic cortex in production of the isolation call of squirrel monkeys. *Brain Research, 450,* 111–123.

Mahler, M. S. (1958). Autism and symbiosis: Two extreme disturbances of identity. *International Journal of Psycho-Analysis, 39,* 77–83.

Mahler, M. S. (1968). *On human symbiosis and the vicissitudes of individuation.* New York: International Universities Press.

Mahler, M. S. (1979). Notes on the development of basic moods: The depressive affect. In M. S. Mahler, *The selected papers of Margaret S. Mahler* (pp. 59–75). New York: Jason Aronson.

Mahler, M. S. (1980). Rapprochement subphase of the separation-individuation process. In R. Lax, S. Bach, & J. A. Burland (Eds.), *Rapprochement: The critical subphase of separation-individuation* (pp. 3–19). New York: Jason Aronson.

Mahler, M. S., & Kaplan, L. (1977). Developmental aspects in the assessment of narcissistic and so-called borderline personalities. In P. Hartocollos (Ed.), *Borderline personality disorders* (pp. 71–85). New York: International Universities Press.

Mahler, M. S., Pine, F., & Bergman, A. (1975). *The psychological birth of the human infant.* New York: Basic Books.

Main, M. (1993). Discourse, prediction, and recent studies in attachment: Implications for psychoanalysis. *Journal of the American Psychoanalytic Association, 41* Supplement, 209–244.

Main, M., Kaplan, N., & Cassidy, J. (1985). Security in infancy, childhood and adulthood: A move to the level of representation. *Monographs of the Society for Research in Child Development, 50,* 66–104.

Main, M., & Solomon, J. (1986). Discovery of an insecure-disorganized/disoriented attachment pattern: Procedures, findings and implications for the classification of behavior. In T. B. Brazelton & M. W. Yogman (Eds.), *Affective development in infancy* (pp. 95–124). Norwood, NJ: Ablex.

Malatesta-Magai, C. (1991). Emotional socialization: Its role in personality and developmental psychopathology. In D. Cicchetti & S. L. Toth (Eds.), *Internalizing and externalizing expressions of dysfunction: Rochester symposium on developmental psychopatholgy* (vol. 2, pp. 203–224). Hillsdale, NJ: Erlbaum.

Malmo, R. B. (1959). Activation: A neurophysiological dimension. *Psychological Review, 66,* 367–386.

Manning, J. T., & Chamberlain, A. T. (1991). Left-side cradling and brain lateralisation. *Ethology and Sociobiology, 12,* 237–244.

Manning, J. T., Trivers, R. L., Thornhill, R., Singh, D., Denman, J., Eklo, M. H., & Anderton, R. H. (1997). Ear asymmetry and left-side cradling. *Evolution and Human Behavior, 18,* 327–340.

Maquet, P., DeGueldre, C., Delfiore, G., Aerts, J., Peters, J.-M., Luxen, A., & Franck, G. (1997). Functional neuroanatomy of human slow wave sleep. *Journal of Neuroscience, 17*, 2807–2812.

Marcus, D. M. (1997). On knowing what one knows. *Psychoanalytic Quarterly, 66*, 219–241.

Marshall, J. C., Halligan, P. W., Fink, G. R., Wade, D. T., & Frackowiak, R. S. J. (1997). The functional anatomy of a hysterical paralysis. *Cognition, 64*, B1–B8.

Marsolek, C. J., Schacter, D. L., & Nicholas, C. D. (1996). Form-specific visual priming for new associations in the right cerebral hemisphere. *Memory and Cognition, 24*, 539–556.

Martin, E., Kikinis, R., Zuerrer, M., Boesch, C., Briner, J., Kewitz, G., & Kaelin, P. (1988). Developmental stages of human brain: An MR study. *Journal of Computer Assisted Tomography, 12*, 917–922.

Martin, J. H. (1989). *Neuroanatomy: Text and atlas.* New York: Elsevier.

Martin, R. A., Berry, G. E., Dobranski, T., & Horne, M. (1996). Emotion perception threshold: Individual differences in emotional sensitivity. *Journal of Research in Personality, 30*, 290–305.

Mason, A. (2000). Bion and binocular vision. *International Journal of Psycho-Analysis, 81*, 983–989.

Massana, G., Gastó, C., Junqué, C., Mercader, J-M., Gomez, B., Massana, J., Torres, X., & Salamero, M. (2002). Reduced levels of creatine in the right medial temporal lobe region of panic disorder patients detected with ^{1}H magnetic resonance spectroscopy. *NeuroImage, 16*, 836–842.

Masterson, J. F. (1981). *The narcissistic and borderline personality disorders.* New York: Brunner/Mazel.

Masterson, J. F. (2000). *The personality disorders: A new look at the developmental self and object relations approach.* Phoenix, AZ: Zeig, Tucker & Co.

Masterson, J. F., & Rinsley, D. B. (1975). The borderline syndrome: the role of the mother in the genesis of psychic structure of the borderline personality. *International Journal of Psychiatry, 56*, 163–178.

Matsui, M., Gur, R. C., Turetsky, B. I., Yan, M. X.-H., & Gur, R. E. (2000). The relation between tendency for psychopathology and reduced frontal brain volume in healthy people. *Neuropsychiatry, Neuropsychology, & Behavioral Neurology, 13*, 155–162.

Matsuzawa, J., Matsui, M., Konishi, T., Noguchi, K., Gur, R. C., Bilker, W., & Miyawaki, T. (2001). Age-related changes of brain gray and white matter in healthy infants and children. *Cerebral Cortex, 11*, 335–342.

Maunder, R. G., & Hunter, J. J. (2001). Attachment and psychosomatic medicine: Developmental contributions to stress and disease. *Psychosomatic Medicine, 63*, 556–567.

Mayberg, H. S., Lewis, P. J., Regenold, W., & Wagner, H. N., Jr. (1994). Paralimbic hypoperfusion in unipolar depression. *Journal of Nuclear Medicine, 35*, 929–934.

McCabe, P. M., & Schneiderman, N. (1985). Psychophysiologic reactions to stress. In N. Schneiderman & J. T. Tapp (Eds.), *Behavioral medicine: The biophysical approach* (pp. 99–131). Hillsdale, NJ: Erlbaum.

McCarley, R. W., & Hobson, A. J. (1977). The neurobiological origins of psychoanalytic dream theory. *American Journal of Psychiatry, 134*, 1211–1221.

McDevitt, J. (1975). Separation-individuation and object constancy. *Journal of the American Psychoanalytic Association, 23*, 713–742.

McDevitt, J. (1980). The role of internalization in the development of object relations during the separation-individuation phase. In R. F. Lax, S. Bach, & J. A. Burland (Eds.), *Rapprochement: The critical subphase of separation-individuation* (pp. 135–149). New York: Jason Aronson.

McDougall, J. (1978). Countertransference and primitive communication. In J. Mc-Dougall, *Plea for a Measure of Abnormality* (pp. 247–298). New York. International Universities Press.

McDougall, J. (1989). The dead father: On early psychic trauma and its relation to disturbance in sexual identity and in creative activity. *International Journal of Psycho-Analysis, 70*, 205–219.

McFarlane, A. C., & Yehuda, R. (2000). Clinical treatment of posttraumatic stress disorder: Conceptual challenges raised by recent research. *Australian and New Zealand Journal of Psychiatry, 34*, 940–953.

McGregor, I. S., & Atrens, D. M. (1991). Prefrontal cortex self-stimulation and energy balance. *Behavioral Neuroscience, 105*, 870–883.

McKenna, C. (1994). Malignant transference: A neurobiologic model. *Journal of the American Academy of Psychoanalysis, 22*, 111–127.

McLaughlin, J. T. (1978). Primary and secondary processes in the context of cerebral hemispheric specialization. *Psychoanalytic Quarterly, 47*, 237–266.

McLaughlin, J. T. (1981). Transference, psychic reality and countertransference. *Psychoanalytic Quarterly, 50*, 639–644.

McLaughlin, J. T. (1991). Clinical and theoretical aspects of enactment. *Journal of the American Psychoanalytic Association, 39*, 595–614.

McLaughlin, J. T. (1996). Power, authority, and influence in the analytic dyad. *Psychoanalytic Quarterly, 63*, 201–235.

Mega, M. S., & Cummings, J. L. (1994). Frontal-subcortical circuits and neuropsychiatric disorders. *Journal of Neuropsychiatry and Clinical Neuroscience, 6*, 358–370.

Mender, D. (1994). *The myth of neuropsychiatry: A look at paradoxes, physics, and the human brain.* New York: Plenum Press.

Merten, J., Anstadt, T., Ullrich, B., Krause, R., & Buchheim, P. (1996). Emotional experience and facial behavior during the psychotherapeutic process and its relation to treatment outcome: A pilot study. *Psychotherapy Research, 6*, 198–212.

Mesulam, M.-M. (1990). Large-scale neurocognitive networks and distributed processing for attention, language, and memory [Review]. *Annals of Neurology, 28*, 597–613.

Mesulam, M.-M. (1998). From sensation to cognition. *Brain, 121*, 1013–1052.

Mesulam, M.-M., & Geschwind, N. (1978). On the possible role of neocortex and its limbic connections in the process of attention in schizophrenia: Clinical cases of inattention in man and experimental anatomy in monkey. *Journal of Psychiatric Research, 14*, 249–259.

Mesulam, M.-M., & Mufson, E. J. (1982). Insula of the old world monkey. I. Architectonics in the insulo-orbito-temporal component of the paralimbic brain. *Journal of Comparative Neurology, 212*, 1–22.

Meyersburg, H. A., & Post, R. M. (1979). An holistic developmental view of neural and psychological processes: A neurobiologic-psychoanalytic integration. *British Journal of Psychiatry, 135*, 139–155.

Migone, P. (1995). Expressed emotion and projective identification: A bridge between psychiatric and psychoanalytic concepts? *Contemporary Psychoanalysis, 31*, 617–640.

Mikulincer, M., Gillath, O., Halevy, V., Avihou, N., Avidan, S., & Eshkoli, N. (2001). Attachment theory and reactions to others' needs: Evidence that activation of the sense of attachment security promotes empathic responses. *Journal of Personality and Social Psychology, 81*, 1205–1224.

Miller, B. L., Seeley, W. W., Mychack, P., Rosen, H. J., Mena, I., & Boone, K. (2001). Neuroanatomy of the self. Evidence from patients with frontotemporal dementia. *Neurology, 57*, 817–821.

Miller, J. P. (1965). The psychology of blushing. *International Journal of Psycho-Analysis, 146,* 188–199.

Miller, L. (1986). Some comments on cerebral hemispheric models of consciousness. *Psychoanalytic Review, 73,* 129–144.

Miller, L. (1991). *Freud's brain: Neuropsychodynamic foundations of psychoanalysis.* New York: Guilford Press.

Miller, S. (1985). *The shame experience.* Hillsdale, NJ: Analytic Press.

Miller, S. (1988). Humiliation and shame. Comparing two affect states as indicators of narcissistic stress. *Bulletin of the Menninger Clinic, 52,* 40–51.

Miller, S. (1989). Shame as an impetus to the creation of conscience. *International Journal of Psycho-Analysis, 70,* 231–243.

Min, S. K., & Lee, B. O. (1997). Laterality in somatization. *Psychosomatic Medicine, 59,* 236–240.

Mlot, C. (1998). Probing the biology of emotion. *Science, 280,* 1005–1007.

Modell, A. H. (1980). Affects and their non-communication. *International Journal of Psycho-Analysis, 61,* 259–267.

Modell, A. H. (1984). *Psychoanalysis in a new context.* New York: International Universities Press.

Modell, A. H. (1993). *The private self.* Cambridge, MA: Harvard University Press.

Modell, A. H. (1994). Fairbairn's structural theory and the communication of affects. In J. Grotstein & D. B. Rinsley (Eds.), *Faribairn and the origins of object relations* (pp. 195–207). New York: Guilford Press.

Mogenson, G. J., Jones, D. L., & Yim, C. Y. (1980). From motivation to action: Functional interface between the limbic system and the motor system. *Progress in Neurobiology, 14,* 69–97.

Moll, J., Oliveira-Souza, R., Bramati, I. E., & Grafman, J. (2002). Functional networks in emotional moral and nonmoral social judgments. *NeuroImage, 16,* 696–703.

Mollon, P. (1996). *Multiple selves, multiple voices: Working with trauma, violation and dissociation.* Chichester, UK: Wiley.

Mollon, P. (2001). *Releasing the self: The healing legacy of Heinz Kohut.* London: Whurr Publishers.

Money, J., & Ehrhardt, A. (1968). *Man, woman, boy, and girl.* Baltimore: Johns Hopkins University Press.

Moorcroft, W. H. (1971). Ontogeny of forebrain inhibition of behavioral arousal in the rat. *Brain Research, 35,* 513–522.

Mordecai, E. M. (1995). Negative therapeutic reactions: Developing a new stance. *Psychoanalytic Psychology, 12,* 483–493.

Morgan, M. A., & LeDoux, J. E. (1995). Differential contribution of dorsal and ventral medial prefrontal cortex to the acquisition and extinction of conditioned fear in rats. *Behavioral Neuroscience, 109,* 681–688.

Morris, J. S., Ohman, A., & Dolan, R. J. (1998). Conscious and unconscious emotional learning in the human amygdala. *Nature, 393,* 467–470.

Morris, J. S., Ohman, A., & Dolan, R. J. (1999). A subcortical pathway to the right amygdala mediating "unseen" fear. *Proceedings of the National Academy of Sciences of the United States of America, 96,* 1680–1685.

Morris, W. N. (1989). *Mood: The frame of mind.* New York: Springer-Verlag.

Morrison, A. P. (1984). Working with shame in psychoanalytic treatment. *Journal of the American Psychoanalytic Association, 32,* 479–505.

Morrison, A. P. (1986). On projective identification in couples' group. *International Journal of Group Psychotherapy, 36,* 55–73.

Morrison, A. P. (1989). *Shame, the underside of narcissism.* Hillsdale, NJ: Erlbaum.

Morrison, N. K. (1985). Shame in the treatment of schizophrenia: Theoretical considerations with clinical illustrations. *Yale Journal of Biological Medicine, 58,* 289–297.

Muir, R. C. (1995). Transpersonal processes: A bridge between object relations and attachment theory in normal and psychopathological development. *British Journal of Medical Psychology, 68,* 243–257.

Muller, M. M., Keil, A., Gruber, T., & Elbert, T. (1999). Processing of affective pictures modulates right hemispheric gamma band EEG activity. *Clinical Neurophysiology, 110,* 1913–1920.

Munder-Ross, J. (1999). Once more on the couch: Consciousness and preconscious defenses in psychoanalysis. *Journal of the American Psychoanlytic Association, 47,* 91–111.

Murphy, S. T., Monahan, J. L., & Zajonc, R. B. (1995). Additivity of nonconscious affect: Combined effects of priming and exposure. *Journal of Personality and Social Psychology, 69,* 589–602.

Murray, L. (1991). Intersubjectivity, object relations theory and empirical evidence from mother–infant interactions. *Infant Mental Health Journal, 12,* 219–232.

Mussen, P. H., Conger, J. J., & Kagan, J. (1969). *Child development and personality.* New York: Harper & Row.

Nagae, S., & Moscovitch, M. (2002). Cerebral hemispheric differences in memory of emotional and non-emotional words in normal individuals. *Neuropsychologia, 40,* 1601–1607.

Nagera, H., & Colonna, A. (1965). Aspects of the contribution of sight to ego and drive development—a comparison of the development and some blind and sighted children. *Psychoanalytic Study of the Child, 20,* 267–287.

Nakamura, K., Kawashima, R., Ito, K., Sato, N., Nakamura, A., Sugiura, M., Kato, T., Hatano, K., Ito, K., Fukuda, H., Schorman, T., & Zilles, K. (2000). Functional delineation of the human occipito-temporal areas related to face and scene processing. A PET study. *Brain, 123,* 1903–1912.

Nakamura, K., Kawashima, R., Ito, K., Sugiura, M., Kato, T., Nakamura, A., Hatano, K., Nagumo, S., Kubota, K., Fukuda, H., & Kojima, S. (1999). Activation of the right inferior frontal cortex during assessment of facial emotion. *Journal of Neurophysiology, 82,* 1610–1614.

Narumoto, J., Yamada, H., Iidaka, T., et al. (2000). Brain regions involved in verbal and nonverbal aspects of facial recognition. *NeuroReport, 11,* 2571–2576.

Nathanson, D. L. (1987). A timetable for shame. In D. L. Nathanson (Ed.), *The many faces of shame* (pp. 1–63). New York: Guilford Press.

Natterson, J. (1991). *Beyond countertransference: The therapist's subjectivity in the therapeutic process.* Northvale, NJ: Jason Aronson.

Nauta, W. J. H. (1971). The problem of the frontal lobe: A reinterpretation. *Journal of Psychiatric Research, 8,* 167–187.

Neafsey, E. J. (1990). Prefrontal cortical control of the autonomic nervous system: Anatomical and physiological observations. *Progress in Brain Research, 85,* 147–166.

Neininger, B., & Pulvermüller, F. (2003). Word-category deficits after lesions in the right hemisphere. *Neuropsychologia, 41,* 53–70.

Neisser, U. (1967). *Cognitive psychology.* New York: Appleton-Century-Crofts.

Nelson, C. A. (1987). The recognition of facial expressions in the first two years of life: Mechanisms of development. *Child Development, 58,* 889–909.

Newman, J. P., & Wallace, J. F. (1993). Diverse pathways to deficient self-regulation: Implications for disinhibitory psychopathology in children. *Clinical Psychology Review, 13,* 699–720.

Nicholls, M. E. R., Wolfgang, B. J., Clode, D., & Lindell, A. K. (2002). The effect of left and right poses on the expression of facial emotion. *Neuropsychologia, 40,* 1662–1665.

Niedenthal, P. M. (1990). Implicit perception of affective information. *Journal of Experimental Social Psychology, 26,* 505–527.

Nieuwenhuys, R., Voogd, J., & van Huijzen, C. (1981). *The human central nervous system: A synopsis and atlas.* New York: Springer-Verlag.

Nijenhuis, E. R. S. (2000). Somatoform dissociation: major symptoms of dissociative disorders. *Journal of Trauma & Dissociation, 1,* 7–32.

Nijenhuis, E. R. S., Vanderlinden, J., & Spinhoven, P. (1998). Animal defensive reactions as a model for trauma-induced dissociative reations. *Journal of Traumatic Stress, 11,* 242–260.

Nishihara, K., Horiuchi, S., Eto, H., & Uchida, S. (2002). The development of infants' circadian rest-activity rhythm and mother's rhythm. *Physiology & Behavior, 77,* 91–98.

Nobre, A. C., Coull, J. T., Frith, C. D., & Mesulam, M. M. (1999). Orbitofrontal cortex is activated during breaches of expectation in tasks of visual attention. *Nature Neuroscience, 2,* 11–12.

Noebels, J. L. (1989). Introduction to structure-function relationships in the developing brain. In P. Kellaway & J. L. Noebels (Eds.), *Problems and concepts in developmental neurophysiology* (pp. 151–160). Baltimore: Johns Hopkins University Press.

Nolde, S. F., Johnson, M. K., & Raye, C. L. (1998). The role of prefrontal cortex during tests of episodic memory. *Trends in Cognitive Sciences, 2,* 399–405.

Oatley, K., & Jenkins, J. M. (1992). Human emotions: Function and dysfunction. *Annual Review of Psychology, 43,* 55–85.

Ogawa, J. R., Sroufe, L. A., Weinfield, N. S., Carlson, E. A., & Egeland, B. (1997). Development and the fragmented self: Longitudinal study of dissociative symptomatology in a nonclinical sample. *Development and Psychopathology, 9,* 855–879.

Ogden, T. H. (1979). On projective identification. *International Journal of Psycho-Analysis, 60,* 357–373.

Ogden, T. H. (1990a). On the structure of experience. In L. B. Boyer & P. L. Giovacchini (Eds.), *Master clinicians on treating the regressed patient* (pp. 69–95). Northvale, NJ: Jason Aronson.

Ogden, T. H. (1990b). *The matrix of the mind.* Northvale, NJ: Jason Aronson.

Ogden, T. H. (1994). *Subjects of analysis.* Northvale, NJ: Aronson.

Ogden, T. H. (2001). Re-minding the body. *American Journal of Psychotherapy, 55,* 92–104.

Olnick, S. (1969). On empathy and regression in the service of the other. *British Journal of Medical Psychology, 42,* 41–49.

Opatow, B. (1997). The real unconscious: psychoanalysis as a theory of consciousness. *Journal of the American Psychoanalytic Association, 45,* 865–890.

Orlinsky, D. E., & Howard, K. I. (1986). Process and outcome in psychotherapy. In S. L. Garfield & A. E. Bergin (Eds.), *Handbook of psychotherapy and behavior change* (3rd ed., pp. 311–381). New York: Wiley.

Ornstein, R. (1997). *The right mind: Making sense of the hemispheres.* New York: Harcourt Brace.

Ostow, M. (1954). A psychoanalytic contribution to the study of brain function: I. The frontal lobes. *Psychoanalytic Quarterly, 23,* 317–328.

Ostrowsky, K., Magnin, M., Ryvlin, P., Isnard, J., Guenot, M., & Maugiere, F. (2002). Representation of pain and somatic sensation in the human insula: A study of responses to direct electrical cortical stimulation. *Cerebral Cortex, 12,* 376–385.

Otto, M. W., Yeo, R. A., & Dougher, M. J. (1987). Right hemisphere involvement in depression: Toward a neuropsychological theory of negative affective experience. *Biological Psychiatry, 22,* 1201–1215.

Ovtscharoff, W. Jr., & Braun, K. (2001). Maternal separation and social isolation modulate the postnatal development of synaptic composition in the infralimbic cortex of *octodon degus. Neuroscience, 104,* 33–40.

Pally, R. (1998). Emotional processing: The mind-body connection. *International Journal of Psycho-Analysis, 79,* 349–362.

Palombo, J. (1992). Narratives, self-cohesion, and the patient's search for meaning. *Clinical Social Work Journal, 20,* 249–270.

Pandya, D. N., & Barnes, C. L. (1987). Architecture and connections of the frontal lobes. In E. Perecman (Ed.), *The frontal lobes revisited* (pp. 41–72). Mahwah, NJ: Erlbaum.

Pandya, D. N., & Yeterian, E. H. (1985). Architecture and connections of cortical association areas. In A. Peters & E. G. Jones (Eds.), *Cerebral cortex. Association and auditory cortices* (vol. 4, pp. 3–61). New York: Plenum Press.

Pandya, D. N., & Yeterian, E. H. (1990). Prefrontal cortex in relation to other cortical areas in rhesus monkey: Architecture and connections. *Progress in Brain Research, 85,* 63–94.

Panksepp, J. (1991). Affective neuroscience: A conceptual framework for the neurobiological study of emotions. In K. Strongman (Ed.), *International reviews of studies in emotions* (vol. 1, pp. 59–99). New York: Wiley.

Panksepp, J. (1998). *Affective neuroscience: The foundations of human and animal emotions.* New York: Oxford University Press.

Panksepp, J. (1999). Emotions as viewed by psychoanalysis and neuroscience: An exercise in consilience. *Neuro-Psychoanalysis, 1,* 15–38.

Panksepp, J., Siviy, S. M., & Normansell, L. A. (1985). Brain opioids and social emotions. In M. Reite & T. Field (Eds.), *The psychobiology of attachment and separation* (pp. 3–49). Orlando, FL: Academic Press.

Pao, P. (1971). Elation, hypomania, and mania. *Journal of the American Psychoanalytic Association, 19,* 787–798.

Pao, P.-N. (1979). *Schizophrenic disorders.* New York: International Universities Press.

Papousek, H., & Papousek, M. (1979). Early ontogeny of human social interaction: Its biological roots and social dimensions. In M. von Cranach, K. Foppa, W. Lepenies, & D. Ploog (Eds.), *Human ethology: Claims and limits of a new discipline* (pp. 456–478). New York: Cambridge University Press.

Papousek, H., & Papousek, M. (1995). Intuitive parenting. In M. H. Bornstein (Ed.), *Handbook of parenting: Vol. II. Ecology and biology of parenting.* Hillsdale, NJ: Erlbaum.

Papousek, H., & Papousek, M. (1997). Fragile aspects of early social integration. In L. Murray & P. J. Cooper (Eds.), *Postpartum depression and child development* (pp. 35–53). New York: Guilford Press.

Papousek, J., & Schulter, G. (2001). Associations between EEG asymmetries and electrodermal lability in low vs. high depressive and anxious normal individuals. *International Journal of Psychophysiology, 41,* 105–117.

Pardo, J. V., Pardo, P. J., & Raichle, M. E. (1993). Neural correlates of self-induced dysphoria. *American Journal of Psychiatry, 150,* 713–718.

Parens, H. (1980). An exploration of the relations of instinctual drives and the symbiosis/separation-individuation process. *Journal of the American Psychoanalytic Association, 28,* 89–114.

Paris, J. (1995). Memories of abuse in borderline patients: True or false? *Harvard Review of Psychiatry, 3,* 10–17.

Park, L. C., & Park, T. J. (1997). Personal intelligence. In M. McCallum & W. E. Piper (Eds.), *Psychological mindedness: A contemporary understanding* (pp. 133–167). Mahwah, NJ: Erlbaum.

Parker, J. D. A., Taylor, G. L., & Bagby, R. M. (1992). Relationship between conjugate lateral eye movements and alexithymia. *Psychotherapy and Psychosomatics, 57,* 94–101.

Parker Lewis, P. P. (1992). The creative arts in transference/countertransference relationships. *The Arts in Psychotherapy, 19*, 317–323.

Parkin, A. (1985). Narcissism: Its structures, systems and affects. *International Journal of Psycho-Analysis, 66*, 143–156.

Parsons, L. M., & Osherson, D. (2001). New evidence for distinct right and left brain systems for deductive versus probabilistic reasoning. *Cerebral Cortex, 11*, 954–965.

Paus, T., Petrides, M., Evans, A. C., & Meyer, E. (1993). Role of the human anterior cingulate cortex in the control of oculomotor, manual, and speech responses: A positron emission tomography study. *Journal of Neurophysiology, 70*, 453–469.

Perna, P. A. (1997). Reflections on the therapeutic system as seen from the science of chaos and complexity: Implications for research and treatment. In F. Masterpasqua & P. A. Perna (Eds.), *The psychological meaning of chaos: Translating theory into practice* (pp. 253–272). Washington, DC: American Psychological Association.

Perry, B. D., Pollard, R. A., Blakely, T. L., Baker, W. L., & Vigilante, D. (1995). Childhood trauma, the neurobiology of adaptation, and "use-dependent" development of the brain. How "states" become "traits." *Infant Mental Health Journal, 16*, 271–291.

Perry, R. J., Rosen, H. R., Kramer, J. H., Beer, J. S., Levenson, R. L., & Miller, B. L. (2001). Hemispheric dominance for emotions, empathy, and social behavior: Evidence from right and left handers with frontotemporal dementia. *Neurocase, 7*, 145–160.

Petrovic, P., Petersson, K. M., Ghatan, P. H., Sone-Elander, S., & Ingvar, M. (2000). Pain-related cerebral activation is altered by a distracting cognitive task. *Pain, 85*, 19–30.

Petrovich, S. B., & Gewirtz, J. L. (1985). The attachment learning process and its relation to cultural and biological evolution: Proximate and ultimate considerations. In M. Reite & T. Field (Eds.), *The psychobiology of attachment and separation*. Orlando: Academic Press.

Pettersson, M., Hulting, A.-L., & Uvnas-Moberg, K. (1999). Oxytocin causes a sustained decrease in plasma levels of corticosterone in rats. *Neuroscience Letters, 264*, 41–44.

Phelps, J. L., Belsky, J., & Crnic, K. (1998). Earned security, daily stress, and parenting: A comparison of five alternative models. *Development and Psychopathology, 10*, 21–38.

Phillips, M. L., Young, A. W., Senior, C., Brammer, M., Andrew, C., Calder, A. J., Bullmore, E. T., Perrett, D. I., Rowland, D., Williams, S. C. R., Gray, J. A., & David, A. S. (1997). A specific neural substrate for perceiving facial expressions of disgust. *Nature, 389*, 495–498.

Piaget, J. (1967). *Six psychological studies*. New York: Random House.

Pick, I. B. (1985). Working through in the countertransfernce. *International Journal of Psycho-Analysis, 66*, 157–166.

Piers, G., & Singer, M. B. (1953). *Shame and guilt*. Springfield, IL: Charles C. Thomas.

Pine, F. (1980). On the expansion of the affect array: A developmental description. In R. Lax, S. Bach, & J. A. Burland (Eds.), *Rapprochement: The critical subphase of separation-individuation* (pp. 217–233). New York: Jason Aronson.

Pine, F. (1985). *Developmental theory and clinical process*. New Haven, CT: Yale University Press.

Pipp, S. (1993). Infant's knowledge of self, other, and relationship. In U. Neisser (Ed.), *The perceived self* (pp. 185–204). New York: Cambridge University Press.

Pipp, S., & Harmon, R. J. (1987). Attachment as regulation: A commentary. *Child Development, 58*, 648–652.

Pistole, M. C. (1995). Adult attachment style and narcissistic vulnerability. *Psychoanalytic Psychology, 12*, 115–126.

Pizzagalli, D. A., Greischar, L. L., & Davidson, R. J. (2003). Spatio-temporal dynamics of brain mechanisms in aversive classical conditioning: high-density event-related potential and brain electrical tomography analyses. *Neuropsychologia, 41,* 184–194.

Pizzagalli, D. A., Lehmann, D., Hendrick, A. M., Regard, M., Pascual-Marqui, R. D., & Davidson, R. J. (2002). Affective judgments of faces modulate early activity (~160 ms) within the fusiform gyri. *NeuroImage, 16,* 663–677.

Pizzagalli, D., Regard, M., & Lehmann, D. (1999). Rapid emotional face processing in the human right and left brain hemispheres: An ERP study. *NeuroReport, 10,* 2691–2698.

Plakun, E. M. (1999). Sexual misconduct and enactment. *Journal of Psychotherapy Practice and Research, 8,* 284–291.

Plakun, E. M. (2001). Making the alliance and taking the transference in work with suicidal patients. *Journal of Psychotherapy Practice and Research, 10,* 269–276.

Plooij, F. X., & van de Plooij, H. (1989). Vulnerable periods during infancy: Hierarchically reorganized systems. Control, stress, and disease. *Ethology and Sociobiology, 10,* 279–286.

Plutchik, R. (1983). Emotion in early development: A psychoevolutionary approach. In R. Plutchik & H. Kellerman (Eds.), *Emotion, theory, research, and experience* (pp. 221–257). New York: Academic Press.

Poeggel, G., & Braun, K. (1996). Early auditory filial learning in degus (*Octodon degus*): behavioral and autoradiographic studies. *Brain Research, 743,* 162–170.

Poeggel, G., Lange, E., Hase, C., Metzger, M., Gulyaeva, N., & Braun, K. (1999). Maternal separation and early social deprivation in *Octodon degus*: quantitative changes in nicotinamide adenine dinucleotide phosphate diaphorase-reactive neurons in the prefrontal cortex and nucleus accumbers. *Neuroscience, 94,* 497–504.

Polan, H. J., & Hofer, M .A. (1999). Psychobiological origins of infant attachment and separation responses. In J. Cassidy & P. R. Shaver (Eds.), *Handbook of attachment: Theory, research, and clinical applications* (pp. 162–180). New York: Guilford Press.

Pollak, S. D., & Kistler, D. J. (2002). Early experience is associated with the development of categorical representations for facial expressions of emotion. *Proceedings of the National Academy of Sciences of the United States of America, 99,* 9072–9076.

Popper, K. (1962). *Conjectures and refutations.* New York: Basic Books.

Porges, S. W. (1976). Peripheral and neurochemical parallels of psychopathology: A psychophysiological model relating autonomic imbalance to hyperactivity, psychopathy, and autism. *Advances in Child Development and Behavior, 11,* 35–65.

Porges, S. W. (1997). Emotion: An evolutionary by-product of the neural regulation of the autonomic nervous system. *Annals of the New York Academy of Sciences, 807,* 62–77.

Porges, S. W. (2001). The polyvagal theory: phylogenetic substrates of a social nervous system. *International Journal of Psychophysiology, 42,* 29–52.

Porges, S. W., Doussard-Roosevelt, J. A., & Maiti, A. K. (1994). Vagal tone and the physiological regulation of emotion. *Monograph of the Society for Research in Child Development, 59,* 167–186.

Porter, R. H., & Winberg, J. (1999). Unique salience of maternal breast odors for newborn infants. *Neuroscience and Biobehavioral Reviews, 23,* 439–449.

Posner, M. I., & Rothbart, M. K. (1998). Attention, self-regulation and consciousness. *Philosophical Transactions of the Royal Society of London B, 353,* 1915–1927.

Post, R. M., Weiss, S. R. B., & Leverich G. S. (1994). Recurrent affective disorder: Roots in developmental neurobiology and illness progression based on changes in gene expression. *Development and Psychopathology, 6,* 781–813.

Potter-Effron, R. T. (1989). *Shame, guilt, and alcoholism: Treatment issues in clinical practice.* New York: The Haworth Press.

Povinelli, D., & Preuss, T. M. (1995). Theory of mind: Evolutionary history of a cognitive specialization. *Trends in Neuroscience, 18,* 418–424.

Powles, W. E. (1992). *Human development and homeostasis.* Madison, CT: International Universities Press.

Pratto, F. (1994). Consciousness and automatic evaluation. In P. M. Niedentahl & S. Kiyayama (Eds.), *The heart's eye: Emotional influences in perception and attention* (pp. 116–143). San Diego, CA: Academic Press.

Preisler, G. M. (1995). The development of communication in blind and in deaf infants—similariites and differences. *Child: Care, Health and Development, 21,* 79–110.

Pribram, K. H. (1960). The intrinsic systems of the forebrain. In *Handbook of Physiology* (vol. II, pp. 1323–1344). Washington, DC: American Physiological Society.

Pribram, K. H. (1981). Emotions. In S. B. Filskov & T. J. Boll (Eds.), *Handbook of clinical neuropsychology* (pp. 102–134). New York: Wiley.

Pribram, K. H. (1987). The subdivisions of the frontal cortex revisited. In E. Perecman (Ed.), *The frontal lobes revisited* (pp. 11–39). Hillsdale, NJ: Erlbaum.

Pribram, K. H. (1991). *Brain and perception: Holonomy and structure in figural processing.* Hillsdale, NJ: Lawrence Erlbaum Associates.

Pribram, K. H., & Gill, M. M. (1976). *Freud's "project" re-assessed.* New York: Basic Books.

Price, J. L., Carmichael, S. T., & Drevets, W. C. (1996). Networks related to the orbital and medial prefrontal cortex; a substrate for emotional behavior? *Progress in Brain Research, 107,* 523–536.

Prigogine, I., & Stengers, I. (1984). *Order out of chaos.* New York: Bantam Books.

Pulver, S. E. (1970). Narcissism. The term and the concept. *Journal of the American Psychoanalytic Association, 18,* 319–341.

Putnam, F. W. (1989). *Diagnosis and treatment of multiple personality disorder.* New York: Guilford Press.

Putnam, F. W. (1997). *Dissociation in children and adolescents: A developmental perspective.* New York: Guilford Press.

Pyszczynski, T., & Greenberg, J. (1987). Self-regulatory perseveration and the depressive self-focusing style: A self-awareness theory of reactive depression. *Psychological Bulletin, 102,* 122–138.

Racker, H. (1968). *Transference and countertransference.* New York: International Universities Press.

Radke-Yarrow, M., & Zahn-Waxler, C. (1984). Roots, motives and patterns in children's prosocial behavior. In E. Staub, D. Bar-Tal, J. Karylowski, & J. Reykowski (Eds.), *Development and maintenance of prosocial behavior* (pp. 81–99). New York: Plenum Press.

Raichle, M. E. (1994). Images of the mind: Studies with modern imaging techniques. *Annual Review of Psychology, 45,* 333–356.

Raine, A. (2002). Biosocial studies of antisocial and violent behavior in children and adults: a review. *Journal of Abnormal Child Psychology, 30,* 311–326.

Raine, A., Park, S., Lencz, T., Bihrle, S., LaCasse, L., Widom, C. S., Al-Dayeh, L., & Singh, M. (2001). Reduced right hemisphere activation in severely abused violent offenders during a working memory task: An fMRI study. *Aggressive Behavior, 27,* 111–129.

Ramachandran, V. S., Levi, L., Stone, L., Rogers-Ramachandran, D., McKinney, R., Stalcup, M., Arcilla, G., Zweifler, R., Shatz, A., & Flippin, A. (1996). Illusions of body image: What they reveal about human nature. In R. Llinas & P. S. Churchland (Eds.), *The mind-brain continuum: Sensory processes* (pp. 29–60). Cambridge, MA: MIT Press.

Ramon y Cajal, S. (1995). *Histology of the nervous system of man and vertebrates* (N. Swanson & L. W. Swanson, Trans.) New York: Oxford University Press. (Original work published 1899.)

Rangell, L. (1997). The unitary theory of Leo Rangell, M.D. *Journal of Clinical Psychoanalysis, 6,* 453–592.

Rapaport, D. (1960). The structure of psychoanalytic theory [*Psychological Issues,* Monograph 6]. New York: International Universities Press.

Rashid, N., & Andrew, R. J. (1989). Right hemisphere advantage for topographical orientation in the domestic chick. *Neuropsychologia, 27,* 937–943.

Rauch, S. C., Savage, C. R., Alpert, N. M., Miguel, E. C., Baer, L., Breiter, H. C., Fischman, A. J., Manzo, P. A., Moretti, C., & Jenike, M. A. (1995). A positron emission tomographic study of simple phobic symptom provocation. *Archives of General Psychiatry, 52,* 20–28.

Rauch, S. L., van der Kolk, B. A., Fisler, R. E., Alpert, N. M., Orr, S. P., Savage, C. R., Fischman, A. J., Jenike, M. A., & Pitman, R. K. (1996). A symptom provocation study of posttraumatic stress disorder using positron emission tomography and script-driven imagery. *Archives of General Psychiatry, 53,* 380–387.

Rauschecker, J. P., & Marler, P. (1987). Cortical plasticity and imprinting: Behavioral and physiological contrasts and parallels. In J. P. Rauscheker & P. Marler (Eds.), *Imprinting and cortical plasticity: Comparative aspects of sensitive periods* (pp. 349–366). New York: Wiley.

Reich, A. (1960). Pathologic forms of self-esteem regulation. *Psychoanalytic Study of the Child, 15,* 215–234.

Reiser, M. F. (1985). Converging sectors of psychoanalysis and neurobiology: Mutual challenge and opportunity. *Journal of the American Psychoanalytic Association, 33,* 11–34.

Reiser, M. F. (1997). The art and science of dream interpretation: Isakower revisited. *Journal of the American Psychoanalytic Association, 45,* 891–905.

Reite, M., & Capitanio, J. P. (1985). On the nature of social separation and attachment. In M. Reite & T. Field (Eds.), *The psychobiology of attachment and separation* (pp. 223–255). Orlando, FL: Academic Press.

Reite, M., Kaufman, I. C., Pauley, J. D., & Stynes, A. J. (1974). Depression in infant monkeys: Physiological correlates. *Psychosomatic Medicine, 36,* 363–367.

Renik, O. (1998). The analyst's subjectivity and the analyst's objectivity. *International Journal of Psycho-Analysis, 79,* 487–497.

Renik, O. (1999). Playing one's cards face up in analysis. An approach to the problem of self-disclosure. *Psychoanalytic Quarterly, LXVIII,* 521–539.

Rheingold, H. L., & Eckerman, C. O. (1970). The infant separates himself from his mother. *Science, 168,* 78–83.

Ribble, M. A. (1944). Infantile experience in relation to personality development. In J. McV. Hunt (Ed.) *Personality and the behaviour disorders* (vol. II) (pp. 621–651). New York: Ronald Press.

Ricciardelli, P., Ro, T., & Driver, J. (2002). A left visual field advantage in perception of gaze direction. *Neuropsychologia, 40,* 769–777.

Rinsley, D. B. (1989). *Developmental pathogenesis and treatment of borderline and narcissistic personalities.* Northvale, NJ: Jason Aronson.

Robbins, M. (1996). The mental organization of primitive personalities and its treatment implications. *Journal of the American Psychoanalytic Association, 44,* 755–784.

Rogers, R. D., Owen, A. M., Middleton, H. C., Williams, E. J., Pickard, J. D., Sahakian, B. J., & Robbins, T. W. (1999). Choosing betweeen small, likely rewards and large, unlikely rewards activates inferior and orbital prefrontal cortex. *Journal of Neuroscience, 20,* 9029–9038.

Rolls, E. T. (1986). Neural systems involved in emotion in primates. In R. Plutchik & H. Kellerman (Eds.), *Emotion: Theory, research, and practice* (vol. 3, pp. 125–143). Orlando, FL: Academic Press.

Rolls, E. T. (1996). The orbitofrontal cortex. *Philosophical Transactions of the Royal Society of London B, 351,* 1433–1444.

Rolls, E. T., Hornak, J., Wade, D., & McGrath, J. (1994). Emotion-related learning in patients with social and emotional changes associated with frontal lobe damage. *Journal of Neurology, Neurosurgery, and Psychiatry, 57,* 1518–1524.

Rosenblum, L. A., Coplan, J. D., Friedman, S., Bassoff, T., Gorman, J. M., & Andrews, M. W. (1994). Adverse early experiences affect noradrenergic and serotonergic functioning in adult primates. *Biological Psychiatry, 35,* 221–227.

Rosenfeld, H. (1971). Contribution to the psychopathology of psychotic states; the importance of projective identification in the ego structure and the object relations of the psychotic patient. In P. Doucet & C. Laurin (Eds.), *Problems of psychosis* (pp. 115–128). The Hague: Excerpta Medica.

Rosenzweig, M. R. (1996). Aspects of the search for neural mechanisms of memory. *Annual Review of Psychology, 47,* 1–32.

Rosenzweig, M. R., Bennet, E. L., & Diamond, M. C. (1972). Brain changes in response to experience. *Scientific American, 226,* 22–29.

Ross, E. D. (1984). Right hemisphere's role in language, affective behavior and emotion. *Trends in Neuroscience, 7,* 342–346.

Ross, E. D., Homan, R. W., & Buck, R. (1994). Differential hemispheric lateralization of primary and social emotions. Implications for developing a comprehensive neurology for emotions, repression, and the subconscious. *Neuropsychiatry, Neuropsychology, and Behavioral Neurology, 7,* 1–19.

Rossi, E. L. (1993). *The psychobiology of mind-body healing.* New York: Norton.

Rotenberg, V. S. (1994). An integrative psychobiological approach to brain hemisphere functions in schizophrenia. *Neuroscience and Biobehavioral Reviews, 18,* 487–495.

Rotenberg, V. S. (1995). Right hemisphere insufficiency and illness in the context of search activity concept. *Dynamic Psychiatry, 150/151,* 54–63.

Rotenberg, V. S., & Weinberg, I. (1999). Human memory, cerebral hemispheres, and the limbic system: A new approach. *Genetic, Social, and General Psychology Monographs, 125,* 45–70.

Rothbart, M. K., Taylor, S. B., & Tucker, D. M. (1989). Right-sided facial asymmetry in infant emotional expression. *Neuropsychologia, 27,* 675–687.

Rubin, S. S., & Niemeier, D. L. (1992). Non-verbal affective communication as a factor in psychotherapy. *Psychotherapy, 29,* 596–602.

Ruby, P., & Decety, J. (2001). Effect of subjective perspective taking during simulation of action: A PET investigation of agency. *Nature Neuroscience, 4,* 546–550.

Rueckert, L., & Grafman, J. (1996). Sustained attention deficits in patients with right frontal lesions. *Neuropsychologia, 34,* 953–963.

Rutter, M. (1987). Temperament, personality and personality disorder. *British Journal of Psychiatry, 150,* 443–458.

Ryan, R. M., Kuhl, J., & Deci, E. L. (1997). Nature and autonomy: An organizational view of social and neurobiological aspects of self-regulation in behavior and development. *Development and Psychopathology, 9,* 701–728.

Ryle, A. (1994). Projective identification: A particular form of reciprocal role procedure. *British Journal of Medical Psychology, 67,* 107–114.

Sable, P. (2000). *Attachment and adult psychotherapy.* New York: Jason Aronson.

Sabshin, M. (1984). Psychoanaylsis and psychiatry: Models for potential future relations. *Journal of the American Psychoanalytic Association, 41,* 473–491.

Sacks, H. S. (1998). Presidential address: New challenges for proven values. *American Journal of Psychiatry, 155,* 1479–1482.

Safran, J. D., & Muran, J. C. (2000). *Negotiating the therapeutic alliance: A relational treatment guide.* New York: Guilford Press.

Sagi, A., Koren-Karie, N., Gini, M., Ziv, Y., & Joels, T. (2002). Shedding further light on the effects of various types and quality of early child care on infant-mother attachment relationship: the Haifa study of early child care. *Child Development, 73,* 1166–1186.

Sander, L. (1977). Regulation of exchange in the infant caretaker system: A viewpoint on the ontogeny of structures. In N. Freedman & S. Grand (Eds.), *Communicative structures and psychic structures* (pp. 13–34). New York: Plenum Press.

Sander, L. (1991). *Recognition process: Specificity and organization in early human development.* Paper presented at University of Massachussetts Conference on The Psychic Life of the Infant.

Sander, L. (1992). Letter to the editor. *International Journal of Psycho-Analysis, 73,* 582–584.

Sandler, J. (1976). Countertransference and role responsiveness. *International Review of Psychoanalysis, 3,* 43–47.

Sandler, J., & Sandler, A.-M. (1978). On the development of object relationships and affects. *International Journal of Psycho-Analysis, 59,* 285–296.

Sandler, J., & Sandler, A.-M. (1996). Psychiatric footnotes on love. In L. Rangell & R. Moses-Hrushovski (Eds.), *Psychoanalysis at the political border: Essays in honor of Rafael Moses* (pp. 23–33). Madison, CT: International Universities Press.

Sands, S. (1994). What is dissociated? *Dissociation, 7,* 145–152.

Sands, S. (1997a). Self psychology and projective identification—whither shall they meet? A reply to the editors (1995). *Psychoanalytic Dialogue, 7,* 651–668.

Sands, S. (1997b). Protein or foreign body? Reply to commentaries. *Psychoanalytic Dialogues, 7,* 691–706.

Sar, V., Unal, S. N., Kiziltan, E., Kundakci, T., & Ozturk, E. (2001). HMPAO SPECT study of regional cerebral blood flow in dissociative identity disorder. *Journal of Trauma and Dissociation, 2,* 5–25.

Sartre, J-P. (1957). *Being and nothingness.* London: Methuen.

Saugstad, L. F. (1998). Cerebral lateralization and rate of maturation. *International Journal of Psychophysiology, 28,* 37–62.

Scaer, R. C. (2001). *Trauma, dissociation, and disease: The body bears the burden.* New York: Haworth Press.

Scalaidhe, S. P., Wilson, F. A. W., & Goldman-Rakic, P. S. (1997). Areal segregation of face-processing neurons in prefrontal cortex. *Science, 278,* 1135–1138.

Schafer, R. (1968). *Aspects of internalization.* New York: International Universities Press.

Scharff, J. S. (1992). *Projective and introjective identification and the use of the therapist's self.* Northvale, NJ: Jason Aronson.

Scharff, J. S., & Scharff, D. E. (1998). *Object relations: Individual therapy.* Northvale, NJ: Jason Aronson.

Scheff, T. J. (1988). Shame and conformity: The deference-emotion system. *American Sociological Review, 53,* 395–406.

Scheflen, A. E. (1981). *Levels of schizophrenia.* New York: Brunner/Mazel.

Schiffer, F., Teicher, M. H., & Papanicolaou, A. C. (1995). Evoked potential evidence for right brain activity during recall of traumatic memories. *Journal of Neuropsychiatry, 7,* 169–175.

Schmahl, C. G., Glzinga, B. M., & Bremner, J. D. (2002). Individual differences in psychophysiological reactivity in adults with childhood abuse. *Clinical Psychology and Psychotherapy, 9,* 271–276.

Schneider, C. D. (1977). *Shame, exposure and privacy*. Boston: Beacon Press.

Schneiderman, N., & McCabe, P. M. (1985). Biobehavioral responses to stress. In T. M. Field, P. M. McCabe, & N. Schneiderman (Eds.), *Stress and coping* (pp. 13–61). Hillsdale, NJ: Erlbaum.

Schnider, A., & Ptak, R. (1999). Spontaneous confabulators fail to suppress currently irrelevant memory traces. *Nature Neuroscience, 2*, 677–681.

Schnider, A., Treyer, V., & Buck, A. (2000). Selection of currently relevant memories by the human posterior medial orbitofrontal cortex. *Journal of Neuroscience, 20*, 5880–5884.

Schnider, A., Valenza, N., Morand, S., & Michel, C. M. (2002). Early cortical distinction between memories that pertain to ongoing reality and memories that don't. *Cerebral Cortex, 12*, 54–61.

Schoenbaum, G., Chiba, A. A., & Gallagher, M. (2000). Changes in functional connectivity in orbitofrontal cortex and basolateral amygdala during learning and reversal training. *Journal of Neuroscience, 20*, 5179–5189.

Schore, A. N. (1991). Early superego development: The emergence of shame and narcissistic affect regulation in the practicing period. *Psychoanalysis and Contemporary Thought, 14*, 187–250.

Schore, A. N. (1994). *Affect regulation and the origin of the self: The neurobiology of emotional development*. Mahwah, NJ: Erlbaum.

Schore, A. N. (1996). The experience-dependent maturation of a regulatory system in the orbital prefrontal cortex and the origin of developmental psychopathology. *Development and Psychopathology, 8*, 59–87.

Schore, A. N. (1997a). A century after Freud's Project—is a rapprochement between psychoanalysis and neurobiology at hand? *Journal of the American Psychoanalytic Association, 45*, 1–34.

Schore, A. N. (1997b). Early organization of the nonlinear right brain and development of a predisposition to psychiatric disorders. *Development and Psychopathology, 9*, 595–631.

Schore, A. N. (1997c). Interdisciplinary developmental research as a source of clinical models. In M. Moskowitz, C. Monk, C. Kaye, & S. Ellman (Eds.), *The neurobiological and developmental basis for psychotherapeutic intervention* (pp. 1–71). Northvale, NJ: Aronson.

Schore, A. N. (1997e, October). *The relevance of recent research on the infant brain to clinical psychiatry*. Grand Rounds at the Columbia University School of Medicine, New York.

Schore, A. N. (1998a). Early shame experiences and infant brain development. In P. Gilbert & B. Andrews (Eds.), *Shame: Interpersonal behavior, psychopathology, and culture* (pp. 57–77). New York: Oxford University Press.

Schore, A. N. (1998b). The experience-dependent maturation of an evaluative system in the cortex. In K. H. Pribram (Ed.), *Fifth Appalachian Conference on Behavioral Neurodynamics, "Brain and Values"* (pp. 337–358). Mahwah, NJ: Erlbaum.

Schore, A. N. (1998c, March). *Projective identification: An intrapsychic mechanism of right brain communication*. Annual memorial lecture presented at the New York University Postdoctoral Program in Psychoanalysis and Psychotherapy, New York.

Schore, A. N. (1998d, July). *Affect regulation: A fundamental process of psychobiological development, brain organization, and psychotherapy*. Paper presented at the Baby Brains: Psychobiological Development of the Infant and Its Implications for Therapy Practice Conference, Tavistock Clinic, London.

Schore, A. N. (1998e, October). *Early trauma and the development of the right brain*. Keynote address delivered at the Royal Australian and New Zealand College of Psychiatrists, Faculty of Child and Adolescent Psychiatry 11th Annual Conference, Sydney, Australia.

Schore, A. N. (1998f, October). *The relevance of recent research on the infant brain to pediatrics.* Paper presented at the Annual Meeting of the American Academy of Pediatrics, Scientific Section on Developmental and Behavioral Pediatrics, Section Program on Translating Neuroscience: Early Brain Development and Pediatric Practice, San Francisco, CA.

Schore, A. N. (1998g, October). *The right brain as a neurobiological substrate of Freud's dynamic unconscious.* Keynote address delivered at the conference "Freud at the Millennium," Georgetown University, Washington, DC.

Schore, A. N. (1998h, October). *The relevance of recent research on the infant brain to clinical psychiatry.* Keynote address delivered at the Royal Australian and New Zealand College of Psychiatrsts Annual Conference, Sydney.

Schore, A. N. (1998i, November). *Early trauma and the development of the right brain.* Keynote address delivered at the C. M. Hincks Institute Conference on Traumatized Parents and Infants: The Long Shadow of Early Childhood Trauma, Toronto, Canada.

Schore, A. N. (1999a). Commentary on emotions: Neuro-psychoanalytic views. *Neuro-Psychoanalysis, 1,* 49–55.

Schore, A. N. (1999c). The right brain, the right mind, and psychoanalysis. [Online]. Available: http:www.neuro-psa.com/schore.htm

Schore, A. N. (1999d, March). *Affect regulation: A fundamental process of psychobiological development, brain organization, and psychotherapy.* Paper presented at the New York Freudian Society, New York.

Schore, A. N. (1999e, March). *The development of a predisposition to violence: The critical roles of attachment disorders and the maturation of the right brain.* Paper presented at the Children's Institute International Conference on Understanding the Roots of Violence: Kids Who Kill, Los Angeles.

Schore, A. N. (1999f, April). *Early trauma and the development of the right brain.* Keynote address delivered at the Boston University School of Medicine Conference on Psychological Trauma: Maturational Processes and Therapeutic Interventions, Boston.

Schore, A. N. (1999g, October). *The enduring effects of early trauma on the right brain.* Paper presented at the Annual Meeting of the American Academy of Child and Adolescent Psychiatry, Symposium on Attachment, Trauma, and the Developing Mind, Chicago.

Schore, A. N. (1999h, December). *Psychoanalysis and the development of the right brain.* Paper presented at The First North American International Psychoanalytic Association Regional Research Conference, "Neuroscience, Development & Psychoanalysis," Mount Sinai Hospital, New York.

Schore, A. N. (1999i, December). *Parent–infant communication and the neurobiology of emotional development.* Unpublished paper presented at the Zero to Three 14th Annual Training Conference, Los Angeles.

Schore, A. N. (2000a). Attachment and the regulation of the right brain. *Attachment & Human Development, 2,* 23–47.

Schore, A. N. (2000b). Attachment, the right brain, and empathic processes within the therapeutic alliance. *Psychologist Psychoanalyst, XX*(4), 8–11.

Schore, A. N. (2000c). Foreword. In J. Bowlby, *Attachment and loss, vol. 1: Attachment.* New York: Basic Books.

Schore, A. N. (2000d). Plenary address: Parent–infant communications and the neurobiology of emotional development. In *Proceedings of Head Start's Fifth National Research Conference, Developmental and Contextual Transitions of Children and Families. Implications for Research, Policy, and Practice* (pp. 49–73). Department of Health and Human Services, Washington, DC.

Schore, A. N. (2000e). The self-organization of the right brain and the neurobiology of emotional development. In M. D. Lewis & I. Granic (Eds.), *Emotion, development, and self-organization* (pp. 155–185). New York: Cambridge University Press.

Schore, A. N. (2000f, March). *Early relational trauma and the development of the right brain.* Paper presented at the Anna Freud Centre, London, England.

Schore, A. N. (2000g, March). *Projective identification—an interface of developmental psychoanalysis, neuropsychoanalysis, and clinical psychoanalysis.* Paper presented at Scientific Meeting, Tavistock Society of Psychotherapists, Tavistock Clinic, London.

Schore, A. N. (2000h, November). *Healthy childhood and the development of the human brain.* Keynote address, Luxembourg and World Health Organization, Healthy Children Foundation Conference, Luxembourg.

Schore, A. N. (2000i). Special section: attachment research and psychoanalytic process. Psychologist Psychoanalyst, XX, No. 3, 20.

Schore, A. N. (2001a). Contributions from the decade of the brain to infant mental health: an overview. *Infant Mental Health Journal, 22,* 1–6.

Schore, A. N. (2001b). The effects of a secure attachment relationship on right brain development, affect regulation, and infant mental health. *Infant Mental Health Journal, 22,* 7–66.

Schore, A. N. (2001c). The effects of relational trauma on right brain development, affect regulation, and infant mental health. *Infant Mental Health Journal, 22,* 201–269.

Schore, A. N. (2001d). The Seventh Annual John Bowlby Memorial Lecture. Minds in the making: Attachment, the self-organizing brain, and developmentally-oriented psychoanalytic psychotherapy. *British Journal of Psychotherapy, 17,* 299–328.

Schore, A. N. (2001e, March). *Early relational trauma and the development of the right brain.* Keynote address delivered at the Joint Annual Conference, Australian Centre for Posttraumatic Mental Health and The Australasian Society for Traumatic Stress Studies, Canberra, Australia.

Schore, A. N. (2001f, March). *Regulation of the right brain—a primary mechanism of attachment development and psychotherapy.* Keynote address delivered at the Joint Annual Conference, Australian Centre for Posttraumatic Mental Health and The Australasian Society for Traumatic Stress Studies, Canberra, Australia.

Schore, A. N. (2001g, June). *Regulation of the right brain: A fundamental mechanism of attachment, trauma, dissociation, and psychotherapy, Parts 1 & 2.* Papers presented at the Conference on Attachment, Trauma, and Dissociation: Developmental, Neuropsychological, Clinical, and Forensic Considerations, University College of London Attachment Research Unit and the Clinic for the Study of Dissociative Disorders, Sponsors, London.

Schore, A. N. (2001h). Special section: the relevance of developmental neuropsychoanalysis to the clinical models of Sandor Fenenczi and Wilfred Bion. Introduction. *Psychologist Psychoanalyst, XXI*(1), 12–13.

Schore, A. N. (2002a). The neurobiology of attachment and early personality organization. *Journal of Prenatal & Perinatal Psychology and Health, 16,* 249–263.

Schore, A. N. (2002b). Clinical implications of a psychoneurobiological model of projective identification. In S. Alhanati (Ed.), *Primitive mental states, vol. lll: Pre- and peri-natal influences on personality development* (pp. 1–65). London: Karnac.

Schore, A. N. (2002c). Dysregulation of the right brain: A fundamental mechanism of traumatic attachment and the psychopathogenesis of posttraumatic stress disorder. *Australian & New Zealand Journal of Psychiatry, 36,* 9–30.

Schore, A. N. (2002d). Neurobiology and psychoanalysis: Convergent findings on the subject of projective identification. In J. Edwards (Ed.), *Being alive: Building on the work of Anne Alvarez* (pp. 57–74). London: Brunner-Routledge.

Schore, A. N. (2002e). The right brain as the neurobiological substratum of Freud's dynamic unconscious. In D. Scharff (Ed.), *The psychoanalytic century: Freud's legacy for the future* (pp. 61–88). New York: The Other Press.

Schore, A. N. (2002f). Advances in neuropsychoanalysis, attachment theory, and trauma research: Implications for self psychology. *Psychoanalytic Inquiry, 22,* 433–484.

Schore, A. N. (2002g, April). *The role of the emotional brain: Attachment, trauma, and clinical implications.* Paper presented at the 8th Annual Self Psychology Conference of the Institute of Contemporary Psychotherapy and Psychoanalysis, Washington, DC.

Schore, A. N. (in press a). Early relational trauma, disorganized attachment, and the development of a predisposition to violence. In D. J. Siegel & M. Solomon (Eds.), *Healing trauma: Attachment, mind, body, and brain* (pp. 107–167). New York: Norton.

Schore, A. N. (in press b). The human unconscious: The development of the right brain and its role in early emotional development. In V. Green (Ed.), *Emotional development in psychoanalysis, attachment theory, and neuroscience.* London: Brunner-Routledge.

Schore, A. N. (in press c). Implications of recent advances in developmental neuroscience and attachment theory. *American Academy of Pediatrics UPDATE,* audiotape and publication. Port Washington, NY: Medical Information Systems.

Schore, A. N. (2003). *Affect dysregulation and disorders of the self.* New York: W.W. Norton.

Schore, J. R. (1983). *A study of the superego: The relative proneness to shame or guilt as related to psychological masculinity and femininity in women.* Unpublished doctoral dissertation, California Institute for Clinical Social Work, Berkeley.

Schore, J. R. (2003). The development of affect regulation in infancy and childhood with possible clues to psychological gender. In J. B. Sanville & E. B. Ruderman (Eds.), *Therapies with women in transition: Toward relational perspectives with today's women* (pp. 77–89). Madison, CT: International Universities Press.

Schuengel, C., Bakersmans-Kranenburg, M. J., & van IJzendoorn, M. H. (1999). Frightening maternal behavior linking unresolved loss and disorganized infant attachment. *Journal of Consulting and Clinical Psychology, 67,* 54–63.

Schulman, M. A. (1999). Book review of *Freud's model of the mind,* by J. Sandler, A. Holder, C. Dare, & A. U. Dreher. *Psychoanalytic Psychology, 16,* 477–480.

Schumann, J. H. (1997). *The neurobiology of affect in language.* Malden, MA: Blackwell.

Schwaber, E. A. (1990). Interpretation and the therapeutic action of psychoanalysis. *International Journal of Psycho-Analysis, 71,* 229–240.

Schwaber, E. A. (1992). Countertransference: The analyst's retreat from the patient's vantage point. *International Journal of Psycho-Analysis, 73,* 349–362.

Schwaber, E. A. (1995). A particular perspective on impasses in the clinical situation: Further reflections on psychoanalytic listening. *International Journal of Psycho-Analysis, 76,* 711–722.

Schwaber, E. A. (1998). The non-verbal dimension in psychoanalysis: "State" and its clinical vicissitudes. *International Journal of Psycho-Analysis, 79,* 667–679.

Schwaber, J. S., Wray, S., & Higgins, G. A. (1979). Vagal cardiac innervation: Contributions of the dorsal motor nucleus and the nucleus ambiguus determined by liquid scintillation counting. *Society of Neuroscience Abstracts, 4,* 809.

Schwartz, A. (1992). Not art but science: Applications of neurobiology, experimental psychology, and ethology to psychoanalytic technique. I. Neuroscientifically guided approaches to interpretive "what's" and "when's." *Psychoanalytic Inquiry, 12,* 445–474.

Schwartz, J. M., Stoessel, P. W., Baxter, L. R., Jr., Martin, K. M., & Phelps, M. E. (1996). Systematic cerebral glucose metabolic rate changes after successful behavior modification treatment of obsessive-compulsive disorder. *Archives of General Psychiatry*, 53, 109–113.

Segalowitz, S. J. (1994). Developmental psychology and brain development: A historical perspective. In G. Dawson & K. W. Fischer (Eds.), *Human behavior and the developing brain* (pp. 67–92). New York: Guilford Press.

Seidman, L. J., Oscar-Berman, M., Kalinowski, A. G., Ajilore, O., Kremen, W. S., Faraone, S. V., & Ming, T. T. (1995). Experimental and clinical neuropsychological measures of prefrontal dysfunction in schizophrenia. *Neuropsychology*, 9, 481–490.

Seinfeld, J. (1990). *The bad object: Handling the negative therapeutic reaction in psychotherapy*. Northvale, NJ: Jason Aronson.

Seligman, S. (1999). Integrating Kleinian theory and intersubjective research. Observing projective identification. *Psychoanalytic Dialogues*, 9, 129–159.

Semple, W. E., Goyer, P., McCormick, R., Morris, E., Compton, B., Berridge, M., Miraldi, F., & Schulz, S. C. (1992). Increased orbital frontal cortex blood flow and hippocampal abnormality in PTSD: A pilot PET study. *Biological Psychiatry*, 31, 129A.

Semrud-Clikeman, M., & Hynd, G. W. (1990). Right hemisphere dysfunction in nonverbal learning disabilities: Social, academic, and adaptive functioning in adults and children. *Psychological Bulletin*, 107, 196–209.

Settlage, C. (1977). The psychoanalytic understanding of narcissistic and borderline personality disorders: Advances in developmental theory. *Journal of the American Psychoanalytic Association*, 25, 805–833.

Settlage, C. F., Curtis, J., Lozoff, M., Lozoff, M., Silberschatz, G., & Simburg, E. J. (1988). Conceptualizing adult development. *Journal of the American Psychoanalytic Association*, 36, 347–369.

Severino, S., McNutt, E., & Feder, S. (1987). Shame and the development of autonomy. *Journal of the American Academy of Psychoanalysis*, 15, 93–106.

Seyle, H. (1956). *The stress of life*. New York: McGraw-Hill.

Shalev, A. Y., Peri, T., Canetti, L., & Schreiber, S. (1996). Predictors of PTSD in injured trauma survivors: A prospective study. *American Journal of Psychiatry*, 153, 219–225.

Shane, P. (1980). Shame and learning. *American Journal of Orthopsychiatry*, 50, 348–355.

Share, L. (1994). *If someone speaks, it gets lighter: Dreams and the reconstruction of infant trauma*. Mahwah, NJ: Analytic Press.

Sherwood, V. R. (1989). Object constancy: The illusion of being seen. *Psychoanalytic Psychology*, 6, 15–30.

Shevrin, H. (1997). Psychoanalysis as the patient: High in feeling, low in energy. *Journal of the American Psychoanalytic Association*, 45, 841–867.

Shiller, V. M., Izard, C. E., & Hembree, E. A. (1986). Patterns of emotion expression during separation in the strange-situation procedure. *Developmental Psychology*, 22, 378–382.

Shin, L. M., Kosslyn, S. M., McNally, R. J., Alpert, N. M., Thompson, W. L., Rauch, S. L., Macklin, M. L., & Pitman, R. K. (1997). Visual imagery and perception in posttraumatic stress disorders. *Archives of General Psychiatry*, 54, 233–241.

Shin, L. M., McNally, R., Kosslyn, S. M., Thompson, W. L., Rauch, S. L., Alpert, N. M., Metzger, L. J., Lasko, N. B., Orr, S. P., & Pitman, R. K. (1999). Regional cerebral blood flow during script-driven imagery in childhood sexual abuse-related PTSD: A PET investigation. *American Journal of Psychiatry*, 156, 575–584.

Shuren, J. E., & Grafman, J. (2002). The neurology of reasoning. *Archives of Neurology*, 59, 916–919.

Siegel, A. M. (1996). *Heinz Kohut and the psychology of the self*. London: Routledge.

Siegel, D. J. (1995). Memory, trauma, and psychotherapy: A cognitive science view. *Journal of Psychotherapy Practice and Research*, 4, 93–122.

Siegel, D. J. (1996). Cognition, memory and dissociation. In D. O. Lewis & F. Putnam (Eds.), *Child and adolescent psychiatric clinics of North America on dissociative disorders* (pp. 509–536). New York: W.B. Saunders.

Siegel, D. J. (1999). *The developing mind: Toward a neurobiology of interpersonal experience*. New York: Guilford Press.

Sifneos, P. E. (1988). Alexithymia and its relationship to hemispheric specialization, affect, and creativity. *Psychiatric Clinics of North America*, 3, 287–292.

Silberman, E. K., & Weingartner, H. (1986). Hemispheric lateralization of functions related to emotion. *Brain and Cognition*, 5, 322–353.

Singer, J. L. (1985). Transference and the human condition: A cognitive-affective perspective. *Psychoanalytic Psychology*, 2, 189–219.

Slap, J. W., & Slap-Shelton, L. J. (1994). The schema model: A proposed replacement paradigm for psychoanalysis. *Psychoanalytic Review*, 81, 677–693.

Smith, C. G. (1981). *Serial dissection of the human brain*. Baltimore: Urban & Scwarzenberg.

Smith, H. F. (1990). Cues: The perceptual edge of the transference. *International Journal of Psycho-Analysis*, 71, 219–227.

Snow, D. (2000). The emotional basis of linguistic and nonlinguistic intonation: Implications for hemispheric specialization. *Developmental Neuropsychology*, 17, 1–28.

Sobótka, S., Grabowska, A., Grodzicka, Wasilewski, R., & Budohoska, W. (1992). Hemispheric asymmetry in event relevant potentials associated with positive and negative emotions. *Acta Neurobiologiae Experimentalis*, 52, 251–260.

Solms, M. (1995). New findings on the neurological organization of dreaming: Implications for psychoanalysis. *Psychoanalytic Quarterly*, 64, 43–67.

Solms, M. (1996). Towards an anatomy of the unconscious. *Journal of Clinical Psychoanalysis*, 5, 331–367.

Solms, M., & Nersessian, E. (1999). Freud's theory of affect: Questions for neuroscience. *Neuro-Psychoanalysis*, 1, 5–14.

Solms, M., & Saling, M. (1986). On psychoanalysis and neuroscience: Freud's attitude to the localizationist tradition. *International Journal of Psychoanalysis*, 67, 397–416.

Solomon, R. C. (1974). Freud's neurological theory of mind. In R. Wollheim (Ed.), *Freud: A collection of critical essays* (pp. 25–52). Garden City, NY: Anchor Press.

Soufer, R., Bremner, J. D., Arrighi, J. A., Cohen, I., Zaret, B. L., Burg, M. M., & Goldman-Rakic, P. (1998). Cerebral cortical hyperactivation in response to mental stress in patients with coronary artery disease. *Proceedings of the National Academy of Sciences of the United States of America*, 95, 6454–6459.

Spence, S., Shapiro, D., & Zaidel, E. (1996). The role of the right hemisphere in the physiological and cognitive components of emotional processing. *Psychophysiology*, 33, 112–122.

Spero, M. H. (1984). Shame: An object-relational formulation. *Psychoanalytic Study of the Child*, 39, 259–282.

Spezzano, C. (1993). *Affect in psychoanalysis: A clinical synthesis*. Hillsdale, NJ: Analytic Press.

Spiegel, L. A. (1966). Affects in relation to self and object: A model for the derivation of desire, longing, pain, anxiety, humiliation, and shame. *Psychoanalytic Study of the Child*, 21, 69–92.

Spitz, R. A. (1958). On the genesis of superego components. *Psychoanalytic Study of the Child*, 13, 375–404.

Spitz, R. A. (1965). *The first year of life: A psychoanalytic study of normal and deviant development of object relations*. New York: International Universities Press.

Sroufe, L. A. (1979). Socioemotional development. In J. D. Osofsky (Ed.), *Handbook of infant development* (pp. 462–516). New York: Wiley.

Sroufe, L. A. (1996). *Emotional development: The organization of emotional life in the early years*. New York: Cambridge University Press.

Sroufe, L. A., & Waters, E. (1977). Attachment as an organizational construct. *Child Development, 48,* 1184–1189.

Stark, M. (1999). *Modes of therapeutic action: Enhancement of knowledge, provision of experience, and engagement in relationship*. New York: Jason Aronson.

Starkstein, S. E., Boston, J. D., & Robinson, R. F. (1988). Mechanisms of mania after brain injury: 12 case reports and review of the literature. *Journal of Nervous and Mental Disease, 176,* 87–100.

Starkstein, S. E., Mayberg, H. S., Berthier, M. L., Federoff, P., Price, T. R., Dannals, R. F., Wagner, H. N., Leiguarda, R., & Robinson, R. G. (1990). Mania after brain injury: Neuroradiological and metabolic findings. *Annals of Neurology, 27,* 652–659.

Starkstein, S. E., & Robinson, R. G. (1997). Mechanism of disinhibition after brain lesions. *Journal of Nervous and Mental Disease, 185,* 108–114.

Stechler, G., & Halton, A. (1987). The emergence of assertion and aggression during infancy: A psychoanalytic systems approach. *Journal of the American Psychoanalytic Association, 35,* 821–838.

Stein, R. (1990). A new look at the theory of Melanie Klein. *International Journal of Psycho-Analysis, 71,* 499–511.

Steklis, H. D., & Kling, A. (1985). Neurobiology of affiliative behavior in nonhuman primates. In M. Reite & T. Field (Eds.), *The psychobiology of attachment and separation* (pp. 93–134). Orlando, FL: Academic Press.

Stellar, E. (1954). The physiology of emotion. *Psychological Review, 61,* 5–22.

Stenberg, G., Wiking, S., & Dahl, M. (1998). Judging words at face value: Interference in a word processing task reveals automatic processing of affective facial stimuli. *Cognition and Emotion, 12,* 755–782.

Stern, D. (1977). *The first relationship*. Cambridge, MA: Harvard University Press.

Stern, D. N. (1983). Early transmission of affect: Some research issues. In J. Call, E. Galenson, & R. Tyson (Eds.), *Frontiers of infant psychiatry* (pp. 52–69). New York: Basic Books.

Stern, D. N. (1985). *The interpersonal world of the infant*. New York: Basic Books.

Stern, D. N. (1989). The representation of relational patterns: Developmental considerations. In A. J. Sameroff & R. N. Emde (Eds.), *Relationship disturbances in early childhood* (pp. 52–69). New York: Basic Books.

Stern, D. N. (2000). Foreword. In J. Bowlby (Au.), *Attachment and loss, vol. III: Loss: Sadness and depression*. New York: Basic Books.

Stern, D. N., Bruschweiler-Stern, N., Harrison, A. M., Lyons-Ruth, K., Morgan, A. C., Nahum, J.P., Sander, L., & Tronick, E. Z. (1998). The process of therapeutic change involving implicit knowledge: Some implications of developmental observations for adult psychotherapy. *Infant Mental Health Journal, 19,* 300–308.

Stern, D. N., Morgan, A. C., Nahum, J. P., Sander, L., & Tronick, E. Z. (1998). The process of therapeutic change involving implicit knowledge: Some implications of developmental observations for adult psychotherapy. *Infant Mental Health Journal, 19,* 300–308.

Stern, D. N., Sander, L., Nahum, J. P., Harrison, A. M., Lyons-Ruth, K., Morgan, A. C., Bruschweiler-Stern, N., &, Tronick, E. Z. (1998). Non-interpretive mechanisms in psychoanalytic therapy. *International Journal of Psycho-Analysis, 79,* 903–921.

Stoll, M., Hamann, G. F., Mangold, R., Huf, O., & Winterhof-Spurk, P. (1999). Emotionally evoked changes in cerebral hemodynamics measured by transcranial Doppler sonography. *Journal of Neurology, 246,* 127–133.

Stolorow, R. D. (1996). The intersubjective perspective. *Psychoanalytic Review, 82,* 181–194.

Stolorow, R. D., & Atwood, G. E. (1992). *Contexts of being: The intersubjective foundations of psychological life.* Hillsdale, NJ: Analytic Press.

Stolorow, R. D., & Atwood, G. E. (1996). The intersubjective perspective. *Psychoanalytic Review, 83,* 181–194.

Stolorow, R. D., & Lachmann, F. M. (1980). *Psychoanalysis of developmental arrests.* New York: International Universities Press.

Stolorow, R. D., Brandchaft, B., & Atwood, G. (1987). *Psychoanalytic treatment: An intersubjective approach.* Hillsdale, NJ: Analytic Press.

Stolorow, R. D., Orange, D. M., & Atwood, G. E. (1998). Projective identification begone! Commentary on paper by Susan H. Sands. *Psychoanalytic Dialogues, 8,* 719–725.

Stone, M. H. (1977). Dreams, free association, and the nondominant hemisphere: An integration of psychoanalytical, neurophysiological, and historical data. *Journal of the American Academy of Psychoanalysis, 5,* 255–284.

Stone, M. H. (1992). The borderline patient: Diagnostic concepts and differential diagnosis. In D. Silver & M. Rosenbluth (Eds.), *Handbook of borderline disorders* (pp. 3–28). Madison, CT: International Universities Press.

Stone, V. E., Baron-Cohen, S., & Knight, R. T. (1998). Frontal lobe contributions to theory of mind. *Journal of Cognitive Neuroscience, 10,* 640–656.

Strachey, J. (1934). The nature of the therapeutic action of psychoanalysis. *International Journal of Psycho-Analysis, 15,* 117–126.

Strachey, J. (Ed.). (1955–1966). *The standard edition of the complete psychological works of Sigmund Freud* (24 vols.). London: Hogarth Press.

Strupp, H. H. (1989). Psychotherapy: Can the practitioner learn from the researcher? *American Psychologist, 44,* 717–724.

Sturm, W., & Wilness, K. (2001). On the functional neuroanatomy of intrinsic and phasic alertness. *NeuroImage, 14,* 576–584.

Stuss, D. T., & Alexander, M. P. (1999). Affectively burnt in: one role of the right frontal lobe? In E. Tulving (Ed.), *Memory, consciousness, and the brain: the Talin conference* (pp. 215–227). Philadelphia: Psychology Press.

Stuss, D. T., Gow, C. A., & Hetherington, C. R. (1992). "No longer Gage": Frontal lobe dysfunction and emotional changes. *Journal of Consulting and Clinical Psychology, 60,* 349–359.

Stuss, D. T., Kaplan, E. F., Benson, D. F., Weir, W. S., Chiulli, S., & Sarazin, F. F. (1982). Evidence for the involvement of orbitofrontal cortex in memory functions: An interference effect. *Journal of Comparative Physiological Psychology, 96,* 913–925.

Suberi, M., & McKeever, W. F. (1977). Differential right hemispheric memory storage of emotional and non-emotional faces. *Neuropsychologia,15,* 757–768.

Suler, J. R. (1989). Mental imagery in psychoanalytic treatment. *Psychoanalytic Psychology, 6,* 343–366.

Sullivan, R. M., & Gratton, A. (1999). Lateralized effects of medial prefrontal cortex lesions on neuroendocrine and autonomic stress responses in rats. *Journal of Neuroscience, 19,* 2834–2840.

Sullivan, R. M., & Gratton, A. (2002a). Behavioral effects of excitoxic lesions of ventral medial prefrontal cortex in the rat are hemisphere-dependent. *Brain Research, 927,* 69–79.

Sullivan, R. M., & Gratton, A. (2002b). Prefrontal cortical regulation of hypothalamic-pituitary-adrenal function in the rat and implications for psychopathology: Side matters. *Psychoneuroendocrinology, 27,* 99–114.

Sulloway, F. S. (1979). *Freud, biologist of the mind: Beyond the psychoanalytic legend.* New York: Basic Books.

Suomi, J. J. (1995). Influence of attachment theory on ethological studies of biobehavioral development in nonhuman primates. In S. Goldberg, R. Muir, & J. Kerr (Eds.),

Attachment theory: Social, developmental, and clinical perspectives (pp. 185–201). Hillsdale, NJ: Analytic Press.

Szatkowska, I., Grabowska, A., & Szymanska, O. (2001). Evidence for the involvement of the ventromedial prefrontal cortex in a short-term storage of visual images. *NeuroReport, 12,* 1187–1190.

Tansey, M. J., & Burke, W. F. (1989). *Understanding countertransference: From projective identification to empathy.* Hillsdale, NJ: Analytic Press.

Tataranni, P. A., Gautier, J.-F., Chen, K., Uecker, A., Bandy, D., Salbe, A. D., Pratley, R. E., Lawson, M., Reiman, E. M., & Ravussin, E. (1999). Neuroanatomical correlates of hunger and satiation in humans using positron emission tomography. *Proceedings of the National Academy of Sciences of the United States of America, 96,* 4569–4574.

Taylor, D. C. (1969, July). Differential rates of cerebral maturation between sexes and between hemispheres. *Lancet,* pp. 140–142.

Taylor, G. (1987). *Psychosomatic medicine and contemporary psychoanalysis.* Madison, CT: International Universities Press.

Taylor, G. J., Bagby, R. M., & Parker, J. D. A. (1997). *Disorders of affect regulation: Alexithymia in medical and psychiatric illness.* Cambridge, UK: Cambridge University Press.

Teasdale, J. D., Howard, R. J., Cox, S. G., Ha, Y., Brammer, M. J., Williams, S. C. R., & Checkley, S. A. (1999). Functional MRI study of the cognitive generation of affect. *American Journal of Psychiatry, 156,* 209–215.

Thatcher, R. W. (1991). Maturation of the human frontal lobes: Physiological evidence for staging. *Developmental Neuropsychology, 7,* 397–419.

Thatcher, R. W. (1993). The self born in intersubjectivity: The psychology of an infant communicating. In U. Neisser (Ed.), *The perceived self: Ecological and interpersonal sources of self-knowledge* (pp. 121–173). New York: Cambridge University Press.

Thatcher, R. W. (1994). Cyclical cortical reorganization: Origins of human cognitive development. In G. Dawson & K. W. Fischer (Eds.), *Human behavior and the developing brain* (pp. 232–266). New York: Guilford Press.

Thatcher, R. W. (1996). Neuroimaging of cyclic cortical reorganization during human development. In R. W. Thatcher, G. R. Lyon, J. Rumsey, & N. Krasnegor (Eds.), *Developmental neuroimaging: Mapping the development of brain and behavior* (pp. 91–106). San Diego, CA: Academic Press.

Thatcher, R. W., & Aitken, K. (1994). Brain development, infant communication, and empathy disorders: Intrinsic factors in child mental health. *Development and Psychopathology, 6,* 597–633.

Thatcher, R. W., Aitken, K., Papoudi, D., & Robarts, J. (1998). *Children with autism: Diagnosis and interventions to meet their needs.* London: Jessica Kingsley.

Thatcher, R. W., & John, E. R. (1977). Neurophysiology and emotion. In R. W. Thatcher & E. R. John (Eds.), *Functional neuroscience 1. Foundations of cognitive processes* (pp. 117–134). New York: Erlbaum.

Thatcher, R. W., Lyon, G. R., Rumsey, J., & Krasnegor, N. (Eds.). (1996). *Developmental neuroimaging: Mapping the development of brain and behavior.* San Diego, CA: Academic Press.

Thatcher, R. W., Walker, R. A., & Giudice, S. (1987). Human cerebral hemispheres develop at different rates and ages. *Science, 236,* 1110–1113.

Thorpe, S. J., Rolls, E. T., & Maddison, S. (1983). The orbitofrontal cortex: Neuronal activity in the behaving monkey. *Experimental Brain Research, 49,* 93–115.

Tomkins, S. (1962). *Affect/imagery/consciousness: Vol. 1, The positive affects.* New York: Springer.

Tomkins, S. (1963). *Affect/imagery/consciousness. Vol. 2, The negative affects.* New York: Springer.

Tomkins, S. (1984). Afffect theory. In P. Ekman (Ed.), *Approaches to emotion* (pp. 165–195). Mahwah, NJ: Erlbaum.

Tomkins, S. (1987). Shame. In D. L. Nathanson (Ed.), *The many faces of shame* (pp. 133–161). New York: Guilford Press.

Trad, P. V. (1986). *Infant depression*. New York: Springer-Verlag.

Tremblay, L., & Schultz, W. (1999). Relative reward preference in primate orbito-frontal cortex. *Nature, 398,* 704–708.

Trevarthen, C. (1990). Growth and education of the hemispheres. In C. Trevarthen (Ed.), *Brain circuits and functions of the mind* (pp. 334–363). Cambridge, UK: Cambridge University Press.

Trevarthen, C. (1993). The self born in intersubjectivity: The psychology of an infant communicating. In U. Neisser (Ed.), *The perceived self: Ecological and interpersonal sources of self-knowledge* (pp. 121–173). New York: Cambridge University Press.

Trevarthen, C. (1996). Lateral asymmetries in infancy: Implications for the development of the hemispheres. *Neuroscience and Biobehavioral Reviews, 20,* 571–586.

Trevarthen, C., Aitken, K., Papoudia, D., & Robards, J. (1998). *Children with autism: Diagnosis and interventions to meet their needs.* London: Jessica Kingsley.

Tronick, E. Z. (1989). Emotions and emotional communication in infants. *American Psychologist, 44,* 112–119.

Tronick, E. Z., Bruschweiler-Stern, N., Harrison, A. M., Lyons-Ruth, K., Morgan, A. C., Nahum, J. P., Sander, L., & Stern, D. N. (1998). Dyadically expanded states of consciousness and the process of therapeutic change. *Infant Mental Health Journal, 19,* 290–299.

Tronick, E. Z., & Cohn, J. F. (1989). Infant–mother face-to-face interaction: Age and gender differences in coordination and occurrence of miscoordination. *Child Development, 60,* 85–92.

Tronick, E. Z., & Weinberg, M. K. (1997). Depressed mothers and infants: Failure to form dyadic states of consciousness. In L. Murray & P. J. Cooper (Eds.), *Postpartum depression and child development* (pp. 54–81). New York: Guilford Press.

Truex, R., & Carpenter, B. A. (1964). *Strong and Elwyn's human neuroanatomy* (5th ed.). Baltimore: Williams & Wilkins.

Tucker, D. M. (1981). Lateral brain function, emotion, and conceptualization. *Psychological Bulletin, 89,* 19–46.

Tucker, D. M. (1992). Developing emotions and cortical networks. In M. R. Gunnar & C. A. Nelson (Eds.), *Minnesota symposium on child psychology. Vol. 24, developmental behavioral neuroscience* (pp. 75–128). Mahwah, NJ: Erlbaum.

Tucker, D. M. (2001). Motivated anatomy: A core-and-shell model of corticolimbic architecture. In G. Gainoti (Ed.), *Handbook of neuropsychology* (2nd ed.). San Diego, CA: Elsevier.

Tucker, D. M., Luu, P., & Pribram, K. H. (1995). Social and emotional self-regulation. *Annals of the New York Academy of Science, 769,* 213–239.

Tucker, D. M., Roth, R. S., Arneson, B. A., & Buckingman, V. (1977). Right hemisphere activation during stress. *Neuropsychologia, 15,* 697–700.

Tulving, E. (1972). Episodic and semantic memory. In E. Tulving & W. Donaldson (Eds.), *Organization of memory* (pp. 381–403). New York: Academic Press.

Turiell, E. (1967). An historical analysis of the Freudian conception of the superego. *Psychoanalytic Review, 54,* 118–140.

Tustin, F. (1981). Psychological birth and psychological catastrophe. In J. Grotstein (Ed.), *Do I dare disturb the universe: A memorial to W. R. Bion* (pp. 181–196). London: Karnac.

Tyson, P., & Tyson, R. L. (1984). Narcissism and superego development. *Journal of the American Psychoanalytic Association, 32,* 75–98.

Tzourio-Mazoyer, N., De Schonen, S., Crivello, F., Reutter, B., Aujard, Y., & Mazoyer, B. (2002). Neural correlates of woman face processing by 2-month-old infants. *NeuroImage, 15,* 454–461.

Ungerleider, L. G., & Haxby, J. V. (1994). "What" and "where" in the human brain. *Current Opinions in Neurobiology, 4,* 157–165.

U.S. Department of Health and Human Services. (2000). *Child maltreatment 1998: Reports from the states to the National Child Abuse and Neglect Data System.* Washington, DC: U.S. Government Printing Office.

Uvnas-Moberg, K. (1997). Oxytocin linked antistress effects—the relaxation and growth response. *Acta Physiologica Scandinavica, 640*(Suppl.), 38–42.

Valent, P. (1998). *From survival to fulfillment: A framework for the life-trauma dialectic.* Philadelphia: Brunner/Mazel.

Valent, P. (1999). *Trauma and fulfillment therapy: A wholist framework.* Philadelphia: Brunner/Mazel.

Vallortigara, G. (1992). Right hemisphere advantage for social recognition in the chick. *Neuropsychologia, 30,* 761–768.

Vanaerschot, G. (1997). Empathic resonance as a source of experience-enhancing interventions. In A. C. Bohart & L. Greenberg (Eds.), *Empathy reconsidered: New directions in psychotherapy* (pp. 141–165). Washington, DC: American Psychological Association.

van der Kolk, B. A. (1996). The body keeps the score. Approaches to the psychobiology of posttraumatic stress disorder. In B. A. van der Kolk, A. C. McFarlane, & L. Weisaeth (Eds.), *Traumatic stress: The effects of overwhelming experience on mind, body, and society* (pp. 214–241). New York: Guilford Press.

van der Kolk, B. A., & Fisler, R. E. (1994). Childhood abuse and neglect and loss of self-regulation. *Bulletin of the Menninger Clinic, 58,* 145–168.

van der Kolk, B. A., Hostetler, A., Heron, N., & Fisler, R. (1994). Trauma and the development of borderline personality disorder. *Psychiatric Clinics of North America, 17,* 715–730.

van der Kolk, B. A., McFarlane, A. C., & Weisaeth, L. (1996). *Traumatic stress: The effects of overwhelming experience on mind, body, and society.* New York: Guilford Press.

van der Kolk, B. A., van der Hart, O., & Marmar, C. R. (1996). Dissociation and information processing in posttraumatic stress disorder. In B. A. van der Kolk, A. C. MacFarlane, & L. Weisaeth (Eds.), *Traumatic stress: The effects of overwhelming experience on mind, body, and society* (pp. 303–327). New York: Guilford Press.

van der Kolk, B. A., Weisaeth, L., & van der Hart, O. (1996). History of trauma in psychiatry. In B. A. van der Kolk, A. C. MacFarlane, & L. Weisaeth (Eds.), *Traumatic stress: The effects of overwhelming experience on mind, body, and society* (pp. 47–74). New York: Guilford Press.

van IJzendoorn, M. H., Juffer, F., & Duyvesteyn, M. G. F. (1995). Breaking the intergenerational cycle of insecure attachment: A review of the effects of attachment-based interventions on maternal sensitivity and infant security. *Journal of Child Psychology and Psychiatry, 36,* 225–248.

van IJzendoorn, M. H., Schuengel, C., & Bakermans-Kranenburg, M. J. (1999). Disorganized attachment in early childhood: Meta-analysis of precursors, concomitants, and sequelae. *Development and Psychopathology, 11,* 225–249.

van Kleeck, M. H. (1989). Hemispheric differences in global versus local processing of hierarchical visual stimuli by normal subjects: New data and a meta-analysis of previous studies. *Neuropsychologia, 27,* 1165–1178.

van Lancker, D. (1991). Personal relevance and the human right hemisphere. *Brain and Cognition, 17,* 64–92.

van Lancker, D. (1997). Rags to riches: Our increasing appreciation of cognitive and communicative abilities of the human right cerebral hemisphere. *Brain and Language*, 57, 1–11.

van Lancker, D., & Cummings, J. L. (1999). Expletives: Neurolingusitic and neurobehavioral perspectives on swearing. *Brain Research Reviews*, 31, 83–104.

van Toller, S., & Kendal-Reed, M. (1995). A possible protocognitive role for odor in human infant development. *Brain and Cognition*, 29, 275–293.

Vaslamatzis, G. (1999). On the therapist's reverie and containing function. *Psychoanalytic Quarterly*, LXVIII, 431–440.

Verfaellie, M., Bowers, D., & Heilman, K. M. (1988). Hemispheric asymmetries in mediating intention, but not selective attention. *Neuropsychologia*, 26, 521–531.

Vergopoulo, T. (1996). Panel report on Bion's contribution to psychoanalytic theory and technique. 39th Congress of IPA (1995). *International Journal of Psycho-Analysis*, 77, 575–577.

Vida, J. E. (1997). The voice of Ferenczi: Echoes from the past. *Psychoanalytic Inquiry*, 17, 404–415.

Vitz, P. C. (1990). The use of stories in moral development. *American Psychologist*, 45, 709–720.

Voeller, K. K. S. (1986). Right hemisphere deficit syndrome in children. *American Journal of Psychiatry*, 143, 1004–1009.

Volkow, N. D., Fowler, J. S., Wolf, A. P., Hitzeman, R., Dewey, S., Bendriem, B., Alpert, R. O., & Hoff, A. (1991). Changes in brain glucose metabolism in cocaine dependence and withdrawal. *American Journal of Psychiatry*, 148, 621–626.

Wagner, H., & Fine, H. (1981). A developmental overview of object relations and ego psychology. In L. Saretsky, G. D. Goldman, & D. S. Milman (Eds.), *Integrating ego psychology and object relations theory*. Dubuque, IA: Kendall/Hunt.

Walker, J. P., Daigle, T., & Buzzard, M. (2002). Hemispheric specialisation in processing prosodic structures: Revisited. *Aphasiology*, 16, 1155–1172.

Wallace, L. (1963). The mechanism of shame. *American Journal of Psychoanalysis*, 32, 62–73.

Waller, G., Hamilton, K., Elliott, P., Lewendon, J., Stopa, L., Waters, A., Kennedy, F., Lee, G., Pearson, D., Kennerley, H., Hargreaves, I., Bashford, V., & Chalkey, J. (2000). Somatoform dissociation, psychological dissociation, and specific forms of trauma. *Journal of Trauma & Dissociation*, 1, 81–98.

Wallerstein, R. (1990). Psychoanalysis: The common ground. *International Journal of Psycho-Analysis*, 71, 3–19.

Wallerstein, R. S. (1998). The new American psychoanalysis: A commentary. *Journal of the American Psychoanalytic Association*, 46, 1021–1043.

Wang, S. (1997). Traumatic stress and attachment. *Acta Physiologica Scandinavica*, 640(Suppl.), 164–169.

Ward, H. P. (1972). Shame—a necessity for growth in therapy. *American Journal of Psychotherapy*, 26, 232–243.

Watanabe, S., Miki, K., & Kakigi, R. (2002). Gaze direction affects face perception in humans. *Neuroscience Letters*, 325, 163–166.

Waters, E. (1978). The reliability and stability of individual differences in infant–mother attachment. *Child Development*, 49, 483–494.

Watson, C. (1977). *Basic human neuroanatomy, an introductory atlas* (2nd ed). Boston: Little, Brown.

Watt, D. F. (1986). Transference: A right hemispheric event? An inquiry into the boundary between psychoanalytic metapsychology and neuropsychology. *Psychoanalysis and Contemporary Thought*, 9, 43–77.

Watt, D. F. (1990). Higher cortical functions and the ego: Explorations of the boundary between behavioral neurology, neuropsychology, and psychoanalysis. *Psychoanalytic Psychology, 7*, 487–527.

Watt, D. F. (1998). Affect and the limbic system: Some hard problems. *Journal of Neuropsychiatry, 10*, 113–116.

Watt, D. F. (2000). The dialogue between psychoanalysis and neuroscience: Alienation and reparation. *Neuro-Psychoanalysis, 2*, 183–192.

Weil, A. P. (1985). Thoughts about early pathology. *Journal of American Psychoanalytic Association, 33*, 335–352.

Weinberg I. (2000). The prisoners of despair: Right hemisphere deficiency and suicide. *Neuroscience and Biobehavioral Reviews, 24*, 799–815.

Westen, D. (1997). Towards a clinically and empirically sound theory of motivation. *International Journal of Psycho-Analysis, 78*, 521–548.

Westen, D., Muderrisoglu, S., Fowler, C., Shedler, J., & Koren, D. (1997). Affect regulation and affective experience: Individual differences, group differences, and measurement using a Q-sort procedure. *Journal of Consulting and Clinical Psychology, 65*, 429–439.

Wexler, B. E., Warrenburg, S., Schwartz, G. E., & Janer, L. D. (1992). EEG and EMG responses to emotion-evoking stimuli processed without conscious awareness. *Neuropsychologia, 30*, 1065–1079.

Wheeler, M. A., Stuss, D. T., & Tulving, E. (1997). Toward a theory of episodic memory: The frontal lobes and autonoetic consciousness. *Psychological Bulletin, 121*, 331–354.

Whitaker, H. A. (1978). Is the right left over? Commentary on Corballis and Morgan, "On the biological basis of laterality." *Behavioral and Brain Sciences, 1*, 1–4.

White, L. E., Lucas, G., Richards, A., & Purves, D. (1994). Cerebral asymmetry and handedness. *Nature, 368*, 197–198.

White, R. (1960). Competence and the psychosexual stages of development. In M. Jones (Ed.), *Nebraska symposium on motivation* (pp. 97–143). Lincoln: University of Nebraska Press.

White, R. (1963). Ego and reality in psychoanalytic theory. *Psychological Issues* [Monograph 11]. New York: International Universities Press.

Wicker, B., Michel, F., Henaff, M. A., & Decety, J. (1998). Brain regions involved in the perception of gaze in PET study. *NeuroImage, 8*, 221–227.

Wiedemann, G., Pauli, P., Dengler, W., Lutzenberger, W., Birbaumer, N., & Buchkremer, G. (1999). Frontal brain asymmetry as a biological substrate of emotions in patients with panic disorders. *Archives of General Psychiatry, 56*, 78–84.

Willock, B. (1986). Narcissistic vulnerability in the hyperaggressive child: The disregarded (unloved-uncared for) self. *Psychoanalytic Psychology, 3*, 59–80.

Wilson, A. (1995). Mapping the mind in relational perspectives: Some critiques, questions, and conjectures. *Psychoanalytic Psychology, 12*, 9–29.

Wilson, A., Passik, S. D., & Faude, J. P. (1990). Self-regulation and its failures. In J. Masling (Ed.), *Empirical studies of psychoanalytic theory* (vol. 3 , pp. 149–213). Hillsdale, NJ: Analytic Press.

Winner, E., & Gardner, H. (1977). The comprehension of metaphor in brain-damaged patients. *Brain, 100*, 717–729.

Winnicott, D. (1956). Primary maternal preoccupation. In J. D. Sutherland (Ed.), *Through pediatrics to psychoanalysis* (pp. 300–305). London: Hogarth [The International Psycho-Analytical Library].

Winnicott, D. (1958a). The capacity to be alone. *International Journal of Psycho-Analysis, 39*, 416–420.

Winnicott, D. (1958b). *Through paediatrics to psycho-analysis*. New York: Basic Books.

Winnicott, D. (1960). The theory of the parent–infant relationship. In D. Winnicott, *The maturational processes and the facilitating environment* (pp. 37–55). New York: International Universities Press.

Winnicott, D. (1965). On communicating and not communicating leading to a study of certain opposites. In D. Winnicott, *The maturational processes and the facilitating environment* (pp. 179–192). New York: International Universities Press.

Winnicott, D. (1971a). *Playing and reality*. New York: Basic Books.

Winnicott, D. (1971b). *Therapeutic consultations in child psychiatry*. New York: Basic Books.

Winnicott, D. (1975). *Through paediatrics to psychoanalysis*. New York: Basic Books.

Winnicott, D. (1986). *Home is where we start from*. New York: Norton.

Winson, J. (1990, November). The meaning of dreams. *Scientific American*, pp. 86–96.

Winston, J. S., Strange, B. A., O'Doherty, J. O., & Dolan, R. J. (2002). Automatic and intentional brain responses during evaluation of trustworthiness of faces. *Nature Neuroscience, 5*, 277–283.

Wittling, W. (1997). The right hemisphere and the human stress response. *Acta Physiologica Scandinavica, 640*(Suppl.), 55–59.

Wittling, W., Block, A., Schweiger, E., & Genzel, S. (1998). Hemisphere asymmetry in sympathetic control of the human myocardium. *Brain and Cognition, 38*, 17–35.

Wittling, W., & Pfluger, M. (1990). Neuroendocrine hemisphere asymmetries: Salivary cortisol secretion during lateralized viewing of emotion-related and neutral films. *Brain and Cognition, 14*, 243–265.

Wittling, W., & Roschmann, R. (1993). Emotion-related hemisphere asymmetry: Subjective emotional responses to laterally presented films. *Cortex, 29*, 431–448.

Wittling, W., & Schweiger, E. (1993). Neuroendocrine brain asymmetry and physical complaints. *Neuropsychologia, 31*, 591–608.

Wolf, E. S. (1988). *Treating the self: Elements of clinical self psychology*. New York: Guilford Press.

Wolf, E. S. (1991). Advances in self psychology: The evolution of psychoanalytic treatment. *Psychoanalytic Inquiry, 11*, 123–146.

Woodman, C. L., & Tabatabai, F. (1998). New-onset panic disorder after right thalamic infarct. *Psychosomatics, 39*, 165–167.

Wright, C. I., Fisher, H., Whalen, P. J., McInerney, S. C., Shin, L. M., & Rauch, S. L. (2001). Differential prefrontal cortex and amygdala habituation to repeatedly presented emotional stimuli. *NeuroReport, 12*, 379–383.

Wright, K. (1991). *Vision and separation: Between mother and baby*. Northvale, NJ: Jason Aronson.

Wrye, H. K. (1998). The embodiment of desire: Rethinking the bodymind within the analytic dyad. In L. Aron & F. Sommer Anderson (Eds.), *Relational perspectives on the body* (pp. 97–116). Hillsdale, NJ: Analytic Press.

Wurmser, L. (1981). *The mask of shame*. Baltimore: Johns Hopkins University Press.

Yakovlev, P. I., & Lecours, A. R. (1967). The myelogenetic cycles of regional maturation of the brain. In A. Minkow (Ed.), *Regional development of the brain in early life* (pp. 3–70). Oxford, UK: Blackwell.

Yamada, H., Sadato, N., Konishi, Y., Kimura, K., Tanaka, M., Yonekura, Y., & Ishii, Y. (1997). A rapid brain metabolic change in infants detected by fMRI. *NeuroReport, 8*, 3775–3778.

Yamada, H., Sadato, N., Konishi, Y., Muramoto, S., Kimura, K., Tanaka, M., Yonekura, Y., Ishii, Y., & Itoh, H. (2000). A milestone for normal development of the infantile brain detected by functional MRI. *Neurology, 55*, 218–223.

Yoon, B.-U., Morillo, C. A., Cechetto, D. F., & Hachinski, V. (1997). Cerebral hemispheric lateralization in cardiac autonomic control. *Archives of Neurology, 54*, 741–744.

Zagon, A. (2001). Does the vagus nerve mediate the sixth sense? *Trends in Neuroscience, 24,* 671–673.

Zaidel, D. W., Esiri, M. M., & Beardsworth, E. D. (1998). Observations on the relationship between verbal explicit and implicit memory and density of neurons in the hippocampus. *Neuropsychologia, 36,* 1049–1062.

Zald, D. H., & Kim, S. W. (1996). Anatomy and function of the orbital frontal cortex, II: Function and relevance to obessive-compulsive disorder. *Journal of Neuropsychiatry, 8,* 249–261.

Zald, D. H., Lee, J. T., Fluegel, K. W., & Pardo, J. V. (1998). Aversive gustatory stimulation activates limbic circuits in humans. *Brain, 121,* 1143–1154.

Zanarini, M. C., Williams, A. A., Lewis, R. E., Reich, R. B., Vera, S. C., Marino, M. F., Levin, A., Yong, L., & Frankenburg, F. R. (1997). Reported pathological childhood experiences associated with the development of borderline personality disorder. *American Journal of Psychiatry, 154,* 1101–1106.

Zeddies, T. J. (2000). Within, outside, and in between. The relational unconscious. *Psychoanalytic Psychology, 17,* 467–487.

Zelazo, P. R. (1982). The year-old infant: A period of major cognitive change. In T. G. Beyer (Ed.), *Regressions in mental development: Basic phenomena and theories* (pp. 47–79). Hillsdale, NJ: Erlbaum.

Zelkowitz, P., Paris, J., Guzder, J., & Feldman, R. (2001). Diatheses and stressors in borderline pathology of childhood: The role of neuropsychological risk and trauma. *Journal of the American Academy of Child and Adolescent Psychiatry, 40,* 100–105.

Zetzel, E. R. (1956). Current concepts of transference. *International Journal of Psycho-Analysis, 37,* 369–376.

Zhang, L.-X., Levine, S., Dent, G., Zhan, Y., Xing, G., Okimoto, D., Gordon, M. K., Post, R. M., & Smith, M. A. (2002). Maternal deprivation increases cell death in the infant rat brain. *Brain Research, 133,* 1–11.

Zillman, D., & Bryant, J. (1974). Effects of residual excitation on the emotional response to provocation and delayed aggressive behavior. *Journal of Personality and Social Psychology, 30,* 782–791.

Zukier, H. (1985). Freud and development: The developmental dimensions of psychoanalytic theory. *Social Research, 52,* 3–41.

Index